SPORT PSYCHOLOGY

THEORY, APPLICATIONS AND ISSUES

EDITED BY
TONY MORRIS
&
JEFF SUMMERS

JOHN WILEY & SONS
BRISBANE • NEW YORK • CHICHESTER • TORONTO • SINGAPORE

First published 1995 by
JOHN WILEY & SONS
33 Park Road, Milton, Qld 4064

Offices also in Sydney and Melbourne

Typeset in 10/12 pt New Baskerville

© Jacaranda Wiley Ltd 1995

National Library of Australia
Cataloguing-in-Publication data

Sport psychology: theory, applications and issues.

Includes index.
ISBN 0 471 33549 5.

1. Sports — Psychological aspects. I. Morris,
Tony (Tony M.). II. Summers, J. (Jeff).

796.01

Cover photograph: Photo Library
Sydney/Dennis O'Clair

Printed in Singapore
10 9 8 7 6 5 4 3 2

This book is dedicated to all those who have worked to create a sport psychology profession in Australia. All of us who share in the benefits in practice and research in the late 1990s owe them a debt. In that respect, it is sad for us to note the passing of Denis Glencross, whose influence on Australian sport psychology will be missed.

CONTENTS

Preface xii

Acknowledgements xv

Contributors xvi

Introduction xxiii
Development of sport psychology   xxiii
Current status   xxv
Theory and practice   xxvii
Major issues   xxx
Sport psychology: Into the future   xxxiii
References   xxxiv

Part 1   Theory and research in sport psychology
Chapter 1   Psychological characteristics and sports behaviour
   Tony Morris   3
   Research on personality and sport   4
   Issues in personality and sport   11
   Future directions   21
   Conclusions   23
   Summary   24
   References   25

Chapter 2   Anxiety
   Mark H. Anshel   29
   Definitions of terms   30
   Trait and state anxiety   31
   Measurement of anxiety in sport   32
   Antecedents of state anxiety in sport: personal and situational factors   35
   Effects of anxiety on motor performance   41
   Anxiety in elite and non-elite athletes   47
   Arousal in sport: brief review of hypotheses and theories   48
   Cognitive–behavioural strategies for anxiety management   52
   Coaching techniques for managing athlete anxiety   54
   Future directions   56
   Conclusions   57
   Summary   58
   References   59

Chapter 3   **Attention in sport**
        Jeff Summers and Stephen Ford **63**

Attention — what is it? 64
Theoretical perspectives 65
Dimensions of attention 70
Models of attention 78
Future directions 81
Conclusions 83
Summary 83
References 85

Chapter 4   **Individual and social motivation in Australian sport**
        Gayelene J. Clews and John B. Gross **90**

Introduction: the relevance of motivational theory to sport 91
Intrinsic and extrinsic motivation 94
Achievement orientation 103
Participation and withdrawal in sport 109
Future directions 114
Conclusions 116
Summary 117
References 118

Chapter 5   **Attribution theory**
        Stephanie Hanrahan **122**

Theories of attribution 123
Attributions and achievement behaviour 127
Additional attributional dimensions 129
Attributional bias 131
Attributional style and intrinsic motivation 133
Measurement issues 134
Future directions 137
Conclusions 137
Summary 138
References 138

Chapter 6   **Self-efficacy in sport and exercise**
        Tony Morris **143**

Definition of self-efficacy 145
Self-efficacy and social cognitive theory 146
Measurement of self-efficacy 147
Antecedents of self-efficacy 150
Research on self-efficacy antecedents 152
Self-efficacy and sports performance 155
Self-efficacy and exercise behaviour 157
Practical applications of self-efficacy in sport and exercise 160
Future directions 162
Conclusions 165
Summary 166
References 168

Chapter 7   **Social facilitation**
        Michelle Pain **173**

Historical perspectives 174
Current perspectives 177
Practical implications of the research 185
Future directions 186
Conclusions 187
Summary 187
References 188

Chapter 8   **Team dynamics**
        Ken Hodge **190**

Historical retrospective 191
Introduction to "the" team 192
Research on team performance 194
Team motivation 196
Cohesion and team performance 197
Current perspectives 200
Future directions 205
Conclusions 207
Summary 207
References 208

Part 2 **Applied sport psychology**

Chapter 9   **Approaches to applied sport psychology**
        Tony Morris and Patrick Thomas **215**

Nature of applied sport psychology 216
Performance enhancement and psychological skills training 220
Approaches to psychological skills training (PST) 225
Performance profiling 243
Role limitations 244
Stages of professional development 246
Future directions 249
Conclusions 251
Summary 252
References 252

Chapter 10   **Goal setting**
        Graham Winter **259**

What is applied goal setting? 259
Why set goals? 260
Principles of goal setting 261
A goal-setting program 262
Goal setting in competition 266
Goals for training 267

Future directions   268
Conclusions   268
Summary   269
References   270

Chapter 11   Stress management
             Catherine Martin   **271**

Applied issues   272
The elite athlete   274
Approaches to treatment   276
The coach   284
Future directions   284
Conclusions   285
Summary   285
References   285

Chapter 12   Ways of coping
             Chris Madden   **288**

A context for coping   288
The development of coping strategies   289
Coping strategies and coping styles   290
Ways of coping with injury   296
Drug use as a way of coping with stress   298
Consequences of maladaptive coping   299
Coping questionnaires and coping skills training programs   299
Training in adaptive coping skills   301
Future directions   305
Conclusions   306
Summary   307
References   307

Chapter 13   Confidence and sporting performance
             Chris Horsley   **311**

Applied issues   312
Theories of self-confidence   313
Self-concept   313
Self-efficacy   315
Self-image   316
Attributions   317
Intervention strategies   319
Future directions   335
Conclusions   336
Summary   336
References   337

Chapter 14   Mental imagery in sport
             Clark Perry and Tony Morris   **339**

Nature of mental imagery   340
Definition of mental imagery   341

Brief review of research   344
Influence of individual differences   347
Imagery orientation or perspective   349
What makes imagery work?   350
Measurement of imagery   355
Uses of imagery   360
How do we begin an imagery-training program?   363
Video modelling as an aid to imagery   372
Flotation as an aid to imagery   373
Relaxation and imagery   375
Future directions   376
Conclusions   378
Summary   379
References   379

Chapter 15   **Concentration skills in sport: an applied perspective**
   Jeffrey Bond and Gregory Sargent   **386**
The importance of focusing on the right thing at the right time   388
The Nideffer attention model   391
The test of attentional and interpersonal style   396
Specific attentional training exercises for athletes   400
Future directions   412
Conclusions   415
Summary   415
References   416

Chapter 16   **Building and maintaining an effective team**
   Neil McLean   **420**
The challenge of team sport   421
Definitions of team building   423
Philosophy or bag of tricks?   423
Effective principles of team development   425
Future directions   432
Conclusions   433
Summary   433
References   434

Part 3   **Issues in sport psychology**
Chapter 17   **An introduction to exercise psychology**
   J. Robert Grove   **437**
A definition of exercise psychology   438
Areas of interest within exercise psychology   440
Consequences of exercise behaviour   445
Future directions   449
Summary   449
References   449

Chapter 18 **Psychological factors in sport injuries**
Rob Kirkby **456**

Personality research 457
Life event research 460
Stress, coping and injury 463
Future directions 467
Conclusions 468
Summary 469
References 470

Chapter 19 **Career transitions in competitive sport**
Sandy Gordon **474**

Theoretical models 476
Career transition research 481
Career assistance programs 489
Prevention and treatment strategies 493
Future directions 495
Conclusions 497
Summary 498
References 498

Chapter 20 **Sport psychology for athletes with disabilities**
Stephanie Hanrahan **502**

Descriptive profiles/assessment 503
Application of mental skills training 504
Disability-specific studies on mental skills training 507
General considerations for athletes with disabilities 511
Future directions 512
Conclusions 513
Summary 513
References 514

Chapter 21 **Children and sport psychology**
Patsy Tremayne **516**

Children's development 517
Why do children play sport? 518
Physical education versus sport 523
Psychological skills training for children 526
Future directions 531
Conclusions 532
Summary 532
References 533

Chapter 22 **Gender and sport**
Vicki Plaisted **538**

Status of the genders in sport 540
Biologically based sex differences 543
Social role 545

Achievement   550
Aspects of sexuality   554
Gender study and men   559
Future directions   560
Conclusions   564
Summary   565
References   566

Chapter 23   The growth of qualitative research in sport psychology
Susan A. Jackson   **575**

The growth of qualitative research   576
Qualitative research   580
Examples of sport psychological qualitative research   584
Future directions   588
Conclusions   590
Summary   590
References   590

Chapter 24   Future directions in sport and exercise psychology
Tony Morris and Jeff Summers   **592**

Future directions in theory and research   593
Future directions for the sport psychology profession   600
The theory–practice nexus   601
Conclusions   602
Summary   602
References   603

Author index   605

Subject index   617

PREFACE

Sport psychology has grown substantially in the last ten to fifteen years. For those who teach it and wish to keep up to date, the literature to be covered is ever expanding. Students are also faced with the prospect of acquiring a range of texts to cover the subjects they can now study as part of expanding undergraduate streams and graduate programs. This curriculum development has culminated in the creation of a number of masters programs which represent the Australian professional training in sport psychology. Talking to each other and colleagues around Australia and New Zealand, we perceived the need for a single text which covers much of this expanding curriculum. Existing books tend to be specific to areas of sport psychology such as theoretical or applied issues. Because most are American imports these books are also quite expensive.

Another issue with these American texts is their emphasis on North American sports. In particular, they tend to focus on the high-profile, professional sports, such as baseball, American football, basketball and hockey, by which they mean *ice*-hockey. While many Australian sports enthusiasts are familiar with at least the rudiments of those sports, Australasian sport has its own culture and flavour, but netball, Australian Rules football, Rugby Union, Rugby League, cricket and the like will rarely get a mention in North American texts.

We were also aware of the maturing of sport psychology in Australasia. Late in 1990, a number of Australian sport psychologists, from different aspects of the field, came together and decided to create a national body and to locate Australian sport psychology firmly within the psychology profession by forming a board within the Australian Psychological Society (APS). This was accomplished by the end of 1991 and the board prognosticated on the appropriate training for sport psychologists, favouring specialist masters programs as the professional training. The combination of enhanced status and credibility of sport psychology and the need to establish masters programs led to an increase in the range and numbers of sport psychology subjects being offered in university psychology and physical education departments. In addition, the shift to a research ethos in the "new" universities (the converted Colleges of Advanced Education) is producing a rapid increase in graduate research in sport psychology. Together these forces have greatly increased the number of sport psychologists employed in the tertiary education sector. The demand for resources, particularly appropriate level texts, has increased and we now have Australasian-based sport psychologists with the expertise to contribute to an edited text.

The present book is a response to all these forces; in fact, when it was planned it anticipated most of them. It is a recognition of the sport psychology talent currently active in Australasia, both in the universities and in the national and State sports institutes. It is also a celebration of the establishment of an Australian national body, to which all the Australian authors belong (at the time of writing, Ken Hodge is president of the New Zealand equivalent), which is providing impetus for the discipline and the profession. Our aim has been to provide, within one volume, an advanced text which covers the major aspects of theoretical and applied sport psychology, including recent developments and with topics addressed by experts, and to offer it at a manageable price for students.

In addition, the book adopts an Australasian perspective. This does not mean that there should be any distortion of the contributions of leading theorists and practitioners, who are often North American. Each chapter and every topic recognises those contributions. Nonetheless, the existence of Australasian research and applied work is justly acknowledged and the authors employ examples from sporting situations familiar to Australasian readers. We believe that the exclusive involvement of Australasian-based contributors and reference to local research and practice will be of value to readers, and we hope many will join the Australasian sport psychology profession in due course. In addition to receiving a thorough grounding in the ideas and activities of sport psychologists generally, readers will also acquire a sense of the topography of sport psychology in this part of the world, which will serve them in good stead when they move into practice.

In a young and fast-changing discipline, it is not possible to include every development. Since the structure of the book was set, topics have emerged which would have been valuable additions. Theoretical issues such as psychological momentum, enjoyment in sport, and the home advantage seem to be emerging as substantive topics, while personal counselling, drugs in sport, overtraining and burn-out, and eating disorders are important issues in practice. A number of texts consider the coach, particularly in terms of relationships with the sport psychologist and athletes' parents. Similarly, the growth in training of sport psychologists throws into relief issues to do with preparation for practice, including ethical and professional issues, and the supervision of practical experience. By the time a second edition of this book is due, we will not be surprised if most of these topics deserve their own space.

Accepting that inevitably there are emerging issues as well as potential contributors we were not able to include, we believe that this book has much to offer. It includes expert contributions on most of the major topics in sport psychology. We are confident that it will be of great value to our academic and applied colleagues and their students. The book has three parts, following a general introduction. The first part considers the orthodox issues in theoretical sport psychology. Part two is concerned with performance enhancement, particularly in terms of psychological skills training. The third and final part covers a range of the issues which have emerged as substantive aspects of sport psychology in recent years. Elements of this structure might echo other texts; the discipline of sport psychology is still small enough to make that inevitable in an inclusive text. The present book is unique in that no general text book we know includes all this between two covers. It is also original in its use of a wide range of expert Australasian-based contributors and its Australasian emphasis. We hope that it further stimulates the emerging profession in this part of the world, an area where the special blend of the love of sport and down to earth professional practitioners and academics has produced arguably the most promising framework for the future health of sport psychology research and practice.

Tony Morris and Jeff Summers

ACKNOWLEDGEMENTS

Our thanks go to all the contributors for their patience and perseverance. Thanks also to Anita Chou and Elise Downes for taking the strain off administrative chores. Our gratitude to Jane Gale and all other staff at Jacaranda Wiley who have helped this book see the light of day. Most of all, our thanks to Felicity, Rachel and Adam and to Avril for living without us for so long.

Photographs: National Sport Information Centre, Australian Sports Commission (pages 1, 435); Sporting Pix/Tony Feder (page 213).

CONTRIBUTORS

Mark H. Anshel

Mark H. Anshel is an associate professor in the Department of Psychology, University of Wollongong (New South Wales). Born and raised in Chicago (USA), Dr Anshel arrived in Australia in July 1988 to teach postgraduate and undergraduate sport and exercise psychology and health psychology. He is the author of over 60 research publications, six book chapters and three books, most notably *Sport Psychology: From Theory to Practice (2nd ed.)*. His current research emphasis is on coping with acute stress in sport, and he has developed the COPE model for providing cognitive and behavioural strategies in response to various sources of acute stress.

Jeffrey Bond

Jeffrey Bond has been Head of the Sport Psychology Unit at the Australian Institute of Sport since 1982. His extensive experience in sport psychology spans some 25 years, culminating in applied work at the elite level. He has been an Olympic Team sport psychologist on six occasions and has worked with numerous sporting groups and individuals at many international and national competitions. Jeffrey's research interests lie in the areas of salt-water flotation, as well as attentional and emotional control in high-performance situations. His clinical interests relate to the management of "at-risk" athletes.

Gayelene J. Clews

Gayelene J. Clews is the Sport and Psychology Consultant to the ACT Academy of Sport. She was awarded the Australian Psychological Society Prize at the completion of her Graduate Diploma course in Psychology. She has served as the Psychology Consultant to national teams for Triathlon Australia and Athletics Australia. Gayelene was a world-ranked triathlete and multiple Australian Champion and national representative in athletics. She has coached athletes to Australian team representation in triathlon, athletics and orienteering, where she combines her coaching and psychology skills. She has contributed to five books and is a regular sport psychology columnist in a number of Australia's national sporting magazines. Gayelene is presently completing her Sports Science Master's thesis on dysfunctional eating behaviours in female· athletes, and is designing an educational intervention program in response to the problem. She works privately with individuals suffering from anorexia, bulimia and obesity.

Stephen Ford

Stephen Ford graduated with Honours in Psychology from the University of Melbourne. Since then, he has been involved in doctoral research with Jeff Summers. His research has addressed the issue of attention in sport, with particular reference to its theoretical construction and measurement. He has a broad interest in sport psychology issues, as well as other aspects of psychology, and a special interest in research methodology and statistics. Stephen has published in major sport psychology journals. He is a Victorian state junior-volleyball coach.

Sandy Gordon

Dr Sandy Gordon is a senior lecturer in the Department of Human Movement, UWA, and teaches sport and exercise psychology and sport sociology. Formerly a Physical Education teacher, his postgraduate studies were in the social psychology of sport and led to interests in Applied Sport Psychology. He is a member of both APS and the Board of Sport Psychologists and works as a certified consultant (AAASP) with VTA-Women and the WA State Cricket Association. His current research interests include the psycho-social aspects of sport injuries, exercise promotion among elderly cohorts, evaluation of mental skills programs, and career transitions in competitive sport.

John B. Gross

John Gross is a senior lecturer and the Director of the Centre for Sports Studies at the University of Canberra. He has been an editor for the sport psychology section of the *Australian Journal of Science and Medicine in Sport* and is currently on the editorial board of the *New Zealand Journal of Sports Medicine*. John has a special interest in the development of quality training programs for sport psychologists and his research interests lie in the area of coaching behaviours. He is also a member of the Board of Sport Psychologists in the Australian Psychological Society.

J. Robert Grove

J. Robert Grove is a senior lecturer in exercise and sport psychology within the Department of Human Movement at the University of Western Australia. He has published more than 30 articles in peer-review journals and has written five chapters for edited books. He is an associate editor for the *Australian Journal of Science and Medicine in Sport* as well as a member of the editorial staff for the *Journal of Sport Psychology* and the *International Journal of Sport Psychology*. His teaching and research interests include attributions in health and sport, personality correlates of sport-related behaviour, and the psychological aspects of exercise.

Stephanie Hanrahan

Stephanie Hanrahan received her Master's degree from the University of Illinois and completed her doctorate at the University of Western Australia.

She is currently a lecturer in the departments of Human Movement Studies and Psychology at the University of Queensland. Her teaching areas include health psychology as well as sport and exercise psychology. Stephanie's main research interests include mental skills training for performance enhancement of individuals not traditionally associated with elite sport, attributional style, and motivation. She works with athletes and coaches from a variety of sports and levels. Her own sporting background includes professional ice-skating and 17 years of representative volleyball.

Ken Hodge

Ken Hodge is a lecturer in sport psychology in the School of Physical Education, University of Otago. His research focuses primarily on the psycho-social effects of participation in sport. In particular, he has investigated issues such as character/morality in sport, sport and psychological well-being, the psycho-social effects of the KiwiSport program, and participation motivation and drop-outs in high school sport. In 1992 he worked as Team Psychologist for the NZ Olympic Team at the Barcelona Games. He was also Team Psychologist for the NZ Commonwealth Games Team at the Victoria Games. Ken is currently President of the NZ Sports Psychology Association and is serving as Deputy-Chairman of the NZ Federation of Sports Medicine in 1993–94.

Chris Horsley

Chris Horsley has worked as a sport psychologist at the Australian Institute of Sport for eight years. Starting his working life with an economics degree, Chris went on to gain an undergraduate degree in psychology (Honours) and a Master's degree in clinical psychology, both from the Australian National University. He has travelled extensively to international competitions with Australian teams, including the Australian Men's Water Polo and Australian Women's Hockey teams. He has worked at the Barcelona Olympic Games, attended four world championships with three sports and been a consultant with two professional teams. His research interest is in the areas of injury and self-concept.

Susan A. Jackson

Sue Jackson is a lecturer in sport and exercise psychology in the departments of Human Movement Studies and Psychology at the University of Queensland. Sue completed her PhD in sport psychology at the University of North Carolina at Greensboro, with Daniel Gould. Her major research interests are in flow states and peak performance, social-cognitive motivational theories, stress and coping in elite performers, and the psychological aspects of health, healing, and wellness. Sue has been involved with a number of qualitative research projects in sport psychology and her research has an applied focus. In addition to her academic involvement in sport psychology, Sue practises as a mental training consultant to athletes in a wide range of sports.

Rob Kirkby

Dr Rob Kirkby is a reader in the School of Behavioural Health Sciences at La Trobe University. He has an extensive background in research, practice and teaching in sport psychology. Coming as he does from a background of health psychology, it is not surprising that his research interests are health-related. These include the investigation of the psychological factors in the vulnerability to and the recovery from sports injuries, variables influencing the involvement of individuals in exercise programs, and sport and exercise for people with disabilities. In the applied area, Dr Kirkby has worked with several national teams and with individuals at international and Olympic levels.

Chris Madden

Dr Chris Madden is a senior lecturer in the School of Behavioural Health Sciences at La Trobe University. As a clinical psychologist, he has skills and training in assessment and intervention. He specialises in Australian Rules Football and basketball, gives talks to AFL and VBA teams on performance enhancement, and works with elite athletes to maximise their potential. He has recently developed a system for examining the effect of coaching communications on game outcome. Chris regularly presents his work at international conferences, and was Secretary of the Board of Sport Psychologists of the Australian Psychological Society in 1993–94.

Catherine Martin

Catherine Martin is the senior psychologist at the South Australian Sports Institute. The institute services around 20 full-time coaches and sports, including the Cricket Academy and track cycling, which are based in Adelaide. Cathy is involved in performance-enhancement programs, which are sport specific and implemented progressively throughout the season. Her work includes the development of resources such as *Sport Psych: Basic Training Program* and *Sport Psych for Tennis* which she co authored. She has accompanied national teams overseas and has herself competed in distance running and triathlons. Cathy also consults privately in health and organisational psychology.

Neil McLean

Neil McLean is a lecturer in Psychology at the University of Western Australia. He is a registered clinical psychologist and a member of the Australian Psychological Society Board of Sport Psychology. He has worked with a range of sporting teams including the Perth Wildcats Basketball Team, the West Coast Eagles AFL Team, the Bond Syndicate America's Cup Team and the Australian Men's Hockey Team. He also works with individuals in sports ranging from cricket to croquet, and is a consultant to a variety of business and professional groups. Neil McLean was one of the sport psychologists attached to the Australian team at the Barcelona Olympic Games.

Tony Morris

Tony Morris was trained in psychology in England and worked as a sport psychologist at the West Sussex Institute of Higher Education. Since his arrival in Australia in 1990, he has been a senior lecturer in sport psychology at the Victoria University of Technology (formerly Footscray Institute). His research interests include imagery processes and applications, flotation for performance and health, motivation in sport and exercise, self-efficacy in sports performance and health promotion, performance enhancement, career transitions, and exercise and well-being across the lifespan. He has presented internationally and published in these areas. Tony has consulted widely, most often in racquet sports. He has coaching qualifications and experience in tennis and table tennis, which he has played competitively. He has been the Foundation Chairperson of the Board of Sport Psychologists from 1991 to 1994.

Michelle Pain

Michelle Pain is a member of the Board of Sport Psychologists, and teaches sport psychology in the Department of Psychology at Monash University. Her doctorate, which examines the predictive ability of the CSAI-2 and salivary cortisol on 1500 m athletes' performance, has been a major research focus in recent years, although she has also published works in the areas of health and education. A participant in track and field and netball for many years, she has worked with athletes and coaches in such diverse sports as three-day equestrian riding, badminton, board paddling, cricket and track and field.

Clark Perry

Clark Perry is from New Jersey and trained in psychology at Trenton State College and in psychology of human movement (MEd and EdD) at Temple University. Since 1990 he has been a full-time sport psychologist at the Australian Institute of Sport. He has worked with a wide range of sports, especially swimming and cycling. He has attended several world championships and was a sport psychologist with Australian swimming and cycling teams at the 1992 Olympic Games and the 1994 Commonwealth Games. His major research interests are in the areas of imagery, flotation REST, immune-system function and self-concept. He has wide experience of using imagery techniques and combining them with flotation.

Vicki Plaisted

Vicki Plaisted lectures in sport psychology and health education at the University of Ballarat, Victoria and is currently undertaking doctoral studies. She has completed a Graduate Diploma in Counselling Psychology and a Master's degree focusing on children's sport. Vicki has played state-level netball and was awarded a scholarship to the Australian Institute of Sport (AIS) in netball. She recently returned to the AIS in

Canberra to take up a Fellowship in Sport Psychology. She has worked as a sport psychology consultant with a wide variety of athletes and coaches, including the Australian Parachute Team.

Gregory Sargent

Gregory Sargent graduated from the University of Melbourne, completing research on 'The Mind of the Marathoner' and on motor control, under the supervision of Jeff Summers. He has since completed sport science qualifications at Deakin University and is currently undertaking a Master's degree at ANU. Greg has been a student counsellor and taught psychology and physical education in secondary schools before taking up a postgraduate appointment at the Australian Institute of Sport under the supervision of Jeffrey Bond. Greg's research interests are in the effects of flotation and the effectiveness of interventions in sport psychology. He has participated in and coached a wide variety of sports including athletics, Australian Rules Football, netball and baseball, and still aspires to breaking three hours for the marathon.

Jeff Summers

Jeff Summers is the Foundation Professor of Psychology and Head of Department at the University of Southern Queensland (USQ). He moved to USQ in 1993 after 18 years at the University of Melbourne. Jeff has published extensively in the fields of motor control and sport psychology. His teaching areas include sport and exercise psychology, and learning and skilled performance. In the sport psychology area, his research interests include attentional mechanisms in sport, stress-performance relationship, predisposition to injury and exercise addiction. He has acted as consultant to individual athletes and sports teams and was the first National Secretary of the Board of Sport Psychologists.

Patrick Thomas

Patrick R. Thomas is a senior lecturer in the Faculty of Education at Griffith University in Brisbane. He is a member of the Australian Psychological Society's Board of Sport Psychologists, and has been a visiting professor in sport psychology at the United States Olympic Training Centre in Colorado Springs. He consults with athletes in various sports and has worked extensively with junior and senior golfers, both amateur and professional. His research on psychological and psychomotor skills in sport and the cognitive processes in learning and performance is supported by faculty and university programme grants.

Patsy Tremayne

Patsy Tremayne is a senior lecturer in Human Movement/Health Education at the University of Sydney. Dr Tremayne's research interests have focused on the arousal–performance relationship, including attention/concentration strategies and biofeedback training, particularly for performance routines in closed skills. Formerly a nationally ranked high-board diver and trampolinist, her applied interests include consulting with a variety of team and individual athletes, from youth sport participants to Olympic-level competitors. She remains an avid fitness enthusiast, and is involved in community fitness activities teaching aerobics and coaching diving. Dr Tremayne is a foundation member of the Australian Board of Sport Psychology.

Graham Winter

Graham Winter is a psychologist who works with sporting and business clients. He established the Sport Psychology Unit at the South Australian Sports Institute and was psychologist to the 1988 Olympic Team. Graham worked as a senior consultant with Coopers and Lybrand and is a director of Winter Consulting International, through which he consults to business on developing world-competitive people. He is the author of *The Business Athlete* and *The Psychology of Cricket* (Pan Macmillan). Graham was a member of winning Sheffield Shield and One-Day Cup cricket teams.

INTRODUCTION

Sport, in its many forms, is one of the most ubiquitous institutions in the world. Through its natural evolution from play and by the more artificial route of the missionary activities of various nations, many peoples from all parts of the globe have come to share a range of activities involving physical effort and skill, played competitively according to widely agreed rules. Sports are enjoyed by children, adults and older people, by males and females, by the able-bodied and people with disabilities. Participation in some form of sport at an appropriate level is denied to few.

It is hardly surprising, given the universal interest in play and games which has been rapidly translated into a world of sport during the last century, that sport has come to play such a significant role in economic and political realms, nor that it has attracted the interest of academic scholars. That this latter interest focused first on the biological and then the mechanical and motor aspects of sport is also predictable; the physical demands and the production of skill being the most obvious elements that many sports have in common. Still, some people recognised that other factors affect sport behaviour, the psychological aspects of sport. Many of us have observed the player with all the skills and physical attributes, the outstanding favourite for an Olympic or world championship gold, fall at the first hurdle against a lesser opponent. We have watched performers in the heat and emotion of competition producing a superhuman feat of endurance or strength to achieve their goals. Everybody knows someone, whether a player, coach, administrator or, even a spectator, who shows a level of commitment to his or her sport which borders on the fanatical, even though these people know they will never achieve fame or glory. What makes millions of people exhibit such devotion to activities which typically have little or no instrumental value? Why does the overwhelming favourite crash in a major competition? How can athletes display resources of strength or endurance way beyond their normal capacities? It is an interest in seeking answers to questions like these which led some scholars to focus on the application of psychological principles to sport, and, thus, to create sport psychology.

DEVELOPMENT OF SPORT PSYCHOLOGY

The relationship between sport and psychology has a long history, going back at least as far as Triplett's (1897) study of coaction effects in racing cyclists, which is acknowledged as the first social psychological experiment. Psychologists studied sport for its own sake or as an exemplar of human behaviour in general for several decades before the field was recognised and expanded into a specialism, originally within Physical Education. It is over the last 30 years that this specialist area of sport psychology has developed from its hesitant beginnings to become a confident, mature academic discipline, supported by a plethora of texts, several international journals, and national and international professional associations. Such associations host conferences, where new theories, research and practice are presented and discussed and where the sport psychology community meets to shape the future of the discipline.

Nonetheless, the academic study of sport psychology was a comparatively late starter. Coleman Griffith, an American coach and academic, is often named as the "grandfather" of sport psychology. Triplett used sport to examine social psychological processes. Griffith was a physical educator and coach. He worked at the University of Illinois in the 1920s, producing two books entitled *Psychology of Coaching* (1926) and *Psychology of Athletics* (1928). His main role was to facilitate the work of university coaches, and he studied motor learning as much as sport psychology (Williams & Straub, 1993). Griffith is not considered to be the "father" of sport psychology, despite his pioneering example, because a whole generation passed by before the field blossomed.

It was in the 1960s that interest developed on the scale which was to provide the foundation for an academic area of study. Although there were a number of developments which occurred concurrently, probably the one which ensured the solid base for the future was the spread of sport psychology among the university physical education departments of North America. This created sufficient momentum for the formation of the North American Society for the Psychology of Sport and Physical Activity (NASPSPA) in 1967. It is interesting to note that this group held its first meeting prior to the conference of the American Alliance for Health, Physical Education, Recreation and Dance (AAPHERD), the professional body for physical educators in the USA. Because the new sport psychologists were largely physical educators who would be congregating for the AAPHERD meeting anyway, it was, no doubt, assumed that this timing would ensure a large attendance of interested parties.

A similar relationship between a nascent sport psychology group and a parent physical education body was the vehicle to establish a sport psychology association in Canada, just two years later in 1969. Here the connection was even closer, as the Canadian Society for Psychomotor Learning and Sport Psychology (CSPLSP) was actually part of the Canadian Association for Health, Physical Education and Recreation (CAHPER) until 1977, when it became independent. It will be noticed that not only was the parent a physical education association, but in both cases the "older sibling" was motor learning.

This was also the case in Europe, where the small cadre of academics interested in sport psychology and led by Miroslav Vanek, came together in 1965 to form the International Society of Sport Psychology (ISSP). Although this body makes no mention of motor learning and control in its title, many of its early adherents worked in motor skill and there is still a substantial contribution from this field, as indicated by the proceedings of the 8th World Congress (Serpa, Alves, Ferreira, & Paulo-Brito, 1993). ISSP was the first body to sponsor a journal specifically on sport psychology. Consistent with its mission to encourage and share research in sport psychology from around the world, this was called the *International Journal of Sport Psychology* (IJSP). The IJSP was first published in 1970 and it was not until 1979 that a specialist journal was established to cater for the strong research tradition which had rapidly developed in North America. Although a small number of texts had been produced in the 1970s, the publication of the *Journal of Sport Psychology* (JSP) by NASPSPA in 1979 possibly signalled the arrival of sport psychology as an academic field of study more than any other single event.

There is no doubt that the establishment of sport psychology owes much to the developments in North America. The USA, in particular, has been the focus of academic sport psychology since the 1960s, both in terms of numbers of trained people involved and quantity of publications produced. It was believed that rapid strides were also being taken in Eastern Europe. Now it is not clear how much of the great success achieved by the old Soviet Bloc countries was attributable to their massive talent development programs, rather than advanced performance enhancement techniques per se.

Certainly on a smaller scale, but all the same pioneering in its conception, has been the progress of sport psychology in Australasia. In Australia, a small cadre of academics has been studying sport psychology since the 1960s, as in North America. Again, many were based in physical education or human movement departments, although there were some whose base was in psychology. The 1978 text *Psychology and Sport* by Glencross was a contemporary of the classic North American texts of Martens (1975), Cratty (1981) and Fisher (1976), for example. Applied sport psychology was a particularly early starter in Australia. Although expert advisers in the sport science area were recruited by the United States Olympic Committee (USOC) in 1978, it was 1983 before an official sport psychology committee was established by the USOC, and only in 1988 that the USOC employed its first full-time sport psychologist at its training centre at Colorado Springs. By comparison, the Australian Sports Commission appointed a sport psychologist in 1982, hard on the heels of its creation of the Australian Institute of Sport (AIS). During the 1990s, there have been four full-time sport psychologists at the AIS and three at the South Australian Sports Institute (SASI).

CURRENT STATUS

Sport psychology in Australia has taken another massive leap forward in the early 1990s with the formation of the Board of Sport Psychologists, a professional body within the Australian Psychological Society (APS). In North America, recognition of the applied field required the practitioners to set up a separate body from the research-oriented North American Society for the Psychology of Sport and Physical Activity (NASPSPA), creating the Association for the Advancement of Applied Sport Psychology (AAASP) in 1985. AAASP has rapidly developed as a national organisation for the promotion of applied sport psychology, gaining sufficient support to establish a certification program for practitioners in 1991. The very demanding criteria for certification, including some form of proposed accreditation of doctoral programs, leads Williams and Straub (1993) to comment that "whether or not the AAASP's certifying criteria and procedures will be widely accepted remains to be seen" (p. 5). While AAASP has generated substantial momentum, it is not formally a part of the organisational structure of either of the "parent" disciplines, namely physical education or psychology. The American Psychological Association (APA), a very large and powerful pressure group, officially recognised sport psychology by establishing Division 47 as an interest group in this area in 1987. AAASP is entirely separate from this body. In Australia, the creation of the Board of Sport Psychologists in the APS in 1991, gave sport psychology direct recognition as one of only eight professional areas of psychological practice. Not only does individual membership of the board confer tacit professional status, but the APS controls accreditation of all tertiary psychology courses and boards approve programs as professional training. The nascent board let it be known that it would follow the APS model of four years of general psychology training followed by a two-year specialist masters degree, and this led to the development of such masters programs around Australia. Those programs, along with the introduction or expansion of sport psychology at other levels, especially in departments of psychology, also led to a virtual doubling of sport psychology positions in tertiary education in Australia in 1993. Sport psychology in Australia now seems in a strong position to build the discipline and the profession on a solid foundation. It will be part of a strong professional society, the Australian Psychological Society (APS), which has more than 7000 members. The APS provides sport psychology with status and credibility in the psychology profession, sport and the community. It also offers an established infrastructure for the operation of a truly national organisation and provides the support of a powerful, national pressure group.

The practice of sport psychology and the theory and research on which it is based, are the bricks and mortar of that professional edifice. Those who practise sport psychology and those who train and are being trained in sport psychology need to have the best possible bricks and mortar to build the highest quality edifice. It is the aim of this book to provide that theoretical and applied knowledge for all those involved in the endeavour of developing the profession, particularly in Australasia. The theoretical base of sport psychology is quite broad, but a number of issues have been of major concern to those conducting research in sport psychology. These issues tend to be reflected in the topics consistently found in sport psychology textbooks. These form the content of Part 1 of this book. The context of applied sport psychology is discussed in Chapter 9. There, it is observed that performance enhancement, through psychological skills training, is the most widely practised element of applied sport psychology. Part 2 of the text considers major aspects of psychological skills training, along with team performance enhancement. The breadth of interest and application of sport psychology has increased rapidly in recent years. Part 3 reflects topics which have been brought to the attention of the sport psychology community and which seem destined to play a significant role in the future development of the discipline. We hope that the inclusion of these three areas within a single text will make it a valuable resource for all those interested in sport psychology.

THEORY AND PRACTICE

The nexus between theory and practice is an issue which is of great concern in sport psychology. The foregoing discussion and the structure of this book itself reflect this concern: theory and research are discussed in one part of the book and the areas of practice, both well-established and developing, are considered in the other two parts. Although we are unaware of any other text which covers all the ground that this one does, other books which cover some of it tend to be structured in the same way. Much consideration was given to alternative ways of presenting sport psychology, particularly thematic approaches which would bring together all the theory, research and practice on, for example self-confidence or stress management, in an integrated discussion. Unfortunately, much of the theory and research on topics related to applied issues was not executed in the applied setting and its applicability is questionable. Conversely, much applied practice is based on what has worked in other areas of psychology or in related areas such as meditation and the martial arts, what has appeared to be intuitively the appropriate action, and what has proved successful on a trial-and-error basis. This is less the case with respect to the topics in Part 3 of the book, because most of these are recent developments which have evolved through the interplay of theory, research and practice.

On the other hand, there is much in the theoretical area which has little directly to do with the applied field, particularly performance enhancement and especially in the context of elite athletes. Theoretical issues frequently concerned mass participation, addressing questions such as:

- What makes people participate in sports and exercise activities, and what makes them stop?
- Do particular types of people play specific sorts of sports?

Theoretical issues were also related to the outcomes of mass participation sport, such as:

- Does sport build character?
- Does sport involvement make people more aggressive?

Even when the issues were relevant to practice, the research has often been of questionable applicability. Much research has employed high-school or college students as subjects and it is doubtful whether they think, feel or behave like Olympic rowers, professional footballers or big-money golfers and tennis players in many of the contexts of interest.

A concern for the lack of articulation between theory and practice was evident in two seminal papers by Martens. In the first issue of the *Journal of Sport Psychology*, Martens (1979) wrote an article entitled "About smocks and jocks". Martens (1980) wrote a similar chapter in an edited text. It was more pointedly entitled "From smocks to jocks: a new adventure for sport psychologists". In these papers Martens argued that it was important for the ecological validity of research in sport psychology, that sport psychology researchers should leave their symbolically white-coated laboratories (smocks) for the training fields and competition pitches of sport (jocks). Some years later, by no coincidence in the first issue of *The Sport Psychologist*, Martens (1987) considered methodological and epistemological issues related to the need for research to be executed in real-world sport. In particular, Martens noted the difficulty which the traditional, positivist paradigm of science has in providing a framework to answer many of the questions of interest to practitioners. He encouraged researchers in sport psychology to consider other ways of knowing about sport which were not based on the positivist construction of the world (see Chapter 23).

One reason for this poor integration between theory and practice in sport psychology lies in the historical development of theoretical and applied sport psychology, which was touched on earlier and is discussed again in Chapter 9. Briefly, it is suggested that many of the early sport psychologists came from a physical education background and a philosophy which related to the value of sport and physical activity for everyone in the population. Hence, sport psychology theory and research reflected this interest in issues such as participation and drop-out, aggression and character. Applied sport psychology had an abrupt start, which was driven by organised, elite sport. The research on performance enhancement was largely absent, because of that broad focus of theoretical sport psychology and there being no time for elaborate research projects; the sports needed action immediately.

Another major factor, particularly in the slow response of sport psychology in establishing research to address the issues of concern in relation to practice, was the nature of elite sport. Although benefits can be gleaned from the application of psychology to the training ground, practitioners appreciate that the crunch comes with competitive performance, especially in major competition. They are also aware that it is in the intensity of the Olympics, world championships, grand finals or grand slam events that the psychological "glue" typically comes unstuck. Many psychologists have ethical reservations about executing invasive research in these situations and, if they didn't, most coaches would oppose any activity the psychologist proposed which might disrupt the performer.

Thus, the best that could often be hoped for was arms-length activity, such as observation or the use of tests or interviews well before or after the event. Similarly, where sport psychologists have the opportunity to apply interventions, it is often not possible to employ traditional experimental designs. First, it would not be ethical, for example, to employ half an Olympic squad as the control group, who were denied a potentially important psychological strategy. Second, as noted in Chapter 9, most practitioners adopt individualised approaches to performance enhancement, that is, interventions vary between individuals who receive them. Clearly, it would be equally unethical to give all athletes exactly the same intervention, whether it is considered to be appropriate for them or not.

These concerns about the difficulty of executing research where it counts, in the major competitive setting of elite performers, reduced the amount of applied research which was done for some years. More recently, a number of developments have increased the potential for such research. Perhaps lacking the confidence of a mature discipline, sport psychology for many years adopted a conservative perspective on what constituted acceptable research. It copied the sciences, and its closer relatives the other sports sciences, by predominantly employing the traditional experimental methods and occasionally using correlational research methods. Aware of the need for research in real-world settings, sport psychologists began to acknowledge the value of other research methods, such as in-depth interviews (e.g., see Chapter 24), and single-case design studies (e.g., Kendall, Hrycaiko, Martin, & Kendall, 1990). Concurrently, the applied sport psychology community has created its own journals to promote the communication of good practice and research in the applied field. *The Sport Psychologist* is now well established, having published four issues a year since 1987. *The Journal of Applied Sport Psychology* is less so, having started two years later, in 1989, and publishing two issues each year. This shift in the ethos of sport psychology does reduce the ethical problems, and many of the logistical ones associated with research on elite athletes. The patient years of practice of many sport psychologists have also developed a high degree of trust in top coaches and administrators. They have seen the benefits which can accrue from the involvement of a sport psychologist, without any threat to their own positions. Such trust is the basis for acceptance of the need for research, and that recognition is helping to resolve problems of access to elite athletes in real competitive environments. Together, these developments should lead to a much richer research base for the applied area in the not too distant future.

Sport and exercise psychology is a dynamic young discipline, now well enough established to have the confidence to develop its own theories and perspectives, to use the broadest range of appropriate research methods, and to generate distinctive modes of practice. As the chapters of the book themselves demonstrate, interest and attention in sport psychology has moved away from less fruitful issues, such as the role of personality in determining sport involvement or the trait of achievement motivation as the key to direction and intensity of sport activity. As well as embracing an interactionist perspective (Williams & Straub, 1993), sport psychology has broadly adopted a cognitive phenomenological approach (Straub & Williams, 1984), in such areas as attribution theory (Weiner 1972, 1979), cognitive evaluation theory (Deci, 1975), and goal orientations (Duda, 1987; Nicholls, 1984). The cognitive phenomenological approach recognises that human behaviour is not based on what is misleadingly called the "objective" situation, that is, the situation as perceived by the psychologist, but on the interpretation of the situation in the head of the performer. Similarly, applied sport psychology, in taking up the broader range of research methods, recognises the importance of the subjective experience of individual athletes and is in its best-ever position to study this in the field. The growing areas covered in Part 3 of this book, further show the way in terms of more integrated research and practice. As a result of these forces, which appear to be acting in the same direction, perhaps we will see a thematic text on sport psychology, which hangs together comfortably, to greet the new century.

MAJOR ISSUES

In each chapter of this book, the contributors will propose the future directions which they believe merit examination by those students moving into practice and research and colleagues already involved in research and applied work. In the final chapter we will synthesise those ideas and draw out any consistent themes with respect to theory and practice. Certain general implications for the future of sport psychology are also raised by the present discussion. These are now briefly addressed.

ACCREDITATION

Sport psychology has suffered as a result of its rather disjointed history and the uncertainty about the appropriate professional direction for it to take. In Australia, this uncertainty has been resolved in favour of professional psychology, whereas in the United States it is in the form of a free-standing association and in the UK it is as part of the sports sciences national organisation. Perhaps the critical point is that one voice should speak for professional sport psychology nationally. Accreditation would seem to be a central pillar of the professional association, whatever its location. In all three major structures referred to here, it has been one of the first issues addressed, leading to accreditation systems now being in place in the USA, the UK and Australia. In the case of the latter, the vast majority of those who would like to call themselves sport psychologists appear to have supported the new Board of Sport Psychologists in the Australian Psychological Society by joining it. The sustained success of the national association in improving the position of sport psychologists is likely to be a crucial factor in the viability of the accreditation systems. Thus the profession will keep membership unified and this will ensure that the accredited route is perceived to be the accepted path for training.

It is our view that the professional groups will facilitate the establishment of the profession, so the working of the accreditation processes will be a major issue for observation in the coming years.

Training is a primary element of each accreditation system mentioned in the previous paragraph. For the profession to emerge in a strong and healthy position in the 21st century, training must not just pay lip-service to the criteria laid down in accreditation papers. On the contrary, training must produce open-minded, thinking practitioners, who do not simply follow established procedures in a mechanistic manner. They must be observant of the needs of their clients and flexible in their practices, being prepared to try new ideas to meet those needs, without going beyond ethical limits. Because of this, examination of the processes involved in training is essential, both in the teaching and the practical experience components. Awareness of a range of research and evaluation techniques, especially those which can be used in the field and in monitoring on-going work, will also be required. Sensitivity to the gamut of ethical issues which face the practitioner will help the newly accredited sport psychologist avoid some of the pitfalls. Research on these issues must become a major thrust in applied sport psychology to provide guidance for those who train sport psychologists, as to the best training methods and professional practice.

Training does not end with the award of a degree certificate in the profession of psychology. As in all other areas of the profession, graduates from the professional training programs will need to undergo a period of supervised practice or internship. In a professional community as small as that of sport psychology in Australia, those currently practising must consider it a professional responsibility to support the supervised practice system. If practitioners fail their responsibility, those dedicated people who have undergone at least six years of full-time training will have no way of qualifying. In the same way, products of the new training programs must be taught their professional responsibility in this area, so that in the future, there are always adequate numbers of supervisors in the field. In addition, sport psychologists must be sensitised to their other professional responsibilities, such as keeping their knowledge up-to-date by attending courses, conferences, seminars and workshops; communicating with colleagues; referring on when issues beyond their competence are raised; and always presenting themselves and the profession in a responsible manner. Examination of the progress of the profession in these terms will be a worthwhile exercise for the future.

SPORTS LINKS

Much of what has been said in this section can be linked to the relationship that the national sport psychology association has with the major sports organisations. In Australia, for example, close working relationships with the Australian Sports Commission, the Australian Olympic Committee and the Australian Coaching Council will ensure that the training and accreditation of sport psychologists meets the needs and expectations of those bodies. This will enhance the applicability of the training received and the confidence of those bodies in the individuals who attain accreditation. The professional organisation can then enhance its standing in the sports community by gaining preferred status with the sports organisations, for example, in the consideration of Olympic and world championship sport psychology appointments and coach educators. Investigation of the needs of these organisations is an important area of research.

THEORY AND PRACTICE

It has been recognised that research on theoretical issues in sport psychology has dominated the field until recently and there is still a need for more integration of theory and research with the main issues being addressed in practice. Working directly with sports organisations will sharpen the perception of sport psychologists to those practical needs. New research directions should reflect concerns of the sports organisations, coaches and athletes. In addition, funding of research is always a concern of those involved in the study of sport psychology. Where the sports organisations perceive that sport psychologists are sensitive to the research questions for which they need answers, more funding may be accessible to the researchers. Funding agencies in sport should also be made aware that sport psychology research to date has not resolved many issues of behaviour, thoughts and feelings in sport. Rather, it has provided a base for the myriad of issues to be addressed, and trained a new generation of research sport psychologists, whose skills and perception should be broader than their predecessors. There is now, in Australasia as well as internationally, a growing number of highly trained researchers, ready to extend our knowledge more rapidly and significantly than ever before. It is important for sport psychology to communicate to funding organisations that this expansion in research potential merits a compatible increase in research support.

At the same time, sport psychology researchers and those who determine the allocation of research funds, often coming from a more conservative positivist science base, must recognise the value of employing a range of qualitative and interpretive research methods, as well as their traditional quantitative methods. While the latter have served sport psychology well in some respects, they have restricted the appreciation of some aspects of sport psychology. Work like that of Scanlan, Ravizza, and Stein (Scanlan, Ravizza, & Stein, 1989; Scanlan, Stein, & Ravizza, 1989, 1991) and of Gould and his colleagues (Gould, Eklund, & Jackson, 1992a, 1992b; Gould, Jackson, & Finch, 1993a, 1993b) demonstrates the richness of research using qualitative techniques with elite sports performers. The field must benefit from the application of a wide range of research approaches to address the real issues in sport.

It was noted that the number of research sport psychologists is increasing. This expansion is equalled, and probably exceeded, by the number of new practitioners emerging from training each year. New and high quality programs have been established in North America for a number of years and it is now the turn of Australia to see such development. The evolution of the tertiary sector has given university status to a number of institutions with a tradition in the sport sciences. This has resulted in a change of ethos and emphasis toward research in these institutions. As a result, opportunities for graduate research study in sport psychology are increasing. The professionalisation of sport psychology has led to the specification of a training route, involving four years of preparation in general psychology, followed by a two-year specialist masters degree in sport psychology. A number of masters programs are being established, thus providing increased opportunities for specialist training. Although the increased opportunities for training are exciting, they carry a responsibility for the profession to support the important practical elements of that training and to create jobs in the field.

Job creation depends on the marketing and promotion of sport and exercise psychology to the community. While various means must be sought to facilitate the development of sport psychology in education and the sports institutes, the majority of new work will be created in the community. It is important for professional organisations and those already occupying sport psychology roles to promote sport psychology to the wider population. A central implication is the need for a greater understanding of what currently represents community knowledge and expectations about sport psychology, and how these might best be enhanced. It also means that the recent expansion in the breadth of sport and exercise psychology must be continued. This is particularly true with respect to areas of work that affect large sections of the population, especially those as yet little touched by sport psychology. Reflection on these pressing issues suggests that exploratory research in the sport and exercise community would be valuable to identify those aspects of behaviour, thoughts and feelings in sport and exercise which are not presently addressed by research or practice in the field.

SPORT PSYCHOLOGY: INTO THE FUTURE

Sport and exercise psychology is an exciting, young field which has a great deal of untapped potential. Its development may have been delayed by a lack of vision and a focus on other priorities, but the ground made up over the last 30 years is significant. Nonetheless, that development has provided only the foundation from which the field must launch itself, in both its theoretical and practical domains. There is a need for a broadening of the issues addressed in research and practice, with greater coherence between the concerns of practice and research activities.

Approaches to research and evaluation must also continue to proliferate, to allow for the most sensitive methods to be used to explore each issue. Self-reflexivity is essential to successful future development. Sport and exercise psychology must continually examine its expectations of training and determine effective modes of preparation for future practitioners and researchers, not losing the essence of the scientist-practitioner model of training common in psychology, but evolving more effective ways of achieving it in practice. Sport and exercise psychology has entered a crucial period for its long-term development. Opportunities and recognition are greater than ever, but so are expectations. It is up to the next generation of sport psychologists to take advantage of the position carved out for them by the pioneers and fulfil those expectations in the world of sport. We hope this book will help, in one sense, to point the way, but also to create bold and confident professionals who are prepared to think of new avenues and new perspectives to follow.

REFERENCES

Cratty, B. J. (1981). *Social psychology in athletics*. Englewood Cliffs, NJ: Prentice-Hall.

Deci, E. L. (1975). *Intrinsic motivation*. New York: Plenum Press.

Duda, J. L. (1987). Toward a developmental theory of children's motivation in sport. *Journal of Sport Psychology, 9*, 130–145.

Fisher, A. C. (1976). *Psychology of sport*. Palo Alto, CA: Mayfield Publishing Company.

Glencross, D. J. (1978). *Psychology and sport*. East Roseville, NSW: McGraw-Hill.

Gould, D., Eklund, R. C., & Jackson, S. A. (1992a). 1988 USA Olympic wrestling excellence I: Mental preparation, precompetitive cognition, and affect. *The Sport Psychologist, 6*(4), 358–382.

Gould, D., Eklund, R. C., & Jackson, S. A. (1992b). 1988 USA Olympic wrestling excellence II: Competitive cognition, and affect. *The Sport Psychologist, 6*(4), 383–402.

Gould, D., Jackson, S. A., & Finch, L. M. (1993a). Life at the top: The experiences of US national figure skaters. *The Sport Psychologist, 7*(4), 354–374.

Gould, D., Jackson, S. A., & Finch, L. M. (1993b). Sources of stress in national champion figure skaters. *Journal of Sport and Exercise Psychology, 15*(2), 134–159.

Griffith, C. R. (1926). *Psychology of coaching*. New York: Scribner.

Griffith, C. R. (1928). *Psychology of athletics*. New York: Scribner.

Kendall, G., Hrycaiko, D., Martin, G. L., & Kendall, T. (1990). The effects of an imagery rehearsal, relaxation, and self-talk package on basketball game performance. *Journal of Sport and Exercise Psychology, 12*, 157–166.

Martens, R. (1975). *Social psychology and physical activity*. New York: Harper & Row.

Martens, R. (1979). About smocks and jocks. *Journal of Sport Psychology, 1*, 94–99.

Martens, R. (1980). From smocks and jocks: A new adventure for sport psychologists. In P. Klavora & K. A. W. Wipper (Eds.), *Psychological and sociological factors in sport* (pp. 20–26). Toronto: Schools of Physical and Health Education, University of Toronto.

Martens, R. (1987). Science, knowledge and sport psychology. *The Sport Psychologist, 1*, 29–55.

Nicholls, J. G. (1984). Achievement motivation: Conceptions of ability, subjective experience, task choice and performance. *Psychological Review, 91*, 328–346.

Scanlan, T. K., Ravizza, K., & Stein, G. L. (1989). Sources of enjoyment in elite figure skaters. *Journal of Sport and Exercise Psychology, 11*, 65–83.

Scanlan, T. K., Stein, G. L., & Ravizza, K. (1989). An in-depth study of former elite figure skaters: Introduction to the project. *Journal of Sport and Exercise Psychology, 11*, 54–64.

Scanlan, T. K., Stein, G. L., & Ravizza, K. (1991). Sources of stress in elite figure skaters. *Journal of Sport and Exercise Psychology, 13*, 103–120.

Serpa, S., Alves, J., Ferreira, V., & Paulo-Brito, A. (Eds.). (1993, June). *Proceedings of the VIII World Congress of Sport Psychology*, Lisbon, Portugal.

Straub, W. F., & Williams, J. M. (1984). *Cognitive sport psychology*. Lansing, NJ: Sports Science Associates.

Triplett, N. (1897). The dynamogenic factors in pacemaking and competition. *American Journal of Psychology, 9*, 507–553.

Weiner, B. (1972). *Theories of motivation: From mechanism to cognition*. Chicago: Rand McNally.

Weiner, B. (1979). A theory of motivation for some classroom experiences. *Journal of Educational Psychology, 71*, 3–25.

Williams, J. M., & Straub, W. F. (1993). Sport psychology. In J. M. Williams (Ed.), *Applied sport psychology: Personal growth to peak performance* (2nd ed.). Palo Alto, CA: Mayfield Publishing Company.

P A R T

1

THEORY AND RESEARCH IN SPORT PSYCHOLOGY

Sport psychology largely became established, as a sub-discipline of physical education, through attempts to understand human behaviour in sport using a psychological perspective. Major issues were typically addressed by theories from mainstream psychology, using well-established research methods, such as experiments and correlational studies. As sport psychology has matured, more theories, models and research tools have been developed in the field and changes in perspectives have taken place. Still, most of these directions, such as interactionism, cognitive theory, and qualitative research methods, originate in general psychology. Part 1 of this book reviews classic work and recent advances in major areas of sport psychology. In the first chapter, Morris considers the popular area of psychological characteristics and sport behaviour. This chapter shows how a pure trait approach was not fruitful and has been replaced by a state-trait-interactionist perspective. The second chapter, by Anshel, considers another major issue from the early work, anxiety. Whereas work on personality has become scarce in recent years, research and theories on stress and anxiety proliferate and sport psychologists are making original contributions to theory and model development in psychology. Summers and Ford illustrate the complexity of the concept of attention in Chapter 3, pointing to the need for more rigorous work to clarify what attention is and how it works. Motivation is a vast and varied area, which is addressed by Clews and Gross in Chapter 4. They summarise the major issues on participation motivation, intrinsic and extrinsic motivation and achievement motivation. Closely related to motivation is the concept of attributions. In Chapter 5, Hanrahan describes the development and significance of this cognitive process. Self-efficacy provides a link between motivation and confidence. Morris argues for the central role of self-efficacy in sport and exercise behaviour, in Chapter 6. Social facilitation, the influence of the presence of others as competitors, team-mates or audience is considered by Pain in Chapter 7. It is widely recognised that a champion team will usually beat a team of champions. In Chapter 8, Hodge discusses issues like cohesion and leadership, which influence team dynamics. Links are made from theory to applications and issues, wherever appropriate.

C H A P T E R

1

PSYCHOLOGICAL CHARACTERISTICS AND SPORTS BEHAVIOUR

TONY MORRIS

Does a certain type of person play sport and another avoid physical activity, especially when it is competitive? Perhaps particular characteristics lead an individual to participate in high physical contact sports, like Rugby and hockey, or those where they are part of a team, such as netball or Australian Rules football, while people with different personalities prefer to play non-contact sports, like tennis or volleyball, or get involved in individual sports, such as swimming or squash? Could it be that success in sport, or in specific sports, depends on the possession of certain personal characteristics? Ideas like these have had intuitive appeal for those interested in sport psychology from the early days of research in the field. Research on personality and sports behaviour was the topic of choice for many sport psychologists during the 1960s and 1970s, the first two decades of concerted activity in the field. Even in the years since then, and in the wake of a number of largely negative reviews, it appears that the idea of a relationship between sport and personality dies hard.

The aims of this chapter are to present a summary of the current position in this field and to raise some critical issues for thought and discussion. The chapter briefly considers the research on personality and sports behaviour, particularly the relationship between personality traits and sport. Recent attempts to find alternatives to the traditional personality trait approach are also briefly discussed. The chapter then reflects on issues which the personality and sport debate has raised. These issues include such questions as what constitutes a relatively enduring aspect of a person's psychological make-up; what is the status of research on psychological characteristics and sport behaviour; what are the practical issues in sport which might make personality and sport such an enduring topic for research; and what might be a fruitful direction for future research to take in this field.

This chapter will not present a substantive review of research on personality and sport. A number of recent texts have reviewed the field and mere repetition of these would serve little purpose. The aim is to summarise the field and raise some critical issues. Others provide much of the material which underpins the issues (e.g., Cox, 1994; Vealey, 1992). A common approach is to consider major perspectives on personality, as identified by introductory psychology books and personality texts. These typically include psychodynamic, dispositional (trait), social learning, and phenomenological views of personality. Work in sport psychology is then described in this context, which tends to show that the breadth of personality research in sport is limited, largely emanating from the trait or trait-state perspectives. What emerges is a view that sport psychology's interest in personality has been myopic or at least very selective. It highlights the potential for consideration of sport from other perspectives, such as the psychodynamic approach, personal construct theory (Kelly, 1955) or self-theory (Rogers, 1961); "potential" because very little research has been carried out in sport using these perspectives to date. Different accounts also reveal a lack of agreement about what should be defined as personality (e.g., Cox, 1994; Vealey, 1992). Reviews of the field typically report very similar literature, but the interpretation of this research can be supportive of the value of studying personality in sport (e.g., Cox, 1994) or clearly indicate the absence of consistent findings, particularly in trait-based research (e.g., Vealey, 1992). The definition of personality and the interpretation of existing research are two major themes to be addressed here. These and related questions will be considered in the context of the history of research on personality in sport, issues which do remain to be resolved in this field, and the status of research on personality and sport, considering the trait and the trait-state approaches. The chapter also reflects on some of the important issues for sport, and particularly its administrators, which tend to keep personality or psychological characteristics on the sport psychology research agenda.

RESEARCH ON PERSONALITY AND SPORT

During the 1960s and 1970s, there was a vast amount of research on various aspects of personality and sports behaviour. Ruffer (1975, 1976a, 1976b) identified 572 examples of research on personality and sport. Fisher (1984) found over a thousand studies less than ten years later. It has been claimed that interest has since waned (e.g., Cox, 1994), although others propose that the attention of researchers has merely shifted away from the dispositional approach, to study personality and sport largely from the cognitive phenomenological perspective (e.g., Vealey, 1992). To place recent trends in personality research in context, it is important to appreciate the nature of the early research on personality traits and sport.

The trait-oriented research carried out during the 1960s and 1970s was prolific. It dominated sport psychology for well over a decade. The idea that personality is related to sports behaviour has long been intuitively appealing. In the 1960s the pre-eminence of the trait perspective in mainstream psychology, along with this intuition that different types of people will choose and excel in different activities, must have made it almost irresistible as an area of research for psychologists interested in sport. To add to these inducements, it was also a relatively clean and easy mode of research. Sport psychologists could easily access personality questionnaires that allowed for the assessment of a range of traits on the basis of a 15 to 30 minute administration. Sports performers were also, typically, readily accessible, as they tend to congregate in clubs and teams or turn up for competitions in large numbers. Thus, a large amount of data could be collected quickly, but, as Martens (1975) and Morgan (1980a, 1980b) pointed out, the studies were often conceptually and methodologically flawed.

Martens (1975) particularly criticised the tendency for atheoretical research of the "shotgun" type. By this he meant that many studies were not based on hypotheses derived from personality theory, but simply applied a questionnaire to a group(s) of athletes to see what significant results would arise. Then they might attempt to interpret those significant findings in terms of theory, after the fact. Based on this approach, many studies did find significant results, but different variables often proved significant in each study. There was no consistent pattern, especially one that matched, let alone was predicted by, theory. One obvious interpretation of this pattern of results across a large number of studies is that significant findings simply represented chance characteristics of the specific samples in individual studies.

Reviews such as those of Ogilvie (1968), Cooper (1969) and Hardman (1973) proposed different personality characteristics of sports performers. Much of the research employed Cattell's (1965, 1973) Sixteen Personality Factor Questionnaire (16PF). This questionnaire measures 16 personality factors or traits, leading to one of Morgan's (1980b) methodological criticisms. It is always possible that one or two traits will reach statistical significance when each is tested separately, that is, using univariate statistics. Morgan recommends the use of multivariate statistics, which examine the significance of all dependent measures together. He also noted that the 16PF version used in much of the research did not include a response distortion scale, so there is no way of knowing whether subjects gave socially desirable, rather than honest, responses, for example.

Other criticisms of the research, made by Morgan (1980a, 1980b), refer to the operationalisation of dependent and independent variables. Studies often tested intact teams or clubs, where many psychosocial factors, such as geographical proximity, socio-economic status, education, or ethnicity, may have systematically operated to bring those people together. These factors gave that group of subjects, who were considered to represent a sport or sport type in the study, a homogeneity not based solely on their choice of that sport. Failure to check on other sports involvement was another weakness of many studies, which assumed that athletes tested in one sport group were "pure" members of that group. In reality, it is often the case that people play several sports. Sometimes they play one sport as a means of preparing for another. For example, a fast winger in Rugby might well do some sprinting in the summer to keep in shape. Researchers who test this Rugby player during the summer at the athletics club could misclassify him as an individual, non-contact sport player, when his major sport is a team, contact sport. Often, individuals do not have a "major sport" among those in which they participate and they frequently mix quite different activities. Several well-known dual internationals have played Australian Rules football or Rugby in the winter and cricket in the summer, while many high level soccer, Australian Rules football and Rugby players are low handicap golfers.

Most of the weaknesses described above relate to research on personality and sport type, but the research on personality and sports success has also suffered from lack of clarity in its independent variables. Frequently this research has made distinctions between performers, whose level of performance is very similar, determining that some are assigned to the successful or high skill group while others are labelled unsuccessful. The line drawn is often quite arbitrary in skill terms. Also, many of the studies do not include genuine elite performers, that is, international athletes, Olympic and world championship competitors. High skill level often means the best in college or club. Perhaps there are not even many state level players in their samples.

A study by Schurr, Ashley, and Joy (1977) exemplifies some of these problems. It is cited here because it has acquired a place in sport psychology mythology as a model study. Certainly it involved a large sample, 1596 subjects to be exact. They came from a range of sports and were classified into team/individual and direct/parallel categories. The latter refers to the nature of contact, so Australian Rules football and boxing would be direct, while volleyball and badminton would be parallel. Schurr et al. also used multivariate statistics and looked at second order factors derived from the 16PF, as recommended by Morgan (1980a) and Kane (1980). Carron (1980) appears to be the first to commend this study in a textbook chapter. Cox (1994) calls the study "signal research" (p. 37) and Vealey (1992) states that it "illustrates a sound methodological approach" (p. 44).

The subjects in the Schurr et al. (1977) study were all university students, whose age, intellectual ability, education, socio-economic status and home background would not make them typical of the whole population. They were also all males. Schurr et al. distinguished between performance levels in terms of whether the individual was a letter winner or not. This relies on a fine distinction where there may be many unlucky players who just miss out when their skills and competitive performance is effectively indistinguishable from some who achieve letters, because there is a limited number of places available. Subjective judgement is also involved here, with coaches preferring certain styles of player or those that make good team players, perhaps even those with whom they get on best. It is doubtful that a big difference existed between the letter and non-letter winners. In fact, it is likely that performance distributions for these groups would have shown substantial overlap. On this variable, not surprisingly, Schurr et al. did not find any difference in personality.

The allocation of subjects to sports was based on the number of awards that individuals had won in each sport they played, subjects being allocated to the sport in which they had the most awards. Again, this suffers from subjective judgement in some cases; coaches' or team awards for best player may include personal and social factors along with skill. It is also the case that awards are very difficult to come by in some sports, whereas they abound in others. Some sports have many events where awards are on offer. Also, to win an award in most individual sports the player must usually be the best, the winner. A moderate, supporting player in a great team could win lots of medals. In any event, what is to say that the sport gleaning the most awards is the sport of choice for that individual? Consider again the dedicated Rugby winger who sprints to keep fit in the summer. All his efforts may be geared to winning a Rugby pennant, the only award available to his team each season. During the summer he may win a hatful of sprints with a medal for each. Classifying that individual as an athlete on the basis of awards gained is still misleading.

Schurr et al. (1977) actually found clearer distinctions between specific sub-groups of athletes and a group of non-athletes, than between different sport groups. For example, direct sport athletes were more extroverted and independent than non-athletes and parallel sport athletes were less anxious and less independent than non-athletes. This supports the proposition made here that larger inter-group differences, based on the characteristics of the group, are more likely to show any significant personality differences. The definition of "non-athlete" in the Schurr et al. study is also questionable, however. Non-athletes were those who did not participate in intercollegiate sport. Again, many performers may miss out on this at a university with a very strong reputation in that sport, but would comfortably make selection at many other universities. Exceptional players may be committed to play for outside clubs at even higher levels. We also know many average performers who are dedicated to their sport, but will never quite make the grade. Are all these individuals "non-athletes"?

Another statistical problem arises with this study. Accepting that multivariate statistics were correctly used, there was still a large number of comparisons between various athlete groups and between each of them and non-athletes. The number of comparisons may still have been sufficiently large to make probable the occurrence of a few chance significant findings. The Schurr et al. study also appears to have no theoretical base, nor are the results interpreted in terms of theory, even *a posteriori*. Readers should consider the criticisms of research levelled by Morgan (1980a, 1980b) and Martens (1975) and judge the original Schurr et al. (1977) article for themselves.

The absence of a theoretical base is a problem shared with most of the research which has used the 16PF as the measure of personality. Cattell (1965) proposed a very general theoretical framework for personality, which also recognised the role of the environment in shaping behaviour. His fundamental argument that B=f(P,E), that is, behaviour (B) is a function (f) of certain aspects of the person (P) and the environment (E), was not elaborated on, as Cattell felt that it was too early to do this in terms of our understanding of these variables. His handling of the 16 personality factors was purely descriptive.

Other research suffered from the weakness that it employed measures not designed for prediction with normal populations. The Minnesota Multiphasic Personality Inventory (MMPI) was developed in the 1940s to assess some of the personality characteristics that affect adjustment in "persons of disabling psychological abnormality" (Cox, 1994, p. 29). Morgan (1980b) and others criticise its use with normal populations, although it has been claimed that such use is legitimate by the authors in the test manual (Hathaway & McKinley, 1967). Most American research uses either the 16PF or the MMPI. Eysenck and Eysenck (1964, 1975) developed the Eysenck Personality Inventory (EPI) to measure personality types rather than traits. Although there was great debate between Eysenck and Cattell over the years, the personality types of Eysenck were very similar to some of the second order factors derived from Cattell's 16 traits and it appears that the two researchers may have preferred to work at different levels. Eysenck (1970) argued for the principle of parsimony, which states that one should employ the simplest explanation that deals with all the information to hand. He claimed that a small number of types best satisfied this principle. Cattell argued that the richness of the trait approach was needed to appreciate relationships between personality and behaviour. The advantage of the EPI, aside from referring to just two dimensions, extroversion–introversion and neuroticism–stability, was that a clear theoretical base was established by Eysenck (1967, 1970). Both variables were linked to the functioning of the nervous system.

Originally, extroversion–introversion was associated with cortical arousal by Eysenck, while neuroticism–stability was associated with lower levels of brain and nervous function more closely linked with emotionality. Eysenck argued that introverts were characterised by a chronically higher level of functioning of the ascending reticular activating system (ARAS). While this may at first seem the wrong way round, since extroverts appear to be the more aroused in terms of behaviour, the relationship between biological function and behaviour is based upon a homeostasis notion.

Level of arousal in the nervous system seeks a balance; too little arousal is experienced as unpleasant, in terms of lack of stimulation, which may be experienced as boredom, while too much arousal is also unpleasant, as the system is over-excited. Because introverts have a high level of internally generated cortical arousal, they rarely need much more to avoid boredom and often find stimulating environments, such as parties, discos and other very noisy, action-filled situations, raise cortical arousal to subjectively unpleasant levels. Extroverts often crave stimulation to raise their chronically low cortical arousal levels, which are experienced as subjectively unpleasant, toward the homeostatic point. A biological explanation, based on the nervous system, is also proposed for neuroticism–stability, except that a higher level of lability in the autonomic nervous system is proposed to be the reason for the greater emotionality of individuals who score higher on neuroticism.

The sociability, impulsivity and stimulus-hungry nature of extroverts, developed by Eysenck (1970) from the nervous system based theory, leads to some clear predictions for sport. Thus, extroverts are predicted to have a greater preference than introverts for team sports because of the sociability and the greater stimulation afforded by the group. They are also predicted to prefer contact sports as they are more directly stimulating via the body contact and also entail greater risk. Thus, high risk sports would also be their choice more than that of introverts. Neurotic individuals prefer high levels of structure and little threat from the environment because their emotions are easily raised to subjectively unpleasant levels. It is predicted from the theory that they would avoid high risk sports and those involving high contact, as well as very unstructured sporting environments. Closed skills would be preferred to open skills where there is greater environmental uncertainty. Unfortunately, these sorts of predictions have rarely been put to the test in the personality and sport research. This is largely because the predominantly American research has typically not employed Eysenck's theoretical framework. Kane (1980), working in England, did find some significant relationships, using Eysenck's variables but not based on the theory per se. Morgan (1980a), a leading American researcher, has also been inclined towards the Eysenckian level of analysis.

There is another weakness which applies to all the trait approaches, but is perhaps best exemplified using Eysenck's work. It has not been commonly presented in the personality and sport literature, but may be more basic to the practical utility of this approach than any raised so far. Eysenck's research, for example, on personality and learning (e.g., Eysenck, 1964, 1973), typically involved tightly controlled experiments. Subjects for these experiments were selected from a pool of individuals screened using the EPI. Where extroversion–introversion was under scrutiny, the 100 most extrovert and the 100 most introvert of a pool of perhaps 2000 subjects were selected. Significant findings in Eysenck's work were, thus, based on the use of extreme groups and were often not replicated by other researchers who did not have access to Eysenck's rich subject pools.

The crucial point about this approach is that many human characteristics, including personality traits, are presumed to be normally distributed in the population. This means that about two-thirds of the population score within one standard deviation to either side of the mean. When researchers take a random sample (or intended random sample) from the whole population, the vast majority of their subjects are not extreme extroverts or extreme introverts; they are largely individuals who score relatively close to the mean on one side or the other and are probably more like each other than they are like the very few extreme extroverts or extreme introverts included in such studies or in the population. This argument also applies to the other trait variables and is an inherent weakness in this whole approach. It also suggests that the orthodox practice of using statistical tests of significant difference is not likely to be as fruitful as the use of regression analyses, which consider patterns across the breadth of a dimension (Morris, 1984).

The regression approach would be even more amenable to research where the sport variable, as well as the personality variable(s), is dimensional rather than dichotomous. Thus, performance would be an obvious area where it would not be necessary to make the arbitrary and often misleading divisions on the basis of team membership, awards or letters. Instead an actual performance level measure could spread people across a dimension, accepting again that the distribution is likely to approximate the normal, rather than the bimodal, which dichotomies implicitly assume.

To summarise the earlier and most substantial work on personality and sport, the trait approach was frequently used with no theoretical base and studies often demonstrated methodological and statistical flaws. The outcome was that no clear relationships emerged between personality and involvement in sport, preference for specific sports, or performance level. One other point which emerges from the literature is that the research was correlational in nature, despite its frequent use of inferential statistics designed to test for differences. This means that it was not possible to determine cause and effect. Subjects were studied in cross-sectional designs, where their personality and sports behaviour were already determined. Had the research indicated that extroversion and team sport were associated, it would not have been possible to conclude that extroverts chose team sports or that playing in a team increased extroversion.

In fact, Kroll's (1970) attrition hypothesis might be more plausible. This states that individuals across the breadth of personality types initially enter sports, but those not suited to the environment gradually opt out, leaving a more homogeneous group. An interesting line of inquiry, following the attrition idea, may be to investigate the role of the specific subculture of a sport as a mediator of the personality and sport relationship. For example, one reason for the inconsistency of results on extroversion and team sport could be that one can play in a hockey, volleyball or netball team as an introvert by simply turning up, playing one's part and departing after the game. In those team sports where involvement in post-game social rituals is seen to be essential, the introvert, while enjoying the game itself, would soon voluntarily drop out, if he or she were not ostracised because of an apparent unwillingness to accept these subcultural norms. It could, thus, be that there is no difference based on introversion–extroversion in team sports where such sociability based subcultures are not prevalent, but extroverts predominate in sports like Rugby and Australian Rules football where they are. The trait based research of the 1960s and 1970s was not able to demonstrate cause and effect relationships, nor did it reveal any enduring associations between personality and sport.

ISSUES IN PERSONALITY AND SPORT

A number of issues are raised by the research which has examined the relationship between personality and sport. Those which appear to be basic issues are the conception of the nature of personality, the interpretation of the status of research, the standing of alternatives to the pure trait approach, and the implications of current thinking for practical work in sport psychology which involves personality.

NATURE OF PERSONALITY

What is considered to be personality and sport research depends on the conception of personality which is supported. For a number of years, the trait approach *was* personality for many sport psychologists. Martens (1975), in a review up to 1974, recommended that the trait approach be superseded by the interactional approach. Vealey (1989), reviewing 1974 to 1988, found that this had indeed occurred in the intervening years, but of the 55% of the personality and sport literature identified as interactional for the period her review covered, only 20% employed a trait-state approach and 35% adopted a cognitive phenomenological approach. This conclusion depends on the interpretation that cognitive phenomenological approaches are personality. If this research were to be classified as referring to motivation and cognitive processes, then the remaining percentages are 45% for trait research and 20% for trait state interactional research. Accepting that a small proportion of the discarded research was interactional, adopting the narrower conception of this term, this still means that during the period in question about twice as much trait research on personality and sport was being executed as interactional work, a very different conclusion than that reached (Vealey, 1989).

A closer look at the debate about what represents personality is warranted, especially with respect to that work labelled "interactional". Mischel (1968) argued that the trait-state approach is overshadowed by the cognitive approach because the trait-state approach is difficult to validate empirically, despite its conceptualisation being logical. The distinction between traits and states is another important conceptual issue in this debate. Fridhandler (1986) proposed four dimensions which define the distinguishing aspects of trait and state concepts. These are temporal duration, continuous versus reactive manifestation, concreteness versus abstractness and situational versus personal causality. Traits are considered to be enduring over time, but not always active, rather they react to certain situations. They are abstract and must be inferred from behaviour and they emanate from within the person. State constructs are transient or short-lived and are manifested continuously in reaction to relevant situations. States are also directly observable and detectable and they result from situational factors.

Two problems with these definitions arise. First, the distinction between continuous and reactive seems confusing. Traits are proposed to be reactive, yet they are abstract and part of the person. This appears to mean that they are only sometimes part of the person and not there when their abstract nature is not manifest. Making traits reactive also seems to contradict the notion that they are personally caused. Conversely, if states are manifested continuously in reaction to relevant situations, this does not seem to distinguish them from traits which are reactions to situations and presumably there all the time that those situations exist. Again, if states were considered to be situationally caused, then they would not be the result of an interaction between a trait and a situation, but a simple situational response.

An alternative conception might be put that traits are certainly enduring, but they are always present as an aspect of the person. However, they are never manifest, rather they are abstract and inferred from people's behaviour, that is, from the pattern of their transient states. For example, a particular sports performer might **usually** appear very nervous before matches, **frequently** displaying **strong** competitive anxiety state. Because it "usually" happens that this performer is highly state anxious before matches, it can be inferred that the person has a high level of competition trait anxiety. A state in this interpretation would be a subjectively experienced feeling, with behavioural concomitants, which is manifested through the interaction of the level of the enduring trait with a specific situation. This interpretation owes a lot to Spielberger's (1966) distinction between state and trait anxiety. What is considered to be "enduring" is still a matter of judgement. Some writers distinguish between traits and dispositions, the latter being less permanent and unchanging (e.g., Vealey, 1992).

The view that includes cognitive concepts, like self-efficacy, intrinsic motivation and perceived ability, in the discussion of personality appears to base the inclusion largely on the consideration of phenomenological approaches to personality:

> Phenomenological approaches to personality focus on individuals' subjective experience and personal views of the world and self; that is, behavior is seen to be determined by the individual's understanding of self and environment rather than by predetermined or dispositional responses to external events (Vealey, 1992, p. 31).

It is through the subjective processing of internal and external events that phenomenological theories explain one of the basic characteristics of personality, its uniqueness in every individual.

Carver and Scheier (1988) distinguish between two categories of phenomenological approach, one based on striving for actualisation or fulfilment and the other based on the processing of external events and their own behaviour to make sense of the world. The latter is labelled the *cognitive approach to personality*. Within the former, actualisation theories like Rogers' (1961) self theory and Maslow's (1943) hierarchy of needs are prime examples. Also cited in some reviews (e.g., Vealey, 1992) are Deci's (1975, 1980) cognitive evaluation theory of intrinsic motivation and the concept of hardiness (e.g., Kobasa, 1979), which has been labelled a theory (Vealey, 1992). Kelly's (1955) personal construct theory exemplifies the cognitive theories category. Vealey also includes cognitive dissonance (Festinger, 1957) and attribution theory (Heider, 1958, Weiner, 1974, 1985).

It could be argued that these examples are not of the same order. In the actualisation category, the heart of Rogers' (1961) self theory is that the self is not only unique, it is also stable. It is when the individual perceives a lack of congruity between the self and aspects of current behaviour that psychological disturbance occurs. It occurs because the self, being the enduring core of the individual's psychological make-up, does not easily change to accommodate behaviours not "typical" of that individual. The self is capable of change, but it is more likely that behaviour will be brought back into line with the stable perception of self. On the other hand, Deci (1975, 1980) does not invest particular aspects of intrinsic motivation with either stability or uniqueness. Deci is describing processes which apply to all individuals; the factors which are intrinsically motivating vary, but they only explain behaviour toward a specific object or in a specific context, and the research indicates that extrinsic rewards alter intrinsic motivation quite easily (e.g., Deci, 1971, 1972). Similarly, Kelly (1955) considers personal constructs to be developed through each individual's unique experience of the world. They are used to make sense of the world and, thus, determine behaviour. Personal constructs originate through experience of the world, so they are subject to change on the basis of further experience. Kelly does, however, refer to core constructs, which are those that are central to that individual's experience of the world. They have been built up from many experiences, mostly confirming the hypotheses, as Kelly called the emerging constructs, established from previous experience. They are, thus, relatively impervious to change on the basis of specific experiences. Like Rogers (1961), Kelly (1955) proposed that a major source of psychological disturbance occurred when experience threatened core constructs.

Dissonance and attribution theories, conversely, refer to psychological processes experienced by everyone. As with intrinsic motivation, the focus is on the consistency of the process in all people, not the stability of the structure. In dissonance theory, for example, any pair of cognitions or cognition-behaviour pairing can create dissonance. It is the two conflicting elements which lead to the experience of dissonance and everyone is presumed to experience dissonance in such circumstances. The theory does not focus on highly dissonant individuals who are different from those with low dissonance. Dissonance affects us all and it comes and goes. A cognition–cognition dissonance could remain unresolved for a long time. Other such conflicts could be resolved in a moment. The transience of many experiences of dissonance also questions any conception of dissonance as a personality variable.

Another characteristic which can be claimed to be an essential element of theories of personality is that the theory refers to the full range of human behaviour. Psychodynamic, trait and social learning theories attempt to account for all the actions of human beings, as do self theory and personal construct theory. Intrinsic motivation, cognitive dissonance, attribution theory and hardiness are specific to one realm of behaviour, whether it be the role of self-determination and perceived competence in motivating behaviour, the resolution of contradictions between cognitions, the effect of explanations for behaviour on future motivation or the sense of control, commitment and flexibility typical of the style of behaviour Gentry and Kobasa (1979) describe in discussing hardiness. Hardiness is a personality *style*, not a personality *theory*.

To summarise this section, it is proposed that reviews of personality and sport should not include theories and concepts referring to psychological processes that lack either one of these two essentials of personality theories, namely a stable structure and an attempt to explain all aspects of human behaviour. It must be stressed that the presence of such a structure does not imply the absence of change. The major theories of personality, including self theory and personal construct theory, involve dynamic elements, but those elements of change operate in the presence of a relatively enduring core structure. This discussion has moved some distance from the central topic of the chapter, the relationship between personality and sport behaviour, but it is important to debate the nature of personality, in considering the relationship between personality and sport. As reviewed by Cox (1994), most of the research on personality and sport uses trait theory or trait-state theory. Vealey's (1989, 1992) view adds a range of cognitive interactional research. What is considered to represent this field is ultimately a matter for interpretation by the reader. This discussion should focus attention on some relevant issues.

STATUS OF PERSONALITY AND SPORT RESEARCH

In his seminal paper, Morgan (1980a) suggested that there were two perspectives on the personality and sport issue, which he termed the *sceptical* and the *credulous* views. Those who believed that personality and sport were related, that it was possible to predict sports participation, preference and/or performance on the basis of personality characteristics were considered to be credulous. Sport psychologists who proposed that personality characteristics had no role in determining sports behaviour were deemed to be sceptical. Morgan actually adopted a position midway between these extremes. Positions in this credulous–sceptical debate could be considered to represent a dimension rather than a dichotomy, with researchers holding views that could be located at various points between the extremes. Morgan argued that the research up to 1980 revealed little. That was partly because it was methodologically weak. Much of it was also conceptually weak, relying totally on first order traits. The essence of personality may more likely lie in second order factors, so these needed to be considered. In any event, prediction was bound to be limited while little notice was taken of the situational factors. Morgan espoused a trait-state approach and developed a mental health model that operationalised it. This will be considered in the next section.

Two substantial reviews adopt different positions along the credulous–sceptical dimension, even if the extreme positions are no longer tenable (Cox, 1994: Vealey, 1992). Cox presents a review which focuses on the trait and trait-state research. He considers athletes versus non-athletes, sport type, skill level and player position. On the first three standard topics he acknowledges the weight of unconvincing research, but manages at least to leave the door open to further research and on some issues to be even more positive or credulous. In considering the possibility of positional effects, Cox cites his own unpublished study (Cox, 1987) of women's volleyball, where only the attentional style variable of broad attentional focus, presumably measured by the Test of Attentional and Interpersonal Style (TAIS), distinguished setters from other positions, with setters scoring higher on this scale, as would be expected. A study by Schurr, Ruble, Nisbet, and Wallace (1984) on Australian Rules footballers also revealed that linemen were more organised and practical, backs were more flexible and adaptable. No mention is made of Maynard and Howe's (1990) study in Rugby Union, which, like Cox (1987) found that the playmakers, the halfbacks in Rugby, scored higher on broad internal than other players. On the whole then, Cox adopts a position which suggests that despite all the non-significant, contradictory and atheoretical results of research, personality is related to sports behaviour, but that it accounts for a proportion of the variance only.

After what appears to be a more positive review, mainly based on the value of the cognitive interactional approach, Vealey (1992) concludes that:

> No distinguishable "athletic personality" has been shown to exist ... No consistent dispositional personality differences between athletic subgroups ... have been shown to exist ... [Vealey's italics] It is noteworthy that personality differences between successful athletes and less successful athletes have been found in mood states, cognitions and coping abilities, as opposed to more enduring personality traits and dispositions. (p. 50)

This seems to locate Vealey in at least a moderately sceptical position on the dimension. Thus, the conclusions in these two substantial reflections on the area do not seem to match the corresponding reviews too closely. Vealey's (1992) conclusions appear to be focused on the trait approach. They appear to present a more accurate assessment of the research on personality traits and sport than does Cox. The earlier statement from Vealey (see page 11) does point to the trait-state approach as potentially more fruitful. Major work in this field will now be considered.

TRAIT-STATE APPROACHES TO PERSONALITY AND SPORT

Martens' (1975) review of personality and sport research is generally recognised as the most influential single stimulus to the shift from trait to trait-state research and theorising in sport psychology. It followed the critical analyses of Endler (1973) and Bowers (1973) in mainstream psychology and the theoretical and research work of Spielberger (1966) on the specific topic of anxiety. Martens led the way by example, again in the area of anxiety, but specific to sport, with the development of the Sport Competition Anxiety Test (SCAT) (Martens, 1977). He did so once more with his theory of multidimensional state anxiety and the Competitive State Anxiety Inventory-2 (CSAI-2) (Martens, Burton, Vealey, Bump, & Smith, 1983, 1990).

The SCAT is a trait measure, based on Spielberger's (1966) conception that trait anxiety is an anxiety disposition, a proneness to become anxious in a range of situations and to react with large increases in state anxiety. The SCAT measures this disposition specifically in the context of competitive sport.

The CSAI-2 is a measure of state anxiety which is a subjectively unpleasant, transient feeling of tension and apprehension. The CSAI-2 assesses the self-reported anxiety in response to upcoming competition in sport. Martens, Vealey, and Burton (1990) report on the development of these conceptions and the associated measures, as well as the large amount of research which has used them. Although Martens' state-trait approach is the best established example in sport, its authors would not claim that it is a personality theory, as it focuses on one aspect of behaviour, anxiety. It does illustrate what can be achieved with the trait-state approach, but no parallel scheme has been applied successfully to personality. Martens' work is discussed in detail in Chapter 2.

Two trait-state approaches which are considered in the realm of personality are Morgan's (1985) mental health model and Nideffer's (1976, 1981) conception of attentional and interpersonal style. Although Nideffer's work is often closely linked to the personality field, it is also perceived to be part of the field of attention. Cox (1994) locates his chapter on attention immediately after the personality chapter and, while discussing a number of other issues in attention and sport briefly, devotes most of the chapter to Nideffer's theory. Nideffer (1981) argues that the theory of attentional and interpersonal style is an attempt to develop a theoretical perspective which avoids many of the pitfalls of previous research on personality or psychological characteristics. Thus, it is focused on a process, attention, which is seen to be important in many aspects of behaviour. This is then linked to another concept, arousal, which is seen to have a pervasive influence on attention and, hence, behaviour. Thus, attention can be described along a number of dimensions of which breadth and direction are the most important. Combinations of the two dimensions lead to four attentional styles. Each attentional style is seen to be optimal for certain situations in sport, and switching rapidly from one style to another is often important in sports contexts. An increase in level of arousal leads to narrowing of attention, involuntary switching to one's attentional strength and involuntary switching to an internal focus, which is an attentional response to the increased intensity of stimulation from physiological functions.

Nideffer (1981) argues that these attentional styles have trait and state components and different attentional profiles will lead to different patterns of behaviour in a wide range of situations. He also includes interpersonal variables in the theory, proposing that these interact with situations to produce varying levels of arousal, which in turn influence attention and thus performance. For example, a performer high on the interpersonal factor of need for control placed in a football team with an autocratic coach, who maintains total control of the players, will experience a high level of arousal, which will cause a narrowing of attentional focus. This is likely to have a negative effect on performance in a game with so many team mates and opponents to monitor.

Nideffer's (1981) attentional theory is considered in some detail in Chapter 3, so that aspect of the work is not dealt with in depth here. Nideffer (1976) has developed a test, the Test of Attentional and Interpersonal Style (TAIS) to measure the attentional and interpersonal variables. Scores on this test are plotted as a profile which can then be interpreted to understand athletes (Nideffer, 1992). This psychological profiling aspect of the TAIS appears to have been exclusively applied to individual diagnosis. The research examining the TAIS has usually focused on the attentional variables independent of the interpersonal scales. In early work (Nideffer, 1976), it was claimed that the attentional profile or specific scales could distinguish between skill levels. Notwithstanding the reports on personality and position cited earlier (e.g., Cox, 1994; Maynard & Howe, 1990), research has more recently concluded that the original TAIS, which is general in nature, asking questions about everyday behaviour, does not predict skill level as well as sport specific versions such as the tennis TAIS (T-TAIS) (Van Schoyck & Grasha, 1981), the baseball-softball TAIS (B-TAIS) (Albrecht & Feltz, 1987) or the basketball TAIS (BB-TAIS) (Summers, Miller, & Ford, 1991).

The theory and the test of attentional and interpersonal style represent an attempt to address personality and sport from a different perspective and to take account of some of the weaknesses of previous work. The theory has stimulated a substantial amount of research, particularly on attention, but its success as a predictor of behaviour in sport is little greater than that of the personality trait approach. Work in the applied field has used the TAIS and the related theory to somewhat better effect (see Chapter 15).

Probably the most successful recent approach to address the relationship between personality and sport has been developed by Morgan (1985) in his "mental health model" and "iceberg" profile of mood states. This approach does not follow the typical one in the trait-state field of proposing that traits are the underlying personal factors which interact with situations to produce states and the states then directly influence behaviour. Rather, Morgan argues that a number of traits and states together reflect the relative mental health of athletes and those with positive mental health will produce superior performance to those with negative mental health. Morgan employs the second order traits or types of extroversion–introversion and neuroticism–stability from Eysenck's (1970) biological theory and the EPI (Eysenck & Eysenck, 1964), with one other trait, anxiety, as measured by the trait scale from Spielberger's (1966) State-Trait Anxiety Inventory (STAI). Morgan also includes Spielberger's (1966) state anxiety scale from the STAI, as a state measure. He proposes that positive mental health is depicted by high extroversion and low neuroticism, trait and state anxiety. The opposite extremes reflect a negative mental health condition.

To this picture, Morgan adds the Profile of Mood States (POMS) (McNair, Lorr, & Droppleman, 1971). In early studies on athletes with this 65-item clinical scale, the POMS distinguished between successful and less successful performers in elite wrestling (Morgan & Johnson, 1977) and college rowing (Morgan & Johnson, 1978). The POMS has six scales which measure tension, depression, anger, vigour, fatigue and confusion. Relatively unsuccessful performers produced a rather flat profile with all six scales around the mean on the standardised scale, with scores on vigour and fatigue a little higher than the other four scales. The successful group presented very low scores on tension, depression and confusion, lower scores than the other group on anger and fatigue and a very high score on vigour, the tip of the iceberg emerging from the sea of the unsuccessful profile.

Thus, the mental health model is completed by the six mood states with high vigour and low scores on the other five scales indicative of positive mental health and related to successful performance. Silva, Shultz, Haslam, and Murray (1981) were able to classify 80% of elite wrestlers into successful and unsuccessful groups, using the mental health model, while Silva, Shultz, Haslam, Martin, and Murray (1985) successfully classified 78% of Olympic wrestlers. It is not clear whether this percentage would be substantially reduced if the POMS scales were used alone, however.

Although the mental health model is rarely criticised, little has been done with the trait variables in the full model, nor with state anxiety, in combination with the mood state scales. As reviewed in this chapter and in Vealey (1992) and Cox (1994), there is little empirical evidence to support the claims made for the trait variables. Theoretically, also, traits are typically conceived to be normally distributed and it is proposed that the very small percentage of individuals with extreme scores at either end of these scales are those who have difficulty in adapting to the range of situations in life where most of us, with moderate levels of the variable, fit in with little or no discomfort. Thus, the person extremely low on neuroticism would appear to be an incredibly cold fish with little emotion in highly stressful sports situations. The lack of reaction of this individual may be just as dysfunctional as the emotional lability of the extreme neurotic in some competitive circumstances. Similarly, the constant stimulus seeking, impulsive and interpersonal behaviour of an extreme extrovert may prove a major disruption to team mates and lead to a lack of appropriate focus in some sports. Trait anxiety is similar to neuroticism in nature and a parallel argument can be presented.

Considering state anxiety, a low level of state anxiety has long been recognised to be detrimental to performance in power, strength, speed and endurance activities which involve few fine motor skills, such as a 100 metre sprint, weightlifting or the prop forward's role in Rugby (although more ball-handling skill is now demanded of this position). A high level of state anxiety is generally accepted to be disruptive to performance of fine motor skill tasks, such as golf putting, archery, snooker, bowls or shooting (see Chapter 2). These theoretical and empirical points make somewhat unlikely the proposition that extreme scores on any of these variables will reflect positive mental health, adaptability or result in optimal performance across a range of sporting activities.

Further evidence for the capacity of the POMS to differentiate between successful and unsuccessful performers has come from a wide range of studies on elite triathlon competitors (Bell & Howe, 1988), rodeo performers (Meyers, Sterling, & LeUnes, 1988), male and female bodybuilders (Fuchs & Zaichkowsky, 1983), swimmers (Furst & Hardman, 1988; Morgan, Brown, Raglin, O'Connor, & Ellickson, 1987), elite cyclists (Hagberg, Mullin, Bahrke, & Limburg, 1979), elite male distance runners (Morgan, O'Connor, Sparling, & Pate, 1987), elite female distance runners (Morgan, O'Connor, Ellickson, & Bradley, 1988) and many more. It has also been seen in elite wheelchair athletes (Greenwood, Dzewaltowski, & French, 1990; Henschen, Horvat, & French, 1984) and elite visually impaired athletes (Gench, Mastro, & French, 1987, cited in Cox, 1994). It does appear that the iceberg profile is a robust finding in elite performers, provided they are not in very heavy training, when the profile can become very flat, a potential sign of the onset of overtraining (Mackinnon & Hooper, 1992).

An important issue which does not typically merit discussion is whether the POMS measures a relatively enduring aspect of personality or a transient state. The standard instructions ask subjects to assess how they have felt for the past week. Alternative instructions can specify the last two or three days or the last 24 hours. In any event, is it likely that respondents are reporting enduring characteristics? The POMS has also been used in studies which have investigated the effects of an intervention (LeUnes,

Hayward, & Daiss, 1988; Morris & Anderson, 1994), suggesting that scores on the POMS scales are relatively transient or at least malleable. It is suggested that the POMS is not a measure of personality, but is useful in predicting performance level on the basis of mood state.

PRACTICAL ISSUES IN SPORT

A number of issues important to sports performers, coaches and administrators have been the driving force behind much of the work in this field. They are largely still to be resolved. Issues which attract the interest of administrators in mass participation sport, that is, those who are charged with attracting participants to the sport, include whether people with certain psychological profiles are attracted to the sport or continue their participation while others drop out. Were this the case, it would be possible to reduce attrition and increase initiation into the sport by promoting the elements of the sport which attract individuals with that personality or psychological profile.

There are two major practical concerns in elite sport, which sport psychologists have addressed through their study of personality and sport: first, whether it is possible to select those who will perform best on any particular occasion based, at least in part, on personality or psychological profiles; and, second, whether it is possible to use psychological characteristics, perhaps alongside physiological, anthropometric and other factors, to select at an early age those who will be the best in the future, so that they can receive all the benefits of coaching and training to maximise their potential.

The scale of attrition from sport, especially in the teenage years, is a major source of worry to sports organisations. It is not surprising that the thought has occurred to many sports administrators that the ability to determine beforehand, on the basis of tests, who would enjoy the sport and be a long-term participant, would soon substantially reduce the number of people who drop out. Recruiting on the basis of psychological profile would also secure the future, as those recruited would reflect the psychological characteristics considered to be important for that sport. Unfortunately, the research to date has not clearly identified any systematic correspondence between personality and sport choice (Vealey, 1992).

When one has had a long association with a group or squad, selection of the team to play in a particularly important game can often be stressful for all concerned, including the coach. Abdicating responsibility to a sport psychologist would be unacceptable, but perhaps the process would be "sanitised" if the psychologist were to give a small battery of tests and the team was then selected from those performers who responded "appropriately". It may be speculative to impute an unconscious desire among some coaches to hand-ball the ultimate responsibility for selection on to a test battery, which could shoulder the blame in the event of failure, but would not snatch the glory from the grasp of the coach should success result. The desire to use every process at the coach's disposal to maximise the probability of success may be a more palatable motive for the use of psychological tests in selection. There is, however, no consistent evidence that any personality or psychological characteristics profile or set of variables is associated with superior performance (Vealey, 1992), with the possible exception of the POMS, which again reflects state rather than trait factors. Sport psychologists are very wary of the use of tests or other psychological techniques in selection, as none has yet attained the level of prediction on which to base decisions which affect individuals in such important respects.

The idea of using psychological characteristics in talent identification possibly holds the greatest attraction of any application of personality to sport. Selection of those who will be the best has two great benefits. First, it means that scarce resources can be allocated to optimal use. Talent identification is closely associated with talent development and it is the use of limited funds on those who will be the Olympic and world champions of the future, rather than the drop-outs, burn-outs or also-rans, which talent identification might deliver, that appeals to sports administrators. Second, provision of all the resources needed for the development of the future champion, some of which would not be forthcoming in a more dissipated system, would make it more likely that those performers would reach their potential.

The Australian Sports Commission has been running a two-year talent identification program, based on a multidisciplinary perspective. Sport psychological factors have been included in the broad ranging program. At the Australian Psychological Society Annual Conference in 1992 a discussion on talent identification, stimulated by this program, revealed a breadth of opinion among psychologists present. Some believed that certain tests could be used judiciously in this cause. Others felt that no psychological tests presently achieve adequate levels of discrimination. It was generally agreed that there had not been any acceptable longitudinal research on personality and related tests which could form the basis for the identification of talent. A plea was made for such longitudinal research to be executed.

It was not the intent of this section to review the areas of promotion in mass participation sport, selection in elite sport, and talent identification in junior sport. The point to be made here is that these issues are of sufficient import in sport to make it easier to understand some of the motives underlying the persistence of research on personality and sport. The issues are still central in sports administration and will certainly emerge in various guises in future sport psychology research.

FUTURE DIRECTIONS

The needs of the sports are not the only reason why research on psychological characteristics and sport behaviour will continue, even in the light of the unsuccessful research of the past. Many would argue that understanding how personal factors influence the behaviour of people in sport is the essence of sport psychology. It can also be proposed that the absence of consistent, significant patterns in previous research can be attributed to conceptual and methodological weaknesses in the previous work. These weaknesses might include application of inappropriate theoretical perspectives, use of tests which lack sensitivity for differentiating between people in sport, selection of samples without sufficient precision in operationalisation, and failure to employ the most powerful statistics to examine the data.

Vealey (1992) points to some new directions which research might take at a conceptual level. The major area she discusses is investigation of the role of moderator variables, that is, variables which are thought to moderate the influence of personality on behaviour. Trait relevance is an important example of this type of variable. It refers to the idea that certain people may not possess a particular trait. This does not simply mean that they are low scorers on the trait, but that it is not relevant to include their score in an analysis of personality–performance relationships because those people do not possess the trait at all. Including them in the analysis results in the overall level of the relationship being an underestimate. Vealey (1992) refers to the work of Baumeister and Tice (1988) who called the characteristic of having versus not having a particular trait, a *metatrait*. Vealey (1992) also refers to two other variables which are likely to affect the way in which personality and behaviour are related. These are self-schema and self-monitoring. Self-schema are knowledge structures which influence the way people process information about themselves (Markus, 1983). Self-monitoring refers to the degree to which individuals monitor and regulate their behaviour, based on the nature of the situation. Behaviour in any situation would, thus, result from personality characteristics moderated by the way information about oneself is interpreted and the way the situation is monitored.

Another approach suggested by Vealey (1992) is to place the personality–performance relationship in the context of the life-span. People learn to think and behave in different ways during different stages of life (Neugarten, 1977). Personality operates within this life-span framework, so that the same personality trait may not lead to the same behaviour in similar contexts during two different stages of the life-span. Much of the trait research has been conducted with college students, but there is enough which has employed adolescents or adults to introduce some variance on the basis of life-span. A similar argument may be made with respect to elite performers. Their whole way of thinking about sport and life may differ from the way the rest of us think.

The emphasis in research on personality and sport has been on determining the personality variables which predict sports behaviour. Put another way, most of the research has adopted a dichotomous or all-or-none perspective. Such a view may be overly restrictive, trying to force an outcome that is too all-embracing to be found in the multifaceted real world. It may be that a more fruitful approach would be to try to understand what influence various personality variables have on sports behaviour and under what circumstances each variable exerts that influence. This would again argue for the use of statistics which reveal patterns or commonalities, rather than significant differences. Standard correlational methods may also be too crude for this type of perspective. Newer approaches such as discriminant function analysis and structural equation modelling may be more appropriate for this type of research.

The field of research which has considered relationships between personality and sport has been dominated by the cross-sectional approach to studying behaviour. Greater understanding of many aspects of this field may be forthcoming from a longitudinal approach, which follows the same individuals over a long period of time. This research method demands much patience and a research program capable of living up to a commitment to follow the subjects for several years. While this does not appeal to many researchers in the present "publish or perish" ethos of academe, it would undoubtedly throw light on issues which cross-sectional research does not easily examine. For many of the practical problems discussed, especially that of talent identification, the longitudinal research approach is essential.

This section may appear to contradict much that goes before it. The review and analysis of the personality and sport field was rather gloomy in outlook. The proposals for future research adopt a more positive position. This is not so much of a contradiction. We have learned a lot from the research on personality and sport, particularly that a simple one-factor solution is inadequate to account for a complex problem in human behaviour. The suggestions presented in this section all propose looking at the issue in a multifaceted way, where personality variables are recognised to operate in concert with other factors. Adopting this approach may throw further light on the relationship between personality and sport.

CONCLUSIONS

This chapter has reflected on the extensive research tradition in the field of personality and sport, raising some issues for consideration and searching for some new directions for research based on our experience of nearly 30 years of endeavour. It is concluded that the attempt to explain sports behaviour on the basis of traits alone has devoured vast amounts of research energy for little in the way of outcomes. It should be used as a means of understanding what researchers should not do in future. The trait-state approach appears to have been more fruitful in developing the area of anxiety; but this has not been extended to a consideration of other aspects of personality in terms of an abstract, underlying trait, representing proneness to a particular style of thought and behaviour, which interacts with the situation to generate a state — that subjectively experienced, transient level of the variable at any moment in time.

Isn't this picture consistent with experience? A basically kind person (trait) will occasionally be a little unkind and very occasionally cruel (manifestations of the state). Similarly, a trustworthy person (trait) will be unreliable under some circumstances (state). It appears that the state provides the sensitivity, measuring the level of a personal characteristic at the time when behaviour is being predicted from it. The trait measures a proneness to think and behave in a particular manner or the average of a large number of measurements of that state, which may or may not correspond to the actual state at the moment of a specific performance. The levels of prediction to be expected when the trait is used as a measure of the characteristic should be anticipated to be variable, at best. Aside from the work in anxiety, only Vealey (1986), in her research on self-confidence, has attempted to develop a state-trait perspective. Her conceptualisation and the measures which operationalise it appear to have received less than their deserved attention from researchers. It would be interesting to see other trait-state approaches in this field and it is certainly premature to write off this approach.

Other directions in personality and sport research seem to hold some promise for exploration. These include the life-span approach and the investigation of moderator variables like trait relevance, self-schema and self-monitoring, as well as use of the longitudinal research paradigm. These views highlight the point that it is unrealistic to expect something as complex as human behaviour in the vast array of sport contexts to be explained purely by personality variables. If there is a role for personality it is surely in interaction with other processes and factors, perhaps only in certain contexts and only explaining a proportion of the variance in performance at best. More sophisticated models are needed, which include personality among the antecedents of sport behaviour. These models should be examined by the application of advanced statistical techniques which seek patterns not obvious to crude levels of analysis.

Perhaps there is still some life in the personality and sport behaviour research field. After all the research that failed to reveal any consistent patterns and the reviews which have warned students off the area, the question may be whether everyone will be too wary of producing yet another inconclusive study to initiate research in this field. It is to be hoped that fresh minds and new ideas will prevail. Even if no definitive answers are produced, knowledge is increased and practice may be enhanced.

SUMMARY

This chapter has adopted a critical approach to the field of personality or psychological characteristics and sports behaviour. It commented on some of the weaknesses of early research, as cited by Martens (1975) and Morgan (1980a), including theoretical, conceptual and methodological problems, adding one or two to the list. The chapter then considered a number of issues in personality research related to sport. Among these were lack of clarity of definition of the personality concept, as well as the trait, state and interactional concepts, and some uncertainty about the use of particular phenomenological concepts in the realm of personality.

The chapter looked at the credulous–sceptical argument, especially in terms of major reviews in the 1990s. Examples of some widely used trait-state approaches were then discussed. These included state and trait anxiety, attentional style and the iceberg profile of the POMS.

Finally, the chapter briefly considered some issues of import to sports administrators and coaches, these being promotion of the sport to those inclined to participate over the long term, use of personality profiles for selection purposes and talent identification. The chapter concluded with a number of future directions, including the study of moderator variables, the promotion of life-span and longitudinal research approaches, and the need for research to look at more sophisticated, multifaceted theories and models.

REFERENCES

Albrecht, R. R., & Feltz, D. L. (1987). Generality and specificity of attention related to competitive anxiety and sport performance. *Journal of Sport Psychology, 9*, 231–248.

Baumeister, R. F., & Tice, D. M. (1988). Metatraits. *Journal of Personality, 56*, 571–598.

Bell, G. J., & Howe, B. L. (1988). Mood state profiles and motivations of triathletes. *Journal of Sport Behavior, 11*, 66–77.

Bowers, K. S. (1973). Situationism in psychology: An analysis and a critique. *Psychological Review, 80*, 307–336.

Carron, A. V. (1980). *Social psychology of sport.* Ithaca, NY: Mouvement Publications.

Carver, C. S., & Scheier, M. F. (1988). *Perspectives on personality.* Boston: Allyn & Bacon.

Cattell, R. B. (1965). *The scientific analysis of personality.* Baltimore: Penguin.

Cattell, R. B. (1973, July). Personality pinned down. *Psychology Today*, pp. 40–46.

Cooper, L. (1969). Athletics, activity, and personality: A review of the literature. *Research Quarterly, 40*, 17–22.

Cox, R. H. (1987). Relationship between psychological variables with player position and experience in women's volleyball. Unpublished manuscript.

Cox, R. H. (1994). *Sport psychology: Concepts and applications* (3rd ed.). Dubuque, IA: Wm Brown & Benchmark.

Deci, E. L. (1971). Effects of externally mediated rewards on intrinsic motivation. *Journal of Personality and Social Psychology, 18*, 105–115.

Deci, E. L. (1972). Intrinsic motivation, extrinsic reinforcement. *Journal of Personality and Social Psychology, 22*, 113–120.

Deci, E. L. (1975). *Intrinsic motivation.* New York: Plenum.

Deci, E. L. (1980). *The psychology of self-determination.* Lexington, MA: D. C. Heath.

Endler, N. S. (1973). The person versus the situation — A pseudo issue? A response to Alker. *Journal of Personality, 41*, 287–303.

Eysenck, H. J. (1964). Personality and reminiscence — an experimental study of the "reactive inhibition" and the "conditioned inhibition" theories. *Life Sciences, 3*, 189–198.

Eysenck, H. J. (1967). *The biological basis of personality.* Springfield, IL: Thomas.

Eysenck, H. J. (1970). *The structure of human personality* (3rd ed.). London: Methuen.

Eysenck, H. J. (1973). Personality and learning. *Studia Psychologica, 15*, 93–106.

Eysenck, H. J., & Eysenck, S. B. G. (1964). *Eysenck Personality Inventory manual.* London: University of London Press.

Eysenck, H. J., & Eysenck, S. B. G. (1975). *Eysenck Personality Inventory manual.* London: Hodder & Stoughton.

Festinger, L. A. (1957). *A theory of cognitive dissonance.* New York: Harper & Row.

Fisher, A. C. (1984). New directions in sport personality research. In J. M. Silva & R. S. Weinberg (Eds.), *Psychological foundations of sport* (pp. 70–80). Champaign, IL: Human Kinetics.

Fridhandler, B. M. (1986). Conceptual note on state, trait, and the state-trait distinction. *Journal of Personality and Social Psychology, 50,* 169–174.

Fuchs, C. Z., & Zaichkowsky, L. D. (1983). Psychological characteristics of male and female bodybuilders: The iceberg profile. *Journal of Sport Behavior, 6,* 136–145.

Furst, D. M., & Hardman, J. S. (1988). The iceberg profile and young competitive swimmers. *Perceptual and Motor Skills, 67,* 478.

Gentry, W. D., & Kobasa, S. C. (1979). Social and psychological resources mediating stress illness relationships in humans. In R. B. Haynes, D. W. Taylor, & D. Sackett (Eds.), *Compliance in health care* (pp. 87–116). Baltimore: Johns Hopkins University Press.

Greenwood, C. M., Dzewaltowski, D. A., & French, R. (1990). Self-efficacy and psychological wellbeing of wheelchair tennis participants. *Adapted Physical Activity Quarterly, 7,* 12–21.

Hagberg, J., Mullin, J., Bahrke, M., & Limburg, J. (1979). Physiological profiles and selected physiological characteristics of national class American cyclists. *Journal of Applied Medicine, 19,* 341–346.

Hardman, K. (1973). A dual approach to the study of personality and performance in sport. In H. T. A. Whiting, K. Hardman, L. B. Hendry, & M. G. Jones (Eds.), *Personality and performance in physical education and sport.* London: Kimpton.

Hathaway, S. R., & McKinley, J. C. (1967). *Minnesota Multiphasic Personality Inventory manual.* New York: Psychological Corporation.

Heider, F. (1958). *The psychology of interpersonal relations.* New York: John Wiley & Sons.

Henschen, K., Horvat, M., & French, R. (1984). A visual comparison of psychological profiles between able-bodied and wheelchair athletes. *Adapted Physical Activity Quarterly, 1,* 118–124.

Kane, J. E. (1980). Personality research: The current controversy and implications for sport studies. In W. F. Straub (Ed.), *Sport psychology: An analysis of athlete behavior* (pp. 330–339). Ithaca, NY: Mouvement.

Kelly, G. (1955). *The psychology of personal constructs.* New York: Norton.

Kobasa, S. C. (1979). Stressful life events, personality and health: An inquiry into hardiness. *Journal of Personality and Social Psychology, 37,* 1–11.

Kroll, W. (1970). Current strategies and problems in personality assessment in athletes. In L. E. Smith (Ed.), *Psychology of motor learning.* Chicago: The Athletic Institute.

LeUnes, A., Hayward, S. A., & Daiss, S. (1988). Annotated bibliography on the Profile of Mood States in sport. *Journal of Sport Behavior, 11,* 213–240.

Mackinnon, L. T., & Hooper, S. (1992). Overtraining: State of the art review No. 26. *Excel, 8,* 3–12.

Markus, H. (1983). Self-knowledge: An expanded view. *Journal of Personality, 51,* 543–565.

Martens, R. (1975). The paradigmatic crisis in American sport personology. *Sportwissenschaft, 1,* 9–24.

Martens, R. (1977). *Sport competition anxiety test.* Champaign, IL: Human Kinetics.

Martens, R., Burton, D., Vealey, R. S., Bump, L. A., & Smith, D. E. (1983). *Competitive State Anxiety Inventory–2.* Unpublished manuscript. University of Illinois at Urbana-Champaign.

Martens, R., Burton, D., Vealey, R. S., Bump, L. A., & Smith, D. E. (1990). Development of the Competitive State Anxiety Inventory–2. In R. Martens, R. S. Vealey, & D. Burton (Eds.), *Competitive anxiety in sport* (pp. 117–190). Champaign, IL: Human Kinetics.

Martens, R., Vealey, R. S., & Burton, D. (Eds.). (1990). *Competitive anxiety in sport.* Champaign, IL: Human Kinetics.

Maslow, A. H. (1943). *Toward a psychology of being.* Princeton, NJ: Van Nostrand.

Maynard, I. W., & Cotton, P. C. J. (1993). An investigation of two stress management techniques in a field setting. *The Sport Psychologist, 7* (4), 375–387.

Maynard, I. W., & Howe, B. L. (1990). Attentional styles in rugby players. *Perceptual and Motor Skills, 69,* 283–289.

McNair, D. M., Lorr, M., & Droppleman, L. F. (1971). *Profile of Mood States manual.* San Diego, CA: Educational and Industrial Testing Service.

Meyers, M. C., Sterling, J. C., & LeUnes, A. D. (1988). Psychological characterization of the collegiate Rodeo Athlete. *Journal of Sport Behavior, 11,* 59-65.

Mischel, W. (1968). *Personality and assessment.* New York: John Wiley & Sons.

Morgan, W. P. (1980a). Sport personology: The credulous–skeptical argument in perspective. In W. F. Straub (Ed.), *Sport psychology: An analysis of athlete behavior* (pp. 330–339). Ithaca, NY: Mouvement.

Morgan, W. P. (1980b). The trait psychology controversy. *Research Quarterly for Exercise and Sport, 51,* 50–76.

Morgan, W. P. (1985). Affective benificence of vigorous physical activity. *Medicine and Science in Sports and Exercise, 17,* 94–100.

Morgan, W. P., Brown, D. R., Raglin, J. S., O'Connor, P. J., & Ellickson, K. A. (1987). Psychological monitoring of overtraining and staleness. *British Journal of Sports Medicine, 21,* 107–114.

Morgan, W. P., & Johnson, R. W. (1977). Psychological characterizations of the elite wrestler: A mental health model. *Medicine and Science in Sports, 9,* 55–56.

Morgan, W. P., & Johnson, R. W. (1978). Psychological characteristics of successful and unsuccessful oarsmen. *International Journal of Sport Psychology, 11,* 38–49.

Morgan, W. P., O'Connor, P. J., Ellickson, K. A., & Bradley, P. W. (1988). Personality structure, mood states, and performance in elite male distance runners. *International Journal of Sport Psychology, 19,* 247–263.

Morgan, W. P., O'Connor, P. J., Sparling, P. B., & Pate, R. R. (1987). Psychological characterization of the elite female distance runner. *International Journal of Sports Medicine, 8,* 124–131.

Morris, T. (1984). *A study of some personality factors in relation to computer based learning.* Unpublished doctoral thesis. University of Leeds.

Morris, T., & Anderson, D. (1994, September). *Career education, perceived performance and mood state in elite athletes.* Paper presented at the Australian Psychological Society Annual Conference, Wollongong.

Neugarten, B. (1977). Personality and aging. In J. E. Birren & K. W. Schaie (Eds.), *Handbook of the psychology of aging* (pp. 626–649). New York: Van Nostrand.

Nideffer, R. M. (1976). Test of attentional and interpersonal style. *Journal of Personality and Social Psychology, 34,* 394–404.

Nideffer, R. M. (1981). *The ethics and practice of applied sport psychology.* Ithaca, NY: Mouvement Publications.

Nideffer, R. S. (1992, December). *Australian Institute of Sport consultants' workshop.* Australian Institute of Sport, Canberra.

Ogilvie, B. C. (1968). Psychological consistencies within the personality of high-level competitors. *Journal of the American Medical Association, 205,* 780–786.

Rogers, C. R. (1961). *On becoming a person.* Boston: Houghton Mifflin.

Ruffer, W. A. (1975). Personality traits in athletes. *Physical Educator, 32,* 105–109.

Ruffer, W. A. (1976a). Personality traits in athletes. *Physical Educator, 33,* 50–55.

Ruffer, W. A. (1976b). Personality traits in athletes. *Physical Educator, 32,* 211–214.

Schurr, K. T., Ashley, M. A., & Joy, K. L. (1977). A multivariate analysis of male athlete characteristics: Sport type and success. *Multivariate Experimental Clinical Research, 3,* 53–68.

Schurr, K.T., Ruble, V. E., Nisbet, J., & Wallace, D. (1984). Myers-Briggs Type Inventory characteristics of more and less successful players on an American football team. *Journal of Sport Behavior, 7,* 47–57.

Silva, J. M., III, Shultz, B. B., Haslam, R. W., Martin, T. P., & Murray, D. (1985). Discriminating characteristics of contestants at the United States Olympic wrestling trials. *International Journal of Sport Psychology, 16,* 79–102.

Silva, J. M., III, Shultz, B. B., Haslam, R. W., & Murray, D. (1981). A psychological assessment of elite wrestlers. *Research Quarterly for Exercise and Sport, 52,* 348–358.

Spielberger, C. D. (1966). *Anxiety and behavior.* New York: Academic.

Summers, J. J., Miller, K., & Ford, S. (1991). Attentional style and basketball performance. *Journal of Sport and Exercise Psychology, 13,* 239–253.

Van Schoyck, S. R., & Grasha, A. F. (1981). Attentional style variations and athletic ability: The advantages of the sports specific test. *Journal of Sport Psychology, 3,* 149–165.

Vealey, R. S. (1986). Conceptualization of sport confidence and competitive orientation: Preliminary investigation and instrument development. *Journal of Sport Psychology, 8,* 221–246.

Vealey, R. S. (1989). Sport personology: A paradigmatic and methodological analysis. *Journal of Sport and Exercise Psychology, 11,* 216–235.

Vealey, R. S. (1992). Personality and sport: A comprehensive view. In T. S. Horn (Ed.), *Advances in sport psychology* (pp. 25–59). Champaign, IL: Human Kinetics.

Weiner, B. (1974). *Achievement motivation and attribution theory.* Morristown, NJ: General Learning.

Weiner, B. (1985). An attributional theory of achievement motivation and emotion. *Psychological Review, 92,* 548–573.

C H A P T E R

2

ANXIETY

MARK H. ANSHEL

Virtually all skilled competitive athletes enter the contest with some degree of concern about their performance success, often in relation to their opponent. As Canadian sport psychologist Terry Orlick (1986) reports, "when an athlete's performance suffers in an important event, it is often a result of too much worry about outcome... the winning focus is likely to heighten anxiety and interfere with proper skill execution in virtually all sports" (p. 12). Orlick is describing the emotion of worry, a feeling of concern and perceived threat about the outcome of some future event, in this case, about the results of participating in competitive sport. What are the sources of worry? We know that athletes are concerned about the quality of their performance, but why? What are the factors that contribute to this worry, and what can be done about it? Researchers have determined that a primary source of worry among athletes is anxiety.

Martens, Vealey, and Burton (1990) raise relevant questions about the study of anxiety in sport. For example, "What causes athletes to become uptight? Why do some athletes rise to the occasion in intense competition while others choke under pressure? What are the short- and long-term effects of competitive stress? How does competitive anxiety affect the performance of the athlete? Can athletes learn to control their emotional states, and will this help them optimise their performance? What can be done to alleviate hyperanxious states? What can be done to prevent athletes from burning out as a result of the tremendous psychological stress from intense competition over extended periods of time"? (p. 4).

The importance of mental skills has been well recognised in the sport psychology literature. For example, in her survey of psychological skills training in the sport psychology literature, Vealey (1988) found that 93% of the authors addressed the area of physical relaxation and thought control. The area of arousal and anxiety control was discussed by 70% of the writers. In particular, researchers have attempted to identify the sources of unpleasant emotions such as stress, anxiety, and fear so that appropriate cognitive and behavioural strategies can be used to reduce their occurrence and intensity. It is thought that identifying the factors contributing to unpleasant thoughts can reduce the athlete's undesirable psychological and physical reactions to them. The answer to these questions is in the proper use of mental skills, discussed later in this chapter. Before these issues can be addressed it is necessary to define the concept of *anxiety*.

DEFINITIONS OF TERMS

The *Dictionary of the Sport and Exercise Sciences* (Anshel, Freedson, Hamill, Haywood, Horvat, & Plowman, 1991) defines anxiety as a "subjective feeling of apprehension or perceived threat, sometimes accompanied by heightened physiological arousal" (p. 9). This definition indicates two characteristics of anxiety. First, it is a psychological process. Although anxiety may be manifested by somatic responses such as heightened heart rate, raised blood pressure, or sweating, feelings of anxiety are derived from the mind. The second characteristic is that anxiety is an unpleasant feeling. As Eysenck (1992) notes, "Anxiety is an unpleasant and aversive state... The key purpose or function of anxiety is probably to facilitate the detection of danger or threat in potentially threatening environments" (p. 4). Thus, feeling anxious may be a necessary part of life, but no-one would ever call it desirable. Despite the relative clarity with which anxiety is defined, it is a construct that has been applied in various ways in the sport psychology literature.

For example, the terms *anxiety* and *arousal* have been used interchangeably by writers, both in the media and the scientific literature. Iso-Ahola and Hatfield (1986), for example, use the term "anxiety" in virtually the same context as Bird and Cripe (1986) apply the term "arousal". However, in more recent years, writers and researchers in sport psychology have recognised that anxiety and arousal are not synonymous. They are measured differently and, in fact, require different techniques to regulate them (Gould & Krane, 1992).

Perhaps one primary cause of using arousal with anxiety interchangeably is that both have been identified from somatic and cognitive measures. Traditionally, arousal has been interpreted and measured strictly as a physiological process on a continuum ranging from sleep to high excitation (Weinberg, 1989). Even in current literature, arousal is often determined by changes in heart and respiration rate, extent of sweating, and other physiological measures. However, Oxendine (1970) and Anshel (1985) have measured emotional aspects of arousal, including positive feelings (e.g., excitement, happiness) and negative feelings (e.g., fear, embarrassment, and depression). Such emotions may or may not correlate highly with physiological responses (Hackfort & Schwenk-mezger, 1989, 1993).

As indicated earlier, anxiety has also been measured based on somatic and cognitive responses. Iso-Ahola and Hatfield (1986, pp. 193–194) take a "multidimensional view of anxiety", asserting that it has "both a physiological and a psychological basis". More recent attempts at measuring state anxiety in sport have incorporated cognitive and somatic components (Hackfort & Schwenkmezger, 1993). Cognitive anxiety consists of negative concerns about performance and other unpleasant feelings, whereas somatic anxiety includes symptoms of autonomic reactions such as stomach upset, sweating, and increased heart rate (Mahoney & Meyers, 1989). At least one research study supports the independent nature of cognitive and somatic anxiety. For example, Anshel, Brown, and Brown (1993) examined the effectiveness of coping strategies on subjects' dart-throwing performance, emotions, and muscular tension immediately after receiving critical verbal feedback. Whereas the intervention strategies resulted in significantly better performance and fewer unpleasant feelings (i.e., reduced cognitive anxiety), muscle tension, as measured by electromyography (somatic anxiety), was uninfluenced by the strategies.

Gould and Krane (1992) contend that "anxiety can be considered the emotional impact or cognitive dimension of arousal" (p. 121). Borkovec (1976) argues that arousal is best measured by the interactions of physiological, cognitive, and behavioural response components. Thus, a review of related literature reveals that arousal and anxiety are multidimensional processes. Both arousal and anxiety contain psychological and physiological properties and manifestations. However, it is also apparent that, based on traditional measures and current definitions, arousal is essentially a physiological response, and that anxiety is primarily a cognitive process. Readers are referred to Chapter 11 for a discussion of stress, another concept often confused with anxiety.

TRAIT AND STATE ANXIETY

Scholars draw a distinction between two types of anxiety, trait and state. Trait anxiety is a personality dimension, whereas state anxiety is "characterised by subjective, consciously perceived feelings of tension and apprehension, and heightened autonomic nervous system activity" (Spielberger, Gorsuch, & Lushene, 1970, p. 3). The *Dictionary of the Sport and Exercise Sciences* (Anshel et al., 1991) defines state anxiety as "an immediate emotional experience that is characterised by apprehension, fear, and tension, and sometimes accompanied by physiological arousal" (p. 145). The dictionary's second definition of state anxiety is the "state of arousal engendered by a stressful or threatening situation" (p. 145). State anxiety, then, reflects both psychological and physiological processes. Trait anxiety, on the other hand, is the "relatively permanent personality predisposition to perceive certain environmental situations as threatening or stressful, and the tendency to respond to these situations with increased state anxiety" (p. 154).

In his review of related literature, Eysenck (1992) asserts that "the state-trait distinction relates mainly to temporal duration: States typically last for relatively short periods of time, whereas traits remain essentially unchanged for considerably longer" (p. 38). Trait anxiety is viewed as a property of an individual that is inferred from predictable responses in the appropriate circumstances. State anxiety, on the other hand, reflects a single event occurrence (Fridhandler, 1986).

MEASUREMENT OF ANXIETY IN SPORT

The multidimensional nature of anxiety requires distinguishing its measurement cognitively, physiologically and behaviourally. Although anxiety is primarily a manifestation of psychological processes such as cognitive appraisal and expectancies (Smith, Smoll, & Schutz, 1990), researchers have also recognised the importance of somatic anxiety in affecting sport performance. The importance of separating cognitive and somatic anxiety is predicated on three lines of evidence.

First, researchers have shown that cognitive and somatic anxiety may be a function of different antecedents. In other words, the factors that precede each type of anxiety may differ. For example, Smith et al. (1990) report that a performer's expectations in evaluative situations and performance evaluation are more related to cognitive anxiety than with somatic anxiety. However, threat of an unpleasant stimulus impacts more on somatic than cognitive anxiety.

Second, cognitive and somatic anxiety influence performance differently. For example, only cognitive anxiety negatively affects performance on purely cognitive tasks such as reading or problem solving. Somatic anxiety, on the other hand, has a more negative effect on refined motor tasks as compared to cognitive anxiety.

The third factor that influences the manner in which anxiety is measured concerns its treatment. Somatic anxiety should respond best to treatments that include reducing physiological arousal (e.g., relaxation, biofeedback). Cognitive anxiety, on the other hand, may work best with cognitively-based strategies (e.g., self-talk, thought-stopping). Chapter 11 includes further discussion of stress management techniques. Still, some disagreement exists among the results of studies examining the link between the type of anxiety and the effectiveness of its treatment (Hackfort & Schwenkmezger, 1993). It is also important to recognise that, in addition to cognitive and somatic features, anxiety also has behavioural manifestations that will be discussed later in this chapter.

COGNITIVE MEASURES

Measuring anxiety in this manner is usually accomplished with a standardised paper-and-pencil questionnaire. Several have been published (see Anshel, 1987, for a list of these surveys). Traditionally, relatively few anxiety inventories were created for sport situations. For example, Taylor's (1953) Manifest Anxiety Scale (MAS) is used to ascertain chronic (trait) anxiety. However, it does not adequately predict differences between high- and low-anxious persons with respect to learning and performing sports skills (Martens, 1971). A more precise measure of A-trait and A-state is the State-Trait Anxiety Inventory (STAI) (Spielberger et al., 1970). It has been used less often in more recent sport psychology literature than in the 1970s and 1980s because the STAI was not developed for, and does not ask the respondent about, their thoughts and feelings in sport situations. Researchers now use newer inventories developed specifically for sport.

To date, two inventories, the Competitive State Anxiety Inventory–2 (CSAI–2) by Martens et al. (1990) and the Sport Anxiety Scale (SAS) by Smith et al. (1990), measure A-state in sport situations. The CSAI–2 and SAS measure two forms of anxiety, cognitive and somatic. Another measure of anxiety, the Sport Competition Anxiety Test (SCAT) (Martens, 1977), also ascertains the athlete's somatic anxiety. However, Smith et al. (1990) contend that SCAT "is primarily a measure of somatic anxiety and not an adequate measure of the cognitive dimensions of sport-specific anxiety" (p. 277).

Trait anxiety in sport, a measure of the athlete's disposition for feeling anxious in competitive situations, has typically been measured by SCAT. Upon reading the SCAT's questions, its use as a measure of trait, not state, anxiety is apparent. Questions such as "Before I compete I am calm", or "I get nervous wanting to start the game", reflect the athlete's tendencies in similar types of sport situations, and do not reflect "right now" (i.e., the athlete's current state) answers. Martens (1977) and Martens et al. (1990) point out that most measures of A-trait predict heightened anxiety only in specific types of stressful situations (e.g., a school classroom rather than a sport situation). This means that a person might have a disposition to feel anxious before school exams but not necessarily in sport-related situations — or vice versa. Yet, the person's subjective feelings about how he or she views the competitive situation is the single most important issue in measuring and in experiencing anxiety.

PHYSIOLOGICAL MEASURES

Anxiety is not usually measured physiologically for several reasons. First, there is no single physiological response to the anxiety state (Sonstroem,

1984). Second, anxiety is typically viewed as a feeling — an individual's interpretation, or appraisal, of a situation. The individual's somatic response (e.g., heart rate, blood pressure) to appraisals of joy may be similar to appraisals of threat or sadness. As Hackfort and Schwenkmezger (1989) point out, "... an increase in heart rate can occur both in the context of the emotion anxiety and in reactions of joy or anger" (p. 59). Third, the relationship between any two measures that are typical physiological measures of anxiety (heart rate and palm sweating, for instance) is quite low, about .10 (Hackfort & Schwenkmezger, 1989). This means that one measure can predict the other measure only about 1% of the time. Fourth, the nervous system response to anxiety differs among individuals. While some persons sweat profusely when nervous, others do not sweat at all.

The final argument against using physiological measures of anxiety is the attempt by scientists to separate emotional from physiological responses to stress (Hackfort & Schwenkmezger, 1993). An individual may experience feelings of stress without experiencing the harmful physiological effects often associated with stress. This is important because an athlete, sport psychologist, or coach may incorrectly assume the athlete is anxious if the conclusion is based on the performer's heart rate rather than on the person's self-reported feelings. Further, the techniques for reducing somatic anxiety (e.g., progressive relaxation or physical activity) and cognitive anxiety (e.g., positive self-talk) often differ.

BEHAVIOURAL MEASURES

Altering a person's emotions need not require the systematic use of mental techniques. For many individuals, anxiety reduction is best handled by engaging in a physical activity. Perhaps the most common — and studied — behavioural technique for reducing anxiety is exercise. In their summary of studies in this area, Folkins and Sime (1981) concluded "the research suggests that physical fitness training leads to improved mood, self-concept, and work behavior" (p. 373). It is important to note, however, that most of the reviewed studies have examined chronically anxious patients in clinical settings rather than athletes. This makes the application of these findings for athletes relatively tenuous. However, Berger and McInman's (1993) more recent review of literature indicates that exercise markedly improves quality of life. Studies indicate that psychological benefits from exercise are more related to aerobic work than other forms of exercise. For example, in addition to lowering acute anxiety, individuals with higher aerobic fitness appear to cope better with stress than aerobically unfit subjects (Fillingim & Blumenthal, 1993). Thus, it appears that exercise does reduce the onset of unpleasant emotions, improve the quality of life, and reduce — perhaps even prevent — state anxiety.

Hackfort and Schwenkmezger (1993), Berger and McInman (1993), and Fillingim and Blumenthal (1993) offer guidelines for using behavioural techniques — physical activity — for coping with stress and anxiety. First, it is important that athletes *enjoy* the activity in which they engage. If an athlete dislikes running, for example, then a running program will not be in his or her best interests. Engaging in an undesirable activity not only leads to dropping out, but may actually increase rather than reduce undesirable feelings. The athlete may prefer weightlifting, yoga, or some other form of activity. The second factor, related to the first, is that the person feels *successful* at the activity. One way to ensure success is to reduce or eliminate the competitive feature of the activity. Behavioural anxiety management should be free of inherent forms of stress such as competition and evaluation by an external source. If the person enjoys competition, then it is important that he or she not equate unsuccessful performance outcomes with low competence. If individuals are concerned about performance quality, then they are replacing one source of anxiety with another source of anxiety.

A third factor is that the activity serves to *distract* the individual from unpleasant thoughts. For example, one reason exercise may benefit psychological well-being is because it distracts the person from other, less pleasant thoughts (Berger & McInman, 1993). Some activities may have a better thought-distracting function than others. One type of activity that meets all of these criteria is aerobic dance, or exercising to music. Anshel and Reeves (1992), based on empirical evidence, contend that exercising to music promotes adherence to the exercise program, meets social needs, and enhances enjoyment from participation, in addition to markedly improving the individual's aerobic fitness. However, Berger and McInman (1993) suggest that most forms of exercise (e.g., recreational swimming, walking) decrease undesirable mood states. See Chapter 11 for a more extensive discussion of this area.

ANTECEDENTS OF STATE ANXIETY IN SPORT: PERSONAL AND SITUATIONAL FACTORS

Identifying the causes of state anxiety leads to the factors that precede and predict it. One cause of state anxiety in sport situations is the extent of a person's trait anxiety. Individuals high in A-trait are more vulnerable to A-state because they possess less adequate coping strategies than persons low in A-trait (Eysenck, 1992). This has two implications for controlling A-state in sport. First, the athlete's level of A-trait must be identified. Only then will the person's susceptibility to A-state be known. Second, it is important that athletes be taught cognitive and behavioural strategies for coping with A-state. The athlete's susceptibility to anxiety, that is, their A-trait level, will often determine the type (i.e., mental or physical) and timing (i.e., pre-game or game) of strategies used. In one non-sport study, Endler and Parker (1990) found that the selection of coping strategies differed between high trait anxious and low trait anxious subjects.

Highly anxious individuals tended to cope with stressful situations in a relatively passive way, using what is referred to as "avoidance-oriented strategies". This is in contrast to low-anxious individuals who more often use active coping interventions, referred to as "task-oriented strategies". Coping techniques will be discussed more extensively later in the chapter.

The antecedents of A-state are a function of personal and situational factors. These factors relate to the individual's personal experiences, predispositions and personality traits. Some of these situational factors include the presence of observers, involvement in a competitive event, expectations of others, and the demands of the task at hand. The antecedents, thoughts, and processes of anxiety that influence behaviour are illustrated in Figure 2.1.

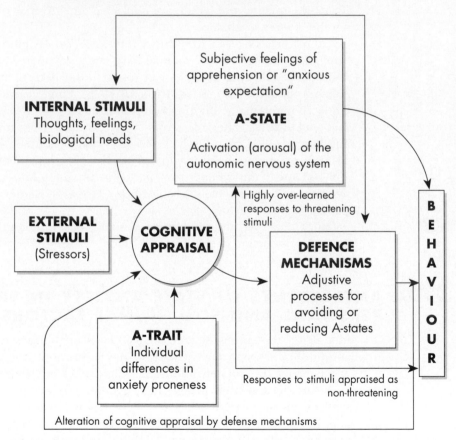

Figure 2.1: Influence of trait and state anxiety on sport performance (*Source: Anxiety and Behavior* (p. 17) by C. D. Spielberger (Ed.), 1966, New York: Academic Press.)

In their study of antecedents of competitive state anxiety in British middle distance runners, Jones, Swain, and Cale (1990) found that five factors markedly contributed to A-state. These were: perceived readiness, attitude toward previous performance, position goal (i.e., the athlete's perception of goal difficulty and capacity to achieve that goal), coach influence, and the external environment (i.e., weather and track conditions). All of these factors contributed to the athlete's performance expectations. These findings partially support Martens et al. (1990) who contend that perceived readiness is the best predictor of self-confidence and competitive state anxiety. Other personal factors that precede and often cause A-state are cognitive appraisal, coping style, A-trait, and perfectionism.

PERSONAL FACTORS

Expectations Athletes maintain certain hopes and dreams about how successful their performance will be. Skilled competitors have a history of success and, based on their previous efforts, expect to perform well in future attempts. These expectancies are a source of anxiety. Past performance forms expectations for future performance (Harris & Harris, 1984). Indeed, previous performance forms the best predictor of future performance outcomes. Athletes worry if they are not playing at a level that is commensurate with their (sometimes unrealistic) expectations. In addition, always feeling responsible for a contest's outcome places an added emotional burden on the competitor. Examples of potential antecedents of anxiety include attributing failure to one's low ability rather than to a superior opponent or bad luck, or explaining success as a result of a poor opponent or good luck, rather than taking responsibility for performance success.

Cognitive appraisal

To understand the causes of anxiety in sport, we must take into account two factors: the thinking processes that intervene between the encounter and the reaction (e.g., "Look at the size/speed of my opponents!!"), and the factors that influence the nature of this interaction (e.g., A-trait, low self-confidence). According to Lazarus and Folkman (1984), "cognitive appraisal reflects the unique and changing relationship taking place between a person with certain distinctive characteristics... and an environment whose characteristics must be predicted and interpreted" (p. 24). The authors contend that appraisal determines emotion. Thus, if an athlete perceives his or her opponent as dangerous or as a source of potential failure, anxiety will likely follow.

Coping style The "tendencies of an individual to use a particular type of coping across a variety of stressful encounters" reflects their coping style (Cohen, 1987, p. 286). This concept differs from episodic coping which refers to "the strategies individuals actually use in coping with a particular situation" (p. 287). A person's coping style, which is a function of episodic coping from situation to situation, has been categorised as approach (also called sensitisation or attentional coping) and avoidance (also referred to as desensitisation or repression coping). Coping style is assessed by a questionnaire, and this instrument is considered as an indicator of the type of coping behaviour the individual would use in a particular stressful situation or in response to a particular stressor (e.g., reacting to making an error, poor performance, receiving a penalty from the referee). Thus, the athlete's use — or non-use — of coping strategies often reflects his or her coping style. Of primary importance here is that the athlete's coping style may lower or even heighten anxiety, depending on the proper use of coping strategies for a given situation.

For example, imagine a basketball player who has just received a penalty from the referee. If he or she has an approach coping style, they will more likely react by attending to the stressor rather than ignoring it. Approach coping strategies include arguing with the call, asking the referee for more information, and/or thinking about the error that caused the penalty. In addition to distracting the athlete from immediate task demands — which, in itself, may impair performance — the tendency to think about a stressor that is out of the athlete's control (e.g., the referee's call) may increase anxiety. Instead, reactions to some stressors are more effective when they are ignored or discounted (i.e., "It's no big deal; just keep playing"). On the other hand, anxiety can also increase if the athlete's avoidance coping style increases his or her frustration due to an inability or unwillingness to express feelings. More research is needed on coping style in sport.

Trait anxiety

As indicated earlier, trait anxiety is a stable and enduring personality characteristic that, if elevated, causes high susceptibility to state anxiety. Having high A-trait does not necessarily ensure performance failure. High A-trait individuals must acknowledge their tendency to feel anxious and take necessary precautions, such as using cognitive and behavioural strategies (discussed later). However, the athlete's motivation and satisfaction as a sport participant and disposition to feel tense prior to and during competition are linked. According to Carron (1984), "the degree to which an athlete finds the whole competitive experience enjoyable is strongly related to his/her trait anxiety level" (p. 134). From his review of this literature, Carron has concluded that trait anxiety has a major impact on how competition is perceived.

Perfectionism

A perfectionist is someone who has trouble discriminating between realistic and idealised standards (Hewitt & Flett, 1991). Perfectionists will set themselves up for failure with extraordinarily high expectations and will engage in self-criticism whether or not they reach their lofty goals. Because perfectionists are rarely happy with their performance and anticipate failure, they tend to be highly anxious. Sport, as well as all other types of physical activities, are perceived as work, not play. In a rare study of perfectionism in sport, Frost and Henderson (1991) found that athletes who scored high in "concern over mistakes" (one dimension of perfectionism) reported more anxiety and less self-confidence in sports. Sadly, the perfectionist tends not to perceive sport competition as a source of enjoyment.

Fear of success/Fear of failure

Sometimes the athlete's previous experiences of success or failure can trigger anxiety. Athletes and non-athletes alike may prefer failure to success to avoid the social consequences, responsibilities, and future expectations that success may bring (Hodapp, 1989). Conversely, and far more common, many athletes fear failure. The social pressure from a "win at all costs" philosophy, combined with fear of injury and the fear of not meeting the expectations of significant others (e.g., coaches, parents, fans), are common sources of anxiety (Cratty, 1989). Perhaps the ultimate source of fear of failure is tied to a person's strong affiliation between sport success and self-esteem (Chu, 1982). Athletes who derive their self-esteem primarily from experiencing success in sport will more likely fear defeat.

Low self-confidence

Vealey (1986) defines sport confidence as "the belief or degree of certainty individuals possess about their ability to be successful in sport" (p. 222). Intuitively, it would appear that athletes high in self-confidence would be less anxious than their low-confident peers. Although research in this area is surprisingly scant, a study by Martin and Gill (1991) partially confirms this hypothesis. They found that distance runners who scored high in self-confidence were relatively low in cognitive state anxiety. They concluded that "low self-confidence, high anxiety, and, ultimately, poor performances are often noted in athletes who hold unrealistic outcome goals. In contrast, athletes who are more concerned with performing well in their sport appear more self-confident and less anxious and may perform closer to their potential" (p. 149). Thus, one approach to reducing A-state is to build sport confidence.

SITUATIONAL FACTORS

Sometimes particular situations or events interact with personal characteristics to produce state anxiety. For example, engaging in recreational sport places far less stress on the individual than performing under the demands of competition. If A-state reflects perceived threat, then situations that are perceived as dangerous or unpleasant will be more anxiety-provoking than situations that appear less threatening. Some of the factors that contribute to these aversive states include competition, pressure to succeed, and expectations or anticipation, referred to here as planned situations.

Competition

The link between anxiety and competition can be found in defining the concept of competition in sport. Martens (1976) defines competition as "a process in which the comparison of an individual's performance is made with some standard in the presence of at least one other person who is aware of the criterion for comparison and can evaluate the comparison process" (p. 14). The process of competition is inherently threatening because it consists of internal and external evaluation of the person's competence. As an achievement situation, competition compares the individual's performance against some standard, and then provides information about that individual's success or failure. In particular, it is the individual's interpretations and appraisals of the competitive situation that influence perceptions of threat (Gill, 1986). Because the need to feel competent is a fundamental and natural motive in life, competition is potentially threatening to the fulfilment of this need. Thus, the extent to which a person defines his or her competence in a given competitive situation is strongly related to feelings of competitive anxiety.

Pressure

Pressure is created when one or more factors increase the importance of performing well on a particular occasion (Baumeister, 1984). These factors may be internal (e.g., the athlete's high need to achieve) or external (e.g., demands and expectations from coaches, team mates, parents, fans). Taken together, pressure creates anxiety due to the importance which the athlete attributes to the competitive situation. Anxiety, then, is a function of two factors, the pressure to be successful, and perceived unpleasant consequences of not meeting internal and external performance expectations.

Planning

Orlick (1986), among others, contends that developing a plan that describes the athlete's thoughts and actions prior to and during the contest helps control anxiety. Orlick explains the importance of a mental plan this way: "You want to avoid the intrusion of self-defeating thoughts. They can raise the level of worry, lower confidence, or interfere with a good event, race, or game focus, thereby hindering your performance. You need to hold your attention away from worry and channel it into doing you the most good" (p. 20). Planning consists of determining one's thoughts and actions before (24–48 hours, depending on the person or situation) and during the event. In addition, Orlick urges the athlete to create a "refocus plan" that consists of implementing cognitive and behavioural strategies if some unexpected event or distraction occurs. For example, what will an athlete do or think to overcome physical discomfort or injury? What if there is broken or missing equipment? What if there is a sudden change of game venue or the competitor experiences early (unexpected) failure? The "mental plan" takes into account alternative strategies so that unpredicted events do not automatically "spell doom" and lead to undesirable consequences. Figure 2.2 illustrates the framework of Orlick's (1986) mental plan.

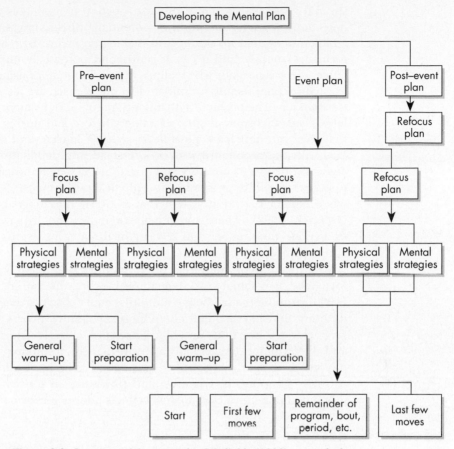

Figure 2.2: Conceptual framework of Orlick's (1986) mental plan

---

EFFECTS OF ANXIETY ON MOTOR PERFORMANCE

Trait anxiety does not influence performing motor skills directly. Because it is viewed as a personality trait, a person with high A-trait will be more susceptible to state anxiety than a person with low A-trait. In this way, A-trait affects the likelihood of experiencing state anxiety in anxiety-provoking situations. What is of primary concern to athletes and coaches is the way in which A-state is controlled. It is important to understand that controlling anxiety does not necessarily mean eliminating it completely.

In many ways, anxiety is a desirable, even necessary, aspect of effective sport performance. To understand its importance, anxiety should be considered from an evolutionary perspective. Feelings of perceived threat have life-saving implications. As Eysenck (1992) points out, "it is clear that rapid detection of the early warning signs of danger possesses considerable survival value" (p. 4). Thus, the key function of anxiety is to improve the detection of danger or threat in potentially threatening situations. Sport competitors would no doubt find making an error, their opponents' performance success, and a coach reprimand potentially unpleasant experiences. This is partially why feelings of self-doubt, appraising an opponent as superior, and feeling intimidated by one's coach are all sources of high state anxiety. The problem with anxiety, then, is not its mere presence. Athletes *should* feel some degree of anxiety before and during the contest so that they can anticipate possible sources of failure, and then effectively deal with the problem if it occurs. Instead, the debilitating influence of anxiety concerns its intensity and duration. Anxiety is unhealthy, and leads to poorer cognitive processing and physical performance, if the individual has a danger detection system that is overly developed or too sensitive (Eysenck, 1992). These individuals then become hypervigilant, grossly exaggerate the number and severity of threatening events in a situation, and appear extremely tense.

When examining the effect of competitive state anxiety on motor performance, it is valuable to determine how it is measured. Martens et al. (1990) propose that anxiety is a multifaceted construct that includes three different and interactional components: cognitive (worry), physiological (e.g., elevated heart rate and blood pressure, increased muscular tension), and behavioural (e.g., poorer performance, trembling, frequent urination). Competitive A-state affects performance by altering the first two of these components, cognitive and physiological processes. The behavioural component of over-anxiety reflects poorer performance.

COGNITIVE EFFECTS

Bird and Horn (1990) studied mental errors in response to cognitive A-state in female softball players. The researchers reasoned that if mental errors occurring during competition are representative of cognitive and attentional disruptions, then individuals who exhibit more mental errors should have higher cognitive anxiety than those who demonstrate fewer mental errors. Questionnaires ascertained the athletes' experience of mental errors (obtained from the athletes' coach after the game) and A-state (derived from the athletes within one hour before the game). The researchers found that higher cognitive anxiety was directly related to mental errors that occur during sport performance. Their study provided further evidence that anxiety has a detrimental effect on performance. Exactly how elevated anxiety affects sport performance is less than certain, but the causes appear related to cognitive functioning.

It is thought that increased A-state can cause disruptions in the athlete's attentional focus or biases in the information the performer receives from the environment (Schmidt, 1988). For example, optimal performance in some tasks requires the competitor to focus externally, searching for a wide array of information in the field. Heightened state anxiety tends to induce a narrowed, internal attentional focus which may be just the opposite of the desirable attentional state (Nideffer, 1990). (See Chapters 3 and 15 for further explanations of the dimensions and examples of Nideffer's attentional focusing model.)

A link between anxiety and attentional narrowing was investigated in a study by Williams, Tonymon, and Andersen (1991). Their study examined the influence of life stress and/or poor coping ability on state anxiety and attentional narrowing in response to a stress condition in the laboratory — the Stroop Colour Word Test. In this test, the subject is to report, quickly and verbally, the colour of ink used to write a word. This is stressful because the word is written in a different colour ink than the colour the word represents (e.g., the word "red" written in green ink). Their results indicated that heightened A-state was related to greater attentional narrowing. More specifically, subjects who were experiencing relatively more life stress had higher state anxiety during the stressful situation and, in turn, exhibited greater narrowing of peripheral vision, as measured by accuracy of subjects' observations of stimuli. The researchers viewed this effect as a counterproductive attentional shift in performing the task.

Another debilitative attentional response to state anxiety is the tendency to focus one's attention internally rather than externally. Anxious athletes, more than their more relaxed peers, are often preoccupied with their uptight feelings (e.g., "I hope I don't lose". "If only it wasn't raining".). Researchers often refer to this process as *self-preoccupation*. According to Sarason (1988), "how well people perform, how anxious they feel in particular situations, and their levels of physiological activation are powerfully influenced by self-related thoughts" (p. 3). Sarason contends that self-preoccupation, per se, is not the problem. After all, anyone performing a task must indulge in some degree of self-talk, imagery and other internal processes. Instead, it is the amount and type of self-preoccupation that influences the person's receptivity to available information.

The highly anxious person is very concerned over his or her inadequacies and shortcomings, about present or potential dangers, threats, and the inability to cope with them. However, danger and threat do not necessarily cause anxious self-preoccupation. Sarason contends that self-preoccupation is a function of the interpretation placed on those events by the individual. Self-preoccupation in sport occurs when the athlete has not learned how to cope with interpretations of dangers and threats.

Thus, anxiety is strongly linked to self-preoccupation in sport when the athlete interprets an actual or potential event as threatening and is distracted from the task at hand by these non-productive thoughts. For example, instead of focusing externally on environmental information needed for optimal performance and going all out (e.g., observing and reacting to the speed and trajectory of the approaching ball or the opponent's position), the overly-anxious competitor focuses internally on non-productive thoughts of self-doubt and possible danger. This can inhibit the processing of relevant information. According to Abernethy (1987), stress may cause the athlete to attend to stimuli not relevant to the task, consequently inhibiting the detection of important information. One aspect of the anxiety–attention relationship that has been studied by researchers concerns athletic injuries (see also Chapter 18).

Over-attending to internal rather than external cues has been shown to increase the likelihood of injury in sport and inhibit the athlete's psychological rehabilitation (Williams & Roepke, 1993). For example, injury may occur due to the athlete's attentional narrowing, in which the athlete focuses exclusively on a particular stimulus or on relatively few, readily apparent stimuli, instead of scanning the peripheral field of vision and anticipating certain stimuli. This may be especially dangerous in contact sports in which the anticipation of body contact allows the performer to either avoid the oncoming opponent or prepare for contact by tightening selected muscles and stabilising joints, all of which reduce the chance or severity of injuries. In their model of stress and athletic injury, Anderson and Williams (1988) assert that "during stress, narrowing of the visual field may occur, leading to a failure to pick up vital cues in the periphery and thus increasing the likelihood of injury" (p. 299). More recently, Williams and Roepke (1993) have concluded that "with increased stress the attentional field involuntarily narrows and becomes more internally focused" (p. 820). The internal focusing aspect also plays an important role in slowing psychological rehabilitation from injury. Instead of concentrating on task-relevant cues and executing skills with optimal effort, injured athletes often focus internally on the rehabilitated injured area and become more tentative in performing at optimal effort (Nideffer, 1983; Williams & Roepke, 1993). Sometimes they just cannot "let go".

In general, then, anxiety in sport ostensibly produces poorer performance because it distracts the athlete emotionally (e.g., negative feelings) and cognitively (e.g., overly narrow and internal attention). In his review of literature, Abernethy (1987) has concluded that expert and novice athletes differ with respect to the quantity and quality of information the performer processes. For instance, experts place fewer demands upon limited attentional resources that are partially taken up by anxiety and other distracting thoughts. As Krohne and Hindel (1988) have surmised in their study of stress and coping with sudden stress in table tennis players:

> High-anxious players should manifest task-irrelevant cognitions (reflections about the consequences of a negative outcome, criticism of one's own performance, distraction due to reactions in the audience), whereas low-anxious players should be capable (of maintaining their concentration). Consequently, high-anxious players should not be able any longer to use all their technical and tactical skills . . . since a great deal of their attention is distracted from the actual contest. (p. 228)

As we will see later, there are certain mental skills that, if used correctly, will reduce — even eliminate — the harmful effects of anxiety on performance.

PHYSIOLOGICAL EFFECTS

As indicated earlier, somatic anxiety results in a change in one or more physiological processes such as heart rate, blood pressure, muscle tension and sweating. For some tasks, a rise in somatic functioning is undesirable. One process that leads to decreased movement coordination is muscular tension. In one early study, Weinberg and Hunt (1976) examined the influence of acute stress on motor performance (dart-throwing) and muscular tension, as measured by electromyography (EMG), as a function of trait anxiety. They found that the high-anxious group exhibited significantly poorer performance accuracy than the low-anxious group. However, perhaps more important, this performance decrement was partially explained by poorer muscular coordination brought on by increased muscular tension used for the task. A similar, more recent, study by Anshel, Brown, and Brown (1993) concurred with Weinberg and Hunt, briefly discussed earlier. Anshel et al. studied the effects of a stress management intervention program in coping with acute verbal stress. They also found that poorer performance on a dart-throwing task was accompanied by more variability in muscular contractions (i.e., less coordination) in the task-related muscles for subjects who did not receive the coping program. In addition, however, subjects' cognitive anxiety scores were statistically similar among groups. Thus, although the stress manipulation elicited higher somatic anxiety, cognitive anxiety was not markedly affected.

Somatic anxiety can also influence heart rate which, in turn, can inhibit sport performance. For example, in a study of elite rifle marksmen, Hatfield, Landers, and Ray (1987) found a consistent deceleration of heart rate within two seconds prior to the trigger pull as well as increased brain wave (electroencephalogram, or EEG) activity in the right hemisphere during shooting. The researchers suggest that these somatic patterns reflect an attentional focus that allows the athletes to filter out distractions and task-irrelevant stimuli. It appears, then, that anxiety influences various physiological processes which, in turn, can help or hinder sport performance.

THE CHOKING PHENOMENON

Athletes differ in their ability to overcome the intense pressures of sport. Competitors who demonstrate competence in practice sessions but fail to perform at similar levels during the contest are often accused of "choking". Choking is defined as the inability to perform up to previously exhibited standards, particularly in pressure situations (Anshel et al., 1991). As indicated earlier, pressure is defined "as any factor or combination of factors that increases the importance of performing well on a particular occasion" (Baumeister, 1984, p. 610).

The causes of choking are both internal and external. Internal causes of choking include overarousal, appraising situations as highly stressful, feelings of little self-control in a situation, and low expectations of success. External causes of choking include high expectations of spectators coupled with low to moderate expectations of the athlete, the performer's fear of success and fear of failure, expectations and actions of the coach (e.g., importance of winning or attaining a certain performance level), and the demands and expectations of team mates.

Similar to acute state anxiety, choking may lead to narrowed attention and slower information processing. A narrowed attentional focus is undesirable when task demands require the athlete to scan the competitive area, looking for the location of opponents and team mates and planning strategy. Slower information processing includes being easily distracted from the task at hand, slow shifting of attention between internal (thinking) and external (scanning) directions, lower and less accurate decision-making, less reliance on automatic responses, and making performance errors.

Choking can also be accompanied by physiological changes. These changes include increased muscle tension, sweating, higher heart rate, nausea, and stomach cramps, any of which can directly influence performing sport skills (Hatfield & Landers, 1983).

Are some athletes more likely to choke than others? Is there a "choking disposition"? Baumeister (1984) examined the extent to which individuals differ in their susceptibility to choking on a disposition called self-consciousness (SC), the tendency to focus attention on oneself. He theorised that pressure increases SC, possibly by means of heightened arousal, and that this focus of attention disrupts skilled performance. He predicted that persons who are habitually self-conscious should find it easier to cope with situations that promote self-consciousness (i.e., high pressure situations) because they are accustomed to performing while self-conscious. Low SC persons, on the other hand, were predicted to choke more easily in pressure situations. This is because low SC persons, who have a greater jump going from low to high pressure situations, would not cope easily with pressure. His findings supported these predictions. Choking, then, is partly dependent on at least one disposition.

Strategies for overcoming "the choke"

Choking in sport is not inevitable. Athletes can use mental and behavioural techniques to prevent and overcome the tendency to not meet expectations. Anshel (1994) offers a few suggestions:

Practise under game-like conditions. This allows athletes to learn to adapt to real pressure under realistic conditions experienced in the contest.

Improve the athlete's self-confidence. The coach should teach skills and strategies under practice conditions until mastery is achieved. Together with positive information feedback on performance quality, self-confidence will markedly improve.

Keep expectations realistic. Choking is partly due to external pressures that, in turn, are generated by high external expectations of coaches and other observers. Keeping expectations in accordance with past performance will reduce pressure and reduce the probability of choking.

Put the game — and sport — in perspective. As indicated earlier, sport is not a matter of "life or death". Athletes compete to win, but it is also true that sport should be fun to play. The phrase, "it's only a game", is a cliché but it is also true.

Coach, avoid pressure statements. "We have to win this game", "The game is now in your hands", "We're counting on you", and other statements that induce guilt coming from coaches, and to a lesser extent from parents, team mates and spectators, add considerable pressure for success and contribute to choking.

Focus externally. Choking is a reaction to aversive thoughts. Athletes should reduce the time spent thinking and, instead, focus on external features in the sport environment. Carver and Scheier (1981) have found that performance and mood are both improved when attention is focused externally when experiencing unpleasant emotions. The author knows of one elite athlete who focused on advertisement signs in the stadium before the game; it relaxed him. Talking with team mates about topics that have nothing to do with the contest may also relax some athletes.

Develop performance routines. Linked to external focusing is engaging in one or more thoughts and actions that prepare the athlete for action. Orlick (1986) refers to this as a "mental plan" (discussed earlier). Many other sport psychology researchers have suggested using a specific routine prior to engaging in a performance or before the contest that will act as a tension reducer and confidence builder.

ANXIETY IN ELITE AND NON-ELITE ATHLETES

The psychological processes that link anxiety to sport performance differ among athletes. Previous research has indicated that individual differences exist concerning sources of stress and worry, the use of coping strategies, and the influence of anxiety on performance. One of the most important factors that contributes to these individual differences is skill level. This section will review how elite athletes differ from their less-skilled peers on the anxiety-performance relationship.

In a series of three experiments, Kerr and Cox (1991) studied individual differences in the level of arousal, psychological preparation, and the players' cognitive reactions under competitive conditions. Subjects were categorised as skilled, average, or novice squash ability. Their primary findings were that skilled players, in contrast to novices, engaged in more planning and other mental strategies related to attention and concentration prior to competition. In addition, elites were more successful at achieving their preferred arousal level, indicating they were better at using arousal-inducing and coping strategies. Finally, successful players appeared to show more stable and more appropriate mood states than less skilled players.

One possible explanation for these findings is that skilled and novice players differ in their respective use of cognitive strategies. For example, the researchers found differences in attentional focusing strategies. Better players were less preoccupied by the general environment, less engrossed with the array of external events, and more able to concentrate on particular environmental demands than average players. In addition, Kerr and Cox surmised that better players "were either less affected by, or perhaps more successful at, minimising negative emotional responses to playing demands than less successful players" (p. 1083). Thus, evidence exists that anxiety is at least partly influenced by the competitor's skill level. However, this is not to suggest that highly skilled athletes do not experience extreme anxiety, especially as the time for competition approaches.

There is considerable evidence suggesting a pattern of experiencing anxiety among skilled athletes. Athletes across all age groups and skill levels report experiencing manifestations of cognitive and somatic anxiety before, during and after competition (Mahoney & Meyers, 1989; Sanderson, 1989). However, higher skilled and experienced competitors tend to initiate a disciplined calmness in the 24 to 48 hours prior to the contest (see Parfitt, Jones, & Hardy, 1990, for a review of related literature). Mahoney and Avener (1977) found that gymnasts who qualified for the Olympics were slightly more anxious than non-qualifiers prior to the competition, but less anxious once the actual meet began.

Based on their review of related literature, Mahoney and Meyers (1989) concluded that skilled athletes, more so than less skilled competitors: (a) are less negatively affected by feeling anxious, (b) tend to "pace" their anxiety more effectively before competition, and (c) are less focused on their anxiety and more focused on immediate task demands during their performance. Thus, previous studies indicate that although all athletes feel anxious at some point before and during the contest, higher quality competitors appear to adapt and cope better with anxiety and, as a result, suffer fewer negative consequences in their performance. It is the effective use of cognitive and behavioural strategies for managing anxiety that apparently separates higher and lesser skilled athletes, an area to which we now turn.

AROUSAL IN SPORT: BRIEF REVIEW OF HYPOTHESES AND THEORIES

Earlier, it was noted that both anxiety and arousal contain physiological and psychological components. However, arousal has been traditionally studied as a physiological response, whereas anxiety has been defined primarily as a cognitive process (Anshel et al., 1991; Gould & Krane, 1992). As indicated earlier, many writers have used the terms arousal and anxiety synonymously. There have been recent developments in arousal theory that may improve our understanding of the ways in which certain thought processes and emotions affect sport performance. These developments are also important in their refutation of earlier theories, specifically drive theory and the inverted-U hypothesis, that purportedly explained the arousal-performance relationship. We begin with a brief overview of these original explanations, then move to the more recent hypotheses — Hanin's (1980) zone of optimal functioning, Hardy's (1990) catastrophe theory, and Kerr's (1985) reversal theory.

DRIVE THEORY

First proposed in 1943 by Hull, drive theory posited that performance was a direct function of drive (a term now equated with arousal). The relationship between motor performance and arousal is positive and linear. In other words, performing a motor task improves as the individual's level of arousal increases. More specifically, increased arousal was thought to increase the likelihood of performing the dominant response. The dominant responses would be incorrect at early learning stages, and correct later when the skill was better learned. These predictions appeared valid when performing relatively easy motor tasks (the type used in the studies that generated drive theory). However, as later research indicated, drive theory was not valid for performing relatively complex motor tasks (see Weinberg, 1979, for a review of this literature). Therefore, more arousal does not necessarily predict improved performance given the uncertainty about the performer's skill level, the level of task difficulty, and what constitutes "correct" and "incorrect" responses.

INVERTED-U HYPOTHESIS

Originally proposed by Yerkes and Dodson in 1908, the inverted-U hypothesis indicates that increased arousal facilitates motor performance to a certain point, followed by poorer performance if arousal continues to climb. This made the relationship between arousal and performance curvilinear instead of linear (see Figure 2.3). Intuitively, this theory makes sense because it takes into account skill complexity. For example, most athletes would contend that feeling too psyched-up before the contest reduces rather than fosters performance. More scientifically, the inverted-U hypothesis has gained support in field research (e.g., Sonstroem & Bernardo, 1982). Its limitation, however, is the failure to explain how, why, or precisely when arousal affects performance (Gould & Krane, 1992). For instance, Hardy (1990), who like many authors juxtaposes the concepts of anxiety and arousal, contends that while the performance of a highly anxious athlete may suffer, performance does not always improve when anxiety comes down, as predicted by the inverted-U hypothesis. As indicated earlier, cognitive anxiety results in prolonged self-preoccupation, a form of internal attentional focusing. Researchers have shown that focusing on unpleasant thoughts (e.g., perceived threat, worry) inhibits performance (Sonstroem, 1984). Thus, given the array of thoughts and somatic responses that are brought on by, and often precede, anxious feelings, it is easy to understand why sudden decreased anxiety would not automatically and quickly lead to improved sport performance. See Weinberg (1990) for a further critique of the inverted-U hypothesis.

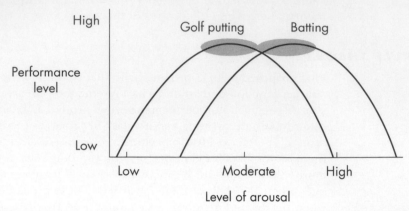

Figure 2.3: Inverted-U hypothesis illustrating optimal arousal level for golf putting and batting

OPTIMAL ZONES OF AROUSAL HYPOTHESIS

Although sport psychologists have recognised that a certain degree of anxiety in sport is a good thing, no-one knows what this "optimal" level of anxiety is for each individual. How much anxiety is too much? Hanin (1980) contends that individual differences exist in determining the competitor's own optimal level of state anxiety that leads to best performance. Rather than searching for a given amount of anxiety, Hanin suggests each competitor has a "zone of optimal functioning" (ZOF). The ZOF is derived from two sources: (a) the athlete's average precompetitive A-state score from Spielberger's et al. (1970) State Trait Anxiety Inventory (STAI), and (b) multiple observations of the athlete's A-state and accompanying performance levels. The "zone" component of Hanin's hypothesis is primarily dependent on plus or minus four points on the STAI scores. Ostensibly, athletes were expected to perform better if their A-state fell within their ZOF than if their A-state was outside their ZOF. The results of several studies support the ZOF concept (see Hanin, 1989, for a review).

The ZOF fills a large void in the anxiety literature in addressing the elusive problem of determining the individual's optimal anxiety. Although intuitively appealing, the ZOF hypothesis awaits further scientific scrutiny in explaining the role of anxiety in sport performance.

CATASTROPHE THEORY

Hardy's (1990) primary criticism of the inverted-U hypothesis is that "if the inverted-U hypothesis is simply a description of the relationship between stress and performance, then it does not seem to fit anecdotal evidence from the field of sport psychology which suggests that this relationship should not be symmetrical" (p. 82). In other words, when competitors choke or become over-excited, their performance often drops markedly rather than gradually. Moreover, it is very difficult to then return performance to a desirable level. All of this is contrary to the predictions of the inverted-U hypothesis.

The inverted-U hypothesis and catastrophe theory are similar in predicting that increases in arousal and A-state will improve performance up to an optimal level. However, the inverted-U predicts that further increased arousal or anxiety will impair performance in an orderly, curvilinear manner. By comparison, catastrophe theory posits that further physiological arousal and cognitive anxiety will result in a large and dramatic decline in performance. The theory predicts that the relationship between physiological arousal and performance is dependent on the performer's level of cognitive anxiety; only when cognitive A-state is high in combination with high physiological arousal will there be "catastrophic" changes in performance. The combination of physiological and cognitive responses, often manifested by "choking", will significantly impair the return to optimal performance level. To date, the only published study testing catastrophe theory (Hardy & Parfitt, 1991) indicated that increased physiological arousal (heart rate) correlated with performance as a function of whether the subject's cognitive anxiety was high or low.

Gould and Krane (1992) recognise two strengths in their critique of catastrophe theory. First, the theory addresses the effects of both physiological and cognitive effects of arousal (and anxiety) on performance. Second, it indicates that actual sport conditions "do not always function in perfectly symmetrical ways" (p. 129). In other words, like all human behaviour, very rarely is sport performance highly predictable. Gould and Krane also list two limitations of catastrophe theory, that it is overly complex, and that there is a need to obtain many assessments of the same athletes over time to test it. Further research testing the efficacy of catastrophe theory is warranted.

REVERSAL THEORY

Although not the "inventor" of reversal theory, Kerr (1985) is noted for examining its application in sport. Reversal theory is based on the premise that a person is capable of interpreting his or her arousal level. High arousal may be perceived as excitement (pleasant) or anxiety (unpleasant), and low arousal may be interpreted as relaxation (pleasant) or boredom (unpleasant). Thus, arousal (high–low) and emotion (pleasant–unpleasant) are each located on a continuum and form four quadrants, as illustrated in Figure 2.4.

The concept of psychological reversals stems from the person's shift in interpreting his or her feelings — what Kerr (1985) calls a change in metamotivational states. For example, engaging in a dangerous, risk-taking task such as rock-climbing or motor bike racing induces heightened arousal, deemed anxiety. However, when the dangerous task or situation is mastered, the anxiety suddenly reverses and becomes excitement. These psychological reversals markedly alter a person's emotional state. One particularly important feature of reversal theory is that the athlete's interpretation of arousal states is viewed as central to the ability to explain and predict the effect of emotion on sport performance. See Kerr (1990) for a review of the several studies that support reversal theory.

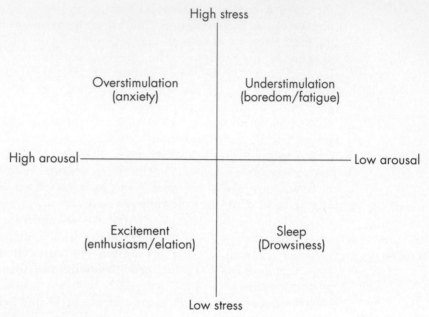

Figure 2.4: Arousal–stress continuum of reversal theory

These new theories are welcome additions to the contemporary sport psychology literature because they contribute to our ability to explain the psychological factors that influence sport performance. Ultimately, only continued research will tell us to what extent these explanations are valid and applicable, and improve our understanding of the role of arousal and anxiety in sport.

 # COGNITIVE–BEHAVIOURAL STRATEGIES FOR ANXIETY MANAGEMENT

The responsibility of controlling an athlete's emotions rests with the individual competitor. There are many books, chapters, and magazine articles that address the proper use of cognitive techniques for reducing undesirable feelings before and during the contest. Certainly some techniques will work better for one athlete than another, and not all of these strategies are valid under all sport conditions. The following recommendations for anxiety management are derived from applied sport psychology researchers. (Also see Chapter 11 for additional suggestions.)

GUIDELINES FOR MANAGING ANXIETY

Focus on what you can control

One primary source of anxiety is worrying about uncontrollable factors such as sustaining an injury, playing a superior opponent, or a successful game outcome. Athletes whose thoughts centre on "what ifs" or "I hopes" are candidates for heightened anxiety. Quality competitors focus on their performance and reflect on the strategies they practised in preparation for the contest. Anxiety lies in fear of the unknown. By focusing on what one can control, athletes become task-oriented and concentrate on immediate performance demands. Focus on strengths, not weaknesses, and what you can do, not what you cannot do.

Think about practice situations

As a sport psychology consultant, I have found these two words to be the most concise, yet powerful message I can give a competitor — "think practice". If high anxiety is due to the performer's perception of a threatening situation, it makes sense to reflect the times when sport skills were executed without these same unpleasant thoughts. These times are practice sessions. When athletes "think practice", they are reflecting a relatively relaxed, non-threatening environment when their sport skills were performed successfully.

Remember the worst case scenario

The worst case scenario reflects this simple question: What is the worst that can happen? If you were to walk across the street blindfolded, the worst case scenario is death if you were struck by a car. Consequently, this sort of behaviour is unthinkable. Fortunately, sport is not a matter of life and death. The reason for competing in sport is the enjoyment and pleasure it brings its participants. If it is not enjoyable, perhaps it is time to think of doing something else for recreation or changing the situation (e.g., a change of team, coach, or sport type). Remember that the contest's outcome is not usually under the performer's control, so on thinking of the worst case scenario, you are placing sport in perspective. Sport should be fun. With very few exceptions, sport competition is not about making the Olympic team.

Keep active

Researchers have shown that engaging in physical activity reduces anxiety. This relaxing effect is one reason for engaging in the pre-game warm-up. Although the physiological basis of this response goes beyond the scope of this book, exercise: (a) provides a physical outlet for heightened emotions such as anxiety rather than "bottling up" these emotions, and (b) focuses the athlete's attention externally on performing a physical task rather than internally on undesirable emotions.

Use pre-packaged interventions

There are numerous approaches to managing anxiety based on a series of cognitive and behavioural strategies executed in a pre-planned and structured manner. Smith's (1980) Anxiety Management Training (AMT), Suinn's (1987) visuo-motor behavioural rehearsal (VMBR), and Meichenbaum's (1985) stress inoculation training (SIT) are examples. Many of these programs have received research support in scientific journals.

Use cognitive strategies

Finally, the sport psychology literature suggests numerous cognitive techniques for managing anxiety. Mental imagery, various forms of relaxation, psyching-up, thought-stopping, positive self-talk, and numerous mental skill packages have been used successfully to reduce unpleasant emotions (see Chapter 11 in this book for an extensive review of these techniques for stress management; and Sachs, 1991, for a reading list of this material).

Develop a mental plan

Perhaps one of the most useful and widely practised approaches to anxiety management comes from Orlick's (1986) concept of developing a mental plan (discussed earlier). While the efficacy of Orlick's mental plan has not been exposed to scientific scrutiny, there is abundant empirical evidence that his conceptual framework is widely used by elite athletes world-wide. See page 40 for a discussion on the mental plan.

COACHING TECHNIQUES FOR MANAGING ATHLETE ANXIETY

The coach, more than any other person, should be in a position to help athletes manage their anxiety. The coach is more aware of the athletes' needs and has more credibility to alter the athletes' thoughts than any other source. However, sometimes the coach actually increases the athletes' anxiety. Examples of using the *wrong* coaching strategies include: (a) communicating unrealistic goals and expectations of player performance; (b) teaching new skills immediately before or during the contest; (c) reminding the athlete about the importance of winning; (d) reminding athletes of who is watching them; (e) embarrassing the athlete by inappropriate or poorly timed reprimanding, or attempts at sarcasm (e.g., "Nice play, butter fingers") and guilt (e.g., "You should know better ..."); and (f) criticising the competitor's character rather than performance (e.g., "That was a dumb play" rather than "You were supposed to cover the wing on that play, John"). See Anshel (1994) for further discussion of this topic.

It is also important to mention here that sometimes increasing anxiety is actually *desirable*. Athletes who take their opponents too lightly, exhibit low energy level, or are not following the coach's directions need to be reminded that maintaining their present status may result in undesirable team and individual performance outcomes. Athletes must feel some degree of danger or threat at the competition in order to establish an optimal level of arousal. So, the coach's role is not always to eliminate anxiety but, rather, to help athletes manage it. Here are some techniques coaches can use for this purpose as suggested in reviews of this literature by Anshel (1994), Cratty (1989), and Fuoss and Troppmann (1981).

SPECIFIC TECHNIQUES FOR COACHES

Be realistic   One of the leading causes of anxiety is athletes' perceptions that others have very high expectations of their performance. There is nothing wrong with teaching athletes to expect success and to feel self-confident. But athletes must feel that the coach is not asking for perfection and will accept the athletes' best efforts. Statements that promise approval such as, "All I can ask of you is your best effort", help reduce athletes' fear of rejection if they do not win.

Have fun   One of the most effective pre-game talks a coach can make, especially before playing a superior opponent, is to remind the athletes to enjoy themselves rather than reminding the athletes about the importance of winning. The effectiveness of this message is supported by a great deal of anecdotal evidence in the media and at professional conferences (see Anshel, 1994). Sport is supposed to be fun. Often, the athletes respond to this message by playing their best game.

Avoid using the W-I-N word

Focusing on contest outcomes does not help athletes feel in control of a situation. Remind athletes of their strategies and skills, perhaps in reference to their opponents. The key message here is to help the athletes feel in control of the situation. Reminding them of the importance of winning has the opposite effect and often induces anxiety. As Cratty (1989) suggests, "the coach, during a pregame talk, may emphasize effort rather than absolute scores" (p. 149).

Use game simulations in practice

Athletes are best prepared for the contest when they have had an opportunity to use — and master — game-related skills and strategies in practice. Coaches should be creative in generating situations in practice that closely approximate game conditions. Among the most anxiety-inducing actions of a coach is to ask athletes to perform new skills and strategies that have not previously been practised, and to expect perfect — even desirable — outcomes.

Teach skills and provide feedback

One way to build self-confidence and reduce anxiety about competing is to improve skilled performance. This can be accomplished over time by providing athletes with feedback on their skill improvement, effort and, if warranted, their performance outcome. Coaches should consider this fundamental to their job.

Remember the injured athlete

One of the saddest outcomes of sport competition is experiencing an injury. The athlete is no doubt experiencing pain and guilt from feelings of letting down the team, or disappointing the coach or parents. The coach's sensitivity and attentiveness is needed more in response to an athlete's injury than at any other time. Immediately following the injury and during the rehabilitation period, coaches should occasionally visit or at least call their injured athletes in the hospital or at home, and remind team members to do the same. Phone calls to injured players and their parents are important reminders that the athlete is a valued team member — and a human being — on and off the field or court.

Keep things in perspective

This point is reserved for the final, and perhaps most crucial, guideline. Coaches need to remind their players about the importance of high *effort* and performance *improvement* rather than reliance on winning as the only sign of success. Physical and mental errors are an inherent part of sport competition. In addition, it is highly unlikely that a particular error is solely responsible for a contest's final outcome. Coaches can help lower anxiety if they keep competitive sport as the enjoyable and healthy activity it is intended to be.

FUTURE DIRECTIONS

There are at least six aspects of the anxiety in sport literature that need further study. First, the internal mechanisms that explain how anxiety negatively influences sport performance are not known. Why do some thoughts negatively affect performance but not others? How do these thoughts influence motor responses that affect performance outcome? Second, the role of an athlete's dispositions (e.g., self-esteem, self-confidence, coping style) in experiencing and coping with anxiety is unknown and understudied. Why are some individuals more susceptible than others to feeling anxious? This leads to the third issue, improving our ability to predict highly anxious individuals. To date, we rely on the athlete's willingness to convey their feelings about their anxiety. The ability to predict a person's susceptibility to anxiety will allow coaches and sport psychologists to initiate strategies to prevent or quickly remedy anxious feelings.

A fourth area of future study concerns the most effective means for coping with anxiety. The effectiveness of stress management programs in controlling stress and anxiety is still a function of trial-and-error. Greater sensitivity to individual differences in examining individual needs is warranted. Sport psychology consultants are not the only ones who need greater awareness of helping athletes cope with anxiety. Coaches also need better training in their ability to recognise and respond properly to an athlete's state anxiety. Researchers (e.g., Hanson & Gould, 1988) have shown that coaches are not aware of the signs of anxiety, and rarely offer appropriate treatment techniques. The fifth issue in anxiety concerns how to determine a person's optimal anxiety level. We know that some anxiety is good — even necessary — for optimal performance. We also know that too much anxiety is not conducive to concentrating on the most relevant information in a situation, and can lead to choking under pressure. There must be a middle ground that meets the needs of a given individual in a particular situation for a specific type of sport or athletic skill. To date, researchers do not know what this middle ground — or optimal level — is. Hanin's (1980) zone of optimal functioning (ZOF) theory is a good start at examining this issue. However, more research is needed in depicting the role of individual differences in influencing ZOF. The final area of future study is that sport psychologists are unsure about the effectiveness of particular cognitive and behavioural techniques in anxiety management. One example of this problem is the overprescription of certain cognitive strategies.

Although there is no published research in this area, it is apparent from a plethora of conference presentations, seminars, and applied manuals, that sport psychology consultants oversubscribe the use of particular cognitive strategies for anxiety management. A good example of this practice is the prolific use of various relaxation techniques. While it is true that various forms of relaxation training have been shown to reduce undesirable feelings and improve the subject's emotional status, there are other reasons for not using relaxation. For example, according to Anshel (1991), "it appears that the purpose of relaxation programs may be misunderstood, overly prescribed, and incorrectly implemented" (p. 23), and he goes on to list specific points against using relaxation techniques.

CONCLUSIONS

The sport environment is one which can be highly stressful and anxiety-inducing. However, sport psychology researchers and practitioners have made great strides in recent years in attempting to describe, explain and understand anxiety, and how this emotion affects sport performance. This is of particular importance because the "causes and cures" for competitive anxiety will benefit sport participants in many ways. In addition to reducing optimal performance, uncontrolled heightened competitive anxiety often leads to dropping out of sport. For these athletes, the primary purpose of competing in sport, its enjoyment, is gone. Further participation serves no further purpose.

Typically, athletes at all skill levels and ages experience some degree of anxiety. In the final analysis, it is the individual's ability to prevent, reduce, or even more important, to cope with or manage anxiety that influences performance quality. According to Smith et al. (1990), "considerable individual variation exists in the tendency for athletes to experience anxiety within the competitive context ..." (p. 265). Thus, each athlete differs with respect to their appraisals of and responses to anxiety-inducing events and situations. Individual differences also exist in terms of each athlete's *need* to feel anxious in order to perform optimally. Some athletes actually thrive on perceptions of threat to possess the necessary emotions for performance success. It is wrong to assume that anxiety is necessarily "bad" and that all athletes should strive to minimise it. For example, to some athletes, pre-game vomiting is an anticipated ritual (Anshel, 1994). Future research is needed to understand the mechanisms that cause anxiety, and why it affects athletes differently. Much still needs to be learned in this area.

SUMMARY

Anxiety, an inherent aspect of sport competition, can be defined in two words, perceived threat. It is the performer's interpretation of the competitive environment as potentially dangerous or threatening to his or her success or to self-esteem that forms the main source of anxiety. The immediate nature of these feelings is called state anxiety.

However, not all individuals feel anxious under all conditions. Each of us differs in our susceptibility to feeling anxious in a given situation. Thus, some individuals are more likely to feel anxious than others based on a segment of their personality. This disposition is called trait anxiety. Trait anxiety is always measured in response to one's thoughts and feelings (cognitive measures). State anxiety, on the other hand, is also measured in terms of physiological processes (somatic anxiety; e.g., heart rate, blood pressure) and the person's behaviours (e.g., frequent or loud talking, pacing, poor performance).

Individuals who are unable to manage their anxiety and perform at lower than expected levels may suffer from a phenomenon called choking. Strategies to overcome choking centre on changing the athlete's ways of interpreting the event or situation, primarily by reducing perceptions of threat in the sport situation. Behavioural techniques to prevent choking include mastering skills in practice and engaging in physical activity.

Anxiety affects sport performance primarily by altering the competitor's attentional focus. Instead of the desirable shifting of attention between broad (scanning) and narrow, internal and external directions, the highly anxious athlete engages in an overly narrow and internal attentional focus.

The other way in which anxiety affects sport performance is by altering physiological processes that counter performance demands. Examples include increased muscle tension and, for sports that demand steadiness, higher than desirable heart rate. Finally, although the sources of anxiety are similar among high- and less-skilled athletes, the better competitors are less influenced by, and apparently cope better with, high state anxiety.

REFERENCES

Abernethy, B. (1987). Selective attention in fast ball sports II. Expert-novice differences. *Australian Journal of Science and Medicine in Sport, 19,* 7–16.

Anderson, M. B., & Williams, J. M. (1988). A model of stress and athletic injury: Prediction and prevention. *Journal of Sport and Exercise Psychology, 10,* 294–306.

Anshel, M. H. (1985). Effect of arousal on warm-up decrement. *Research Quarterly for Exercise and Sport, 56,* 1–9.

Anshel, M. H. (1987). Psychological inventories used for sport psychology research. *The Sport Psychologist, 1,* 331–349.

Anshel, M. H. (1991, December). Relaxation training in sport: Pros and cons. *Sport Health, 9,* 23–24.

Anshel, M. H. (1994). *Sport psychology: From theory to practice* (2nd ed.). Scottsdale, AZ: Gorsuch Scarisbrick.

Anshel, M. H., Brown, J. M., & Brown, D. F. (1993). Effectiveness of an acute stress coping program on motor performance, muscular tension and affect. *Australian Journal of Science and Medicine in Sport, 25,* 7–16.

Anshel, M. H., Freedson, P., Hamill, J., Haywood, K., Horvat, M., & Plowman, S. A. (1991). *Dictionary of the sport and exercise sciences.* Champaign, IL: Human Kinetics.

Anshel, M. H., & Reeves, L. H. (1992). *Aerobics for fitness* (3rd ed.). Minneapolis, MN: Burgess.

Baumeister, R. F. (1984). Choking under pressure: Self-consciousness and paradoxical effects of incentives on skilful performance. *Journal of Personality and Social Psychology, 46,* 610–620.

Berger, B. G., & McInman, A. (1993). Exercise and the quality of life. In R. N. Singer, M. Murphey, & L. K. Tennant (Eds.), *Handbook of research on sport psychology* (pp. 729–760). New York: Macmillan.

Bird, A. M., & Cripe, B. K. (1986). *Psychology and sport behavior.* St. Louis: Mirror-Mosby.

Bird, A. M., & Horn, M. A. (1990). Cognitive anxiety and mental errors in sport. *Journal of Sport and Exercise Psychology, 12,* 217–222.

Borkovec, T. D. (1976). Physiological and cognitive processes in the regulation of arousal. In G. E. Schwartz & D. Shapiro (Eds.), *Consciousness and self-regulation: Advances in research* (Vol. 1, pp. 261–312). New York: Plenum.

Carron, A. V. (1984). *Motivation: Implications for coaching and teaching.* London, Ontario: Sports Dynamics.

Carver, C. S., & Scheier, M. F. (1981). *Attention and self-regulation: A control-theory approach to human behavior.* New York: Springer-Verlag.

Chu, D. (1982). *Dimensions of sport studies.* New York: John Wiley & Sons.

Cohen, F. (1987). Measurement of coping. In S. V. Kasl & C. L. Cooper (Eds.), *Stress and health: Issues in research methodology* (pp. 283–305). Chichester UK: John Wiley & Sons.

Cratty, B. J. (1989). *Psychology in contemporary sport* (3rd ed.). Englewood Cliffs, NJ: Prentice-Hall.

Endler, N. S., & Parker, J. D. A. (1990). Multidimensional assessment of coping: A critical evaluation. *Journal of Personality and Social Psychology, 58,* 844–854.

Eysenck, M. W. (1992). *Anxiety: The cognitive perspective.* Hove, UK: Lawrence Erlbaum.

Fillingim, R. B., & Blumenthal, J. A. (1993). The use of aerobic exercise as a method of stress management. In P. M. Lehrer & R. L. Woolfolk (Eds.), *Principles and practice of stress management* (2nd ed.) (pp. 443–462). New York: Guilford.

Folkins, C. H., & Sime, W. E. (1981). Physical fitness training and mental health. *American Psychologist, 36,* 373–389.

Fridhandler, B. M. (1986). Conceptual note on state, trait, and the state-trait distinction. *Journal of Personality and Social Psychology, 50,* 169–174.

Frost, R. O., & Henderson, K. J. (1991). Perfectionism and reactions to athletic competition. *Journal of Sport and Exercise Psychology, 13,* 323–335.

Fuoss, D. E., & Troppmann, R. J. (1981). *Effective coaching: A psychological approach.* New York: John Wiley & Sons.

Gill, D. L. (1986). *Psychological dynamics of sport.* Champaign, IL: Human Kinetics.

Gould, D., & Krane, V. (1992). The arousal-athletic performance relationship: Current status and future directions. In T. S. Horn (Ed.), *Advances in sport psychology* (pp. 119–142). Champaign, IL: Human Kinetics.

Hackfort, D., & Schwenkmezger, P. (1989). Measuring anxiety in sports: Perspectives and problems. In D. Hackfort & C. D. Spielberger (Eds.), *Anxiety in sports* (pp. 55–74). New York: Hemisphere.

Hackfort, D., & Schwenkmezger, P. (1993). Anxiety. In R. N. Singer, M. Murphey, & L.K. Tennant (Eds.), *Handbook of research on sport psychology* (pp. 328–364). New York: Macmillan.

Hanin, Y. L. (1980). A study of anxiety in sports. In W. F. Straub (Ed.), *Sport psychology: An analysis of athlete behavior* (pp. 236–249). Ithaca, NY: Mouvement.

Hanin, Y. L. (1989). Interpersonal and intragroup anxiety in sports. In D. Hackfort & C. D. Spielberger (Eds.), *Anxiety in sports* (pp. 19–28). New York: Hemisphere.

Hanson, T. W., & Gould, D. (1988). Factors affecting the ability of coaches to estimate their athletes' trait and state anxiety levels. *The Sport Psychologist, 2,* 298–313.

Hardy, L. (1990). A catastrophe model of performance in sport. In J. G. Jones & L. Hardy (Eds.), *Stress and performance in sport* (pp. 81–106). Chichester, UK: John Wiley & Sons.

Hardy, L., & Parfitt, G. (1991). A catastrophe model of anxiety and performance. *British Journal of Psychology, 82,* 163–178.

Harris, D. V., & Harris, B. L. (1984). *The athlete's guide to sports psychology: Mental skills for physical people.* Champaign, IL: Leisure Press.

Hatfield, B. D., & Landers, D. M. (1983). Psychophysiology — A new direction for sport psychology. *Journal of Sport Psychology, 5,* 243–259.

Hatfield, B. D., Landers, D. M., & Ray, W. J. (1987). Cardiovascular–CNS interactions during a self-paced, intentional attentive state: Elite marksmanship performance. *Psychophysiology, 24,* 542–549.

Hewitt, P. L., & Flett, G. L. (1991). Perfectionism in the self and social contexts: Conceptualization, assessment, and association with psychopathology. *Journal of Personality and Social Psychology, 60,* 456–470.

Hodapp, V. (1989). Anxiety, fear of failure, and achievement: Two path-analytical models. *Anxiety Research, 1,* 301–312.

Iso-Ahola, S. E., & Hatfield, B. (1986). *Psychology of sports: A social psychological approach.* Dubuque, IA: Wm. C. Brown.

Jones, J. G., Swain, A., & Cale, A. (1990). Antecedents of multidimensional competitive state anxiety and self-confidence in elite intercollegiate middle-distance runners. *The Sport Psychologist, 4,* 107–118.

Kerr, J. H. (1985). The experience of arousal: A new basis for studying arousal effects in sport. *Journal of Sport Sciences, 3,* 169–179.

Kerr, J. H. (1990). Stress and sport: Reversal theory. In G. Jones & L. Hardy (Eds.), *Stress and performance in sport* (pp. 107–134). Chichester, UK: John Wiley & Sons.

Kerr, J. H., & Cox, T. (1991). Arousal and individual differences in sport. *Personality and Individual Differences, 12,* 1075–1085.

Krohne, H. W., & Hindel, C. (1988). Trait anxiety, state anxiety, and coping behavior as predictors of athletic performance. *Anxiety Research, 1,* 225–234.

Lazarus, R. S., & Folkman, S. (1984). *Stress, appraisal, and coping.* New York: Springer.

Lehrer, P. M., & Woolfolk, R. L. (1993). Specific effects of stress management techniques. In P. M. Lehrer & R. L. Woolfolk (Eds.), *Principles and practice of stress management* (2nd ed.) (pp. 481–520). New York: Guilford.

Mahoney, M. J., & Avener, M. (1977). Psychology of the elite athlete: An exploratory study. *Cognitive Therapy and Research, 1,* 135–141.

Mahoney, M. J., & Meyers, A. W. (1989). Anxiety and athletic performance: Traditional and cognitive-developmental perspectives. In D. Hackfort & C. D. Spielberger (Eds.), *Anxiety in sports* (pp. 77–94). New York: Hemisphere.

Martens, R. (1971). Anxiety and motor behavior; A review. *Journal of Motor Behavior, 3,* 151–179.

Martens, R. (1976). Competition: In need of a theory. In D. M. Landers (Ed.), *Social problems in athletics.* Urbana, IL: University of Illinois Press.

Martens, R. (1977). *The Sport Competition Anxiety Test.* Champaign, IL: Human Kinetics.

Martens, R., Vealey, R. S., & Burton, D. (1990). *Competitive anxiety in sport.* Champaign, IL: Human Kinetics.

Martin, J. J., & Gill, D. L. (1991). The relationships among competitive orientation, sport-confidence, self-efficacy, anxiety, and performance. *Journal of Sport and Exercise Psychology, 13,* 149–159.

Meichenbaum, D. (1985). *Stress inoculation training.* New York: Pergamon.

Nideffer, R. M. (April, 1983). The injured athlete: Psychological factors in treatment. *Orthopedic Clinics of North America, 14,* 373–385.

Nideffer, R. M. (1990). Use of the test of attentional and interpersonal style (TAIS) in sport. *The Sport Psychologist, 4,* 285–300.

Orlick, T. (1986). *Psyching for sport: Mental training for athletes.* Champaign, IL: Leisure Press.

Oxendine, J. B. (1970). Emotional arousal and motor performance. *Quest, 13,* 23–32.

Parfitt, C. G., Jones, J. G., & Hardy, L. (1990). Multidimensional anxiety and performance. In G. Jones & L. Hardy (Eds.), *Stress and performance in sport* (pp. 43–80). New York: John Wiley & Sons.

Sachs, M. L. (1991). Reading list in applied sport psychology: Psychological skills training. *The Sport Psychologist, 5,* 88–91.

Sanderson, F. H. (1989). Analysis of anxiety levels in sport. In D. Hackfort & C. D. Spielberger (Eds.), *Anxiety in sports* (pp. 39–54). New York: Hemisphere.

Sarason, I. G. (1988). Anxiety, self-preoccupation and attention. *Anxiety Research, 1,* 3–7.

Schmidt, R. A. (1988). *Motor control and learning* (2nd ed.). Champaign, IL: Human Kinetics.

Smith, R. E. (1980). Development of an integrated coping response through cognitive-affective stress management training. In I. G. Sarason & C. D. Spielberger (Eds.), *Stress and anxiety* (Vol. 7). Washington: Hemisphere.

Smith, R. E., Smoll, F. L., & Schutz, R. W. (1990). Measurement and correlates of sport-specific cognitive and somatic trait anxiety: The Sport Anxiety Scale. *Anxiety Research, 2,* 263–280.

Sonstroem, R. J. (1984). An overview of anxiety in sport. In J. M. Silva & R. S. Weinberg (Eds.), *Psychological foundations of sport* (pp. 104–117). Champaign, IL: Human Kinetics.

Sonstroem, R. J., & Bernardo, P. (1982). Intraindividual pre-game state anxiety and basketball performance: A re-examination of the inverted-U curve. *Journal of Sport Psychology, 4,* 235–245.

Spielberger, C. D., Gorsuch, R., & Lushene, R. (1970). *The State Trait Anxiety Inventory (STAI) Test manual.* Palo Alto, CA: Consulting Psychologists Press.

Suinn, R. M. (1987). Behavioral approaches to stress management in sports. In J. R. May & J. J. Asken (Eds.), *Sport psychology: The psychological health of the athlete* (pp. 41–58). New York: PMA Publishing.

Taylor, J. A. (1953). A personality scale of manifest anxiety. *Journal of Abnormal and Social Psychology, 48,* 285–290.

Vealey, R. S. (1986). Conceptualization of sport-confidence and competitive orientation: Preliminary investigation and instrument development. *Journal of Sport Psychology, 8,* 221–246.

Vealey, R. S. (1988). Future directions in psychological skills training. *The Sport Psychologist, 2,* 318–336.

Weinberg, R. S. (1979). Anxiety and motor performance: Drive theory vs. cognitive theory. *International Journal of Sport Psychology, 10,* 112–121.

Weinberg, R. S. (1989). Anxiety, arousal, and motor performance: Theory, research, and applications. In D. Hackfort & C. D. Spielberger (Eds.), *Anxiety in sports* (pp. 95–115). New York: Hemisphere.

Weinberg, R. S. (1990). Anxiety and motor performance: Where to go from here? *Anxiety Research, 3,* 227–242.

Weinberg, R. S., & Hunt, V. V. (1976). The interrelationships between anxiety, motor performance, and electromyography. *Journal of Motor Behavior, 8,* 219–244.

Williams, J. M., & Roepke, N. (1993). Psychology of injury and injury rehabilitation. In R. N. Singer, M. Murphey, & L. K. Tennant (Eds.), *Handbook of research on sport psychology* (pp. 815-839). New York: Macmillan.

Williams, J. M., Tonymon, P. & Andersen, M. (1991). The effects of stressors and coping resources on anxiety and peripheral narrowing. *Journal of Applied Sport Psychology, 3,* 126–141.

C H A P T E R

3

ATTENTION IN SPORT

JEFF SUMMERS • STEPHEN FORD

As William James remarked as long ago as 1890, "Everyone knows what attention is" (p. 404). This is particularly true in the sporting arena where the importance of attentional factors in producing optimal performance has long been recognised by coaches, athletes and the sports media. Coaches frequently exhort athletes to "concentrate", "stay alert", "watch the ball". Likewise, athletes often report a lack/loss of concentration as a major factor in a poor performance. The sport media also recognise the importance of attention to performance. For example, one television commentator put the defeat of the Australian Rugby Union team by South Africa, in the second match of the 1993 series, down to "a lack of focus by the Wallabies".

Attention appears to be a fundamental prerequisite for optimal performance in any sporting endeavour. It also plays a key role in the learning of skills. The learner's motivation to attend to the task and exert effort to improve performance has been identified as a key ingredient in the development of expertise in a variety of domains (eg., sport, music, science) (Ericsson, Krampe, & Tesch-Romer, 1993). It is not surprising, therefore, that attention skills training is a major area of applied sport psychology (see Chapter 15). In this chapter we examine the concept of attention, with particular reference to the research and theory underlying the concept. We will show that, despite everyone knowing what attention is, the phenomenon itself is still poorly understood. A brief overview of theoretical perspectives to attention developed in mainstream psychology will be followed by an examination of those aspects of attention most relevant to sport. Finally, some models and metaphors for attentional functioning will be considered that may provide a useful framework for understanding the relationships between the sub-dimensions of attention.

~~~ ATTENTION — WHAT IS IT?

Although we all have an intuitive view of what attention is and how it operates, within the domain of psychology there is no consensus on how to define the concept. Terms such as concentration, alertness, focus, selectivity, arousal, mental set and consciousness have all been associated with the notion of attention. In one of the most cited quotes in psychology, William James (1890) defined attention as:

> ... the taking possession by the mind, in clear and vivid form, of one out of what seem several simultaneously possible objects or trains of thought. Focalization, concentration, of consciousness are of its essence. It implies withdrawal from some things in order to deal effectively with others. (pp. 403–404)

In his definition, James identified an obvious dimension of attention — its selectivity. That is, attention refers to the concentration and focusing of mental effort onto certain sources of information while ignoring others. In sport, the ability to focus attention on task salient cues while simultaneously screening out or ignoring extraneous and irrelevant information is crucial for optimal performance. For example, the golfer attempting to sink a vital putt must focus on the task at hand and be oblivious to potential distractions, such as crowd noise.

It is also clear that the focus of our mental effort is shiftable. Some shifts are involuntary as when our attention is drawn by a sudden change, such as a loud noise or flash of light. Most shifts of focus, however, appear to be under our control, as when the Rugby place kicker shifts attentional focus between the ball and the posts as he prepares for a penalty shot. In fast ball games, such as basketball, the player has to be able to make rapid shifts in attentional focus, often from a broad focus as when scanning the court for the position of opponents, to a narrow focus when shooting.

Shifts of attentional focus can also be from external stimuli to stimuli arising from within the individual, internal attention (e.g., thoughts, sensations).

In addition to being selective and shiftable, under certain circumstances we seem to be able to maintain more than one focus of attention simultaneously. Many sports, for example, require players to perform a number of activities concurrently. This is especially so in fast ball games like basketball, soccer and hockey where players have to look for someone to pass to while dribbling the ball. The limitations we have on performing more than one activity at the same time have been of long-standing interest to researchers in attention.

So, as an initial general definition, attention can be viewed as the concentration and focusing of mental activity; a focus that is selective, shiftable and divisible (Best, 1986). James (1890) equated the focusing of mental effort with consciousness. Understanding attention would be much easier if all decisions about which stimuli to focus upon were made consciously but, unfortunately, this does not appear to be the case. Driving a car while talking to a passenger is the example most frequently used to illustrate this point. While paying conscious attention to your passenger's speech you continue to drive appropriately, focusing your mental effort on continually changing road conditions. However, you seem to make the driving decisions without being aware of these decisions. James (1890) did distinguish between effortful attention (focalisation of consciousness) and habitual (non-conscious) attention. This distinction has become important in contemporary views of attention.

It should be clear from the previous discussion that a single concise definition of attention is impossible. Part of the problem is that attention has been studied from at least three perspectives, with each perspective emphasising a different aspect of attention (Boutcher, 1992). First, within cognitive psychology attention has been seen as a moderating influence on the basic information-processing stages of encoding, response selection and response execution. It is within this framework that most of the theories of attentional functioning have been developed. A second perspective proposes that individuals have a characteristic style of attending to stimuli. Nideffer (1976a), for example, has argued that attentional style can be considered a personality trait or individual difference variable. It is this perspective that has had the greatest influence in the development of attention training programs in sport psychology (see Chapter 15). The third, more recent, perspective has been concerned with identifying the psychophysiological mechanisms underlying attention. In the sport domain this work has primarily involved the examination of electroencephalogram (EEG) and cardiac deceleration patterns in sports people (e.g., archers, shooters) during a performance (see Abernethy, 1993; Boutcher, 1992, for a review of this literature).

THEORETICAL PERSPECTIVES

BOTTLENECK THEORIES

A basic assumption of information-processing theory is that there is a limitation on the amount of information that can be processed at one time. As a consequence we need to be selective in what we process to avoid cognitive overload. It was argued that there is a bottleneck somewhere in the information-processing system that allows us to perceive only a part of what is available in the world around us. Much of the early research from this perspective was concerned with identifying the location of the bottleneck in the processing sequence and under what conditions attention could be divided between two or more tasks (e.g., Broadbent, 1958;

Deutsch & Deutsch, 1963; Keele, 1973; Norman, 1969; see Abernethy, 1993, for a review of this literature). Evidence supporting an attention mechanism located both early and late in the processing sequence argued against attempts to locate attention selection at a particular stage of processing.

RESOURCE THEORIES

Growing dissatisfaction with stage models of attention led to the view that attention may be best conceptualised as the deployment of cognitive resources. The basic assumption is that there is a limited supply of resources which are undifferentiated and unspecialised in nature, and which can be flexibly allocated in varying amounts to different tasks (Allport, 1980; Kahneman, 1973). The performance of any cognitive task, therefore, depends on the amount of resource capacity assigned to that task. Theoretically, two tasks can be performed at the same time if the combined demands of both tasks do not exceed the common pool of resources. However, when the processing requirements exceed available resources, then performance on one or both of the tasks will deteriorate.

The notion of performance being constrained by available resources has important implications for understanding sport performance. In most sporting situations there is a vast amount of information that could be processed, some of it relevant to performance and some of it not (e.g., spectators, negative thoughts). The athlete's problem is to cope with this potential overload. To do this the athlete must learn what to attend to and when, and must shift attention skilfully between events in the environment, monitoring and correcting his or her own actions, planning future actions, and carrying out many other processes that compete for the limited pool of resources.

One way to reduce the resource demands of a task is through practice. Extensive practice on a task is seen as leading to the development of automaticity. Automatic processing refers to the activation of a learned sequence of elements or behaviours in permanent memory (Moates & Schumacher, 1980). Under automatic control performance is fast, effortless and does not require conscious control. The skilled tennis player, for example, is aware when it is time to serve in a match but would not have to consciously think about the serving action itself. Most world champion athletes report being in an automatic or "autopilot" state during their best performances (e.g., Kreiner-Phillips & Orlick, 1993). In contrast, controlled or conscious processing is used during the early stages of learning and when athletes have to make choices and decisions (e.g., which type of serve to use) during a performance. Controlled processing is slow, attention demanding, serial in nature and under voluntary control. There are many examples in sport that appear to support the change from controlled to automatic processing with practice. When first learning to dribble a ball in hockey or soccer a great deal of attention is required to control the process and the player mainly fixates on the ball. The skilled player, in contrast, can dribble the ball and be monitoring the opposition's defenders, or searching for a team mate to pass to. The resources previously devoted to dribbling can be directed to other tasks such as monitoring the periphery or deciding on strategy or tactics. Highly skilled performance in any sport, therefore, involves a combination of controlled and automatic processing. Figure 3.1 shows how these processes interact in a typical sporting situation (fast break in basketball). Nougier, Stein, and Bonnel (1991) suggest that the ability to coordinate and switch between automatic and controlled processes is a characteristic of expert athletes. In closed skills, such as golf, archery and shooting, the overlearned nature of the skill can create a problem because there is ample opportunity for attention to focus on disruptive sources of information such as negative thoughts and irrelevant information.

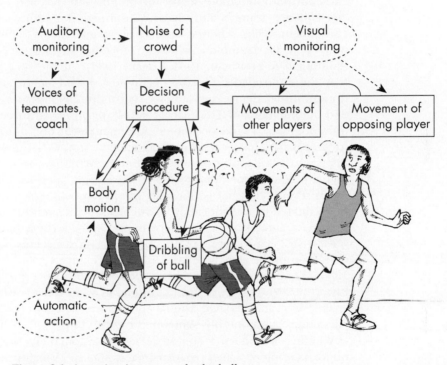

Figure 3.1: Attention in sport — basketball

Although notions of attentional resources, automatic and controlled processes have considerable appeal in describing sport performance, they have been under increasing criticism in recent years. First, there has been a move away from the assumption that resources are undifferentiated in nature and toward the view that there are different types of resources that can be allocated to any task that demands them (Navon & Gopher, 1979). If two tasks do not have resources in common, they can be performed concurrently without interference. For example, specific resources have been proposed for input modality (visual versus auditory), processing stage (early versus late), processing code (spatial versus verbal) and motor control (Gopher & Sanders, 1984; Wickens, 1984, 1992). There have also been attempts to link resources to particular brain structures, such as the cerebral hemispheres (e.g., Friedman & Polson, 1981). Although multiple resource models have been able to account for a wide range of dual task findings, lack of definitional clarity and specific patterns of interference between concurrent motor actions present problems for the attentional resource framework (Barber, 1988; Neumann, 1987; Summers, 1990).

The traditional definition of automatic processing as a fast unconscious process that consumes no attentional capacity (Shiffrin & Schneider, 1977) also has been questioned (Broadbent, 1982; Neumann, 1984). For example, it has been pointed out that in dual-task experiments, even after extensive practice, seldom, if ever, can two tasks be performed concurrently without some degree of mutual interference occurring. As a consequence some writers have questioned the utility of the concept (Broadbent, 1982) whereas others have argued for a redefinition of the unitary term "automaticity" (e.g., Jacoby, Ste-Marie, & Toth, 1992; Kahneman & Treisman, 1984; Logan, 1985). At the very least it is clear that the controlled-automatic distinction should be regarded as a continuum rather than a dichotomy (Abernethy, 1993; Logan, 1985). To this end, Kahneman and Treisman (1984) have proposed three subcategories of strong, partial and occasional automaticity. Strong automaticity refers to processing that is neither facilitated by applying attention to it nor impaired by diverting attention from it. Whether or not strong automaticity can ever be demonstrated, however, is open to question (Peters, 1990). Processing that is normally carried out without attention but can be facilitated by the allocation of attention is referred to as partially automatic. An interesting point here is that some writers have argued that once a skill has become automated, applying conscious attention to the execution of the activity will disrupt performance (e.g., Schneider & Fisk, 1983). For example, the golfer at the tee who is worrying about keeping his or her head down, arm straight etc. may experience what is known as "paralysis by analysis". Occasional automaticity refers to processes that usually require attention but sometimes can be completed without it.

Whether introducing subcategories of automaticity will increase our understanding of skilled performance is unclear. A major problem for this approach is how these degrees of automaticity can be measured and distinguished. In a complex sporting performance containing many processes operating in parallel, it is likely that some of these processes will be strongly automated, others partially automated and still others under volitional control. Furthermore, how attention comes to bear on a strongly automated activity is not understood. In fact, often resources may need to be devoted to inhibiting or controlling the initiation of automatic processing. For example, Reason (1979) has argued that many of the errors (action slips) we make in everyday activities are failures to inhibit automatic sequences of behaviour. Recently, even the assumption that automaticity (without awareness) requires extensive practice on a task to develop has been questioned. Singer, Lidor, and Cauraugh (1993) examined whether beginners could be instructed to adopt a non-awareness strategy similar to that reported by elite performers. Four learning strategies were compared on the acquisition of a self-paced motor task (non-dominant overhand throw at a target) by novices. One group (awareness strategy) was encouraged to consciously attend to the throwing action, the feel of the movement and the noise of the ball hitting the target. Subjects in a non-awareness strategy group were told to focus on one cue (e.g., centre of the target) and then execute the throwing movement automatically, i.e., without consciously attending to it. A third group was taught Singer's (1988) Five-Step Approach (ready oneself, image the act, focus attention on a cue, execute automatically, evaluate the act). Subjects in the fourth (control) group were allowed to adopt their own strategy for the task. The results showed that the Five-Step Approach and non-awareness strategy groups produced superior performance to either the awareness or control groups. The authors conclude that novices can successfully adopt attentional strategies frequently reported by experts. It remains to be seen the extent to which these findings will generalise to more complex sequential motor skills.

The conceptual framework of resource theory still has intuitive appeal in explaining sport performance despite a number of obvious shortcomings. Unfortunately, much of the current thinking about attention has been based on laboratory experiments using relatively simple tasks. Studying attention in more "real world" tasks such as sporting activities may provide important insights into the functions of attention.

A major problem with the concept of attention is that there does not appear to be common language among those involved with studying, and applying the phenomenon. Many times the same labels are used to denote different aspects of attention (e.g., alertness) and different labels are used to denote the same aspect (e.g., narrow, focused, selective, concentrative, are all terms for attending to only a small number of stimuli at once). This situation is compounded by the use of some of these terms in a different sense by participants in sports. For example, the term concentration is commonly used by sports participants simply to mean attend in a manner necessary to complete the task successfully. This may include using a broad attentional focus, being able to switch attention quickly, and staying alert. However, in the attention literature concentration is used rarely but, when it is, it refers to attending to only a small number of task relevant stimuli at one time. Thus confusion can result from use of these terms without defining them.

In the next section we examine some of the suggested dimensions of attention that appear particularly important in sport performance and review the limited amount of research on attention that has been conducted within a sport context. Traditionally, our understanding of the role of attention in sport relied on a form of naive phenomenology in which people described how attention works based on how it seems to work in practice and how it is experienced by the participants. This has resulted in some understanding of attention in sport but has also led to many misinformed beliefs about the function. One example that comes to mind is the command to "watch the ball right onto the racquet" which successful racquet players do not do, nor do they need to. Another example is "never take your eye off the ball if you want to catch it" which is also false because the eyes can be removed from the flight of the ball at some stage without performance decrement (Savelsbergh, Whiting, & Pijpers, 1992). Many of the common notions about attention in sport need to be challenged to further our understanding of the phenomenon.

DIMENSIONS OF ATTENTION

The functioning of attention involves three major aspects: where is attention directed (direction), how much attention is devoted to that direction (intensity), and the alteration of intensity and direction as required (flexibility). The first two aspects can be broken down to reveal further distinctions that are useful in guiding our understanding of attention and its application to sport. For example, whether attention is directed to a number of stimuli, or only a few, relates to the span or width of attention (i.e., distributed or focused attention). Which particular stimuli receive attention, as some have greater relevance for the task, relates to the selectivity of attention. Concepts such as mental workload, alertness and overall processing capacity are related to the intensity of attention. Attentional flexibility, in a more refined sense, can usually be conceived as altering attention along any of these subdimensions.

DIRECTION

The direction dimension refers to the source of the stimuli attended. That is, whether the stimuli originate in the environment, referred to as external attention or whether they originate internally from within the individual (Nideffer, 1976a). Examples of external attention would be watching a ball, focusing on a target and watching a play develop. Internal attention refers to thoughts, self-talk, imagery and internal sensations (e.g., kinaesthetic cues). Becoming too focused on thoughts and feelings appears to be one cause of an athlete "choking" when under pressure.

Width

The width of attention refers to the number of cues that receive attention at one time. Nideffer (1976b) views width as a continuous dimension ranging from broad (many cues receiving attention) to narrow (small number of cues attended).

Some writers have suggested that broad attention should be broken into scanning and broad "snapshot" forms (Wachtel, 1967). Scanning relates to searching serially across a field of cues while broad attention relates to a snapshot form that processes a great number of cues in one glance. Narrow attention is usually equated with the notion of focused attention.

Selectivity

As noted at the beginning of this chapter a major feature of attention is its selectivity. Selective attention is not, however, merely reducing the number of stimuli that receive further processing (narrowing or focusing attention), it also relates to the task relevance of the cues attended. For example, a soccer goalkeeper defending a penalty could focus on the ball as the kick is taken, or on the kicker's leg angle and foot orientation before contact. In both instances attention is selective. However, focusing on the leg swing may be more beneficial for successful task performance (defending the goal) because it would yield earlier information on the likely direction of the ball. Thus, selective attention involves two major aspects: the ability to focus attention without being overloaded or distracted and the ability to direct that focus to the most important stimuli for successfully performing the task. Wickens (1992) suggests the essential difference between selective and focused attention is that failures of selective attention result from an "intentional but unwise choice to process non-optimal environmental sources" (p. 75). In contrast, failures of focused attention result from processing non-optimal sources "driven" by the stimuli despite attempts to block them out; i.e., unintentional processing. Stimuli attract attention when they are novel, moving, or salient.

Over the last decade, selectivity has been the main focus in sport research on attention. Most of these studies have centred on comparing elite versus novice participants on visual perception to examine differences in selective attention. The basic task used in this research is to show subjects films of an athlete performing various sporting actions (e.g., tennis serve and forehand drive, badminton smashes and drop-shots, volleyball offensive plays), with the task of responding as quickly as possible when the outcome of the action is determined. For example, Abernethy and Russell (1987a, b) had badminton players watch films of a player (seen from the perspective of an opponent) performing various badminton shots. In a temporal occlusion condition, the film was cut at various times prior to and after racquet contact. In a spatial occlusion condition, different regions of the player's body were occluded by masking (e.g., arm and racquet, head and face). The eye movements of subjects were also recorded. The subjects' task was to predict the direction of the shot and record where they believed the opponent's shot would land by marking it on a scaled version of the court (see Abernethy, 1991 for a review of this research).

Consistent across studies of badminton and squash was the finding that experts were able to use earlier cues than novices to predict the flight of the ball or shuttle. In particular, experts were attuned to movement of the player's arm and racquet, whereas novices typically relied on racquet cues alone. The use of earlier cues led to faster decision times and superior accuracy for experts. It was notable that early flight path cues of the ball or shuttle did not greatly improve accuracy for either novices or experts. Experts, therefore, are better able to recognise the redundancy of many cues (such as the ball) and focus on extracting meaning from more pertinent cues. This effectively reduces the quantity of information to manageable proportions within the time constraints. The ability to use earlier cues also results in more time to choose, organise and execute a response.

Interestingly, in the Abernethy and Russell studies both the experts and novices showed similar visual search patterns. Visual scanning differences between experts and novices, however, have been reported in other studies. For example, in studies examining the pick-up of anticipatory information in tennis, experts made more eye fixations on the racquet and arm of opponents than novices (Goulet, Bard, & Fleury, 1989) and had longer fixation times than novices (Cauraugh, Singer, & Chen, 1993). Expert–novice differences have also been found in team sports. Williams, Davids, Burwitz, and Williams (1993) examined expert–novice differences in anticipation and visual search strategies within "open-play" in soccer. Inexperienced players tended to fixate mainly on the ball and the player passing the ball, whereas experienced players fixated more frequently on players "off the ball".

Prediction accuracy and decision times have been found to depend on a number of factors. Salmela and Fiorito (1979), for example, found that ice hockey goal-keepers' accuracy in determining the terminal location of the puck in a goal shot attempt depended on the type of shot viewed. Similarly, Glencross and Paull (1993) in a study of baseball batters found that there were different trends in decision times and outcome accuracy for curve balls and slide pitches compared to fast balls. The differences suggested that the earlier cues for curve balls and sliders were misleading with respect to the final outcome of the pitch, whereas the earlier cues could be used to reliably predict the path over the home plate of fast balls.

The role of the player in team games has also been shown to influence selective attention. Ripoll (1988) had volleyball players predict the position along the net where the opposing team would make the attack. Coaches were the fastest and most accurate, followed by the setters (the playmakers on volleyball teams), and finally the spikers (attacking players). Another factor that has recently been shown to affect prediction accuracy is the strategic state of the game. In the study of baseball batters (Glencross & Paull, 1993), a game context was described for some of the film clips but not others. It was found that knowing the strategic context decreased decision time and errors in predicting the final position of the pitch over the plate, for both experts and novices, although experts were still superior on both aspects. Thus it appears that strategic knowledge helps players in setting up prior probabilities for certain types of pitches.

Importantly, the above findings are unlikely to be due to "hardware" differences between elite and novice athletes. That is, elite athletes do not appear to possess a superior nervous system to less talented sportspersons. There is little empirical evidence, for example, to support the link between visual-perceptual abilities such as stereoacuity, dynamic visual acuity, or processing speed (e.g., reaction time) and sport skill (Starkes & Deakin, 1984). It is possible, of course, that the "hardware" factors previously examined may not be the same as those used by the central nervous system in skilled performance. For example, Bootsma (1993) has argued that the expert performer may be someone who has learned to pick up, accurately, relevant optical information directly (e.g., "tau" — visual information specifying time to contact).

Some caution must be exercised in interpreting the findings of film occlusion studies, however, because of the questionable ecological validity of this approach. For example, these simulated situations do not contain factors known to affect attentional processes such as contextual information and the stressors or the motivation encountered in a competitive situation. Moreover, determining the direction of attention from eye movements and fixations may be problematic. There is increasing evidence that the locus of attention can be detached from the locus of fixation (e.g., Posner, Nissen, & Ogden, 1978). Studies of covert attentional orienting (determining the direction of attention when the focus of the eyes does not move) have found that the focus of attention need not be where the eyes are centred and that attention can move flexibly during a fixation. Castiello and Umilta (1992), for example, found that professional volleyball players could split focal attention between noncontiguous regions of space better than novices. Ripoll (1991) has also argued that experts use a synthetic mode of visual scanning, consisting of directing the gaze to a position from which the maximum number of events can be seen and grouping from one fixation (a type of visual chunking). Despite the above reservations, studies using the film occlusion paradigm do suggest that cognitive skills, such as selective attention and memory, differentiate elite from non-elite athletes, at least for fast action sports.

INTENSIVE ASPECTS OF ATTENTION

Capacity limits on attention

How much attention is devoted to a task is related to the assumption that the information-processing system has limits on the amount of information that can be processed at one time. As previously discussed, capacity limitations evident under controlled processing, may not apply when the task becomes automated. It is not clear, however, how a task goes through the transition from being a controlled to an automatic process. One possibility is that part of the automatisation process involves chunking, or perceptual grouping; organising separate stimuli into meaningful units or wholes.

The advantage of chunking is that a number of stimuli, previously processed independently and serially, are processed as one stimulus group. This not only speeds up processing because more can be taken in at a glance, but the patterns of stimuli can be more easily interpreted. Furthermore, grouping the discrete stimuli can result in emergent features that are not evident if the stimuli are viewed in isolation, but are present if the different stimuli are treated as a whole.

Research into "chunking" by athletes in sport has used the paradigm originally developed by de Groot (1965) and Chase and Simon (1973) to study chess masters. Most of this research has compared elite and non-elite athletes on how much information can be extracted in a short period of time. For example, Allard, Graham, and Paarsalu (1980) had basketballers and non-basketballers view slides of structured and unstructured basketball situations for four seconds and then recall the position of the players on a scaled-down version of the court. They found that the basketballers were more accurate in their recall of the positions for players in structured (e.g., a point guard about to initiate a play from the top of the key) but not unstructured (e.g., a scramble for a loose ball) situations. Starkes and Deakin (1984) found similar results comparing Canadian National Hockey players to physical education students on structured and unstructured hockey situations. The same pattern of results has been reported for coaches: elite coaches were able to extract more information about the technical quality of a shot-put throw, particularly in the critical phase of the shot-put action, than novice coaches (Pinheiro, 1993).

Support for the hypothesis that the stimuli are being perceptually chunked has come from investigating how the game elements are recalled. Allard and Burnett (1985) had elite and non-elite basketballers recreate game situations but allowed them as many five-second glances at the slides as they needed. They found that elite players needed fewer glances and that they recreated more elements of the play after each glance. Thus elite players encoded larger chunks than novices. However, this was only the case for structured situations, but not unstructured, suggesting that it was not a general cognitive ability that divided elite and novices. This greater ability to chunk information was explained by memory rather than attention factors. That is, elite players had greater declarative knowledge and had superior retrieval systems for this knowledge.

Chunking studies may be uncovering the processes that allow automaticity to develop. Logan (1988) suggests that the reason automaticity develops, and is generally unrelated to attention resource use, is because it depends on the acquisition of domain specific knowledge. Briefly, Logan suggests that novices' performance is limited by their lack of knowledge rather than scarcity of resources. With increased practice (repeated instances of a task) memory improves in various ways (e.g., better encoding, organisation, retrieval). Further increases in experience lead to learning specific solutions to specific problems. Automaticity, according to this view is memory retrieval, performance is automatic because it is based on a single-step direct-access retrieval of past solutions from memory. Chunking studies appear to support this view, in that chunking depends on the level of an athlete's declarative knowledge; processing is faster because the pattern of cues is treated as a single stimulus and so memory retrieval occurs for fewer stimuli and no integration is required. Furthermore, structured situations would be encountered more frequently than unstructured situations in a game, so practice effects would occur and structured situations (as opposed to unstructured) contain elements that are consistent across repetitions, a necessary condition for developing automaticity (Schneider & Shiffrin, 1977). Chunking, therefore, may simply be a part of the automatisation process. Regardless of the underlying causes, however, chunking does appear to ease the processing burden on the athlete and allow other tasks to be accomplished.

Alertness

The term alertness has been used in many ways in the attention literature. Most commonly, alertness has been defined as the responsivity or sensitivity of a person to stimuli. Martens (1987), for example, refers to the concept as "a person's awareness to the stimuli impinging on the senses, or a person's responsiveness to the environment" (p. 147). Other writers suggest that the development and maintenance of optimal sensitivity over a period of time is a further aspect of alertness (e.g., Posner & Boies, 1971). Clearly, momentary increases in alertness (e.g., when receiving a serve in tennis) and sustained alertness (e.g., over a long, five-set tennis match) are crucial requirements in many sports.

In the laboratory, sustaining alertness has been typically studied using vigilance tasks. In a vigilance task subjects' ability to detect stimuli that occur infrequently and irregularly over a long period of time is measured (e.g., watching a clock face for occasional jumps of the sweep hand). In sport, outfielders in cricket, baseball, and softball are engaged in vigilance tasks, as are line and net cord judges in tennis (Abernethy, 1993). The ability to maintain sufficient sensitivity to the environment (or maintain general awareness) is also important for open sports where events can take an unexpected direction, or provide an opportunity to take advantage of an unexpected situation.

Fluctuations in a person's level of alertness have been seen as being related to, or synonymous with (Abernethy, 1993), changes in arousal level. Arousal refers to the physiological and psychological activation of the person. Kahneman (1973), for example, suggests that, although attentional capacity is limited, the amount of available capacity (resources) for processing fluctuates as a function of arousal. In particular, increases in arousal lead to activation of additional resources and hence the capacity limits of the person increase. Kahneman refers to the situational capacity of an individual as "alertness" (the amount of available capacity at any one time), or the amount of conscious sensitivity to task-related stimuli. With greater alertness, individuals have more acute attentional capabilities. An athlete's level of arousal is, therefore, important in ensuring that maximum attentional capacity is available to optimise attentional functioning.

AROUSAL AND ATTENTION

Any discussion on the attentional processes in sport needs to consider the profound effect arousal has on attention. In most sports, arousal level is affected by not only the physical exercise involved but also other factors such as anxiety, emotions, and motivation.

The relationship between arousal and performance has typically been hypothesised to follow the shape of an inverted-U curve (see Chapter 2). That is, as arousal increases it facilitates performance up to a point beyond which further increases lead to decrement in performance. The most common explanation of the inverted-U curve suggests that changes in arousal level produce changes in attentional processes. Easterbrook's (1959) cue utilisation theory, for example, suggests that poor performance when underaroused is a result of indiscriminate processing of stimuli. As arousal increases, attention narrows to cues pertinent to the task and irrelevant stimuli (e.g., crowd movement) are ignored, hence performance improves. Further increases in arousal produce further attentional narrowing and eventually important task-relevant cues (e.g., position of team mates) begin to be neglected leading to a decrement in performance. Strong support for the attention narrowing explanation has come from a number of studies, including a study of rifle shooters (Landers, Wang, & Courtet, 1985), showing a narrowing of peripheral vision under stress (e.g., Bacon, 1974; Hockey, 1970). However, attentional narrowing is not simply a reduction in the spatial area attended with peripheral stimuli automatically filtered, as Easterbrook's hypothesis suggests. Rather, a high state of arousal impairs the process of discrimination (ability to distinguish relevant from irrelevant stimuli) and consequently the ability to focus on relevant external stimuli is impaired (Broadbent, 1971). Thus, even though attention becomes more selective (narrowed) when arousal increases, the effectiveness of the selections is likely to deteriorate producing a decline in performance.

The effects of arousal on attentional processes are clear, although the mechanisms that underlie these effects are not well understood. One problem is that much of the research has been based around optimal arousal theory proposing an inverted-U relationship between arousal and performance. It is clear, however, that high arousal does not always have a deleterious effect on performance. Rather, it is the athlete's interpretation of his or her arousal level that is important. For example, high risk sporting activities (e.g., motor racing, mountaineering, hang gliding) involve extremely high levels of arousal, but are experienced as exciting and pleasant by most participants (Kerr, 1985). As a consequence of increasing criticism of the inverted-U hypothesis, other models such as multidimensional anxiety theory (Martens, Burton, Vealey, Bump, & Smith, 1990), reversal theory (Kerr, 1990) and catastrophe theory (Hardy, 1990) have been proposed (see Chapter 2 for further discussion of these models). These models may help refine our understanding of the attention-arousal relationship further.

FLEXIBILITY

Flexibility, or switching, of attention is vital in almost any sporting context (Nideffer, 1976a). It is particularly important in sports where there are fast environmental changes and it is the attentional "glue" that allows athletes to move or alter their attention to meet the changing attentional requirements of the environment or task. In more static sports such as pistol shooting, the performer must shift attention between internal cues (monitoring the body's state of relaxation) and external cues such as the target.

Etzel (1979) defined attentional flexibility as the ability to direct and alter the scope (width) and focus (direction) of attention (i.e., along a broad to narrow as well as internal to external continuum). It is reasonable to extend this definition to include two other aspects that also require flexible use. The first is the ability to switch between cues that are optimally task-relevant, including refocusing after becoming distracted. For example, an athlete must learn to quickly regain control and focus on the task at hand following errors during a performance (e.g., missed shots, double faults). The second is the regulation of mental energy in order to prolong the maintenance of attention/alertness (Martens, 1987). To concentrate for extended periods of time is very energy consuming so an athlete must be able to relax, or lower the intensity of his or her focus (reduce the mental workload) whenever possible to conserve energy, but be able to increase the intensity when necessary. For example, a batter in cricket often has to concentrate for four to eight hours to make a good score. It is not possible, however, to maintain an intense attentional focus for so long without mentally tiring so the batter learns to relax mentally between balls to delay mental fatigue. However, turning attention to focus on the next delivery is crucial after this "time-out". Flexibility of attention, then, is needed to alter the intensity of attention to meet the task demands and regulate mental energy (e.g, switching between controlled and automatic processes).

A person's ability to shift attention can be viewed as lying along a continuum ranging from complete control over the alteration of attentional processes to perseveration, the inability to relinquish a particular attentional focus or state despite wanting to do so. Nideffer (1976a) has argued that detriments in performance may occur because an individual is dominated by a particular attentional style and is unable to adopt the attentional style more appropriate to the situation. Nideffer uses the attentional dimensions, originally developed by Easterbrook (1959) and Wachtel (1967), of width (broad to narrow) and direction (external to internal) to form a four quadrant matrix of attentional styles: broad–external, broad–internal, narrow–internal and narrow–external. Individuals who prefer a broad-internal style are the "thinkers", good at analysing game situations and planning strategies but can over-analyse a situation and neglect events in the environment. Those athletes who predominately operate in a broad–external mode are good at taking in a lot of information quickly, a necessity in fast action sports. Such individuals, however, can become overloaded by information and experience difficulty staying focused on a task. A narrow–external attentional style is necessary when executing actions (e.g., hitting or kicking a ball) and is the preferred style in most aiming sports (e.g., golf, archery, shooting, bowls). Adoption of this attentional style in inappropriate situations (e.g., when the environment is rapidly changing) can lead to tunnel vision. Finally, a narrow–internal style is good for diagnosing performance errors and is adopted when an athlete mentally prepares for competition. It can lead, however, to a preoccupation with one's own thoughts, often negative, and a slowing of reactions to external events. Increases in arousal are seen as causing a breakdown in the ability to shift attentional focus when appropriate, with the athlete relying on his/her preferred attentional style. High arousal can also lead to a narrowing of attention, and a tendency to become more internally focused.

Effective attention, therefore, results from adopting the appropriate style for the task requirements at a particular time. To maintain control over attention, Martens (1987) identifies two important factors: the first is being able to identify which stimuli require attention for effective task performance and the second is the efficient timing of shifts or alterations of attention. Shifting attention too early or too late can have a degrading effect on performance. For example, a netballer receiving a pass may take her eyes off the ball too early in search of a team mate to pass to and fumbles the ball because she switched her attention to the next task prematurely. In contrast, a tennis player may be taken by surprise by an opponent's return of serve because he/she failed to switch attention fast enough from serving mode to receiving mode.

Despite the obvious importance of flexible attention in sport, little research has been conducted on this aspect of attention within the sporting context. Some support for the role of attentional flexibility in highly skilled performance was obtained in two studies by Kahneman and colleagues (Gopher & Kahneman, 1971; Kahneman, Ben-Ishai, & Lotan, 1973). They found that low accident bus drivers and successful pilots (completed pilot training) performed better on dichotic listening tasks requiring switching of attention than high accident bus drivers and less successful pilots. It was proposed that laboratory tests of attentional flexibility, such as dichotic listening, could be used to predict success in tasks requiring divided attention. However, attempts to show that attentional flexibility is a generalisable ability have met with limited success (e.g., Keele & Hawkins, 1982).

MODELS OF ATTENTION

It is useful to consider models and metaphors for attentional functioning as they attempt to integrate knowledge on attention and provide a basis for analogical reasoning about the unknown aspects of attention. However, most models have been developed to explain narrow aspects of, what is presumed to be, attention. For example, many models explain mainly visual attention but auditory attention which appears to operate differently is often neglected.

Covert attentional orienting studies have also derived models which help illuminate the operation of selective attention. These models are referred to as the spotlight, zoom-lens and gradient models. The spotlight metaphor likens visual attention to the beam of a spotlight or searchlight. It illuminates cues (selectively attends) in the field by focusing the spotlight onto those cues, with cues outside the beam receiving little or no processing. To reorient attention the beam is moved to the stimuli of interest. There is some evidence that expert athletes (e.g., boxers, tennis players, fencers) are able to respond almost as fast to expected (i.e., within the attentional beam) and unexpected (outside the beam) cues, whereas nonexperts are much faster at responding to expected than unexpected cues (Nougier, Stein, & Bonnel, 1991). That is, experts are quicker at disengaging attention from one location and reorienting to another in response to an unexpected event. This ability would clearly be an advantage in sports containing a high level of uncertainty such as boxing and fencing.

The zoom-lens model (Eriksen & Yeh, 1985), an extension of the spotlight model, suggests the beam can be broadened or narrowed like adjusting the focus on a camera. It can be broadened to take in a wider field of stimuli (diffuse attention) or narrowed to focus on only a very small field (focal attention). The model assumes that a finite pool of attentional resources is evenly distributed across the beam. Therefore, altering the width of the beam acts to dilute or concentrate the distribution of resources across the beam. If attention is focused narrowly, the resources become concentrated and so more detailed processing can occur. If the beam is broadened then the same number of resources must be "stretched" across the beam, thus reducing the ability to perceive and process detail. This redistribution of resources has been described as the resolving power of the zoom-lens. It has been suggested that optimal attentional beam width may differ across different sports, across ability levels within a sport, and in team sports it may vary according to an individual's role in the game (Nougier, Stein, & Bonnel, 1991).

Both the spotlight and zoom-lens models predict a boundary for the focus of attention, outside which stimuli receive very little or no processing. The gradient model (La Berge & Brown, 1989), in contrast, proposes no distinct boundary, rather resources are distributed like a bell-shaped curve; most resources are concentrated around the focal point and gradually drop-off as a function of the distance from the focal point. This model predicts, therefore, that cues at and very near the focal point receive the most processing but cues in the periphery also receive some processing. This model appears to be able to accommodate most of the attentional phenomena observed in sporting situations.

Although far from complete, these models of covert attention may be useful in increasing our understanding of attentional operation. The models, however, suffer (as all attention models do) from an inability to provide a satisfactory explanation of what orients attention (the beam). Peters (1990) has argued that whichever way one looks at the problem of attention, "one does not really get around the concept of a central unitary scheduler, the unitary acting self" (p. 564), that assigns priorities and determines the contents of focal attention.

A further problem with searchlight models of attention is that they deal exclusively with attending externally to cues in the environment. Indeed, much of our knowledge and theorising about attention relates to external attention. Internal attention, attention to cues that originate within the individual, has been largely neglected. Yet, in sport psychology much of the work done by practitioners involves helping athletes to control their emotions and thoughts through the use of techniques such as relaxation and imagery. There is also some evidence that the type of internal attention may be important in endurance sports such as marathon runnning. Morgan and Pollock (1977) interviewed elite and non-elite marathon runners and concluded that elite runners predominantly use an associative strategy to adjust pace while running, involving the continual monitoring of body signals such as breathing and feelings in the legs. Non-elite runners, in contrast, use a dissociative strategy in which they try to divert attention away from the discomfort of running by thinking of other things. Subsequent research, however, has failed to substantiate this dichotomy and it appears that runners of all levels use both types of strategies during a long run (Schomer, 1986; Summers, Machin, & Sargent, 1983; Summers, Sargent, Levey, & Murray, 1982). The use of either an associative or dissociative strategy depends on a number of factors, such as whether it is a training or competition run, the length and stage of the run and the topography of the terrain.

One approach that attempts to incorporate both internal and external attention within the same framework is Nideffer's (1976a) attentional style theory, discussed previously. Nideffer (1976b) developed the Test of Attentional and Interpersonal Style (TAIS) to measure a person's attentional style. The TAIS and sport-specific versions of the instrument have been used extensively in examining expert–novice differences in attentional style in a variety of sports (e.g., Albrecht & Feltz, 1987; Maynard & Howe, 1989; Summers & Maddocks, 1986; Summers, Miller, & Ford, 1991; Vallerand, 1983; Van Schoyck & Grasha, 1981).

Although attentional style theory has done much to further the understanding of the role of attention in sport, a number of questions and criticisms have been raised about aspects of the theory. First, there is little direct evidence to support a basic assumption of the theory that preferred attentional styles exist in normal populations. Second, as Martens (1987) has pointed out, attention is either external or internal, not a little more or less of one or the other, so the direction dimension should be dichotomous rather than continuous as proposed. Third, there are other dimensions of attention seemingly neglected by the theory (e.g., intensity, capacity, alertness, maintenance). Similarly, adopting the appropriate width and direction of attention (appropriate style) is not necessarily sufficient for effective attention. For example, a narrow external focus may be required but, if this focus is not on the cues that are task relevant, then performance will be poor. The addition of a further orthogonal dimension to the theory relating to the task relevance of stimuli may, therefore, be necessary. Fourth, the application of the generalised theory to the sporting domain is questionable because of the sport-specific nature of cues used by athletes. The consistent finding that elite athletes make better and faster use of cues than novices in sport-specific contexts but not in non-specific contexts, or even unstructured sport-specific contexts, suggests that it is not some attentional style or trait that determines cue use or effective attention in sport. Finally, recent criticisms of the psychometric properties of the TAIS (e.g., Ford & Summers, 1992; Summers & Ford, 1990, Van Schoyck & Grasha, 1981) suggest that the test may have limited value in assessing attentional processes in athletes.

Although we believe that attentional style theory is an incomplete model of macro-attentional operation (as opposed to micro-attentional operation that deals with the specific details, such as covert attention) it has provided a good starting point for the development of future models of attentional processes in sport performance.

FUTURE DIRECTIONS

Our current understanding of the concept of attention has come predominantly from the information processing framework within cognitive psychology. This laboratory-based approach has focused on three major aspects of attention: alertness, capacity, and selectivity (Posner & Boies, 1971). As a consequence, much has been learned about the role of these attentional factors in the performance of relatively simple laboratory tasks. There have been, however, few attempts to integrate the various facets of attention into a unified theory of attentional functioning. What is also not clear is the extent to which the findings obtained with contrived tasks will extend to "real-world" activities such as sport performance.

There is a clear need for detailed analyses of the attentional demands of various sports. The sporting arena seems to provide an ideal environment for the study of attentional processes. For example, experts in many domains appear to have overcome many of the limitations on attention that have been identified in laboratory situations (Ericsson et al., 1993; Summers, 1990). One promising research direction has been the marrying of cognitive psychology and psychophysiology in the investigation of cognitive processes involved in athletic performance. Cognitive psychophysiologists have begun to examine the relationship between physiological measures such as electroencephalogram (EEG), event-related potentials (ERPs), contingent negative variation (CNV), and heart rate and athletic performance. For example, hemispheric asymmetries in the direction of increased left hemisphere EEG alpha activity have been observed just prior to trigger pull in elite rifle shooters (Hatfield, Landers, & Ray, 1984, 1987) and arrow release in archers (Salazar, Landers, Petruzzello, Crews, & Kubitz, 1988; Salazar, Landers, Petruzzello, Crews, Kubitz, & Han, 1990). The changes in EEG activity have been interpreted as reflecting a transition of control from the verbal-based left hemisphere to the more visual-spatial right hemisphere prior to response execution. It has been suggested that the inhibition of left hemisphere activity may reduce the intrusion of unwanted cognitions during performance of the activity (Boutcher, 1992).

ERPs are changes in EEG activity that are directly related to the occurrence of discrete events (Donchin, 1979) and CNV is a slow negative potential that seems related to stimulus anticipation and preparation for movement. Some researchers argue for a direct relationship between ERPs and human information processing stages (e.g., Zani & Rossi, 1991) whereas others are more sceptical (e.g., Timsit-Berthier, 1991). Zani and Rossi (1991), for example, report reliable differences between clay-pigeon shooters specialising in either trap or skeet in the early latency N2 component (elicited by rare and unexpected events) and the late latency P300 component (reflecting the operation of attention) of the ERP. Of particular importance is that these differences were obtained in a simple laboratory task unrelated to clay-pigeon shooting. These findings suggest that elite athletes develop attentional strategies (styles) specific to their sport and that these strategies are generalisable to other non-sport tasks that demand controlled attention. This generalisability of attentional strategies contrasts with the specificity of sport related declarative knowledge discussed earlier.

Heart rate changes also seem to be related to attentional processes in athletes. Cardiac deceleration has been observed immediately prior to response execution in closed skill sports such as rifle shooting (Konttinen & Lyytinen, 1992) and golf putting (Boutcher & Zinsser, 1990). Furthermore, the degree of cardiac deceleration appears to be related to skill level and performance with highly skilled performers exhibiting greater deceleration than less skilled performers and, within an individual, the best trials in a performance being preceded by greater cardiac deceleration than the poorest trials (Boutcher, 1992; Boutcher & Zinsser, 1990). It has been suggested that the greater the cardiac deceleration the more efficient the attentional control (Boutcher, 1992). Alternatively, heart rate deceleration/acceleration patterns may reflect the direction of attention (Abernethy, 1993) with deceleration accompanying the intake of information (external focus), while acceleration may accompany an internal focus of attention (Lacey, 1967).

Cognitive psychophysiology is still in its infancy and there remains uncertainty in measuring, defining and describing electrophysiological phenomena. Future research must endeavour to establish, unambiguously, the relationship between the physiological changes observed during performance and attentional processes. So far, the collection of physiological measures has been limited to static sports such as rifle shooting and archery, however, recent advances in technology should allow for the accurate measurement of physiological variables in more dynamic sports. Another exciting technological advance that should provide important insights into the phenomenon of attention is functional brain imagery, such as the positron emission tomography (PET) scan. Recent work using the PET has identified specialised cortical areas of the frontal and parietal lobes that perform different functions of selective attention (Posner & Dehaene, 1994).

As indicated, most of our knowledge about attention in sport has been gained within an information-processing perspective. In the last decade the motor control field has seen the emergence of a radically different approach to the study of motor behaviour. The dynamic or emergent properties approach, exemplified in the work of Kelso and Turvey (e.g., Kelso & Schoner, 1988; Kugler & Turvey, 1987), seeks to explain goal directed behaviour in terms of physical laws without recourse to cognitive constructs. Furthermore, central themes of this approach are the coupling between perception and action in natural tasks, and the action system's capacity for self-organisation. This approach is just beginning to address issues such as intentionality and attention. It seems likely, however, that the phenomenon we have called attention will be viewed very differently by theorists from the dynamic perspective.

CONCLUSIONS

We started this chapter with the quote from William James that everyone knows what attention is. Certainly, the vital role of attention in sports performance is acknowledged by both coaches and athletes. A review of the literature on attention, however, has revealed a lack of consensus not only regarding terminology but also about the actual function(s) of attention. Furthermore, much of our knowledge about attention has been gained using contrived tasks in laboratory situations and the extent to which this knowledge can be applied to "real world" activities is unclear. The systematic study of attention in applied settings such as sport, therefore, should provide valuable information toward a better understanding of the phenomenon.

In ending the chapter, we are forced to conclude that while everyone may think they know what attention is, we are only beginning to understand what it really is.

SUMMARY

In this chapter we have given an overview of the theoretical perspectives and research related to the concept of attention. In attempting to define attention it became clear that attention is a multifaceted phenomenon that has been studied from a variety of perspectives. Within cognitive psychology, attention has assumed a major role in information processing models of human behaviour. From this perspective, attention has been conceptualised as the allocation of cognitive resources from a limited undifferentiated pool of resources. More recent models have proposed multiple resource pools with each pool being concerned with a particular aspect of information processing.

One of the most useful aspects of resource models for the understanding of skilled performance has been the distinction between controlled and automatic processing. Automaticity develops as a function of practice and leads to fast, effortless and non resource demanding performance. Some writers have proposed levels of automaticity; strong, partial, and occasional. Controlled processing, in contrast, is slow, serial and attention demanding. It was argued that highly skilled performance requires a delicate balance between controlled and automatic processes.

Although a great deal of research effort has been devoted to the topic of attention, much of it has been laboratory based and the generalisability of the findings to sport performance is questionable. In the next section of the chapter, therefore, we speculated on the dimensions of attention that may be important in sport performance and reviewed some of the research that has examined these dimensions within a sport context. We saw the functioning of attention as involving three main aspects: direction (where attention is directed), intensity (how much attention is devoted to a task), and flexibility (the shifting of attention).

Within the sport domain, most of the research examining the direction dimension has used a film occlusion paradigm to identify the visual cues used by elite athletes in a variety of sports to anticipate the actions of opponents. In general, experts were able to make use of earlier cues than novices and often the two groups exhibited different eye scan patterns. The ecological validity of these simulated situations, however, was questioned.

With regard to the intensive aspects of attention, it was suggested the transition from controlled to automatic processing may involve the chunking or perceptual grouping of discrete stimuli into meaningful units. Another concept that seems related to intensity is alertness. Alertness refers to the sensitivity or acuteness of the attentional system and is best operationalised as the ability to detect infrequent or unexpected events. A person's level of alertness was seen to be directly related to their level of arousal. Decrements in performance accompanying increases in arousal above some optimal level have been explained in terms of attentional narrowing leading to the neglect of important task relevant cues. It was argued that in addition to the physical narrowing of attention, high arousal also impairs the ability to discriminate between task relevant and irrelevant cues and that it is the latter effect that is mainly responsible for performance decline.

Attentional flexibility was seen as the ability to direct and alter the width (broad to narrow), direction (external to internal), and intensity (mental energy) of attention. Effective performance in many sports (e.g., fast ball games) necessitates the continual shifting of attentional focus to match the constantly changing task requirements. Nideffer's (1976a) theory of attentional style was outlined and the consequences of inappropriate attentional style adoption described. Although flexibility is one of the most important attentional aspects for sport performance, little sport-related research has, to date, been conducted on this dimension.

Some models and metaphors of attentional functioning were then considered. Comparing attention to a beam of light which can be broadened and narrowed as it selectively explores the environment was seen as a useful metaphor for describing visual attention. The concept of attentional style

(Nideffer, 1976a) is one attempt to incorporate both types of attention within the same framework. Despite a number of problems with the concept and its operationalisation, the theory provides a useful description of some of the attentional processes important in sport performance.

When the future directions for research on attention were considered, three main directions were advocated. The first was the need for more research on attention to be conducted within the sporting environment and the development of models specifically related to sport performance. The second was the investigation of cognitive processes involved in athletic endeavours using physiological measures such as EEG and heart rate. Finally, it was suggested that a recent radically different approach to the study of motor behaviour, the dynamic approach, may offer some new insights into the operation of the phenomenon known as attention.

REFERENCES

Abernethy, B. (1991). Visual search strategies and decision-making in sport. *International Journal of Sport Psychology, 22,* 189–210.

Abernethy, B. (1993). Attention. In R. N. Singer, M. Murphey, & K. Tennant (Eds.), *Handbook of research on sport psychology* (pp. 127–170). New York: Macmillan.

Abernethy, B., & Russell, D. G. (1987a). Expert-novice differences in an applied selective attention task. *Journal of Sport Psychology, 9,* 326–345.

Abernethy, B., & Russell, D. G. (1987b). The relationship between expertise and visual search in a racquet sport. *Human Movement Science, 6,* 283–319.

Albrecht, R. R., & Feltz, D. L. (1987). Generality and specificity of attention related to competitive anxiety and sport performance. *Journal of Sport Psychology, 9,* 231–248.

Allard, F., & Burnett, N. (1985). Skill in sport. *Canadian Journal of Psychology, 39,* 294–312.

Allard, F., Graham, S., & Paarsalu, M. E. (1980). Perception in sport: Basketball. *Journal of Sport Psychology, 2,* 14–21.

Allport, D. A. (1980). Attention and performance. In G. Claxton (Ed.), *Cognitive psychology: New directions* (pp. 112–156), London: Routledge & Kegan Paul.

Bacon, S. J. (1974). Arousal and the range of cue utilization. *Journal of Experimental Psychology, 102,* 81–87.

Barber, P. (1988). *Applied cognitive psychology.* London: Methuen.

Best, J. B. (1986). *Cognitive psychology.* New York: West.

Bootsma, R. J. (1993). Simple laws of control for interceptive actions. In S. Serpa, J. Alves, V. Ferreira, & A. Paula-Brito (Eds.), *Proceedings of the VIII World Congress of Sport Psychology* (pp. 973–976). Lisbon.

Boutcher S. H. (1992). Attention and athletic performance: An integrated approach. In T. S. Horn (Ed.), *Advances in sport psychology* (pp. 251–265). Champaign, IL: Human Kinetics.

Boutcher, S. H., & Zinsser, N. (1990). Cardiac deceleration of elite and beginning golfers during putting. *Journal of Sport and Exercise Psychology, 12,* 37–47.

Broadbent, D. A. (1958). *Perception and communication.* New York: Pergamon.

Broadbent, D. A. (1971). *Decision and stress.* London: Academic Press.

Broadbent, D. A. (1982). Task combination and selective intake of information. *Acta Psychologica, 50,* 253–290.

Castiello, I., & Umilta, C. (1992). Orienting of attention in volleyball players. *International Journal of Sport Psychology, 23,* 301–310.

Cauraugh, J. H., Singer, R. N., & Chen, D. (1993). Visual scanning and anticipation of expert and beginner tennis players. In S. Serpa, J. Alves, V. Ferreira, & A. Paula-Brito (Eds.), *Proceedings of the VIII World Congress of Sport Psychology* (pp. 336–340). Lisbon.

Chase, W. G., & Simon, H. A. (1973). Perception in chess. *Cognitive Psychology, 4,* 55–81.

de Groot, A. D. (1965). *Thought and choice in chess.* The Hague: Mouton.

Deutsch, J. A., & Deutsch, D. (1963). Attention: Some theoretical considerations. *Psychological Review, 70,* 80–90.

Donchin, E. (1979). Event-related brain potentials: A tool in the study of human information-processing. In H. Begleiter (Ed.), *Event potentials and behavior* (pp. 13–75). New York: Plenum Press.

Easterbrook, J. A. (1959). The effect of emotion on cue utilization and the organization of behavior. *Psychological Review, 66,* 183–201.

Ericsson, K. A., Krampe, R. T., Tesch-Romer, C. (1993). The role of deliberate practice in the acquisition of expert performance. *Psychological Review, 100,* 363–406.

Eriksen, B., & Yeh, Y. Y. (1985). Allocation of attention in the visual field. *Journal of Experimental Psychology: Human Perception and Performance, 11,* 583–597.

Etzel, E. F. (1979). Validation of a conceptual model characterizing attention among international rifle shooters. *Journal of Sport Psychology, 1,* 281–290.

Ford, S. K., & Summers, J. J. (1992). The factorial validity of the TAIS attentional style subscales. *Journal of Sport and Exercise Psychology, 14,* 283–297.

Friedman, A., & Polson, C. M. (1981). Hemispheres as independent resource systems: Limited-capacity processing and cerebral specialization. *Journal of Experimental Psychology: Human Perception and Performance, 7,* 1031–1058.

Glencross, D. J., & Paull, G. (1993). Expert perception and decision making in baseball. In S. Serpa, J. Alves, V. Ferreira, & A. Paula-Brito (Eds.), *Proceedings of the VIII World Congress of Sport Psychology* (pp. 356–359), Lisbon.

Gopher, D., & Kahneman, D. (1971). Individual differences in attention and the prediction of flight criteria. *Perceptual and Motor Skills, 33,* 1335–1342.

Gopher, D., & Sanders, A. F. (1984). S-Oh-R? Oh stages! Oh resources! In W. Prinz & A. F. Sanders (Eds.), *Cognition and motor processes* (pp. 231–253). Heidelberg: Springer-Verlag.

Goulet, C., Bard, C., & Fleury, M. (1989). Expertise differences in preparing to return a tennis serve: A visual information processing approach. *Journal of Sport and Exercise Psychology, 11,* 382–398.

Hardy, L. (1990). A catastrophe model of performance in sport. In J. G. Jones & L. Hardy (Eds.), *Stress and performance in sport* (pp. 81–106). Chichester: John Wiley & Sons.

Hatfield, B. D., Landers, D. M., & Ray, W. J. (1984). Cognitive processes during self-paced motor performance: An electroencephalographic profile of marksmen. *Journal of Sport Psychology, 6,* 42–59.

Hatfield, B. D., Landers, D. M., & Ray, W. J. (1987). Cardiovascular-CNS interactions during a self-paced, intentional state: Elite marksmanship performance. *Psychophysiology, 24,* 542–549.

Hockey, G. R. (1970). Signal probability and spatial location as possible bascs for increased selectivity in noise. *Quarterly Journal of Experimental Psychology, 22,* 37–42.

Jacoby, L. L., Ste-Marie, D., & Toth, J. P. (1992). Redefining automaticity: Unconscious influences, awareness, and control. In A. Baddeley & L. Weiskrantz (Eds.), *Attention: Selection, awareness, and control: A tribute to Donald Broadbent* (pp. 261–282). Hillsdale, NJ: Erlbaum.

James, W. (1890). *Principles of psychology.* New York: Holt.

Kahneman, D. (1973). *Attention and effort.* Englewood Cliffs: Prentice-Hall.

Kahneman, D., Ben-Ishai, R., & Lotan, M. (1973). Relation of test attention to road accidents. *Journal of Applied Psychology, 58,* 113–115.

Kahneman, D., & Treisman, A. (1984). Changing views of attention and automaticity. In R. Parasuraman & D. R. Davies (Eds.), *Varieties of attention* (pp. 29–61). London: Academic Press.

Keele, S. W. (1973). *Attention and human performance.* Pacific Palisades, CA: Goodyear Publishing.

Keele, S. W., & Hawkins, H. L. (1982). Explorations of individual differences relevant to high level skill. *Journal of Motor Behavior, 14,* 3–23.

Kelso, J. A. S., & Schoner, G. (1988). Self-organization of coordinative movement patterns. *Human Movement Science, 7,* 27–46.

Kerr, J. H. (1985). The experience of arousal: A new basis for studying arousal effects in sport. *Journal of Sports Sciences, 3,* 169–179.

Kerr J. H. (1990). Stress and sport: Reversal theory. In J. G. Jones & L. Hardy (Eds.), *Stress and performance in sport* (pp. 107–131). Chichester: John Wiley & Sons.

Konttinen, N., & Lyytinen, H. (1992). Physiology of preparation: Brain slow waves, heart rate, and respiration preceding triggering in rifle shooting. *International Journal of Sport Psychology, 23,* 110–127.

Kreiner-Phillips, K., & Orlick, T. (1993). Winning after winning: The psychology of ongoing excellence. *The Sport Psychologist, 31–48.*

Kugler, P. N., & Turvey, M. T. (1987). *Information, natural law, and the self-assembly of rhythmic movement.* Hillsdale, NJ: Erlbaum.

LaBerge, D. L., & Brown, V. R. (1989). Theory of attentional operations in shape identification. *Psychological Review, 96,* 101–124.

Lacey, J. I. (1967). Somatic response patterning and stress: Some revision of activation theory. In M. H. Appley & R. Trumbull (Eds.), *Psychological stress: Issues in research* (pp. 170–179). New York: Appelton-Century-Crofts.

Landers, D. M., Wang, M. Q., & Courtet, P. (1985). Peripheral narrowing among experienced and inexperienced rifle shooters under low- and high-time stress conditions. *Research Quarterly for Exercise and Sport, 56,* 122–130.

Logan, G. D. (1985). Skill and automaticity: Relations, implications, and future directions. *Canadian Journal of Psychology, 39,* 367–386.

Logan, G. D. (1988). Toward an instance theory of automatization. *Psychological Review, 95,* 492–527.

Martens, R. (1987). *Coaches guide to sport psychology.* Champaign, IL: Human Kinetics.

Martens, R., Burton, D., Vealey, R. S., Bump, L. A., & Smith, D. E. (1990). The Competitive State Anxiety Inventory-2 (CSAI-2). In R. Martens, R. S. Vealey, & D. Burton (Eds.). *Competitive anxiety in sport* (pp. 117–190). Champaign, IL: Human Kinetics.

Maynard, I. W., & Howe, B. L. (1989). Attentional style in rugby players. *Perceptual and Motor Skills, 69,* 283–289.

Moates, D. R., & Schumacher G. M. (1980). *An introduction to cognitive psychology.* Belmont, CA: Wadsworth.

Morgan W. P., & Pollock, M. L. (1977). Psychologic characterization of the elite distance runner. *Annals of the New York Academy of Sciences, 301*, 382–403.

Navon, D., & Gopher, D. (1979). On the economy of the human processing system. *Psychological Review, 86*, 214–255.

Neumann, O. (1984). Automatic processing: a review of recent findings and a plea for an old theory. In W. Prinz & F. Sanders (Eds.). *Cognition and motor processes* (pp. 256–293). Berlin: Springer-Verlag.

Neumann, O. (1987). Beyond capacity: A functional view of attention. In H. Heuer & F. Sanders (Eds.), *Perspectives on perception and action* (pp. 361–394). Hillsdale, NJ: Erlbaum.

Nideffer, R. M. (1976a). *The inner athlete: Mind plus muscle for winning.* New York: Crowell.

Nideffer, R. M. (1976b). Test of Attentional and Interpersonal Style. *Journal of Personality and Social Psychology, 34*, 394–404.

Norman, D. A. (1969). *Memory and attention.* New York: John Wiley & Sons.

Nougier, V., Stein, J. F., & Bonnel, A. M. (1991). Information processing in sport and "orienting of attention". *International Journal of Sport Psychology, 22*, 307–327.

Peters, M. (1990). Interaction of vocal and manual movements. In G. E. Hammond (Ed.). *Cerebral control of speech and limb movements* (pp. 535–574). Amsterdam: North-Holland.

Pinheiro, V. E. D. (1993). Chunking: Perceptual advantage in motor skill diagnosis. In S. Serpa, J. Alves, V. Ferreira, & A. Paula-Brito (Eds.). *Proceedings of the VIII World Congress of Sport Psychology* (pp. 375–378). Lisbon.

Posner, M. I., & Boies, S. J. (1971). Components of attention. *Psychological Review, 78*, 391–408.

Posner, M. I., & Dehaene, S. (1994). Attentional networks. *TINS, 17*, 75–79.

Posner, M. I., Nissen, M., & Ogden, W. (1978). Attended and unattended processing modes: The role of set for spatial location. In H. L. Pick & E. Saltzman (Eds.), *Modes of perceiving and processing information* (pp. 128–181). Hillsdale, NJ: Erlbaum.

Reason, J. T. (1979). Actions not as planned: The price of automatization. In G. Underwood & R. Stevens (Eds.), *Aspects of consciousness. Vol. 1, Psychological issues* (pp. 67–89). London: Academic Press.

Ripoll, H. (1988). Analysis of visual scanning patterns of volleyball players in a problem solving task. *International Journal of Sport Psychology, 19*, 9–25.

Ripoll, H. (1991). The understanding-acting process in sport: The relationship between the semantic and the sensorimotor visual function. *International Journal of Sport Psychology, 22*, 221–243.

Salazar, W., Landers, D. M., Petruzzello, S. J., Crews, D. J., & Kubitz, K. (1988). The effects of physical/cognitive load on electrocortical patterns preceding response execution in archery. *Psychophysiology, 25*, 478–479.

Salazar, W., Landers, D. M., Petruzzello, S. J., Crews, D. J., Kubitz, K., & Han, M. W. (1990). Hemispheric asymmetry, cardiac response, and performance in elite archers. *Research Quarterly for Exercise and Sport, 61*, 351–359.

Salmela, J. H., & Fiorito, P. (1979). Visual cues in ice hockey goaltending. *Canadian Journal of Applied Sport Sciences, 4*, 56–59.

Savelsbergh, G. J. P., Whiting, H. T. A., & Pijpers, J. R. (1992). The control of catching. In J. J. Summers (Ed.), *Approaches to the study of motor control and learning* (pp. 313–342). Amsterdam: North-Holland.

Schneider, W., & Fisk, A. D. (1983). Attention theory and mechanisms for skilled performance. In R. A. Magill (Ed.), *Memory and control of action* (pp. 119–143). Amsterdam: North-Holland.

Schneider, W., & Shiffrin, R. M. (1977). Controlled and automatic human information processing: I. Detection, search, and attention. *Psychological Review, 84,* 1–66.

Schomer, H. (1986). Mental strategies and the perception of effort of marathon runners. *International Journal of Sport Psychology, 17,* 41–59.

Shiffrin, R. M., & Schneider, W. (1977). Controlled and automatic human information processing: II. Perceptual learning, automatic attending, and a general theory. *Psychological Review, 84,* 127–190.

Singer, R. N. (1988). Strategies and metastrategies in learning and performing self-paced athletic skills. *The Sport Psychologist, 2,* 49–68.

Singer, R. N., Lidor, R., & Cauraugh, J. H. (1993). To be aware or not aware? What to think about while learning and performing a motor skill. *The Sport Psychologist, 7,* 19–30.

Starkes, J. L., & Deakin, J. (1984). Perception in sport: A cognitive approach to skilled performance. In W. F. Straub & J. M. Williams (Eds.), *Cognitive sport psychology* (pp. 115–128). New York: Sport Sciences Associates.

Summers, J. J. (1990). Temporal constraints on concurrent task performance. In G. E. Hammond (Ed.), *Cerebral control of speech and limb movements* (pp. 661–680). Amsterdam: North-Holland.

Summers, J. J., & Ford, S. K. (1990). The Test of Attentional and Interpersonal Style: An evaluation. *International Journal of Sport Psychology, 21,* 102–111.

Summers, J. J., Machin, V. J., & Sargent, G. I. (1983). Psychosocial factors related to marathon running. *Journal of Sport Psychology, 5,* 314–331.

Summers, J. J., & Maddocks, D. (1986). Attentional style profiles and sport performance. *Behaviour Change, 3,* 105–111.

Summers, J. J., Miller, K., & Ford, S. K. (1991). Attentional style and basketball performance. *Journal of Sport and Exercise Psychology, 13,* 239–253.

Summers, J. J., Sargent, G. I., Levey, A. J., & Murray, K. D. (1982). Middle-aged, non-elite, marathon runners: A profile. *Perceptual and Motor Skills, 54,* 963–969.

Timsit-Berthier, M. (1991). Toward a dynamic and integrative approach in sport psychology. *International Journal of Sport Psychology, 22,* 399–401.

Vallerand, R. J. (1983). Attention and decision making: A test of the predictive validity of the Test of Attentional and Interpersonal Style (TAIS) in a sport setting. *Journal of Sport Psychology, 5,* 449–459.

Van Schoyck, R. S., & Grasha, A. F. (1981). Attentional style variations and athletic ability: The advantage of a sport-specific test. *Journal of Sport Psychology, 3,* 149–165.

Wachtel, P. (1967). Conceptions of broad and narrow attention. *Psychological Bulletin, 68,* 417–429.

Wickens, C. D. (1984). Processing resources in attention. In R. Parasuraman & R. Davies (Eds.), *Varieties of attention* (pp. 63–101). New York: Academic Press.

Wickens, C. D. (1992). *Engineering psychology and human performance* (2nd. ed.). New York: HarperCollins.

Williams, M., Davids, K., Burwitz, L., & Williams, J. (1993) Proficiency-related differences in anticipation and visual search strategy in soccer (NASPSPA abstract). *Journal of Sport and Exercise Psychology, 15* supplement, S91.

Zani, A., & Rossi, B. (1991). Cognitive psychophysiology as an interface between cognitive and sport psychology. *International Journal of Sport Psychology, 22,* 376–398.

C H A P T E R

4

INDIVIDUAL AND SOCIAL MOTIVATION IN AUSTRALIAN SPORT*

G A Y E L E N E   J.   C L E W S   •   J O H N   B.   G R O S S

The study of motivation is the investigation of the "energization and direction of behaviour" (Roberts, 1992, p. 6). Roberts says that theories which describe the direction of behaviour without specifying why the behaviour was energised are not motivational theories. In this context, we believe it is important to discuss motivational theories in sport not only with respect to the individual, but also within the wider social perspective.

An individual's intrinsic and extrinsic motivation, achievement orientation, participation, adherence and withdrawal from sport are affected by the uniqueness of the individual and by the wider social values inherent in the infrastructure of his or her society. The individual does not exist in a vacuum; we are social beings and, as such, the environment in which we live exerts both a passive and dynamic influence on our behaviour.

It is important, as suggested by Roberts (1992), to not only understand the direction of behaviour, but also the drive behind that behaviour. To do this, we need to examine individual motivation within the context of the individual's social infrastructure, and the "why" behind the development of that infrastructure. We believe this has not been adequately discussed in previous motivational literature. Therefore, the term "social

* The authors wish to acknowledge Dr Tony Morris's contribution towards the summary and concluding statements in this chapter.

motivation" in this chapter refers to the motivation of a society at a political, administrative and educational level to develop an infrastructure for the enhancement and development of sport from a recreational to an elite level of participation.

This chapter is intended to review motivational research in sport and the Australasian experience from an individual and social perspective. Such information has a far-reaching impact on coaching, administration, funding, policy and planning. In understanding its impact, sport psychologists, educators and students may be better equipped to focus on the essential research needs in Australian sport.

INTRODUCTION: THE RELEVANCE OF MOTIVATIONAL THEORY TO SPORT

What motivates thousands of people to seek sporting challenges? The answer varies for each and every individual. Motivation is a complex topic that involves identifying a number of personal and social factors that reflect some form of valued reward or incentive. The drive that motivates people to excel in sport is similar to the drive that enables them to excel in life.

In understanding the relationship between motivation and sport, we can begin by looking at the theories of some of the world's most accomplished psychologists. Freud (1920) believed people were driven by sexual and aggressive impulses struggling for expression. Erikson (1963) saw developmental processes as central to human behaviour. Rogers (1951, 1963) saw within us a striving for self-enhancement and growth. Skinner (1938, 1971) seemed to "view humans as little different from animals in the way they respond to rewards and punishment" (Phares, 1988, p. 38). From these theories parallels can be drawn to the sporting domain.

For years, major national and international sporting organisations took what would appear to be a Freudian approach to sport. They restricted female participation on the basis of biological differences between the genders. Sporting participation was deemed more appropriate for men as an expression of innate aggressive impulses, and the motivation to participate in sport was seen as a "natural" expression of male sexuality.

Phillips (1992), in his book *Australian Women at the Olympic Games*, stated that Baron Pierre de Coubertin, the father of the modern Olympic Games, was totally against the idea of women in sport. de Coubertin saw male participation in the Olympics erected around the "manly" and "virile" image of sport. In the July 1912 edition of the *Review Olympique*, de Coubertin saw the motivation for the Olympics as "the solemn and period exaltation of male athleticism and internationalism as a base, loyalty as a means, art for its setting, and female applause as reward" (cited in Leigh, 1974, p. 12).

Neo-Freudians such as Erikson (1963), on the other hand, viewed human physical and cognitive developmental phases as having differing motivational emphasis. This is echoed in Horn and Hasbrook (1986, 1987) and Horn and Weiss (1991), who found that children of different ages relate to information about physical ability differently. Younger children tend not to discriminate between the concepts of ability and work and see these two very different constructs as one. Younger children of eight to nine years of age are also found to be more influenced by adult feedback than children of 10 to 11 years who identify peer comparison and evaluation as more important (Longhurst & Spink, 1987).

Rogers (1951, 1963) held that life motivational forces resulted from a need for positive regard. Rather than sexual impulses motivating a need to play sport, Rogers' theory suggested we are motivated to play out of an encompassing need for love, acceptance and respect from ourselves and significant others. Sport provides an environment where successful participation is rewarded with admiration and acceptance from others. This provides the individual with an opportunity to build confidence and respect for self, through the setting and obtaining of goals, hence, striving for self-enhancement and growth, by achieving a sense of competence and self-determination.

Support for such an interpretation is extensively addressed in the literature on motivational orientations that look at mastery versus outcome orientations. In their review of literature, Weiss and Chaumeton (1992) found support for Rogerian thinking, where desirable motivational objectives are born from an athlete's desire to demonstrate ability through engagement in mastery attempts. These individuals choose challenging goals and activities in order to maximise, (self-realise) their athletic abilities.

Skinner (1938, 1971) believed rewards and punishment directed behaviour, and identified factors outside the individual, such as extrinsic rewards, which motivate people to participate in sport. The effect of extrinsic rewards on behaviour has been well documented and in some cases has been said to undermine sustained interest and participation in sport (Greene & Lepper, 1974; Lepper & Greene, 1975; Lepper, Greene, & Nisbett, 1973; Orlick & Mosher, 1978). While the research in this area is not conclusive (Thomas, 1978), external rewards and punishment alone cannot account for the motivational precipitators to sporting involvement.

The complexity and multidimensional nature of motivation in sport is highlighted by extensive research in numerous subject areas on the topic. Needless to say, Freud, Erikson, Rogers and Skinner all had theories that contribute to understanding of human motivation, on the basis of biological, developmental, intrinsic and social factors. Parallels between their theories and more contemporary research on motivation in sport can be found, but it is the multidimensional nature of the individual's personality and social/cultural environment that holds the key.

Research on motivational factors in sport helps us understand why people play sport, why they choose one sport over another and what factors encourage persistence as opposed to withdrawal and drop-out. All these factors essentially deal with the motivation of the individual, but what about social motivation? What motivates a nation to form an extensive support structure for its athletes? A little more than a decade ago Australia's elite athletes were essentially self-determining. Today, they have the extensive support of government, coaching, sports science and medicine, administration and business.

Keeping this in mind, this chapter will focus on two broad issues in motivation theory in sport: the personal qualities of the individual, and their social reinforcers. These personal qualities may involve physical and mental maturity, gender, affiliation, fitness, an orientation towards self-actualisation and personal improvement. For example, a lack of persistence may not be indicative of a decline in motivation, but rather a change in direction. Growth and ageing necessitates a constant reprioritisation of goals, incentives and values. Motivation enhancement in this sense may be a matter of redirection of personal investment.

The social reinforcers that are present in our environment — social status, recognition, rewards and social approval — have an impact on motivation. Both individual and social reinforcers impact upon the choices we make, the intensity by which we play and our desire to remain involved or withdraw from sport.

Although little research has been done on the issue of social motivation, the impact it has on the individual is undeniable. What motivates a society to play an assisting role rather than an actual participation role in sporting performance is an important area for consideration and future research. Millions of dollars each year are spent on sport in Australia. Servicing of athletes has become a full-time occupation for many, in the areas of medicine, physiotherapy, massage, exercise physiology, psychology, biomechanics, nutrition, career training, coaching, education, travel and administration. Many more millions of hours are dedicated on a voluntary basis in the form of coaching and coaching education. As this servicing continues to increase, so have Australia's athletic performances, but it becomes inevitable that this servicing will impact on the social reinforcers experienced by our athletes.

Birch and Veroff's (1966) view of motivation concerns three basic aspects of human behaviour. The first aspect is the direction of behaviour, to approach or avoid goals. Direction refers to the choice we make among a set of alternatives that are usually governed by goals and incentives. Second, the intensity of behaviour ranges from low to high levels of arousal and refers to the extent to which one is active. The third aspect is the duration of behaviour, either persisting over long periods through the pursuit of a meaningful challenge, or persisting for shorter periods due to the absence of a challenge. Persistence also provides a basis for continued involvement in sport. Maehr (1984) points out that persistence cannot fully be distinguished from direction. A lack in persistence may be indicative not of a decline in motivation, but rather a change in direction.

When any activity is directed toward clearly-defined goals which are experienced as arousing and worthy of persistent effort, that activity is said to be "highly motivating". The motivation to pursue any goal depends on the identification of some form of valued reward or incentive. Watson (1984) states that all sports tend to be potentially motivating because they present opportunities for attaining a wide range of these incentives.

Knowing why people participate in, stay involved, switch sports, drop out, or return to sport, as well as the impact sport has on their life, has practical implications for improving mass participation, talent identification and higher levels of elite performances, all of which are interrelated (Robertson, 1988).

INTRINSIC AND EXTRINSIC MOTIVATION

DEFINITIONS

Along with essential requirements for successful sporting participation, it is often held that athletes choose to participate in sport from both intrinsic and extrinsic motives. Intrinsic motives are said to be primarily determined by the inherent desire and curiosity of embracing optimal skill challenges in the sport settings, while extrinsic incentives are said to be primarily determined by external sources, such as adult and peer approval, material rewards, and a competitive emphasis on winning.

Individuals who are involved in sport for the sheer fun, pleasure and personal mastery derived from the experience are classified as *intrinsically motivated individuals*. The enjoyment of physical movement is valued for its own sake, for both the pleasurable chemical and physiological effect exercise has on the body, and the positive experiences the athlete receives through personal achievement, a sense of competency, perceived control, self-confidence and positive self-regard.

The extrinsic motives for an individual's choice to be involved in sport, such as social approval from adults and peers, material rewards and social status, may occur alongside intrinsic motives, or dominate the athlete's sporting experience. The subsequent intrinsic and extrinsic motivational changes that individuals experience have a substantial effect on their perceived competence, control and tendencies to approach or avoid achievement situations.

COGNITIVE EVALUATION THEORY

It is believed that intrinsic motivation is maximised when individuals feel competent and self-determining in dealing with their environment. Deci and Ryan (1985) proposed Cognitive Evaluation Theory. They believe that sport settings provide opportunities for individuals to compare their skills and competencies against a standard, thus enhancing the likelihood of meaningful feedback and positive changes in intrinsic motivation. For example, a basketball player who wishes to improve his or her free throw average is likely to be more motivated in practice to work on a free throw routine if there is a standard by which to judge improvement. A success rate may have started at four goals in ten tries but with practice increases to eight goals out of ten. The player then feels in control of the improvement, by devoting more practice time to goal shooting. A sense of internal control increases intrinsic motivation and leads to positive changes in self-determination.

However, sport can also be structured to provide negative feedback about one's competencies and apply pressure on individuals to conform to standardised rules and behaviour. This can result in a loss of intrinsic motivation and internalising a more extrinsic orientation, for example, the soccer team that is made to feel incompetent because it lost a game, rather than identifying aspects of the game that went well, and attributing the loss to inexperience or lack of effort rather than lack of ability.

Weiss and Chaumeton (1992) describe the Cognitive Evaluation Theory position that any event that affects an individual's perception of competence and feelings of self-determination will impact on their intrinsic motivation. These events may include rewards, feedback and reinforcement. Depending on how this information is structured it can convey messages that are controlling or informational. The controlling aspect relates to the individual's perceived locus of causality within the situation. If an event or situation is seen as controlling one's behaviour, then an external locus of causality and a low level of self-determination are developed. For example, a young gymnast who only receives praise from her coach for the successful execution of a difficult tumbling routine, and not for her effort in unsuccessful attempts, may see this verbal reinforcement as controlling her behaviour. This perception of external control is likely to reduce her feeling of self-determination, because the athlete perceives she has less control over her ability than her effort. These negative self-perceptions cause a decrease in intrinsic motivation. However, if the coach acknowledges effort, over which the athlete does have control, and emphasises the components of the exercise that the gymnast executes well, while continuing to offer correctional information, the athlete is more likely to feel she has control over the outcome result. If information relates to the athlete's competence and effort, then intrinsic motivation may be enhanced.

This is an important factor to keep in mind, when one considers the potential impact extensive social servicing has on athletes. If the assistance afforded to our elite athletes via scholarship programs is presented in a way that reinforces athletes' confidence, for example, they feel they have earnt the scholarship because of their sporting prowess and the scholarship is an acknowledgement of the level of expertise they have obtained, then intrinsic motivation of the individual may be enhanced. Conversely, if social support is used coercively as a way of controlling the athlete, where the athlete is threatened with losing the scholarship unless certain performances are forthcoming irrespective of commitment and effort, intrinsic motivation may be reduced in that the athlete feels a loss of self-determination. This may, or may not, benefit the athlete's future performance.

PERSONAL AND SOCIAL FACTORS

Intrinsic and extrinsic factors will have an impact on an athlete's motivation, but as Chalip (1989) reflects, there does not appear to be any one ideal personality type, or environment, motivating athletes towards success. Motivation is both dynamic and varied. She concludes that we are socialised to expect that personalities rather than situations account for outcomes, although in Australia it can definitely be shown that both are essential ingredients.

Chalip (1989) quotes writer Robyn Langwell's comments on New Zealand marathon runner, Lorraine Moller. Langwell portrays Moller as a person with a "hankering for the weird" and "inadequate self control", who "is easily influenced by others"... "Moller has not got the right stuff anymore" (p. 26). The assumption is that motivation is internal to the athlete and that personality provides the link between ability and greatness; that an athlete who possesses or demonstrates the appropriate personality will compete successfully.

Several years after Langwell's article, the New Zealand Olympic Federation told Moller it didn't believe she had what it takes to compete successfully in her third Olympics. It omitted her from the 1992 Olympic team, but after some discussion with the New Zealand Athletic Federation, Moller was added to the team. The athlete who "didn't have what it takes" became New Zealand's first Olympic track and field medallist in 12 years, when she took out the bronze medal in the women's marathon. At 37 years of age, Lorraine was the oldest track and field medallist in Barcelona from all countries. After the event, Moller commented to the first author of this chapter, "Why would I want to be like the norm, to run like everybody else? It is what makes me different, that sets me apart from others athletically" (personal communication, Lorraine Moller, 30 June 1993).

To continue with Chalip's argument further, she says it is a fundamental error for countries to only attribute sporting success to factors internal to the athlete — talent and personality. In doing so, countries underrate the need for sports policies that pay sufficient heed to social motivation, coaching and development of sport infrastructure. The challenge for Australia was to create administrative policy and programs that facilitate motivation, support individual differences and not constrict intrinsic motivation.

It is this infrastructure that was lacking in Australia until recently. Through nearly a century of Olympic competition Australia had relied on the motivation of the individual for its international sporting success. After a successful Olympics in Melbourne in 1956, in which Australia won 35 medals, its international performances began a rapid downward slide, hitting an all-time low in 1976, when Australian athletes gained a meagre five medals.

DEVELOPMENT OF SPORTS INSTITUTES AND ACADEMIES IN AUSTRALIA

Australia had been left behind. World-wide, nations were making substantial contributions towards their sporting programs, seeking the most up-to-date training methods, using research and science to understand and improve athletic performance. For every Australian athlete who succeeded, through determination and motivation, many more were lost through the lack of social support and recognition. Australia had always taken pride in its internationally successful sporting profile, which, by the late 1970s, had significantly dwindled. As a result, the Australian Institute of Sport was established in 1981 to get Australia back into world contention.

Other countries were already making substantial investments in their athletes. Australia, motivated by the importance of sport to the community in improving health and fitness, and providing inspiration to the nation, started to provide greater opportunities for its athletes. Initially, programs were established to assist our elite competitors, but the whole infrastructure was eventually revised, with programs for talent identification and greater participation.

The Australian Institute of Sport (AIS) started on a small scale — a director, one sports scientist and several administrative staff, people who wanted to be part of a new era. The sceptics said the AIS was a white elephant and was not going to help lift Australia's sporting profile, but with patience and a long-term approach the AIS moved from strength to strength.

In the beginning, professional support staff had to be enticed to Canberra, athletes had to be solicited to join the institute. Elite national coaches were sought domestically and internationally to design and run the programs. Sports medical practitioners and scientists had to be talked into leaving their private practices and university jobs to join the program. There were no guarantees and a lot of risks.

Why were these support personnel motivated to take those risks? Eccles and Harold (1991) tell us that the value individuals attach to options, and the expectations of success, have a tremendous influence on the choices we make. Working with elite athletes is an opportunity for professionals to take their expertise from the domestic market into the international arena. Eccles also specifies that the value we place on what we do derives from cultural norms, the experiences one has growing up, aptitude and a set of personal beliefs and attitudes (Eccles (Parsons), Adler, Futterman, Goff, Kaczala, Meece, & Midgley, 1983).

Keeping this in mind it is easy to see why administrative, science and medical professionals were interested in a close association with the athletes, their coaches and sport. With the extensive media coverage sport is given in Australia, it is not surprising it is valued so highly. Athletes receive positive feedback for displays of assertiveness, strength, power, grace and agility, increasing the value placed on sport. So pervasive is sport's cultural appeal that Eccles and Harold (1991) found in their study of 3000 American adolescents that school-age girls and boys value doing well in sports, in their free time, more highly than maths and English.

Cultural values may have a direct effect on social motivation. Danish, Kleiber, and Hall (1987) found that the social appropriateness of any activity will obviously dictate its ultimate acceptability. Hence, sport is a highly acceptable activity in Australia because being actively involved in sport is seen as socially desirable. However, Danish et. al. add that this extrinsic reinforcer must be married with the individual's intrinsic motivation for the ultimate sporting performance to be realised.

Within Australia the social desirability and motivation were present for the establishment of the AIS and other State institutes and academies. Developing them into the successful institutions that they are today required careful planning, insight and a long-term approach towards success.

Intrinsic and extrinsic motivation strategies were then combined to motivate the individual. Athletes and coaches imbued with a motivation to succeed were recruited for the academies and institutes of sport. Coaches were encouraged to run their own programs. To do this they had to be innovative and keep abreast with the rest of the world, developing international contacts and networks to make sure Australia's athletes were serviced with the best technology, equipment, facilities and competition. As part of this process, both athletes and coaches were made accountable and responsible for their performances and programs.

This accountability of performance has an extrinsic motivating quality that, when combined with the intrinsic qualities of the individual, can enhance performance. Numerous studies have been conducted showing that people tend to exert less effort in a collective performance than they do as individuals (Hardy, 1989; Hardy & Latane, 1988; Latane, Williams, & Harkins, 1979). To counter these findings, it has been discovered that individual accountability (Bartis, Szymanski, & Harkins, 1988; Harkins & Jackson, 1985; Williams, Harkins, & Latane, 1981), task difficulty (Harkins & Petty, 1982; Jackson & Williams, 1985), indispensability (Kerr & Bruun, 1983; Weldon & Mustari, 1988), task attractiveness (Zaccaro, 1984) and group size (Widmeyer, Brawley, & Carron, 1990) are all important.

Therefore, to ensure intrinsically motivated athletes and motivated support staff, individuals have to be given responsibility and made accountable for their own performances and programs. For example, if a distance running coach is to incorporate a foundation fitness phase with weights and conditioning and biomechanical analysis into a training program, followed by a pre-competition training phase that emphasises flexibility, threshold and some anaerobic work, before a short season racing phase, every component in that program should be thought out and have a purpose. Coaches, athletes and support staff need to believe that their own contributions are indispensable, value their involvement in sport, and possess realistic, but challenging, goals that can be periodically evaluated.

Individuals must have a standard against which to strive, and a large part of sporting success is realised in competition. For many athletes that standard is found in performing better than others, for some it may be performing better than their own previous best (see pages 103–109). However, a good illustration of a personal orientation towards achievement was given by Australia's 1992 Olympic 1500 metre swimming champion and world record holder, Kieren Perkins. When Kieren received his 1992 Sports Star of the Year award, he commented, "I always race against myself to improve my own performances, the fact that sometimes I set world records in the process is a bonus. My personal best performance is the goal, not necessarily the world record".

Danish et al. (1987) give a good description of how this personal orientation towards achievement provides a clear structure within which the athlete works. They say that when the participant feels in control but somewhat challenged and the activity is complex enough to demand complete attention, while still in the realm of the athlete's competence (as was the case in Kieren's Olympic final), the centring of the attention on the action (swimming) and the merging of this action with awareness is accompanied by a loss of self-consciousness and ego-involvement.

One may assume from Kieren's comment (above), that he focused on the kinesthetic feel of his swimming, his stroke technique, while monitoring his effort. As soon as an athlete steps back for self-appraisal and/or comparison with others, the flow is lost and the task is made more difficult. But to the extent that task involvement is maintained, athletes report feelings of enjoyment based on a growing sense of competence. The perception of competence is a direct consequence of task involvement rather than being mediated by a secondary interpretation process, for example, how someone else would rate the athlete's performance.

By 1992, Australia had forged a path to its most successful away-from-home Olympic Games, finishing ninth out of 172 countries in the medal tally, with 27 Olympic medals to its credit. However, equally impressive was the depth of performances across the board, with 66 finishers in the top eight and a further 119 finishing in the top 16 in their events. The depth in performance in Barcelona was the real show of Australia's success. With its small population, Australia cannot afford high attrition rates and low participation numbers in its sporting programs. With so many sporting choices, the nation's athletic talent is spread thinly across many sports. Understanding what motivates the elite athletes to be involved in sport, what the social motivators are, and what motivates individuals to become involved, is all part of the process of building a sporting infrastructure that enables continued success.

Some literature on extrinsic motivation for sports participation questions the use of extrinsic rewards (Lepper & Green, 1975; Orlick & Mosher, 1978), viewing it as controlling and undermining the individual's desire to remain interested in participation in the future. A good argument, however, can be put forward for the use of extrinsic reward in encouraging participation and effort in sport, when used as a bonus for activities that are already fun, or an acknowledgment of competency.

FIVE STAR AWARD SCHEME

Children who have not experienced sport, or for that matter adults who have limited sporting experience, may not choose to engage in sport on their own. However, external rewards such as tangible commodities, social support or status may be seen as a motivator to initiate participation. In sport, external rewards are usually given contingent on a minimal participation level or quality of performance. Rewards given in this manner usually convey positive information about the individual's competence and should increase intrinsic motivation.

The incorporation of the Five Star Award Scheme in Australian athletics is a good example of the use of extrinsic reward that complements intrinsic motivation of children involved in this program (Cook, 1980). The scheme started in Australia in 1974, after its success in the United Kingdom. The scheme caters for young athletes from seven to 16 years of age and is designed to help every young athlete become a winner, by striving to improve their own personal performances. Motivation for continued participation comes from each athlete, based on fun and challenge, combined with a sense of achievement that comes with improvement.

Students in the scheme are encouraged to select five events from track and field, for example, 70 metres, 100 metres, 200 metres, together with shot-put and long jump. Their performances for each event are compared with the scoring tables which show a number of points achieved for age and gender. The total number of points are added and on the next occasion students contest those five events, they attempt to earn more points than on the previous occasion. If the improvement is by the required margin, a one-star certificate is earnt. The young athlete is encouraged to keep working through his or her age group until all five star awards have been obtained.

The Five Star Awards Scheme is designed to benefit all participants because it offers incentives to the whole population and not merely a gifted minority. It encourages an all-round test, rather than one specialist quality. It combines the use of internal standards with extrinsic reward. Initially the external reward is a big motivator, but as the children develop their athletic ability they are more likely to become absorbed by the challenges athletics has to offer. From a developmental perspective, it may well be that the social reward system is the best way to encourage sporting involvement.

This scheme was not essentially developed to make champions, but to get students involved in an activity that was enjoyable. In this program Athletics Australia have identified the motivational factors that encourage children to play sport — fun, friends and reward. This approach is a major step towards building the pyramid base from where Australia's future track and field champions are likely to come.

A broad-based effort was needed to mobilise athletic participation. With greater participation and updated philosophies and attitudes, Australia has rebuilt its sporting profile worldwide through a unified national effort.

Different researchers have found that with age and maturity the motives for sporting involvement change. Sporting involvement is a function of both the individual's physical growth and maturation. The athlete must have enough motor skills to engage in the particular sport, adequate fitness to complete the event/match, the social competency to relate to peers, the psychological capacity to cope with the emotional demands of the sport, and the cognitive ability to understand the rules of the game (Robertson, 1988).

DEVELOPMENT OF INTRINSIC AND EXTRINSIC MOTIVATION IN SPORT

The development of intrinsic and extrinsic motivation also appears to be influenced by social and cultural factors. This is exemplified by a comparison of developmental patterns in the United States and Australia. In the United States, Gould and Horn's (1984) research suggests six motives which promote the sporting involvement of North American children aged 8–19 years:
- the potential for improving skills
- having fun
- playing with friends
- experiencing certain thrills and pleasures
- achieving and maintaining a level of fitness
- achieving success in a socially desirable realm.

Gould (1987) further suggests that children continue their involvement in sport until such a time as their motives are no longer being met, or other activities are seen as even more desirable. As children move into adolescence and the pressures of sport achievement become greater, there may be a shift from the intrinsic to extrinsic motives such as status and entitlement (Gould & Horn, 1984).

It is interesting to note that a reverse shift in motivation occurs in Australian children. Australian studies have shown children to move from an extrinsic motivation in childhood to a more intrinsic orientation in adolescence.

Longhurst and Spink (1987) examined the participation motives of Australian youth, from eight to 18 years of age and concluded, in contrast to American sporting participants, that younger children endorsed extrinsic and social motives for sporting participation, to a greater extent than older participants. This is supported by Watson, Blanksby, and Bloomfield (1984), who found that social motives rated highest amongst elite junior swimmers for sporting involvement. In older children or adolescents, however, Longhurst and Spink found that the most important reasons for participation in sport were "to improve skills", "be physically fit", "compete", "learn new skills" and "to be challenged" (p. 24).

Further support for the idea that Australian adolescents are not as extrinsically motivated as their North American counterparts comes from the study by Watkin and Youngen (1988), which looked at cross-cultural comparisons of motivation participation in sport between Australian and American adolescents. Watkin and Youngen (1988) compared 1353 year 10 students from Australian secondary schools with 591 subjects from a North American sample. They found that American adolescent males are more "win oriented", while Australian males are more motivated to play sport for the opportunity to "develop or improve physical skills".

"Success and status" were found to rate more highly among American males and females than Australian participants. Watkin and Youngen (1988) support Gould and Horn's (1984) remarks that American youth are "status and entitlement" oriented. An explanation for these cross-cultural differences was not proposed. However, the American culture is win-oriented and a heavily extrinsic reward component exists in American high schools for sporting performances. American college athletic scholarships offer athletes free tuition in exchange for successful sporting performances. This may account for the shift from intrinsic motivation to a greater emphasis on extrinsic motivation for the North American adolescent. (Passer (1981) says that as players get older, those who are attracted to sport because of extrinsic factors and/or who no longer find competition attractive are more likely to drop out.)

Few Australian universities offer free tertiary education in exchange for sporting participation. Ryan (1977, 1980) compared the intrinsic motivation of scholarship and non-scholarship athletes. Ryan (1977) put a questionnaire assessing intrinsic motivation to a group of male athletes, some of whom were on athletic scholarships and some of whom were not. The scholarship athletes reported less intrinsic motivation than the non-scholarship holders. One may pose the question here: if the American university sporting scholarship system reduces the athlete's intrinsic motivation, then do Australia's national, State and academy sporting institutes do likewise? Fortunately, later research indicates scholarships may have more positive effects on athletes' intrinsic motivation.

In Ryan's (1980) study, a larger survey of both male and female athletes in several sports at several universities was made. The findings of the first study were replicated as scholarship football players reported less intrinsic motivation than non-scholarship players. However, further comparisons revealed more complex relationships. Among male wrestlers and female athletes in all sports, scholarship athletes report greater intrinsic motivation than non-scholarship holders. Ryan suggests two possible reasons for these varying results. First, if virtually "all" good football players receive scholarships, then scholarships provide no confidence information to their recipients. However, if only the top wrestlers and top female athletes receive scholarships, then the scholarships provide positive information about competence and are more intrinsically motivating. Second, Ryan notes that football coaches may use scholarships in a more controlling manner than coaches in other sports.

In Australia, there are relatively few athletic scholarships available in each sport at the AIS, State institutes or academies. Therefore, an Australian athlete receiving such recognition is more likely to view the scholarship as providing positive information on competency, reinforcing intrinsic motivation.

Rather than the AIS having a coercive effect on Australian athletes it amalgamated with the Australian Sports Commission and helped facilitate the development of State institutes and academy programs; and the Australian Coaching Council was able to mobilise extensive coach education programs, and programs for disabled and women's sports were established. However, as these social support infrastructures continue to grow, it is vital that their present and future impact on sporting participation is closely examined. For example, researchers need to look at the impact scholarship and talent identification programs have on the motivation of both the individuals identified as possessing talent and on those missing out; whether those identified stay in the program or withdraw, whether those not selected continue to play the sport, change sports or drop out all together.

ACHIEVEMENT ORIENTATION

Achievement motivation purports to explain behaviour intensity (trying hard), persistence (continuing to try hard), choice of action possibilities, and performance outcomes, although it should be noted that this is not a complete list of all the consequences or correlates of motivation. Roberts (1992) states that an individual's motivation is inferred from assessing intensity, persistence, choice and performance. Achievement orientation refers to the motive states of individual behaviour. For example, is the individual motivated out of a fear of failure or from a desire to succeed? Achievement orientation is a function of individual differences, development, situational factors and the athlete's environment.

Research on achievement orientation — the motive to achieve success and the motive to avoid failure — was conceptualised by Alfred Adler at the turn of this century. He believed that all humanity shared the same basic motivation, a striving for superiority. This is a drive that propels us towards perfection. It grows out of our need to compensate for our feelings of inferiority and represents an attempt to attain power or strength, so that we can better control the environment. Adler saw the striving for superiority as innate, but each individual places on it their own individual stamp of idiosyncratic personality (Adler, 1924).

To overcome feelings of inferiority, a person develops a style of life unique to each personality. Adler believed that all of us struggle to overcome our feelings of infantile helplessness. We all pursue the same basic goal, but none of us takes exactly the same route. Influential research in the area of sport began with Murray (1938) and was further developed by McClelland and Atkinson and their colleagues (Atkinson, 1957; McClelland, 1961; McClelland, Atkinson, Clark, & Lowell, 1953). They believe that motive states — the motive to achieve success and the motive to avoid failure — are the mainsprings of action.

TO ACHIEVE SUCCESS OR AVOID FAILURE

The motive to achieve success is the capacity to experience pride or satisfaction in accomplishment, while the motive to avoid failure is the capacity to experience shame or humiliation in failure. These behaviours are believed to interact with cues in the environment that arouse affective states, for example, pride and shame, which elicit instrumental approach or avoidance behaviour. To some degree everyone has both characteristics. We all feel good when we achieve things or disappointment when we do not.

Most of the theoretical models of achievement behaviour have been formulated in the academic domain. However, several of these theories have been applied to the physical domain with common themes. These themes are, first, the individual's perceived ability. Does the individual perceive that he or she has the competency to meet the demands of the activity? Second, achievement behaviour is multidimensional, an interaction of the individual's salient personality characteristics, the social environment and development parameters. Finally, it is generally agreed that "goals" are central determinants of achievement behaviour, with individuals defining success or failure depending on how these goals are obtained.

Watson (1986) looked at approach and avoidance behaviour in senior and junior Australian national hockey players. Some of the psycho-social ingredients of players high in approach behaviour (and by implication the reverse for the player high in avoidance behaviour) were:

• they possess a high sense of competence experience during competition (i.e., heightened intrinsic motivation)
• they are attracted by tasks of intermediate difficulty (rather than high or low levels of difficulty)
• they tend to lose motivation after prolonged success (that is, they require meaningful challenge)
• they tend to increase the intensity of approach behaviour after failure on tasks related to high levels of difficulty
• they are more likely to attribute success to their own ability and persistence
• they generally have the capacity to learn about self (as distinct from task alone) through involvement in achievement situations
• they tend to prefer to work with a partner on the criterion of ability level rather than affiliation
• they tend to learn faster, perform more efficiently, and recall their errors more effectively.

ACHIEVEMENT BEHAVIOUR

One of the most noted researchers on achievement motivation is Atkinson (1974). Atkinson's theory predicted three general categories of achievement behaviour:

• choice — the individual's decision to approach or avoid the achievement situation
• intensity — the effort the individual applies in the sporting situation
• persistence — whether or not the individual continues to try hard.

Atkinson's theory suggests high achievers are attracted to the most challenging situations, while low achievers have a tendency to avoid all achievement situations, especially challenging ones.

Choice

Choice, whether made consciously or unconsciously, is assumed to be guided by one's expectations for success in the various sporting options available. However, the value of one goal over another must also be considered. Eccles and Harold (1991) link choice to performance expectations and the value individuals attach to the available options. Their model is built on the assumption that it is one's interpretation of reality, rather than reality itself, that directly influences activity choices. For example, a young girl may decide not to choose a male-oriented sport like Australian Rules football, even if she is competent athletically, because the value she places on her football skills may be outweighed by other social influences that steer her towards a more "socially acceptable" sporting choice.

Intensity

The second characteristic in Atkinson's (1974) achievement motivation theory is behavioural intensity. In sport we often recognise and praise the individual who displays a high level of effort and we assume the individual is highly motivated. Duda (1988) found that individuals who are high in task orientation are more likely to practise in their free time. In a study looking at adherence to athletic injury rehabilitation, Duda, Smart, and Tappe (1989) reported that task-orientation was positively related to the effort exerted by athletes while completing their prescribed exercises.

Task orientation refers to one of two goal perspectives — ego-involvement and task-involvement. Nicholls (1984a, 1984b) says that these two goal perspectives relate to different ways of construing one's level of competence. He says that ego- and task-involvement are based on a differentiated conception of ability. Ego-involvement entails a concern with being judged competent, displaying ability by being successful when out-performing others, or by achieving success with little effort. Task-involvement places an emphasis on developing new skills. The process of learning itself is valued, and the attainment of mastery is seen as dependent on effort.

Trying hard when playing sport is a critical ingredient to improvement, in recovery from a setback or injury, or to ultimate performance. Certainly, encouraging words such as "give it your best shot" and "try your hardest" are words frequently heard in the sporting arena. Duda (1992) writes that although behavioural intensity is not an easy variable to operationalise, much more work on the interdependence between goals and exerted effort in the physical domain is needed.

An individual's achievement orientation (task- or ego-involvement) in a particular setting is held to be a function of not only individual differences, but also situational factors. Dispositional differences in goal perspectives determine the priority individuals place on adopting and displaying a particular behavioural pattern, and situational factors are seen as potentially altering these probabilities. Therefore, in situations characterised by interpersonal competition, public evaluation, normative feedback and/or testing of valued skills, a state of ego-involvement is more likely to occur (Duda, 1992). As discussed previously, university scholarships in the United States awarded on athletic achievement may encourage an ego-involved achievement orientation. On the other hand, environments which place an emphasis on the learning process, participation, individualised skill mastery, and/or problem solving tend to invoke task-involvement, for example, Australia's Aussie Sports Programs.

In Australia, several programs have been developed by the Australian Sports Commission, under "Aussie Sports", to encourage and enhance a task-involved achievement orientation. The motivation for the development of these programs arose from research conducted by the commission that showed up to 40% of eight to 12-year-old children were not playing sport. Children, in general, lacked skill development and had restricted sporting choices; there were fewer opportunities for girls. Children seemed to enjoy sport less than adults because sport was too adult oriented, with few well-trained instructors (Australian Sports Commission, 1990).

In response to these findings, several programs were initiated. The "Ready Set Go" modified sports program took adult sports and scaled everything down. Equipment and rules were modified so that children could experience a sense of competency as they developed and acquired new skills. T-ball, for example, is a modified game of softball/baseball. Children play on a smaller diamond, with a larger ball, and hit the ball off a stationary tee rather than a pitched ball. All children bat before side away is called. "Ready Set Go" emphasises the learning process, skill development, participation and fun essential in task-involved sport. The sporting experience, therefore, can be considered more or less task- or ego-involved depending on the demands of the social environment.

Maehr and Nicholls (1980) discussed the attributions that may accompany goal-orientations and social approval behaviours. Ability-oriented behaviour is the desire to maintain favourable perceptions of ability. If performance outcomes are attributed to high ability, rather than luck, the athlete is likely to derive a positive feeling about his or her ability and expectations of future success in similar situations. Conversely, if performance outcomes are perceived as failure with future negative expectancies, future attempts may result in the demonstration of low ability. Ability-oriented behaviour is mostly derived from social comparison and in sport that most often means competition.

Competitive sport is a form of achievement motivation. Competitiveness is defined as a disposition to strive for satisfaction when making comparisons with some standard of excellence in the presence of evaluative others in sport (Martens, 1976). Competition is the most common achievement situation in sport, but achievement also occurs in non-competitive situations when individuals compare their performances to personal standards.

Task-oriented behaviour focuses on personal standards — the process, rather than the outcome; how well an athlete performed, rather than the finishing result. The Five Star Award Scheme (see page 99), for example, assesses personal standards rather than win/loss. Task-oriented behaviour is also seen within Australia's swimming associations, where clubs run swim meets that challenge young developing swimmers to compete against their previous best times. In these meets children are grouped together on time, rather than age or gender.

Persistence
Atkinson's (1974) third characteristic in achievement motivation centres on persistence. Roberts (1984) was the first to attempt to assimilate work on dropping out (or lack of persistence) in sport, within social cognitive theories of achievement motivation. He argued that individuals with high ego-involvement will not persist in sport if their high ability goals are not met.

Keeping in mind Atkinson's theory on achievement motivation, it is pertinent to examine the Australian Sports Commission's Sports Search program initiated in 1993, and its possible effect on motivational choices, intensity and persistence.

SPORTS SEARCH

Sports Search was designed for adolescents who were not participating in sport, because they perceived themselves to be lacking in personal ability. The program, after identifying the individual's unique physical attributes, encourages individuals to select a sport for which they are better suited. In doing so, Sports Search considers the individual's need to anticipate and experience a level of competency and enjoyment. When these expectations are increased, individuals are more likely to initiate sporting participation and maintain an on-going involvement.

In Sports Search, Australian adolescents between the ages of 11 and 15 years complete a series of ten tasks which include height, sitting height, weight, arm span, catch (limb–eye coordination), basketball throw, vertical jump, agility run, 40 metre sprint and shuttle run (multi-stage fitness). The tasks are easily administered, with results entered into a computer program. Students then answer some questions about sporting preferences and the Sports Search package provides the following:

- a fitness and skill profile for individual students
- a list of sports, derived from some 80 sporting choices, that the individual's personal attributes are suited to
- a description of any sport in the program and information on how to contact the sporting organisation.

In this program we can see how a social reinforcer presented in the Australian environment can positively impact on the choices individuals make. The flow-on effect from this initial sport selection may increase both the intensity and adherence of Australians to sporting participation.

The social motives of the Sports Search program are clear:

- to mobilise the general population towards greater participation in sport in an endeavour to obtain a healthier population
- to develop a broader participation base and match individuals to sports they are most physically suited to, thereby more readily identifying our future world and Olympic champions.

Individuals are motivated to participate in the Sports Search program out of an increased expectation that they will display competency in their chosen sport. The program claims to direct students towards activities for which they have already shown a suitability. When initial success is experienced, individuals are more likely to increase the intensity of their efforts and explore more fully their sporting potential.

For intensity of effort in achievement situations, Atkinson (1974) says the higher the achievement orientation the greater the effort directed towards achieving the desired goal, and the better the performance. However, the tendency that inhibits intense effort, such as a fear of failure, also impairs performance while increasing the individual's anxiety. In the Sports Search program the increased likelihood of success is expected to reduce anxiety, by encouraging individuals to focus their energies into activities they have already shown a potential for. This cyclic pattern, then, of poor experience, increased anxiety and possible withdrawal seen in sporting situations may be reduced.

Sports Search then offers part of a solution to low participation. Our on-going personal assessments of ability continue to impact on the intensity with which athletes strive to achieve their athletic goals. Let's look at two Australian females training to complete their first marathon. The athletes, Jane and Sue, have identical physiological ability and the same goal. Both athletes fail to finish the event. However, Jane is a high achiever and she has a strong work ethic. She believes she is capable of training harder, getting fitter, improving her muscle-to-weight ratio and is prepared to spend more time learning how to carbohydrate load and heat acclimatise before her second attempt. Sue, on the other hand, is not as dedicated or persistent in her effort to achieve her goal. She is reluctant to increase her effort, for fear it may be wasted if she fails to complete the marathon for a second time. In fact, Sue is less likely than Jane to make a second attempt.

This on-going personal assessment of ability and the value of achieving the desired goal involves Atkinson's (1974) third general category of achievement behaviour, persistence. If Sue is an under-achiever, she is less likely to persist with a task that she feels she has less than a 50% chance of achieving. Once having failed at the task, she is even less motivated to try again. Jane, on the other hand, may be particularly persistent in her attempt to complete the marathon if she has come close in the first attempt, because she can see the work she has already done and is able to more readily concentrate efforts to assure success in her second attempt. She may believe, with this new knowledge, that her chance of achieving success has increased from 50% in the first attempt to 60–70% in the second.

It is not the success or failure per se, but the interpretation one puts on them, that really reflects an individual's achievement orientation. As such, Sports Search may significantly increase the child's initial expectations for success, to get them involved. But to stay involved, children will continually assess their own values, abilities and potential, to determine both the intensity and duration of their participation. This may be aided by coach and teacher education emphasising a task-oriented approach to sporting education, in which children learn that work and persistence lead to improvement and effort is valued, rather than a win- or ego-orientation.

In general, achievement orientation looks at the individual's motive to succeed, the ability to experience pride or satisfaction, shame or doubt in sporting accomplishments, goal perspectives (task- or ego-involved) and the impact of the environment. The expectations that arise from these affective states elicit approach or avoidance behaviour, which in turn is reflected in the choice, intensity and duration of an individual's athletic involvement. Consequently, Australia should be endeavouring to develop athletes high in intrinsic motivation with internal control and an orientation towards task mastery with a view to learning about one's personal capacity. Australian initiatives have been taken, through programs such as Sports Search, to identify and develop positive expectations from sporting involvement and to increase general participation and enjoyment.

PARTICIPATION AND WITHDRAWAL IN SPORT

Chalip (1989) comments that too often sporting event outcomes are described as resulting from internal or personal attributes. She quotes Ross (1977), who labels this propensity the "fundamental attribution error", defines it as the "general tendency to overestimate the importance of the personal factors ... relative to environmental influences" (p. 184). In other words, motivational factors in sport are too frequently stated in terms of personality traits or motives, rather than in terms of situations or external contingencies. Chalip says that in the media, individual identity and social existence are not important. Athletes are presented as devoid of ethical convictions, political concerns, and non-sport agendas. Further, the significance of coaching, sport administration, facilities and other forms of requisite infrastructure are never salient.

Central to this is the notion that if the athlete demonstrated or possessed the appropriate personality, then he or she would compete successfully. Chalip's concern about the underrating of external influences on sports motivation can be seen in an unpublished letter by Australian Olympian, Carolyn Schuwalow, to her running sponsors, who gave her the motivation to persist with running after her 1992 Olympic Games exclusion.

> I haven't been this excited about my running since the 1988 Seoul Olympics, when I set the Australian record. Thank-you ... for renewing a great enthusiasm with me again.

Carolyn's loss of motivation in running occurred after administrators showed a loss of confidence in her athletic ability and dropped her from the 1992 Olympic team:

> I really have no idea what happened... I had performed very well in the domestic season and had shown good form in Europe. My time

ranked me in the top fifteen in the world (a requirement for Olympic selection). Then I was left out of the team. I still can't figure out what happened.

Carolyn's enthusiasm was rekindled the following year, after a shoe sponsor expressed confidence in her athletic ability, providing her with the financial assistance to continue training and racing. In 1993, she raced through the American road racing circuit, defeating a number of Olympic finalists from Barcelona, including the Olympic gold medallist from the women's marathon. Obviously, both administrators and sponsors can have significant influence on an athlete's career and motivation to withdraw or persist in sport. It is, therefore, important to consider both factors internal and external to the athlete's motivation to continue or withdraw from sport.

INTERNAL FACTORS IN PARTICIPATION AND DROP-OUT FROM SPORT

When looking at internal factors regarding athletes' motivation, Watson's (1986) research into leading Australian hockey players discovered that some individuals approached achievement situations while others avoided failure. His results showed that unique properties were associated with sporting participants and that in observing elite junior and senior national players, it appeared that one recurring behaviour necessary for success is a motivation to approach — to play free from a fear of failure or unknown consequences.

These competitors were competitive, felt competent during competition, were attracted to tasks that were of intermediate difficulty (rather than too hard or too easy). They were more likely to attribute success to their own ability and persistence, feeling that being involved in an achievement situation gave them an opportunity to learn about themselves, not just about the task. This self-awareness occurs because greater challenges are sought as abilities expand, making the process inherently growth-producing.

Avoiders have a high need for the social incentives of power and aggression, with a need to maintain control over others. Perhaps the key difference found by Watson was that the approacher focuses on the task, while the avoider, who is generally higher in trait and state anxiety, focuses on the social situation as reflected in the need for power and control.

How does this information help us understand the motivation to participate or withdraw from sport participation? It identifies a number of characteristics that need to be inherent in the task in order for the task to be seen as challenging and enjoyable for prolonged participation. For example, the prospect of failure, reduced social affiliation and high adult expectations may all result in negative experiences that result in child and adolescent drop-out.

Robertson (1988) suggests that this information reinforces the need for interventions in sporting communities to modify the expectations, attitudes and values of some behaviour in adults who have a leadership role in junior sport. When we have a good understanding as to what motivates individuals to participate in, stay involved, drop out or change sports, then we can help reverse the drop-out trend.

As has been discussed earlier (see page 99), a developmental process is taking place in Australian sport to change children's involvement in sport from being extrinsically motivating to intrinsically motivating. Children encouraged to participate in athletics through the Five Star Award Scheme are given the opportunity to see their own performances improve, deriving a sense of competency. As the child matures he or she has a choice to give up certain social activities to invest more time in training and competition. This choice involves a self-examination of predispositions and potential if the individual is to have a long-term commitment to sport.

The potential of the athletes is assessed by the level of competency they have experienced in their initial contact with the sport. For athletes to make a long-term commitment, they must be given challenging athletic goals. If greater challenges are not present, intensity drops and the individual becomes bored and may withdraw from the activity. However, a child or adolescent provided with challenges too great for his or her ability may suffer from excessive demands which are anxiety-producing, making concentration and investment too difficult; for example, the child who is zealously supported to make a State Age Group Swimming Championship, by parents and/or their coach, when the child doesn't realistically have the ability to do so. The fear of disappointing themselves and letting down others may be considered stakes that are too high. There are too many risks, or so much to be accomplished that the swimmer is overwhelmed and the outcome performance remains a constant, stressful distraction.

The child/adolescent may find this increased stress reduces feelings of competency and significantly reduces the enjoyment derived from the participation. Failure to achieve these outcomes may be a source of discouragement and the child drops out.

It is important to remember here that persistence is a matter of direction that the individual finds motivating and this will differ across the lifespan. What is often termed as drop-out in Australian sport may in fact be a reflection of an individual's inability, the administration, or the sporting organisation's inability to help the individual move through a particularly difficult transition period.

SOCIAL FACTORS AND AUSTRALIAN SUPPORT PROGRAMS

In the area of social motivation, numerous programs have been developed by the Australian Sports Commission to address these issues, in order to minimise drop-out. In designing these programs, the commission had to identify the de-motivators and counter them. Some of the issues identified were:

- *Concerns about education and future employment.* These concerns resulted in full-time, live-in tutors residing and working with residential athletes at the AIS. Reduced academic workloads were established in targeted schools for scholarship athletes, enabling athletes to take extra time to complete their education. Reducing the educational commitment helps minimise the risk of poor grades that can result because of the amount of time athletes are absent from class to train and compete.

SportsLEAP (Life Skills for Elite Athletes Program) was designed to help athletes with education and career opportunities. It includes periodic personal development seminars to assist individuals with a variety of personal skills, such as curriculum vitae preparation, time management, media skills and public speaking.

- *Isolation.* Younger athletes at the AIS, living away from home, have house parents to care for and supervise them in order to minimise absent parent stress. Athletes who are on full-time scholarships at the AIS, are married and/or have children, may be accommodated at the institute with their families, or receive assistance for housing outside the institute.
- *Financial difficulties.* Scholarships are afforded to athletes who have reached a required standard in their sport, to help them off-set training and competition expenses. After the completion of the scholarship period, the commission is looking at "exit counselling", to help keep the athletes motivated to continue their sporting involvement.

MOTIVATING SPORT THROUGHOUT LIFE

Developmental factors and priorities impinge upon an athlete's decision to remain in, or withdraw from, sport. A child's motivation to play sport is likely to be different from that of the adolescent and adult athlete. The greater the understanding of these phases, the increased likelihood that sporting organisations, government and business will be able to make the sporting experience a positive one for individuals across their life-span.

Developmental and transitional phases have been well documented in psychological literature and are most readily identified with the following psycho-social crises:

- infancy — trust versus mistrust
- toddlerhood — autonomy versus shame and doubt
- early school age — initiative versus guilt
- middle school age — industry versus inferiority
- early adolescence — group identity versus alienation
- later adolescence — individual identity versus role confusion
- early adulthood — intimacy versus isolation
- middle adulthood — generativity versus stagnation
- later adulthood — integrity versus despair (Erikson, 1963).

As we move through these stages, certain demands and social expectations are placed upon us. The effort to adjust to these demands is the psychological crisis. It would seem to suggest, then, that the direction one chooses in sport is most likely going to be related to these different life stages. So we see children identifying friendship and social integration as the greatest motivators for their sporting participation (Watson, Blanksby,

& Bloomfield, 1984), while adults identify goal achievement and personal worth as their strongest motivators (Barrell, Holt, & MacKean, 1988).

We are in fact seeing a developmental shift in the importance and place sport has in the life experience of the individual. However, what is difficult during these transition periods is how to facilitate the redirection in motivation. The individuals themselves may only be aware of a drop in motivation and reduced desire to participate, but not consciously be aware that what motivated them in the past is no longer sufficient to sustain their immediate interest. The athletes may be looking for new and challenging goals and see these in other endeavours.

The opposite can also occur when individuals get stuck. They are so motivated by the enjoyable aspects of their sport — the "flow experience" — that they cannot see a suitable replacement and become addicted to continued participation. An example of this is the athlete who finds it painfully difficult to retire from elite competition.

The problem of transition that faces athletes does not mean that individuals should not specialise in activities. Selective optimisation of skills builds a sense of competence and provides a tremendous source of personal gratification. Rather, athletes need to prepare for these transitions. As former World Marathon Champion and record holder, Robert de Castella, said: "Most athletes spend years training and preparing to deal with success in competition, it comes upon us slowly, but for retirement they receive no apprenticeship, it just happens" (de Castella & Clews, 1993).

Retirement from elite sport is inevitable for every athlete (Clews, 1993). However, the reasons for retirement are varied. Athletes retire because they can no longer sustain maximal performance, they have suffered a debilitating injury, are burned out, have financial difficulties, or have other priorities such as personal, family or career demands. The transition process may be a long one, from the initial recognition that they can no longer sustain the workload or actual performances needed for exceptional performances, to the actual withdrawal.

How the athlete copes with this transition depends on a number of factors:

- Is the withdrawal from elite sport a self-imposed choice, or a premature one due to external consequences?
- Can the athlete redirect his or her energies into other facets of life?
- Can the athlete remain in sport by attributing a new set of values to sporting involvement? For example, future involvement may no longer be for status and accomplishment, but for general health and self-confidence.
- Does the athlete have a satisfactory support network which can be of assistance through this transition period?

If athletes are not psychologically or emotionally ready for this transition, they may experience one, or several, of the following four stages of retirement, outlined by Svoboda and Vanek (1982):

- In the first stage, athletes often report an increased motivation to train harder in an effort to regain former levels of performance.

- In the second stage, when athletes are unable to sustain the desired level of performance, they may suffer from denial and anger. Although denial and anger are painful, they are usually only temporary.
- In the third stage — depression and withdrawal — athletes may feel alone and isolated, having withdrawn from a lifestyle that once provided so much meaning and purpose, to one that is without direction or aim.
- If the process is effectively completed, athletes will reach a fourth stage — a level of acceptance — and be able to redirect their energies into other aspects of their life that they find, over time, to be equally fulfilling.

In keeping this in mind, Danish et al. (1987) suggest that the task of coaches and administrators is to attempt to enhance motivation developmentally. They can help athletes to identify alternative activities which might replace their involvement in sport at the previous level and intensity. The replacement activities must provide individuals with challenges that are compatible with their interests, knowledge and skills. This allows retiring athletes to gain feelings of competence and satisfaction from their new activities.

Transitional activities are important for athletes moving from junior sport into open competition. These will enable athletes to maintain the motivation to play sport, during a period where it may be a number of years before they are realistically competitive in open competition. It is important that, during this transitional time, individuals be encouraged to set personal best goals that require discipline and concentration, but are also enjoyable and supply satisfaction and meaning.

Danish et al. (1987) summed up the underlying process needed for continued sporting involvement when they said "the intent is to encourage individuals to be producers of their own development, to be active problem solvers and planners, and to develop a sense of self-efficacy" (p. 232). Central to this are an athlete's ability to set goals and to focus his or her intensity and effort with direction, where the direction is the sporting goal. When goals are defined in terms of eliminating a given problem, it instils confidence and empowers the individual. With this empowerment comes the motivation to persist, the motivation to achieve, the motivation to excel.

FUTURE DIRECTIONS

The possibilities for further research into the motivation variables that are involved in sporting participation and withdrawal are great. To date most of the research done in this area has been based in the United States and Canada. While North American, Canadian and Australian cultures are similar, they are not identical, and further research is needed with specific consideration to the Australian experience.

Research in the area of motivation in sport needs to be addressed from a developmental perspective, in consideration of other life changes occurring within the individual. Long-term studies may be useful in that they would enable the researchers to view changes that occur within individual development, across time, rather than cross-sectional studies that may be more reflective of the social environment at the time.

We need more comprehensive studies on why children choose to participate or withdraw from sport. It is quite possible that an absence of factors that encourage participation may not be reasons for withdrawal but, in fact, withdrawal may result from a completely separate set of circumstances. It would also be useful to look at the dynamic changes that take place between participation and adherence. The motives involved in adherence may be different from those that encourage initial participation.

Follow-up research on the impact of the Australian Sports Commission's Sports Search program and its impact on general participation and adherence levels, along with the flow-on effect to talent identification, will be of great interest.

Robertson (1988) suggests that a more detailed consideration of the differing types of sport participants and withdrawers could be examined. He suggests the following possible categories in youth sport, but they may be applicable across all ages:

- the super-tuned-in athlete who has specialised in one sport from a young age with intense commitment
- the tuned-in athlete who has sought continual involvement in several sports over a period of time
- the shifting athlete who has displayed a consistent involvement in sport in general, characterised by continually changing involvement
- the athlete who drifted into sport with a casual interest
- the inducted athlete whose participation reflects more of the influence of others, such as parents or teachers, than of their own motivation
- the athlete who has been cut out as a consequence of the selection process in sport and so denied the opportunity to participate
- the athlete who has been sat out for a period of time either through illness or a sport-related injury
- the athlete who has suffered burn-out from excessive sport involvement.

In all of the above, the perceptions of the individual as to the personal cost and benefits of sporting involvement need to be considered, because ultimately it is the cost–benefits ratio that enhances or reduces an individual's motivation to play.

The impact of the various social support networks on motivation and participation, such as State and national institutes and academies, needs to be examined. There is a fine line between external reinforcers being viewed as an acknowledgment of an individual's competency and, therefore, increasing intrinsic motivation, or being used coercively and detracting from the individual's intrinsic motivation. The "buzz" words in Australia now are *talent identification*. Sporting organisations are keen to identify new athletic talent. In Australia, talented athletes have many sporting options through which they may express their abilities. Sports are now competing against each other to access this talent. Identifying the talent is not as difficult as retaining it. Further research is still needed on persistence versus withdrawal, why an athlete who may be physiologically and psychologically suited to several sports chooses one over the other.

Before large sums of money are spent on identifying this new talent, sporting organisations need to be selective in their talent identification and to be able to target those who are most likely to remain in their sport, rather than suffering the large withdrawal rates currently experienced.

The effectiveness of our current support structures depends on their ability to reflect positive information to athletes about their personal competency, thereby reinforcing their intrinsic motivation, and to evaluate the success of programs. For example, is a talent identification program considered successful if it identifies elite talent, but that talent is not retained? The infrastructure of Australian sport must be examined to determine its impact on the intrinsic motivation of the individual.

CONCLUSIONS

Motivation is a broad topic, which has been addressed in a number of ways by psychologists. A range of these approaches have attracted sport psychologists. Two of the perspectives are addressed in chapters which follow. The application of attribution theory to sport is considered in Chapter 5 and self-efficacy in sport and exercise is the topic in Chapter 6. Three other approaches to motivation have been widely applied to sport. They are intrinsic and extrinsic motivation, achievement motivation and participation motivation. A general review of the literature in these areas was thought to be inappropriate, since contemporary reviews are available elsewhere (e.g., Cox, 1994; Roberts, 1992; Weiss & Chaumeton, 1992). Instead, while referring to the theoretical and research literature, the emphasis of the present chapter has been on the implications for sport and sports performers, especially in the context of Australasia, of current thinking about motivation.

It can be concluded from the discussion of a range of Australasian initiatives that there is great potential for motivating people at all levels of sport, provided that these programs are developed in the light of our current understanding of what motivates people to initiate and to continue participation in sport. The chapter provides some observations on the implementation of various programs, based on the importance of developing intrinsic motivation and ensuring that extrinsic motivation is presented in a manner that complements the intrinsic. The importance of developing a task-involved goal orientation in sports performers at all levels is also emphasised. It is recognised, however, that there is a need for much more research, especially with Australasian samples.

The approach to sport implied above is developmental in nature. Research must also examine motivation in sport and exercise developmentally across the life-span, in the way that Brodkin and Weiss (1990) extended the work on participation motivation in youth sport (e.g., Gill, Gross, & Huddleston, 1983; Gould, Feltz, & Weiss, 1985). The Participation

Motivation Questionnaire (PMQ) was developed by Gill et al. (1983) in the investigation of adolescent motives for participation in sport. Brodkin and Weiss (1990) used it developmentally to examine reasons for participation in sport of people from under ten years old to more than 70 years of age. While this sort of developmental research is important, there must be reservations about results gained from cross-sectional studies, which will only be resolved by the execution of longitudinal research. Commitment to study the same sample for many years is critical to our understanding of what motivates people to participate in sport at different points in their lives. Research must also be conducted in the field, especially in association with the formal programs set up by Federal and State agencies.

There is much to admire about the way in which Australasian sports organisations have approached the promotion of sport at all levels, for example the Sports Search program, the various initiatives on talent identification, and the support for elite and potential elite performers through the sports institutes and academies. Also promising is the recent emergence of programs intended to help athletes facing transitions in sport, such as the SportsLEAP program and the Victorian Institute of Sport (VIS) Athlete Career Education (ACE) program (see Chapter 19). This is reflected in the positive social attitudes and motivation toward sport in Australasia, which provide the solid base on which to build, as psychologists understand motivation in sport more fully in the future.

SUMMARY

This chapter considers three major aspects of motivation applied to sport: intrinsic/extrinsic motivation, achievement motivation, and participation motivation. It first places these in the context of major psychological perspectives on motivation, noting that the major approaches tend to focus on internal sources of motivation. The chapter also considers social factors which influence motivation in sport. In examining intrinsic and extrinsic motivation, the terms are defined and the major theoretical perspective, Cognitive Evaluation Theory, is described. Examples are presented from sport and implications are pointed out for issues such as sports scholarships and other awards. These aspects of social infrastructure are seen to counterbalance personal sources of motivation. The focus of the following section is achievement orientation. Emphasis is placed on the intensity, choice and persistence elements of motivation in sport contexts, particularly how these are differently affected by the adoption of a task-involved or ego-involved orientation. Again, such practical issues as the effectiveness of Aussie Sports and Sports Search programs are considered in this context. Participation in and withdrawal from sport are addressed next. In this section some stress is placed on the role of the culture in determining participation and withdrawal, especially by contrasting research results from the United States and Australia. Implications are drawn for programs like the SportsLEAP program in Australia, which aims to smooth the transition from elite sport on retirement. The chapter concludes with comments on future directions, which include the need for developmental and longitudinal research, the need to address initiation, continuation and withdrawal as independent processes, the need for research and evaluation to monitor and follow up on the likes of the Sports Search and talent identification programs, as well as the need for wide-ranging examination of the impact of the sports institutes and academies. The chapter concludes that infrastructure and social attitudes for sport are positive and provide great potential for the future.

REFERENCES

Adler, A. (1924). *The practise and theory of individual psychology.* New York: Harcourt, Brace.

Atkinson, J. W. (1957). Motivational determinants of risk taking behaviour. *Psychological Review, 64,* 359–372.

Atkinson, J. W. (1974). The mainsprings of achievement oriented activity. In J. W. Atkinson & J. O. Raynor (Eds.), *Motivation and achievement* (pp. 13–41). New York: Halstead.

Australian Sports Commission. (1990). *Sport for young Australians.* (Market research report). Canberra: Australian Sports Commission.

Barrell, G. V., Holt, D., & MacKean, J. M. (1988). In E. F. Broom, R. Klumpner, B. Pendleton, & C. A. Pooley (Eds.), *Comparative physical education and sport: Vol. 5* (pp. 131–137). Chicago, IL: Human Kinetics.

Bartis, S., Szymanski, K., & Harkins, S. G. (1988). Evaluation and performance: A two edged knife. *Personality and Social Psychology Bulletin, 14,* 242–251.

Birch, D., & Veroff, J. (1966). *Motivation: A study of action.* Belmont, CA: Brooks/Cole.

Brodkin, P., & Weiss, M. R. (1990). Developmental differences in motivation for participating in competitive swimming. *Journal of Sport and Exercise Psychology, 12,* 248–263.

Chalip, P. (1989). Athletes as personalities: Policy implications of the fundamental attribution error. *New Zealand Journal of Sports Medicine, 17*(2), 25–28.

Clews, G. J. (1993). Mind matters. In R. Cedaro (Ed.), *Triathlon into the nineties.* Sydney: Murray Child.

Cook, B. (1980). An athletics programme incorporating the Five Star Award Scheme. *Sports Coach, 4*(4), Spring, 20–25.

Cox, R. H. (1994). *Sport psychology: concepts and applications.* (3rd ed.). Dubuque, IA: Wm C. Brown.

Danish, S. J., Kleiber, D. A., & Hall, H. K. (1987). Developmental intervention and motivation in the context of sport. In M. L. Maehr & D. A. Kleiber (Eds.), *Advances in Motivation and Achievement: Enhancing Motivation: Volume 5* (pp.211–238). Greenwich, CT: JAI Press Inc.

De Castella, F. R., & Clews, G. J. (1993). *Life after sport.* Unpublished manuscript.

Deci, E. L., & Ryan, R. M. (1985). *Intrinsic motivation and self determination in human behaviour.* New York: Plenum.

Duda, J. L. (1988). The relationship between goal perspectives and persistence and intensity among recreational sport participants. *Leisure Sciences, 10,* 95–106.

Duda, J. L. (1992). Motivation in sports settings: A goal perspective approach. In G. C. Roberts (Ed.), *Motivation in sport and exercise* (pp. 57–91). Champaign, IL: Human Kinetics.

Duda, J. L., Smart, A., & Tappe, M. (1989). Personal investment in rehabilitation of athletic injuries. *Journal of Sport and Exercise Psychology, 11*, 367–381.

Eccles, J. S., & Harold, R. D. (1991). Gender differences in sport involvement: Applying the Eccles' expectancy-value model. *Journal of Applied Sport Psychology, 3*, 7–35.

Eccles (Parsons) J., Adler, T. F., Futterman, C. A., Goff, S. B., Kaczala, C. M., Meece, J. L., & Midgley, C. (1983). Expectations, values and academic behaviours. In J. T. Spence (Ed.), *Achievement and achievement motivation* (pp. 75–146). San Francisco: W. H. Freeman.

Erikson, E. H. (1963). *Childhood and society* (2nd ed.). New York: Norton.

Freud, S. (1920). *Beyond the pleasure principle.* New York: Norton.

Gill, D. L., Gross, J. B., & Huddleston, S. (1983). Participation motivation in youth sports. *International Journal of Sport Psychology, 14*, 1–14.

Gould, D. (1987). Promoting positive sport experiences for children. In J. R. May & M. J. Asken (Eds.), *Sport psychology: The psychological health of the athlete.* New York, NY: PMA Publishing Corp.

Gould, D., Feltz, D., & Weiss, M. (1985). Motives for participation in competitive youth swimming. *International Journal of Sport Psychology, 16*, 126–140.

Gould, D., & Horn, T. S. (1984). Participation motivation in young athletes. In J. M. Silva & R. S. Weinberg (Eds.), *Psychological foundations of sport* (pp. 359–370). Champaign, IL: Human Kinetics.

Greene, D., & Lepper, M. R. (1974). Effects of extrinsic rewards on children's subsequent intrinsic interest. *Child Development, 45*, 1141–1145.

Hardy, C. J., & Latane, B. (1988). Social loafing in cheerleaders: Effects of team membership and competition. *Journal of Sport and Exercise Psychology, 10*, 109 114.

Hardy, C. J. (1989). Social loafing: Economizing individual effort during team performance. In L. R. Brawley, A. W. Carron, W. N. Widmeyer, & C. J. Hardy (Eds.), *Group size in physical activity: Psychological and behavioural impacts.* Proceedings of the symposium of the North American Society of the Psychology of Sport and Physical Activity. Kent, OH: Kent State University.

Harkins, S. G., & Petty, R. E. (1982). Effects of task difficulty and task uniqueness on social loafing. *Journal of Personality and Social Psychology, 43*, 1214–1229.

Harkins, S. G., & Jackson, J. M. (1985). The role of evaluation in eliminating social loafing. *Personality and Social Psychology Bulletin, 11*(4), 457–465.

Horn, T. S., & Hasbrook, C. A. (1986). Informational components influencing children's perceptions of their physical competence. In M. R. Weiss & D. Gould (Eds.), *Sport for children and youths* (pp. 81–88). Champaign, IL: Human Kinetics.

Horn, T. S., & Hasbrook, C. A. (1987). Psychological characteristics and the criteria children use for self-evaluation. *Journal of Sport Psychology, 9*, 208–221.

Horn, T. S., & Weiss, M. R. (1991). A developmental analysis of children's self-ability judgements in physical domain. *Paediatric Exercise Science, 3*, 310–326.

Kerr, N. L., & Bruun, S. E. (1983). Dispensability of member effort and group motivation losses: Free-rider effects. *Journal of Personality and Social Psychology, 44*, 78–94.

Jackson, J. M., & Williams, K. D. (1985). Social loafing on difficult tasks: Working collectively can improve performance. *Journal of Personality and Social Psychology, 49*(5), 937–942.

Latane, B., Williams, K. D., & Harkins, S. G. (1979). Many hands make light work: The causes and consequences of social loafing. *Journal of Personality and Social Psychology, 37*, 822–832.

Leigh, M. H. (1974). *The evolution of women's participation in the Summer Olympic games, 1900–1948.* Unpublished doctoral dissertation, Ohio State University, Ohio.

Lepper, M. R., & Greene, D. (1975). Turning play into work: Effects of adult surveillance and extrinsic rewards on children's intrinsic motivation. *Journal of Personality and Social Psychology, 31,* 479–486.

Lepper, M. R., Greene, D., & Nisbett, R. E. (1973). Undermining children's intrinsic interest with extrinsic rewards: A test of the "overjustification" hypothesis. *Journal of Personality and Social Psychology, 28,* 129–137.

Longhurst, K., & Spink, K. S. (1987). Participation in motivation of Australian children involved in organized sport. *Canadian Journal of Sport Science, 12*(1), 24–30.

Maehr, M. L. (1984). Meaning and motivation: Toward a theory of personal investment. In R. Ames & C. Ames (Eds.), *Research on motivation in education: Vol. 1 Student motivation* (pp. 115–144). New York: Academic Press.

Maehr, M. L., & Nicholls, J. G. (1980). Culture and achievement motivation: A second look. In N. Warren (Ed.), *Studies in cross cultural psychology* (Vol. 3, pp. 221–267). New York: Academic.

Martens, R. (1976). *Competitiveness and sport.* Paper presented at the International Congress of Physical Activity Sciences, Quebec City.

McClelland, D. C. (1961). *The achieving society.* New York: Free Press.

McClelland, D. C., Atkinson, J. W., Clark, R. A., & Lowell, E. W. (1953). *The achievement motive.* New York: Appleton-Century-Crofts.

Murray, H. A. (1938). *Explorations in personality.* New York: Oxford University Press.

Nicholls, J. G. (1984a). Achievement motivation: Conceptions of ability, subjective experience, task choice, and performance. *Psychological Review, 91,* 328–346.

Nicholls, J. G. (1984b). Conceptions of ability and achievement motivation. In R. Ames & C. Ames (Eds.), *Research on motivation in education: Vol. 1. Student motivation.* New York: Academic Press.

Orlick, T. D., & Mosher, R. (1978). Extrinsic rewards and participant motivation in a sport related task. *International Journal of Sports Psychology, 9,* 27–39.

Passer, M. N. (1981). Children in sport: Participation motives and psychological stress. *Quest, 33*(2), 231–244.

Phares, E. J. (1988). *Introduction to personality* (2nd ed.). Glenview, IL: Scott, Foresman & Company.

Phillips, D. H. (1992). *Australian women at the Olympic Games.* Kenthurst, NSW: Kangaroo Press.

Roberts, G. C. (1984). Toward a new theory of motivation in sport: The role of perceived ability. In J. M. Silva & R. S. Weinberg (Eds.), *Psychological foundations of sport.* Champaign, IL: Human Kinetics.

Roberts, G. C. (1992). Motivation in sport and exercise: Conceptual constraints and convergence. In G. C. Roberts (Ed.), *Motivation in sport and exercise.* Champaign, IL: Human Kinetics.

Robertson, I. (1988). *The sports drop-out: A time for change? A review of literature.* (A report presented to the Applied Sports Research Program.) Canberra: Australian Sports Commission.

Rogers, C. R. (1951). *Client-centred therapy.* Boston: Houghton-Mifflin.

Rogers, C. R. (1963). The actualizing tendency in relation to motives and to consciousness. In M. Jones (Ed.), *Nebraska symposium on motivation.* Lincoln: University of Nebraska Press.

Ross, L. (1977). The intuitive psychologist and his shortcomings: Distortions in the attribution process. *Advances in Experimental Social Psychology, 10,* 184–237.

Ryan, E. D. (1977). Attribution, intrinsic motivation and athletics. In L. I. Gedvilas & M. E. Kneer (Eds.), *Proceedings of the NAPECW/NCPEAM National Conference, 1977* (pp. 346–353). Chicago: Office of Publications Services, University of Illinois at Chicago Circle.

Ryan, E. D. (1980). Attribution, intrinsic motivation, and athletics: A replication and extension. In C. H. Nadeau, W. R. Halliwell, K. M. Newell, & G. C. Roberts (Eds.), *Psychology of motor behavior and sport — 1979* (pp. 19–26). Champaign, IL: Human Kinetics.

Skinner, B. F. (1938). *The behaviour of organisms.* New York: Appleton-Century-Crofts.

Skinner, B. F. (1971). *Beyond freedom and dignity.* New York: Knopf.

Svoboda, B., & Vanek, M. (1982). Retirement from high level competition. In T. Orlick, J. T. Partington, & J. H. Salmela (Eds.), *Mental training for coaches and athletes* (pp. 166–175). Ottawa, Canada: Coaching Association of Canada.

Thomas, J. R. (1978). Attribution theory and motivation through reward: Practical implications for children's sports. In R. A. Magill, M. J. Ash, & F. L. Smoll (Eds.), *Children in sport: A contemporary anthology* (pp. 149–158). Champaign, IL: Human Kinetics.

Watkin, B., & Youngen, L. (1988). Cross national comparisons of motivation for participation in physical activity of Australian and American adolescents. In E. F. Broom, R. Clumpner, B. Pendleton, & C. A. Pooley (Eds.), *Comparative physical education and sport: Volume 5* (pp. 267–275). Chicago, IL: Human Kinetics.

Watson, G. G. (1984). Intrinsic motivation and competitive anxiety in sport: Some guidelines for coaches and administrators. *The Australian Journal of Science and Medicine in Sport, 16* (4), 14–20.

Watson, G. G. (1986). Approach-avoidance behaviour in team sports: An application to leading Australian national hockey players. *International Journal of Sports Psychology, 17,* 136–155.

Watson, G. G., Blanksby, B. A., & Bloomfield, J. (1984). Reward systems in children's sport: Perceptions and evaluations of elite junior swimmers. *Journal of Human Movement Studies, 10,* 123–156.

Weiss, M. R., & Chaumeton, N. (1992). Motivational orientation in sport. In T.S. Horn (Ed.), *Advances in sport psychology* (pp. 61–100). Champaign, IL: Human Kinetics.

Weldon, E., & Mustari, E. L. (1988). Felt dispensability and explicit anonymity on cognitive effort. *Organizational Behaviour and Human Decision Processes, 41,* 330–351.

Widmeyer, W. N., Brawley, L. R., & Carron, A. V. (1990). The effects of group size in sport. *Journal of Sport and Exercise Psychology, 12,* 177–199.

Williams, K., Harkins, S., & Latane, B. (1981). Identifiability as a deterrent to social loafing: Two cheering experiments. *Journal of Personality and Social Psychology, 40,* 303–311.

Zaccaro, S. J. (1984). Social loafing: The role of task attractiveness. *Personality and Social Psychology Bulletin, 10*(1), 99–106.

C H A P T E R

5

ATTRIBUTION THEORY

S T E P H A N I E   H A N R A H A N

Attributions are reasons that people use to explain cause and effect relationships. Individuals generate these causes or explanations to make sense of their world. We make attributions because we are predisposed to predict, explain, and understand the behaviours of ourselves and others. This attributional activity occurs spontaneously, especially when we experience unexpected events or the non-attainment of goals (Weiner, 1985a).

Attributions are not necessarily the actual causes of particular events, but rather the perceived causes of those events. For example, if you are in a basketball team in a club competition and find that you spend a lot of time on the bench, you may attribute your lack of playing time to your poor basketball skills or to the poor judgement of the coach who you perceive is biased against you. Similarly, if you are playing in a Rugby team and find that you are not performing well, you might make one of a number of attributions to explain your poor performance. The attributions you make will affect your future thoughts, feelings and behaviour. For example, if you attribute your poor performance to poor fitness, you may begin a running program to augment your training sessions. If you make an attribution of poor technique you might ask the coach or another player for extra instruction. If, however, you attribute your poor performance to a general lack of coordination and ability, you might quit Rugby entirely.

Attributions are also made regarding the behaviour of other people. When someone we know who has been a couch potato for years suddenly turns into an avid exerciser, we try to understand why. When teams we support lose we try to understand why by making attributions. Attributions, however, are not only made for poor performances or losses. If a team which was last in the competition last year suddenly turns around to win the grand final this year, people spontaneously engage in attributional activities to explain the situation.

THEORIES OF ATTRIBUTION

Attribution theory is the systematic study of the processes involved in assigning causality and the consequences of this causal ascription. A variety of theories have been proposed, but the founder of attribution theory is generally acknowledged to be Fritz Heider. Heider initiated this area of study with the publication of his article "Social perception and phenomenal causality" in 1944. This article focused on the perceptions humans have of other people and their behaviour. It also presaged future attributional research by suggesting that not only does the state of the individual influence his or her attributions, but that attributions may influence the dynamic state of the person.

In his "common-sense psychology", Heider (1958) believed that behaviour is determined by the additive combination of internal and external forces. Personal or internal factors include ability, effort and fatigue, whereas environmental or external factors include task difficulty, opportunity and luck. Heider tried to explain the thought processes that people use to make sense out of everyday events in the world around them. He discussed subjective or "common-sense" features that guide people's perceptions of others and of themselves. These features include judgements about intentions, causal responsibility, and motives. We try to find invariant conditions to help us explain what is happening around us.

CORRESPONDENT INFERENCES

Although Heider's model is difficult to test, it did lay the intellectual background for future work by Jones and Davis (1965) and Kelley (1973). Jones and Davis (1965) offered a theoretical framework for dispositional attributions or inferring the traits of other persons from their behaviour. They postulated that information about the consequences of alternative actions could be used to infer the intention behind a particular act. Jones and Davis introduced the principle of noncommon effect. This principle holds that the intention underlying a voluntary act is most clearly evident when it has a small number of effects or consequences that are unique or noncommon to that act. For example, it could be inferred that an individual has chosen to participate in cricket because of the enjoyment of being outdoors with a group of people. If, however, it is learned that the individual also had the options of going whitewater rafting with an outdoor recreation group or attending a family barbecue, then it might be deduced that the individual participates in cricket for other reasons (e.g., the opportunity to compete or improve specific skills). No longer would it be inferred that the individual has chosen to play cricket just because it allowed for outdoor participation with others. Effects that are common across all choices give no information about dispositional attributes. On the other hand, if one choice of action has a lot of noncommon effects, dispositional attribution is also weak. The strongest dispositional attributions are made when one choice of action has just one or two noncommon effects.

Limiting themselves to the case in which the action is known to be intentional, Jones and Davis (1965) suggested that actions which are performed for only one reason and which are unlike those performed by most people are most useful in understanding the individual's personal traits. An illustration of this is an athlete who chooses to attend training camps instead of going on holidays and trains daily even in the rain or cold. Conclusions about this person's attitudes or goals would be much more accurate than if the person was just seen training on a beautiful day with a group of friends.

Inferences concerning the traits of others which are achieved with a high degree of confidence are termed "correspondent inferences" (Fiske & Taylor, 1984). The likelihood of making a correspondent inference is increased when there are few noncommon effects and when the person's behaviour is seen as undesirable or non-normative. Success in inferring the traits, motives and intentions of others was believed to stem from careful attention to certain key aspects of their behaviour (Jones & Davis, 1965).

The correspondent inference model proposed by Jones and Davis (1965) is a significant extension of Heider's model. The correspondent inference model notes the importance of choices available to the individual, specifies variations of processes that will affect the strength of attributions, and provides an overall more testable model. This model, however, does not address self-attributions and is limited to personal explanations of behaviour. Environmental forces are not considered.

COVARIATION

To determine whether another person's behaviour stems from internal or external causes, Kelley (1973) felt that people focus on three different factors of covariation:

- consensus — the extent to which other persons react in the same manner to a particular stimulus
- consistency — the degree to which an individual reacts to a particular stimulus in the same manner on a number of occasions
- distinctiveness — the extent to which an individual reacts in the same manner to other, different stimuli.

The basic premise of Kelley's model is that the cause of an event is seen to be that factor which is present when the event is present and absent when the event is absent. In other words, the event is attributed to the factor with which it covaries.

Kelley's theory suggests that an individual's behaviour is most likely to be attributed to internal causes under conditions of low consensus, high consistency and low distinctiveness. On the other hand, external attributions will most likely be made under conditions of high consensus, high consistency and high distinctiveness. For example, if an athlete makes a formal protest against an official, information about consensus, consistency and distinctiveness will help observers determine the cause of that behaviour. If this individual is the only person who complains about the official, complains about that official on numerous occasions, and generally complains about all officials, then the protest would be likely to be attributed to the athlete personally not liking officials (an internal cause). If, however, many athletes and coaches complain about that official on a regular basis, yet rarely complain about other officials, the protest would be likely to be attributed to the poor performance of that particular official (an external cause).

The logical analysis used in the principles of noncommon effects and covariation requires the synthesis of considerable information and selection among a large number of causal explanations. There are many situations where all of the information on consensus, distinctiveness and consistency is not available. Even when all of the information is available, people may not put the time into attributions required by this model except for cases that are very important to them. Therefore, on some occasions causal attributions may depend on the earliest or most salient information available to the individual (Kelley & Michela, 1980).

The factors which influence this process have been termed the *primacy effect* and the *salience effect*. The primacy effect occurs when a person scans and interprets information only until that time when an attribution is obtained. Once an attribution for an event has been determined, all later information is disregarded. The salience effect occurs when an effect is attributed to the cause that is most salient in the perceptual field at the time the effect is observed. No matter which method of information processing is utilised by an attributor, however, the causal beliefs, motives and expectations that the attributor brings to the situation will affect the attributional process.

The attribution theories of Heider, Jones and Davis, and Kelley have been given little direct attention in sport psychology. The theory which underpins most of the attribution research in sport psychology is Weiner's model of achievement attributions. Weiner based his model on Heider's work, and although the model initially focused on achievement in the classroom, it has since been expanded to include achievement behaviours in a variety of domains including sport.

FOUR BASIC ATTRIBUTIONS

Weiner (1972) developed a specific attributional model for achievement behaviour. Following Heider, Weiner stated that four causal elements generalise to all achievement tasks. These causal elements are ability, effort, task difficulty and luck. The four perceived causes of success and failure are analysed within two causal dimensions:

- locus of control (whether the cause of the performance was due to something inside the person (internal) or something outside the person (external))

- stability (whether the cause of the performance will rarely if ever be present again (unstable) or will always be present in the future (stable)).

Ability is internal and stable, effort is internal and unstable, task difficulty is external and stable, and luck is external and unstable (see Figure 5.1). These four attributions soon came to be regarded by researchers of achievement attributions as the basic attributional factors.

	Stable	**Unstable**
Internal	Ability	Effort
External	Task difficulty	Luck

Figure 5.1: Weiner's (1972) two-dimensional model of attributions

In sport settings, however, these four attributions have not always been found to fit Weiner's original dimensional model. Using Little League baseball players as subjects, Iso-Ahola (1977) measured attributions using effort, ability, task difficulty and luck as possible responses. He proposed that effort has a different attributional meaning in the cases of success and failure. The results of a principle component analysis indicated that effort was loaded highly with ability in the win situation, whereas in the loss condition effort tended to load highly with luck and task difficulty. Iso-Ahola interpreted this as meaning that when losing, effort is treated as an external factor; and when winning, effort tends to be interpreted as an internal factor.

Similarly, ability may not always be perceived as a stable factor, as traditionally considered. Carron (1984) suggested that ability related to fitness may be viewed as relatively unstable. The ability to run a certain distance, for example, is dependent on fitness which may not remain at a constant level over time. Deaux (1976) has also argued that task difficulty is not always as stable as suggested by Weiner's (1972) original model. The instability of task difficulty in sporting situations is logical. The difficulty of performing particular skills in soccer, for example, would be dependent on changeable factors such as field conditions, the ability of the opposition, and the weather. In other sports, however, task difficulty may remain relatively constant. For example, in diving competitions each dive has been assigned a specific degree of difficulty which is not influenced by the ability of other competitors.

Limitations of the four attributions

The stringent use of Weiner's traditional four attributions may be constraining in the sporting situation. In a laboratory study investigating attributions for performance on a motor maze task, Iso-Ahola and Roberts (1977) found that lack of practice was a more important external reason for failure than the traditional reasons of luck and task difficulty. Similarly, Bukowski and Moore (1980) found that the traditional attributions of luck and task difficulty were perceived as having little importance in boys' attributions of possible causes for success and failure in athletic events. In addition to the traditional factors of effort and ability, officiating and interest in competing were rated as important causes for success and failure in athletics.

Using an open-ended questionnaire with hypothetical situations to determine the causal elements used in sport, Roberts and Pascuzzi (1979) found that the four traditional elements were used only 45% of the time. A Japanese study investigating attributions made for performances in soft tennis also revealed that more than four attributions are needed to explain success and failure in sport (Yamamoto, 1983). Thirteen attributional factors were extracted from winners and 14 from losers. Weiner (1979) himself has pointed out that the four attributions of ability, effort, task difficulty and luck were never intended to be the only attributions used in achievement situations. Generally speaking, competition in sport is likely to elicit more diverse attributions than academic situations because of its interactive nature. Research in sport, therefore, should focus on causal dimensions rather than the four basic attributions (Gill, Ruder, & Gross, 1982).

CONTROLLABILITY AS A THIRD DIMENSION

In 1979 Weiner added a third dimension to his two-dimensional model of attributions. Locus of control was split into the two dimensions of locus of causality and controllability. Locus of causality is very similar to the old locus of control and refers to whether the cause was internal or external. Controllability is a fairly self-explanatory dimension which ranges from causes which are not at all controllable to causes which are completely controllable. Locus of control was split into two separate dimensions because a cause such as aptitude or body build could be internal yet uncontrollable, and a cause such as evaluator bias could be external but still controllable (Weiner, 1979). Weiner (1985b) expanded his three-dimensional model of attributions to an attributional theory of achievement motivation and emotion. He stated that the perceived stability of causes influences future expectancies of success, and that all three dimensions affect a variety of emotions. This attributional theory of achievement motivation will be explored before describing additional attributional dimensions which have been proposed by others.

ATTRIBUTIONS AND ACHIEVEMENT BEHAVIOUR

EXPECTANCY OF SUCCESS

The perceived stability of causes influences individuals' expectancies of future success which in turn influence future achievement behaviour (Weiner, 1985b). An individual who fails and attributes the failure to stable causes will expect to fail in the future. An individual who succeeds and attributes the success to stable causes will expect to succeed in the future. An individual who fails and attributes the failure to unstable causes will expect that future success is possible. An individual who succeeds and attributes that success to unstable causes will expect that future failure is possible. (See Figure 5.2.) This expectancy of future success can determine whether or not a person chooses to continue to participate in a particular task.

Outcome	Stability of attribution	Expectancy of future success
Success	Stable	Success
Success	Unstable	Success or failure
Failure	Stable	Failure
Failure	Unstable	Success or failure

Figure 5.2: Attributions and expectancy of success

To illustrate the above, two individuals may have the same level of performance, but attribute that performance to different causes, resulting in different behaviour. If Jane attributes her poor performance in basketball to a total lack of ability (a stable cause), she will expect to continue to have poor performances in basketball in the future. Since she perceives that she has no chance of experiencing future success, Jane will probably stop participating in that activity when given a choice. If Joan, however, attributes her own poor performance in basketball to a particular injury or choosing an inappropriate strategy for the specific situation (unstable causes), she will expect that future performances may be better, resulting in continued effort and participation. Attributions influence athletes' expectancies for future success, which in turn can determine whether or not a person chooses to participate in a particular task (Weiner, 1985b).

EMOTIONS

Attributions may also influence emotions, which in turn also influence achievement behaviour (Weiner, 1985b). When a positive outcome is attributed internally, an athlete usually feels pride and positive self-esteem. When individuals feel good about themselves in particular situations they are likely to maintain involvement in those situations. When a negative outcome is attributed internally, an athlete usually experiences negative self-esteem, which in turn may lead to a decrease in voluntary involvement.

Simple internal attributions, however, are not the limit of the influence of attributions on emotions. Hopelessness, guilt and shame are all related to attributions. If a negative outcome is attributed to stable causes (e.g., John performs poorly in platform diving and attributes his poor performance to the immense difficulty of the task), hopelessness is often experienced. Hopelessness-related emotions result in quitting. Shame-related emotions also tend to result in withdrawing and giving up. Shame is experienced when a negative outcome is attributed to internal and uncontrollable causes (e.g., Lisa attributes poor performance in netball to her poor depth perception which leads to poor hand–eye coordination). Guilt, however, is experienced when a negative outcome is attributed to internal and controllable causes (e.g., Tom attributes his poor hockey performance to a lack of effort). Guilt-related emotions often result in increased motivation and retribution. In summary, attributions influence emotions which influence future achievement behaviour (Weiner, 1985b). See Biddle (1993) for a summary of attribution–emotion studies in sport.

ADDITIONAL ATTRIBUTIONAL DIMENSIONS

GLOBALITY

While studying the "depressive attributional style", Seligman, Abramson, Semmel, and von Baeyer (1979) included the dimensions of internality, stability and globality in their investigations. A depressive attributional style involves attributing uncontrollable bad events to internal, stable and global causes. The globality dimension measures the breadth of the impact of a particular cause. In other words, it measures whether the cause only influences one particular situation or a wide variety of situations. Attributing lack of control to global factors will probably lead to an expectation of uncontrollability in future situations, thereby extending helplessness and depressive deficits across situations (Abramson & Martin, 1981). For example, if a footballer attributes poor officiating in a game to the general lack of concern of officials and the poor training they receive as officials (a global attribution), he is likely to perceive that things will not improve for other games at other venues with different officials. If, however, a footballer attributes poor officiating in a game to the ill health of a particular official (a specific attribution), the expectancy of quality officiating in other games at other venues is much more positive.

In a study of learned helplessness in sport, Prapavessis and Carron (1988) suggested that tennis players who exhibited symptoms of learned helplessness attributed losses to internal, stable and global factors to a greater extent than players not exhibiting these symptoms. This finding suggests that globality may be an important dimension in sport-related attributional style.

INTENTIONALITY

The idea of intentionality in causal attributions was introduced by Heider (1958). A person will assign more responsibility to acts which are attributed to intentional causes than for those believed to be the result of unintentional factors. Elig and Frieze (1975) included the intentionality dimension in their three-dimensional coding scheme of causality, but defined intentional causes as those that are under conscious control of the individual. In this case intentionality appears to be confounded with controllability.

Intentionality and controllability have been integrated by Russell (1982). He developed a questionnaire to measure attributions along the dimensions of internality, stability, and controllability. The dimension of controllability was measured with questions about responsibility, controllability and intentionality. Therefore, according to Russell intentionality is not a separate dimension, but rather one facet of controllability. Biddle and Jamieson (1988), however, did separate analyses on the three controllability sub-scales proposed by Russell and found that winners were higher than losers in responsibility and intentionality but not controllability. As a result, they have suggested that a distinction between intentionality and control may be necessary for sport-related attributions.

It is logical to consider that not all controllable actions are also intentional in sporting situations. For example, an athlete performs poorly in a competition and attributes that poor performance to the fact that he or she was distracted by a group of friends in the stands. The cause of the poor performance was unintentional (the athlete did not intend to become distracted), but it could be controllable (the athlete will work on attention and concentration skills to be able to block out similar distractions in the future).

ENDOGENOUS/EXOGENOUS

An endogenous/exogenous distinction has also been proposed to replace the frequently used distinction between internal and external causes (Kruglanski, 1975). An action is said to be endogenously attributed when it is judged to constitute an end in itself and exogenously attributed when it is judged to serve as a means to a further end (Kruglanski, 1978). Actions are assumed to be determined by the will, the will is internal to the person; therefore all actions are determined internally. These actions, however, can be either endogenous or exogenous.

Logically, Kruglanski's proposal makes sense, but his underlying assumption may not be applicable to the competitive sport situation. Actions may be determined by the will, but in competitive sport situations the outcome of one's actions, whether objective win/loss or subjective perception of success/failure, is usually the target of causal thinking. Outcomes in sport are often affected by factors which are external to the will of the individual competitor such as weather, injuries, officiating, luck, and the skill and determination of the opponent (Gill, Ruder, & Gross, 1982; Roberts & Pascuzzi, 1979; Yamamoto, 1983). Therefore, investigations of attributional style in sport should perhaps focus on the traditional internal/external dimension rather than the proposed endogenous/exogenous dimension.

CHOSEN/NOT CHOSEN

Miller, Smith, and Uleman (1981) also believed that there are problems with the internal/external dimension, but suggested that it should be replaced with a chosen/not chosen distinction rather than the endogenous/exogenous distinction. Miller, Smith, and Uleman (1981) cited four problems with the internal/external dimension:

(1) The diversity of causes within each category is too broad.

(2) The distinction between the two categories can rest on arbitrary phrasing of sentences (for example, "I lost because my skills weren't good enough" (internal attribution) versus "I lost because the skills of the opposition were outstanding" (external attribution).

(3) There is low convergent validity of various closed-ended attribution measures.

(4) It is incorrectly assumed that internality and externality are inversely linked.

Their study implies that subjects define dispositional or internal causality as denoting acts chosen freely by the individual, and situational or external causality as denoting acts for which choice and responsibility are limited. Miller, Smith, and Uleman (1981) suggested that in future studies of causal attribution, researchers may want to explicitly measure the degree to which acts are deliberately chosen by the actor instead of the degree of internality or externality.

If only one dimension is going to be investigated, then the idea of using the chosen/not chosen dimension in place of the internal/external dimension may be of value. However, when the dimensions of stability, intentionality and controllability are included, the usefulness of the chosen/not chosen dimension becomes questionable. The chosen/not chosen distinction would appear to measure the same dimensions as the intentional/unintentional distinction. If an act was intentional, it would have to have been chosen. Similarly, if an act was unintentional, it would not have been chosen.

ATTRIBUTIONAL BIAS

There is a tendency for individuals to attribute their success to their own efforts, abilities or dispositions while attributing failure to luck, task difficulty or other external factors (Heider, 1958; Kelley, 1971). If this bias holds true in sport, then most athletes who perform well will claim that their performances were due to their natural ability, their dedicated training or the intense amount of effort they put into the performances. If, however, they fail, performances would more often be attributed to poor officiating, bad weather or the incredible skill of the opposition.

Two explanations have been offered to rationalise this attributional bias. The ego-defensive explanation states that the attributional bias allows individuals to maintain or enhance their general self-esteem or positive opinion of their specific dispositions and abilities (Miller & Ross, 1975). Taking credit for success and finding external factors to blame for failure allows people to feel good about themselves.

An alternative explanation is a cognitive explanation. Successful outcomes are intended and failures are unintended. If things go as planned, there is a tendency to attribute the result to one's effort or ability. If, however, things do not go as planned, the result is assumed to be due to some outside interfering factor (Miller & Ross, 1975). People do not intend to fail, so if failure occurs it is attributed to external factors. People are not trying to protect their egos, they are just being logical.

In sporting situations the attributional bias has most often been investigated by comparing the attributions of winners and losers. A few studies have obtained the attributional bias, with athletes making more internal attributions for success than failure (e.g., Iso-Ahola, 1977). Much of the more recent research, however, has focused on multiple attributional dimensions rather than just the locus of causality. McAuley and Gross (1983), for example, found that the attributions of winners of table tennis matches were more internal, stable and controllable than those made by the losers. Winners in both squash and racquetball (Mark, Mutrie, Brooks, & Harris, 1984) and volleyball (Gill, Ruder, & Gross, 1982) were found to have perceived the causes of their performances to be more stable and controllable than did losers. However, both winners and losers tended to make internal attributions. Similarly, Grove, Hanrahan, and McInman (1991) found that winning outcomes in basketball were attributed to more stable and controllable causes than losing outcomes. Once again, relatively internal attributions were made for both winning and losing. These basketball attributions were made by players, coaches and spectators and were not affected by how close the game scores were. The attributional bias has been referred to as the "self-serving bias". The results of Grove, Hanrahan, and McInman (1991) extend the scope of the bias to include coaches and spectators.

Instead of just defining success and failure as winning and losing in sport, some researchers have suggested that ability levels delineate good and bad performers. Tenenbaum and Furst (1985) found that athletes with high perceived ability made more internal, stable and controllable attributions than athletes with low perceived ability. Mark et al. (1984), however, found no apparent differences between attributions made by players involved in open competition versus those in B and C grade competition in racquetball or between B and C grade versus D grade competitors in squash.

Additional research with competitive squash players has investigated dimensional ratings of attributions according to outcome (win/loss) and skill level (Grove & Prapavessis, in press). Winners made more stable and global attributions than losers. The internality of attributions, however, was influenced by the interaction between outcome and ability level. High ability players made more internal attributions for success than failure, but low ability players tended to make more internal attributions after failure than success (Grove & Prapavessis, in press).

Although the bias represented by the above research is not necessarily ego-defensive in the traditional sense of making internal attributions for success and external attributions for failure, it still may be a type of self-serving bias. By generally attributing success to internal, stable, global and controllable factors, athletes can take credit for their successes, expect those successes to be obtainable in the future, feel that success is possible in a variety of situations, and sense that they have the power to determine if they are successful. By attributing failure to internal, unstable and specific causes, athletes can believe that future success is possible, and that they may be able to change whatever caused the failure.

ATTRIBUTIONAL STYLE

There are relatively stable, individual differences in the kinds of causal attributions people make (Ickes, 1980). Attributional style is the generally consistent manner in which people tend to account for outcomes. In familiar situations, this pattern of making causal attributions is especially well established. Attributional style has been explored as a personality characteristic of alcoholics (Dowd, Lawson, & Petosa, 1986), gamblers (McCormick & Taber, 1988), and rodeo cowboys (McGill, Hall, Ratliff, & Moss, 1986).

Individual differences in attributional style have also been associated with psychological variables other than personality. Snodgrass (1987), for example, reported that duration of loneliness is related to attributional style. Anderson and Arnoult (1985) found that not only loneliness, but also shyness and depression are related to attributional style. Attributional style best predicted these factors when assessed in relevant situations (Anderson & Arnoult, 1985). For example, attributional style for interpersonal situations was the best predictor of shyness. It logically follows that attributional style for sporting situations would be more useful than a general measure of attributional style when investigating sport-related behaviours.

Other researchers have found a significant relationship between depression and attributional style (Feather, 1983; Seligman, Abramson, Semmel, & von Baeyer, 1979; Sweeney, Anderson, & Bailey, 1986), as well as between learned helplessness and attributional style (Fincham, Diener, & Hokada, 1987; Mikulincer, 1988). Attributional style has also been associated with combat-related stress disorder (Mikulincer & Solomon, 1988), general mental health (Ostell & Divers, 1987), and self-esteem (Belgrave, Johnson, & Carey, 1985).

ATTRIBUTIONAL STYLE AND INTRINSIC MOTIVATION

Attributional style also appears to be related to levels of intrinsic motivation in sporting situations. Thomas (1977) suggested that by changing the attributional processes of the young athlete so that effort becomes the causal determinant of success and failure, fewer individuals would drop out because of feelings of little hope for future success. Similarly, McHugh, Duquin, and Frieze (1978) felt that training athletes to make effort attributions would increase their pride in success and also lead to increased persistence. Controlled laboratory studies have in fact found that effort attributions enhance the practice behaviour of subjects with low achievement tendencies (Grove & Pargman, 1984).

Fisher (1978) determined that personal control over performance was a very important determinant of intrinsic motivation. She argued that one must be responsible for one's own success in order to feel intrinsic rewards like pride. Similarly, failure is not meaningful if it is caused by external events beyond one's control. This argument suggests not only that internal attributions for success and external attributions for failure promote intrinsic motivation, but also that intrinsic motivation is related to the dimension of controllability. Making attributions to controllable causes, however, appears to be beneficial for intrinsic motivation regardless of whether the outcome is positive or negative.

Roberts (1978) stated that attributional retraining programs are important for maintaining or heightening the motivation of children to participate in physical activities and organised sport, but that it is imperative that such programs are founded on sound and appropriate attributional assumptions. Currently there is no clear conceptual basis for intervention so that persistence is enhanced (Roberts, 1984). Should athletes be trained to focus on internal attributions for success, external attributions for failure, controllable attributions for both success and failure, or unstable attributions for failure?

Preliminary research into pre-existing attributional styles of athletes and levels of intrinsic motivation suggests that the relationship between attributional style and intrinsic motivation is different for males and females (Hanrahan & Grove, 1989). Male athletes with higher levels of intrinsic motivation made more controllable attributions for positive events than did less motivated males. On the other hand, intrinsically motivated female athletes made more stable attributions. More research needs to be done to determine if this relationship is causal. In other words, it may be that having high levels of intrinsic motivation causes athletes to make certain attributions, rather than particular attributional styles leading to increased intrinsic motivation.

 ## MEASUREMENT ISSUES

A number of questionnaires and surveys have been developed to measure attributions or attributional style. A large percentage of these are not specifically developed for use in the sport context, but have occasionally been used by researchers in sport psychology.

NON-SPORT MEASURES

The Intellectual Achievement Responsibility Scale (IAR) forces a choice between internal and external responses (Dweck & Repucci, 1973; Weiner, Heckhausen, Meyer, & Cook, 1972; Weiner & Kukla, 1970). To help differentiate between two internal responses, Dweck (1975) developed a five-question scale to differentiate between effort and ability to supplement the IAR. The IAR, however, has not been shown to be predictive of the causal dimensions that people employ in actual behaviour (Andrews & Debus, 1978).

A variety of questionnaires have been used to measure the four basic attributions of ability, effort, task difficulty and luck in non-sport settings. These questionnaires have involved imaginary vignettes (e.g., Fielstein, Klein, Fischer, Haman, Koburger, Schneider, & Leitenberg, 1985), paired comparisons (e.g., Fyans & Maehr, 1980; McMahan, 1973), explanations of other people's performances (e.g., Fontaine, 1975) and explanations of subjects' own performances (e.g., Gollwitzer, Earle, & Stephan, 1982).

Probably one of the most commonly used measurement instruments in attribution research is the Causal Dimension Scale (CDS) (Russell, 1982). The CDS assesses causal perceptions in terms of the dimensions of internality, stability and controllability by having the respondents place their attributions into the causal dimensions as they see fit. The CDS format is very effective when used in a particular situation, however, it is not designed to measure an overall attributional style.

For measuring attributional style in non-sport settings, the Attributional Style Questionnaire (ASQ) (Abramson & Martin, 1981) has been found to have considerable construct, criterion and content validity (Peterson, Semmel, von Baeyer, Abramson, Metalsky, & Seligman, 1982). The ASQ requires subjects to name causes for hypothetical situations and then rate those causes along the dimensions of internality, stability and globality. To ensure that individuals are rating the same types of situations for both positive and negative events, Feather and Tiggeman (1984) developed the Balanced Attributional Style Questionnaire (BASQ). The BASQ has a similar format to the ASQ, but matches positive and negative events for content.

SPORT MEASURES

The Wingate Sport Achievement Responsibility Scale (WSARS) (Tenenbaum, Furst, & Weingarten, 1984) is a sport-specific measure of attributions. Like the IAR, the WSARS only measures causal attributions along the internal/external dimension. This test does, however, have separate scales for successful and unsuccessful events. This is an important consideration as athletes are likely to make very different attributions for success and failure.

Just as a variety of instruments have been used to measure the four basic attributional factors in non-sport situations, many questionnaires have also been devised to measure these four factors in sport settings (e.g., Bird, Foster, & Maruyama, 1980; Iso-Ahola, 1977; Scanlan & Passer, 1980). However, realising that stringent use of Weiner's traditional four attributions could be constraining, some researchers have added additional attributions to their measures. For example, Iso-Ahola and Roberts (1977) included items such as amount of practice and mood. Similarly, Bukowski and Moore (1980) included the attributions of good officiating and being interested in competing.

With the wide use of Russell's (1982) Causal Dimension Scale (CDS), Leith and Prapavessis (1989) constructed a sport-specific version of the CDS. The Performance Outcome Survey (POS) assesses the causal attributions athletes give to explain their successes and failures when competing in sport by having them rate the causes on the dimensions of internality, stability and controllability.

When measuring attributional style in sport, as opposed to attributions about single events, the Sport Attributional Style Scale (SASS) (Hanrahan, Grove, & Hattie, 1989) is an appropriate instrument. The SASS has respondents decide upon the most likely causes for positive and negative events which are matched for content. The athletes then rate those causes on the dimensions of internality, stability, globality, controllability and intentionality. A short form of the SASS is also available (Hanrahan & Grove, 1990).

GENERAL MEASUREMENT CONSIDERATIONS

Whether measuring attributions about specific events or attributional style, the individual's subjective interpretations of success and failure should be used instead of the objective outcomes of win and lose (Bird, Foster, & Maruyama, 1980; Ickes, 1980; Tenenbaum & Furst, 1985). Individuals' perceptions of success are distinct from objective outcome information. A person may not necessarily perceive all losses as failures and all wins as successes. For example, a social tennis player could consider a 4–6, 5–7 loss to an internationally ranked player as a success. Similarly, the internationally ranked player may consider the 6–4, 7–5 win over a local tennis hack as a terrible failure.

As mentioned previously, attributional measurements should also allow for a wide variety of causal attributions rather than being limited to Weiner's traditional four (Bukowski & Moore, 1980; Gill, Ruder, & Gross, 1982; Yamamoto, 1983). Careful consideration should be made to the dimensions upon which these attributions are then rated. If one is interested in studying depression or learned helplessness, the dimension of globality may be of interest. However, if the matter of interest is the expectancy of future success, the attributional dimension of stability may be more appropriate.

The measurement of causal attributions should allow for separate attributions for positive and negative events because combining positive and negative events reflects an implicit assumption that people perceive positive and negative outcomes to be the result of the same types of causes (Ickes, 1980; Tenenbaum, Furst, & Weingarten, 1984). Additionally, these positive and negative events should be matched for content so that if one pattern of causal attributions emerges to account for positive events and a different pattern emerges to account for negative events, the difference could not be the result of corresponding differences in event content (Feather & Tiggeman, 1984).

Lastly, if attributional style is being measured rather than attributions about a single event, a multi-item questionnaire must be used (Peterson & Seligman, 1984). Attributional style is a multidimensional construct which requires domain-specific measurement. Individuals may make very different attributions about the success or failure of their social lives than they do about the success or failure of their competitive sporting experiences.

FUTURE DIRECTIONS

Attributions have been found to influence achievement behaviour. Future research needs to investigate the application of much of the attribution theory. For example, it would be well worth investigating whether practical programs designed to change children's attributions are effective in decreasing drop-out behaviour in sport. Similarly, it would be useful to know if attribution retraining could constructively enhance the self-efficacy or self-confidence of athletes. With the introduction of any attribution retraining programs, it is imperative to understand which attributional styles are most effective. More research needs to determine which attributional dimensions and/or which specific attributions have the most impact on the factors of interest.

In addition to the impact that attributions may directly have on achievement behaviour in sport, it may be valuable to apply attribution research from health psychology to the sporting situation. For example, the importance of attributions in patients' psychosocial adjustment to chronic illness has been highlighted in research into cancer, arthritis and heart disease (Lewis & Daltroy, 1990). It is logical to consider that similar processes may be in place for athletes with chronic injuries. Similarly, health psychology research has demonstrated that symptom attributions influence medication compliance (Leventhal, Safer, & Panagis, 1983). Sport psychology could apply the same principles to injury attributions and rehabilitation compliance.

It is also obvious that an athlete's general state of health can influence his or her level of sporting performance. Therefore, attributions influencing general health behaviours may be of interest. For example, Grove (1993) has recently investigated the role that attributional processes play in one's perceived ability to refrain from smoking.

CONCLUSIONS

Attributions are a common occurrence in the sporting environment. Participants, coaches, spectators and the media continually propose causal explanations for outcomes and performances. By listening to post-competition conversations or reading the sports pages in the newspaper, one becomes aware of how often attributions are made for both positive and negative situations. We generate these attributions to help us understand, explain and predict both our behaviour and the behaviour of others.

Attributional style is the relatively stable manner in which individuals make causal attributions. If different attributional styles can be associated with different behaviours or attitudes, then it may be possible to change these behaviours or attitudes by modifying individuals' attributional styles. More research is needed before it can be stipulated which specific attributional styles are of most benefit. Similarly, longitudinal studies are needed to determine the efficacy of any attribution retraining programs.

SUMMARY

This chapter began by describing attributions. Different theories of attributions were then presented beginning with Heider's (1958) "commonsense psychology", the correspondent inference model (Jones & Davis, 1965) and Kelley's (1973) model of covariation. This was followed by the introduction of Weiner's (1972) two-dimensional model (i.e., internality and stability), which includes the four basic attributions of effort, ability, task difficulty and luck. Limitations of these four basic attributions were discussed followed by the expansion of Weiner's model to include controllability as a third dimension (Weiner, 1979).

The role of attributions in achievement behaviour as proposed by Weiner (1985b) was addressed by examining attributions in terms of both emotions and the expectancy of success. The function of attributional dimensions was then expanded to include the globality dimension as it relates to learned helplessness. Next, the additional attributional dimensions of intentionality, endogenous/exogenous, and chosen/not chosen were presented. This was followed by a discussion of the attributional bias.

Attributional style was introduced and related to a variety of psychological variables, with the greatest emphasis placed on the relationship between attributional style and intrinsic motivation. The chapter finished with a review of measurement issues and a brief introduction of possible areas of future research in the attribution area.

REFERENCES

Abramson, L. Y., & Martin, D. J. (1981). Depression and the causal inference process. In J. H. Harvey, W. J. Ickes, & R. F. Kidd (Eds.), *New directions in attribution research* (Vol. 3). Hillsdale, NJ: Erlbaum.

Anderson, C. A., & Arnoult, L. H. (1985). Attributional style and everyday problems in living: Depression, loneliness, and shyness. *Social Cognition, 3*(1), 16–35.

Andrews, G. R., & Debus, R. L. (1978). Persistence and causal perceptions of failure: Modifying cognitive attributions. *Journal of Educational Psychology, 70*, 154–166.

Belgrave, F. Z., Johnson, R. S., & Carey, C. (1985). Attributional style and its relationship to self-esteem and academic performance in Black students. *Journal of Black Psychology, 11*(2), 49–56.

Biddle, S. J. H. (1993). Attribution research and sport psychology. In R. N. Singer, M. Murphey, & I. K. Tennant (Eds.), *Handbook of research on sport psychology* (pp. 437–464). New York: Macmillan.

Biddle, S. J. H., & Jamieson, K. J. (1988). Attribution dimensions: Conceptual clarification and moderator variables. *International Journal of Sport Psychology, 19,* 47–59.

Bird, A. M., Foster, C. D., & Maruyama, G. (1980). Convergent and incremental effects of cohesion on attributions for self and team. *Journal of Sport Psychology, 2,* 181–194.

Bukowski, W. M., & Moore, D. (1980). Winners' and losers' attributions for success and failure in a series of athletic events. *Journal of Sport Psychology, 2,* 195–210.

Carron, A. V. (1984). Attributing causes to success and failure. *The Australian Journal of Science and Medicine in Sport, 16*(2), 11–15.

Deaux, K. (1976). Sex: A perspective on the attribution process. In J. H. Harvey, W. J. Ickes, & R. F. Kidd (Eds.), *New directions in attribution research* (Vol. 1). Hillsdale, NJ: Erlbaum.

Dowd, E. T., Lawson, G. W., & Petosa, R. (1986). Attributional style of alcoholics. *International Journal of the Addictions, 21,* 589–593.

Dweck, C. S. (1975). The role of expectations and attributions in the alleviation of learned helplessness. *Journal of Personality and Social Psychology, 31,* 674–685.

Dweck, C. S., & Repucci, N. D. (1973). Learned helplessness and reinforcement responsibility in children. *Journal of Personality and Social Psychology, 25,* 109–116.

Elig, T., & Frieze, I. H. (1975). A multidimensional scheme for coding and interpreting perceived causality for success and failure events: The SCPC. *Catalog of Selected Documents in Psychology, 5,* 313. (Ms No. 1069)

Feather, N. T. (1983). Some correlates of attributional style: Depressive symptoms, self-esteem, and Protestant ethic values. *Personality and Social Psychology Bulletin, 9*(1), 125–135.

Feather, N. T., & Tiggeman, M. (1984). A balanced measure of attributional style. *Australian Journal of Psychology, 36*(2), 267–283.

Fielstein, E., Klein, M. S., Fischer, M., Haman, C., Koburger, P., Schneider, M. J., & Leitenberg, H. (1985). Self-esteem and causal attributions for success and failure in children. *Cognitive Therapy and Research, 9,* 381–398.

Fincham, F. D., Diener, C. I., & Hokada, A. (1987). Attributional style and learned helplessness: Relationship to the use of causal schemata and depressive symptoms in children. *British Journal of Social Psychology, 26*(1), 1–7.

Fisher, C. F. (1978). The effects of personal control, competence and extrinsic reward systems on intrinsic motivation. *Organizational Behavior and Human Performance, 21,* 273–288.

Fiske, S. T., & Taylor, S. E. (1984). *Social cognitions* (pp. 20–45). Sydney: Addison-Wesley.

Fontaine, G. (1975). Causal attributions in simulated versus real situations: When are people logical and when are they not? *Journal of Personality and Social Psychology, 32,* 1021–1029.

Fyans, L. J., & Maehr, M. L. (1980). Attributional style, task selection and achievement. In L. J. Fyans (Ed.), *Achievement motivation: Recent trends in theory and research.* New York: Plenum Press.

Gill, D. L., Ruder, M. K., & Gross, J. B. (1982). Open-ended attributions in team competition. *Journal of Sport Psychology, 4,* 159–169.

Gollwitzer, P. M., Earle, W. B., & Stephan, W. G. (1982). Affect as a determinant of egotism: Residual excitation and performance attributions. *Journal of Personality and Social Psychology, 43,* 702–709.

Grove, J. R. (1993). Attributional correlates of cessation self-efficacy among smokers. *Addictive Behaviors, 18,* 311–320.

Grove, J. R., Hanrahan, S. J., & McInman, A. (1991). Success/failure bias in attributions across involvement categories in sport. *Personality and Social Psychology Bulletin, 17,* 93–97.

Grove, J. R., & Pargman, D. (1984). Behavioral consequences of effort versus ability orientations to interpersonal competition. *The Australian Journal of Science and Medicine in Sport, 16*(2), 16–20.

Grove, J. R., & Prapavessis, H. (in press). The effect of skill level and sport outcomes on dimensional aspects of causal attributions. *Australian Psychologist.*

Hanrahan, S. J., & Grove, J. R. (1989). Intrinsic motivation and attributional style in sport: Does a relationship exist? In C. K. Giam, K. K. Chook, & K. C. Teh (Eds.), *Proceedings of the VII World Congress of Sport Psychology* (pp. 51–52). Singapore: International Society of Sport Psychology.

Hanrahan, S. J., & Grove, J. R. (1990). A short form of the sport attributional style scale. *Australian Journal of Science and Medicine in Sport, 22*(4), 97–101.

Hanrahan, S. J., Grove, J. R., & Hattie, J. A. (1989). Development of a questionnaire measure of sport-related attributional style. *International Journal of Sport Psychology, 20*(2), 114–134.

Heider, F. (1944). Social perception and phenomenal causality. *Psychological Review, 51,* 358–374.

Heider, F. (1958). *The psychology of interpersonal relations.* New York: John Wiley & Sons.

Ickes, W. (1980). Attributional styles and the self-concept. In L. Y. Abramson (Ed.), *Attributional processes and clinical psychology.* New York: Guilford Press.

Iso-Ahola, S. E. (1977). Immediate attributional effects of success and failure in the field: Testing some laboratory hypotheses. *European Journal of Social Psychology, 7,* 275–296.

Iso-Ahola, S. E., & Roberts, G. C. (1977). Causal attributions following success and failure at an achievement motor task. *Research Quarterly, 48,* 541–549.

Jones, E. E., & Davis, K. E. (1965). From acts to dispositions: The attribution process in person perception. In L. Berkowitz (Ed.), *Advances in experimental social psychology* (Vol. 2). New York: Academic Press.

Kelley, H. H. (1971). *Attribution in social interaction.* New York: General Learning Press.

Kelley, H. H. (1973). The processes of causal attributions. *American Psychologist, 28,* 107–128.

Kelley, H. H., & Michela, J. L. (1980). Attribution theory and research. *Annual Review of Psychology, 31,* 459–501.

Kruglanski, A. W. (1975). The endogenous-exogenous partition in attribution theory. *Psychological Review, 82,* 387–406.

Kruglanski, A. W. (1978). Endogenous attribution and intrinsic motivation. In M. R. Lepper & D. Greene (Eds.), *The hidden costs of reward* (pp. 85–108). Hillsdale, NJ: Lawrence Erlbaum Associates.

Leith, L. M., & Prapavessis, H. (1989). Attributions of causality and dimensionality associated with sport outcomes in objectively evaluated and subjectively evaluated sports. *International Journal of Sport Psychology, 20,* 224–234.

Leventhal, H., Safer, M. A., & Panagis, D. M. (1983). The impact of communications on the self-regulation of health beliefs, decisions, and behavior. *Health Education Quarterly, 10,* 3–29.

Lewis, F. M., & Daltroy, L. H. (1990). How causal explanations influence health behavior: Attribution theory. In K. Glanz, F. M. Lewis, & B. K. Rimer (Eds.), *Health behavior and health education: Theory research and practice.* San Francisco: Jossey-Bass.

Mark, M. M., Mutrie, N., Brooks, D. R., & Harris, D. V. (1984). Causal attributions of winners and losers in individual competitive sports: Toward a reformulation of the self serving bias. *Journal of Sport Psychology, 6*, 184–196.

McAuley, E., & Gross, J. B. (1983). Perceptions of causality in sport: An application of the Causal Dimension Scale. *Journal of Sport Psychology, 5*, 72–76.

McCormick, R. A., & Taber, J. I. (1988). Attributional style in pathological gamblers in treatment. *Journal of Abnormal Psychology, 97*(3), 368–370.

McGill, J. C., Hall, J. R., Ratliff, W. R., & Moss, R. F. (1986). Personality characteristics of rodeo cowboys. *Journal of Sport Behavior, 9*(4), 143–151.

McHugh, M. C., Duquin, M. E., & Frieze, I. H. (1978). Beliefs about success and failure: Attribution and the female athlete. In C. A. Oglesby (Ed.), *Women and sport: From myth to reality*. Philadelphia: Lea & Febiger.

McMahan, I. (1973). Relationships between causal attributions and expectancy of success. *Journal of Personality and Social Psychology, 28*, 108–114.

Mikulincer, M. (1988). Reactance and helplessness following exposure to unsolvable problems: The effects of attributional style. *Journal of Personality and Social Psychology, 54*(4), 679–686.

Mikulincer, M., & Solomon, Z. (1988). Attributional style and combat related post-traumatic stress disorder. *Journal of Abnormal Psychology, 97*(3), 308–313.

Miller, D. T., & Ross, M. (1975). Self-serving biases in the attribution of causality: Fact or fiction? *Psychological Bulletin, 82*(2), 213–225.

Miller, F. D., Smith, E. R., & Uleman, J. (1981). Measurement and interpretations of situational and dispositional attributions. *Journal of Experimental Social Psychology, 17*, 80–95.

Ostell, A., & Divers, P. (1987). Attributional style, unemployment and mental health. *Journal of Occupational Psychology, 60*(4), 333–337.

Peterson, C., & Seligman, M. E. P. (1984). Causal explanations as a risk factor for depression: Theory and evidence. *Psychological Review, 91*(3), 347–374.

Peterson, C., Semmel, A., von Baeyer, C., Abramson, L. Y., Metalsky, G. I., & Seligman, M. E. P. (1982). The Attributional Style Questionnaire. *Cognitive Therapy and Research, 6*, 287–299.

Prapavessis, H., & Carron, A. V. (1988). Learned helplessness in sport. *The Sport Psychologist, 2*, 189–201.

Roberts, G. C. (1978). Children's assignment of responsibility for winning and losing. In F. Smoll & R. Smith (Eds.), *Psychological perspectives in youth sports* (pp. 145–171). Washington DC: Hemisphere Corporation.

Roberts, G. C. (1984). Achievement motivation in children's sport. In J. G. Nicholls & M. L. Maehr (Eds.), *Advances in motivation and achievement* (Vol. 3, pp. 251–281). Greenwich, CT: JAI Press.

Roberts, G. C., & Pascuzzi, D. (1979). Causal attributions in sport: Some theoretical implications. *Journal of Sport Psychology, 1*, 203–211.

Russell, D. (1982). The Causal Dimension Scale: A measure of how individuals perceive causes. *Journal of Personality and Social Psychology, 42*, 1137–1145.

Scanlan, T. K., & Passer, M. W. (1980). Self-serving biases in the competitive sport setting: An attributional dilemma. *Journal of Sport Psychology, 2*, 124–136.

Seligman, M. E. P., Abramson, L. Y., Semmel, A., & von Baeyer, C. (1979). Depressive attributional style. *Journal of Abnormal Psychology, 88*, 242–247.

Snodgrass, M. A. (1987). The relationships of differential loneliness, intimacy, and characterological attributional style to duration of loneliness. *Journal of Social Behavior and Personality, 2*(2), 173–186.

Sweeney, P. D., Anderson, K., & Bailey, S. (1986). Attributional style in depression: A meta-analytic review. *Journal of Personality and Social Psychology, 50*(5), 974–991.

Tenenbaum, G., & Furst, D. (1985). The relationship between sport achievement responsibility, attribution, and related situational variables. *International Journal of Sport Psychology, 16*(4), 254–269.

Tenenbaum, G., Furst, D., & Weingarten, G. (1984). Attribution of causality in sport events: Validation of the Wingate Sport Achievement Responsibility Scale. *Journal of Sport Psychology, 6*, 430–439.

Thomas, J. R. (1977). Attribution theory and motivation through reward: Practical implications for children's sports. *Motor Skills: Theory into Practice, 1*, 123–129.

Weiner, B. (1972). *Theories of motivation: From mechanism to cognition.* Chicago: Rand McNally.

Weiner, B. (1979). A theory of motivation for some classroom experiences. *Journal of Educational Psychology, 71*, 3–25.

Weiner, B. (1985a). Spontaneous causal thinking. *Psychological Bulletin, 97*(1), 74–84.

Weiner, B. (1985b). An attributional theory of achievement motivation and emotion. *Psychological Review, 92*(4), 548–573.

Weiner, B., Heckhausen, H., Meyer, W. N., & Cook, R. E. (1972). Causal ascriptions and achievement motivation: A conceptual analysis of effort and reanalysis of locus of control. *Journal of Personality and Social Psychology, 21*, 239–248.

Weiner, B., & Kukla, A. (1970). An attributional analysis of achievement motivation. *Journal of Personality and Social Psychology, 15*, 1–20.

Yamamoto, Y. (1983). A study on causal attribution for coaching. *Japanese Journal of Sport Psychology, 10*(1), 36–42.

C H A P T E R

6

SELF-EFFICACY IN
SPORT AND EXERCISE

TONY MORRIS

Confidence is an essential element of successful performance in any sphere, not least sport and exercise. In sport, examples abound of players and teams who have demonstrated their ability, but go through troughs of performance, which seem like they will never end. A recent example in team sport was the ascendancy of Australia over England in the 1993 Ashes tests. Australia certainly had a better balanced team and it was probably more skilful, man for man, but the stranglehold which permitted Australia to turn around the few difficult situations they met surely illustrates the difference in confidence between the teams during that summer. When they found themselves under pressure, Australia did not think about defeat and they pulled things around, while England did not believe they could win, so they let their chances slip.

A prime example in individual sport is the performance of golfer Greg Norman. He ended a succession of losses in "the Majors", at the 1993 British Open. Although golfers are particularly prone to look to technical deficiencies when performance declines, there was no doubting Norman's great ability. During the lean time, however, Norman frequently stayed with the pace, or even made it, for three rounds, only to fade in the final and crucial round. The turn around in Norman's fortunes since the "Open" once again demonstrates the role of confidence in sport.

In the more general area of exercise activity, rehabilitation from heart attack provides a ready example of the role of confidence. Although knowledge is gradually increasing in the community, the reaction of many people to suffering a heart attack is that they are invalids. The last thing they would imagine they can do in the future is vigorous exercise. Their confidence for exercise is very low and their return to exercise or, for many heart attack sufferers who were previously sedentary, to a much higher level of exercise than before, must be a slow, gradual process in which confidence is built on the achievement of small step-by-step goals.

While sport and exercise psychologists have long been aware of the important role of confidence, it is only recently that any conceptual frameworks have begun to emerge from within sport psychology. Martens (Martens, Burton, Vealey, Bump, & Smith, 1983; Martens, Vealey, & Burton, 1990) identified a state self-confidence construct in his work on multidimensional state anxiety, but has done little to develop the concept, his focus being on somatic and cognitive anxiety. Vealey (1986), one of Martens' colleagues, developed a state-trait conceptualisation of self-confidence in sport and scales to measure the trait and the state components separately. While the underlying rationale for this approach seems promising, researchers have been slow to take it up.

One conceptualisation of self-confidence, which has proved fruitful in sport is the concept of self-efficacy, which has gained substantial support from research. Self-efficacy comes from mainstream psychology. It was developed by Bandura (1977, 1982) in his social learning theory and then in his reframed social cognitive theory (Bandura, 1986). Feltz applied self-efficacy to sport as early as 1979 (Feltz, Landers, & Raeder, 1979) and she has since been a major contributor to the development of the concept (e.g., Feltz, 1982, 1988a; Feltz & Mugno 1983; Feltz & Riessinger, 1990; George, Feltz, & Chase, 1992). She has written a substantial review of the theoretical base and the empirical work in sport (Feltz, 1988b) and a more specific review of self-efficacy in the context of motivation in sport (Feltz, 1992). Self-efficacy has also been the subject of promising research in exercise psychology, particularly in relation to sedentary populations, obesity, heart problems and diabetes (McAuley, 1992a). McAuley (1992c) also reviews the sport and exercise research, making some interesting links with attribution theory. It is the substantial and generally positive work published on self-efficacy in sport and exercise which makes it the appropriate subject for detailed consideration in the theoretical section of a sport psychology text. Other conceptions of self-confidence are considered in Chapter 13.

In the present chapter, self-efficacy will be defined and placed in its theoretical context as a subjective perception of the individual's confidence, but one which is task-specific. The measurement of self-efficacy, as proposed by Bandura (1977, 1986), will be described and alternatives will be discussed. The development of self-efficacy will then be considered, focusing on the influence of antecedents on the level of self-efficacy. Research will then be examined which relates level of self-efficacy to sports performance, also considering the reciprocal relationship between self-efficacy and performance, as well as the influence of the other main antecedents. The research demonstrates the influence of this construct of task-specific confidence on sports performance, as well as pointing to some important factors which enhance confidence in sport. The role of self-efficacy in exercise initiation and adherence will be considered, with an emphasis on the need for research in this area and its potential in community health. Research on exercise initiation and adherence will be exemplified by a focus on self-efficacy and diabetes, an area which does not appear to be covered in any detail by recent reviews of self-efficacy in the sport psychology literature. Practical implications of the research on self-efficacy in sport and exercise for the development of self-confidence in sports performers will be briefly considered and future research directions for self-efficacy in sport will be discussed.

DEFINITION OF SELF-EFFICACY

Bandura (1986) has defined self-efficacy as the belief that a person has in their capability of performing a particular task. It is a cognitive process, whereby the person forms a subjective judgement of their ability to meet certain environmental demands. The point that self-efficacy is a subjective perception, that is, it reflects what the person believes, rather than accurately representing the true state of affairs, is crucial to the role of self-efficacy as a conceptualisation of self-confidence. Thus, a person standing on a diving board may well have the physical capability to perform an acceptable dive, but while they believe that they cannot, that is, while their self-efficacy is low, they are unlikely to launch off towards the water. Observers would probably say that the person lacked the confidence to perform the dive. Conversely, many people whose self-efficacy is clearly higher than their capability are observed to jump from the diving board. This is obvious from their disorganised and often painful entry to the water, a state of affairs commonly called "overconfidence"!

Self-efficacy and true capability are not usually very different for tasks with which the person is familiar, as previous performance is a major source of information for the cognitive, self-reference process of self-efficacy. Thus, for example, the gymnast who performed several successful back somersaults on the beam in her previous training session is likely to have a high level of self-efficacy for the back somersault when asked to perform it in the present session. It is the gymnast who fell on her last attempt in the previous session or the one who is being asked to perform this advanced move for the first time whose self-efficacy is likely to be low, with a consequent negative effect on performance.

Self-efficacy is considered by Bandura (1977, 1986) to be task-specific. A person can have high self-efficacy for tennis and low self-efficacy for football, perhaps based on self-assessment that, while their ball skills are strong, they find it difficult to pay attention to all the stimuli operating in a football match and their fear of hard physical contact makes them hesitant. Further, it is a rare performer of a multiskill task like tennis, whose confidence in performance of every skill in the game is equally high. For example, a great serve and volley exponent like Pat Cash may well have felt much lower self-efficacy for his backhand drive from the baseline, if pinned back there on a clay court by the hard, deep groundstrokes of a player of the style and class of Andre Agassi.

As well as being an indicator of self-confidence, self-efficacy is also considered to bear a close relationship with motivation. Bandura (1986) argues that level of self-efficacy will influence individuals' choice of activity, high self-efficacy tasks being preferred to low ones; the amount of effort they expend on the activity, greater self-efficacy leading to greater effort; and the level of persistence in the activity when faced with adversity, higher self-efficacy being associated with greater persistence. Choice, effort and persistence are all major elements of motivation.

To summarise, self-efficacy refers to an individual's belief in their capability to execute a specific task or sub-component of a multi-component task. It influences both motivation and actual performance. A person's perception of their self-efficacy for a task, at any time, results from a cognitive process, involving past experience and the current context. That cognitive process is part of a larger network of processes, which Bandura (1986) described as social cognitive theory.

SELF-EFFICACY AND SOCIAL COGNITIVE THEORY

Self-efficacy is part of a complex social cognitive theory, within which its action is linked to a number of other variables. In sports research, self-efficacy has frequently been examined independently, that is, without accompanying analysis of the other major aspects of Bandura's (1986) theory (e.g., Feltz & Riessinger, 1990; Fitzsimmons, Landers, Thomas, & van der Mars, 1991; McAuley, 1985a; Weinberg, Gould, & Jackson, 1979). Less often, what Bandura calls self-efficacy expectation has been considered alongside another major element of the social cognitive theory, outcome expectation, although this is more common in exercise research (e.g., Barling & Abel, 1983; Dzewaltowski, 1989; Godding & Glasgow, 1985; Manning & Wright, 1983).

Bandura has long argued that for behaviour to be produced, it is not sufficient that the behaviour has been learned, or that the individual believes it has; in addition, it is essential for the person to be motivated to perform the behaviour (Bandura, 1977). In social cognitive theory, Bandura (1986) refers to the need for an incentive to be present. That incentive is based on outcome expectancy. An outcome expectation is the belief a person has that their behaviour will lead to certain outcomes. Dzewaltowski (1989) argues that in certain activities, like exercise, individuals differ in the outcomes they expect to receive and whether they perceive certain outcomes to be desirable or not. For example, a person may not particularly enjoy running five kilometres, three times a week at six o'clock in the morning, but if that person believes that maintaining such an exercise schedule will substantially reduce the risk of having a heart attack or contracting diabetes, which are outcome expectancies, and that individual considers reduced risk of such illnesses as highly desirable, that is, it has a high outcome value, then the person will probably be motivated to keep up the exercise regimen. Thus, Dzewaltowski has measured outcome expectation as a multiplicative function of the expected outcomes and their respective values to the individuals being studied.

One reason why outcome expectation has not often been considered in the competitive sports context could be that it is not likely to vary greatly among those who have voluntarily chosen to engage in an activity, because their goals are usually clear and highly valued. To put it another way, most sports performers, especially at the elite level, would be expected to have high outcome expectancy and when a variable is uniformly high or low it can hardly act as a sensitive predictor. The research on self-efficacy in areas other than sport, which has employed outcome expectations in addition to efficacy expectations, has been equivocal. Outcome expectation has been found to add to the variance explained by efficacy expectations (Desharnais & Godin, 1986), but most investigations have found that only efficacy expectations play a significant explanatory role (e.g., Barling & Abel, 1983; Dzewaltowski, 1989; Godding & Glasgow, 1985; Kingery & Glasgow, 1989; Manning & Wright, 1983). The nature of the situation might influence the role of outcome expectations. In circumstances where outcome expectations probably vary quite widely, such as outcomes for exercise in healthy adults, outcome expectations are likely to influence behaviour. In situations where there is general agreement about outcomes, such as for cigarette smoking, outcome expectations are not likely to add much information.

Bandura (1986) expresses a similar view that in activities where efficacy perceptions are directly linked to task outcomes, outcome expectation will not add information, but where efficacy and outcome are dissociated, outcome expectation may add significant variance. So far, as Dzewaltowski (1989) concludes, research on exercise has not revealed the expected dissociation. It remains to be seen whether outcome expectation is a useful concept in competitive sport, where individuals' incentive level is generally high. Other aspects of Bandura's (1986) social cognitive theory have not generally been applied to sport and exercise.

 ## MEASUREMENT OF SELF-EFFICACY

Measurement is a crucial factor in the successful development of any concept. Bandura (1977, 1986) has taken special care to delineate the way in which self-efficacy should be measured. He proposed that a microanalytic technique should be used to assess self-efficacy cognitions. This involves measuring three aspects of self-efficacy — level, strength and generality — for each specific task or each component of a multi-component skill.

Level of self-efficacy is a measure of the number of the tasks or subskills which make up the total behaviour, which the individual believes they can attain. In competitive sport, for example, a free program in figure skating involves a combination of jumping and gliding movements which require strength, agility and flexibility, balance and grace. A performer may believe she has good balance and grace, so rates herself high on level for the smooth, dance-inspired elements of the program. She considers that her agility and flexibility are developing, but still need further work, so the level of her technical production is limited. Finally, she has not yet developed the body strength to perform the eyecatching jumps, like double axels and triple salkos, so she would rate herself low on this level of self-efficacy.

Another example, this time from exercise, more clearly illustrates the idea that the tasks are levels of performance. A self-efficacy questionnaire on aerobic exercise for older adults might ask whether a person believes they can walk one kilometre twice a week, two kilometres twice a week, five kilometres twice a week and ten kilometres twice a week. This represents four levels of self-efficacy for aerobic exercise specific to walking. Further levels could be included by increasing the frequency for the same distances, thus three, five and seven days a week might be used. Following Bandura (1986), a list of levels of the task is presented to the individual and they simply check those which they believe they can perform or answer "yes" to these and "no" to the levels they believe to be beyond them. Choice of levels is an important process, as it limits the responses which people can make. Substantial pilot work should typically be carried out to ensure the levels are meaningful to the subject population. For example, asking patients who have recently suffered heart attacks whether they can jog five, seven, ten or 12 kilometres would clearly be inappropriate, probably receiving "no" responses for all levels for every subject.

A problem which has not received adequate attention in the measurement of self-efficacy, especially when the frequency of performing the task is included (such as in the example of walking two, three, five or seven times a week) is the distinction between ability and intention. It is possible that the typical instructions of self-efficacy level scales do not make it clear that the issue is whether the person is *capable* of performing the activity, not whether they intend to do it. This could add variability to responses, as those making an interpretation based on their intention would say "no" to levels which they believe themselves capable of performing, but which they have no intention of doing, producing misleadingly low scores on level compared with those making the ability interpretation.

Although the list of levels is already a grading of the task, Bandura (1986) recognised that people do not move from the simplest version of the task up to their limit of self-assessed capability with an equal level of assurance in their ability to perform, and then suddenly have no belief at all in being able to perform one step higher. To reflect the way in which confidence varies for different levels which an individual expresses some capability to perform, Bandura included a measure of **strength of self-efficacy**. Strength of self-efficacy assesses the certainty the individual has that they will successfully attain each level or component task. It is usually measured on a scale from ten to 100, where response is made at ten-point intervals, representing the person's strength of confidence as a percentage. A score of zero is excluded in Bandura's original scoring method, because only those levels of the activity to which the person answered "yes" are included in the strength measure. Bandura's decision to restrict response to the ten-point intervals is something of an anachronism. It means that a person cannot have a 45% or 73% strength of confidence. Because only the 10% steps are used, it is questionable whether the scores can be considered as true percentages. An alternative which has been used in research is to employ a scale from −100 to +100 (e.g., Kingery, 1988; Kingery & Glasgow, 1989). Kingery and Glasgow (1989) argued that in their study of exercise in type 2 diabetics this was done to reflect the situation that negative expectations might exist.

It is also not entirely clear whether tasks which a person indicates they cannot perform in the level assessment should be included in the strength assessment. McAuley (1992a), for example, indicates that "overall strength of self-efficacy is determined by summing the confidence ratings and dividing by the total number of items comprising the target behavior" (p. 109). By omitting the possibility of giving a zero rating on the scale, Bandura (1986) seems to be indicating that the strength rating should only include items for which some degree of confidence has been assessed from the levels, not the total number of items comprising the target behaviour. Inclusion of the zero scoring items in the final arithmetical division will make a big difference for those with low levels of self-efficacy, greatly reducing their final scores relative to more efficacious respondents, which may be what was originally intended. Dzewaltowski (1989) cites the results from two studies by Bandura (Bandura & Cervone, 1983, 1986) as support for his decision to exclude level and simply measure strength on a 100-point scale with a zero point.

The level and strength of self-efficacy refer to specific behaviours and reflect the microanalytic approach which Bandura espouses. He has also considered **generality of self-efficacy** as a measure of the number of domains in which individuals believe they are capable of successful performance. For a highboard diver, level and strength of self-efficacy may be assessed for each specific dive they are required and choose to perform. From this, it is possible to obtain a measure of that individual's general diving self-efficacy. This is a more recent aspect of Bandura's thinking and is less well supported than other elements of self-efficacy theory, although some evidence does support generalisation of self-efficacy across sports events (Brody, Hatfield, & Spalding, 1988; Holloway, Beuter, & Duda, 1988; McAuley, Courneya, & Lettunich, 1991). Ryckman, Robbins, Thornton, & Cantrell (1982) produced a global measure of physical self-confidence, the Physical Self-Efficacy Scale. This 22-item scale, assessing two sub-scales, perceived physical ability and physical self-presentation confidence, contradicts Bandura's (1986) advice that a microanalytic approach is most effective. Research has generally supported Bandura's position with the global measure less predictive than task-specific measures (e.g., McAuley & Gill, 1983; Mueller, 1992).

Measurement is a critical component of any research testing theories or concepts. Bandura's (1977, 1986) approach to the measurement of self-efficacy is certainly thorough and this may, in some circumstances, account for the demonstrated utility of self-efficacy as a predictor of behaviour and performance. Nonetheless, there are some ambiguities in the measurement technique, reflected in the unorthodox manner of its use in some research on self-efficacy to date.

ANTECEDENTS OF SELF-EFFICACY

Self-efficacy has been shown to be a key variable in successful performance in sport and of health and exercise behaviours in general (Feltz, 1992; McAuley, 1992a, 1992c). Thus, the issue of raising self-efficacy is central to interventions designed to increase confidence and enhance performance. Bandura (1986) proposes four major antecedents of self-efficacy, that is, factors which influence the level and strength of self-efficacy. These are performance accomplishments, vicarious experience, verbal persuasion, and physiological state.

PERFORMANCE ACCOMPLISHMENTS

The most convincing source of information in the cognitive process of self-assessment or self-persuasion (Feltz, 1992) which produces self-efficacy beliefs is *performance accomplishments*. One's own experiences of success provide direct evidence of capability, while failure experiences raise doubts about one's ability to perform the task under consideration. Bandura (1986) also proposes that success in a more difficult task will enhance self-efficacy to a greater extent than success in an easy one. Similarly, achieving success independently will be more efficacious than the same level of success, with support from others. When success is attained without expending a great deal of effort, it implies greater ability than when great effort must be expended. Tasks performed well on the first few attempts engender greater efficacy than those where failures occur early in learning. In all of these cases the mastery or lack of it is experienced personally and the effect on self-efficacy is, Bandura (1986) claims, strong.

VICARIOUS EXPERIENCE

During learning in sport and exercise settings, individuals often have to perform skills which they have never performed before. The skills might involve an element of risk or a new technique. In competition a person may face an opponent for the first time. Self-efficacy in these situations cannot be based on the individual's own previous experience. Observing somebody else perform the new skill successfully or beat the unknown opponent can enhance that observer's self-efficacy for the task, especially if the person observed is similar to the observer in skill and other relevant characteristics. This social comparison process is called *vicarious experience* and it is an area in which Bandura did a great deal of research (e.g., Bandura, 1969; Bandura, Blanchard, & Ritter, 1969; Bandura, Ross, & Ross, 1961) prior to the first publication of his social learning theory (Bandura, 1977). The potency of vicarious experiences is diminished when the individual has some personal experience of the task, but it is important in situations like those described earlier, where the person is going into unknown territory. Gould and Weiss (1981) found that similarity of sex and ability of the model to that of the subject enhanced the effect of the model's actions on the self-efficacy of the subject. George, Feltz, and Chase (1992) further demonstrated that when the model had a level of ability similar to that of the subject, ability was a more important characteristic than the sex of the model.

VERBAL PERSUASION

Coaches and team mates often spend time persuading a player that the player has the capability to meet specific task demands, such as to beat the next opponent or to make the next qualifying standard. This is a common application of Bandura's (1986) third antecedent of self-efficacy, *verbal persuasion*. The persuasion is likely to be more effective if the person presenting it is perceived to be trustworthy as a source of information and credible, that is, is perceived to possess the knowledge or expertise requisite to make the judgement. The potential for achievement of the task must also be realistic. Even when all these criteria apply, the effect of verbal persuasion is still likely to be weaker than performance accomplishments. Feltz (1992) also considers self-talk and imagery to be persuasive techniques, along with "other cognitive strategies" (p. 94). Positive self-talk is certainly a widely used technique for building confidence (Bunker, Williams, & Zinsser, 1992) and many sports performers do talk to themselves as if they were one person, like a coach, talking to another.

Imagery, again involving successful performance of the target activity, is another means of communicating ideas and the intent would certainly be to persuade in cases where it is used to enhance confidence; but imagery defined as a rich multi-modal process which reintegrates reality experiences (Suinn, 1984) could also be categorised, for an individual who is a practised exponent, somewhere between performance accomplishment and vicarious experience.

PHYSIOLOGICAL STATE

A common experience in sport is the heightened physiological arousal which is associated with the period immediately prior to performance. Performers often interpret this as a sign that they are anxious about the performance and thus they begin to suffer from self-doubts. In other words, such physiological arousal can lead to reduced self-efficacy. Where the same physical sensations are interpreted as a signal that the body has been activated and the person is, thus, ready to perform optimally, self-efficacy can be enhanced. Feltz (1992) notes that other physiological states, such as fitness, fatigue and pain, can influence judgements of self-efficacy. McAuley (1985a) has examined the possibility that level of anxiety is not an antecedent, but a consequence, of self-efficacy. A causal modelling approach was employed in that study and analyses did support such a contention.

Bandura (1977) proposed that a reciprocal relationship exists between self-efficacy and performance accomplishments, that is, previous experience of performance influences present level of self-efficacy and this in turn affects the person's next performance and so on. He called this phenomenon in which self-efficacy is affected by and affects other variables, **reciprocal determinism**. In her path analysis research, Feltz (1982) found that, while self-efficacy was a strong predictor of the first performance of a back dive, for the second and succeeding dives previous performance became the strongest predictor. More recently, Bandura (1989, 1990) has suggested that a similar reciprocal relationship exists between self-efficacy and thought processes. Because the influence of all four antecedents is cognitively mediated, it is likely that all the antecedents of self-efficacy at one point in time become consequences of self-efficacy later. Thus, it is possible that physiological state at any time is a result of a variety of physical and psychological factors, which would include existing self-efficacy, and that this current state will influence self-efficacy in the immediate future.

RESEARCH ON SELF-EFFICACY ANTECEDENTS

Because self-efficacy is an important factor influencing performance, the determination of techniques which reliably enhance self-efficacy becomes a central issue for sport psychologists interested in performance enhancement. It is, therefore, not surprising that research has been executed on the effects of all four antecedents on self-efficacy in a range of sport and exercise settings. Least studied in this respect is the area of physiological state and most of the findings regarding this antecedent come from investigations of other antecedents, where measures of emotional state were included. In fact, a number of studies have looked at more than one antecedent, some actually comparing their relative influence on self-efficacy.

Research considering the influence of performance accomplishments on self-efficacy has consistently found that techniques involving performance accomplishments enhance self-efficacy (Brody, Hatfield, & Spalding, 1988; Feltz, Landers, & Raeder, 1979; Hogan & Santomier, 1984; McAuley, 1985b; Weinberg, Sinardi, & Jackson 1982). Feltz, Landers, and Raeder (1979) also found that performance accomplishments, in the form of participant modelling, where the learner makes an attempt after the model, strengthened self-efficacy more than modelling alone, whether that modelling was live or recorded on videotape. McAuley (1985b) and Weinberg, Sinardi, and Jackson (1982) found similar results.

Vicarious experience has been the subject of much research, in part because physical education had a well-established interest in modelling and related observational learning techniques. Again, most of these studies found results which supported the role of modelling as an antecedent of self-efficacy (George, Feltz, & Chase, 1992; Gould & Weiss, 1981; Lirgg & Feltz, 1991; McAuley, 1985a). George, Feltz, and Chase (1992) required female college students to watch a videotaped model perform a leg-extension endurance task and then perform the same task themselves. The subjects completed self-efficacy questionnaires on two occasions. Only those subjects who indicated that it was at least moderately important for them to do well were included in the study. The five conditions were an athletic male model, an athletic female model, a non-athletic male model, a non-athletic female model and a no-model control condition. Results replicated Gould and Weiss's (1981) finding that self-efficacy was enhanced more by the similar model, but extended the previous work by determining that similarity of ability was more influential than similarity of sex.

Another type of study has placed subjects in a competition against an opponent, who is in fact a confederate of the researcher, allowing manipulation of the subjects' self-efficacy by the provision of information about the opponent. Thus a social comparison process has been established (Weinberg, Gould, & Jackson, 1979). Having shown the confederate performing poorly or well on a related strength task, Weinberg, Gould, and Jackson (1979) showed that subjects' self-efficacy for a muscular endurance task was greater when they had seen their opponent perform poorly on a similar task and that this led to longer endurance.

Few studies have looked at the effect of persuasion on self-efficacy directly. Wilkes and Summers (1984) used a combination of persuasory techniques to enhance confidence and redirect arousal interpretations. They found that strength performance was enhanced, but concluded that self-efficacy did not appear to mediate that effect. Feltz (1992) includes research on the use of self-talk and imagery in her review of "persuasory efficacy information" (p. 98). These seem, at best, to be examples of self-persuasion. A more obvious and commonly occurring form of persuasion in sport is verbal persuasion by a coach. Related to the persuasory influence a high status source like a coach may have is the research which has presented false feedback. The results of the studies reported are equivocal. Yan Lan and Gill (1984) tried to persuade subjects in one group that heightened arousal levels were indicative of superior performance. There was no effect of increasing self-efficacy through this manipulation, but it may have been that the false feedback given was not believed by the subjects in the context of their experience of performance.

Recently, Fitzsimmons, Landers, Thomas, and van der Mars (1991) considered the self-efficacy of experienced weightlifters to see if false feedback affected experienced performers, arguing that much of the previous work was done with novices and may not transfer easily to experienced performers. Their male subjects performed six sessions of one maximum bench press, having been pilot tested for performance, to set believable levels of false feedback in an attempt to minimise that problem found in the previous work. The subjects were randomly assigned to one of three conditions: accurate performance information, false positive feedback (that they lifted more than they actually had) or false negative feedback (that they lifted less than was really the case). Fitzsimmons et al. (1991) found that performance was enhanced by the false positive manipulation, but that previous weightlifting performance accounted for most of the variance in subsequent performance. They argue that it is difficult to extend the findings of research on verbal persuasion to performers who are experienced or who gain experience on repeated training trials.

Feltz and Riessinger (1990) assigned college males and females to one of three conditions: "in vivo" mastery imagery with feedback, feedback alone, or a control condition, following loss to a confederate on a strength task. In a different but related strength task which followed, the subject lost to the confederate by ten seconds, a clear defeat, on each of two trials. Results indicated that only after the imagery treatment did subjects' self-efficacy increase, but the experience of another failure reduced self-efficacy levels to below their levels before treatment. Two interesting elements of this study were the measurement of self-efficacy in two contexts and the use of an open-ended question to explore the information on which subjects based their efficacy beliefs. Feltz and Riessinger asked subjects to provide an ego-oriented assessment of their efficacy, by comparing themselves to their opponent, and a standard mastery-oriented rating, based on their own previous performance. Results were equivalent for the two ratings. The examination of subjects' sources of efficacy information revealed that they largely based their assessment on their own experiences or comparisons with the competitor, rather than the imagery treatment.

It is clearly difficult to persuade a person to raise their self-efficacy, when they know what their typical capability is from past experience, especially if continuing experience contradicts the persuasory information. In a questionnaire study on antecedents, Weinberg and Jackson (1990) surveyed 222 high school tennis coaches to examine their view of the most effective strategies for enhancing self-efficacy. The responses emphasised modelling confidence, positive self-talk, and verbal persuasion. It would appear that these coaches were not aware that the experience of their players could counteract these devices, while the most potent strategies are likely to be associated with ensuring performance accomplishments.

Bandura's (1986) fourth antecedent, physiological states, has rarely been systematically examined. The work of Feltz (Feltz, 1982, 1988a; Feltz & Mugno, 1983) on the high avoidance task of performing a back dive measured physiological arousal and perceived autonomic arousal. The former did not significantly predict self-efficacy, but the latter did. Since perceived physiological arousal involves cognitive processing as does self-efficacy, it is not surprising that the two are related in the same context, but it does suggest that contextual factors might be used to bias the interpretation of actual level of physiological arousal in a positive direction. In any event, performance accomplishments again had a much greater effect on self-efficacy. Induction of happy and sad moods was used by Kavanagh and Hausfeld (1986) in an attempt to manipulate self-efficacy in strength tasks. They did not find any consistent pattern of change in self-efficacy associated with the mood changes.

In summary, research suggests that self-efficacy is influenced by the four antecedents which Bandura (1986) has identified. The evidence clearly indicates that performance accomplishments provide the most potent information for judgements of self-efficacy. In many situations where other aspects have been manipulated, incidental information about actual performance has overridden the experimental manipulation. Vicarious experience seems to be a fairly reliable source of effective information to the self-efficacy process, but the research on persuasion and physiological states is unconvincing, especially when the most positive effects cited in this area by Feltz (1992) involve imagery and might arguably be classified as a special case of vicarious experience.

SELF-EFFICACY AND SPORTS PERFORMANCE

As has often been the case in sport psychology, a substantial proportion of the research on self-efficacy has considered sport and physical activity tasks outside of actual sports competition. The number of studies carried out in competitive sport is increasing, as critics continue to question the validity of generalising from non-competitive to competition contexts. Feltz (1988b) performed a substantial review of the literature. Although research continues to be done, a CD-ROM literature search suggests that the focus of research on self-efficacy has shifted to the exercise area.

The work of Feltz (Feltz, 1982, 1988a; Feltz & Mugno, 1983) on backdiving stands out among that research on performance of sports skills out of competition, not only because of its seminal position in determining the roles of self-efficacy and performance accomplishments, but also for its early use of then sophisticated methods and analysis. Based on Bandura's (1977) social learning theory, Feltz (Feltz, 1982, 1988a; Feltz & Mugno, 1983) examined the relationship between self-efficacy, performance accomplishments and physiological arousal in college students. Feltz employed a causal modelling approach, her model predicting that self-efficacy would be the strongest predictor of performance on each of four dives. Also consistent with Bandura's (1977) view, she proposed a reciprocal relationship between self-efficacy and back-diving performance. Results of path analyses revealed that self-efficacy was indeed the major determinant of diving performance on the first dive. For dives two, three and four, however, the major predictor of performance on a particular dive was the subject's performance on the previous dive. From trial to trial, previous performance of the backdive became a stronger predictor of self-efficacy than self-efficacy was of performance. Feltz (1992) noted that "although a reciprocal relationship between self-efficacy and diving behavior was evidenced, they were not equally reciprocal" (p. 100).

Another study which tested models was executed by McAuley (1985a). He examined the relationship of self-efficacy and state anxiety to performance of a high avoidance task, a dive forward roll onto the gymnastics beam, by 39 female undergraduates, who were novices at gymnastics and were selected because their pre-task anxiety was high. Two forms of modelling were used: aided participant, where the model demonstrated the task and then supported the subject physically during four training trials; and unaided participant, where the same demonstration was made, but subjects had to attempt the move with no physical support during training. These conditions were compared with a control group, shown an instructional film on uneven bar exercises. A task-specific self-efficacy measure, constructed in accordance with Bandura's (1977) instructions, and the Competitive State Anxiety Inventory (CSAI) developed by Martens, Burton, Rivkin, and Simon (1980) were employed. Performance was scored by ratings of three expert coaches. Results of multivariate and univariate analysis of variance showed that both aided and unaided modelling increased self-efficacy, reduced state anxiety and enhanced performance. McAuley (1985a) also compared two models of the process. The self-efficacy model, based on Bandura (1977), proposed that self-efficacy is the direct mediator between the modelling treatments and performance. Reduced anxiety is simply a result of increased self-efficacy. For high avoidance tasks, others, notably Eysenck (1978), have proposed that anxiety is the mediating variable and self-efficacy is an epiphenomenon, that is, it is a by-product of the anxiety reduction process. Using path analysis, McAuley (1985a) examined these models and also tested the fully recursive models generated by the variables. Fully recursive models consider all the possible connections between variables in one direction, as opposed to only those links predicted by the theory to be significant. The path analyses favoured the interpretation that self-efficacy was the direct mediating variable. One weakness in this otherwise exemplary study was the use of the CSAI, which never demonstrated adequate reliability and validity and was replaced by the conceptually and psychometrically superior CSAI-2 (Martens, Burton, Vealey, Bump, & Smith, 1983).

A number of studies have considered the relationship between self-efficacy and performance in competitive sport (Barling & Abel, 1993; Feltz, Bandura, & Lirrg, 1989; Gayton, Matthews, & Burchstead, 1986; Lee, 1982; McAuley & Gill, 1983; Weiss, Weise, & Klint, 1989). In general, these studies have indicated that higher levels of self-efficacy are associated with superior performance. Weiss, Weise, and Klint (1989) measured self-efficacy and performance in young female gymnasts. The gymnasts were competing in state championships, a relatively high level of competition in the context of much research in sport psychology. A significant correlation (r = 0.57) was found between self-efficacy and performance.

The causal modelling research of Feltz (1982) indicates that as personal experience of performance increases, the predictive influence of that experience on further performance increases relative to the causal influence of self-efficacy. At the same time, because performance accomplishment is the most potent antecedent of self-efficacy expectations, self-efficacy becomes a much closer reflection of previous performance, as the individual has more experience of performance. This would explain the correlation found by Weiss, Weise, and Klint (1989) between self-efficacy and competitive performance in high-level sports performers.

SELF-EFFICACY AND EXERCISE BEHAVIOUR

Physical activity in the shape of sport and exercise is now recognised as an important factor in primary health care (Dishman, 1988; Haskell, 1984), that is, in preventing a range of health problems and reducing the risk of contracting debilitating and life-threatening diseases. It is also a specific component of the treatment in a number of common diseases, that is, in secondary health care, in such illnesses as coronary heart disease, diabetes, stroke and hypertension (National Heart Foundation, 1989). In addition, substantial research now indicates that exercise positively influences mood state (Dyer & Crouch, 1988; Frazier, 1988; Weinberg, Jackson, & Kolodny, 1988) and psychological well-being (Hayden, Allen, & Camaione, 1986; Hayes & Ross, 1986), although there is some debate (e.g., Gauvin, 1989). Thus, sport and exercise play a significant role in the prevention of illness, the treatment of disease and the promotion of a positive quality of life. Nonetheless, while people of all ages and backgrounds do play sport or take regular exercise by choice, many with passion and dedication, there is still a large proportion of the population which does not participate in regular health-promoting physical activity of any kind. Often these people are precisely those most at risk for the diseases already mentioned, because they are overweight, sedentary and older or because they lead hectic, stressful lives, or both. As sport psychology has expanded its interest into the general exercise area, the application of self-efficacy to the problems of initiation of and adherence to exercise has proved to be a very fruitful avenue for research and applied interventions.

McAuley (1992a) presents a substantial review of the research on self-efficacy and exercise behaviour. Among the most prominent findings here are those which relate to the influence of self-efficacy on exercise in cardiac rehabilitation. Ewart, Stewart, Gillian, Keleman, Valenti, Manley, and Kaleman (1986) found that postmyocardial infarction patients with higher levels of self-efficacy for exercise complied with prescribed exercise programs more closely than those with lower self-efficacy. The finding that the physical capabilities of these patients did not predict their compliance supports Bandura's (1986) proposal that it is the individual's belief in what they are able to do, rather than their actual physical capabilities, which is the important factor. Further support for the influence of self-efficacy on effort in treadmill exercise (Ewart, Taylor, Reese, & DeBusk, 1983) and cardiac rehabilitation (Taylor, Bandura, Ewart, Miller, & DeBusk, 1985) has come from Ewart's group.

Research has also shown self-efficacy to be related to exercise activity in middle-aged and older adults (McAuley, 1991, 1992b; Sallis, Haskell, Fortnam, Vranisan, Taylor, & Solomon, 1986), sedentary adult women and self-professed "unfit" young females (McAuley & Jacobson, 1991; McAuley & Rowney, 1990). It has also been shown that self-efficacy is related to adherence to an exercise program (McAuley, 1989). In addition, self-efficacy explained a significant amount of the variance in studies where self-reported exercise behaviour was the independent variable (Dzewaltowski, 1989; Dzewaltowski, Noble, & Shaw, 1990). The study by McAuley (1989) used structural equation modelling to examine exercise participation during a ten-week program. Subjects were followed up three months later. Self-efficacy was found to positively affect not only attendance during the program, but also perceptions of success when it was over. In addition, self-efficacy influenced self-reported exercise behaviour, when the subjects were questioned about this after three months.

SELF-EFFICACY AND EXERCISE IN DIABETICS

While research on self-efficacy and exercise behaviour in healthy individuals and in those with heart disease is widely reported, the sport and exercise literature rarely reports research on the important role of self-efficacy in the exercise behaviour of individuals with another chronic disease, diabetes. In Australia there are over 250,000 people who have been diagnosed as diabetic and 85% of these are type 2 diabetics (Simmons & Owen, 1992). People at high risk from type 2 diabetes, also known as non-insulin dependent diabetes mellitus (NIDDM), are typically obese, sedentary and older, usually over 40 and often not diagnosed until they are over 50 or 60 (Cantu, 1987; Kemmer & Berger, 1980; Stepanas, 1991). In this form of the disease, unlike type 1, the pancreas does produce insulin, but it is not absorbed through cell walls from the bloodstream into the cells. Thus, it cannot metabolise the fats and sugars. Research indicates that regular exercise does enhance this metabolic process (Sherman & Albright, 1992) and regular exercise has therefore become one of the standard elements in the treatment of type 2 diabetes (Gordon, 1993). Adherence to exercise in type 2 diabetics is low, largely because they are usually older people, who are overweight and have not been exercising for some years. Research has addressed the barriers to exercise perceived by type 2 diabetics and has considered the role of efficacy expectations and outcome expectations in adherence to exercise.

Glasgow and his colleagues have examined the barriers to exercise, psychosocial factors associated with self-care and the role of self-efficacy and outcome expectations in type 2 diabetics. Ary, Toobert, Wilson, and Glasgow (1986), using an open-ended questionnaire, found the most common reason for non-adherence was negative physical feelings, that is, exercise made diabetics feel bad, partly because many had not exercised for so long. Other reasons were being too busy, inappropriate weather, criticism by others and no partner with whom to exercise. Wilson, Ary, Biglan, Glasgow, Toobert, and Campbell (1986) found that a set of psychosocial factors, among which self-efficacy was prominent, predicted self-care behaviour, including exercise, but did not predict glycemic control. Kingery (Kingery, 1988; Kingery & Glasgow 1989) examined Bandura's (1986) social cognitive theory. He measured self-efficacy following Bandura's (1977) methods, except that he used a scale with the range −100 to +100 to allow for the measurement of negative as well as positive self-efficacy and outcome expectancies. Results indicated that self-efficacy was lower for exercise than for diet or glucose testing, but that outcome expectations were highest for exercise. Both self-efficacy and outcome expectancies predicted exercise self-care, prospectively and concurrently, but outcome expectation added very little to the stepwise multiple regression, when included after self-efficacy, while the reverse was not the case.

These results indicate that even though the diabetic subjects believed that exercise would be of more benefit to their condition than careful diet or regular glucose testing, because they did not believe that they were capable of exercising as prescribed, they did not adhere to exercise regimens. Following these earlier descriptive studies, an intervention study dubbed the "Sixty Something Study" was conducted (Glasgow, Toobert, Hampson, Brown, Lewinsohn, & Donnelly, 1992). Glasgow et al. (1992) recruited 102 type 2 diabetics over 60 years old and gave half of them a ten-session self-management training program based on social learning variables, especially self-efficacy. Goal setting and coping strategies were the main techniques employed to raise self-efficacy. Although exercise did not improve significantly in the short term, it had, but only for the intervention group, at a six-month follow-up. There was no improvement in self-efficacy, however. Glasgow, Toobert, and Hampson (1991) examined the manner of recruitment of the sample for the "Sixty Something Study" and noted that the sample were largely under 70 years old and self-initiated. Type 2 diabetics over 70 years of age and those invited to take part by the researchers did not participate. Initial self-efficacy scores for exercise in this self-initiated sample were relatively high and it was suggested that the failure to obtain a significant increase in self-efficacy may have been due to a ceiling effect. The approach adopted by Glasgow and his colleagues is to be encouraged. They explored the field descriptively first, then they tested for relationships between variables identified in the earlier work. Finally, they examined the efficacy of interventions to change important mediating variables, such as self-efficacy. This research program did suffer from several methodological problems. The group acknowledge that they had sampling problems. These led to indefinite conclusions about the role of self-efficacy. There was also a concern that outcome expectations are not likely to vary greatly in a diabetic group. Immediately after being diagnosed, type 2 diabetics learn that exercise is an important element of their treatment. This should give them a uniform outcome expectation that exercising will lead to better control of blood glucose. A uniformly high (or low) score for a sample makes that variable uninformative in correlational statistics. Thus, it is not surprising that outcome expectation fails to account for a substantial proportion of the variance in these circumstances.

The increase in attention which has been given to the role of self-efficacy in exercise activity reflects the potential health benefits to special groups and the general population if interventions can be applied to increase self-efficacy for exercise, thus raising confidence and motivation with one intervention. The results of research to date appear to be promising, clearly indicating that self-efficacy is frequently linked to exercise behaviour. Intervention studies are still limited in number and their success is unconvincing. Care particularly needs to be taken in selection of the sample. Ethical, as well as logistical, problems exist when working with special groups, but it is likely that volunteers for exercise studies will have higher self-efficacy for exercise than those who do not volunteer. The role of outcome expectations in exercise behaviour is still not clear. The research on diabetes suggests that the influence of outcome expectations on exercise behaviour may depend on knowledge, education or attitudes about the particular behaviour in the population under study. This will affect the degree of variability of outcome expectations in that population. When the variability is small, outcome expectations are unlikely to be a potent predictor of behaviour. Thus, outcome expectations might be found to be of greater import as a factor interacting with self-efficacy in primary health care, where the general population varies widely in its information and attitudes about exercise-related health benefits.

 ## PRACTICAL APPLICATIONS OF SELF-EFFICACY IN SPORT AND EXERCISE

Enough is now known about the antecedents and consequences of self-efficacy to draw out some practical applications for sport and exercise. At the same time, Horsley in Chapter 13 focuses on applied work in the area of self-confidence, so the present section will be indicative only. Enough evidence from research supports the claim that self-efficacy for a task enhances performance of that task, for the development of self-efficacy (especially when it is low) to be an important issue in applied sport psychology. Bearing in mind what is also known about the antecedents of self-efficacy, they would seem to represent a sensible starting point for the enhancement of self-efficacy.

1. Performance accomplishment. This is the most potent antecedent of self-efficacy and should be considered where possible. An important precursor to the use of performance accomplishment is to determine what is perceived to represent performance accomplishment for that athlete. In other words, it is important to set appropriate goals, through a process of negotiation, goals which are challenging enough to be beyond previous performance, yet which lead to sufficient success for the individual to perceive goal attainment, which reflects performance accomplishment and leads to increased self-efficacy. Winter describes a range of goal-setting techniques in Chapter 10. Goal setting may be used alone in situations where the task is predefined, such as in an Olympic competition. If a gold medal or a medal of any colour is clearly beyond the current capability of the athlete, aiming for a personal best or the successful completion of the event may be an appropriate goal. Where there is some control over the task itself, performance accomplishment can be achieved by setting the task at an attainable level. For example, in the early stages of cardiac rehabilitation, when the patient has low self-efficacy for any form of exercise, walking round the block or completing a light weight-training circuit, would represent performance accomplishment.

2. Vicarious experience. Research indicates that seeing somebody else execute the task one is expected to perform can enhance one's self-efficacy for that task. Again this can be expected to apply across the full range of sport and exercise: from the Olympic level diver watching the only person yet to perfect a highly complex dive, a dive that she herself must execute if she is to defeat that opponent, to the person who has recently suffered a heart attack seeing other cardiac rehabilitation patients working out at the rehabilitation centre. These experiences will be especially effective if the models are perceived by the observers to be similar to them in relevant ways. The use of vicarious experience should be carefully considered, particularly in terms of model similarity. If the person perceives the model to be unlike herself, this may further justify her belief that she cannot do the task. Used judiciously, vicarious experience can increase self-efficacy for tasks not previously performed. Persuasion can be used to the same effect.

3. Persuasion. Bandura (1977) used the term "verbal persuasion" and considered persuasion to represent others telling the person that they are capable of performing the task. Feltz (1992) uses the term "persuasion" and includes other forms of persuasion, such as imagery. As in the case of modelling, persuasion should come from a convincing source and must be presented in an assured manner to be successful. Verbal persuasion may well come from the coach, as a high status source, but again needs to be used selectively. Even the utterings of a highly respected coach will lose their effect if the coach simply claims "You can win this one" before every game. The performer can use imagery to increase self-efficacy by developing images of successful performance in the real setting and against the actual opponent. Imagery is a skill which becomes more potent with practice and especially as the images become more vivid and are controlled by the athlete. Care must be taken that success imagery is achieved, otherwise the intervention will again be counterproductive. Perry and Morris discuss a range of imagery exercises in Chapter 14.

4. Physiological state. The fourth antecedent of self-efficacy proposed by Bandura (1977) focused on the interpretation which people make of their physiological state. Where increased level of arousal, felt in terms of rapid heart rate and respiration, increased sweating, tight muscles and churning of the stomach are interpreted as signals reflecting anxiety about the situation, it is likely that self-efficacy will be reduced. Recognition that these bodily changes accompany appropriate preparation for action, that is, that they indicate that the body is ready for the physical exertion to follow, can reassure the performer and enhance self-efficacy. In events which do not involve the exertion of strength, speed or endurance, such as archery, pistol shooting or darts, this interpretation is not suitable. Pre-performance routines should be used to minimise the increase in arousal level. At the same time, some arousal may be interpreted as a sign that attention is becoming focused on the task (see also Martin, Chapter 11, and Madden, Chapter 12).

According to Bandura's (1977) notion of reciprocal determinism, self-efficacy enhances performance, just as performance accomplishments are the most powerful influence on self-efficacy. In sport, Feltz (1982) demonstrated that while vicarious experience played a significant causal role in the first attempt at a high avoidance task, the back dive, once success had been attained previous performance was the strongest predictor of self-efficacy. This is reassuring for the sport psychologist developing self-efficacy in sports performers or exercisers, because it means that vicarious experience, persuasion and physiological state interpretation can be used sparingly, restricted to situations where past performance cannot be invoked and then quickly removed once they have encouraged successful performance. This is consistent with an important principle in sport psychology, which is to make the athlete/exerciser self supporting. The range of interventions which can be used to enhance self-efficacy is large, involving all the areas discussed in part 2 of this book. It is most important for the sport psychologist to understand the antecedents of self-efficacy, so that the specific application may be generated to meet the circumstances most effectively.

FUTURE DIRECTIONS

Bandura's (1977, 1986) theoretical development of the concept of self-efficacy has proved to be valuable to sport and exercise psychology. The research to date has demonstrated that self-efficacy frequently plays a central role in sport and exercise behaviour, but there are several directions for future research on self-efficacy, some to refine understanding and others to extend it.

While the definition of self-efficacy is clear, there is still some uncertainty about its measurement. Bandura (1977, 1986) has maintained that the measurement of self-efficacy should involve the microanalytic approach, measuring each component of a task separately, although his concept of generality is some concession to those who argue for a more global measure of self-confidence for a task (e.g., Vealey, 1986). Some sport and physical activity researchers have used the more general Physical Self-Efficacy Scale (Ryckman, Robbins, Thornton, & Cantrell, 1982), although comparisons favour task-specific measures (Mueller, 1992). In addition, the distinction between level and strength in the measurement of self-efficacy (Bandura, 1977) has not been applied in some work. This has required subjects to respond to all items (or levels) on a confidence (or strength of self-efficacy) scale, where a zero score is included to indicate a perception of no capability to perform any specific task or component of the task (e.g., Dzewaltowski, 1989). These variations in measures across studies make direct comparisons difficult. Research which focuses on the different types of measure, with the aim of understanding how they affect response, could arrive at a conclusion in favour of one mode of measurement, which researchers could then be encouraged to use consistently. Research on the measurement of self-efficacy also needs to examine the potential for confusion between capability and intention.

With respect to social cognitive theory, the interaction between self-efficacy, the outcomes which subjects expect, and the value which they place on those outcomes has not been clarified by research (e.g., Dzewaltowski, 1989; Kingery & Glasgow, 1989). It appears that other factors affect the influence of these variables on behaviour. Research needs to carefully monitor issues like the initial level of self-efficacy for volunteer subjects, education, knowledge and attitudes of subjects, regarding the behaviour of interest and previous experience of the task. It would be valuable for research to be directed specifically at manipulating these variables to determine their pattern of influence. In addition to refining the theory, this information would increase the precision of interventions. One approach which has been used is the pre-selection of subjects who are assumed, or have been shown, to have low self-efficacy. For example, in his study on the dive forward roll mount, McAuley (1985a) states that:

> Bandura has taken great care to ensure that subjects selected for treatment were highly anxious and avoidant of the behavior under study. For this study, only those subjects who had had no previous gymnastics experience or training were selected for participation. It was reasoned that this would provide a sufficiently anxious sample when confronted with the task. (pp. 284–285)

High anxiety is often associated with low self-efficacy and the results of the study support this relationship. It is much more likely that a treatment intended to increase self-efficacy will produce a statistically significant effect with subjects who are low on self-efficacy at the start. Where it is intended to use interventions with low self-efficacy individuals, this approach seems to be acceptable, provided that it is acknowledged. Looked at from another perspective, concluding that interventions are not effective, based on non-significant results from studies using high self-efficacy samples, subject to ceiling effects, could deny treatments to low self-efficacy individuals who might benefit from them. Screening of populations to select low self-efficacy samples, thus, appears to be justified.

Variations in the influence of self-efficacy, due to amount of experience of the task were demonstrated in the early sports research on back diving by Feltz (1982). This seems to be an important area of inquiry which has not received substantial attention, particularly over long time periods, such as weeks or months, rather than the several trials on one day in that study. An obvious cross-sectional approach to examine the influence of level of experience would be to compare the role of self-efficacy in novices and experts performing the same task. The back diving research would suggest a reduced role for self-efficacy in experts, because they have much more performance accomplishment information on which to directly base their expectation for their next performance. Another approach, which has not been evident in the research, is the longitudinal study of the relationships between self-efficacy, outcome expectations and performance. Kingery and Glasgow (1989) found that a prospective measure of self-efficacy, that is, self-efficacy measured before the start of a six months monitoring period, was a significant predictor of exercise activity over that six-month period, as was a concurrent measure of self-efficacy, taken at the end of the six months, when self-report of exercise was also measured. In that study there was only one measure of behaviour, that for the whole six-month period. Periodic measurement of self-efficacy, outcome expectations and performance would provide a rich source of information to examine changes in the variables over time, the relationships between the variables, any changes in these relationships over time and the role of other variables, such as type of measurement instrument, initial level of the variables or specific interventions. Combined with this, the use of more sophisticated analytical techniques is essential. McAuley's (1989) application of structural equation modelling is a rare example here. The use of multiple measures, which, in combination, determine latent variables in structural equations, should also circumvent some of the measurement problems.

Ultimately, measuring self-efficacy sensitively and understanding its relationship to sport and exercise behaviour will benefit applied sport and exercise psychology by providing clearer guidance to those administering interventions. The amount of research which has examined the efficacy of interventions to enhance self-efficacy is limited. While intervention research must feed off state-of-the-art theory, it is important for more work in this area to be produced. Accepting that it still needs refining, the theoretically driven research to date gives enough positive support to the central role of self-efficacy in sport and exercise behaviour to encourage practitioners to intervene to enhance it. The techniques they use will depend on intuition and experience to a large degree, until there is a substantial body of research to direct them. Research on educational interventions to increase exercise in type 2 diabetics has not proved successful (Bloomgarten, Karmally, Metzger, Brothers, Nechemias, Bookman,

Faierman, Ginsberg-Fellner, Rayfield, & Brown, 1987; Dunn, Beeney, Hoskins, & Turtle, 1990; Kingery, 1988) and new directions might be determined by considering the experiences of these researchers.

This section on future directions has, in common with the chapter as a whole, focused on self-efficacy and related social cognitive theory variables. A number of new lines of research have begun to link self-efficacy to other cognitive variables associated with motivation. McAuley (1992c) reviews the close relationship between self-efficacy and attributions for behaviour. Research examining this association can be expected to follow McAuley's seminal example. Similarly, connections are being made between the motivational orientations work of Duda (Duda, 1987, 1989, 1992) and self-efficacy (e.g., Ames & Archer, 1988; Feltz & Riessinger, 1990). This, again, seems to be a fruitful development. It is not surprising that associations between cognitive variables are emerging and it is likely that all of these variables will ultimately be included in one theoretical network. There is still much to be done within the area of self-efficacy, however, and contributions to the future directions suggested here will undoubtedly help to determine those broader issues.

CONCLUSIONS

Bandura's (1977, 1986) concept of self-efficacy was quickly taken up by researchers in sport psychology, notably Feltz (Feltz, 1982; Feltz, Landers, & Raeder, 1979), based on its evident potential in this performance-oriented field. It has also been widely researched in the context of exercise behaviour. Defined as a person's belief in their capability of performing a particular task or sub-component of a complex task, it has been conceived as a highly specific form of self-confidence. Although the measurement of self-efficacy has been the focus of some disagreement, research has generally produced results which support the important mediating role of this variable in sports performance and exercise behaviour. At the same time, there are still many aspects of the role of self-efficacy which remain unresolved. There is great potential for future research on theoretical issues concerning the relationships between self-efficacy and other cognitive variables. Perhaps even more urgent is the need for research on the nature of interventions designed to enhance self-efficacy, refining the practitioner's ability to apply treatments effectively.

It might be claimed that the concept of self-efficacy has actually hampered the development of a theoretical framework to consider confidence in the sport setting. Reflection on the literature certainly suggests some ambivalence on the part of sport psychologists to propose alternative models or theories of self-confidence. A sport-specific approach to self-confidence, proposed by Vealey (1986), is the only major published work generated in sport psychology. Based, both structurally and in terms of methods of development, on the very successful trait-state approach to anxiety, proposed by Martens and colleagues (e.g., Martens, 1977; Martens, Burton, Vealey, Bump, & Smith, 1983; Martens, Vealey & Burton,

1990), this apparently promising model was quickly criticised in a major review by Feltz (1988b), who compared the nascent self-confidence model to the well-established self-efficacy approach. Researchers appear to have been reluctant to commit themselves to the sport confidence model in the face of the evidence accumulated on self-efficacy.

Much of the research in sport has tended to investigate self-efficacy independent of the theoretical framework of social cognitive theory. More of the work in the exercise behaviour field has included measures of outcome expectations and outcome value. This may reflect the assumption in some cases that competitive athletes uniformly expect successful performance to be associated with money, prizes and fame, which are highly valued, that is, their outcome expectations and outcome values are clear and generally high. In other cases, the failure to include measures of outcome expectation and value may occur because the research is focused on self-confidence alone, as opposed to the intricate network of social cognitive variables which together might mediate performance. In these studies, self-efficacy is employed as the operationalisation of self-confidence with the most substantial theoretical and empirical base. Research which considers the network of cognitive factors, extending beyond the major variables of social cognitive theory, is still needed.

Self-efficacy is an important concept in sport and exercise psychology. It has certainly been shown to play a pivotal role in influencing the performance of athletes and the exercise behaviour of special groups, as well as the general population. Interventions which can reliably and effectively enhance self-efficacy may be among the most potent available to the applied sport and exercise psychologist and efforts to understand and control self-efficacy in sport and exercise should be continued and increased.

SUMMARY

This chapter examined the concept of self-efficacy. The nature of self-efficacy as a cognitive variable mediating behaviour in sport and exercise was indicated by its definition as the belief one has in one's capability to perform a task. This reflects the close association between self-efficacy and self-confidence. It was also noted that self-efficacy is closely related to motivation, in terms of choice, effort and persistence.

The location of self-efficacy in Bandura's (1986) social cognitive theory was discussed, along with its relationship to other variables in that theory, particularly outcome expectancy and outcome value. It was noted that these variables had not frequently been examined in sport, but that many would assume that they are consistently high in competitive, especially elite, sports performers.

Bandura's (1977, 1986) system of measurement based on the microanalytic approach was discussed, the measurement of level, strength and generality being explained. Questions were raised about the need to measure level and strength separately and about the issue of more general or global measures of self-efficacy, addressed by the concept of generality, but not to the satisfaction of many.

The antecedents of self-efficacy were considered, these being performance accomplishments, vicarious experience, persuasion and physiological arousal, according to Bandura (1977). Research was reported which supported the role of each in the derivation of self-efficacy, also showing that previous performance is the most powerful antecedent. As well as being the most potent antecedent of self-efficacy, previous performance was shown to become a stronger predictor of next performance, reducing the role of self-efficacy progressively as more experiences of performance give performers a direct indication of their capability at the task.

Research which has examined the relationship between self-efficacy and sports performance has generally supported the conclusion that higher self-efficacy is associated with superior performance, and a small number of studies have shown improved performance following the enhancement of self-efficacy. It was noted that there is still a need for studies using statistical modelling techniques to confirm the role of self-efficacy in this respect. One such study, by McAuley (1989), does not seem to have stimulated further work of this kind.

It was observed that a substantial literature has been developed more recently in the area of self-efficacy and exercise behaviour, perhaps to the detriment of sports-based research. Issues like adherence to exercise in special groups and in the general population were characterised as very worthy research pursuits, and also as being more likely than high level sports performance to yield encouraging results, with careful design, because the groups would probably have low, or at least relatively variable, levels of initial self-efficacy.

Considering future directions for research on self-efficacy, several possibilities were put forward:
- refinement of the measurement of self-efficacy
- investigation of personal and situational factors which affect the influence of self-efficacy
- examination of the role of experience in the efficacy-performance relationship, via expert–novice comparisons and longitudinal studies
- using statistical modelling procedures to examine the relationships between self-efficacy, outcome expectancy, outcome value and performance
- determining the effectiveness of a range of interventions suggested to enhance self-efficacy for sport or exercise.

This chapter concluded by emphasising that self-efficacy has an important, possibly pivotal, role to play in the future of sport and exercise psychology. Practitioners know it is important and are using whatever techniques are available to enhance self-efficacy for sports performance and exercise activity. It is critical that research effort be focused on the issues which will give the practitioners clear guidance about how to effectively enhance self-efficacy for the benefit of sports performers and the health of the community.

REFERENCES

Ames, C., & Archer, J. (1988). Achievement goals in the classroom: Students' learning strategies and motivational processes. *Journal of Educational Psychology, 80*, 260–267.

Ary, D. V., Toobert, D., Wilson, W., & Glasgow R. E. (1986). Patient perspective on factors contributing to nonadherence to diabetes regimen. *Diabetes Care, 9*, 168–172.

Bandura, A. (1969). *Principles of behavior modification.* New York: Holt, Rinehart & Winston.

Bandura, A. (1977). Self-efficacy: Toward a unifying theory of behavior change. *Psychological Review, 84*, 191–215.

Bandura, A. (1982). Self-efficacy mechanism in human agency. *American Psychologist, 37*, 122–147.

Bandura, A. (1986). *Social foundations of thought and action.* Englewood Cliffs, NJ: Prentice Hall.

Bandura, A. (1989). *Perceived self-efficacy in the exercise of human agency.* Coleman Griffith Memorial Lecture at the Annual Conference of the Association for the Advancement of Applied Sport Psychology, Seattle, September.

Bandura, A. (1990). Perceived self-efficacy in the exercise of human agency. *Journal of Applied Sport Psychology, 2*, 128–163.

Bandura, A., Blanchard, E. B., & Ritter, B. (1969). The relative efficacy of desensitization and modeling approaches for inducing behavioral, affective and attitudinal changes. *Journal of Personality and Social Psychology, 13*, 173–199.

Bandura, A., & Cervone, D. (1983). Self-evaluative and self-efficacy mechanisms governing the motivational effects of goal systems. *Journal of Personality and Social Psychology, 45*, 1017–1028.

Bandura, A., & Cervone, D. (1986). Differential engagement of self-reactive influences in cognitive motivation. *Organizational Behaviors and Human Decision Processes, 38*, 92–113.

Bandura, A., Ross, D., & Ross, S. (1961). Transmission of aggression through imitation of aggressive models. *Journal of Abnormal and Social Psychology, 63*, 575–582.

Barling, J., & Abel, M. (1983). Self-efficacy beliefs and tennis performance. *Cognitive Therapy and Research, 7*, 265–272.

Bloomgarten, Z. T., Karmally, W., Metzger, J., Brothers, M., Nechemias, C., Bookman, J., Faierman, D., Ginsberg-Fellner, F., Rayfield, E., & Brown, W. V., (1987). Randomized, controlled trial of diabetic patient education: Improved knowledge without improved metabolic status. *Diabetes Care, 10*, 263–272.

Brody, E. B., Hatfield, B. D., & Spalding, T. W. (1988). Generalization of self-efficacy to a continuum of stressors upon mastery of a high-risk sport skill. *Journal of Sport and Exercise Psychology, 10*, 32–44.

Bunker, L., Williams, J. M., & Zinsser, N. (1992). Cognitive techniques for improving performance and building confidence. In J. M. Williams, (Ed.), *Applied sport psychology: Personal growth to peak performance* (2nd ed.) (pp. 225–242). Mountain View, CA: Mayfield.

Cantu, R. C. (Ed.). (1987). *The exercising adult.* New York: Macmillan.

Desharnais, R. B., & Godin, G. (1986). Self-efficacy and outcome expectations as determinants of exercise adherence. *Psychological Reports, 59*, 1155–1159.

Dishman, R. K. (Ed.). (1988). *Exercise adherence: Its influence on public health.* Champaign, IL: Human Kinetics.

Duda, J. L. (1987). Toward a developmental theory of motivation in sport. *Journal of Sport Psychology, 9,* 130–145.

Duda, J. L. (1989). The relationship between task and ego orientation and the perceived purpose of sport among male and female high school athletes. *Journal of Sport and Exercise Psychology, 11,* 318–335.

Duda, J. L. (1992). Motivation in sport settings: A goal perspective approach. In G. C. Roberts (Ed.), *Motivation in sport and exercise* (pp. 57–91). Champaign, IL: Human Kinetics.

Dunn, S. M., Beeney, L. J., Hoskins, P. L., & Turtle, J. R. (1990). Knowledge and attitude change as predictors of metabolic improvement in diabetes education. *Social Sciences in Medicine, 31,* 1135–1141.

Dyer, J. B., & Crouch, J. G. (1988). Effects of running and other activities on moods. *Perceptual and Motor Skills, 67,* 43–50.

Dzewaltowski, D. A. (1989). Toward a model of exercise motivation. *Journal of Sport and Exercise Psychology, 11,* 251–269.

Dzewaltowski, D. A., Noble, J. M., & Shaw, J. M. (1990). Physical activity participation: Social cognitive theory versus the theories of reasoned action and planned behavior. *Journal of Sport and Exercise Psychology, 12,* 388–405.

Ewart, C. K., Stewart, K. J., Gillian, R. E., Keleman, M. H., Valenti, S. A., Manley, J. D., & Kaleman, M. D. (1986). Usefulness of self-efficacy in predicting overexertion during programmed exercise in coronary artery disease. *American Journal of Cardiology, 57,* 557–561.

Ewart, C. K., Taylor, C. B., Reese, L. B., & DeBusk, R. F. (1983). Effects of early post myocardial infarction exercise testing on self-perception and subsequent physical activity. *American Journal of Cardiology, 51,* 1076–1080.

Eysenck, H. J. (1978). Expectations as causal elements in behavioural change. In S. Rachman (Ed.), *Advances in behaviour research and therapy* (Vol. 1). Oxford: Pergamon Press.

Feltz, D. L. (1982). Path analysis of the causal elements of Bandura's theory of self-efficacy and an anxiety-based model of avoidance behavior. *Journal of Personality and Social Psychology, 42,* 764–781.

Feltz, D. L. (1988a). Gender differences in the causal elements of self-efficacy on a high avoidance motor task. *Journal of Sport and Exercise Psychology, 10,* 151–166.

Feltz, D. L. (1988b). Self-confidence and sports performance. In K. B. Pandolf (Ed.), *Exercise and Sports Science Reviews, 16,* 423–458.

Feltz, D. L. (1992). Understanding motivation in sport: A self-efficacy perspective. In G. C. Roberts (Ed.), *Motivation in sport and exercise* (pp. 93–105). Champaign, IL: Human Kinetics.

Feltz, D. L., Bandura, A., & Lirrg, C. D. (1989, August). Perceived collective efficacy in hockey. In D. Kendzierski (Chair), *Self-perceptions in sport and physical activity: Self-efficacy and self-image.* Symposium conducted at the meeting of the American Psychological Association, New Orleans.

Feltz, D. L., Landers, D. M., & Raeder, U. (1979). Enhancing self-efficacy in high avoidance motor tasks: A comparison of modeling techniques. *Journal of Sport Psychology, 1,* 112–122.

Feltz, D. L., & Mugno, D. A. (1983). A replication of the path analysis of the causal elements in Bandura's theory of self-efficacy and the influence of autonomic perception. *Journal of Sport Psychology, 5,* 263–277.

Feltz, D. L., & Riessinger, C. A. (1990). Effects of in vivo emotive imagery and performance feedback on self-efficacy and muscular endurance. *Journal of Sport and Exercise Psychology, 12,* 132–143.

Fitzsimmons, P. A., Landers, D. M., Thomas, J. R., & van der Mars, H. (1991). Does self-efficacy predict performance in experienced weightlifters? *Research Quarterly for Exercise and Sport, 62*, 424–431.

Frazier, S. E. (1988). Mood state profiles of chronic exercisers with differing abilities. *International Journal of Sport Psychology, 19*, 65–71.

Gauvin, L. (1989). The relationship between regular physical activity and subjective well-being. *Journal of Sport Behavior, 12*, 107–114.

Gayton, W. F., Matthews, G. R., & Burchstead, G. N. (1986). An investigation of the validity of the Physical Self-efficacy Scale in predicting marathon performance. *Perceptual and Motor Skills, 63*, 752–754.

George, T. R., Feltz, D. L., & Chase, M. A. (1992). Effects of model similarity on self-efficacy and muscular endurance: A second look. *Journal of Sport and Exercise Psychology, 14*, 237–248.

Glasgow, R. E., Toobert, D. J., & Hampson, S. E. (1991). Participation in outpatient diabetes education programs: How many patients take part and how representative are they? *Diabetes Educator, 17*, 376–380.

Glasgow, R. E., Toobert, D. J., Hampson, S. E., Brown, J. E., Lewinsohn, P. M., & Donnelly, J. (1992). Improving self-care among older patients with Type I diabetes: The "Sixty Something..." study. *Patient Education and Counseling, 19*, 61–74.

Godding, P. R., & Glasgow, R. E. (1985). Self-efficacy and outcome expectancy as predictors of controlled smoking status. *Cognitive Therapy and Research, 9*, 591–593.

Gordon, N. F. (1993). *Diabetes: Your complete exercise guide.* Champaign, IL: Human Kinetics.

Gould, D., & Weiss, M. (1981). Effect of model similarity and model self-talk on self-efficacy in muscular endurance. *Journal of Sport Psychology, 3*, 17–29.

Haskell, W. L. (1984). Overview: Health benefits of exercise. In J. D. Matarrazzo, S. M. Weiss, J. A. Herd, W. E. Miller, & S. M. Weiss (Eds.), *Behavioral health: A handbook of health enhancement and disease prevention* (pp. 409–423). New York: John Wiley & Sons.

Hayden, R. M., Allen, G. J., & Camaione, D. N. (1986). Some psychological benefits resulting from involvement in an aerobic fitness program from the perspectives of participants and knowledgeable informants. *Journal of Sports Medicine, 26*, 67–76.

Hayes, D., & Ross, C. E. (1986). Body and mind: The effect of exercise, overweight, and physical health on psychological well-being. *Journal of Health and Social Behavior, 27*, 387–400.

Hogan, P. I., & Santomier, J. P. (1984). Effects of mastering swim skills on older adults' self-efficacy. *Research Quarterly for Exercise and Sport, 56*, 284–296.

Holloway, J. B., Beuter, A., & Duda, J. L. (1988). Self-efficacy and training for strength in adolescent girls. *Journal of Applied Social Psychology, 18*, 699–719.

Kavanagh, D., & Hausfeld, S. (1986). Physical performance and self-efficacy under happy and sad moods. *Journal of Sport Psychology, 8*, 112–123.

Kemmer, F. W., & Berger, M. (1980). Exercise and diabetes mellitus: Physical activity as a part of daily life and its role in the treatment of diabetic patients. *International Journal of Sports Medicine, 4*, 77–88.

Kingery, P. M. (1988). *Self-efficacy and outcome expectations in the self-regulation of non insulin dependent diabetes mellitus.* Unpublished doctoral dissertation, University of Oregon Microfiche, Eugene, Oregon.

Kingery, P. M., & Glasgow, R. E. (1989). Self-efficacy and outcome expectations in the self-regulation of non-insulin dependent diabetes mellitus. *Health Education, 20*, 13–19.

Lee, C. (1982). Self-efficacy as a predictor of performance in competitive gymnastics. *Journal of Sport Psychology, 4*, 405–409.

Lirgg, C. D., & Feltz, D. L. (1991). Teacher versus peer model revisited: Effects on motor performance. *Research Quarterly for Exercise and Sport, 62*, 217–224.

Manning, M. M., & Wright, T. L. (1983). Self-efficacy expectancies, outcome expectancies, and the persistence of pain control in childbirth. *Journal of Personality and Social Psychology, 45*, 421–431.

Martens, R. (1977). *Sport competition anxiety test.* Champaign, IL: Human Kinetics.

Martens, R., Burton, D., Rivkin, F., & Simon, J. (1980). Reliability and validity of the Competitive State Anxiety Inventory (CSAI). In C. H. Nadeau, W. R. Halliwell, K. M. Newell, & G. C. Roberts (Eds.), *Psychology of motor behavior and sport — 1979.* Champaign, IL: Human Kinetics.

Martens, R., Burton, D., Vealey, R. S., Bump, L. A., & Smith, D. E. (1983). *The Competitive State Anxiety Inventory–2.* Unpublished manuscript, University of Illinois, Urbana-Champaign.

Martens, R., Vealey, R. S., & Burton, D. (1990). *Competitive anxiety in sport.* Champaign, IL: Human Kinetics.

McAuley, E. (1985a). Modeling and self-efficacy: A test of Bandura's model. *Journal of Sport Psychology, 7*, 283–295.

McAuley, E. (1985b). Success and causality in sport: The influence of perception. *Journal of Sport Psychology, 7*, 13–22.

McAuley, E. (1989). *Efficacy cognitions and exercise behaviour in young females.* Unpublished manuscript, University of Illinois, Department of Kinesiology.

McAuley, E. (1991). Efficacy and attributional determinants of affective reactions to exercise participation. *Journal of Sport and Exercise Psychology, 14*, 237–248.

McAuley, E. (1992a). Understanding exercise behavior: A self-efficacy perspective. In G. C. Roberts (Ed.), *Motivation in sport and exercise* (pp. 107–127). Champaign, IL: Human Kinetics.

McAuley, E. (1992b). The role of efficacy cognitions in the prediction of exercise behavior in middle aged adults. *Journal of Behavioral Medicine, 15*, 65–88.

McAuley, E. (1992c). Self-referent thought in sport and physical activity. In T. S. Horn (Ed.), *Advances in sport psychology* (pp. 101–118). Champaign, IL: Human Kinetics.

McAuley, E., Courneya, K. S., & Lettunich, J. (1991). Effects of acute and long-term exercise responses in sedentary, middle-aged males and females. *The Gerontologist, 31*, 534–542.

McAuley, E., & Gill, D. L. (1983). Reliability and validity of the physical self-efficacy scale in a competitive sport setting. *Journal of Sport Psychology, 5*, 410–418.

McAuley, E., & Jacobson, L. B. (1991). Self-efficacy and exercise participation in sedentary adult females. *American Journal of Health Promotion, 5*, 185–191.

McAuley, E., & Rowney, T. (1990). The role of efficacy cognitions in adherence and intent to exercise. In L. VanderVelden & J. H. Humphrey (Eds.), *Psychology and sociology of sport: Current selected research* (Vol. 2, pp. 3–15). New York: AMS.

Mueller, L. M. (1992). The effect of general and task specific self-efficacy on the performance of a fine motor task. *Journal of Sport Behavior, 15*, 130–140.

National Heart Foundation (Australia). (1989). *Risk factor prevalence survey no. 3.* Canberra: National Heart Foundation (Australia).

Ryckman, R. M., Robbins, M. A., Thornton, B., & Cantrell, P. (1982). Development and validation of a physical self-efficacy scale. *Journal of Personality and Social Psychology, 42*, 891–900.

Sallis, J. F., Haskell, W. L., Fortnam, S. P., Vranisan, M. S., Taylor, C. B., & Solomon, D. S. (1986). Predictors of adoption and maintenance of physical activity in a community sample. *Preventive Medicine, 15*, 331–341.

Sherman, W. M., & Albright, A. (1992). Exercise and Type II diabetes. *Sports Science Exchange, 4*(37).

Simmons, M. W., & Owen, N. (1992). Perspectives on the management of Type I diabetes. *Australian Psychologist, 27*, 99–102.

Stepanas, T. V. (1991). Types of diabetes. In P. Moffitt, P. Phillips, & B. Ayers (Eds.), *Diabetes and you: An owner's manual.* Canberra: Diabetes Australia.

Suinn, R. M. (1984). Imagery in sport. In W. F. Straub & J. M. Williams (Eds.), *Cognitive sport psychology.* Lansing, NJ: Sport Science Associates.

Taylor, C. B., Bandura, A., Ewart, C. K., Miller, N. H., & DeBusk, R. T. (1985). Exercise testing to enhance wives' confidence in their husbands' cardiac capabilities soon after clinically uncomplicated acute myocardial infarction. *American Journal of Cardiology, 55*, 6335–6338.

Vealey, R. S. (1986). Conceptualization of sport confidence and competitive orientation: Preliminary investigation and instrument development. *Journal of Sport Psychology, 8*, 221–246.

Weinberg, R. S., Gould, D., & Jackson, A. (1979). Expectations and performance: An empirical test of Bandura's self-efficacy theory. *Journal of Sport Psychology, 1*, 320–331.

Weinberg, R. S., & Jackson, A. (1990). Building self-efficacy in tennis players: A coach's perspective. *Journal of Applied Sport Psychology, 2*, 164–174.

Weinberg, R. S., Jackson, A., & Kolodny, K. (1988). The relationship of massage and exercise to mood enhancement. *The Sport Psychologist, 2*, 202–211.

Weinberg, R. S., Sinardi, M., & Jackson, A. (1982). Effect of bar height and modeling on anxiety, self confidence and gymnastic performance. *International Gymnast, 2*, 11–13.

Weiss, M. R., Weise, D. M., & Klint, K. A. (1989). Head over heels with success: The relationship between self-efficacy and performance in competitive youth gymnastics. *Journal of Sport and Exercise Psychology, 11*, 444–451.

Wilkes, R. L., & Summers, J. J. (1984). Cognitions, mediating variables and strength performance. *Journal of Sport Psychology, 6*, 351–359.

Wilson, W., Ary, D. V., Biglan, A., Glasgow, R. E., Toobert, D. J., & Campbell, D. R. (1986). Psychosocial predictors of self-care behaviors (compliance) and glycemic control in Non-Insulin-Dependent-Diabetes-Mellitus. *Diabetes Care, 9*, 614–622.

Yan Lan, L., & Gill, D. L. (1984). The relationships among self-efficacy, stress responses, and a cognitive feedback manipulation. *Journal of Sport Psychology, 6*, 227–238.

C H A P T E R

7

SOCIAL FACILITATION

MICHELLE PAIN

In training and in competition, athletes never perform alone. Whether "relying on one's own ability to perform" or even being "bodily" alone with no other person in sight, athletes carry a burden that cannot be relieved until they stop being athletes (and sometimes, not even then!) They learn that one cannot escape that "voice in their head" when they analyse their performance against their own expectations. As well, any performance is also usually open to comparisons made by others (including spectators, judges, coaches, team mates or other competitors).

This chapter reviews the collective body of research which has been termed "social facilitation" by Allport in 1924, and suggests ways in which the theory can be adapted in practice for athletes, coaches and sport psychologists. Social facilitation research may be classified in terms of two experimental paradigms — the extent to which the actions and presence of other competitors (coaction effects) and the actions and presence of non-competitors (audience effects) influence an individual's learning or motor performance. Among the research of audience effects is a review of the effects of performing in front of a home crowd.

The experience of the athletes, in terms of frequency and duration of exposure to performing in front of crowds; the impact of performing in front of talent scouts (or other knowledgeable people) versus an audience largely ignorant of the intricacies of the performance; the audience size and the "atmosphere" of the venue; and the interactivity and perceived support of the audience with the competitors are all factors thought to add pressure on an athlete. As anxiety theories postulate, too much anxiety can lead to poor performance, and as can be seen in the following pages, social facilitation research is strongly allied with anxiety research.

Triplett's (1897) pioneering work demonstrated that the presence of another contestant improved subjects' performances, although subsequent findings over the next 70 years produced results which were far from clear-cut. Zajonc's (1965) review of the literature, in which he differentiated between research in which subjects were to perform simple or complex tasks, in both learning and performance phases, led to his theory of social facilitation, which was based on Drive Theory (Hull, 1943; Spence, 1956). Zajonc proposed that the presence of an audience created arousal, which enhanced the emission of dominant responses, such that "... the emission of well-learned responses is facilitated by the presence of spectators, while the acquisition of new responses is impaired,... [that is] ... performance is facilitated and learning is impaired by the presence of spectators" (p. 270). This had much support, although modifications to the theory (notably, an "evaluation apprehension" component, first postulated by Cottrell in 1968) have been quite accepted.

The second related area of the social facilitation research examines the effect on performance of playing in front of a home crowd. Athletes' perceptions of the relationship between themselves and the audience have been recognised as a factor contributing to the performance level (Borden, 1980). The strength and consistency of the advantage has been found to differ across and within sports, with relevant factors being identified as crowd size and behaviour, familiarity with the venue, the rules of the game, travel, and the competitors' and officials' psychological and behavioural states (Courneya & Carron, 1992). The future of social facilitation research appears to be, as with the anxiety/performance research, in the acceptance of the role of cognition in behaviour and performance change.

HISTORICAL PERSPECTIVES

A study by Triplett (1897) of the effect of co-performers on motor performance has been credited with being the first scientific experiment in sport psychology ever published, although earlier studies of reaction time, and the effects of play on development, are correctly identified as contributions to motor learning and social psychology, respectively, rather than to sport psychology directly (Iso-Ahola & Hatfield, 1986).

Triplett's (1897) investigation contained an archival study of the official bicycle records of three types of professional races and found that competitors who raced against others cycled faster than those who competed alone, with a gain in favour of the paced over the unpaced of nearly 20%. To test whether increased speed was due to the pacing per se, or was an artifact due to the kind of men who chose to take part in racing, Triplett advanced seven theories:

- the suction theory
- the shelter theory

- the encouragement theory
- the brain worry theory
- the theory of hypnotic suggestion
- the automatic theory
- the theory of dynamogenic factors.

Intuitively, he selected the dynamogenic factor theory to be tested, which suggests that "... the bodily presence of another rider is a stimulus to the racer in arousing the competitive instinct" (p. 516), and designed a laboratory experiment, using a task in which the other theories could not conceivably significantly contribute, to prove the validity of the dynamogenic theory.

Triplett's (1897) second experiment was conducted in a laboratory in which two fishing reels, a stopwatch, and a stylus of a recorder tracing a line on the drum of a kymograph (to illustrate the change in rate of reel turning) were utilised to measure the speed in which a subject could reel a four-metre long silk cord through four circuits of the apparatus. The kymograph recordings were used to measure "the force of competition", "the effects of adverse stimulation", "fatigue" and "other phenomena". His subjects were 40 children with an average age of 11.6 years, and these were divided into two groups of 20. Both groups performed six trials, although the order in which they carried out the reel-turning task (either alone or in competition) was varied. Triplett discovered that those who were in competition performed faster than those who were alone. Using the kymograph recordings, he was able to identify that 20 of the 40 subjects were "positively stimulated by the competition", ten were "little affected by the competition" and the remaining ten were "adversely stimulated by the competition". With the latter group, Triplett claimed this was due to over-stimulation caused by an intense desire to win, as evidenced by their behaviour, where some subjects' records showed that "decided gains were sometimes lost by the subject 'going to pieces' at the critical point of the race, not being able to endure the nervous strain" (p. 525). An examination of the data by sex of the subject revealed that "when (the girls) were stimulated and they had control they made greater gains than the boys and when over-stimulated their losses were greater than those made by the boys" (p. 529).

Although Triplett (1897) concluded that the dynamogenic factors were influencing performance, he was unable to distinguish whether it was the "bodily presence of others" or "other (unknown) factors" that caused the beneficial effects, nor what it was about the presence of others that elicited the improved performances. In spite of this, his work is lauded for its scientific ingeniousness and rigour. His attempt to combine field observations with laboratory experimentation in order to make his explanation more resistant to competing theories is commendable; however, criticism of his work centred around the inability of the laboratory study to replicate the social conditions of the field study and there was suspicion that there was a "treatment effect" from the competition to the non-competition conditions (Wankel, 1984). In spite of Triplett's research, social facilitation experimentation was not stimulated to go much beyond his findings until after World War I.

During the 1920s and 1930s, studies assessing dynamogenic factors on performance produced mixed findings, although thorough reviews by two researchers ensured significant advances in determining requisite conditions for facilitation. Allport (1924) extended Triplett's (1897) study when he attempted to differentiate between the effects of competition and the coaction effects, as well as refine the nature of the benefits for coactors. For example, he recognised that susceptibility to facilitation effects depended on the age of the participant, the task difficulty, and "individual differences" between subjects. Allport noted that good performers were less likely to be affected by coaction than those who were poor performers. He also observed that coaction enhanced the speed of the action (quantity) rather than increasing the accuracy of the movement (quality), and that while muscular performance improved under coaction, mental performance suffered.

One of Allport's former students, Dashiell (1935), reviewed the social facilitation literature, extending Allport's (1924) review by including research examining audience effects, and noted the problems of using conventional statistical methods for dealing with group data.

> When the scores of the respective individuals are treated as such ... many of them show a difference in one direction or the other within his own results, certain strong, "populational" trends, heavy majorities of individuals, among those small differences may become marked. (p. 1103)

Also, Dashiell (1935) claimed that because the type of skills tested by the experiments varied so widely between researchers it was impossible to generalise the findings, and this pessimism appeared to discourage most facilitation research (using human subjects) until the 1960s.

Church (1962) saw a relationship with Drive Theory and noted that measures of "motivation", such as skin conductance and a self-rating of "alertness", both increased during the competition phase, but were not related to a decrease in reaction time. His experimental hypothesis, that "in a simple reaction time task, the competitive situation resulted in a decrease in response latency; in a discrimination reaction time task, the competitive situation resulted in a decrease in response latency and an increase in errors" (p. 35) was supported.

Although, in his classical review of the social facilitation literature, Zajonc (1965) observed that coactors facilitated the performance of simple or well-learned tasks but inhibited the acquisition of new responses, he was the first to frame this within the context of an already established psychological theory. Thus, the generalisation became "the presence of others, as spectators or coactors, enhances the emission of dominant responses" (p. 273), and the link between social facilitation and the Hull-Spence model of behaviour (performance) under conditions of "drive" became formally established.

CURRENT PERSPECTIVES

COACTION EFFECTS

Zajonc (1965) noted that the discrepancy of results from the previous literature seemed to depend on whether the task was simple or complex, and even whether subjects were tested during the learning phase of the task or at the stage when the task was well-learnt. In this, he saw links with Drive Theory (Hull, 1943; Spence, 1956), and suggested that the presence of others increased an individual's level of generalised drive, thus enhancing the individual's dominant response tendency more than competing response tendencies. For a simple task, he reasoned, the subject's dominant response is the correct one, but for a complex task, the dominant tendency is toward an incorrect response. So, when the dominant response is enhanced through increased drive, the presence of others should facilitate simple task performance and impair complex task performance. Three general lines of inquiry have opened for research in this area:

- an augmentation perspective, where the relative strengths of the correct and incorrect response tendencies for a task are identified, either by examining the current levels of performance and pattern of responses or by creating habit strength hierarchies via training procedures
- examining the usefulness of the construct "arousal" as a measure of drive
- determining the minimum social conditions necessary to trigger the drive (Bond & Titus, 1983; Wankel, 1984).

The "augmentation of dominant responses" research has rarely focused on sport settings. The ease of identifying dominant responses in a simple laboratory task has led to support for Drive Theory to be the underlying model to explain behaviour with and without coactors. In the case of complex motor tasks, the issue of determining the dominant response amongst many competing responses means it is difficult to attribute the positive performance effects to one response alone, or the combination of responses that needed to "trigger" the improved performance. Because sport mostly consists of complex tasks involving significant cognitive and motor processing, this line of inquiry has not proved popular.

In looking at the usefulness of the arousal construct as an explanation for "drive", researchers have attempted to use physiological and psychological indicators of arousal to demonstrate the effect that others being present has on a performer. In a later paper, Zajonc (1980) spelt out his interpretation of the "drive" in his social facilitation model as being similar to the hypothetical construct "arousal" in classical Hullian theory. He saw it to be a heightened state of alertness and preparedness for response which could be generated by the presence of others, including those who were not competing with or evaluating the individual in any way.

To gain an understanding of the degree of cognitive anxiety an athlete is experiencing, researchers using self-report questionnaires must be sure that the athlete: (a) is capable of appraising the degree of threat he/she is under; (b) can interpret the symptoms experienced; and (c) can report these symptoms accurately. The researcher has to be aware of the forces that may encourage the athlete to over- or under-report the symptoms, since the validity of the instrument relies significantly on such factors as honesty and openness. An additional problem in dealing with child athletes is that they may not understand the meaning of the statements, or may even attribute different meanings than would adults to the statements.

Physiological indicators of anxiety can be roughly classified as being (a) respiratory and cardiovascular; (b) biochemical; or (c) electrophysiological indicators. These relate to one of three systems in the human organism: (a) the autonomic nervous system; (b) the central nervous system; and (c) the muscular system. Parameters usually studied in anxiety literature include: pulse rate; blood pressure; respiration rate; adrenaline, noradrenaline and cortisol concentrations; muscle potentials; EEG correlates; and galvanic skin resistance.

The benefit of using physiological indicators of anxiety is that the measures do not rely on the subjects' verbal or conscious interpretations and can sometimes be monitored continuously during performance. The disadvantages appear to outweigh the advantages. They include the fact that physiological measures are method-dependent, and the collection method may be stressful in itself. Also, it is difficult to distinguish the valence of the emotion using biochemical indicators (e.g., an increase in heart rate can occur for reactions of excitement or anxiety). However, physiological parameters change in response to physical activity (Djarova, Ilkov, Varbanova, Nikiforova, & Mateev, 1986; Kraemer, 1988; Sharp & Parry-Billings, 1992), which makes it impossible to determine the effects of exercise from emotion. Physiological processes can be influenced by climate, general well-being, and daily rhythm. Intra-individual differences also account for a wide variation in response to a stressor. For example, one person may respond to a stressor by increased heart rate and unchanged skin resistance, while another might respond with increased skin resistance but unchanged heart rate. For all of these reasons, it is not unexpected that low correlations with other physiological indicators or psychological constructs have been reported.

Until researchers can confidently distinguish between the valence of the physiological indicators, these can only be, at best, of secondary importance in understanding the arousal processes. Hackfort and Schwenkmezger (1989) observed:

> ... some authors suggest it may be possible unequivocally to determine the presence of fear and anxiety and to distinguish between them on the basis of catecholamine, adrenaline and noradrenaline levels (e.g., Schildkraut & Kety, 1967), other authors feel that catecholamine secretion can only be regarded as an indication of the size of the emotional reaction and not as an indicator of the quality of the emotion (e.g., Levi, 1967; Frankenhauser, 1969). (p. 60)

The relevance of this whole line of inquiry to Zajonc's (1965) social facilitation theory is tenuous, since the Hullian version of Drive Theory (Hull, 1943; Spence, 1956) "... makes no reference to neurophysiological equivalents of drive and, hence, such arousal changes paralleling increased drive are not essential to (nor indeed predicted by) the theory" (Wankel, 1984, p. 302). As such, it is not a recommended avenue for research.

The third line of inquiry stimulated by Zajonc's (1965) theory — the "minimum social conditions necessary for social facilitation effects" — examines the sources and sufficient conditions of drive. The simplicity of Zajonc's proposal, that the mere presence of others is sufficient for triggering an innate source of drive, was questioned by Cottrell (1968, 1972) who suggested that it was not just the mere presence of others but the evaluation of others which caused anticipation in the mind of the athletes and became the source of the generalised drive. Others (Landers & McCullagh, 1976; Sanders, Baron, & Moore, 1978, cited by Bond & Titus, 1983) attributed it to the attentional conflict which arose when an individual attempted to derive social comparison information from others. This was thought to reduce the attention available to the task (which then led to a decrease in performance). Also, the heightened arousal a player might feel under pressure situations (e.g., playing in a Grand Final) might cause an athlete to revert to a well-learned attentional focus pattern that may be inappropriate for the time and situation. Football commentators have reported that players competing in a grand final often appear dazed and distracted at the commencement of the match, owing to the importance of the occasion and the size of the crowd, and take several minutes to "settle down" to their regular style of play.

To summarise, Drive Theory (Hull, 1943; Spence, 1956) is the most parsimonious explanation for processes underlying social facilitation, although it has been criticised for being too simplistic in accounting for complex human behaviour. The model is used to explain the effects of the mere presence of coactors or an audience on a performer's behaviour and physiological arousal. According to Zajonc (1965), the increased drive leads to an increase in the likelihood of the dominant response. Cottrell's (1968, 1972) evaluation theory suggested that the presence of an audience is arousing only if the audience is capable of making an evaluation of the performance. It was the "threat" of the evaluation which caused the increased drive. Other explanations for the level of drive experienced by a performer involving their cognition, e.g., such as anticipation, have been suggested.

AUDIENCE EFFECTS, AND THE HOME GROUND ADVANTAGE

Other alternatives to Drive Theory as an explanation for social facilitation, especially for the effect of the audience on performance, have been mooted but not fully explored (Wankel, 1984). They recognise a cognitive element to the athlete's level of "drive". Duval and Wicklund's (1972, cited in Bond & Titus, 1983) self-awareness theory explained drive as a function of the discrepancy between the individual's actual task performance and expected performance. Guerin and Innes' (1982, cited in Bond & Titus, 1983) social motivation theory attributed drive to the anxiety felt by being unable to visually monitor reactions of others rather than by distraction, such that individuals are less affected by the presence of coactors (whom they judge to be predictable) than by the presence of spectators (judged to be unpredictable). Bond's (1982) self-presentational awareness theory results from the extent to which an individual is motivated to present and sustain an image of competence in the presence of others.

By linking perceived failure to task complexity, Bond's model follows Drive Theory (Hull, 1943; Spence, 1956) in predicting the social facilitation of simple performances and the social impairment of complex performances. However, drive theorists who equate drive with physiological arousal (e.g., Zajonc, 1980) predict that the presence of others will invariably increase an individual's physiological arousal. The self-presentational analysis depicts arousal as a correlate of embarrassment, implying that the presence of others should heighten arousal only if the individual is attempting a complex (i.e., embarrassing) task (Bond & Titus, 1983).

Attempting to unravel the relative merits of each of the theories has been difficult. Most of the literature reviews of the social facilitation research included studies involving animals, and Geen and Gange (1977) noted that while research using human subjects confined the dependent variables measuring social facilitation to change in rate, frequency, intensity or latency of responses, animal researchers have used other behaviour characteristics, making comparisons difficult. Furthermore, Geen and Gange criticised the way in which some investigators have equated drive with physiological activity, without involving any assumptions concerning possible underlying physiological mechanisms. Although it is legitimate to examine the correlation between physiological arousal and performance, most experiments with a physiological dependent measure have not also included a behavioural measure. Geen and Gange recommended a demonstration of covariance between one or more measures of arousal and some of the behavioural measures.

Bond and Titus (1983) noted that reviews of social facilitation literature prior to their own were narrative reviews, with some categorising the effect of the presence of others in a non-scientific manner, by counting the number of studies with a statistically significant effect, ignoring the dependence of these studies on sample size and the possibility of a "file drawer" problem. A "file drawer" problem occurs when authors "file" their research away without attempting to have it published because the findings do not support a popular way of thinking. Alternatively, a research paper may be submitted to a journal, but the bias of editors toward findings which show statistically significant results means that the research is rejected, causing the author to have it "filed". To avoid the "file drawer" problem, a researcher using meta-analysis has to attempt to discover those findings which remain unpublished. One does this by contacting the known authors who usually publish in this field and asking them to disclose the findings of their unpublished work, as well as the names of others whom they know to be working in that field.

Bond and Titus (1983) carried out a systematic meta-analysis of studies in which "the behavior or physiology of humans who were alone (was compared to) the behavior or physiology of humans who were in the presence of others" (p. 269). In all, 241 English-language articles written prior to 1982 were identified (202 published and 39 unpublished works) and use of the statistically reliable meta-analytic Z allowed an attempt to estimate where the "file drawer" problem influenced results.

Initial analyses of the social facilitation effect across all 241 studies revealed a small to moderate effect due to the presence of others. The largest effect was for subjects who performed a complex task, although this accounted for only 3.1% of the between-subjects variance in performance quality. The effect of the presence of others seems, then, not to have a reliable effect on the physiology of the individual performing a simple task, although the effect is strengthened for subjects carrying out a complex task, as predicted by Bond's (1982) self-presentational analysis theory. In contrast, Zajonc's (1965) social facilitation theory predicts that individuals will invariably experience higher levels of arousal in the presence of others, irrespective of the task complexity. Although Drive Theory predicted that the speed of a simple task performance will be increased by enhancing the correct response when in the presence of others, it made no predictions about the speed of carrying out complex task performance. Non-Drive theories also predict that simple performance accuracy will be facilitated and complex performance accuracy impaired.

Although the facilitation of simple performance quality appeared reliable, Bond and Titus (1983) noted that nearly 40% of the reported effects of the presence of others on simple performance were negative in direction, suggesting that the apparent facilitation may result from the selective reporting of theory-predicting results. When the 194 studies which reported null effects were added to those 112 studies which reported facilitation, they determined that social facilitation effect for simple tasks was, in fact, statistically non-significant.

The wide variability of effect reported by researchers between studies means that a performance ceiling effect cannot be an explanation for the results for simple tasks. It is possible that the operational definition of task complexity adopted by researchers may have affected the findings. The different ways in which arousal (as an indicator of drive) can be measured has also led to suspicion about the strength of the social facilitation effect. Bond (1982, cited in Bond & Titus, 1983) was able to demonstrate that the performance of a simple task was facilitated, without a corresponding increase in physiological arousal, and that the performance of a complex task was inhibited, with an increase in physiological arousal. He attributed this rise in arousal levels to the embarrassment felt by an individual who appeared to be performing a task without mastery, causing a reduction in self-presentation. Bond and Titus' (1983) meta-analysis of other studies which used physiological measures of arousal supported Bond's finding regarding the direction of the effect, and concluded that "... the asymmetry of social effects within tasks suggests that speed and accuracy are not interchangeable measures of performance" (p. 282). They claimed that complex tasks were performed poorly, in general, with physiological arousal accounting for 3.1% of the variance, with subjects losing accuracy before they lost the speed of responses. Like Bond's findings, Bond and Titus' meta-analysis revealed that the speed of performance of simple tasks was facilitated, with accuracy unchanged, and that only .3% of the variance could be attributed to physiological arousal.

According to Zajonc (1980), the mere presence of non-evaluative others increases a person's level of drive, while Cottrell (1972) argued that it was only when these "others" could evaluate the performance that the performer's drive level rose. Bond and Titus' (1983) meta-analysis found little to support Cottrell's learned drive account, instead, favouring Zajonc's position:

> ... directional differences... (show) ... both across and within studies, evaluation potential seems to reduce the mean effect of the presence of others nearly as often as it magnifies the effect... (and furthermore) ... observer status does not influence social effects on complex performances (though only peer presence reliably reduces complex on the quantity), nor does observer status significantly moderate the physiological consequences of the presence of others (though only expert presence increases a complex performer's arousal), (p. 278)

and,

> ... Others who have the power to evaluate task performance should arouse more apprehension than others who lack evaluation potential, but (when all the evidence is examined) they have no greater effect on the individual's task performance or physiology. Expert audiences should arouse more apprehension than peer audiences. Experts may have greater effects on physiology and performance accuracy than do peers. Peers, though, have the larger effect of performance speed. Despite proponents' contentions, evaluation apprehension does not reliably sum with the presence of others to determine the size of social effects. (p. 283)

Cox (1990) suggested that Cottrell's (1972) extension does not contradict Zajonc's (1965) social facilitation theory. He argued that it was the "psychological presence" of the audience which created the arousal in the mind of the performer, and was not the evaluation per se which caused the drive.

One explanation which goes beyond the simple social facilitation paradigm and Cottrell's (1968, 1972) "evaluation apprehension" modification, followed from Borden's (1980) review of the literature. Performers, Borden reasoned, respond to the cues given by the audience proactively. These cues are able to create an expectation in the mind of the athlete for a certain type of behaviour (e.g., aggressive) and a particular performance level (i.e., superior or inferior), as well as affect the athlete's motivation level. This suggestion sits well with past research showing that the interactivity of the audience with performers has a marked effect on the quality and style of performance. The recognition that the audience's input (both verbal and non-verbal) can change an athlete's performance level leads on to the discussion of the effect of the home ground advantage.

There are three interrelated factors which suggest that "home ground" factors are likely to affect the performance of a team to a far greater extent than an individual:

- team sports usually have a season in which half their games are played at home and half are played "away", whereas individual athletes may never play "at home", nor even have a "home ground"
- spectators find it easier to identify and "bask in the reflected glory" of a team than with individual athletes
- team sports, due to the nature of the game, allow spectators to participate in the action (e.g., by loudly supporting their team, waving flags and streamers to distract an opposition player) in order to "help" their team to victory (Iso-Ahola & Hatfield, 1986).

There is, however, one occasion when an individual may experience the same "home ground advantage" support that teams enjoy, and that is when the lone performer is competing for his or her country. Raelene Boyle commented after her gold medal performance (and new Games and Commonwealth record time) in the 400 metres at Brisbane in 1982 that she "grew wings on her feet" when she heard the cheers of the Australian spectators, urging her on down the home straight. It is also not an uncommon phenomenon that the host Olympic country manages to secure more medals than usual. Not only does the home ground advantage work in favour of the home players, it can work against the non-locals. The media sometimes report golfers or tennis players attributing their failure to the distracting crowd, or playing in an unfamiliar or "hostile" territory.

The effect of the home ground advantage was really only first documented in the 1970s. Edwards (1979, cited by Iso-Ahola & Hatfield, 1986) analysed 349 professional and 577 US college football games played during the 1974, 1975 and 1976 seasons and found that the majority were won by the home team. Additionally, he selected 100 games from the 1976 professional football season, comparing performance variables for home and visiting teams but controlling for the win and loss records and concluded that the strength of the home ground advantage was at least as effective as a winning record. However, Edwards' examination of National and American League baseball games found that although 55.6% of home teams were winners, the home ground advantage was not a reliable factor in determining baseball outcomes and performances, since having a winning record was found to be more important than the venue.

The differences between sports was again emphasised by Schwartz and Barsky (1977, cited by Iso-Ahola & Hatfield, 1986), who "... found that the decisiveness of the home advantage varies considerably from one sport to another with the effect being most pronounced in ice hockey and basketball and least so in baseball" (p. 315). In support of this, Irving and Goldstein (1990) examined the extraordinary feats of baseball pitchers classified as "no hitters" and found a home ground advantage did seem to exist for these players in isolation.

Although many people believe that teams have a significant psychological advantage playing in front of their home audience compared to their visiting opponents, research shows that there can be a "home ground disadvantage", depending upon the time of the season. Baumeister and Steinhilber (1984) used archival data from baseball's World Series and basketball's National Basketball Association, and found that the home field was an advantage in the early games but a disadvantage in the deciding games. Further analyses showed that the home team tended to win when facing elimination but choked when facing final victory. The authors noted the dangers of relying purely on archival data, since their research was unable to include manipulation checks to verify hypothesised mediating variables. An examination of professional ice hockey records, however, showed no statistical difference in performance outcome for home teams in the early games compared to the final games (Gayton, Matthews, & Nickless, 1987). Gayton, Matthews, and Nickless attributed this to the different attentional demands of hockey compared to baseball and basketball, with ice hockey players rarely having the opportunity to adopt a narrow focus of attention associated with choking, compared to the free throw shooters in basketball, or the batters waiting for the pitch in baseball.

Social facilitation theory (Zajonc, 1965) cannot predict whether a home ground advantage will exist or not for a particular game, since it appears that other variables have an impact on players' performance. These are thought to include: attention (Irving & Goldstein, 1990); the "special relationship" between spectators and the home team; the level of aggression and motivation of the players (Iso-Ahola & Hatfield, 1986); and the importance of the game (Edwards, 1979, cited by Iso-Ahola & Hatfield, 1986). Naturally, the difference between the skill levels of the competitors is a major contributing factor to the determination of a winner, but these other factors have been proposed to affect a competitor's mental disposition such that an "upset" is always possible and that skill alone cannot always predict the winner of a contest.

A review of the literature by Courneya and Carron (1992) attempted to address the underlying mechanisms responsible for the home ground advantage. They proposed a conceptual framework for game location research that incorporated as many constructs as possible from the many theoretical interpretations (e.g., theories of social facilitation, self-presentation, ritual integration, and perceived social support). Five primary dependent variables were suggested, together with several secondary factors (identified in parentheses): game location (home, away); game location factors (crowd, learning, travel, rules); critical psychological states (competitors, coaches, officials); critical behavioural states (competitors, coaches, officials); and performance outcomes (primary, secondary, tertiary). The latter were defined as: primary measures reflect fundamental skill execution (e.g., penalties per game, free throws); secondary measures reflect the scoring necessary to win a contest (e.g., points scored, runs average); tertiary measures are the traditional outcome measures indicating the outcome of the contest (e.g., win/loss match ratio). Courneya and Carron (1992) concluded that a home ground advantage existed in major team sports but there were no differences in the degree of home advantage between college and professional sport levels. They claimed that the magnitude of the advantage within each sport is consistent and has remained relatively stable over time and the degree of the home advantage varies among sports.

To summarise this section on audience effects and the home ground advantage, the addition of a cognitive component to social facilitation theory extends its usefulness because it recognises that athletes are not automatons and that they are capable of evaluating and acting upon their own and others' emotional states. Research has shown that the disposition of the audience toward the performer can markedly affect the performance standard, and the benefits of performing in front of a supportive audience are thought to be at least as valuable as a winning record. Unfortunately, the effects are not equal across all sports and may also depend on other factors such as the time of the athletic season as well as the importance of the match, so the predictive nature of the model is reduced.

PRACTICAL IMPLICATIONS OF THE RESEARCH

Social facilitation research can help sport psychologists identify the type of stressors within a particular sport and, with input from the athlete and/or coach, develop a strategy that will help the athlete cope with expected (and unexpected) pressures of performance. For example, a beginner athlete would not be expected to perform maximally under conditions of stress (e.g., in front of an audience). Coaches need to expect these athletes to make mistakes under these circumstances, and help the athlete to understand that mistakes may occur and are part of the mastery process. An experienced athlete is likely to find that competing in front of an audience is arousing, and they will be unaffected by the extra stress (or revel in the occasion). If a flawless or inspiring performance is required in a pressure situation, the experienced athlete — not necessarily the most skilled — should be the one to whom the coach turns. The research also suggests that the performers who require speed and strength will respond better to the presence of an audience than performers whose task requires accuracy.

To be able to control the level of arousal required for the task under conditions of stress, players should practise their physical and mental skills in a non-stressful environment (i.e., at training) until they are mastered. Before they are put to the test in competition, these skills should be practised in conditions which simulate the likely competition environment. This is the sort of preparation with which athletes at the Australian Institute of Sport, and the various State institutes, are familiar. The identification of stressors and the development of strategies to combat increased and decreased stress levels are skills which should be taught to teams, athletes and coaches of all levels to increase their potential for success.

FUTURE DIRECTIONS

The social facilitation paradigm has been strengthened by researchers recognising the contribution of cognition to performance, such as Borden (1980), who built on the work of Cottrell (1968, 1972) to suggest that motivation effects (which act as the "drive") as well as evaluation apprehension can explain a performer's actions in front of an audience. Borden's work has specific applicability to sport research and deserves further attention.

Other recommendations for future research tend to continue, in the tradition of Drive Theory, to link arousal (and sometimes anxiety) to "drive", although the evidence of the importance of arousal as an underlying mechanism in the social facilitation paradigm is equivocal at best. For those pursuing this avenue of research, the use of multiple measures of arousal is recommended, but more importantly, a clearer conceptualisation of the role of arousal, as well as the means by which it is measured, are imperative. The examination of personality differences, particularly sport-specific measures of state and trait anxiety, and their effect on learning and performance in front of an audience has been suggested (Underwood, 1976). The development of multidimensional anxiety measures such as the CSAI-2 (Martens, Burton, Vealey, Bump & Smith, 1990) and the Sport Anxiety Scale (Smith, Smoll, & Schultz, 1990, cited by Gould & Krane, 1992) for state and trait anxiety, respectively, would greatly aid knowledge of the ways in which different types of anxiety are manifest under conditions of stress.

The impact of two new areas of anxiety research using reversal theory (Kerr, 1990) and catastrophe theory (Hardy, 1990) as theoretical models has not been examined empirically. These models recognise a cognitive element in the determination of the level of arousal (which, directly and indirectly, takes into account expectations, trait levels of hedonism, goal-setting style, etc.) that has been absent from previous anxiety inventories. Both of these models rely on the performer's interpretation of the situation, and have much to offer researchers in idiographic studies over the long term.

As Borden (1980) discovered, the substitution of "motivation" for "drive" in the Drive Theory is a useful extension to the model and provides impetus for a range of new sport psychology research and practices, including establishing levels of commitment to the task and teaching appropriate and realistic goal-setting strategies.

With regard to research into the effects of the home ground advantage, Courneya and Carron (1992) hypothesised that travel and rule factors, as well as the absolute crowd size and the level of aggression between "home" and "away" players, made a minimal contribution to any advantage. They suspected officials gave decisions which favoured the home team, and that competitors perceived their psychological states to be altered when playing away, compared to playing at home. They suggested specific hypotheses regarding their conceptual framework, noting that it was no longer relevant to identify whether a home ground advantage exists. Researchers must adopt the assumption that one does, and focus their inquiry on the "when" and "why" questions, such as selecting various game location factors and assessing the impact of each of these on performance outcomes, varying for home and away teams with different levels of each factor. Giving operational definitions to, and identification of, crowd factors to determine the influence these have on performance outcomes was also recommended by Courneya and Carron. An examination of players' cognitive states at the time of each game of interest (rather than relying on recall) is another fruitful avenue of research. Potential cognitive and affective states to be investigated include: anxiety, confidence, moods, expectations (Courneya & Carron, 1992), attentional focus (Irving & Goldstein, 1990) and motivation (Iso-Ahola & Hatfield, 1986).

CONCLUSIONS

By examining the literature, this chapter has identified those factors which affect how a person is likely to perform in front of other competitors (coactors) and non-competitors (audience). Behaviourally-based theories that account for performances, based on arousal levels at the time of competition, have been strengthened by the recognition of the role of cognition in performance outcome. Central to the approaches which include the role of the performer's view of the competitive situation is the perception of evaluation by audience or competitors.

Social facilitation research suggests to athletes, coaches and sport psychologists ways in which an athlete may be trained (both mentally and physically) so that arousal levels and cognitions are recognised and monitored, and sometimes changed, thus moderating audience effects. This helps athletes to produce a performance that is representative of their ability.

SUMMARY

This chapter discussed the dominant theoretical model for explaining how the presence of others affects performance which comes from the observations made by Zajonc (1965). Based on the work of Triplett, Allport, Dashiell and others, Zajonc re-phrased the features of an existing and accepted psychological theory (Drive Theory, proposed by Hull, 1943 and modified by Spence, 1956) to show that "the presence of others, as spectators or coactors, enhances the emission of dominant responses" (Zajonc, 1965, p. 273). The chapter then examined the three types of research that were inspired by this model, and found that while Drive Theory was an appropriate explanation for simple tasks and behaviours, it was limited in the degree of explanation offered for complex tasks or behaviours.

The chapter then considered more recent views, particularly Bond and Titus's (1983) meta-analysis of the social facilitation literature. It was concluded that the presence of others does impair the performance of a person carrying out a complex task (in terms of accuracy, to a greater extent, and speed), although the size of the effect is small. The chapter also noted that the presence of others does facilitate improved performance for a subject carrying out a simple task, but only in terms of speed, and not in terms of accuracy. It was pointed out that for researchers attempting to explain the mechanisms of social facilitation (i.e., the how and why of performance inhibition or enhancement), advancement will be slow until the performer's cognitions are taken into account, rather than an over-reliance on the overt behavioural and physiological signals. The chapter then considered Borden's (1980) "proactive performer" explanation, where the knowledge that the perception an athlete has of the audience's level of support affects their performance. Borden's conception has been supported by experimental and anecdotal evidence. This line of inquiry is directly relevant for the research into home ground advantages and audience effects.

The chapter then applied audience research to the home ground advantage which has been found for all major team sports and is a function of fan support. Teams that play at home tend to be more assertive in front of their home crowd, although their apparent improved performance record may stem from the visiting teams' increase in dysfunctional behaviour. Other factors thought to assist home teams and work against visiting teams include: the relative size of the audience, compared to the stadium's audience capacity; crowd hostility; and the audience's knowledge of the rules.

The chapter concluded with some suggested practical implications and future directions for research.

REFERENCES

Allport, F. (1924). *Social psychology*. Boston, MA: Houghton Mifflin.

Baumeister, R. F., & Steinhilber, A. (1984). Paradoxical effects of supportive audiences on performance under pressure: The home field disadvantage in sports championships. *Journal of Personality and Social Psychology, 47*(1), 85–93.

Bond, C. F. Jr. (1982). Social facilitation: A self-presentational view. *Journal of Personality and Social Psychology, 42*, 1042–1050.

Bond, C. F. Jr., & Titus, L. J. (1983). Social facilitation: A meta-analysis of 241 studies, *Psychological Bulletin, 94*(2), 265–292.

Borden, R. J. (1980). Audience influence. In P. B. Paulus (Ed.), *Psychology of group influence*. Hillsdale, NJ: Erlbaum.

Carron, A. V. (1980). *Social psychology of sport*. Ithaca, NY: Mouvement Publications.

Church, R. M. (1962). The effects of competition on reaction time and palmar skin conductance. *Journal of Abnormal Psychology, 65*(1), 32–40.

Cottrell, N. B. (1968). Performance in the presence of other human beings: Mere presence audience and affiliation effects. In E. C. Simmel, R. A. Hope, & G. A. Milton (Eds.), *Social facilitation and imitative behavior*. Boston, MA: Allyn & Bacon.

Cottrell, N. B. (1972). Social facilitation. In C. G. McClintock (Ed.), *Experimental social psychology*. New York, NY: Holt, Rinehart & Winston.

Courneya, K. S., & Carron, A. V. (1992). The home advantage in sport competitions: A literature review. *Journal of Sport and Exercise Psychology, 14*(1), 13–27.

Cox, R. H. (1990). *Sport psychology: Concepts and applications* (2nd ed.). Dubuque, IA: Wm. C. Brown Publishers.

Dashiell, J. F. (1935). Experimental studies of the influence of social situations on the behavior of individual human adults. In C. Murchison (Ed.), *A handbook of social psychology*. Worcester, MA: Clark University Press.

Djarvora, T., Ilkov, A., Varbanova, A., Nikiforova, A., & Mateev, G. (1986). Human growth hormone, cortisol, and acid-base changes after hyperventilation and breath-holding. *International Journal of Sports Medicine, 7,* 311–315.

Gayton, W. F., Matthews, G. R., & Nickless, C. J. (1987). The home field disadvantage in sports championships: Does it exist in hockey? *Journal of Sport Psychology, 9*(2), 193–185.

Geen, R. G., & Gange, J. J. (1977). Drive Theory of social facilitation: Twelve years of theory and research. *Psychological Bulletin, 84*(6), 1267–1288.

Gould, D., & Krane, V. (1992). The arousal-athletic performance relationship. In T. S. Horn (Ed.), *Advances in sport psychology*. Champaign, IL: Human Kinetics.

Hackfort, D., & Schwenkmezger, P. (1989). Measuring anxiety in sports: Perspectives and problems. In D. Hackfort & C. D. Spielberger (Eds.), *Anxiety in sports: An international perspective*. New York: Hemisphere.

Hardy, L. (1990). A catastrophe model of performance in sport. In J. G. Jones & L. Hardy (Eds.), *Stress and performance in sport*. Chichester, England: John Wiley & Sons.

Hull, C. L. (1943). *Principles of behavior*. New York: Appleton-Century-Crofts.

Irving, P. G., & Goldstein, S. R. (1990). Effect of home-field advantage on peak performance of baseball pitchers. *Journal of Sport Behavior, 13*(1), 23–27.

Iso-Ahola, S. E., & Hatfield, B. (1986). *Psychology of sports: A social psychological approach*. Dubuque, IA: Wm. C. Brown Publishers.

Kerr, J. H. (1990). Stress and sport: Reversal theory. In J. G. Jones & L. Hardy (Eds.), *Stress and performance in sport*. Chichester, England: John Wiley & Sons.

Kraemer, W. J. (1988). Endocrine responses to resistance exercise. *Medicine and Science in Sports and Exercise, 20,* 152–157.

Landers, D. M., & McCullagh, P. D. (1976). Social facilitation of motor performance. *Exercise and Sport Sciences Reviews, 4,* 125–162.

Martens, R., Burton, D., Vealey, R. S., Bump, L. A. & Smith D. E. (1990). Development and validation of the Competitive State Anxiety Inventory 2. In R. Martens, R. S. Vealey and D. Burton (Eds.), *Competitive anxiety in sport*. Champaign, IL: Human Kinetics.

Moore, J. C., & Brylinsky, J. A. (1993). Spectator effect on team performance in college basketball. *Journal of Sport Behavior, 16*(2), 77–84.

Sharp, C., & Parry-Billings, M. (1992, 15 August). Can exercise damage your health? *New Scientist*, pp. 33–37.

Spence, K. W. (1956). *Behavior theory and conditioning*. New Haven, CT: Yale University Press.

Triplett, N. (1897). The dynamogenic factors in pacemaking and competition. *American Journal of Psychology, 9,* 505–523.

Underwood, G. L. (1976). Social facilitation of individual learning and performance. *International Journal of Sport Psychology, 7*(3), 143–157.

Wankel, L. (1984). Audience effects in sport. In J. M. Silva III & R. S. Weinberg (Eds.), *Psychological foundations of sport*. Champaign, IL: Human Kinetics.

Zajonc, R. B. (1965). Social facilitation. *Science, 149,* 269–274.

Zajonc, R. B. (1980). Compresence. In P. B. Paulus (Ed.), *Psychology of group influence*. Hillsdale, NJ: Erlbaum.

C H A P T E R

8

TEAM DYNAMICS

KEN HODGE

In sport psychology the "interactional" model is often used as a general framework for examining social psychological issues in sport (B = f[P × E]: that is, Behaviour = a function of the Person interacting with the social Environment). However, the situational or "environmental" elements (e.g., team/group setting) have not been investigated with as much diligence as the individual or "person" elements of this model. Given that this "interactional" model is grounded in social learning theory it would seem logical that sport issues should be examined not only from a person perspective, but also from an environmental perspective, as well as the interactional perspective (Silva & Weinberg, 1984). Yet, sport psychology has been guilty over the years of an almost exclusive interest in the "person" and to some extent the "interactional" issues. On the other hand, the "environmental" aspects of sport have typically been relegated to the level of a means-to-the-end for understanding the individual, rather than as an important "end" to be investigated in their own right.

Despite this comparative lack of research interest the issue of team/group dynamics is central to many topic areas in the social psychology of sport, and it is particularly applicable to team sports (Anshel, 1994; Schellenberger, 1990). Consequently there is a need for more research examining the environmental, group/team setting influences on behaviour in sport. There is certainly no shortage of topics to investigate. For example, team/group influences are the basis of social facilitation and audience effects (see Pain, Chapter 7); while group setting influences such as team mates, the coach and spectators are significant sources of stress for many players (Schellenberger, 1990). In addition, teams/squads/groups play an important role in creating a "motivational climate" for individual athletes (Ames, 1992; Walling, Duda, & Chi, 1993); and groups/teams are important "socialising situations" since they act as significant reference groups in sport socialisation (Estrada, Gelfand, & Hartmann, 1988; Greendorfer, 1992). Finally, many sports are indeed team sports, so by definition successful performance of the team, and of individuals within the team, is dependent upon effective team/group processes (e.g., team motivation, cohesion, leadership, communication, audience effects). Even sports that are not team sports, such as swimming and track and field, are often organised to include team events (e.g., relays). In addition, most sportspeople train and practise in squads/teams even if their sport or event is an individual performance situation.

Notwithstanding the clear conceptual rationale for considering the role of group/team dynamics in a number of areas of sport psychology, it has been neglected for the most part in multivariate investigations. As Widmeyer, Brawley, and Carron (1992) point out, sport psychologists often fail to recognise that the group/team has a major influence on individual behaviour and also performance in sport. Many of the "individualised" topic areas in sport psychology, such as achievement motivation, competition, goal orientations, attributions, self-confidence, stress and anxiety, are directly influenced by group processes such as social evaluation, social facilitation, expectations by significant others, and team cohesion. Indeed, Widmeyer et al. (1992) conclude that the failure to examine the influence of the group on the individual excludes a major source of variance in the sport behaviour equation.

This chapter has a clear theoretical base, grounded in both pure and applied research (see Carron, 1988, and Widmeyer, Brawley, & Carron, 1992, for extensive reviews of this literature). Consequently, this chapter is readily able to provide the reader with links to "practice" and with applied suggestions for improving team/group processes and ultimately team/group performance.

HISTORICAL RETROSPECTIVE

> In a team sport I am a great believer in attitude. Now, how do you motivate a team, considering that all of us have so many different reasons for doing things? For me, that's where the fun was, getting all the players linked together and thinking as one in a game... It's always back to attitude. You can always improve your skills, as a player or a coach, if you've got an open mind, but at international level the key thing is mental.
>
> Lois Muir (NZ netball coach, 1974–1987)

In this section the historical literature regarding team dynamics will be reviewed as a precursor to a discussion of current research perspectives in team dynamics. Compared to other topic areas in sport psychology, team/group dynamics has been relatively under-studied (see Carron, 1990). Nevertheless, there is a significant amount of research, and some clear and important conclusions can be drawn from this literature.

INTRODUCTION TO "THE" TEAM

Most sport activities involve groups or teams. Even individual sports such as golf and lawn bowls are often conducted as team competitions (e.g., pairs, fours). In addition, athletes who compete in fully individual sports usually practise and train in groups or squads. So we need to understand how teams work from a psychological perspective in order to increase enjoyment, enhance participation and achieve peak performance. The issue of team dynamics is clearly appropriate for all athletes in team sports, but it is particularly useful for leaders (i.e., captains and coaches) in team sports (Horn, 1992; Murray & Mann, 1993). Finally, to be able to achieve effective team building we need to understand the principles underlying team work and team spirit in sport (see McLean, Chapter 16). However, before examining team dynamics it is necessary to understand the broader issue of group dynamics since most of the research has examined team issues in sport from a group dynamics perspective.

DEFINITION OF A GROUP

Cartwright and Zander (1968), in their classic work, defined a group as "a collection of individuals who have relations to one another that make them interdependent to some significant degree" (p. 46). The key requirements of a group are interaction, mutual awareness, interdependence and continuity over time. In addition, Carron (1993) states that "groups are dynamic not static. They exhibit life and vitality, interaction and activity" (p. 112).

A collection of individuals is not necessarily a group (Zander, 1982). The defining characteristic of a group is interaction and mutual awareness; group members must be aware of each other and able to interact and communicate with each other (Gill, 1986; McGrath, 1984). Consequently, a collection of swimmers who swim for fitness during their lunch hour is not a group — they are not necessarily aware of each other nor do they interact in a structured manner. On the other hand a collection of competitive swimmers who meet for early morning swim training is a group — they have a shared purpose (training for competition), they are aware of each other (they belong to the same swim team/club), and they interact with each other (they pace each other and share coaches and training programs).

WHAT IS A TEAM?

A team is a special type of group. A team is a group of players who have a well-developed collective identity and who work together to achieve a specific goal or set of goals: the goal(s) makes the team members interdependent to some significant degree. Miller (1992), former sport psychology consultant at the Australian Institute of Sport primarily working with team sports, claims that "a team must have a shared sense of purpose, structured patterns of interaction, interpersonal attraction, personal interdependence, and a collective identity" (p. 165). Membership of the team must be viewed by each team member as being rewarding and satisfying, and that such rewards and satisfaction could not be attained without membership of the team.

> Rugby is also the contentment of being part of a team which has through mental collusion and diligent training been able to coordinate its action to overcome that of 15 men with the same ideal... Rugby to the players is not just the game, it is the complete atmosphere surrounding the enjoyment of a team sport... Afterwards having shared such a self-inflicted stressful situation, what more human thing is there than to share and enjoy each other's company, especially if the match has been satisfactorily resolved?

> Graham Mourie (1982) (former NZ Rugby captain)

A COMMON ASSUMPTION ABOUT TEAM PERFORMANCE

"The best players/individuals make the best team": This assumed relationship between individual abilities and team performance is not always accurate. Simply summing the abilities of individual team members does not accurately describe the team performance. One must consider the team/ group process as well as individual ability in order to understand team performance (Gill, 1984, 1986; Steiner, 1972). For example, team motivation (Zander, 1975), team cohesion (Carron, 1982, 1988) and leadership (Chelladurai, 1984) are processes that have a significant impact on team performance.

General observation of any team sport reveals that few teams consistently perform to their potential. On paper, the team may appear to have the best players and be expected to perform well, but that is often not the case. Team dynamics research focuses on explaining why teams do not always effectively harness the individual abilities of their players for consistent team performance. One useful model applied in team dynamics research has been Steiner's (1972) model of group performance.

STEINER'S (1972) MODEL OF GROUP PERFORMANCE

This general model has been useful in providing a framework for team dynamics research in sport; it is expressed in the following equation.

Actual productivity = Potential productivity − Losses due to faulty process

Actual productivity (or performance) is what the group actually does. Potential productivity is the group's best possible performance given its resources which are relevant to the task and the demands of that task.

Process is everything the group does while transforming its resources into a product or performance (Gill, 1986; Steiner, 1972). In sport, process is basically each player's individual skill development combined with team work skills developed by the coach, including team tactics and strategies.

> It is essential for a team to communicate and work together as one unit rather than each doing their own thing and have limited success.
>
> Robin Dillimore (1992) (NZ netball player)

Faulty process is the ineffective use of available resources to meet task demands, and can result from two types of loss — coordination losses and motivation losses. Coordination losses include poor timing, team work or strategy. Motivation losses occur when all or some members of the team lack effort and desire (Steiner, 1972).

Steiner's (1972) model has been effectively used in sport to assess team performance (Ingham, Levinger, Graves, & Peckham, 1974; Latene, Williams, & Harkins, 1979). Nevertheless, while Steiner's conceptualisation of group productivity is a useful heuristic device it lacks sufficient detail to be able to fully explain and predict team performance. In particular, the general categories of coordination losses and motivation losses are loosely defined and difficult to operationalise for assessment in the sport setting. This lack of specificity poses a serious problem for explanatory and predictive research. Notwithstanding these problems, Steiner's model has been useful as a general description of team productivity. It is the role of team leaders and coaches to decrease faulty process by developing and practising organisational strategies that reduce coordination losses (i.e., team work) and maintain optimal motivation levels (i.e., team motivation). If you have been a coach or a captain you will know that this is *not* as easy to achieve as it sounds. So why do teams not always perform up to their potential?

RESEARCH ON TEAM PERFORMANCE

TEAM PROCESS AND TEAM PERFORMANCE

Steiner's (1972) model has been used to investigate the relationship between individual performance or ability and group performance (e.g., Ingham et al., 1974; Latene et al., 1979). The classic work commonly referred to as a precursor to this research is that of a French psychologist, Ringelmann, who examined individual and group performance in a rope-pulling task (i.e., tug-of-war). He discovered that the average individual performance decreased with increases in group size — this finding is commonly referred to as the Ringelmann effect.

Steiner (1972) interpreted the Ringelmann effect as being the result of coordination losses; that is, as the group size increases it becomes more difficult to coordinate effort and skill execution. However, considerable research demonstrates that the Ringelmann effect is primarily the result of motivation losses (e.g., Ingham et al., 1974; Latene et al., 1979; Hardy & Crace, 1991; see Hardy, 1990, for a review). This phenomenon is commonly referred to as social loafing. Social loafing means that the average individual performance decreases with increases in team size. Although the number of coordination losses may also increase as the number of people in the team increases, social loafing is usually not the result of coordination losses. Coordination losses may be part of the reason, but the key psychological reason seems to be motivation losses, especially social loafing (Hardy, 1990).

SOCIAL LOAFING

Social loafing occurs when the identifiability of individual performances is lost in a team/group performance, performances decrease because of the diffusion of responsibility (e.g., Hardy & Latene, 1988; Harkins, 1987; Harkins & Szymanski, 1987; Williams, Harkins, & Latene, 1981). When the identifiability of individual performances is "lost" in a team performance, performances decrease because each player has less apparent responsibility for the overall performance. If individuals believe that their own performance within the team can be identified (e.g., individual statistics, lap times, assists, tackles), and that they will be held accountable for their contribution, then social loafing typically does not occur (Latene et al., 1979). Therefore, players need to have their individual performances monitored and they need to be made accountable for their personal contribution to the team performance.

If monitoring individual performances can eliminate social loafing, then clearly other factors can increase individual effort in teams. Teams can provide social incentives such as peer pressure and social support from team mates. For example, studies in swimming have found that when individual lap times were announced (high identifiability), individuals swam faster in relays than in individual race situations (Latene et al., 1979). When lap times were not announced (low identifiability), individuals swam faster in the individual race situation than they did in the relays (Latene et al., 1979).

GENERAL IMPLICATIONS FOR SPORT TEAMS

Individual skill performance should **not** be the only factor for team member selection. Most team sports require high interaction and communication skills that are not present in individual performance. Also, motivation losses can be avoided by identifying and rewarding the individual and team work behaviours that contribute to desired team performance. Contrary to the common coaching cliché, it may be useful to put the "I" back into "team" so that individual contributions are identified and desired team work behaviours (e.g., positive communication, assists) are recognised, encouraged and rewarded for each team member.

⟁ TEAM MOTIVATION

Team work and team process are necessary but not sufficient for peak performance in team sports. We also need to consider team motivation if a team is to consistently perform to its potential. The basis of team motivation is the team's goal(s) and the team members' "desire for group success".

THE DESIRE FOR GROUP SUCCESS (DGS)

Desire for group success (Dgs) is a team-oriented motive or goal, the basis of which is the team members' desire to derive pride and satisfaction with the team if it is successful in accomplishing its goal(s) (Zander, 1971, 1975). Unlike the analogous "motive to approach success" (Ms) in Atkinson's (1966, 1974) model of achievement motivation, the Dgs is situation-specific. Like the Ms trait, however, the Dgs causes team members to set and strive to achieve a challenging goal(s).

The fundamental factor to consider in developing team motivation is the identification of **one** single, unifying team goal; that is, a goal that all team members agree upon and commit themselves to achieving (Larson & LaFasto, 1989). The team members have to freely agree to redefine their self-esteem to include membership of the team as being important to them as individuals.

Developing Dgs

To develop Dgs, or increase team motivation, first, emphasise a "pride-in-team" approach (Zander, 1975). With input from each team member set a unifying team goal and objectives to achieve that single goal (performance, not outcome objectives: see Winter, Chapter 10). Second, ensure that each member's individual contribution is valued and recognised by both the coach and team mates (Zander, 1975). Keep reserves and substitutes involved. Third, place strong emphasis on good leadership from the coach, and from the team captain(s) (Carron, 1982; Westre & Weiss, 1991). Fourth, actively work to encourage and develop team cohesion; that is, both social cohesion (team spirit) and task cohesion (team work). Fifth, encourage unified commitment to the team effort; team members have to be prepared to invest time and energy to achievement of the overall team goal (Zander, 1975). Expect and reward the pursuit of high standards of excellence. Finally, it is vital that effective communication is utilised to keep all team members informed and feeling "part of the team" (Yukelson, 1993).

> It helps young guys to come into a team containing players who've got it right mentally and to be surrounded by guys who've achieved and are successful . . . To be able to communicate and help guys through is one of the big things about team unity.
>
> John Wright (1990) (former NZ cricketer)

However, while the team members need to feel a strong identification with the team they also need to feel accountable and responsible for playing their key part in the team's success of achieving its unifying goal. This sense of responsibility is also related to the important issue of team cohesion.

COHESION AND TEAM PERFORMANCE

DEFINITION OF COHESION

Team cohesion is a "dynamic process which is reflected in the tendency for a group to *stick together* and remain united in the pursuit of its *goals*" (Carron, 1982, p. 124) [Emphasis by Hodge.]. Indeed, Carron (1993) concluded that the "terms 'cohesion' and 'group' are tautological — if a group exists, cohesion is present" (p. 112). Cohesive teams are able to ignore distractions and avoid disruptions while staying firmly focused on their team goal(s) (Brawley, Carron, & Widmeyer, 1988).

There are two general dimensions associated with team cohesion. **Social cohesion** (interpersonal attraction) reflects the degree to which the members of a team like each other and enjoy each other's company (Brawley, 1990; Carron, 1988). **Task cohesion** reflects the degree to which members of a team work together to achieve a specific and identifiable task (Brawley, 1990; Carron, 1988). The task is usually associated with the purpose for which the team was formed. "Most organized sports have successful task completion as the basis for team member selection and the organization of training" (Brawley, Carron, & Widmeyer, 1987, p. 283).

ANTECEDENTS OF COHESION

Carron (1982, 1988) has developed a model of cohesion that offers four general antecedents of cohesion: environmental (situational), personal, leadership, and team factors (see Carron, 1988; and Widmeyer et al., 1992 for reviews).

Environmental

These include potential factors such as the availability of team sports, eligibility, geographic restrictions, and sporting body organisational structures. Aspects of the social environment also play a role, such as family expectations, peer pressures and socialisation. Another social environmental variable is team size (Carron, 1990; Widmeyer, Brawley, & Carron, 1990). Brawley (1990) contends that team size affects the level of cohesion (i.e., small to moderate sized groups, less than nine members, have higher interaction and therefore greater cohesion) and the type of cohesion (i.e., task or social).

Personal

Each team member's personal characteristics influence the type of cohesion developed, and the "perceived cohesion" of team members (Granito & Rainey, 1988). Brawley (1990) reports that social background, gender, attitudes, ability, level of competition, commitment and person-ality have differential influences on cohesion. Significant similarity on any or all of these factors creates the opportunity for consensus on the goals and tasks of the team. Cohesion rests on agreement on these issues among team members.

> The first thing you have to remember as captain is while Rugby is very much a team concept you are dealing with individuals, who are all dif-ferent in attitudes, temperament and experience. Thus you have to find out each person's strengths and weaknesses... And you have to find out which players best respond to the carrot and which to the stick.
>
> Andy Dalton (1986) (former NZ Rugby captain)

Leadership The role of leaders is vital in developing team cohesion (Brawley, 1990; Westre & Weiss, 1991). Clear, consistent, unambiguous communication from coaches and captains regarding the team goal(s), team tasks, and team member roles plays a very influential role in cohesiveness (Carron, 1993; Yukelson, 1993). In addition, leaders who involve team members in team decisions (e.g., goal setting, selection of tactics) help to develop cohesion by increasing each player's feelings of "ownership and invest-ment" in the team (Westre & Weiss, 1991).

> Be a clear decision maker and give positive cues to team players.
>
> Sandra Edge (1992) (NZ netball player)

Team Finally, Brawley (1990) outlines the role that shared team experiences play in developing or maintaining cohesion. For example, common experi-ence of a series of successes or failures creates a "shared experience", and the act of unifying as a team to counter the threat of the opposing team can create a climate for increased cohesion. Moreover, Carron (1993) claims that aspects of the team such as team structure, position, status, roles, norms, stability and communication significantly affect cohesion.

CONSEQUENCES OF COHESION

While considerable research has examined the antecedents of cohesion, the focus of most research in this area has addressed the consequences of cohesion; in particular, the consequences of team performance and suc-cess. Although numerous studies have investigated the relationship between cohesion and performance success, the results are equivocal. Some studies have found a positive relationship, with greater cohesion leading to success (e.g., Ball & Carron, 1976; Carron & Chelladurai, 1981; Davids & Nutter, 1988; Shangi & Carron, 1987); while other studies have revealed lesser levels of cohesion leading to success (e.g., Landers & Lueschen, 1974; Lenk, 1969), and some studies have not found any rela-tionship (e.g., Melnick & Chemers, 1974; Williams & Hacker, 1982). The inconsistency in this research has led investigators to consider the possible mediating variables in the cohesion–performance relationship. Mediating variables such as satisfaction, collective efficacy and team motivation will be considered later.

Team motivation is another possible consequence of cohesion — team motivation is usually dependent upon a strong sense of cohesion within the team (Carron, 1988). Team cohesion basically means the tendency for a team to stick together and remain united in the pursuit of its goals (i.e., team work, team spirit, team unity). As mentioned previously, social cohesion (often referred to as **team spirit**) and task cohesion, which is the basis of **team work**, are two distinct and independent aspects of team cohesion. They are both important for the ongoing success of the team.

TEAM HARMONY: KEEPING EVERYONE FOCUSED AND HAPPY

Anshel (1994) discusses team harmony using the term "team climate" to describe team members' perceptions of the conditions and the relationships among team members. Team climate perceptions dictate the level and type of cohesion within the team and also have a major influence on team motivation and team member satisfaction. With respect to team climate there are a number of reasons why players are attracted to team sports and to particular teams. Coaches and leaders need to understand each team member's reasons for being involved with the team if they are to build trust among team members and effectively harness their skills and enthusiasm (McClure & Foster, 1991). Some of the major reasons are as follows:

- **Interpersonal attraction** among members refers to the level of friendship within the team. It is often the case that the stronger the friendship, the more cohesive the team (e.g., Klein & Christiansen, 1969).

  I'm very, very strong on team spirit. If the guys play for each other they do well. They don't have to be the best players in the world... A happy side is a winning side, and a winning side is a happy side... They should also enjoy their cricket. Sure it's a first class sport, but if they don't enjoy it they won't perform. It comes back to that happy thing.

  Lance Cairns (1992) (former NZ cricketer; Otago Provincial Cricket Coach)

- **Attractiveness of the team** as a whole refers to the benefit each player receives from being a member of the team. This is sometimes but not always related to the level of interpersonal attraction (e.g., Carron, Widmeyer, & Brawley, 1985; Brawley, Carron, & Widmeyer, 1987).

  ... only those who play a team sport can fully appreciate the sense of pride in belonging to a team of renown, the trust in the ability of your teammates.

  Graham Mourie (1982) (former NZ Rugby captain)

- **Closeness of identification with the team** refers to the extent to which someone describes herself or himself as a member of the team. The greater the sense of belonging, identification and team integration, the greater the cohesiveness of the team (Carron et al., 1985), for example, proudly describing yourself as a member of the "Riversdale Netball Team".

There is no doubt that I will miss Rugby and there is also a vague suspicion that nothing I may do in the next 10 years will cause me the same pleasure. The sense of belonging, of comradeship through a common team aim with its ability to meld many diverse personalities into a cohesive group is a rare thing; one which I imagine many people never experience.

Graham Mourie (1982) (former NZ Rugby captain)

Cohesiveness undoubtedly involves a combination of the above components and more as well. Indeed, thinking of team cohesion solely in terms of attraction is often not enough for consistent peak team performance. Teams form for reasons other than attraction. For example, the team goal must be compatible with each individual's goals, and a person may expect personal pay-offs or rewards as a result of a team's endeavours (e.g., selection in representative teams/squads, winning a championship).

CURRENT PERSPECTIVES

In this section the most recent research developments are discussed as well as the most promising theoretical perspectives. Finally, this current work will be used as the basis for a number of recommendations regarding future research in the area of team dynamics.

SOCIAL LOAFING

Hardy (1990) suggests that social loafing is consistent with the social facilitation phenomenon in that "evaluation" of performance is the key issue. In social loafing the absence of performance evaluation contributes to motivation losses, whereas in social facilitation the presence of others (i.e., co-actors) increases performance evaluation and therefore contributes to an increase in motivation (see also Pain, Chapter 7). However, the important issues of coactor/partner ability, cohesion, task difficulty, and the incentive value of the task need to be investigated further to determine the full extent of the complementary relationship between social loafing and social facilitation (Hardy, 1990). Moreover, social loafing may not be the only form of possible motivation losses in sport (Hardy, 1990).

It has been suggested that social loafing can be controlled so that team performance is maintained or increased (Hardy, 1990). First, the coach and team leaders need to develop ways to identify, recognise, evaluate, and reward each team member's role and her/his individual contributions to the team performance (see also Carron, 1988). Second, leaders need to seek to increase each team member's sense of responsibility for the team performance by increasing team interaction, commitment to the team goal(s), and task cohesion (see also Yukelson, 1984). Third, leaders should ensure that the team effort and team success is personally involving for each team member by developing a sense of team pride and a collective team identity (Yukelson, 1984; Zander, 1975). Fourth, systematic goal setting needs to be utilised for the team as a whole and for individual team members (Zander, 1975; see also Winter, Chapter 10).

THE RELATIONSHIP BETWEEN TEAM COHESION AND PERFORMANCE

Despite the lack of consistency in the cohesion-performance research, there is a definite feeling among those involved in sport that there is a connection between team cohesion and the quality of performance. The common assumption is that it is a direct and positive relationship; that is, greater cohesion is associated with greater success. There are at least two problems with this assumption. First, sometimes high cohesion is related to success, but sometimes it is not. The relationship is more complex than it first appears (Rainey & Schweickert, 1988). It has been assumed that there is a cause–effect relationship, with cohesion as the cause and success as the effect. However, research has demonstrated that this assumption may not always be valid. Indeed the relationship may be circular rather than linear (see Carron, 1988 for a review). Second, the relationship between cohesion and performance seems to depend on the type of sport task (Williams & Widmeyer, 1991). For example, East German Olympic and world championship rowing teams experienced success despite strong internal conflicts and minimal social cohesion (Lenk, 1969). The rowers had high task cohesion, however.

When considering the different types of sport tasks, one can distinguish between sport tasks involving independence, coactive dependence, reactive/proactive dependence, and interactive dependence (Carron, 1988; Gill, 1986). **Independent** tasks do not require coordinated action between individuals for performance success (e.g., archery, rifle shooting, triathlon). **Coactive dependent** tasks are those in which members perform similar tasks simultaneously and a collective performance contributes directly to team effectiveness (e.g., rowing). In **reactive and proactive dependent** tasks one member of a team initiates the action while another completes the action (e.g., cricket bowler and wicketkeeper; softball pitcher and catcher). Finally, **interactive dependent** tasks are those in which members are mutually dependent on each other (e.g., Australian Rules football, netball, hockey).

For independent, coactive dependent, and proactive/reactive dependent sports, cohesion and performance appear to be relatively unrelated (Carron, 1988; Gill, 1986). Nevertheless, recent research by Williams and Widmeyer (1991) has provided preliminary evidence that cohesion can be positively related to performance in a coacting sport (i.e., golf). For interactive dependent sports there is a clear positive relationship between task cohesion and performance (e.g., Davids & Nutter, 1988). Interaction between members enhances the opportunity for team success.

Finally, for interactive team sports, where each team member is dependent upon their team mates for mutual success via continuous interaction (e.g., soccer, Rugby, basketball, volleyball), social cohesion and performance also appear to be positively related (e.g., Klein & Christiansen, 1969). Social interaction between members in these types of team sports appears to enhance the opportunity for team success. Carron (1993) claims that "there is no doubt that even in individual sports such as golf, greater cohesiveness is associated with more effective team performance" (p. 120).

Nevertheless, even when cohesion and performance are positively related, the issue of whether or not cohesion is the cause and team success the effect is not clear. Indeed, the relationship seems to be circular: cohesion contributes to performance success, and with performance success there is an increase in cohesion (Carron, 1993).

Williams and Hacker (1982) have suggested that satisfaction may be a mediating variable between team cohesion and performance success. Both cohesion and satisfaction can be either a cause or effect of performance. Successful teams express greater satisfaction with participation, and a consequence of satisfaction is increased cohesiveness. Playing on a cohesive team may be more satisfying than playing on a non-cohesive team.

Carron (1988) in his extensive review of the group/team dynamics literature concludes that cohesion is a vital aspect of group and team effectiveness (i.e., success, performance). He states that: "An examination of the consequences of group cohesion clearly shows that it is an important group property worth developing" (p. 174). While the results of these cohesion–performance studies do not provide consistent findings regarding the cause–effect relationship between cohesion and team effectiveness or performance, Carron (1988) claims that "the overall pattern of results does support a conclusion that when groups are more cohesive they are more effective" (p. 170).

A MODEL OF TEAM COHESION

This model of cohesion is based on the premise that cohesion is **dynamic**; it develops and then declines slightly, renews itself and increases again, and then declines slightly (Brawley, Carron, & Widmeyer, 1987; Carron, Widmeyer, & Brawley, 1985). According to Carron (1993) this pattern is repeated throughout the course of a team's existence. Cohesion has a number of dimensions: "It is perceived in multiple ways by different groups and their members" (Carron, 1993, p. 112).

The model of team cohesion proposed by Carron et al. (1985) and Brawley et al. (1987) suggests that these multiple perceptions of the team are organised and integrated by team members into two general categories:
• group integration, representing each individual's perceptions of the team as a total unit
• individual attractions, representing each individual's personal attractions to the team.

Both of these categories of cohesion are assumed to consist of "task" and "social" aspects of the team. As Figure 8.1 demonstrates, team cohesion is considered to have four facets: individual attractions to the group — task (ATG–T), individual attractions to the group — social (ATG–S), group integration — task (GI–T), and group integration — social (GI–S).

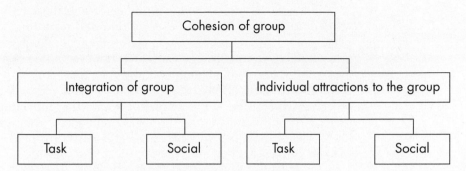

Figure 8.1: Conceptual model of group cohesion
Note: From *The measurement of cohesion in sport teams: The Group Environment Questionnaire* (p. 18) by W. N. Widmeyer, L. R. Brawley and A. V. Carron, 1985. Eastbourne, U. K.: Spodym Publishers. Copyright 1985 by Spodym Publishers. Reprinted by permission.

Group integration represents "the closeness, similarity, and bonding within the group as a whole — the degree of unification of the group" (Carron et al., 1985, p. 248). *Individual attractions* to the group represent "the interaction of the individual member's feelings about the group, their personal role involvement, and involvement with other group members" (Carron et al., 1985, p. 248). It is assumed that these four facets of cohesion are correlated due to the perceived interaction of the various task and social aspects of the group by team members (Carron et al., 1985).

These two important distinctions — the individual versus the group and task versus social — are vital aspects of this model of team cohesion. The model predicts that team members possess views of what personally attracts them to the team, and also how the team functions as a total unit. These combined perceptions help to bind the team into a cohesive unit. Brawley (1990) concludes that it is recognised that the four related dimensions of the cohesion model are likely to be the product of a complex person–environment interaction. The team athlete develops these perceptions over time during the course of a sport season(s). "It is assumed that the process of a team becoming cohesive is one that is dynamic and socially learned" (Brawley, 1990, p. 365).

Carron et al. (1985) and Brawley et al. (1987) developed the Group Environment Questionnaire (GEQ) as an operationalised measure of their model. The GEQ is an 18-item, four-scale instrument with demonstrated psychometric properties of reliability and validity (Brawley, Carron,

& Widmeyer, 1987; Carron, et al., 1985). It has been used to examine issues in both sport (e.g., Brawley et al., 1988; McClure & Foster, 1991; Westre & Weiss, 1991) and exercise contexts (e.g., Carron & Spink, 1992; Carron, Widmeyer, & Brawley, 1988; Spink & Carron, 1992, 1993).

COHESION AND COLLECTIVE EFFICACY

As Spink (1990a) points out, a number of explanations have been forwarded to explain the inconsistent findings regarding the cohesion–performance relationship (e.g., measurement and methodological reasons; difficulty in establishing causality); however, little research has examined the role of mediating variables in the cohesion–performance relationship. Spink (1990a) suggests that one such mediating variable may be collective efficacy. For example, he found that individual perceptions of team/group cohesiveness (both task and social cohesion) were positively related to collective efficacy for elite volleyball players, but not for recreational players.

Collective efficacy

"Collective efficacy is a term coined by Bandura (1982, 1986) to reflect the fact that groups often have collective expectations for success" (Spink, 1990b, p. 381). While Bandura (1982, 1986) developed the motivational concept of self-efficacy to describe an individual's confidence and expectations of success at a particular task, the concept of collective efficacy is the group level equivalent of such confidence and expectations of success. Spink (1990b) suggests that the desire for group success (Dgs) can be construed as a general measure of collective efficacy. Consequently, collective efficacy is a useful concept to employ in a discussion of team motivation. Indeed, Spink (1990b) claims that collective efficacy is particularly germane to the sporting situation as it influences each individual's choice of team goal(s), how much effort individuals will expend in pursuit of that goal(s), and their persistence in the face of slow progress toward the goal(s) or failure in achieving the goal(s).

Preliminary research indicates that collective efficacy is positively related to team performance (e.g., Feltz, Bandura, Albrecht, & Corcoran, 1988; Feltz, Corcoran, & Lirigg, 1989; Spink, 1990a). Nevertheless, while a positive relationship appears to exist considerable research is still needed to fully determine the nature of this relationship and to identify specific methods or strategies to develop collective efficacy. For example, collective efficacy appears to be more than just the summation of the confidence/efficacy levels of individual team members (Bandura, 1986; Feltz et al., 1989; Gould, Hodge, Peterson, & Giannini, 1989). If, as Spink (1990b) claims, collective efficacy is found to represent more than the sum of individual efficacies then the issue of **team cohesion** seems a clear area of investigation to pursue in an attempt to understand the relationship between team performance and collective efficacy. Spink (1990b) believes that the area of cohesiveness holds the most promise due to the commonality between cohesion and collective efficacy. Indeed, the concepts of cohesion and collective efficacy have both been linked to performance success (Spink, 1990a).

FUTURE DIRECTIONS

Brawley (1990) and Widmeyer, Brawley, and Carron (1992) outline the following "research pitfalls" that need to be avoided if team dynamics research is to advance significantly. First, there is a need to consistently base studies on a guiding theory or conceptual framework (see Widmeyer, 1986; and Widmeyer et al., 1992 for greater detail).

Second, longitudinal studies over the period of a complete sport season are needed if the **dynamic**, social learning aspects of team dynamics are to be fully investigated. Moreover, Widmeyer (1986) advocates the use of more sophisticated statistical techniques such as path analysis to directly examine issues of causality in longitudinal research.

Third, team dynamics research needs to investigate multiple aspects of the team dynamics equation concurrently rather than in univariate, discrete studies of single issues such as cohesion, team process or leadership (Widmeyer, 1986). Multivariate team dynamics research is clearly lacking. For example, Brawley (1990) points out that much of the research regarding cohesion focuses on **performance success**, yet the complex outcome referred to as "performance success" is typically dependent on far more than cohesion alone. There is an implicit one-to-one relationship being assumed when in reality team performance is dependent on more than one factor. For example, cohesion, tactics, strategies, and skill/ability level (e.g., Grove & Webb, 1990) all play a role in performance success. Consequently, it is important to differentiate the team's cohesive behaviour from other team factors involved in producing the desired performance (Brawley, 1990). This need for multivariate research applies to all the areas within team dynamics (Widmeyer, 1986).

Fourth, as Brawley (1990) concludes, researchers need to carefully consider the appropriate "unit of analysis" for their particular research question. That is, should the researcher use individual athletes on a team or the team itself as the unit of analysis? For example, the average task cohesion score for a team may be quite different to the "collective efficacy" for that team as a whole — the whole may represent something quite different from the sum of its parts. As Widmeyer (1986) points out:

> Recognizing that the group is more than its mean score is not only recognizing that variations in member characteristics are significant and that compatibility of member characteristics are important. It is also recognizing that the group exhibits properties of its own rather than simply being the sum of its members. (p. 186)

Finally, there is a need to study a variety of "teams"; that is, different sports, different levels of competition, and non-sport groups in the sport/physical activity environment (e.g., exercise groups, recreational activity groups, physical education classes, dance classes). Non-sport groups differ significantly from sport teams. Sport teams are unique and different from other groups since sport is competitive by definition, possesses unique and specified rules, is time-bound, and is formally organised via sporting bodies, clubs and leagues. Consequently, as Widmeyer, Brawley, and Carron (1992) state, "the study of teams alone leads to a narrow view of group dynamics in physical activity" (p. 177).

FUTURE RESEARCH QUESTIONS

Some specific question areas are still in need of concerted investigation. For example, the broad issue of team motivation is poorly understood, as are the specific relationships between cohesion and team motivation, and cohesion and the motivation of individual team members. Team dynamics during training and practice is another area of interest that we know very little about. Is the training/preparation phase for sport different from the competition phase with respect to team dynamics? In addition, we know virtually nothing about inter-team dynamics in sport — do relationships between opposing, competing teams significantly influence intra-team dynamics?

Another issue in need of investigation is the phenomenon of **team momentum**. Many individual athletes report the perception of being "on a roll" in the sense of gaining control, feeling confident, and capturing the initiative in the game, event or race (Vallerand, Colavecchio, & Pelletier, 1988). The concept of psychological momentum is defined as a perception on the athlete's part that she or he is progressing toward her/his goal. Generally such a goal is winning, although personal best performance is also a common goal. Vallerand et al. (1988) contend in their model of psychological momentum that such a perception of "progression toward the goal is associated with heightened levels of motivation and enhanced perceptions of control, confidence, optimism, energy, and synchronism" (p. 94). Vallerand et al.'s model posits that the crucial variable that determines whether psychological momentum will be perceived is the degree of perceived **control** inherent in the situation. One volatile "control" variable in team sports is the performance of team mates and the effectiveness of "team processes" — thus the possibility of a group level **team momentum** perception is one that needs to be investigated.

In addition, the related psychological construct of **flow** or **peak performance** in sport is one that has received considerable attention at the individual level of analysis (e.g., Csikszentmihalyi & Csikszentmihalyi, 1988; Jackson, 1992; Jackson & Roberts, 1992). Yet we know little about this phenomenon at the group/team level of analysis.

A final aspect of sport where a team dynamics perspective needs to be employed is the area of psychological aspects of injury. There is significant evidence to support the important role of **social support** as a mediating variable in the life stress–injury relationship (e.g., Hardy, Richman, & Rosenfeld, 1991; Petrie, 1993). Social support has also been recognised as an important facet of an athlete's psychological rehabilitation and recovery from sporting injury (e.g., Rotella & Heyman, 1993). Nevertheless, while social support has been identified as an important variable in this area of sport, studies so far have not directly investigated social support from a team dynamics perspective.

Finally, Widmeyer et al. (1992) advocate the development of a **strategic** research program in team/group dynamics, that is, the formulation of a systematic line of research questions to be addressed in a logical, hierarchical sequence. They suggest a three-generation hierarchy of research questions. First generation questions focus on one-to-one relationships — is "x" related to "y" ? For example, does a relationship exist between cohesion and performance success? On the other hand, second generation questions focus on the likely mediating variables or moderating conditions of the "apparent" one-to-one relationship. For example, **when** is "x" related to "y"? The third generation of research questions addresses the causes of these observed relationships which may occur under some conditions but not others — this level of research directly examines *why* "x" is related to "y". In order to develop this type of systematic research it is necessary to utilise existing theories or conceptual frameworks, or if no adequate framework exists it may be necessary to develop a conceptual model.

CONCLUSIONS

The literature reviewed in this chapter has provided a clear theoretical and empirical basis for links to "practice" and with applied suggestions for improving team/group processes and ultimately team/group performance (see Carron, 1988, and Widmeyer, Brawley, & Carron, 1992 for extensive reviews of this literature). Thus, this chapter has particular application to team sports and training squads (Anshel, 1994; Carron, 1993; Schellenberger, 1990). However, it also has implications for any "group" in the sport/physical activity environment — the practical focus should not just be on elite sport or on sport performance enhancement. For example, school physical education classes (Martinek, 1991), exercise groups (Carron & Spink, 1993; Carron, Brawley, & Widmeyer, 1990; Spink & Carron, 1992, 1993), recreation groups (Shivers, 1986) and dance classes can all benefit from the practical implications of team dynamics.

SUMMARY

As Carron (1993) concludes, "groups are dynamic, not static; they exhibit life and vitality, interaction, and activity" (p. 120). Sports teams are a special type of group, consequently "teams" are open to frequent change, growth, and improvement. The team captain or coach who wishes to exert some control over this dynamic team/group process and produce positive improvements needs to be aware of the principles of team dynamics outlined in this chapter. Team dynamics issues discussed in this chapter such as team process and performance (Steiner, 1972); social loafing (Hardy, 1990); team motivation (Carron, 1982; Zander, 1971, 1975); cohesion and team performance (Carron, 1982, 1988, 1993); and cohesion and collective efficacy (Spink, 1990a, 1990b) all need to be considered if team effectiveness and performance is to be maximised. The practical aspects of achieving this through "team building" are covered in detail in Chapter 16 (McLean, 1994).

REFERENCES

Ames, C. (1992). Achievement goals, motivational climate, and motivational processes. In G. Roberts (Ed.), *Motivation in sport and exercise* (pp. 161–176). Champaign, IL: Human Kinetics.

Anshel, M. (1994). *Sport psychology: From theory to practice* (2nd ed.) Scottsdale, AZ: Gorsuch Scarisbrick.

Atkinson, J. (1966). *A theory of achievement motivation.* New York: John Wiley & Sons.

Atkinson, J. (1974). The mainsprings of achievement-oriented activity. In J. W. Atkinson & J. O. Raynor (Eds.), *Motivation and achievement* (pp. 13–41). New York: Halstead.

Ball, J., & Carron, A. (1976). The influence of team cohesion and participation motivation upon performance success in intercollegiate ice hockey. *Canadian Journal of Applied Sport Sciences, 1,* 271–275.

Bandura, A. (1982). Self-efficacy mechanism in human agency. *American Psychologist, 37,* 122–147.

Bandura, A. (1986). *Social foundations of thought and action: A social cognitive theory.* Englewood Cliffs, NJ: Prentice-Hall.

Brawley, L. R., (1990). Group cohesion: Status, problems and future directions. *International Journal of Sport Psychology, 21,* 355–379.

Brawley, L. R., Carron, A. V., & Widmeyer, W. N. (1987). Assessing the cohesion of teams: Validity of the Group Environment Questionnaire. *Journal of Sport Psychology, 9,* 275–294.

Brawley, L. R., Carron, A. V., & Widmeyer, W. N. (1988). Exploring the relationship between cohesion and group resistance to disruption. *Journal of Sport and Exercise Psychology, 10,* 199–213.

Cairns, L. (1992). *Otago Daily Times,* 18 November 1992, 29.

Carron, A. V. (1982). Cohesiveness in sport groups: Interpretations and considerations. *Journal of Sport Psychology, 4,* 123–138.

Carron, A. V. (1988). *Group dynamics in sport: Theoretical and practical issues.* London, Ontario: Spodym.

Carron, A. V. (1990). Group size in sport and physical activity: Social psychological and performance consequences. *International Journal of Sport Psychology, 21,* 286–304.

Carron, A. V. (1993). The sport team as an effective group. In J. Williams (Ed.), *Applied sport psychology: Personal growth to peak performance* (2nd ed.) (pp. 110–121). Mountain View, CA: Mayfield.

Carron, A. V., & Chelladurai, P. (1981). Cohesion as a factor in sport performance. *Intentional Review of Sport Sociology, 16,* 21–41.

Carron, A. V., & Spink, K. S. (1992). Internal consistency of the Group Environment Questionnaire modified for an exercise setting. *Perceptual and Motor Skills, 74,* 304–306.

Carron, A. V., & Spink, K. (1993). Team building in an exercise setting. *The Sport Psychologist, 7,* 8–18.

Carron, A. V., Brawley, L. R., & Widmeyer, W. N. (1990). The impact of group size in an exercise setting. *Journal of Sport and Exercise Psychology, 12,* 376–387.

Carron, A. V., Widmeyer, W. N., & Brawley, L. R. (1985). The development of an instrument to assess cohesion in sport teams: The Group Environment Questionnaire. *Journal of Sport Psychology, 7,* 244–266.

Carron, A. V., Widmeyer, W. N., & Brawley, L. R. (1988). Group cohesion and individual adherence to physical activity. *Journal of Sport and Exercise Psychology, 10,* 127–138.

Cartwright, D., & Zander, A. (1968). *Group dynamics: Research and theory.* New York: Harper & Row.

Chelladurai, P. (1984). Leadership in sports. In J. Silva & R. Weinberg (Eds.), *Psychological foundations of sport* (pp. 329–339). Champaign, IL: Human Kinetics.

Csikszentmihalyi, M., & Csikszentmihalyi, I. S. (1988). *Optimal experience: Psychological studies of flow in consciousness.* New York: Cambridge University Press.

Dalton, A. (1986). In L. Knight, *Knight, Dalton, Ashworth: The geriatrics.* Auckland, NZ: Moa.

Davids, K., & Nutter, A. (1988). The cohesion–performance relationship of English National League Volleyball Teams. *Journal of Human Movement Studies, 15,* 205–213.

Dillimore, R. (1992). *Tips from top players.* Auckland, NZ: Netball New Zelaland.

Edge, S. (1992). *Tips from top players.* Auckland, NZ: Netball New Zealand.

Estrada, A. M., Gelfand, D. M., & Hartmann, D. P. (1988). Children's sport and the development of social behaviours. In F. L. Smoll, R. A. Magill, & M. J. Ash (Eds.), *Children in sport* (pp. 251–262). Champaign, IL: Human Kinetics.

Feltz, D., Bandura, A., Albrecht, R., & Corcoran, J. (1988). Perceived team efficacy in collegiate hockey. *Psychology and motor behaviour in sport — 1988: Abstracts.* North American Society for the Psychology of Sport and Physical Activity.

Feltz, D., Corcoran, J., & Lirigg, C. (1989). Relationships among team confidence, sport confidence, and hockey performance. *Psychology and motor behaviour in sport — 1989: Abstracts.* North American Society for the Psychology of Sport and Physical Activity.

Gill, D. L. (1984). Individual and group performance in sport. In J. Silva & R. Weinberg (Eds.), *Psychological foundations of sport* (pp. 315–328). Champaign, IL: Human Kinetics.

Gill, D. L. (1986). *Psychological dynamics of sport.* Champaign, IL: Human Kinetics.

Gould, D., Hodge, K., Peterson, K., & Giannini, J. (1989). An exploratory examination of strategies used by elite coaches to enhance self-efficacy in athletes. *Journal of Sport and Exercise Psychology, 11,* 128–140.

Granito, V. J., & Rainey, D. W. (1988). Differences in cohesion between high school and college football teams and starters and nonstarters. *Perceptual and Motor Skills, 66,* 471–477.

Greendorfer, S. (1992). Sport socialisation. In T. Horn (Ed.), *Advances in sport psychology* (pp. 201–218). Champaign, IL: Human Kinetics.

Grove, J. R., & Webb. S. (1990). Descriptive models for team performance in international baseball competition. *Australian Journal of Science and Medicine in Sport, 22,* 44–48.

Hardy, C. J. (1990). Social loafing: Motivational losses in collective performance. *International Journal of Sport Psychology, 21,* 305–327.

Hardy, C. J., & Crace, R. K. (1991). The effects of task structure and teammate competence on social loafing. *Journal of Sport and Exercise Psychology, 13*, 372–381.

Hardy, C. J., & Latene, B. (1988). Social loafing in cheerleaders: Effects of team membership and competition. *Journal of Sport and Exercise Psychology, 10*, 109–114.

Hardy, C. J., Richman, J. M., & Rosenfeld, L. B. (1991). The role of social support in the life stress/injury relationship. *The Sport Psychologist, 5*, 128–139.

Harkins, S. G. (1987). Social loafing and social facilitation. *Journal of Experimental Social Psychology, 23*, 1–18.

Harkins, S. G., & Szymanski, K. (1987). Social loafing and social facilitation: New wine in old bottles. In C. Hendrick (Ed.), *Review of personality and social psychology: Vol. 9* (pp. 167–188). Beverly Hills, CA: Sage.

Horn, T. S. (1992). Leadership effectiveness in the sport domain. In T. Horn (Ed.), *Advances in sport psychology* (pp. 181–199). Champaign, IL: Human Kinetics.

Ingham, A., Levinger, G., Graves, J., & Peckham, V. (1974). The Ringelmann Effect: Studies of group size and group performance. *Journal of Experimental Social Psychology, 10*, 371–384.

Jackson, S. A. (1992). Athletes in flow: A qualitative investigation of flow states in elite figure skaters. *Journal of Applied Sport Psychology, 4*, 161–180.

Jackson, S. A., & Roberts, G. C. (1992). Positive performance states of athletes: Toward a conceptual understanding of peak performance. *The Sport Psychologist, 6*, 156–171.

Klein, M., & Christiansen, G. (1969). Group composition, group stucture and group effectiveness of basketball teams. In J. Loy & G. Kenyon (Eds.), *Sport, culture, and society* (pp. 397–408). Toronto: MacMillan.

Landers, D., & Lueschen, G. (1974). Team performance outcome and the cohesiveness of competitive coaching groups. *International Review of Sport Sociology, 9*, 57–71.

Larson, C., & LaFasto, F. (1989). *Teamwork: What must go right/What can go wrong.* Newbury Park, CA: Sage.

Latene, B., Williams, K., & Harkins, S. (1979). Many hands make light work: The cause and consequences of social loafing. *Journal of Experimental Social Psychology, 37*, 822–832.

Lenk, H. (1969). Top performance despite internal conflict: An antithesis to a functional proposition. In J. Loy & G. Kenyon (Eds.), *Sport, culture, and society* (pp. 393–397). Toronto: MacMillan.

Martinek, T. J. (1991). *Psycho-social dynamics of teaching physical education.* Dubuque, IA: Wm C. Brown.

McLean, N. (1994). Building and maintaining an effective team. In T. Morris & J. Summers (Eds.), *Sport psychology: Theory, application, and issues* (pp. 420–434). Brisbane: John Wiley & Sons.

McClure, B. A., & Foster, C. D. (1991). Group work as a method of promoting cohesiveness within a women's gymnastics team. *Perceptual and Motor Skills, 73*, 307–313.

McGrath, J. (1984). *Groups: Interaction and performance.* Englewood Cliffs, NJ: Prentice-Hall.

Melnick, M., & Chemers, M. (1974). Effects of group social structure on the success of basketball teams. *Research Quarterly, 45*, 1–8.

Miller, B. (1992). Team athletes. In J. Bloomfield, P. Fricker, & K. Fitch (Eds.), *Textbook of science and medicine in sport* (pp. 165–175). Melbourne: Blackwell.

Mourie, G. (1982). *Graham Mourie: Captain.* Auckland, NZ: Moa.

Muir, L. (1987). In J. Romanos, *Great New Zealand coaches: Makers of champions.* Lower Hutt, NZ: Mills.

Murray, M., & Mann, B. (1993). Leadership effectiveness. In J. Williams (Ed.), *Applied sport psychology: Personal growth to peak performance* (2nd ed.) (pp. 82–98). Mountain View, CA: Mayfield.

Pain, M. (1994). Social facilitation. In T. Morris & J. Summers (Eds.), *Sport psychology: Theory, application, and issues* (pp. 173–189). Brisbane: John Wiley & Sons.

Petrie, T. A. (1993). The moderating effects of social support and playing status on the life stress–injury relationship. *Journal of Applied Sport Psychology, 5,* 1–16.

Rainey, D. W., & Schweickert, G. J. (1988). An exploratory study of team cohesion before and after a spring trip. *The Sport Psychologist, 2,* 314–317.

Rotella, R. J., & Heyman, S. R. (1993). Stress, injury, and the psychological rehabilitation of athletes. In J. Williams (Ed.), *Applied sport psychology: Personal growth to peak performance* (2nd ed.) (pp. 338–355). Mountain View, CA: Mayfield.

Schellenberger, H. (1990). *Psychology of team sports.* Toronto: Sport Books.

Shangi, G., & Carron, A. (1987). Group cohesion and its relationship with performance and satisfaction among high school basketball players. *Canadian Journal of Sport Sciences, 12,* 20.

Shivers, J. S. (1986). *Recreational leadership: Group dynamics and interpersonal behavior* (2nd ed.). Princeton, NJ: Princeton Publishers.

Silva, J., & Weinberg, R. (1984). *Psychological foundations of sport.* Champaign, IL: Human Kinetics.

Spink, K. S. (1990a). Group cohesion and collective efficacy of volleyball teams. *Journal of Sport and Exercise Psychology, 12,* 301–311.

Spink, K. S. (1990b). Collective efficacy in the sport setting. *International Journal of Sport Psychology, 21,* 380–395.

Spink, K. S., & Carron, A. V. (1992). Group cohesion and adherence in exercise classes. *Journal of Sport and Exercise Psychology, 14,* 78–86.

Spink, K. S., & Carron, A. V. (1993). The effects of team building on the adherence patterns of female exercise participants. *Journal of Sport and Exercise Psychology, 15,* 39–49.

Steiner, I. (1972). *Group processes and group productivity.* New York: Academic Press.

Vallerand, R. J., Colavecchio, P. G., & Pelletier, L. G. (1988). Psychological momentum and performance inferences: A preliminary test of the antecedents – consequences psychological momentum model. *Journal of Sport and Exercise Psychology, 10,* 92–108.

Walling, M., Duda, J., & Chi, L. (1993). The perceived motivational climate questionnaire: Construct and predictive validity. *Journal of Sport and Exercise Psychology, 15,* 172–183.

Westre, K. R., & Weiss, M. R. (1991). The relationship between perceived coaching behaviors and group cohesion in a high school football team. *The Sport Psychologist, 5,* 41–54.

Widmeyer, W. N. (1986). Theoretical and methodological perspectives of group dynamics in the study of small groups in sport. In C. R. Rees & A. M. Miracle (Eds.), *Sport and social theory* (pp. 171–187). Champaign, IL: Human Kinetics.

Widmeyer, W. N., Brawley L. R., & Carron, A. V. (1985). *The measurement of cohesion in sport teams: The Group Environment Questionnaire.* Eastbourne, UK: Spodym Publishers.

Widmeyer, W. N., Brawley, L. R., & Carron, A. V. (1990). The effects of group size in sport. *Journal of Sport and Exercise Psychology, 12*, 177–190.

Widmeyer, W. N., Brawley, L. R., & Carron, A. V. (1992). Group dynamics in sport. In T. Horn (Ed.), *Advances in sport psychology* (pp. 163–180). Champaign, IL: Human Kinetics.

Williams, J., & Hacker, C. (1982). Causal relationships among cohesion, satisfaction, and performance in women's intercollegiate field hockey teams. *Journal of Sport Psychology, 4*, 324–337.

Williams, K., Harkins, S., & Latene, B. (1981). Identifiability as a deterrent to social loafing: Two cheering experiments. *Journal of Experimental Social Psychology, 40*, 303–311.

Williams, J. M., & Widmeyer, W. N. (1991). The cohesion-performance outcome relationship in a coacting sport. *Journal of Sport and Exercise Psychology, 13*, 364–371.

Winter, G. (1994). Goal setting. In T. Morris & J. Summers (Eds.), *Sport psychology: Theory, application, and issues* (pp. 259–270). Brisbane: John Wiley & Sons.

Wright, J. (1990). *Christmas in Rarotonga: The John Wright story.* Auckland, NZ: Moa.

Yukelson, D. (1984). Group motivation in sport teams. In J. Silva & R. Weinberg (Eds.), *Psychological foundations of sport* (pp. 229–240). Champaign, IL: Human Kinetics.

Yukelson, D. (1993). Communicating effectively. In J. Williams (Ed.), *Applied sport psychology: Personal growth to peak performance* (2nd ed.) (pp. 122–136). Mountain View, CA: Mayfield.

Zander, A. (1971). *Motives and goals in groups.* New York: Academic Press.

Zander, A. (1975). Motivation and performance of sports groups. In D. M. Landers (Ed.), *Psychology of sport and motor behaviour II.* University Park, PA: Pennsylvannia State University Press.

Zander, A. (1982). *Making groups effective.* San Francisco, CA: Jossey-Bass.

PART

2

APPLIED SPORT
PSYCHOLOGY

Development of applied work in sport psychology lagged behind theory and research concerned with understanding sports behaviour. Applied sport psychology is the application of psychological principles and techniques to sport. It consists of a range of applications, where new directions are always possible. First, an area of sport may be addressed which has not previously been the subject of systematic psychological attention, for example, the recent interest in work with disabled athletes. Second, principles and techniques may be applied which have not previously been employed in sport. Performance enhancement and, more particularly, Psychological Skills Training (PST), is the firmly established area of work, with a substantial literature and major programs within the sports institutes in Australia and their equivalents in other parts of the world.

Part 2 discusses the area of performance enhancement, through psychological skills training. Chapter 9, by Morris and Thomas, overviews the development of applied work in sport psychology, examines current models and their limitations, and explores future directions in the delivery of services. Part 2 then considers major areas of PST in detail. In Chapter 10, Winter describes the role of goal setting in PST and more broadly in athlete preparation. This chapter refers to the theoretical base for goal setting and then considers a number of practical approaches which are soundly based on theory and research. Chapter 11 addresses the issue of stress management. Martin considers a range of techniques and gives examples of how they might be applied. Madden, in Chapter 12, examines ways in which athletes cope with stressful situations. Such strategies can be employed to help others cope more effectively. Self-confidence was not widely considered in the earliest applied work. In Chapter 13, Horsley examines the possible role of self-confidence and a number of techniques for developing it. Imagery has been recognised as the most widely used technique in PST with elite athletes (see Chapter 9). Perry and Morris discuss the nature of imagery, the range of uses of imagery and the practical application of imagery in Chapter 14. Bond and Sargent, in Chapter 15, present a variety of ways to develop attentional skills and be able to focus on performance relevant information. Concluding Part 2 is a consideration of the team. McLean, in Chapter 16, discusses team-building techniques. This is one of the areas of performance enhancement which has received less attention than it deserves.

Part 2 includes excellent contributions from the top practitioners in Australia, but it does not represent an integrated approach, which must be an important aim for the future.

C H A P T E R

9

APPROACHES TO APPLIED SPORT PSYCHOLOGY

TONY MORRIS • PATRICK THOMAS

The discipline of sport psychology has much of practical value to offer sport, particularly sports performers. Of the various functions that it serves, undoubtedly the most prominent is that of enhancing performance. This is reflected in the interests and professional activities of sport psychologists throughout the world (AAASP Newsletter, 1990; Salmela, 1992). Largely as a result of the efforts of those who are practising in the area and have developed effective psychological skills training programs, the role of the applied sport psychologist is now widely accepted and valued by athletes, coaches and administrators (Gould, Murphy, Tammen, & May, 1991; Sullivan & Hodge, 1991). Nowhere is this recognition more evident than in Australia, where the Olympic Commission responded to positive feedback from such groups as participants in the 1988 Olympics by appointing two sport psychologists to its 1992 winter games team for Albertville and five sport psychologists to the team for the 1992 summer games in Barcelona. The main roles of these psychologists were the provision of performance enhancement and personal development services (Bond, 1992).

This chapter first delineates the nature of applied sport psychology, thus placing performance enhancement and psychological skills training in context. In considering the breadth of applied sport psychology, the chapter reflects on the diverse developments occurring within the profession. A detailed analysis of approaches to mental or psychological skills training, as the most prominent aspect of performance enhancement, is then presented. This considers:

(i) literature which has presented each psychological skill as an independent area — a common practice in texts
(ii) accounts of programs conducted with specific groups of athletes
(iii) programs presented as packages of skills
(iv) models which attempt to trace the process of psychological skills training, typically in terms of a number of discrete stages.

The chapter draws together some of the consistencies and highlights significant contradictions in this literature on the application of mental skills training, and raises related issues or problems presently facing practitioners. The chapter then outlines a stage theory of professional development and considers the implications of this theory for the development of expertise in applied sport psychology. Finally, based on the foregoing analysis, the chapter proposes a number of future directions for the practice of applied sport psychology in the performance enhancement area and suggests several areas of research which should be addressed with some urgency. While this chapter attempts not to pre-empt the discussion of specific aspects of applied sport psychology in the second part of this text, it is hoped that it provides a context within which the chapters which follow in this section can be better understood.

NATURE OF APPLIED SPORT PSYCHOLOGY

Sport and exercise psychology is now considered by many researchers and practitioners to be a diverse discipline, involving psychological theory and research directed to the understanding of human behaviour in and through sport. As noted in the Introduction, *applied sport and exercise psychology* is just one part of the discipline, that part which is concerned with the application of theories, principles and techniques from psychology to the enhancement of performance and the personal growth of athletes and exercisers (Williams & Straub, 1993). There has been, and continues to be, a rapid development in the breadth and depth of applied sport and exercise psychology. Some sport psychologists have counselled in favour of tight definitions (e.g., Rejeski & Brawley, 1988), while others argue for this increasing diversity to expand professional development and opportunities (e.g., Morris, in press). Those practising in the area have recently been urged to contribute to this debate (Williams, 1994). The experiences of sport psychologists in the applied field have been a substantial source of issues and problems. Some new aspects of applied sport psychology have arisen as a consequence of the awareness of sport psychologists that a viable profession with jobs to offer must diversify its product. Some comment on the current development of sport psychology, especially in Australia, and how it relates to future employment is appropriate. This section, thus, discusses the major areas where practice of applied sport psychology is well-established. It then considers some fields in which sport psychologists are beginning to apply their skills. The section raises issues about current and future practice which are especially pertinent to future employment prospects in applied sport psychology.

Although occasional consultations for the purpose of crisis intervention in the case of a personal problem or injury rehabilitation may have occurred for some time in sport, the first substantial application of sport psychology was in the area of performance enhancement and this is still the biggest area of consultant involvement with Olympic athletes (Gould, Tammen, Murphy, & May, 1989). While performance can be enhanced by removing a personal problem or an injury worry, the most widely practised approach to performance enhancement is mental or psychological skills training. Research identified a limited number of psychological characteristics which appeared to be associated with peak performance (Highlen & Bennett, 1979; Mahoney & Avener, 1977; Ravizza, 1977). The psychological skills training approach instructs performers in a range of techniques which are intended to emulate these psychological characteristics. The aim is to replicate the peak performance state, based on the assumption that this makes superior performance more likely. The following sections will discuss the performance enhancement and mental skills training field in some detail. To put the performance enhancement area in context, a number of the other areas of applied sport psychology will now be addressed briefly.

Sports injuries cost the Australian community around $1 billion a year and injuries are still growing despite advances in technique, safety of equipment, new technology to reduce risks, physical fitness and preparation (Bond, Miller, & Chrisfield, 1988; Gordon, Milios, & Grove, 1991). A similar picture has emerged from North America (Heil, 1993; Pargman, 1993). Prevention of injuries would save individuals from pain and inactivity and reduce the nation's medical bill. Various psychological factors are important, particularly life stress levels, coping resources and social support (Andersen & Williams, 1988). Interventions involving stress management techniques, coping strategies and mobilisation of social support, for example, through education, can help. Faster rehabilitation would also achieve the aims cited earlier. Research is limited here, as noted in Green's (1992) consideration of the area, but there is preliminary evidence that some applied sport psychology techniques can speed up recovery (e.g., Ievleva & Orlick, 1991) and support for the application of psychology in sports injury rehabilitation from a survey of athletic trainers (Wiese, Weiss, & Yukelson, 1991). Whether it happens to an elite player just before the Olympic trials or to a daily jogger, injury in sport can be very distressing. An understanding of the psychological processes involved and a number of techniques which can help the injured person to cope have provided sport psychologists with a start in this field, but much remains to be done. Finally, an athlete may be considered by medical experts to be recovered from injury, but may still be unable to perform adequately. Psychological readiness for return from injury is an important consideration, alongside physical recovery. Rotella and Heyman (1993) discuss problems with psychological readiness to return from injury, but do not cite one study on this important issue. Kirkby reviews work on sports injury in Chapter 18 of this text. For those interested in more detailed examination of the area, it has developed sufficient lines of study to be the subject of two recent major texts by Heil (1993) and Pargman (1993).

In many sports, endurance, power, speed, technique or a combination of them is critical to success. As sports have become more professional and human limits have been pushed ever further, training demands have been relentlessly forced upwards. This has led to the identification of a new phenomenon called overtraining. Ironically, it is the sheer weight of training to be faster, stronger or more accurate which leads to a reduction in physiological functioning, a downturn in performance at training and in competition, and a negative psychological profile. A range of techniques has been developed or applied to minimise the chance of becoming overtrained and to cope with and recover from it. Again, prevention is considered to be preferable to cure. If it is not recognised quickly, overtraining can increase in severity to the state referred to as burn-out, which requires a much longer rehabilitation period and can lead to permanent drop-out. This area is not the subject of substantial consideration in the present text, but is treated by Henschen (1993) in Williams's (1993) text on applied sport psychology. Australian work on overtraining from a physiological perspective which includes psychological factors is being executed by Mackinnon and her colleagues (Mackinnon & Hooper, 1992).

Many sports performers envy the few who spend their early adulthood playing sport full time, that is, our professional sport heroes in sports like tennis, golf, football, cricket and basketball, and the elite "amateurs" with sports institute scholarships and sponsorships from big companies, like Olympic swimmers, track and field athletes, rowers, hockey players and gymnasts. It is only recently that sport psychologists became aware that all but the most astute of these suffer from doubts during their careers and experience serious problems in adapting to life after sport (e.g., Blann & Zaichkowsky, 1986, 1988, 1989; Petitpas, Danish, McKelvain, & Murphy, 1992). During their careers, many athletes worry about what they will do when their time at the top inevitably comes to an end. The ethos of many top level sports environments has focused on total commitment to sports success. Taking time to study, get work experience or career training would have been unthinkable in some regimes; perhaps considered to be an admission that one was not wholehearted about achieving in sport. The irony is that worrying about lack of career preparation could actually lead to inferior performance because of the stress felt by the individual athlete. In addition to the effects on the performance of elite athletes during their careers, many outstanding sports performers find the transition out of elite sport to be traumatic, as a consequence of the lack of career preparation. The degree of personal investment in their sport can also present problems for some athletes. Elite sport has been alerted to these phenomena now and responses are being made, such as the Lifeskills Education for Athletes Program (LEAP) run by the AIS and the Athlete Career Education (ACE) program of the VIS, but there is still much to be done in this field. See Gordon, Chapter 19, for a detailed review of career transitions and career training.

These issues of injury, overtraining and retirement originally came to light when sport psychologists became intimately involved with elite sports performers and teams. As discussed in the section on performance enhancement to follow, these practitioners found that often an athlete's urgent need was not for educational mental skills training, but for ways of coping with worries about a recurring injury, the feeling of apathy and staleness brought on by heavy training or the stress of approaching thirty and having no skills outside sport. Similarly, applied sport psychologists report being sensitised to the group dynamics in particular elite sport contexts. Once trust was established, athletes, either individually or as a group, often looked to the psychologist to resolve problems with coach or administrator or with other athletes, while coaches were concerned with disunity in their squads. This has led to an interest in the application of a number of principles of group dynamics to sports teams. Research and applied work is now well established on the facilitation of communication within teams, and between players and officials, the development of leadership styles that are most effective in specific situations, and the creation and maintenance of cohesion within teams. Hodge considers the basic theory and research on this issue in Chapter 8 and McLean discusses applications in this growing area of team building in Chapter 16.

The experiences gained from working with elite athletes also led to an awareness that organisational issues at various levels sometimes limit the potential of the team or individual athletes. Again, some applied sport psychologists have begun to address issues of organisational structure, training and competition schedules, time management, when and how to travel, where to stay when on tour or overseas, how to spend time when not training and competing, how to minimise the effects of jet lag, and so on.

The origins of sport psychology are in physical education and the promotion of physical activity as part of a healthy lifestyle for all. The focus has tended to fall on certain high profile elements of society, elite sport being the obvious one. Applied sport psychologists are now beginning to recognise the needs of others, particularly groups that can benefit from different kinds of psychological support to help them compete at the highest level and those who may require special support to undertake any type of physical activity. The feats of high-level disabled athletes match anything able-bodied performers achieve, as does their dedication. It is not yet clear, however, whether they require the same psychological support as elite able-bodied athletes, or when such support is best provided. The current state of research and applied work with disabled athletes receives attention from Hanrahan in Chapter 20. While youth sport, as the

Americans call it, has been the focus of substantial research in theoretical sport psychology, particularly with respect to issues of motivation, it has received little systematic attention in the applied area. Tremayne reports on the issues and current activities in this field in Chapter 21. Sport or exercise is prescribed in the treatment of a number of chronic diseases, such as heart disease, diabetes, and asthma. As Morris points out with reference to diabetics in Chapter 6, many lack the confidence to undertake physical activities, while compliance with regimens also presents problems. These are issues which can be addressed by practitioners in sport psychology.

It is widely recognised that the physical and psychological benefits of sport and exercise apply to everybody, not just to people with chronic illnesses. Research has indicated that, in addition to producing positive change in physical indicators of health, sport and exercise are associated with psychological well-being (e.g., Hayden, Allen, & Camaione, 1986; Morgan & Goldston, 1987). This appears to be the case with some clinically depressed groups (McCullagh, North, & Mood, 1988; North & McCullagh, 1988), as well as with those who are considered to be psychologically healthy. At the same time, there is a recognition that there are many barriers to adherence to exercise in the general population, similar to the compliance problems in special groups. Exercise psychology is becoming a substantial interdisciplinary area, with contributions from sport psychology and from health psychology as well as other areas of psychology. Sport psychology is currently playing a major role in theory and practice, as demonstrated by recent texts from Biddle and Mutrie (1991), Willis and Campbell (1992) and Seraganian (1993). The potential of this area for future applied work is immense. It is considered by Grove in Chapter 17.

Undoubtedly, new applications of sport and exercise psychology are emerging as this is written and those who practise sport psychology in areas not mentioned here will alert the discipline to their activities, but the examples presented are broad enough to make the point that there is not just one area where applications can be made and research needs to be executed. It is this diversity which holds out the hope for those enthusiasts of sport, who also have an interest in human behaviour and mental processes, to train to become sport psychologists in a vibrant profession in the future.

 PERFORMANCE ENHANCEMENT AND PSYCHOLOGICAL SKILLS TRAINING

Sport psychology was an established discipline, albeit relatively undeveloped, for some time before the substantive involvement of sport psychologists in performance enhancement at the elite level of sport. The study of human behaviour in sport was largely the realm of those physical educators interested in the application of a psychological perspective to physical activity and sport. They primarily aimed to understand this aspect of human activity, rather than to manipulate and control it. The desires of sports performers to achieve even greater heights than their predecessors and the various political and economic pressures for sport success on the international arena led to demands on athletes, coaches and administrators alike for higher levels of performance. In general, sports first looked to their coaches for increased success. The 1960s was a time when it was believed that superior technique, produced by the most knowledgable coaches, was the key to world championship and Olympic medals. Developing the best technique was thought to be the answer, but it did not necessarily bring that extra swag of medals. The mixed fortunes of this technique-focused approach led many sports administrators to believe that their athletes were not as physically well prepared as they could be. As a consequence, the 1970s witnessed the reign of the physiologists. They analysed the physical demands of sports and attempted to make physical conditioning work more specific to meet those demands. With increasing professionalism and specificity in the technical and physical preparation of elite sports performers, many athletes arrived at Olympics and world championships with superb technique and excellent physical conditioning, and still performed poorly.

Technique developments did occasionally give a temporary advantage, for example, the Fosbury Flop in high jump, the double-handed backhand in tennis or the high toss service in table tennis, but soon all the elite players would develop the new technique, modify or counter it. Similarly, some short-lived advantages have been gained by enhanced physical conditioning, such as the effect of training at altitude in middle and long distance running. In general, these developments led to elite sports performers, all over the world, preparing full-time to the highest levels of technique and conditioning, thus, ironically, producing greater homogeny, rather than the intended winning edge. Success still seemed to lie elsewhere. It was at this point that sport began to look to psychology for the mental advantage, as Weinberg (1988) later called his applied text on performance enhancement. Claims like "sport at the elite level is 90 percent mental" were soon heard from coaches and athletes alike.

When the sports finally turned to sport psychology to help elite performers attain their potential, few sport psychologists had ready answers. Most were academics who had been developing theories and executing research on the issues discussed in Part 1 of this book, most of which were not directed at producing the consistent achievement of peak performance or maximum potential by elite athletes. Often the theories and research were concerned with youth sport and mass participation, as was seen in Part 1 of this book. Otherwise, the population studied was frequently college students. There was little systematic research on elite performers and a paucity of work examining the efficacy of interventions used to enhance elite sports performance. Also, there were few published or widely disseminated performance enhancement programs.

Feeling the need to respond quickly to the call of the sports, some sport psychologists adopted an approach commonly used in their profession. To find out what psychological factors help athletes to perform at their best, they asked the athletes. The psychologists investigated the factors that were associated with peak performance by asking elite athletes what they felt and thought and did before and during performing at their peak. Mahoney and Avener (1977) employed a questionnaire approach with United States Olympic gymnasts. Highlen and Bennett (1979) used a similar questionnaire to study Canadian National wrestlers. Meyers, Cooke, Cullen, and Liles (1979) studied a university racquetball team, using a similar design. The use of interviews to address similar questions originated around the same time. Ravizza (1977) interviewed athletes from a number of sports about their "greatest moments". Loehr (1984) and Garfield and Bennett (1984) employed interviews on a large scale, involving hundreds of performers. The studies that employed interviews typically examined the subjective experience of elite performers in depth, to determine the psychological characteristics that occur during peak experiences in sport. The questionnaire studies, on the other hand, largely addressed the issue of what psychological factors distinguished successful from unsuccessful performers. They provided lists of behaviours, thoughts and feelings in their questionnaires and tried to determine those factors that distinguished between successful and unsuccessful performers, as operationally defined in their study.

Williams and Krane (1993) describe these and related approaches in greater detail. Such approaches appear to be based on the assumption that what the elite performers subjectively experience, think about and do must be the best psychological preparation for peak performance. They did beg the question whether these performers had reached the top because of other personal and/or social factors, regardless of their mental skills. Fortunately, the results revealed a consistent pattern. A number of characteristics were repeatedly associated with elite performance. These are summarised by Williams and Krane (1993) to be:

• self-regulation of arousal (being energised but relaxed and not fearful)
• higher levels of confidence
• better concentration (being focused on the relevant cues)
• in control, but not forcing it
• positive preoccupation with sport (through imagery and thoughts)
• determination and commitment.

Williams and Krane (1993) do observe:

> Thus, even though adequate cause-and-effect data are lacking, current thinking and practice in applied sport psychology tend to assume that level of performance is a direct reflection of the way one is thinking and feeling rather than that the emotional state is a consequence of performance outcome. In actuality, both could be correct: a circular relationship would be quite logical — that is, optimal mental states lead to better performance, and being successful enhances desirable mental states. (p. 145)

In any event, these characteristics became established as the main elements of the mental state which it was perceived that performers needed to attain as a basis for achievement of peak performance. That is to say, attainment of this mental state did not guarantee peak performance, but it made it possible, or even quite likely, that it would occur. The "Ideal Performance State" as Loehr (1983) dubbed it, was considered to be a necessary, but not sufficient, condition for optimal performance. It should be noted that, what quickly became the basic working principle for applied sport psychology in the area of performance enhancement, was generated from self-report questionnaire and interview-based research, using retrospective techniques. Substantial experimental research in support of these claims has long been lacking. The sports were appealing for psychological support quickly and it would appear that the view of some sport psychologists, at least, was that a positive response was needed for the successful future development of the discipline, particularly as a professional activity.

The major preoccupation of applied sport psychologists for some time to come was the development of techniques to increase those mental characteristics identified by the research into peak performance. Mental skills training was considered primarily to involve *stress management* for the attainment of the relaxed, but energised state; various *confidence-building* techniques, including positive self-talk and positive imagery; techniques to enhance *concentration* or focus attention, such as centring and attention control training; *imagery*, as a technique to see oneself in control, without great effort, as well as to mentally rehearse performance; and *goal setting* to increase determination and commitment (e.g., Gould, Tammen, Murphy, & May, 1989). Research on the efficacy of various techniques, particularly that done on competitive performers in their sports, has increased recently, but it is not clear to what extent it is affected by the perspectives which have pervaded the field for the last fifteen years. It is possible that the breadth of application of relaxation and imagery techniques in applied work could bias researchers to choose to study these techniques. While it may seem logical to determine whether these techniques work, as they have been the most widely used techniques, there may be many other techniques which would work much more effectively, but are not being studied, because the spotlight remains on relaxation and imagery.

Reflection and early experience in consulting with teams and individuals indicated that it is important to gain commitment from performers who are undergoing mental skills training early in the process. This is to ensure that the athletes understand why the psychological work on performance enhancement is important for them. This is a major aspect of what is called the orientation stage in a number of programs and models to be discussed. Presenting the characteristics as mental skills which can be developed, just as physical skills are learned, is one way of placing them in a context which performers readily understand. This approach also emphasises the positive nature of the process. Thus the focus of the training exercise is on developing new skills to optimise performance, not on finding ways to overcome problems or covering up for weaknesses. Perhaps because the term "mental" retains an undesirable, colloquial meaning, it has been replaced, latterly, by the term "psychological", to produce the phrase which is now usually employed to describe the core of performance enhancement work, namely Psychological Skills Training (PST).

The methods and techniques which have come to be standard elements of PST were, in the first instance, gleaned in eclectic fashion from a wide range of sources. These included other applied areas of psychology, such as behaviour modification (e.g., Wolpe, 1958), cognitive theory and therapy (e.g., Beck, 1967, 1976), and rational emotive therapy (Ellis, 1958, 1962), as well as from Eastern mystical traditions, like yoga and meditation, and even the martial arts. For example, probably the most widely used technique in PST has been Progressive Muscle Relaxation (Jacobson, 1930), which has long been employed in Wolpe's (1958) behavioural process of Systematic Desensitisation, as well as being a major induction technique in hypnosis (e.g., Karle & Boys, 1987; Waxman, 1989). The Relaxation Response, which is another popular relaxation technique in sport, was developed by Benson (1975) from his study of transcendental meditation and then adopted by sport psychology. Nideffer's (1985) process of centring emerged from his personal experience with the martial arts.

Thus, the central methods and techniques of the performance enhancement area developed in a somewhat piecemeal fashion from the urgent needs of the new practitioners. They aimed to create the conditions identified by the questionnaire and interview-based research, using the best methods of which they were aware. A number of characteristics of a typical PST program, which are, at least in part, consequences of this historical development process are worthy of note. First, many of the general approaches to PST which are reported in the literature reflect procedures associated with the development of particular skills, such as relaxation and imagery for stress management, or positive self-talk and imagery for confidence. However, there is little or no mention of how the techniques can be effectively implemented in practice, that is, during training and competition. Second, the specific way in which an intervention is to be learned and practised often reflects a consistency that is based on imitation of earlier monographs by more recent publications, rather than empirically determined principles. Thus, for example, many writers who describe relaxation procedures follow the original Jacobson (1930) approach closely, without questioning whether this is appropriate with active athletes. This then becomes the normal procedure, which cannot be questioned on the grounds of research, because little exists, being rejected only by reference to this consensual orthodoxy. These specific skills-based approaches are reviewed first in the following section.

A third characteristic of PST is the manner of delivery of specific programs, which often reflects the exigencies of the particular situation, as the second part of the following review indicates. Thus, it might be that administrators determine that training camps present the only opportunity for the sport psychologist to see the athletes. These only occur every six weeks, artificially elongating particular stages of practice of mental skills. Fourth, there have not been many attempts to produce a general framework or model for PST. Those models which have been produced tend to describe broad stages without referring to the actual procedures involved. Often the models themselves may be too general to be of great practical value. This is reflected in the third part of the review of approaches. Finally, it may be that the PST approach which emerged from the urgent demands of sport and the response of those sport psychologists who were prepared to try to put their skills and knowledge into practice, is not the most appropriate way to approach performance enhancement services. Some problems of the current approach are, therefore, identified and alternative approaches are considered.

APPROACHES TO PSYCHOLOGICAL SKILLS TRAINING (PST)

Information on PST can be found in at least four different types of literature. A number of sport psychologists have written texts on the performance enhancement area. Most of these are basic, often couched in lay language and intended for athletes and coaches more than scientific colleagues (e.g., Gauron, 1984; Harris & Harris, 1984; Orlick, 1986; Weinberg, 1988). Some adhere more to the academic conventions, being intended, like this book, for the use of students in training and colleagues in the profession (e.g., Williams, 1986, 1993). Practitioners have reported the nature of programs which they have offered to specific groups. Until recently it proved difficult to find an appropriate forum for the publication of such material. The development of applied journals in the field has opened one avenue for this valuable type of communication, as exemplified by the papers in special issues (e.g., Botterill, 1990, Gordon, 1990; Gould, Tammen, Murphy, & May, 1989; Halliwell, 1989, 1990; Loehr, 1990; Nideffer, 1989; Orlick, 1989). Some practitioners have published the materials developed in their PST programs, providing athletes, coaches and sport psychologists with training manuals, worksheets, audiocassettes and videotapes. Although there is great diversity in these training materials, they nevertheless represent another useful source of information on PST. General models have been proposed in a range of contexts, occasionally, but not frequently, within texts, sometimes in a wider ranging review of the field, and, again, only rarely in specific papers (e.g., Boutcher & Rotella, 1987; Martens, 1987; Morris, 1991, 1992; Thomas, 1990; Vealey, 1988.) These four types of literature reflect rather different approaches and are, thus, considered separately.

SKILLS WITHOUT A FRAMEWORK

Much of the applied sport psychology literature, at least until relatively recently, consisted of texts written by eminent or high-profile sport psychologists, especially those with strong credentials of practice in the elite sphere. Sachs (1991) produced a useful bibliography of sources in the area. Although various approaches have been adopted in these books to retain the reader's attention or to make books more readily applicable, typically the basic structure is to assign one, occasionally two, chapters to each of the major areas identified in the peak performance literature. Usually this material includes an explanation of the importance of the characteristic, whether it be anxiety or attention, in optimal sports performance, followed by a description of a number of techniques to enhance the athlete's functioning in terms of that characteristic, often with examples. Some or all of the techniques might then be presented in the form of exercises.

Frequently, it is at this point that the book leaves that topic. The exercises are usually to be done outside the sport context. There is little guidance as to how to integrate the techniques into practice or competition, also, aside from whatever examples of typical situations are used to explain the importance of the skill for optimal functioning, it is not made very clear when to use the technique. Many of these texts have been pioneering work, providing thorough and well-informed material as far as they go, but they miss an important link between the development of the basic skill and its effective application in that performer's sport context (e.g., Gauron, 1984; Harris & Harris, 1984). Weinberg (1987) writes specifically in the context of tennis and, as such, his examples are more relevant to practice, but the text still stops short in many cases. Orlick (1986), as much as anyone spends time considering more specific implementation, with chapters on mental plans, pre-competition plan, competition focus plan, pre-competition refocusing, refocusing at the event and implementing the plans. Williams's (1986) book *Applied sport psychology: Personal growth to peak performance* was widely accepted as the outstanding academic text on applied sport psychology. It included a chapter, Chapter 20, on the implementation of psychological skills training, written by Williams herself, but even this seemed to skirt the nuts and bolts of implementation, preferring to concentrate on general principles. It is interesting that in the excellent second edition of the text (Williams, 1993), that chapter is co-authored with Weinberg and does contain much more specific detail on the integration and implementation of PST programs (Weinberg & Williams, 1993).

Perhaps the evolution of that chapter over no more than seven or eight years illustrates the rapid development of applied sport psychology in the 1980s, at least in the premier area of psychological skills training. It may also reflect the more critical and analytical literature emanating from the new applied journals. The heart of Williams's (1993) three part text, Part 2 on "Mental training for performance enhancement", provides perhaps the strongest evidence available that the peak performance based approach still dominates PST. Following an updated version of the chapter on psychological characteristics of peak performance (Williams & Krane, 1993) and one on awareness in athletics (Ravizza, 1993), chapters consider goal setting, arousal, stress and relaxation, imagery, confidence, and attention, before concluding with the implementation chapter. While updated, these chapters reflect little change in the orthodoxy. For some time it has been recognised that there is a need for field-based research on PST, using competitive athletes as subjects. The advent of the applied journals encourages such research and provides a forum for its dissemination. Intervention-based research is now increasing and there is a body of literature on each psychological skill. Nonetheless, it is difficult to draw any firm conclusions on the optimal conditions for the application of any of the psychological skills or to confidently identify the mechanisms upon which their action is based. There is room for much more research on PST, particularly carefully designed and theoretically based work. Understanding the underlying mechanisms of psychological skills well will provide the most flexible and adaptable interventions.

SPECIFIC PROGRAMS

For many years, there was little alternative to the publication of a text as a means to present ideas about applied work or reports of practice. The major journals in the field, the *Journal of Sport Psychology* and the *International Journal of Sport Psychology*, were primarily empirical in nature, reporting formal research. Much of that research, moreover, did not address applied issues. The need for publications which encouraged discussion of topics relevant to applied sport psychology was recognised in the late 1980s by the International Society of Sport Psychology, which became affiliated with *The Sport Psychologist (TSP)* from its inception in 1987, and the Association for the Advancement of Applied Sport Psychology, which began publication of the *Journal of Applied Sport Psychology* in 1989. *The Sport Psychologist* included major sections specifically for Applied Research, which often involves evaluation of programs or techniques, and Professional Practice, which encourages the report of innovative programs, packages or methods, with no requirement to include a research or evaluation component. The early issues of the *Journal of Applied Sport Psychology* addressed the status of sport psychology around the world and specific issues, such as training stress and gender in sport. More recently it has focused on such issues as flow in sport and applying social psychological theories to health and exercise.

Typical of the content of *TSP* is the applied research paper by Gould, Murphy, Tammen, and May (1991) which evaluated the effectiveness of sport psychologists associated with the United States Olympic effort in Seoul in 1988. This research was able to report that individualising sport psychology strategies was considered to be important by athletes and administrators, as well as by sport psychologists and other sport scientists.

Drawing on athletes' strengths was seen to be a positive characteristic of consultants, as was fitting in with the team. That research was able to throw light on the applied process by evaluating a cross-section of sport psychologists operating at the highest level, whereas other research has examined specific programs. Elko and Ostrow (1991) investigated the effects of a Rational-Emotive Therapy (RET) program on the anxiety levels of female gymnasts. A single-case design was used, allowing flexibility in the application of RET and monitoring of the effects of the program in the competitive setting. Although RET principles are widely used in sport psychology, few studies have examined a formal program and the originator, Ellis (1958, 1962), typically receives no formal recognition for the use of his techniques. Elko and Ostrow (1991) selected high anxiety gymnasts as subjects and were able to show that the RET program reduced cognitive anxiety in five of the six gymnasts, while not affecting somatic anxiety.

Ravizza and Osborne's (1991) description of the University of Nebraska football team's "3 R's" pre-performance routine exemplifies contributions to the Professional Practice section of *TSP*. The 3 Rs, refers to "Ready", a cue to focus attention, "Respond", switch to automatic response, and "Refocus", a brief period to review the play, including acknowledging positive and negative feelings, and then move on to the next play. Ravizza and Osborne (1991) go on to apply this routine in a "one-play-at-a-time" (p. 260) technique, describing a number of typical situations where it can enhance performance, such as dwelling on mistakes, coping with distractions and not paying attention in a huddle.

Particularly interesting in the context of the present discussion are the special theme issues published by *TSP*. In 1989, the journal dedicated a whole issue to the delivery of sport psychology services at the two 1988 Olympic Games in Calgary and Seoul. To start the issue, Gould, Tammen, Murphy, and May (1989) presented a general examination of services and to end it Murphy and Ferrante (1989) described the on-site services at the Summer Games, a somewhat different situation, where a small number of sport psychologists are thrown together with a large number of athletes, with most of whom they are not familiar, in the most intense cauldron of sport on earth. In between, there were papers on the specific Olympic preparation programs offered to the Canadian sailing team (Halliwell, 1989), the U.S.A. Alpine ski team (May & Brown, 1989), the U.S.A. women's volleyball team (Gipson, McKenzie, & Lowe, 1989), the Canadian men's gymnastics team (Salmela, 1989), the U.S.A. track and field team (Nideffer, 1989), and the U.S.A. women's gymnastics team (Gordin & Henschen, 1989). Orlick (1989) also contributed a paper based on his experience with "athletes in a dozen different sports over the past 2 Olympic games" (p. 358). Most of these papers discussed the philosophy underlying their service delivery, the range of services provided and problems they encountered, as well as giving specific details of programs.

A year later, the December 1990 issue of *TSP* was devoted to working with professional athletes. A brief, similar in general to that followed by the Olympic contributors, was given to the nine authors. Several contributors wrote papers specific to one sport, these being about baseball (Dorfman, 1990; Ravizza, 1990; Smith & Johnson, 1990), ice hockey (Botterill, 1990; Halliwell, 1990) and tennis (Loehr, 1990). Two authors reported on their work across a number of athletes, teams and sports (Neff, 1990; Rotella, 1990). The final paper was also sport specific; it was about cricket and was by the only Australian-based sport psychologist to make a contribution to these special issues, Gordon (1990), who discussed his work with the West Australian team.

The two sets of papers collected in the *TSP* on Olympic preparation (*TSP,* December 1989) and working with professionals (*TSP,* December 1990) do represent a rich source of information on the thoughts and practices of highly experienced applied sport psychologists in Western sport. The contributors were asked to comment on a number of issues including their service philosophy, their use of psychological tests, the manner in which they gained entry, group versus individual work, use of a model or program, sport psychology philosophy, their effectiveness, problems they have encountered, and the services they offer. Gould et al. (1989), in the first paper of the Olympic issue, report that a survey of all sport psychologists working with US Olympic squads at that time indicated that performance enhancement was their most frequent occupation, although crisis intervention, counselling for personal (non-sport) problems, dealing with injuries and counselling on careers and retirement were growing. In the rest of that issue, and its equivalent on professional sport, mental skills training repeatedly appears as a central aspect of the sport psychologist's role. The papers reveal a number of other interesting patterns.

Over 76% of the contributors claimed to employ an educational philosophy of sport psychology, based on athletes' learning skills. The style of work described in the four papers which did not mention the word "educational", suggested that education played a major role. Four of the educational sport psychology papers indicated that clinical work was also done, but played a subsidiary role, while two said the same about the organisational perspective. Most of the educational sport psychologists commented on the need for a sound referral system for the infrequent occasions when they did identify clinical problems.

It was noteworthy that more than half of the sport psychologists who commented on the use of psychological tests, indicated that they avoided the use of formal tests, although several did acknowledge employing their own customised questionnaires, mainly on pre-performance and performance behaviours, thoughts and feelings. Reasons commonly given were that tests were not effective, that the athletes did not like them or were turned off by them, that a lot of testing wasted valuable time, and that more could be got from interviews and observation, the preferred methods, especially when a feeling of trust had developed. Three more contributors, including the test's author, cited only one test, Nideffer's (1976) Test of Attentional and Interpersonal Style (TAIS) and only two papers referred to more than two tests. It is perhaps surprising that there has not been more debate in the literature about the value of psychological tests following these revelations. They certainly suggest limited scope for formal psycho-metrics in applied work, while others have questioned the validity of such major tests as Nideffer's (1976) Test of Attentional and Interpersonal Style (TAIS) (e.g., Ford & Summers, 1992; Summers, Miller, & Ford, 1991) and Mahoney, Gabriel, and Perkins' (1987) Psychological Skills Inventory for Sport (Hardy & Nelson, 1992) for use in research. It may also appear to be somewhat at odds with the survey findings of Gould et al. (1989). They listed five tests which were those most widely used by their sample of 44 consultants, of whom nearly 20% used the TAIS and around 10% used the PSIS, giving them very high usefulness ratings of 8.0 and 8.8 respectively on a ten point scale. Approximately a quarter of their sample reported using McNair, Lorr, and Droppleman's (1971) Profile of Mood States (POMS), which was mentioned by only one contributor in the two *TSP* issues. The other two tests referred to in the survey results of Gould et al. (1989) were Martens' (1975) Sport Competition Anxiety Test (SCAT), used by nearly 19% of respondents and the Competitive State Anxiety Inventory-2 (CSAI-2) developed by Martens, Burton, Vealey, Bump, and Smith (1983), which was used by 14% of these Olympic applied sport psychologists. Neither of these tests is mentioned by any of the consultants writing in the same issue as Gould et al. (1989) or the next year's professional issue. Presumably, those who contributed to the two special issues were invited because of a recognition that they are among the leading and most expe-rienced exponents of applied sport psychology. They represent at least an overlap with the Gould et al. (1989) sample, if not a subset of it. Their views on the value of psychological tests, however, appear to vary from those of some of their colleagues, who are also working with elite performers and teams in North America. This may arise because the individual contributors were typically the most experienced practitioners. Their reliance on more intuitive and interpretive methods is consistent with a theory of expertise to be proposed later in the present chapter.

When asked to compare a group approach to the delivery of sport psy-chology services with individual or one-to-one work, only Gipson et al. (1989) wholeheartedly supported group work, while Gordin and Henschen (1989) and Rotella (1990) saw a role for both. Neff (1990) adopted some small group practices, Botterill (1990) used groups at the start of a consultancy and Loehr (1990) used them with large tennis school numbers, but not with the top professional players. All the other consultants operated primarily on a one-to-one basis. Gordon (1990) acknowledged using group sessions earlier in his consultancy career, but stated that, from experience, he now preferred working with performers individually. Many of the contributors to the special issues stressed the importance to the success of their work, of developing a relationship with individual athletes. They referred to the need for trust and honesty, as well as confidentiality, all of which are likely to be more readily generated in one-to-one consultations. In addition, a number of authors emphasised the need to individualise or personalise programs offered to elite per-formers, who all have their unique needs.

The use of one-to-one consultations and individualised programs is consistent with another pattern clearly shown in the descriptions of their work by the experts contributing to these special journal issues. Very few of the papers proposed structured programs or models for the delivery of performance enhancement or mental skills training work to elite Olympic or professional sports. Orlick (1989) claimed that he entered consultancy contexts with no preconceived ideas, Ravizza (1990) stressed the need for flexibility and Rotella (1990) talked about "going with the flow" (p. 416). Some appeared to allow the program to emerge, such as Halliwell (1989), who arrived at an 18 part Olympic Preparation Plan for the Canadian sailors and Salmela (1989), who developed a Paired Psychological Skills Program for Canadian male gymnasts.

A number of consultants produced models for the presentation of the areas of training available in at least a part of their program. Several of these (e.g., Gipson et al., 1989; Orlick, 1989; Salmela, 1989) were based on Orlick's (1986) book *Psyching for sport* and the accompanying coaches' workbook. Paradoxically, in view of his "no preconceived ideas" philosophy of practice, Orlick's books probably provide the clearest frameworks for the application of mental skills training. Smith and Johnson (1990) adopted a goal-setting approach, involving technical and psychological goals, Halliwell (1990), in his work with professional ice hockey players adopted an "ICE" model, where intensity, intelligence, concentration, confidence, composure, control, emotion, enthusiasm and enjoyment were mental skills introduced through the word ice, so central to these athletes' interests.

Gordon (1990) presents a substantial model of services presented to the Western Australian cricket team. This covered a range of "Life Domains" of which cricket was only one. Cricket then divided into three "Skill Areas", physical/technical/tactical, "hidden curriculum", such as sleeping and eating behaviour and travel skills, and the mental area. Three desirable mental characteristics were then emphasised. These were confidence, enthusiasm, and mental toughness, the latter a term used by many of the psychologists in their consultancy work. Six areas of mental skills are seen to provide the basis for these mental characteristics, namely self-regulation, concentration and attention, arousal control, visualisation, confidence and consistency, pre-, during- and post-game activities. Loehr (1990) provides a similar model of the areas to be considered under the headings of on and off court, during and between points, and physical and mental. For example, the most directly applicable component is the on court, between points mental area, where a four stage plan is used, consisting of positive physical response, relaxation response, preparation response and ritual response. This is one of the few clear statements in the two special issues of ways to actually apply the mental skills, to which there is frequent, general reference. Gordon's (1990) discussion of the "pre-delivery routine" (p. 397) for batters is another.

This issue of how to apply the mental skills in the game is not addressed thoroughly in discussion by the contributors and there are no general models proposed. A number of authors refer to pre-game (Halliwell, 1990), pre-delivery (Gordon, 1990), pre-performance and performance (Gould & Finch, 1990) routines or performance rituals (Gordin & Henschen, 1989). Game plans, competition plans and pre-competition strategies are also mentioned (Botterill, 1990; Salmela, 1989). What these consist of and how they can be developed is not considered, however. A number of papers also refer to the use of simulations (e.g., Gipson et al., 1989; Nideffer, 1989; Orlick, 1989) or the integration of the mental skills training into the game, usually in training (e.g., Gordon, 1990; Loehr, 1990), but do not describe how this is done.

While it is thought to be beneficial to integrate sport psychology into training to encourage players to perceive it as a part of the training, rather than an add-on, some of the contributors believe that sport psychology should be a part of a player's skills before the elite level is reached. Halliwell (1990), in the context of ice hockey, noted that his most effective work can be done in the minor league teams, preparing players for the major league. Loehr (1990) argued that it is important to teach psychological skills at the junior level in tennis, a point echoed in sailing by Halliwell (1989) and cricket by Gordon (1990). Nideffer (1989) proposed that mental skills training should be introduced in senior, or even junior, high school. There is a suggestion that juniors are also likely to be more flexible, more amenable to new ideas, than some established performers.

The discussion of problems encountered is perhaps the most variable section across the papers in these two special issues. A consultant needs to have a very well-established relationship with a team to list, in print, problems residing in the team. A few confident individuals do this, while others claim they have had no problems and the rest only discuss things they did wrong. Nonetheless, by far the most widely cited problem concerned lack of sufficient time with the players. This could be due to logistical, financial or organisational difficulties or just the commitments of psychologist and players. Rotella (1990) claimed that five weeks between sessions should be the absolute maximum. Other frequently cited issues were situations in which the coach was not supportive, that the program was slow to get going or that the athletes were turned off, perhaps because the program took time to show results. Here it was likely that the consultant could lose credibility with the players. These issues are of concern in any approach to PST.

Those who espoused a philosophy of their involvement in applied sport psychology tended to be consistent in their message. May and Brown (1989) emphasised the importance of the general well-being of the athlete in their broad spectrum systems approach. To maximise talents by mental skills (Dorfman, 1990), "to become the best ... they could become" (Gordin & Henschen, 1989, p. 369), to help individuals learn and grow as a function of their Olympic experience (Murphy & Ferrante, 1989), to help people come closer to their potential (Botterill, 1990) and "to help people's dreams come true" (Rotella, 1990, p. 409) are statements which reflect the commitment these sport psychologists had to fulfilment in the athletes.

Orlick (1989) felt he was most effective when he was committed to the people he was working with and cared about what happened to them. Several contributors indicated that success was usually associated with a focus on the athletes' actualisation, not the consultant's own aggrandisement. The sort of thinking that underlies these philosophies could well provide a litmus test for aspiring sport psychologists.

TRAINING MATERIALS AND RESOURCES

Various psychological skills training programs have been developed in North America. Suinn (1986) was one of the first to produce a mental training manual for athletes. The seven steps in his program begin with training in relaxation techniques. Progressive muscle relaxation is followed by instruction in centring techniques which are then implemented in different situations including competition. The second step trains the athlete to recognise the signs of stress, prevent stress from getting out of hand, and learn how to use centring techniques to control high levels of stress. Step 3 provides training in a number of thought-control techniques including using negative thoughts to trigger positive and corrective action, changing negative thoughts to positive thoughts, countering, reframing, and thought stopping. Training is also provided in developing and using positive affirmation statements. Personal best performances are reviewed in Step 4 in order to develop self-regulation skills. Training in visual-motor behaviour rehearsal — relaxation followed by visualisation of performance in competition and achievement of goals — is provided in Step 5. Step 6 incorporates earlier developed relaxation and mental rehearsal techniques in a routine for controlling and directing concentration at competition, and for refocusing attention after distraction. Finally, Suinn trains athletes to recognise their own energy and to harness this energy so that it can be directed for maximum use.

Martens (1987) published a psychological skills training program primarily for the use of Level 2 coaches in the American Coaching Effectiveness Program. The accompanying study guide and workbook were produced by Bump (1989). After units on the philosophy of coaching, motivation in sport, leadership and communication skills, there is an overview of psychological skills training and useful information on how to introduce the program to athletes. Martens (1987) distinguishes between clinical sport psychologists and educational sport psychologists, arguing that the former deal with abnormal behaviours in athletes such as psychoses and neuroses, whereas the latter are concerned with helping "normal" athletes execute superior physical skills in extremely demanding competitive environments. In order for coaches to function as educational sports psychologists, training materials are provided in six major areas: imagery skills, managing psychic energy, stress management, attentional skills, self-confidence, and goal setting. Martens (1987) provides a coherent account of research in each of these areas and discusses the implications and applications of those findings. In the study guide and workbook, Bump (1989) presents questions and exercises which further develop understanding in each area and provide a range of useful resource materials.

Rushall (1992) has recently produced a psychological skills training manual for use by athletes, coaches and sport psychologists, extending his previous handbook on imagery training in sports (Rushall, 1991). Rushall adopts a behaviourist orientation in the procedures recommended for modifying mental behaviour. These procedures include overt and covert positive reinforcement, maintaining progressive records of behaviour, self-control behaviours, and the use of discriminative and instructional stimuli. Training is provided by way of a series of exercises in each of the following areas: promoting a positive approach to the sporting experience, goal setting, the development of commitment, performance enhancement imagery, relaxation skills, pre-competition mental skills, competition mental skills and team building. Pre-competition strategies include waking with a positive attitude, thorough planning of events and activities prior to competition, establishing appropriate mind-sets on arrival at the contest site and the development and implementation of suitable pre-competition routines. Training in competition strategies includes exercises on performance segmenting, task-relevant thinking, using mood words to control action, positive thinking, switching attention, coping with the unexpected and combating fatigue. This area concludes with a performance debriefing exercise which trains athletes to evaluate the adequacy of their pre-competition preparations and use of competition strategies.

In Britain, Hardy and Fazey (1990) have produced a mental training program for the National Coaching Foundation. This program consists of four audiocassettes and accompanying booklets covering goal setting, anxiety control, mental rehearsal and concentration training. Training in goal setting consists of six sessions each lasting about 30 minutes. These sessions aim to introduce different types of goals, develop understanding of the goal-setting process, illustrate how to plan and structure goals and deal with problems that are commonly experienced in goal setting.

Relaxation training consists of 18 sessions each lasting about 30 minutes and spread over a three week period. After an introduction to topics such as stress, activation, anxiety and relaxation, the athlete in the first week is trained in four relaxation techniques: progressive muscular relaxation, meditative relaxation, centring techniques, and imagery-based relaxation strategies. Athletes are then encouraged to select one of these techniques and to practise it for a week before spending another week on a suggested complementary technique that is likely to achieve both physical and mental relaxation.

The mental rehearsal materials consist of seven sessions, each taking about 30 minutes to complete. After an introductory session on mental rehearsal, athletes are helped to create vivid images, use images to predict courses of action, experience different imagery perspectives, implement rehearsal strategies, and combine imagery and self-talk techniques to supply energy and handle difficult situations in their sport. The last session on reviewing and interpreting performances is aimed at building confidence and deriving maximum benefit for subsequent performances.

Finally, the concentration training materials comprise six sessions each of about 30 minutes. The initial session emphasises the need to focus attention on the present and introduces training in dissociation techniques for use with distractions. The subsequent training exercises promote a narrow focus of attention and further desensitise the athlete to distractions. Athletes are encouraged to simulate competition conditions at practice and develop skills in handling negative feedback during performance. The final session directs the athlete's attention to performance or process-oriented goals and recommends the use of competition tapes containing appropriately positive statements and verbal triggers associated with effective concentration.

In Australia, Winter and Martin (1991) have produced a basic training program in sport psychology for the South Australian Sports Institute. The program, which is expected to take between five and ten weeks to complete, consists of seven modules presented to athletes through a workbook and accompanying audiocassette tapes. A practical guide for coaches has also been prepared. After an introduction to sport psychology, the initial module provides athletes with a systematic approach to goal setting. Athletes are encouraged to identify their short- and long-term goals in sport, select those that are most important, set time-frames for achieving these goals and determine the activities needed to accomplish them. Athletes are shown how to incorporate sessional goals in a training diary.

The second module presents a discussion about the relationship between arousal and performance in different sports, before providing training in progressive muscular relaxation techniques. It is recommended that athletes undergo relaxation training once a day for 10 days, listening to the accompanying relaxation tape at least three days a week. Each of the sessions takes less than half an hour and athletes are encouraged to keep a record of their relaxation training experiences.

The module on concentration provides instruction on focusing skills. Included in the information and suggestions put forward are the importance of being mentally prepared for particular competitions, simulating competition situations at practice and establishing consistent pre-performance routines. Other information refers to breaking competition events into natural segments and ensuring attention is focused on the present moment, and to developing skill in refocusing attention after distractions using focused breathing (centring) techniques and specific cues.

To build self-confidence, athletes are encouraged to identify and record their strengths in three areas: attitude and mental approach, technical skills and knowledge, and physical fitness. After discussion of how thoughts and feelings influence reactions to situations, athletes are taught to recognise instances of negative thinking in sport and learn how to use affirmations to change their own thoughts and feelings and develop confidence in difficult situations.

Athletes are expected to spend about 30 minutes a day for a minimum of six days practising the basic skill in the visualisation module. For each of the six sessions they plan what they want to see, hear and feel in training and competition situations, visualise those situations, record the vividness of their imagery experiences and determine what needs to be improved in subsequent sessions.

The program materials stress the importance of self-motivation in sport, arguing that this is something athletes can learn to control. The goal-setting and visualisation techniques covered in previous modules figure prominently in motivation training. Long-term, short-term, and daily goals provide incentive for training and a record of progress accomplished. Visualisation techniques can be implemented at practice to facilitate development of new skills, and in competition to maintain concentration and enhance performance. Goal visualisation combines these two techniques and plays an important role in developing and maintaining motivation.

The final module combines the skills of relaxation, visualisation and planning to establish a mind-set that is conducive to optimal performance in competition. Athletes are encouraged to reflect on previously successful performances to identify effective pre-competition routines. They are encouraged to plan their pre-competition schedule carefully, beginning with positive thoughts and feelings from the moment they wake on the day of competition. In preparing for competition, athletes implement relaxation techniques as they mentally rehearse important aspects of their performance in the specific competition environment. One objective of these mental rehearsals is to establish a set of performance cues which will later trigger appropriate reactions in competition.

Other useful resources include a number of videotapes that can be integrated very effectively in a psychological skills training program. Some of these videotapes address general skills (e.g., Curtis, 1988; Jacobs, 1988), while others focus on specific skills such as visualisation (Botterill, 1988). Videotapes have also been produced for training psychological skills in specific sports such as Australian football (Stewart, 1990), figure skating (Martin, 1989), golf (Fine, 1993; Hogan, 1988), and tennis (Loehr, 1989). *The Sport Psychologist* regularly includes reviews of new books and videotapes. Other excellent sources of training materials are the *Sport Psychology Bulletin* published by the Australian Institute of Sport, and the *Sport Psychology Training Bulletin*, edited by Hardy and Crace at the University of North Carolina.

GENERAL MODELS

Applied sport psychology practitioners have not proposed many general models of the performance enhancement or PST process. Perhaps, again, there was not enough accrued experience from which to generalise until quite recently. Three of the earliest attempts to be found are those of Martens (1987), Boutcher and Rotella (1987) and Vealey (1988). Martens's proposed program has three phases. In the first, the *education* phase, athletes learn about various psychological skills, how they influence performance, and how they can be developed. The second phase is called *acquisition* and involves structured training on the skills required. Phase two is assumed to take place away from the sport, as the third phase involves practice of the skills to make them habitual and integrate them into competition. It is called the *practice* phase. The training materials that have since been produced to accompany Martens's (1987) model of PST were briefly described in the previous section of this chapter.

Vealey (1988) also proposes a three-phase approach. Her first phase, *attainment*, covers the education and acquisition phases in Martens's conceptualisation, covering understanding and the development of proficiency in the skills. *Sustainment*, then involves incorporation into daily practice and competition routines, like Martens's practice phase. Vealey (1988) adds a *coping* phase, where strategies are developed for coping with situations where the skill proves inadequate or when skills weaken, that is, lose their effectiveness. She emphasises the importance of preparing athletes for the possibility that established competition plans will fail under certain circumstances and back-up coping strategies will be needed. Vealey (1988) also stresses that it is important to distinguish between skills and the methods or techniques used to develop them. Thus, the attainment of optimal arousal for performance or arousal control is a skill which may be supported by a range of techniques such as muscular relaxation, the relaxation response, imagery to reduce or increase arousal level, positive self-talk, thought stopping, centring, meditation and listening to stirring or relaxing music. It is not appropriate to analyse Vealey's model too intensely, as it was a short aside in a discussion of other issues. It should be noted, however, that in that light, it is very general in nature, not giving much guidance on how to do psychological skills training.

Boutcher and Rotella (1987) refer their educational program to the enhancement of closed skills, although they acknowledge that much of it would apply to open skills as well. They state that the program has four phases: sport analysis, assessment, conceptualisation and skill development, but their diagramatic representation also includes a program evaluation at the end. The *sport analysis* phase involves an analysis of the skills needed in the sport from a number of disciplinary perspectives, including sport psychology. Based on this, *assessment* is conducted to determine the individual's strengths and weaknesses, which can be profiled. From the profile it is possible to draw out implications for performance, leading to the use of a goal-setting strategy in the *conceptualisation* phase to gain commitment from the athlete to behaviour change. The fourth stage involves the *development of the skills* identified in the conceptualisation phase, first as general skills, then applying them specifically to the performer's situation and, finally, incorporating them in performance routines. Boutcher and Rotella (1987) propose the use of routines before, during, after and between performances. Interestingly, although Boutcher and Rotella (1987) espouse an educational philosophy, the flavour of their description is problem-oriented, especially the example interview schedule they present.

Drawing on these general models as well as his observations of the practices of prominent North American sport psychologists, Thomas (1990) outlined seven phases of performance enhancement processes as shown in Figure 9.1. Where an athlete seeks the help of a sport psychologist to enhance performance, then the initial *orientation* meeting needs to clarify the purpose of the consultation, set objectives to be achieved, and determine whether the level of commitment to the task is sufficient. Often there is no "quick fix" to the problem identified, and the athlete needs to know and accept that time and effort will be required to understand, develop and integrate psychological skills to the point where they can be utilised effectively in competition.

Once the task has been defined, the sport psychologist needs a detailed *analysis* of the specific domain involved, an analysis that draws on research in psychology, biomechanics, and exercise physiology, as well as knowledge of the situation drawn from personal experience. Boutcher and Rotella (1987) argue that the sport psychologist needs to be skilled, for example, in determining whether a flawed golf swing derives from an underlying biomechanical problem, or as the golfer may initially suggest, something resulting from ineffective concentration. Because the performance enhancement process sometimes begins with an analysis by the athlete (or coach) that precedes the request for help from a sport psychologist or some other professional, dual arrows are shown between the first two phases in Figure 9.1.

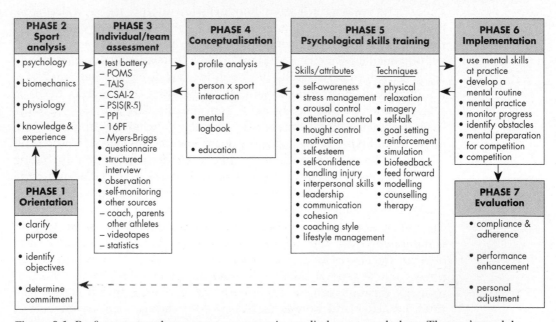

Figure 9.1: Performance enhancement processes in applied sport psychology: Thomas's model

Before beginning a skill training program, many sport psychologists conduct *individual/team assessments* in order to draw up a profile of the strengths and weaknesses. The profile may be based in part on the results of selected tests and inventories. As discussed earlier in this chapter, these often include the Profile of Mood States, Test of Attentional and Interpersonal Style, Competitive State Anxiety Inventory-2, Psychological Skills Inventory for Sports, or Psychological Performance Inventory, although the validity of some of these measures was questioned. Detailed descriptions of these and other tests used by sport psychologists may be found in Anshel (1987) and Ostrow (1990).

There is currently some consensus that sport-related tests are to be preferred over non-sport tests, but there are divergent opinions as to whether the content of those test instruments should refer to sports generally or target situations in specific sports. Test results are usually supplemented with material gleaned from interviews with the athlete. Personal observation of the athlete performing in competition provides valuable insights, but videotapes, diaries, and performance statistics can also be used. Other sources of information for this profiling exercise include the coach and close associates of the athlete.

When analysing and interpreting an athlete's profile, a sport psychologist needs to consider personal characteristics in conjunction with the situational demands of a particular sport. It might be argued that this is best done through use of tests specifically designed to measure these person × situation interactions. At the very least, there ought to be some checking with the athlete as to the accuracy of profile interpretation when more general tests are used. This feedback process enhances *conceptualisation* and provides a foundation for the athlete's education in psychological skills. At this point, athletes are often receptive to the idea of keeping a mental logbook as outlined by Ravizza (1993).

Martens (1987) argues that the *psychological skills training* phase should begin by developing an athlete's self-awareness. The process of feedback and verification of the athlete's assessment profile outlined in Phase 4 serves an important role in improving self awareness. At the same time, skills training may reveal the need for further assessment of an athlete's strengths and weaknesses. Vealey's (1988) distinction between psychological skills and training techniques is evident in Phase 5, although thought control is considered a skill like other aspects of self-control rather than a technique. Relaxation, imagery, self-talk and goal setting are probably the main techniques currently being used to enhance performance through helping athletes cope with stress, find an optimal arousal level, focus attention on the task, develop appropriate motivation for training and competition and improve self-efficacy.

Psychological skills need to be practised extensively before their *implementation* in competition. Most athletes have well-developed behavioural routines associated with their sport, ranging from consistent patterns of activity during the morning of a competition, through to the waggle of a golf club or the wiping of perspiration from the forehead before kicking a goal. Performance enhancement processes frequently involve the development of mental routines that may be combined with existing behavioural routines. Thus the golfer or the footballer may routinely take a centring breath, visualise the ball reaching its target, and mentally rehearse the feel of the shot prior to its execution.

Athletes are encouraged to mentally practise their performance skills away from the competition arena or training track. There is no doubt that mental practice significantly enhances performance, although it is a supplement rather than an alternative to physical practice (Feltz & Landers, 1983). Mental practice is particularly important for those athletes prevented from training through injury. The athlete's progress in implementing psychological skills needs to be constantly monitored, the mental logbook proving useful in identifying obstacles. Those obstacles may range from inadequate understanding of the basic techniques, through to an inability to handle other team members or the coach. Once again, information such as this may lead to alternative activities in the *implementation* phase. Ultimately the psychological skills are implemented to enhance performance in competition, but the period immediately prior to competition has a substantial effect on the subsequent outcome. Psychological skills need to be implemented during this period of preparation to ensure optimal performance. Ravizza (1988) and Weinberg (1984) provide useful accounts of various mental preparation strategies.

Sound *evaluation* of the performance enhancement processes used by sport psychologists is needed for the good of the athlete and the discipline (Greenspan & Feltz, 1989). Various evaluation procedures can be used, ranging from large group studies (e.g., Gould, Petlichkoff, Hodge, & Simons, 1990) to single-subject designs (Bryan, 1987; Smith, 1988). In evaluating the effectiveness of intervention processes, it is essential to determine initially the athlete's level of compliance and adherence to aspects of the training program. Ideally, one would wish to find clear evidence of performance enhancement in those athletes participating fully in the program. But other goals of the program should not be overlooked, such as evidence of improved personal adjustment in athletes. The end result of such evaluations will subsequently help the athlete and sport psychologist set appropriate objectives in the initial *orientation* phase.

The model developed by Morris (1991, 1992) proposes five stages in the process of psychological skills training. These he calls assessment, basic skills training, routine development, routine application and, finally, evaluation. In the *assessment* phase, a range of methods is suggested, based on the principle of triangulation, whereby reliability of the process is indicated, and confidence increased, by the consistency between data acquired from different sources or by varying techniques. Specifically, Morris refers to observation of the player in training and before, during and after competition; interview, possibly on more than one occasion and involving the critical incident technique to access thoughts, feelings and behaviour associated with success and failure; discussion with coach, parents, team mates, as appropriate; psychological tests, preferably sports specific and including measures of traits and states; and diaries or log-books kept by the player. It is proposed that the methods chosen and their sequence should be determined by the circumstances.

In the second stage, *basic skills training*, a range of techniques is used to develop the essential psychological skills, in a way similar to other approaches described, typically including relaxation and other stress management skills, imagery used for a variety of purposes, positive self-talk, focusing exercises for attention control, and so on. Morris stresses the importance of a feedback and individualised program planning session at the end of the assessment phase. In this session the psychologist presents the profile of the performer which has emerged from assessment and elicits reactions from the athlete. This might lead to some modification of the athlete's profile. When relative strengths and weaknesses are agreed upon, an individualised program is developed on the basis of this common understanding. This approach also facilitates the very important process whereby the psychologist explains how the skills training will contribute to performance enhancement for that individual. It is designed to elicit athlete commitment, through involvement in the program development process.

Once the techniques are well practised and the skills developed, two stages ensue which, in Morris's view, are crucial. These are *routine development* and *routine application*. Morris argues that many texts and papers describing psychological skills stop short of integration of the skills into the pre-event preparation and competitive behaviour of athletes. It is interesting that the use of routines to achieve integration was arrived at independently by Boutcher and Rotella (1987) and has been more widely discussed in recent publications on aspects of PST (e.g., Boutcher, 1992; Gordon, 1990; Halliwell, 1990; Loehr, 1990). Routine development is the process of creating pre-performance and competition routines, in which the psychological skills are integrated with administrative, technical and physical necessities, until they become an habitual part of pre-event preparation or the athlete's behaviour during play. *Segmenting* is a process recommended to identify essential activities and existing habits, as well as opportunities for psychological input to create the pre-competition or pre-event routine. In many sports, a scaled-down version, which Morris calls the pre-game routine, may be used in situations where total mental cool down has not occurred between games within the same competition. This occurs in many individual sports and some team tournaments, where a round robin or knockout competition lasts all day or for several days and players must wait for a period of time between matches. It also occurs in sports like diving or athletic field events, where there are several attempts, swimming or athletics, where a competitor may be in several events on the same day, and gymnastics, where the performer moves around several pieces of apparatus. In sports which consist of only one game each day, only the pre-event routine is necessary.

Until the routines have been applied in the performer's usual training and the individual feels comfortable practising with those behaviours integrated into play, the introduction of those psychological techniques into competition is likely to prove counterproductive, according to Morris. The routines should also be tested in simulated competition, to instil confidence in their robustness. Still further trialing in minor competition should precede use in a major event. This process allows the routines to become an habitual part of the performer's pre-game or in-game behaviour.

In-game monitoring and control routines are distinguished from specific incident-handling routines in that the former are structured systematically into the moment-by-moment progress of the game, while the latter are used in impromptu fashion when the athlete's performance is disrupted by a specific unusual occurrence. The in-game monitoring and control routine is practised in training before every serve in tennis, every shot in golf, or every dive, for example, so it becomes part of the pre-performance procedure. Specific incident-handling routines, once developed through practice away from the game, must be tested with a range of simulated, but unexpected, disruptive events. In-game monitoring and control is structured into the performance, whereas specific incident-handling is a response to unpredictable occurrences.

Evaluation in this model refers to the continued monitoring of the effectiveness of the routines for the athlete. Where routines prove ineffective it could be because they were based on erroneous initial assessment, the most effective techniques were not employed for that person, the routines were structured incorrectly or the routines were not applied to the extent that they had become habitual. Once identified, any of these problems can be remedied. Morris focused on the PST process, assuming, as have others (e.g., Neff, 1990; Rotella, 1990; Smith & Johnson, 1990), that evaluation of the psychologist would take place by the players, coaches and administrators and was reflected in evaluation of the program. He also assumed an orientation process for the squad and assessment of the nature of the sport prior to the commencement of the assessment phase of the program.

LIMITATIONS OF MODELS

The general models of psychological skills training share some of the same limitations as the specific programs discussed earlier. There are common logistical difficulties, for example, in getting quality time with individuals and balancing this with sessions for the whole team. Fitting the training program around the schedules of other professionals working with the athletes can also pose difficulties. Working in with the team coach is essential. Initially the sport psychologist might experience difficulty in gaining acceptance from both the coach and the players and a relationship of trust needs to be developed before any meaningful assessment can be conducted. Ravizza (1988) has some particularly sound advice on gaining acceptance as a consultant.

Not all athletes will be well served by formal assessment in the initial phases of intervention. Indeed, appropriate assessment instruments often do not exist. Initially, slow progress in performance enhancement is just as much a problem with the general models as the specific programs. This problem may arise if the orientation, assessment and program design stages are protracted, thus preventing the athlete from actually getting to practise any psychological skills. Similarly, frustration will be experienced by some athletes who have worked on developing stress management skills through progressive muscle relaxation techniques, or thinking more positively through self-talk exercises, only to find little evidence of immediate improvement in their sport performance.

The general models may not adequately represent the performance enhancement processes appropriate in some sports, nor should it be assumed that the same processes are appropriate for elite athletes and beginners. This is perhaps the greatest limitation of the general models — their implicit suggestion that performance enhancement through psychological skills training is accomplished through a single, sequential set of procedures. This lack of flexibility predisposes the sport psychologist to one approach, when others may be more suited to the demands of a particular situation. In situations where the proposed sequence is hard to maintain because of logistical or personal circumstances, applying the model may be both difficult and ultimately ineffective. A number of alternative perspectives on psychological skills training have been published recently and these warrant careful consideration.

PERFORMANCE PROFILING

The performance-profiling approach advocated by Butler and Hardy (1992) and illustrated by Jones (1993) and Butler, Smith, and Irwin (1993) includes most of the processes typically found in psychological skills training programs. The approach begins with an orientation meeting between sport psychologist and athlete, followed by an assessment phase. The athlete identifies characteristics required by elite performers in their sport and receives a visual profile of their self-ratings on each of these characteristics. Discussion of the results of this assessment provides guidelines for the design of a psychological skills training program that meets each athlete's specific needs. There follows a phase in which the newly learned skills are implemented in practice prior to their use in competition. Finally the effectiveness of the intervention is evaluated.

The performance-profiling approach is distinctive in the assessment phase. Sport psychologists typically exercise professional judgement in selecting appropriate techniques to assess the athlete's initial strengths and weaknesses and subsequent changes in those areas. They may choose to use standardised tests or questionnaires developed specifically for sport, interview the athlete, observe performance in competition, or consider information obtained from other sources (coaches, performance records, etc.). The performance-profiling approach, on the other hand, shifts the responsibility for determining which constructs will be assessed from the sport psychologist to the athlete.

There are both advantages and disadvantages in this approach to psychological skills training. Athletes are actively engaged rather than passive participants in the assessment phase. It is argued that this will lead to the identification of pertinent needs and avoid irrelevant measurement. The process of goal setting is likely to increase the athlete's motivation to bring about improvement in selected areas. Adherence and compliance to the training program are thus likely to increase. However, the constructs are subjective and tacitly defined by the athlete. Whereas the items on a questionnaire explicitly define the constructs selected by the sport psychologist, the athlete's interpretation of constructs will need further elaboration. Those interpretations may well change over time, making it difficult to measure progress in an area. Subjective interpretations also make it difficult if not impossible to compare and contrast self-ratings among athletes or to refute an athlete's inaccurate self-ratings.

Inviting athletes to identify the attributes to be assessed assumes that they have knowledge of the skills required for high levels of performance in their sport. Although such knowledge may develop with expertise, it is often the case that athletes are unaware of some psychological skills that may well enhance their performance. How are these skills or attributes to be included in the program?

ROLE LIMITATIONS

Apart from limitations to the models of psychological skills training, there is the much broader issue of limitations to the role of psychological skills trainer. It is clear from the thrust of this chapter, and indeed that of other chapters in this book, that psychological skills training is a crucial role of the applied sport psychologist. However, Jeff Bond, Head of the Sport Psychology Department at the Australian Institute of Sport, has recently cautioned psychologists not to restrict themselves to this role:

> "If Australian sport psychologists continue to see themselves and/or promote themselves as purely educational sport psychologists or performance enhancement mental skills trainers, then in my opinion, they are selling themselves and their profession short and are doomed as far as future involvement in elite sport is concerned ... Our training must surely have equipped us with knowledge and competencies which enable us to offer something more than basic mental skills training ... it is no longer appropriate for sport psychologists to hang their professional hat on, or be seen to be the teachers of basic mental skills for sport. We must continue to do some of that work, continue to teach coaches to do some of that work, but we must practise *psychology* if we are to continue to advance our profession and to contribute to Australian sport."

(Bond, 1993, pp. 8–9)

This issue is addressed further in reports on the changing roles of sport psychologists working with gymnasts in the British national squads (Parfitt & Hardy, 1993). Prior to 1990, the role of the sport psychologist was predominantly that of an expert psychological skills trainer who initially assessed the gymnasts' needs and then provided training that was appropriate to individual needs. Evaluations of the psychological skills training clearly demonstrated its effectiveness. Similarly, evaluation of the effectiveness of sport psychologists indicated they were highly regarded by both gymnasts and coaches. Nevertheless, the feedback obtained from participants, combined with the experience gained and professional development of the applied sport psychologists, led to a new approach being adopted after 1990. In this approach, the psychologists acted as consultants, responding to gymnasts' and coaches' perceived needs rather than being prescriptive about those needs. The approach also acknowledged that the expertise and experience of all individuals involved would prove valuable in solving the problems they faced.

Parfitt and Hardy (1993) describe six roles performed by the sport psychologists in the revised, consultancy approach. As *educators* they taught specific psychological skills, as required, to individuals who had determined their own needs. Coaching workshops and clinics were also conducted throughout the country to develop an understanding of sport psychology at all levels of the sport, enabling others to perform this role. The psychologists acted as *facilitators*, building group cohesion and a social support network among gymnasts and coaches, and assisting them to construct personal profiles that would be used to develop performance enhancement strategies. As *mediators* the psychologists addressed difficulties that threatened effective interactions among gymnasts and coaches. As *counsellors* they worked with gymnasts experiencing a range of problems including injury, disappointing performances in competition, non-selection for a team, and low motivation. As *problem-solvers* they were instrumental in helping gymnasts overcome psychological difficulties in performing certain moves. Performance profiles proved helpful in this role, discrepancies between a gymnast's self-ratings and those provided by the coach being used to devise appropriate training programs. Finally, Parfitt and Hardy (1993) acknowledge the '*tea person*' role in which psychologists performed a range of menial tasks, from fetching pop-corn to minding baggage, tasks which were much appreciated and helpful in the development of friendly relations with their clients.

Evaluations of the effectiveness of the sport psychologists adopting this revised, consultant approach were very positive with many items showing significant improvement from the more traditional approach initially adopted. Relative to the ratings provided by other Olympic teams, the consultants scored particularly highly on flexibility and readiness to collaborate, the ease with which performers could relate to them, and the clarity and practicality of their suggestions. The consultants themselves found this approach to be quite demanding in that they had to make themselves easily accessible and needed to be completely trusted by gymnasts and their coaches. Nevertheless, they found this approach to their work much more satisfying in that it successfully harnessed the expertise of all involved in catering for their perceived needs.

STAGES OF PROFESSIONAL DEVELOPMENT

Clearly there are important differences in how applied sport psychologists approach the task of helping athletes. In part, those differences reflect alternative premises on which the approaches are based. Equally important, however, are the differences that emerge as practitioners develop expertise within a specific domain. Berliner (1988) has proposed a general theory of the development of expertise, based on the model presented by Dreyfus and Dreyfus (1986). Berliner proposes five stages in skill development as ignorance is overcome and expertise is achieved. His theory has implications beyond the field of pedagogy in which it was formulated. We would contend that it provides a useful framework for understanding the professional development of applied sport psychologists.

Stage 1: Novice. In order to perform tasks that will be expected of them, students and beginning practitioners focus initially on learning the meanings of terms and concepts. They acquire a set of context-free rules and procedures that guide behaviour which they tend to follow, relatively inflexibly. The novice seeks the objective facts and features of situations and typically places higher value on gaining real-world experience than on verbal information.

Stage 2: Advanced Beginner. After two or three years of work experience, many practitioners begin to allow contexts to guide their behaviour. As episodic knowledge develops with experience and combines with verbal knowledge, the practitioner recognises similarities across contexts and starts to act strategically — knowing when to break or ignore rules and when to follow them. But like the novice, the advanced beginner often acts in a detached way, having no sense of what is important and often failing to accept personal responsibility for what is happening.

Stage 3: Competent. After three or four years of work experience, competent practitioners have two distinctive characteristics. Firstly, they make conscious choices about their activities, setting priorities and rational goals and planning how those goals will be achieved. Secondly, they exercise judgement about what is important and draw on experience to determine what to attend to and what to ignore. Competent practitioners tend to feel personally responsible for what happens, but at this stage they are not yet fast, fluid, or flexible in their behaviour.

Stage 4: Proficient. Some practitioners reach the proficient stage of development after about five years of work experience. Intuition or know-how becomes prominent at this stage. The proficient individual develops an intuitive sense of a situation and can predict events more precisely through an holistic awareness and recognition of similarities and patterns. However, the proficient individual is typically analytic and deliberative when deciding what to do.

Stage 5: Expert. Experts have the ability to perform a task effortlessly and fluidly. They grasp a situation intuitively and seem to sense the appropriate action to take in non-analytic, non-deliberative ways. In contrast to novices, advanced beginners and competent performers who are rational, and proficient performers who are intuitive, Berliner (1988) describes experts as "arational" in that their behaviour typically involves neither calculation nor deliberative thought. Experts rarely appear to reflect about their performance when things are going smoothly, but bring deliberate analytical processes to bear when anomalies occur.

In concluding his account of this theory of the development of expertise, Berliner (1988) makes some important observations. As in other stage theories of development, wide variations are to be expected in the duration of time individuals spend in a stage. Someone who is typically at one stage of development may display characteristics associated with another stage in particular situations. Finally, expertise is thought to be highly contextualised. Expertise in one domain may not transfer very well to another, unrelated domain.

If we extrapolate Berliner's (1988) theory to the development of skills in the applied sport psychologist, we can see how different interpretations may be placed on the training models and programs we have presented. Those new to the field of applied sport psychology may well use the materials to familiarise themselves with the terms and concepts that define the field. Initially they are likely to expect to learn rules and procedures for intervening with athletes that can be adopted regardless of the specific features of the context in which they are working. However, as practitioners become more knowledgeable in their field, comfortable with their techniques, and more confident in their professional role, their expertise develops. Work experience is integrated with subject knowledge and the professional behaviour of applied sport psychologists becomes much more strategic and flexible. In many cases they are capable of getting quickly to the nub of the problem without recourse, for example, to the results of diagnostic tests. Clearly they do not work in the same way with all athletes. They are sensitive to how athletes prefer to process information and consequently are able to offer suggestions that readily effect improvement in the targeted area.

It is helpful if novices have an understanding of how expertise develops. Students in the field of applied sport psychology who are aware of the limited functioning of novices and beginning practitioners can take steps in their formative years to advance their professional development. It begins with the approaches they adopt to learning at university. There is now considerable research on the different ways students approach learning tasks and set assessments. There is clear evidence that some approaches are much more effective than others. Thomas and Bain (1984) identified three approaches to learning. The skimming approach serves simply to filter information. Information is processed superficially with no deliberate attempt to remember or understand it. Students adopting a reproductive approach view learning as being able to regurgitate study material in the terms and format in which it was presented. They carefully select terms and concepts which they intend to memorise and later reproduce in assessments. Although some students adopt such an approach in an effort to meet course requirements minimally, it is also clear that many students believe that such activities will ultimately lead to an understanding of the study material. The notion of acquiring set rules or procedures that can be applied across contexts is consistent with a reproductive approach to learning.

The transformational approach to learning identified by Thomas and Bain (1984) is based on the view that learning involves something other than just reproducing information or applying procedures. Information presented by lecturers, authors, practitioners and athletes needs to be changed, altered, or transformed in a way that makes it personally meaningful. That might involve expressing the ideas in your own words, relating concepts presented in courses to prior knowledge from other courses, or linking those concepts to your own experiences. Analogies are developed to capture the fundamental principles of what you are studying. This is a much more flexible notion of what it is to learn, in which you go beyond the information given and internalise the underlying principles and perspectives. Such flexibility is characteristic of more advanced stages of professional practice, but importantly the behaviours involved can be developed during the formative years. There is ample evidence to suggest that the processes characterising a transformational approach usually result in highly effective learning.

At advanced levels of professional development, applied sport psychologists engage in their tasks in ways that are qualitatively different from those in earlier stages. In many respects their work displays the "flow" characteristics documented by Csikszentmihalyi (1990). These characteristics have been widely publicised in research on athletes' peak experiences in sport (Cohn, 1991; Garfield & Bennett, 1984; Jackson, 1992; Ravizza, 1984). Csikszentmihalyi's (1990) analysis of flow in work is probably less familiar to sport psychologists, although he reports that people are much more likely to experience flow when they are working than when engaged in leisure activities.

To conclude this section of the chapter, therefore, let us consider the characteristics of flow within the work context of the applied sport psychologist. Optimal experience at work occurs when the tasks are challenging but achievable, given the skills of the performer; the level of involvement in the task is such that activity becomes spontaneous, effortless and almost automatic; the goals are clear and feedback immediate and unambiguous; complete attention is given to the task at hand; there is the sense of exercising control in difficult situations; there is a loss of self-consciousness when actively engaged in performance, though the self is subsequently stronger for the experience; and time is often distorted during a state of complete involvement.

The work of an applied sport psychologist meets all the prerequisites for the experience of flow. The task of enhancing sport performance is as challenging as it is rewarding. The goals can be clearly defined in the orientation phase, though subsequently modified as necessary. Performance data provide clear, unambiguous records of progress achieved, though other achievement criteria are just as important. The tasks to be performed vary greatly and the work itself is usually of high intrinsic interest. Few practitioners have difficulty becoming immersed in a task when working with individuals who are highly competent in their own fields. Equally important, if not more so, are those consultations with athletes who are not performing well because of poorly developed psychological skills. These cases frequently result in immense professional satisfaction.

Csikszentmihalyi's (1990) analysis makes it clear that, although the nature of the work is important, it does not guarantee that the person performing that job will find enjoyment in it. A number of personal characteristics are also required. These characteristics permit the cognitive restructuring of work situations, enabling difficult or bleak conditions to be turned into subjectively controllable experience. Individuals need to recognise initially hidden opportunities for action that match their skills and available resources. By learning to set appropriate goals and by closely monitoring feedback on progress accomplished, practitioners are able to set increasingly complex challenges for themselves. In this way professional skills are honed and expertise develops.

FUTURE DIRECTIONS

Applied sport psychology is a recent addition to the practice of psychology. It has developed rapidly to meet the demands of sport and exercise. There is still much to be done, however. This is particularly the case in the area of performance enhancement, where sport psychologists have had their widest experience of practice in psychological skills training. The present chapter has focused on books, book chapters and journal papers which have attempted to provide some framework or guidelines for the practice of PST. A consistent theme in the more recent writing of applied sport psychologists is that highly structured approaches are unlikely to be optimal across a number of sports situations, because each player and every situation has unique characteristics.

Parfitt and Hardy (1993) recognised some of the limitations of the highly structured PST approach in their long association with the British Amateur Gymnastics Association. One issue they raise, which must be a focus for research, is the necessity for a needs analysis in the early stages of work with a squad or an athlete. It is by no means safe to assume that PST is the treatment of choice in all situations. There may, for example, be coach–athlete communication problems, time management or personal life difficulties, a psychological barrier left over from a major injury or anxiety about lack of preparation for a career after sport. Failure to check for such concerns may lead to wasted effort providing ineffective PST; training which is not effective because the primary problem pre-empts attention to PST. Research which explores the issues and concerns which athletes and coaches do face will sensitise practitioners to the range of needs of athletes. Techniques to accomplish quick but thorough needs analysis should also be an outcome of this line of enquiry. It is likely that more consistent success would accompany PST that follows needs analysis and the resolution of pre-eminent problems.

When PST is determined to be the appropriate intervention, there is still a need for greater flexibility in the approach which is employed. Each performer is different and the situations athletes face also vary. What is highly effective in one situation may be the worst thing to do in another. Again, approaches need to be examined where athletes' perceptions of their circumstances are sought and interpreted effectively. The sensitivity of sport psychologists to client needs is an important issue for research into practice. Not only will performers be poorly served by practitioners who do not respond to those performers' reports of their subjective experience of the problem, but the negative impression given may lose the practitioner valuable credibility in the athletes' eyes.

In addition to listening sensitively and responding appropriately, sport psychology practitioners who employ a long, initial-assessment phase or a sequence of orientation sessions must develop a more flexible approach when athletes are eager to start learning psychological skills. Research is needed to establish ways of introducing skills early in the practitioner's relationship with the team or player, while orientation and assessment are integrated into the ongoing activity, so they are less conspicuous. It is noteworthy that most of the highly experienced practitioners who contributed to the special issues of *TSP*, discussed earlier, employed a less formal approach to assessment than was expected. On reflection, the wisdom of this approach becomes clear. Research is needed to translate flexibility of operation into a form amenable to practical training.

While practitioners freely acknowledged the need to evaluate their activities and other reviewers of the PST field have stressed the importance of this process (Greenspan & Feltz, 1989), few tools for such evaluation have been developed or established through practice. Evaluation of programs takes place at a range of levels. These include the perceptions of the players and the coaches, as well as the administrators, and the more specific changes that take place in thoughts, feelings and behaviour, especially those which influence performance. Research should address the most effective ways of evaluating programs, so that the maximum amount of information is gathered with the least disruption to the program. One dilemma long recognised by applied sport psychologists is to work out who is the client in those cases where it is the athlete whose psychological growth is the objective, but the coach is directly responsible for the performer's overall physical, psychological and performance state and the administrators of the association pay the bills. It is important to study evaluations by these different groups to understand better what they expect, whether there must inevitably be conflict between the goals of the groups, and how they may all be satisfied by the same program, if this is possible.

The future directions for research on practice which have been discussed to this point all reflect the need for practitioners to be able to operate in a highly flexible manner. This allows them to adapt to new or changing situations as they arise and to use the opportunities for training players effectively as they present themselves. The way in which many of the practitioners in the *TSP* special issues described their mode of operation suggests that they were functioning at Berliner's (1988) *Stage 5: Expert* level of professional practice. For the most effective future training of applied sport psychologists, it is important for research to examine the process of acquiring this level of expertise in sport psychology. In the future, it should not be a matter of chance whether practitioners operate in the expert mode. All stages of training should be directed to move novice sport psychologists through Stages 1 to 4 of Berliner's model and on to Stage 5.

Applied sport psychology has not been the subject of sufficient research on the process of PST, performance enhancement or personal growth. The focus has been on the functioning of specific techniques and the development of a small range of skills. The need to examine the process of delivery and the process of training the deliverers is pressing. It is anticipated that future generations of researchers will recognise the importance of such research on practice.

CONCLUSIONS

This chapter has addressed the development and current status of applied sport psychology. While it acknowledged the central role of performance enhancement, and especially psychological skills training, recent trends toward diversification were recognised and supported for the future viability of the profession. In accepting Rejeski and Brawley's (1988) call for tighter definition of the field of sport psychology, it is argued that careful definition of function and an increasing range of applications within that function are not incompatible. There is a great diversity of contexts in which sport psychologists can and should function, but they should always use the skills and knowledge which they have been trained to apply; they must practise sport psychology in those diverse contexts.

In reviewing books on applied sport psychology, programs proposed in journal articles and models of the PST process, the recurring theme was of the flexible and adaptive mode of operation of the most experienced practitioners, as compared to the rather rigid sequences represented by current models. Greater flexibility is needed in future models, yet there must be enough structure for the novice practitioner to lean on. Moving new applied sport psychologists through the stages of development of expertise in professional practice is a challenge which research-minded sport psychologists should address as soon as possible. Recognition of the needs of performers and coaches is essential for effective consultancy in applied sport psychology. This must be accompanied by an adaptability to different needs and contexts. That adaptability should come from the professional training which practitioners receive, a training which must encourage practitioners to become innovative problem-solvers in the field of sport psychology.

SUMMARY

This chapter sets the scene for Part 2 of the book by considering some of the essential elements of applied sport psychology. It begins by examining the nature of applied sport psychology, distinguishing it from the field as a whole and then pointing to the range of issues now considered in an applied context. The chapter then focuses on the major area of performance enhancement and particularly psychological skills training (PST). It reflects on a number of approaches to the communication of PST, including the description of skills without a framework for their operation, common to earlier texts in the applied field, the description of programs designed specifically for a particular sports context, such as work with an Olympic or professional team, and the presentation of a general program, which it is intended will apply to many contexts. Resources and materials developed for training and available to applied sport psychologists are then briefly described. The chapter points out some of the limitations of the PST approach, especially noting the importance of carrying out a needs analysis to determine whether PST is the priority need or whether the person is ready for PST. Performance profiling as a means of examining needs and monitoring progress is also briefly discussed. The chapter then raises a number of limitations of the applied sport psychologist's role. Finally, a model of professional development is described, which appears to be applicable to applied sport psychology, where novice professionals are likely to depend on models of procedure, whereas expert professionals use their experience of many applied contexts to generate original programs, adapting to each new situation they meet. Applied sport psychology is a relatively new area of professional practice and it is recognised that structures and procedures will continue to evolve for the forseeable future.

REFERENCES

AAASP Newsletter. (1990). Membership data. *Association for the Advancement of Applied Sport Psychology Newsletter,* 5(1), 2.

Andersen, M. B., & Williams, J. M. (1988). A model of stress and athletic injury: Prediction and prevention. *Journal of Sport and Exercise Psychology, 10,* 294–306.

Anshel, M. H. (1987). Psychological inventories used in sport psychology research. *The Sport Psychologist, 1,* 331–349.

Beck, A. T. (1967). *Depression.* New York: Hoeber-Harper.

Beck, A. T. (1976). *Cognitive therapy and the emotional disorders.* New York: International Universities Press.

Benson, H. (1975). *The relaxation response.* New York: Avon Books.

Berliner, D. C. (1988, February). *The development of expertise in pedagogy.* Charles W. Hunt Memorial Lecture at the Annual Meeting of the American Association of Colleges for Teacher Education. New Orleans, LA.

Biddle, S., & Mutrie, N. (1991). *Psychology of physical activity and exercise.* London: Springer-Verlag.

Blann, W., & Zaichkowsky, L. (1986). *Career/life transition needs of National Hockey League Players.* Report prepared for the National Hockey League Players Association.

Blann, W., & Zaichkowsky, L. (1988). *Major League baseball players' post-sport career transition needs.* Report prepared for the Major League Baseball Players Association.

Blann, W., & Zaichkowsky, L. (1989). *National Hockey League and Major League baseball players' post-sport career transition surveys.* Final report for the National Hockey League Players Association.

Bond, J. (1992, September). *Sport psychology — State of the art, 1992.* Keynote address at the 27th Annual Conference of the Australian Psychological Society. Armidale, NSW.

Bond, J. (1993). Controversy corner. *Australian Sport Psychology Association Bulletin,* 2(1), 8–9.

Bond, J. W., Miller, B. P., & Chrisfield, P. M. (1988). Psychological prediction of injury in elite swimmers. *International Journal of Sports Medicine, 9,* 345–348.

Botterill, C. (1988). *Visualization; What you see is what you get.* Ottawa, Ontario: Coaching Association of Canada.

Botterill, C. (1990). Sport psychology and professional hockey. *The Sport Psychologist, 4,* 358–368.

Boutcher, S. (1992). Developing consistency. *Sport Psychology Training Bulletin, 3(6),* 1–7.

Boutcher, S. H., & Rotella, R. J. (1987). A psychological skills educational program for closed-skill performance enhancement. *The Sport Psychologist, 1,* 127–137.

Bryan, A. J. (1987). Single-subject designs for evaluation of sport psychology interventions. *The Sport Psychologist, 1,* 283–292.

Bump, L. (1989). *Sport psychology study guide and workbook.* Champaign, IL: Human Kinetics.

Butler, R. J., & Hardy, L. (1992). The performance profile: Theory and application. *The Sport Psychologist, 6,* 253–264.

Butler, R. J., Smith, M., & Irwin, I. (1993). The performance profile in practice. *Journal of Applied Sport Psychology, 5,* 48–63.

Cohn, P. J. (1991). An exploratory study on peak performance in golf. *The Sport Psychologist, 5,* 1–14.

Csikszentmihalyi, M. (1990). *Flow: The psychology of optimal experience.* New York: Harper Perennial.

Curtis, J. (1988). *The mindset for winning.* Bloomington, MN: Athletic Visions.

Dorfman, H. A. (1990). Reflections on providing personal and performance enhancement consulting services in professional baseball. *The Sport Psychologist, 4,* 341–346.

Dreyfus, H. L., & Dreyfus, S. E. (1986). *Mind over machine.* New York: Free Press.

Elko, P. K., & Ostrow, A. C. (1991). Effects of a rational-emotive education program on heightened anxiety levels of female collegiate gymnasts. *The Sport Psychologist, 5,* 235–255.

Ellis, A. (1958). Rational psychotherapy. *Journal of General Psychology, 59*, 35–49.

Ellis, A. (1962). *Reason and emotion in psychotherapy.* Secaucus, NJ: Lyle Stuart.

Feltz, D. L., & Landers, D. M. (1983). The effects of mental practice on motor skill learning and performance: A meta-analysis. *Journal of Sport Psychology, 5*, 25–57.

Fine, A. (1993). *Mind over golf.* London: BBC Enterprises.

Ford, S. K., & Summers, J. J. (1992). The factorial validity of the TAIS attentional-style subscales. *Journal of Sport and Exercise Psychology, 14*, 283–297.

Garfield, C. A., & Bennett, H. Z. (1984). *Peak performance: Mental training techniques of the world's greatest athletes.* Los Angeles: Tarcher.

Gauron, E. F. (1984). *Mental training for peak performance.* Lansing, NY: Sport Science Associates.

Gipson, M., McKenzie, T., & Lowe, S. (1989). The sport psychology program of the USA women's national volleyball team. *The Sport Psychologist, 3*, 330–339.

Gordin, R. D., & Henschen, K. P. (1989). Preparing the USA women's artistic gymnastics team for the 1988 Olympics: A multimodel approach. *The Sport Psychologist, 3*, 366–373.

Gordon, S. (1990). A mental skills training program for the Western Australian state cricket team. *The Sport Psychologist, 4*, 386–399.

Gordon, S., Milios, D., & Grove, R. (1991). Psychological aspects of the recovery process from sport injury. *Australian Journal of Science and Medicine in Sport, 6*, 53–59.

Gould, D., & Finch, L. (1990). Sport psychology and the professional bowler: The case of Michelle Mullen. *The Sport Psychologist, 4*, 418–430.

Gould, D., Murphy, S., Tammen, V., & May, J. (1991). An evaluation of U.S. Olympic sport psychology consultant effectiveness. *The Sport Psychologist, 5*, 111–127.

Gould, D., Petlichkoff, L., Hodge, K., & Simons, J. (1990). Evaluating the effectiveness of a psychological skills educational workshop. *The Sport Psychologist, 4*, 249–260.

Gould, D., Tammen, V., Murphy, S., & May, J. (1989). An examination of the U.S. Olympic sport psychology consultants and the services they provide. *The Sport Psychologist, 3*, 300–312.

Green, L. B. (1992). The use of imagery in the rehabilitation of injured athletes. *The Sport Psychologist, 6*, 416–428.

Greenspan, M. J., & Feltz, D. L. (1989). Psychological interventions with athletes in competitive situations: A review. *The Sport Psychologist, 3*, 219–236.

Halliwell, W. (1989). Delivering sport psychology services to the Canadian sailing team at the 1988 summer Olympic games. *The Sport Psychologist, 3*, 313–319.

Halliwell, W. (1990). Providing sport psychology consulting services in professional hockey. *The Sport Psychologist, 4*, 369–377.

Hardy, L., & Fazey, J. (1990). *Mental training programme.* Beckett Park, Leeds: National Coaching Foundation.

Hardy, L., & Nelson, A. (1992). The development and validation of the Sports Psychological Skills Inventory. Manuscript submitted for publication.

Harris, D. V., & Harris, B. L. (1984). *The athlete's guide to sports psychology: Mental skills for physical people.* Champaign, IL: Leisure Press.

Hayden, R. M., Allen, G. J., & Camaione, D. N. (1986). Some psychological benefits resulting from involvement in an aerobic fitness program from the perspectives of participants and knowledgeable informants. *Journal of Sports Medicine, 26*, 67–76.

Heil, J. (1993). Sport psychology, the athlete at risk, and the sports medicine team. In J. Heil (Ed.), *Psychology of sport injury* (pp. 1–13). Champaign, IL: Human Kinetics.

Henschen, K. P. (1993). Athletic staleness and burnout: Diagnosis, prevention and treatment. In J. M. Williams (Ed.), *Applied sport psychology: Personal growth to peak performance* (2nd ed.) (pp. 328–337). Palo Alto, CA: Mayfield.

Highlen, P. S., & Bennett, B. B. (1979). Psychological characteristics of successful and nonsuccessful elite wrestlers: An exploratory study. *Journal of Sport Psychology, 1*, 123–137.

Hogan, C. (1988). *"Nice Shot"*. Sedona, AZ: Sports Enhancement Associates.

Ievleva, L., & Orlick, T. (1991). Mental links to enhanced healing: An exploratory study. *The Sport Psychologist, 5*, 25–40.

Jackson, S. A. (1992). Athletes in flow: A qualitative investigation of flow states in elite figure skaters. *Journal of Applied Sport Psychology, 4*, 161–180.

Jacobs, A. (1988). *Sports psychology: The winning edge in sports.* Kansas City, MO: The Winning Edge.

Jacobson, E. (1930). *Progressive relaxation.* Chicago: University of Chicago Press.

Jones, G. (1993). The role of performance profiling in cognitive behavioral interventions in sport. *The Sport Psychologist, 7*, 160–172.

Karle, H. W. A., & Boys, J. H. (1987). *Hypnotherapy: A practitioner's handbook.* London: Free Association Books.

Loehr, J. E. (1983). The ideal performance state. *Science periodical on research and technology in sport.* Ottawa: Coaching Association of Canada.

Loehr, J. E. (1984, March). How to overcome stress and play at your peak all the time. *Tennis,* 66–76.

Loehr, J. (1989). *Mental toughness training for tennis: "The 16 second cure".* Miami, FL: FTM Sports.

Loehr, J. E. (1990). Providing sport psychology consulting services to professional tennis players. *The Sport Psychologist, 4*, 400–408.

Mackinnon, L. T., & Hooper, S. (1992). Overtraining: State of the Art Review No. 26. *Excel, 8*, 3–12.

Mahoney, M. J., & Avener, M. (1977). Psychology of the elite athlete: An exploratory study. *Cognitive Therapy and Research, 1*, 135–141.

Mahoney, M. J., Gabriel, T. J., & Perkins, T. S. (1987). Psychological skills and exceptional athletic performance. *The Sport Psychologist, 1*, 181–199.

Martens, R. (1975). *Social psychology and physical activity.* New York: Harper & Row.

Martens, R. (1987). *Coaches guide to sport psychology.* Champaign, IL: Human Kinetics.

Martens, R., Burton, D., Vealey, R. S., Bump, L. A., & Smith, D. E. (1983). *Competitive State Anxiety Inventory–2.* Unpublished manuscript, University of Illinois at Urbana-Champaign.

Martin, G. (1989). *Sport psyching for figure skaters.* Winnipeg, Manitoba: Communication Systems.

May, J. R., & Brown, L. (1989). Delivery of psychological services to the U.S. alpine ski team prior to and during the Olympics in Calgary. *The Sport Psychologist, 3*, 320–329.

McCullagh, P., North, T. C., & Mood, D. (1988). *Exercise as a treatment for depression: A meta-analysis.* Paper presented at the meeting of the North American Society for the Psychology of Sport and Physical Activity, Knoxville, TN.

McNair, D. M., Lorr, M., & Droppleman, L. F. (1971). *Profile of mood states manual.* San Diego, CA: Educational and Industrial Testing Service.

Meyers, A. W., Cooke, C. J., Cullen, J., & Liles, L. (1979). Psychological aspects of athletic competitors: A replication across sports. *Cognitive Therapy and Research, 3,* 361–366.

Morgan, W. P., & Goldston, S. E. (1987). Summary. In W. P. Morgan, & S. E. Goldston (Eds.), *Exercise and mental health* (pp. 155–159). New York: Hemisphere.

Morris, T. (1991). *A model for psychological skills training in table tennis.* International Table Tennis Federation Second World Congress of Science and Table Tennis, Tokyo.

Morris, T. (1992). Psychological skills training for table tennis. *Accredited Coach, 1,* 5–11.

Morris, T. (in press). Sport psychology in Australia: Recent developments.

Murphy, S. M., & Ferrante, A. P. (1989). Provision of sport psychology services to the U.S. team at the 1988 summer Olympic games. *The Sport Psychologist, 3,* 374–385.

Neff, F. (1990). Delivering sport psychology services to a professional sport organization. *The Sport Psychologist, 4,* 378–385.

Nideffer, R. M. (1976). Test of Attentional and Interpersonal Style. *Journal of Personality and Social Psychology, 34,* 394–404.

Nideffer, R. M. (1985). *Athletes' guide to mental training.* Champaign, IL: Human Kinetics.

Nideffer, R. M. (1989). Psychological services for the U.S. track and field team. *The Sport Psychologist, 3,* 350–357.

North, T. C., & McCullagh, P. (1988, October). *Aerobic and anaerobic exercise as a treatment for depression.* A meta-analysis. Paper presented at the meeting of the Association for the Advancement of Applied Sport Psychology, Nashua, NH.

Orlick, T. (1986). *Psyching for sport: Mental training for athletes.* Champaign, IL: Leisure Press.

Orlick, T. (1989). Reflections on sportpsych consulting with individual and team sport athletes at summer and winter Olympic games. *The Sport Psychologist, 3,* 358–365.

Ostrow, A. C. (Ed.). (1990). *Directory of psychological tests in the sport and exercise sciences.* Morgantown, WV: Fitness Information Technology.

Parfitt, G., & Hardy, L. (1993). Sport psychology and the BAGA. *Coaching Focus, 22,* 22–23.

Pargman, D. (Ed.). (1993). *Psychological bases of sport injuries.* Morgantown, WV: Fitness Information Technology.

Petitpas, A., Danish, S., McKelvain, R., & Murphy, S. (1992). A career assistance program for elite athletes. *Journal of Counseling and Development, 70,* 383–386.

Ravizza, K. (1977). Peak experiences in sport. *Journal of Humanistic Psychology, 17,* 35–40.

Ravizza, K. (1984). Qualities of the peak experience in sport. In J. M. Silva, & R. S. Weinberg (Eds.), *Psychological foundations of sport* (pp. 452–462). Champaign, IL: Human Kinetics.

Ravizza, K. (1988). Gaining entry with athletic personnel for season-long consulting. *The Sport Psychologist, 2,* 243–254.

Ravizza, K. (1990). Sportpsych consultation issues in professional baseball. *The Sport Psychologist, 4,* 330–340.

Ravizza, K. (1993). Increasing awareness for sport performance. In J. M. Williams (Ed.), *Applied sport psychology* (2nd ed.) (pp. 148–157). Palo Alto, CA: Mayfield.

Ravizza, K., & Osborne, T. (1991). Nebraska's 3 R's: One-play-at-a-time preperformance routine for collegiate football. *The Sport Psychologist, 5*, 256–265.

Rejeski, W. J., & Brawley, L. R. (1988). Defining the boundaries of sport psychology. *The Sport Psychologist, 2*, 231–242.

Rotella, R. J. (1990). Providing sport psychology consulting services to professional athletes. *The Sport Psychologist, 4*, 409–417.

Rotella, R. J., & Heyman, S. R. (1993). Stress, injury, and the psychological rehabilitation of athletes. In J. M. Williams (Ed.), *Applied sport psychology* (2nd ed.) (pp. 338–355). Palo Alto, CA: Mayfield.

Rushall, B. S. (1991). *Imagery training in sports.* Spring Valley, CA: Sports Science Associates.

Rushall, B. S. (1992). *Mental skills training for sports.* Spring Valley, CA: Sports Science Associates.

Sachs, M. L. (1991). Reading list in applied sport psychology: Psychological skills training. *The Sport Psychologist, 5*, 88–91.

Salmela, J. H. (1989). Long-term intervention with the Canadian men's Olympic gymnastic team. *The Sport Psychologist, 3*, 340–349.

Salmela, J. H. (1992). *The world sport psychology sourcebook* (2nd ed.). Champaign, IL: Human Kinetics.

Seraganian, P. (Ed.). (1993). *Exercise psychology: The influence of physical exercise on psychological processes.* New York: John Wiley & Sons.

Smith, R. E. (1988). The logic and design of case study research. *The Sport Psychologist, 2*, 1–12.

Smith, R. E., & Johnson, J. (1990). An organizational empowerment approach to consultation in professional baseball. *The Sport Psychologist, 4*, 347–357.

Stewart, A. (1990). *Psychology and motivation in football.* Melbourne: National Australian Football Council.

Suinn, R. M. (1986). *Seven steps to peak performance.* Toronto: Hans Huber Publishers.

Sullivan, J., & Hodge, K. P. (1991). A survey of coaches and athletes about sport psychology in New Zealand. *The Sport Psychologist, 5*, 140–151.

Summers, J. J., Miller, K., & Ford, S. (1991). Attentional style and basketball performance. *Journal of Sport and Exercise Psychology, 13*, 239–253.

Thomas, P. R. (1990). *An overview of performance enhancement processes in applied sport psychology.* Unpublished manuscript. Colorado Springs: United States Olympic Training Centre.

Thomas, P. R., & Bain, J. D. (1984). Contextual dependence of learning approaches: The effects of assessments. *Human Learning, 3*, 227–240.

Vealey, R. S. (1988). Future directions in psychological skills training. *The Sport Psychologist, 2*, 318–336.

Waxman, D. (1989). *Hartland's medical and dental hypnosis* (3rd ed.). London: Balliere Tindall.

Weinberg, R. S. (1984). Mental preparation strategies. In J. M. Silva & R. S. Weinberg (Eds.), *Psychological foundations of sport* (pp. 145–156). Champaign, IL: Human Kinetics.

Weinberg, R. S. (1988). *The mental advantage.* Champaign, IL: Leisure Press.

Weinberg, R. S., & Williams, J. M. (1993). Integrating and implementing a psychological skills training program. In J. M. Williams (Ed.), *Applied sport psychology* (2nd ed.) (pp. 274–298). Palo Alto, CA: Mayfield.

Wiese, D. M., Weiss, M. R., & Yukelson, D. P. (1991). Sport psychology in the training room: A survey of athletic trainers. *The Sport Psychologist, 5*, 15–24.

Williams, J. M. (Ed.). (1986). *Applied sport psychology*. Palo Alto, CA: Mayfield.

Williams, J. M. (Ed.). (1993). *Applied sport psychology* (2nd ed.). Palo Alto, CA: Mayfield.

Williams, J. M. (1994). How should we define sport psychology? *Association for the Advancement of Applied Sport Psychology Newsletter, 9*(1), 1.

Williams, J. M., & Krane, V. (1993). Psychological characteristics of peak performance. In J. M. Williams (Ed.), *Applied sport psychology* (2nd ed.) (pp. 137–147). Palo Alto, CA: Mayfield.

Williams, J. M., & Straub, W. F. (1993). Sport psychology: Past, present, future. In J. M. Williams (Ed.), *Applied sport psychology* (2nd ed.) (pp. 1–10). Palo Alto, CA: Mayfield.

Willis, J. D., & Campbell, L. F. (1992). *Exercise psychology*. Champaign, IL: Human Kinetics.

Winter, G., & Martin, C. (1991). *SASI Psych: Basic training program*. Adelaide: South Australian Sports Institute.

Wolpe, J. (1958). *Psychotherapy by reciprocal inhibition*. Stanford, CA: Stanford University Press.

C H A P T E R

10

GOAL SETTING

GRAHAM WINTER

Goal setting is the most researched and, arguably, most used sport psychology technique. Even those coaches and athletes who are most sceptical about the value of psychological training in sport will usually acknowledge the importance of athletes having a clear, specific and realistic set of goals. Their impressions are solidly backed by research on the efficacy of goal setting as a regulator of human action across many areas of human endeavour (Locke & Latham, 1990).

While goal setting is commonly seen as a "motivation tool" (Silva & Weinberg, 1984), it is also widely used as an applied technique to enhance concentration, build self-confidence and to manage time and other resources efficiently.

This chapter focuses on ways in which goal setting can be applied as a technique to enhance the performance of athletes. References are made to research findings; however, the main emphasis is on explaining how the sport psychology consultant might use goal setting to enhance the performance of athletes. Further details on research have been covered in Burton (1992) and Gould (1993).

WHAT IS APPLIED GOAL SETTING?

Goal setting is the process of selecting desirable targets or objectives. The targets or objectives are usually called goals and can include such achievements as winning a medal, gaining a personal best score or developing a skill.

In the context of applied sport psychology it is also important to recognise the distinction between outcome or end-result goals, such as winning a tennis match, and process goals, such as getting 70% of first serves into play or attacking the net on short returns. Research (Burton, 1984, 1989) has shown that the best and most consistent (competition) performances occur when athletes set process goals over which they have control, rather than outcome goals (e.g., winning) which are dependent on the performance of others. Athletes who commence using process goals regularly report that the reduced emphasis on the outcome makes them feel more confident, less anxious and better able to concentrate.

Most leading athletes select technical, tactical, psychological and physiological goals which they strive to achieve in training and competition. Figure 10.1 shows this concept applied to canoeing.

Technical
"Achieve full body twist throughout the 500 metres effort."
Tactical
"Win the race."
Psychological
"Maintain total focus on executing my race plan."
Physiological
"Reduce body fat by 2% before the National Championships."

Figure 10.1: Goals in different domains

The sport psychology consultant can use the process of goal setting to assist athletes greatly in focusing their resources. The goals themselves may range from a (long-term) four-year, detailed written goal program which an aspiring Olympic athlete might choose, to the countless small, short-term goals which a runner might select along the way during a long training session.

WHY SET GOALS?

A goal provides a focus. This allows the athlete to direct limited time and energy into the most productive activities. Any one who has ever developed a "things-to-do-list" knows how this simple list of goals can help to focus attention and energy in a much more efficient way.

Goals provide motivation (Silva & Weinberg, 1984). A typical example of a goal which provides motivation is that which most football teams have at the start of the season, that is, to win the premiership.

Goals provide direction (Locke & Bryan, 1969). Just as a "things-to-do-list" helps us to focus on a task and thereby use our time more productively, so too do sporting goals help the athlete to eliminate potential distractions and to focus on what is important. A common example here is the talented young athlete who must choose between sports in which he or she is equally proficient, (e.g., netball and volleyball). On reflection the athlete may determine that the main goal is to represent his or her country at an Olympic Games and, therefore, the athlete chooses to focus on volleyball because it is an Olympic sport.

Goals produce better results. Research has consistently shown that performance can be enhanced through the effective use of goal setting (Bandura & Cervone, 1983; Locke & Latham, 1990). Goals can increase the athletes' feelings of control, raise their self-esteem and help them to focus on the key elements of the task under highly competitive conditions.

Many coaches see goal setting as the most important psychological technique for athletes to develop. When coaches train young athletes to regularly set and review goals for training and competition, they also develop those athletes' abilities to control their own actions. This is an important attribute as athletes move into senior ranks.

For the sporting coach, goal setting also provides additional ways of developing their athletes. These can come from a greater involvement by athletes in the planning and implementation of the goal-setting process, from the opportunity it provides for enhanced communication during the process, and from the positive reinforcement which comes from setting and achieving meaningful goals.

PRINCIPLES OF GOAL SETTING

Findings from the numerous research studies into goal setting have been extensively described by Locke and Latham (1990). These, together with the accumulated experiences of applied sport psychologists, have created a set of clear, effective guidelines for using goal setting.

MAKE GOALS SPECIFIC

Specific goals, such as the tennis example of achieving 75% of first serves into play, lead to better performance than goals of "do your best" or no goals at all. Goals such as running 4000 metres in 15 minutes are quite specific, but technical skills, (e.g., rowing stroke) and psychological skills, (e.g., concentration) are more difficult to specify. One way to deal with this is to give each skill a "benchmark" percentage. For example, the rowing stroke may be rated at 80% of what is required and a goal to get it to 90% in one month makes this a more specific target.

SET SHORT-TERM GOALS WITH DEADLINES

Long-term goals are more likely to be achieved when they are divided or broken down into a series of short-term goals. Athletes can be encouraged to set major goals (e.g., making the final at the National Championships) and then shown how to set sub-goals (technical, tactical, physical, psychological, competitive) which act like stepping stones towards the "big" goal.

PROVIDE CLEAR, REGULAR FEEDBACK

Goal setting is only effective when there is performance feedback. Good coaches regularly tell athletes how they are performing. This can include statistical information from physiological tests, reports on competition performance and comments on attitude and related areas. One of the most important aspects of coaching is to provide timely and accurate feedback to athletes.

MAKE GOALS CHALLENGING BUT ACHIEVABLE

The goals which lead to best performance are those which are difficult or challenging, rather than moderate or easy. This means finding the balance between a target which the athlete thinks is easy and one on which he or she gives up because it is too hard (i.e., beyond the athlete's perceived ability level). As a guide, it is perhaps wise to err on the side of making the goals harder for the more confident athletes and easier for the less confident ones.

BE FLEXIBLE

The value of goals lies in their ability to interest, challenge and direct the athlete. In the real world, circumstances change and, therefore, goals can become too easy or too difficult. At these times it is best to discuss an alternative goal with the athlete.

SET GOALS TOGETHER

When coaches and athletes set goals together, the commitment of the athletes towards the chosen goals is likely to be higher.

WRITE GOALS AND SET PRIORITIES

By documenting the plan, deciding on priorities and setting clear time frames, the whole goal-setting process can be much more effective. It is often most effective for the athlete to record goals in a diary because this encourages on-going monitoring of progress.

A GOAL-SETTING PROGRAM

There is no single, universally accepted way to introduce a full goal-setting program for athletes. What follows is an approach which has been used successfully with athletes up to and including Olympic and World Champion level.

This approach has been set out in such a way that a sport psychology consultant can follow and adapt it for his or her own needs. For example, at the South Australian Sports Institute these steps have been built into goal-setting workbooks which athletes and coaches can use without the need for an interview with a sport psychologist.

There are seven key steps involved in this goal-setting process.
1. Develop an inventory of possible goals.
2. Select priorities and time-lines.
3. Assess the current position.
4. Set sub-goals.
5. Program the goals.
6. Create action.
7. Monitor and modify the goals and behaviour.

Develop an inventory of possible goals

The first step in goal setting is to encourage the athlete to develop a broad list of possible goals. Often this means encouraging the athlete to expand his or her thinking about what might be possible. Questions such as those which follow can be helpful in drawing out a broad list of sporting goals.

> - At the end of your sporting career, and as you look back, what do you want to have accomplished?
> - What do you most want to achieve in your sport?
> - If you could accomplish anything in your sport what would you aim for?
> - What do you most enjoy about playing sport?

At this stage it is also important to draw out key goals from other life areas and these include career/study, relationships, spiritual, family and personal aspects. It is best not to rush this part of the process because the aim is to ensure that the athlete has had time to consider the full range of available options.

It is also important to point out that most athletes select achievement-type goals. However, they should also consider things like recognition, affiliation (friendship, team-orientation) and the intrinsic enjoyment of sport because these are the elements which often keep athletes in the sport.

At the conclusion of this step, the athlete will ideally have written a detailed list of possible goals. These will include short-, medium- and long-term goals.

Select priorities and time-lines

Once the inventory has been developed the athlete can be encouraged to work through the list, identifying those which are personally the most meaningful. A convenient way to do this is to have the athlete rate each goal according to the following system:

A — most important goals
B — important goals
C — somewhat important goals
D — not important goals
E — goals of no interest.

The sport psychology consultant can play a useful role at this stage by encouraging the athlete to fully consider the reasons for his or her choice of priorities.

Assess the current position

If the athlete is to achieve his or her most important goals, it is likely that improvement will be needed in the following three areas:
1. Skill level
2. Psychological capacity
3. Physiological capacity.

Accordingly, it is necessary that the athlete establishes his or her current level of capacity in these areas. A simple way to do this is to have the athlete and coach develop a list of the key skills, psychological capacities and physiological capacities which are required for the sport. Figure 10.2 shows a list which might be developed by a cricket coach for a batter.

Skills	Psychological capacity	Physiological capacity
Forward defensive	Batting under pressure	Flexibility
Driving off-side	Control of emotions	Strength
Playing quick bowling	Contribution to team	Body fat percentage
Running between wickets	Consistency	Endurance

Figure 10.2: List of skills, psychological and physiological capacities for cricket batters

For those elements which can be measured, such as flexibility, body fat percentage and endurance, the coach can develop tests. For those which are not as readily measured, it is suggested that a rating scale of 1 to 10 points be used. The specific instruction to the athlete can be as follows: "Consider each aspect and give yourself a rating out of ten to describe your present level on that aspect. Assume that a score of ten is the level required to reach the goal that you are currently working towards." For example, a cricketer with the goal to play Sheffield Shield cricket may rate himself at "8" for "consistency", based on his understanding that "10" is required to play successfully at Shield level.

Set sub-goals

Young, achievement-oriented athletes are often inclined to focus on the "top of the mountain" when they might be better served by dividing it into smaller, more manageable steps. Sub-goals provide a more immediate focus and can help athletes through some of the more difficult stages of training.

Many top level athletes have very well-defined, goal-setting processes and they can readily explain how one activity at training is part of the process of achieving a major goal some months or years ahead.

The sport psychology consultant can often have an immediate positive effect on the performance of the young, ambitious athlete by helping the athlete to select small daily and weekly goals which are stepping stones to the "big" goals.

Program the goals

Programming the goals means making them an integral part of the athlete's overall training and competition program. In most cases this requires the coach to institute a goal-oriented approach to training and competition.

Under these conditions the coach will provide the opportunity for the athlete to set goals for all training and competition activities, to review the goals after each activity and to regularly discuss progress towards the major goals.

The sport psychology consultant can assist the coach by providing simple layouts for training and competition diaries and by providing suggestions on ways in which the athlete(s) can best be fully involved in the process. This will at times involve discussions with athletes.

Create action Goal setting is nothing without action. The top athletes are generally proactive people. They waste little time in pondering over their goals once they have set them. They know that planning without action is a waste of their precious time and energy.

Sometimes the challenge for the sport psychology consultant is to extract enough time for the athlete to do justice to the goal-setting process. This is less of a problem now than it was a few years ago. Athletes and coaches are aware that the time spent on planning can ensure that they are not just doing things right but more importantly, they are doing the right things!

Sport psychology consultants need to be wary that they don't fall into the trap of making the goal-setting process an "intellectual" exercise. When all is said and done, the aim of goal setting is to produce action in a certain direction. The consultant can assist this by encouraging athletes to select up to three action plans to go with any goal that they might select. Figure 10.3 illustrates this approach.

- **Goal**
  Run 800 metres in sub 2 minutes.
- **Immediate action plans**
  Train one extra night per week.
  Do hill sprints on Wednesdays.
  Practise visualisation every night this week.

Figure 10.3: A goal and related action plans in athletics

Monitor and modify the goals and behaviour

An essential part of the goal-setting process is the regular checking of progress. As previously mentioned, this is best done as an integral part of the athlete's program. The use of a diary or journal can greatly assist this process. By encouraging young athletes to develop a ritual of setting and reviewing goals prior to and following training and competition, there is every likelihood that a goal-oriented, mind-set can be developed.

The sport psychology consultant can assist this process by meeting regularly with the athlete to discuss his or her progress and by frequently reminding coaches to provide feedback to athletes on their progress. It is this feedback which helps athletes to make realistic modifications to their goals and behaviour.

As a general comment, the "weak link" in goal setting is the post-achievement review. When a goal is not achieved there is often a detailed "post-mortem", but sometimes a valuable learning opportunity can be missed if this is not also done after success.

GOAL SETTING IN COMPETITION

One of the great challenges for the sport psychology consultant is to convince athletes and coaches of the merit in selecting process or performance goals (instead of outcome goals). Many athletes and coaches still focus mainly on the goal "to win", rather than on the performance processes which might allow this to be achieved.

We know from research (Burton, 1984, 1989) that performance goals can positively enhance performance in competition. Such goals might include aspects of technique, applying certain strategies and maintaining concentration in pressure situations. Examples are given for two sports in Figure 10.4.

- **Basketball**
  - get 3 assists each game
  - limit passing errors to 2 per game
  - get 10 rebounds
  - relax before free throws
  - make 50% from the floor.
- **Canoeing**
  - over 10 × 1000 m maintain a time of 4 min. 30 sec. with a 2 minute break between each 1000 m.
  - maintain stroke rate at 85 strokes per minute for 6 minutes.
  - for anaerobic threshold training, maintain heart rate at 175 beats per minute for 5 x 15 minutes with 1 minute rest between each of the 5 segments.
  - focus on every stroke being long and powerful.

Figure 10.4: Performance goals for basketball and canoeing

The use of goals as a means of modifying athletes' mental state predates the existence of sport psychology as an applied science. Accordingly, it is important for the sport psychology consultant to recognise that many coaches and athletes have firm and somewhat rigid views about how goals should be employed. While this may frustrate the consultant, it is often necessary to accept that coaches and athletes will want to set outcome goals because, at the end of the day, this is the basis on which they are selected and rewarded. Nevertheless, it is up to the skill of the consultant to find a way to help athletes to focus on those aspects of the performance which are most likely to produce the result that they seek.

One way that this can be achieved is by simply asking athletes to identify two or three aspects of the performance, which are in their influence to control, and which will give them the best chance of winning.

The example in Figure 10.5 illustrates this point.

(Consultant)	"What is your goal for this tournament?"
(Golfer)	"To win, of course!"
(Consultant)	"What are the two most important things for you to focus on in order to give yourself the best chance of winning?"
(Golfer)	"Hitting 80% of the fairways and following my pre-shot routine for every shot".

Figure 10.5: Developing process goals from an outcome goal

Both the sport psychology consultant and the coach have an important role to play in encouraging athletes to focus on goals which are within their influence. In the example, in Figure 10.5, it is likely that the golfer will perform at a consistently higher level if he or she is able to maintain focus on the processes which are generally under the golfer's control, rather than on winning, which is greatly dependent on the performances of other players.

GOALS FOR TRAINING

The discussion earlier in the chapter highlighted the many benefits for athletes who set goals for training. Ideally, an athlete will have planned and written his or her goals before each training session. Unfortunately this happens all too rarely (often because the coach hasn't planned the session).

For a training session to be truly effective it is necessary for each athlete to know what he or she is doing, the reason for doing it and how he or she is doing. The following questions represent a useful format for coaches and sport psychology consultants to employ when checking with athletes during a session.

- What goals are you working towards in this session?
- How are you doing at the moment?
- How do you know?
- What are you doing to improve it?

Figure 10.6: Questions to ask before a training session

Training diaries are widely used by leading athletes, particularly in individual sports. While the format of the diary can vary enormously, the overall aim is to create a record of goals set and achieved and of the athlete's experiences. This can be an invaluable method of storing information on how a problem was solved (thereby saving time when it occurs again at a later date).

One of the best ways of encouraging athletes to use a training diary is to explain that top athletes use them on a regular basis. A simple way to introduce the diary is to have athletes purchase a blank exercise book which they divide into three sections, headed as follows:

1. "My goals" (allow five pages)
2. "My training record" (allow two-thirds of remainder of book)
3. "My competition record" (allow remainder of book).

Athletes can write their overall goals in the first section and use the remaining two sections to record goals and experiences from training and competition. The coach or sport psychology consultant will ideally check the diaries and encourage the athletes to use the diaries for planning and to record the things which they learn. When used in this way, the diary becomes a valuable resource for the athlete.

FUTURE DIRECTIONS

The trend in the use of goal setting in applied sport psychology is towards greater reliance on process goals as a method of modifying an athlete's psychological state. At international level this practice is widespread; however, there will always be pressure placed on coaches and athletes to produce results (outcomes). Fortunately, we are also likely to see an increased understanding amongst coaches of young athletes, of the value of these athletes working towards goals which are under their control. This will lead to the development of athletes who are able to perform more reliably under changing conditions.

Alongside this trend we may again see more emphasis on what we could call the "Olympic ideals", that is, the use of sport as a method for developing character. This would mean a greater integration of goals for all areas of life, into a total "person-development" strategy. This trend will also have the effect of reducing the importance of the outcome or result and focus athletes' attention onto a broader purpose. It may be that this will reduce anxiety and enhance concentration in a similar way to that achieved through process goals. Further research will no doubt be attracted to the general question of whether having a broader purpose, be it self development, spiritual or whatever, has an influence on performance in various sporting activities.

CONCLUSIONS

Goal setting is a widely used psychological technique which has application across all sports and all ages. In no way can it be considered "new". However, research and practical experience have shown that there are ways in which goal setting can be applied for maximum results.

While the technique of goal setting is relatively straightforward, this might also be one of its main weaknesses, because athletes sometimes consider the idea of goal setting to be rather trite. Equally, there are many who have quite rigid views on the importance of setting outcome goals.

The experience of sport psychologists suggests that there are relatively few athletes who actually use the technique of goal setting as well as they might. The most common experience is that athletes' goals are not specific enough and, for the sport psychology consultant, this is often a "non-controversial" place to start consulting with an athlete.

Ideally, an athlete can be encouraged to develop a goal-setting program which contains both a challenging and meaningful target, for example, "be selected in next year's national team", and a series of sub-goals or stepping stones, that is, technical, tactical, psychological, physiological and competition goals. Goals also need to be set for other life areas and priorities arranged accordingly.

For goal setting to be truly effective it also needs to be an integral part of the athlete's total program. This requires the coach to allocate time for planning and reviewing of training and competition goals.

Finally, it is likely that the most consistent competitive performances will occur when the athlete has developed the capacity to focus on the process, rather than the outcome. The use of performance or process goals presents an ideal vehicle for creating this focus.

SUMMARY

This chapter has focused on how the technique of goal setting can best be applied to assist athletes to enhance their sporting performances. Research and practical experience has demonstrated that goal setting is a powerful technique for influencing the behaviour of athletes at training, in competition and in their daily lives.

Goal setting is generally most effective when goals are selected in a way which ensures that they are specific, measurable, meaningful and challenging for the athlete. Also of importance is the involvement of the coach in providing feedback on goals and building the athlete's goals into the total training and competition plan.

There are various ways in which a goal-setting program can be introduced for an athlete. However, it is recommended that it begin with a broad examination of possible goals. This inventory can then be prioritised and the athlete helped to assess his or her current position in relation to the goal. Given that athletes will generally choose some long-term goals, it is important that they be assisted to break these into sub-goals. It is also important that athletes be encouraged to act on their goals, to monitor their progress and to modify the goals if circumstances change.

Many top athletes make use of training diaries in which they record their progress towards their goals. Such diaries can be a valuable source of information and can help athletes to better understand what set of conditions lead to their better performances.

There is a tendency amongst athletes to select outcome goals for competition. However, research has shown that more consistent performances result when athletes are helped to focus on the process. Accordingly, the use of performance or process goals is encouraged and this trend is spreading through all levels of sport.

REFERENCES

Bandura, A., & Cervone, D. (1983). Self-evaluative and self efficacy mechanisms governing the motivational effects of goal systems. *Journal of Personality and Social Psychology, 45*, 1017–1028.

Burton, D. (1984). Evaluation of goal setting training on selected cognitions and performance of collegiate swimmers. Dissertation Abstracts International. *45* (1), July 1984.

Burton, D. (1989) Winning isn't everything: Examining the impact of performance goals on collegiate swimmers' cognitions and performance. *The Sport Psychologist, 3*, 105–132.

Burton, D. (1992). The Jekyll/Hyde nature of goals: Reconceptualizing goal setting in sport. In T. S. Horn (Ed.), *Advances in sport psychology*. Champaign, IL: Human Kinetics.

Gould, D. (1993). Goal setting for peak performance. In J. M. Williams (Ed.), *Applied sport psychology: Personal growth to peak performance* (2nd ed.). Mountain View, CA: Mayfield.

Locke, E. A., & Latham, G. P. (1990). A theory of goal setting and task performance. Englewood Cliffs, NJ: Prentice-Hall.

Locke, E. A., & Bryan, J. F. (1969). The directing function of goals in task performance. *Organisational Behaviour and Human Performance, 4*, 35–42.

Silva, J. M. (III), & Weinberg, R. S. (1984). *Psychological foundations of sport*. Champaign, IL: Human Kinetics.

C H A P T E R

11

STRESS
MANAGEMENT

CATHERINE MARTIN

The literature suggests that in the general population, physical activity has been regarded as one of the most important lifestyle factors which positively contributes towards both physical health and psychological well-being (Bouchard, Shephard, Stephens, Sutton, & McPherson, 1990). Because of the amount of exercise elite athletes undertake, they have traditionally been regarded as the epitome of both physical and psychological health.

However, it has become increasingly apparent that we cannot make generalisations about the relationship between exercise, fitness and health of the elite athlete in training. Elite athletes engage in exercise to achieve a high performance level, not necessarily to achieve optimal health. Whilst the general public continues to gain many benefits from engaging in regular and moderate levels of exercise, sports scientists, in applied settings, have increasingly raised concerns about the health of elite athletes. Researchers have since focused their attention specifically on elite athletes in order to investigate their physical and psychological health status.

Elite athletes are continually searching for a competitive edge in their performance and maintain very rigorous training regimes. As a result of this highly intensive and specific training, they are commonly regarded as being in peak physical and psychological condition. However, recent research suggests that exercise of a prolonged and intensive nature is not necessarily associated with optimal health. Many elite athletes consistently extend themselves both physically and psychologically, with some showing signs of chronic fatigue, injury and illness, in an attempt to obtain a competitive edge.

The rigours of regular and intense training combined with a range of other non-sporting pressures can often mean that elite athletes are prone to the effects of stress. Common stressors include producing a personal best or winning performance at the right time; social, relationship, financial and time pressures; developing a career outside sport; and overcoming the impact of chronic physical injury. However, stress for elite athletes can also relate to the stress of competition, for example, "psyching-up" for an important event. Performance anxiety levels can differ for individuals and vary from event to event as athletes attempt to perform at their best.

Elite coaches may also experience the effects of stress because of the many and varied functions they are increasingly required to perform. The coach's responsibilities can include:
- the training and effective competition preparation of a number of athletes
- dealing with extreme parental expectations
- financial management of budgets
- counselling athletes to overcome personal or performance-related problems
- non-sporting career demands
- family or relationship commitments.

In many instances, the coach's career is in jeopardy if these athletes do not perform successfully.

For these reasons, both elite athletes and coaches can experience the effects of stress and require specialist psychological assistance in both preventing and managing stress in their sporting and non-sporting lives.

This chapter explores the concept of stress in more detail and will outline a variety of stress management techniques available to elite athletes and coaches to manage stress and anxiety.

APPLIED ISSUES

The research differentiates between stress, anxiety and arousal and Chapter 2 by Anshel discusses these differences in more detail, from a theoretical perspective. The elite athlete, however, often uses these terms interchangeably when referring to how he or she is coping with the pressures in his or her life and when talking about the level of "psych-up" needed for optimum performance. The applied sport psychologist often uses similar techniques when dealing with stress, anxiety and arousal issues, but must apply them in a manner specific to each individual athlete and to the particular situation being addressed. The following examples illustrate some of these differences between stress, anxiety and arousal for the elite athlete.

STRESS   Ann Smith, a long jumper, reports that she has been quite "stressed" over the past month. Ann has school exams in the near future and is considerably behind in her study, having been focusing her efforts on training for the Commonwealth Games selection trials. When Ann talks about her highly stressed state, she is referring to the specific situations and demands that she faces combined with her own perception of her ability to handle those situations and demands.

The term "stress" involves a number of components including the cognitive appraisal of a situation, perceived coping abilities and the subsequent stress symptoms.

The much-researched area of stress has predominantly focused on the physiological effects of the "stress response", the resulting stress symptoms and the effects on both the psychological and physical health status. Stress has become a general descriptor referring to both anxiety and arousal. In the athletic population, however, the effects of the stress response have predominantly been examined in the context of stress as pre-competition state, rather than the effect of stress on the athlete's life in general.

The work of Cannon (1932) and Seyle (1951–1956) focused on the body's defence alarm mechanism or "fight or flight" response to stressful situations. The concept of stress was developed further to include an individual component whereby stress occurred as a result of the interaction between the individual and the environment.

The idea that stress was an individual response which could be influenced by other processes was introduced by Ellis (1962), who acknowledged that individuals differed in their perceptions of situations as stressful or non-stressful. Lazarus (1966) acknowledged a broader definition of stress which included "cognitive appraisal". He introduced the idea that the individual's assessment or appraisal of his or her ability to cope with the stressor affected how each individual reacted to it. McGrath (1970) consolidated the research by conceptualising stress as a process encompassing four stages. Firstly, stress is viewed as an objective demand which is placed on the individual. Secondly, the individual perceives and judges the demand and forms a response to it. Thirdly, the actual response occurs and finally, consequences arise as a result of the response.

More recent research has further developed the role of appraisal of and response to stressors (Anshel, 1990), as well as examining the importance of psychosocial factors, such as recent life events and social support.

ANXIETY   Peter Anderson is a cricketer who confides in his coach general feelings of anxiety. Peter may be referring to a temporary state in which he feels worried or apprehensive in response to a specific situation such as a difficult training session, or he may be referring to a more permanent feeling of agitation and uncertainty which he experiences much of the time. It is likely that Peter's coach will perceive his anxiety as a "negative" influence affecting his ability to concentrate and possibly affecting his energy levels.

Spielberger (1976) acknowledged the individual nature of responses to stress and introduced the importance of the concept of threat. Some situations will be regarded objectively as stressful by most people, whereas the interpretation of a situation as threatening will depend to a large degree on the individual's subjective appraisal of the situation. The concepts of "state" and "trait" characteristics (Spielberger, 1976) determine to some extent how likely it is that the situation will be perceived as stressful or threatening. Individuals with a high trait anxiety are more likely to perceive a stressor as threatening than individuals with low trait anxiety, as their body is already in a heightened state of anxiety which can easily become exacerbated.

Anxiety is generally regarded as a negative characteristic whether the person exhibits short-term state anxiety or whether he or she has a general predisposition of reactivity to situations (trait anxiety). Researchers also differentiate between the symptoms of cognitive and somatic anxiety (Borkovek, 1976; Davidson & Schwartz, 1976; Horn, 1992; Martens, Vealey, & Burton, 1990). Somatic anxiety refers to various physical symptoms such as sweating, increased heart rate, whereas cognitive anxiety refers to psychological symptoms of worry, disrupted concentration and negative thought processes.

AROUSAL   When coach Sue Jordan refers to her players as "lazy and slow" or "alert and ready", she may be referring to their arousal levels and their general state of alertness and activation.

Arousal refers to a state ranging from sleep to intense alertness (Martens, 1977). Whilst the term anxiety is generally considered to have many negative connotations, arousal elicits images of activity, alertness and activation on a continuum from low to high without any negative overtones. The terms competitive anxiety (Martens et al., 1990) and arousal are commonly used to refer to the lift in intensity required for successful competitive performance (Gould & Krane, 1992). At its optimal level, this state is seen as a positive contributor to performance.

The concepts of stress, anxiety and arousal are discussed in more detail by Anshel in Chapter 2. He also expands on coping styles and the influence of positive and negative thought processes on performance.

THE ELITE ATHLETE

Considerable time, effort and sacrifice go into the training of an elite athlete. The success or failure of many years of training often comes down to a single race, event or championship. It is, therefore essential that athletes learn to recognise and control stress, anxiety and arousal that may affect their preparation or their ability to perform at their personal best. Stress management techniques can assist the elite athlete to recognise and control general stress and anxiety responses as well as to regulate pre-competition arousal levels so that the body is ready to respond to the challenge ahead.

LIFE STRESS

The elite athlete may face similar pressures to those experienced by the general public, for example, financial, work and relationship difficulties. For the elite athlete, however, these pressures can be compounded by the demands of his or her chosen sport. The elite athlete may train anywhere from 20–40 hours a week leaving little time or energy for work, social and recreational activities. Training demands and time spent away at competition can mean financial strain and employment instability. Many athletes devote so much time to their athletic career that they do not have a regular income or a reliable career path, whereas others work hard at establishing a sports and working career, placing additional and often unrealistic time demands and pressures on themselves. Professional athletes may be supported financially by sponsors, but this may bring additional pressures in promoting and successfully representing the sponsor on the sporting field.

TRAINING STRESS

Exercise itself is a stressor to which the athlete must adapt physiologically over time. Training sessions are designed to improve the physical and physiological ability of the athlete. As athletes regularly extend themselves physically, they may experience extreme fatigue as well as face the discipline of regular and often demanding training sessions. Not only are training sessions physically demanding, but athletes often extend themselves mentally to push through pain, tiredness or fear. Athletes may also experience injury or illness which may interfere with their training or competition goals. Stress management techniques can assist athletes to cope with the physical and psychological demands, as well as aid in recovery from training and injury.

COMPETITION STRESS

In the lead-up to an important competition, athletes often report feeling edgy, irritable and mentally occupied with thoughts of the imminent competition. Thoughts of the physical and psychological demands of the event, combined with the possibility of achieving, or not achieving the desired performance level, assist some athletes to lift themselves physically and psychologically to cope with the demands. For others, however, it can cause unnecessary worry and anxiety prior to the event and "choking" during important competitions.

BURN-OUT "Burn-out", which is characterised by a range of psychological, physical and behavioural symptoms, refers to a state of emotional exhaustion which results from pressures on the athlete or coach which have built up over an extended period of time. Elite athletes commit themselves to rigorous training demands for many years, in many instances with little or no achievement of the goals that they and others may have expected of them. Individuals can lose energy and drive because they see little reward for their efforts and they can no longer cope with the demands being placed on them.

Freudenberger (1974) originated work in the area of burn-out, predominantly with teachers. Specific research which has since focused on athletes and coaches has also examined which other factors, such as emotional adjustment, may mediate the potential effects of burn-out (Botterill, 1988; Feigley, 1984; Fender, 1989; Saffer & Crawford, 1988). Athletes and coaches who experience burn-out, may require periods of time away from their sport for re-assessment of their goals and implementation of stress management strategies.

APPROACHES TO TREATMENT

In the applied setting the treatment of stress can generally be categorised into three main areas.

1. Athletes who need stress management to assist them in effectively coping with stressful situations affecting them in the short term. Such stress could be life related, such as a family crisis or an overload of work or study.

2. Athletes, particularly those with high levels of trait anxiety and poor coping skills, for whom stress and anxiety is of concern in their daily lives. This anxiety manifests itself as a personality characteristic which affects their attitude to training and other areas of their life. Typically, such athletes report feeling fine when training is progressing well and when there are no other perceived life pressures.

3. Athletes who face debilitating pre-competitive anxiety or an inability to handle stress during the competition. This may cause them to "choke" or to become over-reactive emotionally and lose sight of their perform-ance goals.

When choosing treatment techniques, it is important to choose techniques which meet the needs of the individual and the type of stress being experienced. Programs, however, which include techniques to reduce the physical tension as well as providing mental strategies, are considered the most effective (Jones & Hardy, 1990).

STRESS MANAGEMENT TECHNIQUES

Whether an athlete is seeking stress management techniques for life-related stress, for performance-related pressures or in an attempt to modify personality characteristics which may be influencing his or her behaviour, these techniques will assist the athlete to become more aware of personal stress levels and, as a result, to gain greater control over them.

Researchers differ on how techniques should be categorised. However, the practitioner will want to assist athletes in three main ways.

1. To reduce or control their physiological responses to the stress
2. To control, redirect or re-frame their thoughts and attention
3. To initiate positive and constructive changes in their behaviour.

Changes in behaviour may come spontaneously as a result of the other interventions.

Researchers have recommended that most successful intervention programs are those which combine several different treatment modalities to help athletes manage their stress (Anshel, 1994; Davidson & Schwartz, 1976; Jones & Hardy, 1990; Meichenbaum, 1977, 1985; Smith, 1980; Smith & Ascough, 1985; Smith & Rohsenow, 1987).

Brief descriptions of commonly used stress management techniques are given below and include physiological, cognitive and behavioural interventions.

Relaxation techniques

Several well-known relaxation techniques assist athletes to recognise the build up of tension and to learn to release it. Techniques vary slightly in their emphasis, for example, Progressive Muscle Relaxation, PMR (Jacobson, 1929, 1938), involves the tensing and then relaxing of the muscles in the body. Differential (Jacobson, 1938) and Systematic Relaxation (Wolpe, 1958) involve more passive release of tension when focusing on one or more muscle groups. Benson's Relaxation Response (Benson, 1974) contains an attention control element whereby the individual sits in a comfortable position and focuses on slow and rhythmical breathing. Each breath is combined with the repetition of a single meaningless word to achieve a state of focused relaxation.

The Progressive Muscle Relaxation approach has some advantages for athletes in that it is a physical technique to which athletes may relate more readily. Once familiar with the technique, they can progress to shorter and more specific forms of relaxation.

Techniques need to be practised regularly to begin with in order to gain maximum benefits. The athlete may experience a sense of relaxation immediately after completing the exercise, but after being practised three or four times a week for several weeks, the athlete may feel calmness and control in general day-to-day situations. Individuals will also spontaneously learn to recognise and release the build up of tension in their bodies before it becomes debilitating. General physiological benefits of relaxation techniques include reductions in blood pressure, heart rate and anxiety measures.

The Progressive Muscle Relaxation is a good technique to start with and Benson's Relaxation Response is especially useful as a shorter technique which also assists in focusing concentration. These techniques are available in a script form which can be memorised, read or put onto a cassette tape. They can be obtained from the original texts, and many libraries, as well as the Australian Institute of Sport and the South Australian Sports Institute, are likely to have copies for loan.

Hypnosis, meditation and autogenic training

Techniques such as hypnosis, meditation and autogenic training are commonly used in sport. Hypnosis is a deeper form of relaxation in which the mind is in a more focused state. Unestahl (1979) coined the phrase "ideal performance state" and likened peak performances in sport to the hypnotic state. He suggests that athletes who can learn to achieve a hypnotic state, easily, may be able to achieve a greater control over their sporting performances (Unestahl, 1986). Hypnosis can be used to provide general confidence building suggestions and to incorporate post-hypnotic suggestions which focus on future performance. Success depends on the receptiveness of the athlete to hypnosis and on correctly identifying the key issues that need addressing.

Autogenic training was developed as a means of self-hypnosis (auto means self). In it, the individual learns to create a number of physical concomitants of the hypnotic state, that is, phenomena commonly experienced during hypnosis. These include heavy and warm limbs, rhythmical breathing and heartbeat, a warm solar plexus and a cool forehead. As in many meditation techniques, a passive attitude is also a key element of autogenics. The full method can take several months to develop, but warmth and heaviness can be induced much more quickly and may often be enough for the needs of athletes.

There is a variety of meditation techniques, the most commonly recognised being that of Transcendental Meditation (Maharishi Mahesh Yogi, 1966). In this form of meditation, a "mantra" is recited twice a day for about 15 minutes, to achieve a state of inner awareness, yet wakefulness. Other meditation exercises often encompass focusing on an external object. By practising this attentional control, the athlete can learn to control and narrow his or her concentration onto more specific performance cues or the technique can be used to block out performance distractions such as noise or negative thoughts.

Massage, exercise, flotation and biofeedback

These techniques are seen as more active or physical forms of relaxation. Many sports, but particularly endurance sports, are very demanding on the muscles in the body. Many athletes find that relaxation exercises alone are not sufficient to give them the reduction in muscle tension that they need. The muscle tension may result from stress, but can also result from sore muscles from training. Massage combined with a program of general relaxation can be very effective, particularly after the massage has reduced muscle tension which may have built up over time.

Exercise has been recommended as useful in stress reduction as a "tension release" (Nideffer, 1981) and a variety of physiological and psychological benefits from regular, moderate exercise have been put forward (Breslow, 1990; Paffenbarger, Hyde, & Wing, 1990). However, the elite athlete who already engages in high levels of physical activity may not benefit in the same way from exercise as the non-elite athlete. The elite athlete may already be too tired physically from training to engage in further aerobic exercise and it may increase the risk of physical injury. Elite athletes, however, who are not involved in endurance sports or those in the "off-season" may find aerobic exercise of benefit in improving their general state of well-being.

Flotation Restricted Environmental Stimulation Therapy or REST (Suedfeld, 1980) has become increasingly popular as a form of stress release and performance enhancement for athletes. Most institutes of sport have flotation tanks available to their athletes and they are considered useful to enhance performance, through the use of mental rehearsal, as well as to assist in recovery from demanding training sessions (Hutchison, 1984; Stanley, Mahoney, & Reppert, 1987; Suedfeld, Collier, & Hartnett, 1993). By floating in a tank filled with warm, saline solution, the athlete experiences reduced sensory input due to the quiet environment. Physiological changes which occur, such as reductions in heart rate, blood pressure, muscle tension, fatigue and depression make flotation a useful stress management tool.

Biofeedback enables greater control over bodily processes such as heart rate and blood pressure (Miller, 1969). In its simplest form, biofeedback may mean learning to control your own heart rate by listening to your heart and slowing down your breathing. More complex equipment is also used to let you know when your body is responding in the way that you want it to. For example, the athlete receives "feedback" in the form of an auditory tone when alpha waves associated with relaxation are present, or when the muscles in the body are relaxed. Because stress often produces changes in the body such as racing heart rate and tense muscles, biofeedback techniques are useful in helping to control these symptoms. For example, just before an event, an athlete may want to steady his or her racing heart in order to concentrate better on the task ahead, rather than becoming too nervous before the race.

Stress is not only manifest in physiological symptoms, such as increased heart rate and sweating but, also, in how the athlete focuses and controls his or her thoughts, mood and actions. The following techniques are more cognitively and behaviourally oriented assisting the athlete in controlling thoughts and actions.

Thought stopping and inner game

These mental strategies are based on Meichenbaum's (1977) work aimed at altering "private" cognitive processes. These specific techniques assist the athlete to re-focus away from negative and destructive thought processes onto positive thoughts which assist performance. Thought stopping has been used by sport psychologists (Ziegler, 1980) to reduce stress. When the stressful situation arises or is rehearsed mentally, the athlete shouts "stop", combined with a physical cue to interrupt the thought process. After regular practice the athlete learns to control and reduce negative or intrusive thoughts.

The "inner game" technique (Gallwey, 1975, 1976; Gallwey & Kriegel, 1977) discusses the concept of relaxed concentration and identifies Self 1, the analytical problem solver, and Self 2, the intuitive and emotional self.

The individual is taught to discriminate between the two and to utilise the most appropriate for the most effective handling of the situation. This technique has been popularised in sports such as golf and tennis.

Mental rehearsal, visualisation and visuo-motor behaviour rehearsal

Techniques such as mental rehearsal and visualisation are commonly used in sport to enhance performance and reduce stress and tension. An athlete who wants to reduce stress and tension may visualise his or her self in a favourite relaxing scene, whereas the athlete who is mentally rehearsing a performance may picture his or her self performing in the way that he or she wants or expects to. The mental rehearsal of new skills can hasten the learning of these skills simply through becoming more familiarised with them, as well as through small movements in "neuromuscular activity" of the muscles that would be used if the skill were actually being performed (Mackay, 1981; Ulich, 1967). Mental rehearsal may also assist athletes to picture their "ideal" performance as well as to rehearse handling difficulties or setbacks in a positive way.

Visuo-motor Behaviour Rehearsal (Suinn, 1976, 1987) encompasses a shortened version of Jacobson's Progressive Relaxation, the practice of imagery skills, as well as the specific use of imagery for enhancing mental and physical skills. The athlete masters each technique before progressing on to the next one.

Attention control training

Nideffer (1981), Nideffer and Sharpe (1978) popularised the field of attention control in sports performance. The aim of the intervention is to assist athletes to learn to control their attention, to focus it more effectively and as a result, to avoid undue stress.

Centring is a technique used to interrupt a stressful situation and recover attention control (concentration). It involves a deep abdominal breath, with the individual focusing attention on the breath and then back out to a positive external cue. Centring harnesses concentration and offers the athlete a period of brief relaxation. After the breath it is important that the athlete re-focus on an appropriate performance-related cue or positive thought. In learning to control attention, it is important:

1. to learn to recognise the different types of attention
2. for each person to understand individual attention strengths and weaknesses
3. to identify the attention demands of the athlete's particular sport.

For more information on these important areas refer to Chapter 3.

Performance planning and routines

Once regularly practised and mastered, many relaxation and cognitive techniques can be incorporated into competition strategies which assist the athlete to control performance-related stress and enhance general sporting performance. Most sports and coaches emphasise the use of a competition strategy or a performance plan. The purpose of the plan is to minimise the detail on which the athlete is required to focus. A performance plan can often encompass the following aspects:

- key segments
- task and mood relevant cues and words
- simple stress control triggers or routines.

Most performance plans will incorporate the use of simple routines which keep the athlete focused on important performance-related feelings and cues. Routines often include the following key components:

- a word or an action to help control the athlete's actions or thoughts
- a brief stress management or attention control technique
- a re-focusing element to direct thoughts and feelings more positively.

Routines and performance plans are invaluable for the elite athlete and can be very creative in the elements of cognitive and somatic control they provide the athlete. They can be considered crucial in maximising performance. However, routines and plans must be well rehearsed and practised to be most effective under pressure.

All these techniques assist athletes in managing general stress in their lives. They also help to control pre-competition arousal levels and contribute towards enhanced performance. Many of these techniques are taught through cassette tapes and workbook exercises, such as Winter and Martin's "Sport Psych: Sport Psychology Basic Training Program", Lars-Eric Unestahl's "Inner Mental Training" and Dodd and Unestahl's, "The Inner Champion".

CASE STUDIES

The applied sport psychologist often combines many of the above-mentioned techniques in a treatment program for the athlete. Looking at several case studies may help to show how this is done.

CASE STUDY 1

A gymnastics coach asks the sport psychologist to assist an eleven-year-old gymnast with a skill that she is having difficulty mastering. Evidently, she is becoming increasingly "stressed and negative" at training over her inability to perform the skill.

Background

The first session involves a meeting between the coach, gymnast and sport psychologist to discuss the situation. The skill she is having difficulty with is the "flip flip" which is performed on the ground, low, medium and high beams. It involves two backward flips in succession. During the first session the following important information is gathered from discussion with the coach and gymnast.

Information gathering

- The gymnast completes the skill on the ground and low beam but not on the medium and high beams.

- She tries to control the skill rather than letting it flow.
- She holds on too tight which slows her down.
- She fell once when learning the skill but did not seriously hurt herself.
- She rarely completes the skill, pausing to check that her positioning is perfect before going into the second flip (it should be one continuous movement).

Particularly in young athletes, it is important to discuss their strengths as well as the difficulties they are experiencing. This young athlete was found to be particularly flexible, strong, the correct body height, a "crowd pleaser" in dance routines and "happy and proud" when she masters a new skill.

Problem identification

The following points were identified as contributing towards the problem:
- The gymnast may be experiencing a fear of falling as a result of her previous fall.
- She tenses her muscles which causes her to control the skill and slow down.
- She loses rhythm and balance as a result of slowing and controlling the skill.
- Just prior to attempting the skill, her concentration is outcome focused ("Will I fall or not?").

Intervention

The following approach was taken over 4–6 sessions to assist her mastery of this skill.

1. Increase general confidence and teach her how to reduce muscle tension and feelings of anxiety currently associated with the skill.
2. Through the use of hypnosis or visualisation, assist her to recall the time when she fell and to "re-frame" that as less concerning.
3. Break the skill into its important components and outline the "ideal performance". For example:
   - *Before* — Deep breath, relaxed and confident, spot the end of the beam, 1 . . . 2 . . . 3 . . . go for it!
   - *Take off* — Shoulders drop forward, small sit and hips square, finish with legs straight
   - *Flip* — Legs together, push up in the handstand, stand shoulders up and keep them moving back
     Repeat flip.
4. Visualise the skill in slow motion several times until the steps are correct then continue the visualisation at normal speed to gain feel and rhythm. A video of the skill being performed correctly can be used to assist the visualisation. When the visualisation is well practised, the step-by-step visualisation is replaced by the use of one or two "key" words which are associated with rhythm, confidence and technique. A short routine is developed which incorporates these key words and this routine is used prior to performing the skill.
5. The "ideal visualisation" and confidence building suggestions are recorded on a cassette tape for the gymnast to listen to regularly at home or prior to training sessions.
6. This approach could also be combined with systematic desensitisation where visualisation of skill mastery, relaxation training and actual practice of the skill are combined with a gradual progression to the higher beams.

As is evident in this case study, a combination of techniques including stress management, is generally most effective.

CASE STUDY 2

A middle-distance runner approaches the sport psychologist after the Nationals as he did not perform as well as he would have liked.

Background

When qualifying for the Nationals he performed personal bests but was disappointed with his performance at the National Championships. He reported that it was increasingly common for him to "fail to perform". He also reported feeling constantly "uptight", trying to train as well as fit in work and study.

Information gathering

- He saw himself coming towards the end of his athletic career and was keen to achieve his major goal of qualifying for the Commonwealth Games.
- His parents saw his athletic career as a waste of time and were keen for him to pursue his university studies and "get a real job".
- His fiancée was supportive of his athletics, however, marriage plans were on hold until they had more money to establish themselves.
- He was sponsored by a shoe company who, despite reportedly being happy with his performances, was having to decrease the number of athletes they sponsored due to economic conditions.

Problem identification

The following points were identified as contributing towards the problem:

- A high level of pressure to perform "to make it all worthwhile", from himself, sponsors and family.
- Difficulty organising priorities between study, work, athletics and relationships.
- He presented as the type of person who experiences a high level of day-to-day tension in his life.
- He has set general goals for his study and athletics but does not have specific time frames on these.
- He also reported being frustrated by recurring injuries which interrupted his training.

Intervention

The following approach was taken to assist this athlete to organise and prioritise the goals in his life, as well as to learn how to be more relaxed in general. To teach the following techniques, the psychologist and athlete initially met five times. Follow-up sessions were then arranged throughout the season to check progress.

1. A personality profile was conducted to assess overall tension levels and personality traits which may be contributing towards his stress.
2. Discussions with his fiancée enabled him to prioritise his life and sporting goals. The sport psychologist and the athlete then allocated realistic time frames to each of these goals and detailed the short and medium term steps necessary to achieve them.
3. He learnt and practised muscle relaxation, "thought stopping" and brief relaxation techniques to reduce the day-to-day tension and negativity that he was increasingly experiencing.
4. A diary was collated which allocated time to training, work, study and recreation.
5. Injury prevention strategies were discussed.

6. Adaptions were made to his training diary to include psychological goals and to highlight the progress he was making towards his goals.

7. Race preparation was discussed and performance segmenting and routines were developed to ensure that his concentration at important meets was focused on the controllable aspects of this performance rather than worrying unnecessarily about the result.

This approach enabled the athlete to learn how to control some of the anxiety he experienced as a result of his personality, as well as to learn to focus his energies and concentration in training and races more constructively.

THE COACH

This chapter has predominantly discussed stress in light of the elite athlete but most of the stressors encountered by athletes, including pre-competitive anxiety, are also relevant for the coach. Successful coaching relies on interpersonal and communication skills as well as a technical understanding of the sport. The successful coaches are often those who can manage their own stress levels and provide a positive role model to their athletes. All the stress management techniques discussed are relevant to the coach, including mental rehearsal and performance planning. Many coaches visualise themselves coaching in a positive and constructive way as well as developing strategies and routines that they can use to handle the stress of important competitions and poor performances by their athletes.

FUTURE DIRECTIONS

1. The concepts of stress, anxiety and arousal require further clarification in the general and sports literature. Whilst the elite athlete is rarely concerned about terminology, clarity of terms will ensure that applied programs accurately represent the research.

2. Although the concepts of stress and anxiety have broadened to encompass the interaction of the individual with his or her environment, research models must expand further to consider other mediating characteristics including, a broader range of personality influences, motivation and psycho-social factors.

3. Sport-specific measures need to be further developed as current measures of stress cannot necessarily be generalised to the sport setting.

4. Prevention of burn-out in athletes can be addressed by identifying more clearly those athletes who are likely to be susceptible to its effects. Preventative programs can then be implemented with those athletes.

5. Stress management techniques need to be creatively applied by practitioners and further integrated to meet each individual's needs in terms of training and competition regimes.

6. Multi-modal approaches and programs ideally lead the athlete through a series of processes whereby the individual can ultimately use simple cues and triggers to readily control responses to anxiety and stress.

CONCLUSIONS

It is essential that elite athletes learn to effectively manage the many demands placed on them. As technological advances in sport continue and as financial incentives become increasingly available to athletes, the pressure to perform is intensified. The repercussions from "not performing" have already become far greater than "loss of pride" and disappointment. Athletes need mental discipline to keep their focus on their training and performance goals, as well as mental strength and resolve to deal with the inevitable set backs. Managing stress for athletes and coaches is an essential life skill as well as a performance enhancement tool.

SUMMARY

This chapter considered applied aspects of stress management. To clarify terms, examples were given illustrating the effects of stress, anxiety and arousal. The chapter then considered various sources of stress which can be imposed on elite performers, including life stress, training stress, competition stress, and burn-out. The chapter focused on the treatment of stress, considering a range of stress management techniques, such as relaxation, autogenic training, and flotation. Cognitive techniques, including thought-stopping, mental rehearsal and performance routines, were also discussed. A number of case studies were presented to illustrate the nature of stress and its management. The chapter concluded with a word about the coach and some future directions were suggested.

REFERENCES

Anshel, M. H. (1990). Toward validation of a model for coping with acute stress in sport. *International Journal of Sport Psychology, 21,* 58–83.

Anshel, M. H. (1994). *Sport psychology: From theory to practice* (2nd ed.). Scotsdale, AR: Gorsuch Scarisbrick.

Benson, H. (1974). The relaxation response. *Psychiatry, 37,* 34–46.

Borkovek, T. D. (1976). Physiological and cognitive processes in the regulation of arousal. In G. E. Schwartz & D. Shapiro (Eds.), *Consciousness and self-regulation: Advances in research, 1,* 261–312. New York: Plenum Press.

Botterill, C. (1988). Preventing burnout and retirement problems. *Canadian Academy of Sport Medicine, 8,* 28–29.

Bouchard, C., Shephard, R. J., Stephens, T., Sutton, J. R., & McPherson, B. D. (1990). Exercise, fitness and health: The consensus statement. In C. Bouchard, R. J. Shephard, T. Stephens, J. R. Sutton, & B. D. McPherson (Eds.), *Exercise, fitness and health: A consensus of the current knowledge.* Champaign, IL: Human Kinetics.

Breslow, l. (1990). Lifestyle, fitness and health. In C. Bouchard, R. J. Shephard, T. Stephens, J. R. Sutton, & B. D. McPherson (Eds.), *Exercise, fitness and health: A consensus of the current knowledge.* Champaign, IL: Human Kinetics.

Cannon, W. B. (1932). *The wisdom of the body.* New York: W. W. Norton.

Davidson, R. J., & Schwartz, G. E. (1976). The psychobiology of relaxation and relaxed states: A multi-process theory. In D. I. Mostofsky (Ed.), *Behaviour control and modification of physiological activity.* Englewood Cliffs, NJ: Prentice-Hall.

Dodd, T., & Unestahl, L. (1993). *The inner champion*. HDA/Monash, Australia.

Ellis, A. (1962). *Reason and emotion in psychotherapy*. New York: Lyle Stuart.

Feigley, D. E. (1984). Psychological burnout in high level athletes. *The Physician and Sportsmedicine, 12*, 109–119.

Fender, L. K. (1989). Athlete burnout: Potential for research and intervention strategies. *The Sport Psychologist, 3*, 63–71.

Freudenberger, H. (1974). Staff burnout. *Journal of Social Issues, 34* (4), 111–123.

Gallwey, G. T. (1975). *The inner game of tennis*. London: Jonathan Cape.

Gallwey, G. T. (1976). *Inner tennis*. New York: Random House.

Gallwey, G. T., & Kriegel, B. (1977). *Inner skiing*. New York: Random House.

Gould, D., & Krane, V. (1992). The arousal-athletic performance relationship: Current status and future directions. In T. S. Horn (Ed.), *Advances in sport psychology*. Champaign, IL: Human Kinetics.

Horn, T. S. (1992). *Advances in sport psychology*. Champaign, IL: Human Kinetics.

Hutchison, M. (1984). *The book of floating*. New York, NY: Quill.

Jacobson, E. (1929). *Progressive relaxation*. Chicago: University of Chicago Press.

Jacobson, E. (1938). *Progressive relaxation* (2nd ed). Chicago: University of Chicago Press.

Jones, J. G., & Hardy, L. (Eds.). (1990). *Stress and performance in sport*. Chichester: John Wiley & Sons.

Lazarus, R. S. (1966). *Psychological stress and the coping process*. New York: McGraw-Hill.

MacKay, D. (1981). The problem of rehearsal or mental practice. *Journal of Motor Behavior, 13*, 4, 274–285.

Maharishi Mahesh Yogi (1966). *The science of being and the art of living*. London: International SRM Publications.

Martens, R. (1982). *Sport competition anxiety test*. Champaign, IL: Human Kinetics.

Martens, R., Vealey, R. S., & Burton, D. (1990). *Competitive anxiety in sport*. Champaign, IL: Human Kinetics.

McGrath, J. E. (1970). A conceptual formulation for research on stress. In J. E. McGrath, *Social and psychological factors in stress*. New York: Holt, Rinehart and Winston.

Meichenbaum, D. (1977). *Cognitive-behaviour modification* (2nd ed.). New York: Plenum Press.

Meichenbaum, D. (1985). *Stress inoculation training*. New York: Pergamon.

Miller, N. (1969). Learning visceral and glandular responses. *Sciences, 163*, 434–445.

Nideffer, R. (1981). *The ethics and practice of applied sport psychology*. Ithaca, New York: Mouvement.

Nideffer, R., & Sharpe, R. (1978). *ACT: Attention control training*. New York: Stein and Day.

Paffenbarger, R. S., Hyde, R. T., & Wing, A. L. (1990). Physical activity and physical fitness determinants of health and longevity. In C. Bouchard, R. J. Shephard, T. Stephens, J. R. Sutton, & B. D. McPherson (Eds.), *Exercise, fitness and health: A consensus of the current knowledge*. Champaign, IL: Human Kinetics.

Saffer, D., & Crawford, S. A. G. M. (1988). Burnout: Its effects on athletics. *NIS Scientific Journal, 11* (3), 15–19.

Seyle, H. (1951–1956). *The annual report of stress*. New York: McGraw-Hill.

Seyle, H. (1956). *The stress of life*. New York: McGraw-Hill.

Smith, R. E. (1980). Development of an integrated coping response through cognitive affective stress management training. In I. G. Sarason & C. D. Spielberger (Eds.), *Stress and anxiety*. Washington, DC: Hemisphere.

Smith, R. E. (1984). Theoretical and treatment approaches to anxiety reduction. In J. M. Silva III & R. S. Weinberg (Eds.), *Psychological Foundations of Sport.* Champaign, IL: Human Kinetics.

Smith, R. E., & Ascough, J. C. (1985). Induced affect in stress management training. In S. R. Burchfield (Ed.), *Stress: Psychological and physiological interaction.* New York: Hemisphere.

Smith, R. E., & Rohsenow, D. J. (1987). Cognitive-affective stress management training: A treatment and resource manual. *Social and Behavioural Sciences Documents, 17,* 2.

Spielberger, C. D. (1976). The nature and measurement of anxiety. In C. D. Spielberger & R. Diaz-Guerrero (Eds.), *Cross-cultural anxiety.* Washington D.C.: Hemisphere/John Wiley & Sons.

Stanley, J., Mahoney, M., & Reppert, S. (1987). REST and the enhancement of sports performance: A panel presentation and discussion. In J. W. Turner & T. H. Fine (Eds.), *Proceedings of the Second International Conference on REST.* Toledo, OH: International REST Investigators Society.

Suedfield, P. (1980). *Restricted environmental stimulation: Research and clinical applications.* New York: John Wiley & Sons.

Suedfeld, P., Collier, D. E., & Hartnett, D. G. (1993). Enhancing perceptual motor accuracy through flotation REST. *The Sport Psychologist, 7,* 151–159.

Suinn, R. M. (1976). Psychology for olympic champions. *Psychology Today* (USA), *10*(2), 38–43.

Suinn, R. M. (1987). Behavioural approaches to stress management in sports. In J. R. May & M. J. Asken (Eds.), *Sport psychology: The psychological health of the athlete.* New York: PMA Publishing Corporation.

Ulich, E. (1967). Some experiments in the function of mental training in the acquisition of motor skills. *Ergonomics, 10,* 411–419.

Unestahl, L. (1979). *Inner mental training.* Orebro, Sweden: Veje.

Unestahl, L. (1986). The ideal performance state. In L. Unestahl (Ed.), *Sport psychology: In theory and practice.* Orebro, Sweden: Veje.

Winter, G., & Martin C. (1993). *Sport psych: Sport psychology basic training program.* South Australian Sports Institute, Australia.

Wolpe, J. (1958). *Psychotherapy by reciprocal inhibition.* Stanford: Stanford University Press.

Ziegler, S. G. (1980). An overview of anxiety management strategies in sport. In W. F. Straub (Ed.), *Sport pyschology: An analysis of athlete behaviour* (2nd ed.). Ithaca, NY: Mouvement Publications.

C H A P T E R

12

WAYS OF COPING

CHRIS MADDEN

There are many ways in which individuals cope with competitive sport. Competition, by definition, entails rivalry and a striving to perform better than other competitors. Striving to perform at one's peak can be stressful in itself, quite apart from the stress caused by the performance or behaviour of other competitors. Some individuals are challenged by competitive situations, while others are overwhelmed by anxiety. Individual differences in knowledge, experience, skills, cognitive style or mental outlook can underlie differences in the way competitors cope with the many and changing situations that occur in sport. Coping strategies can be learnt much the same as specific skills in sport can be acquired. Moreover, practising coping strategies, either mentally or in sporting situations, can make those strategies more accessible and effective, similar to the way that training and practice of physical strategies can lead to better performance. As coping strategies enable an individual to manage potentially stressful situations in sport, they therefore represent an important feature of any textbook on theory and practice of sport psychology. In this chapter, the nature and function of various coping strategies in relation to specific sports is discussed, effective coping strategies are described, and an iterative model for training athletes in adaptive or effective coping strategies is outlined.

A CONTEXT FOR COPING

The transactional model of stress and coping, developed by Richard Lazarus and his colleagues reflects current theory and research into stress. Within this model, stress is conceptualised as a relationship between the person and the environment, in which a situation is appraised by the person as taxing or exceeding the person's resources and as endangering well-being (Folkman, Lazarus, Gruen, & DeLongis, 1986). Coping is seen as a mediating process between stressful events and indicators of adaptation such as psychological and somatic health (Khantzian, 1974; Folkman et al., 1986; Folkman, Bernstein, & Lazarus, 1987). Other investigators (Anthony & Liberman, 1986) hold that the development of adaptive coping can buffer the individual against stress. Given that adaptive coping facilitates adjustment (Folkman et al., 1986; Folkman et al., 1987), maladaptive coping might be implicated in under-achievement and dropping out of sport.

THE DEVELOPMENT OF COPING STRATEGIES

Athletes typically become informed about or are introduced to a range of sports in childhood. Although the emphasis in the early years is on sport as a fun activity, competitiveness is often encouraged at an early age. Many factors can influence the extent to which the child experiences sport as play or fun, or as a serious activity in which one has to strive for success. Most of the sporting role models that the child is exposed to through the media (mainly through television) are strongly committed to sport as a serious activity, often reflecting attitudes that convey a "win at all costs" mentality. Parents, coaches, spectators and others can influence the developing attitude and behaviour of the child.

The ways that the child and the adolescent cope with stress will be influenced by the messages they receive, and the behaviour of parents, coaches and others. As the child enters adolescence, the emphasis placed on "winning" in sport typically increases. This is usually associated with a sense of "pressure to perform". This process has been described by Watson (1984) as one in which the evaluative influence of competition is perceived as a potential source of interference in the "flow of motivated behaviour". According to Watson (1984), this process inevitably leads to stress and psychological conflict. However, the child and the adolescent have not yet developed a repertoire of coping responses (Patterson & McCubbin, 1987) that can be drawn upon to manage these experiences.

As Konopka (1980) points out, adolescents typically possess intense energy, yet have minimal experience. Many of the situations they face in life represent new demands on them, but because of their lack of years their reactions may be extreme. This places them at risk of potentially serious consequences to their behaviour (Konopka, 1980). The increased emphasis on winning or on performing at a very high standard is potentially a highly stressful situation that may persist throughout adolescence, and indeed throughout adulthood. According to Valliant (1977), the coping style which develops or emerges during adolescence shapes the coping style of adulthood. It is therefore important that attempts to develop adaptive ways of coping with competitive sport be introduced as early as possible, preferably in childhood and adolescence.

The highly competitive approach to organised sport today has intermittent and often chronic effects on the self-esteem and emotional state of participants. At a more concrete level, the costs can be a determination to behave in a highly competitive and often aggressive or hostile manner and, in some sports, to risk the consequences of the aggressive and hostile behaviour of opponents. In modern parlance, we say that participants in competitive sports are subject to the effects of stress.

In the adult sporting environment, participants are required to manage individual demands on them by drawing on their capabilities. Successful coping in team sports involves an adaptation in which the performer or athlete achieves a "fit" within the team environment. Coping in sporting situations involves the use of cognitive, emotional, and behavioural skills. On a broader level team-sport situations can be viewed within the conceptual framework of Patterson and McCubbin (1987), in which the athlete is one member of a system which includes the individual, the team, and the network of teams in that competition. Each of these systems comprises demands (stressors) and capabilities (resources, coping behaviours).

COPING STRATEGIES AND COPING STYLES

EXERCISE Jogging, running, exercise and sport, through their recreational effects and their effects on physical fitness, are held to be important factors in maintaining good health (Adams, 1979; Powell, 1988). Indeed, physical exercise and, by implication, sport, may be viewed as a way of coping with stress or life generally. Exercise can elicit relaxation and reduce symptoms of anxiety, including muscular tension; in a recent review article, Lariviere and Sydney (1992) argue that physical exercise may prove to be an effective coping mechanism for reducing the symptoms of fear and anxiety in children.

The relaxing and stress-reducing effects of exercise (DeBenedette, 1988) and the positive effects of exercise on mood state (Berger & Owen, 1988; Nieman, 1989) have been recognised for many years. More recently, Brown and Siegel (1988) provide a compelling conceptualisation of exercise as a buffer against life stress. Exercise can be said to fortify the body against stress through the increased strength and hardiness that individuals gain from the physical fitness that results from exercise (Tucker, Cole, & Friedman, 1986). Therefore, exercise in itself can be regarded as a way of coping with stress. While the exercise component in sport is likely to be beneficial for participants, these positive effects can become outweighed by stress and tension caused by overly high or unrealistic expectations for success, or by extremely competitive behaviour.

RELAXATION

The use of relaxation as a means of moderating arousal level or reducing stress is, perhaps, the coping technique most advocated by practitioners and used by individual athletes. Theoretically, relaxation training in preparation for a potentially stressful situation (sport or event) rests soundly on Wolpe's principle of reciprocal inhibition. This principle assumes that maladaptive responses (e.g., tension caused by stress) can be eliminated by the presence of a response which is presumably antagonistic to the initial one. Thus, if one can induce one state (relaxation), then it is logically inconsistent to experience the opposing physiological state (tension) at the same time. Relaxation has many apparent benefits. These may include decreased muscle tension (and improved ease of movement and coordination) as well as increased emotional control. A decrease in oxygen consumption and blood lactate levels, which can lead to a lowering of stress-induced high respiration rate, has also been reported (Wilks, 1991). Relaxation may also have psychological benefits. These include greater concentration and increased confidence. Chapter 11 includes a more detailed discussion of the importance of relaxation as a stress management technique.

ASSOCIATIVE AND DISSOCIATIVE COPING

In long distance and marathon running, strategies can be used to enable the runner to cope with fatigue; to persist and endure against the impulse to slow down or stop running (Sachs, 1984). These cognitive strategies — which are generally categorised as *associative* and *dissociative* — relate to the runner focusing attention on factors relevant to his or her performance (associative strategies), or on thoughts and feelings that may help to take attention away from the runner's physiological condition (dissociative strategies). The research assessing the relative efficacy of these two categories of coping currently yields no clear indication of which strategy is the most efficacious. Indeed, a third thought-focus category has been identified. This "environmental" category consists of stimuli perceived or focused on by the athlete in the course of the event (J. Summers, personal communication, June 24, 1993).

PROBLEM-FOCUSED AND EMOTION-FOCUSED COPING

Coping strategies that involve an attempt to change the player–environment relationship are termed *problem-focused* coping strategies. Problem-focused coping may lead to a resolution of the problem in that the stressful situation may be resolved as a direct result of the threatened player's behaviour. For example, a player may analyse his or her performance in order to come up with a different strategic play to offset an opponent's move. In basketball, for example, a player can decide to use team mates as a "screen" to evade a close-checking opponent.

Emotion-focused coping is a form of coping which involves emotional regulation or reappraisal of stressful situations or experiences. The emotional reaction provoked by the stressful event can be altered by the player reinterpreting the event or turning attention away from it. Emotion-focused strategies can generally be placed under the headings of *emotionality, detachment, denial, wishful thinking,* and *emphasising the positive.* These strategies can be adaptive or maladaptive depending on the way they are used and on the timing and context in which they are used.

Emotions that are not controlled can be detrimental to a player. For example, in football, a player may respond to a situation with *uncontrolled aggression*. This may lead to the giving away of a vital free kick or to suspension of the player from the competition for a number of weeks. When an athlete has lost emotional control, it is unlikely that he or she will be acting in the most effective way. Training in *controlled aggression* (using anger management techniques) can lead to an athlete competing in a vigorous and effective way yet minimising the likelihood of negative consequences of the type described above.

Detachment and *denial* can be effective ways of coping with strong emotional reactions to situations in competitive sport. Detachment strategies include behaviour whereby athletes avoid other players or situations. This can be a way of diminishing contact with a source of potential stress. While the avoidance inherent in detachment strategies would seem to be a behaviour that reduces opportunities for interaction and development — and hence learning — there may be times when detachment can prevent inappropriate responses such as uncontrolled aggression.

Denial can, in some situations, prevent an individual from receiving important feedback from others, including a coach. However, like detachment, it too can be an effective coping strategy if used in appropriate circumstances. An athlete can be said to use denial when he or she refuses to acknowledge or think about a situation. An important and sometimes very effective use of denial in competitive sport is for the athlete to deny or deflect perceived negative evaluation by others. Competitive sport usually creates a situation in which athletes are under close scrutiny from a number of people who represent sources of potential evaluation and criticism. These can include the coach, team mates, opposition players, spectators, and the media. If an athlete is receptive to inappropriate input from others (especially negative input) at critical times during a competition, concentration and subsequent performance can be adversely affected. Athletes can learn or be trained to be selectively open to the input from others; to maintain a strong, positive, task-oriented focus, and thus refuse to allow themselves to perceive potentially distracting input. By being open to the input of others *after* an event or competition is completed, the athlete can take in this information without it interfering with performance.

Wishful thinking would appear to be a largely fruitless coping strategy. It is difficult to imagine wishful thinking as anything but a strategy used when all others have failed. This strategy would seem to best illustrate the point made by Folkman and Lazarus (1985) that when attempts to use problem-focused coping are unsuccessful, the individual will resort to emotion-focused coping. Yet it can be argued (Madden, 1987a; Madden, Summers, & Brown, 1990a, 1990b) that if wishful thinking is accompanied by images or fantasies of successful performance, then such a strategy may have a direct and positive effect. When used in this way, wishful thinking can be said to be a problem-focused as well as emotion-focused coping style.

The fact that the above-mentioned ways of coping can be seen as either adaptive or maladaptive, depending on how, when, and in what context they are used, adds to the view that coping is a dynamic, unfolding process; that particular styles of coping can be used at different times by an individual in similar and dissimilar situations, with different outcomes.

SOCIAL SUPPORT

Social support seeking behaviour is regarded as both a problem-focused and emotion-focused coping strategy (Folkman & Lazarus, 1985). Rosenfeld, Richman, and Hardy (1989) examined the social support networks of athletes. The types and amount of social support were identified, and comparisons were made between low-stressed and high-stressed athletes. It was found that coaches, team mates, friends and parents all provided social support to the athletes in the study. Support in the form of expert sports information and training was provided by coaches and team mates, whilst parents and friends gave complementary types of support which did not require any particular expertise. Low-stressed and high-stressed athletes had similar social support-network characteristics. It was concluded that coaches, team mates, friends, and parents each provided a unique contribution to the athlete's social support network. While there has been good documentation of the role of social support and social support networks as an important form of coping, there is an associated cost for the recipient in terms of the increased contact and effort involved in initiating and maintaining these relationships (Hobfoll, 1991).

Two theories relate to the way social support is considered to influence coping. These theories relate to the hypothesised *buffering* and *direct* effects of social support. The buffering model maintains that social support has a protective function against the negative effects of stress (Cohen & Wills, 1985). This is thought to occur through the person being "helped" to redefine the problem or by the agent of social support providing a solution to it (Terry, Nielsen, & Perchard, 1993). Within the buffering model, the degree of stressfulness is thought to affect the extent to which social support reduces stress. It is also thought that social support can function in a direct and beneficial way to enhance social integration and well-being (Cohen & Wills, 1985), irrespective of the level of stress a person faces.

It follows from the above propositions that, depending on whether the knowledge and communication skills of the coach and club or team personnel match the support requirements of a given situation for the athlete, they ought to be able to reduce the negative effects of stress for the athlete. The more open or receptive the athlete is to significant others in the sports domain (and the more significant others can promote an open and receptive communication position in the athlete), the more effective this style of coping is likely to be for the athlete. The role of the applied sport psychologist in facilitating these processes would appear to be germane to enhancing this way of coping for athletes.

An aspect of social support that has particular relevance to enhancing performance and coping with stress in sport is the use of encouragement.

Encouragement by coaches and significant others can be viewed as a passive form of persuasion that can increase the motivation of athletes. Persuasion is one of the four major antecedents of self-efficacy, as proposed by Bandura (1986). The other three are performance accomplishments, vicarious experiences, and physiological states. As discussed in Chapter 6, coaches and team mates may attempt to persuade players that they have the capability to meet specific task demands, and this is more likely to be effective if the source of the persuasion is viewed by the athlete as trustworthy and credible. Moreover, *performance accomplishments* are considered to have the most influence on self-efficacy. (Feltz, 1992). It is the position of the author of the current chapter that performance accomplishments consist of information derived from an *internal locus of belief* (arising from internal processes, including the memory the individual has of previous experiences). Persuasion and encouragement could be best described as information derived from an *external locus of belief*: the information conveyed to the athlete in the form of persuasion or encouragement purports to be information known by the other rather than the self, and it reflects the other's belief about the athlete's ability.

The above-mentioned distinction is made in order to highlight the importance of cognitions that reflect an *external* locus of belief in enhancing self-efficacy and coping. In the domains of sport and individual accomplishments, self-doubt would appear to be one of the overriding negative cognitions that is experienced. Self-doubt is both pervasive and debilitating, having negative consequences on behaviour. Despite an athlete's knowledge of successful past performances, self-doubt can still re-emerge in the lead-up to important events. Some athletes yield to this type of pressure with an uncharacteristic plummeting of performance. Social support which enhances an external locus of belief would provide additional effects on coping beyond the buffering and direct effects of social support. These effects can best be referred to as the *external efficacy-engendering effects* of social support derived from the athlete's external locus of belief. Self-efficacy is thus likely to peak in the athlete who introjects the belief that significant others believe in his or her capacity to perform a task that will lead to a desired outcome.

It follows from the above line of thinking that there are two perspectives relating to efficacy beliefs. First, there is the belief an individual has in his or her capacity to perform a task that will lead to a desired outcome (self-efficacy). Second, there is the belief a person has about whether significant others believe he or she can perform that task (the individual's external locus of belief about the task). Further to these considerations, a strategy that enhances a person's external locus of belief will enhance self-efficacy. It therefore follows that the more open or receptive an athlete is to positive messages from a coach (or a sport psychologist), the more effective this style of influence is likely to be for the athlete. If athletes are able to avail themselves of this support, this attribute becomes a way of coping for these athletes.

THE COMPLEXITY AND VARIABILITY OF COPING

Coping is a complex process in which an individual may use different strategies at different times as a stressful situation unfolds. Different sports involve different demands and skills, and hence may require different coping strategies. The same measurement device may be used in an attempt to explore differences in coping style across different sports. For instance, the Ways of Coping with Sport [WOCS], which was initially used with basketball players, has been used to measure coping responses across a range of sports (Madden, 1987a; Madden et al., 1990a, 1990b; Kello & Madden, 1993). The WOCS measures problem-focused coping, seeking social support, general emotionality, increased effort and resolve, detachment, denial, wishful thinking, and emphasising the positive coping styles. The different WOCS profiles obtained in the above-mentioned studies reflect the relative frequency of use of these coping styles for different sports. Alternatively, questionnaires can be used for specific purposes with the one sport. For instance, Thomas and Over (1994) developed a golf-specific instrument (the Golf Performance Survey). The use of this sport-specific instrument revealed skills and strategies pertaining to golf. Thomas and Over (1994) found that skilled golfers reported greater mental preparation, higher concentration, fewer negative emotions and cognitions, greater psychomotor automaticity, and more commitment to golf than less skilled golfers.

Predicting how an individual will cope — even when the situation is, for all intents and purposes, the same — is problematic. This is due to the coping process itself, in that an individual can choose to use a different strategy than that previously used in the same or similar situation. Therefore, the exercise of determining test-retest reliability of a coping process test instrument might be a fruitless and meaningless task. Contradicting this view is the notion that individuals have preferred or habitual ways of coping. The latter view holds that the performer has a relatively stable coping style that will consistently manifest itself over time and situations. Thus, it is argued that while different individual strategies can be used in similar situations, a consistent style of coping (for example, associative rather than dissociative) is likely to be manifested by the same person.

While the research evidence on this issue is equivocal at present, Kello and Madden (1993) have shown that similar coping styles are relevant to different task demands (playing football as compared with umpiring football) in the same sport. Yet the saliency and relative frequency of use of different coping styles differs according to the different roles taken in that sport. Kello and Madden (1993) held the environmental factor relative to a sporting domain (Australian Rules Football) constant. Separate factor analyses conducted on data using the same test instument (the WOCS) yielded similar factor structures but different coping profiles — reflecting that the relative frequency of use of these coping styles differed for the two populations (football players and football umpires).

On a broader level, these results demonstrated that the actual coping styles relevant to a sport are qualitatively different from those identified in performers competing in a different domain (basketball competition). In the case of football (whether the performers are players or umpires), proactive problem-focused coping, seeking social support, acceptance, reactive problem-focused coping, positive focus, emotionality, self-blame, and wishful thinking were the eight coping styles identified. A comparison of these styles with those identified for basketball (as described earlier in this chapter), reveals different styles of coping. The major differences in the coping styles relevant to the two separate domains is that a distinction arose in the way problem-focused coping strategies were used. Elite football players used proactive (in preparation for, or anticipation of an event or situation) or reactive (in response to a situation that occurs in competition) styles of problem-focused coping. Although basketball players used problem-focused coping, no such distinction was found.

Overall, the findings of Kello and Madden (1993) support the view that coping is a dynamic and unfolding process in which the frequency of use of coping styles differs in relation to the task demands on the individual in a given environment. While the individual is likely to have a preferred or habitual style of coping, the apparently fluid nature of coping indicates that it is realistic to make significant change in the coping style of an individual; that channelling resources into providing interventions aimed at teaching or training adaptive rather than maladaptive coping styles is a worthwhile exercise.

WAYS OF COPING WITH INJURY

It has been claimed that stress can not only negatively influence performance, but also can increase the likelihood of injury. Indeed, Wilks (1991) maintains that manifestations of stress in the body may be the primary risk factor for injury in sport. An explanation for this is that high arousal leads to reduced concentration, the experience of negative emotions, leading to increased muscle tension, poor execution of skills, and subsequent injury. The research in this area is covered in Chapter 18, and will not be discussed here.

Just as people in the general community show a wide range of responses to pain, athletes differ in the way they respond to pain following injury. A Sports Inventory for Pain (SIP) has been developed (Meyers, Bourgeois, Stewart, & LeUnes, 1992) to measure differences in the response of athletes to pain. Five pain response subscales have been identified, including *coping, cognitive, avoidance, catastrophising,* and *body awareness*. All of these categories represent different ways of coping with the pain of injury.

The way athletes react to sports injury ranges from an athlete responding positively to the injury and viewing it as a challenge to recover quickly, to an athlete responding in such an extreme way that psychiatric intervention is required. The importance to athletes of avoiding serious injury can be very high, with tangible losses in income, lifestyle, and health being at stake, depending on the level of competition. Serious injury can be devastating for the elite athlete. Notwithstanding the above, Smith, Scott, and Wiese (1990) question the hypothesis that the emotional responses of athletes to injury parallel existing "loss of health models" such as that for the terminally ill. Smith et al. (1990) argue that it is important to know the psychosocial dynamics accompanying sport injury so that steps can be taken to ensure psychological recovery. Consequently, these authors emphasise the need for research on the athlete's post-injury response.

Though little has been done to date on the identification of ways of coping with injury, this is an important and potentially fruitful area of research. Research by Madden, Kirkby, and McDonald (1989a, 1989b) with elite middle-distance runners has shown that the number of injuries reported by athletes and the gender of athletes are strong predictors of the extent to which athletes utilise emotionality as a way of coping with a slump in personal performance. Together, these two characteristics of the subjects accounted for over 50% of the variance in the General Emotionality scale of the WOCS. This finding would suggest that elite athletes — particularly elite female athletes — resort to emotional reactions when they have had a high number of injuries. The severity of reported injuries was found to be a relatively good predictor of the use of strategies in which the athlete focuses on or emphasises the positive in order to cope with a slump in personal performance. Athletes who have experienced serious injury might well feel a sense of being unable to control their fate. Serious injuries, by definition, cannot be taken lightly since a considerable degree of debilitation has been suffered. In such cases the athlete may have little recourse but to focus attention on the positive aspects of the situation, perhaps feeling unable to directly change it.

Research conducted by Kirkby, Kolt, and Lindner (1993) supports the notion that severity of injury correlates with the use of emotion-focused coping. Kirkby et al. (1993) administered the WOCS to 115 adolescent gymnasts. A distinction was made between more-injured and less-injured subjects based on the number of injuries sustained. Subjects in the less-injured category (three or fewer injuries) indicated they were more likely to use an *increased effort and resolve* coping style and less likely to use a denial coping style to cope with performance slumps than subjects in the more-injured category. McDonald and Madden (1991) have devised a psychometric instrument for monitoring the ways athletes cope with injury. The Ways of Coping with Injury [WOCI] is comprised of thoughts and actions used by athletes and performers to deal with an injury incurred during training or competition. However, this questionnaire is still in the early stages of development.

Mood disturbance and lowered self-esteem are two correlates of injury in athletes. Smith et al. (1990) argue that a concrete, problem-focused, behaviourally oriented program which minimises uncertainty is "theoretically ideal for injured athletes". This approach is consistent with the emphasis on goal setting and performance outcome which is commonly used in exercise and sport training programs. However, these authors suggest caution, as the effectiveness of these strategies for injured athletes has not yet been clearly established. Cognitive behavioural programs that have been designed to help individuals cope with pain (for example, Turk, Meichenbaum, & Genest, 1983) could well be adapted and tailored to the injuries commonly suffered by athletes.

DRUG USE AS A WAY OF COPING WITH STRESS

The use of alcohol, drugs, medications, and other substances is a common way for athletes to cope with stress (Madden et al., 1990a, 1990b). It is generally agreed that there are many reasons why individuals use drugs (Crundall, 1988). Drug abuse, on the other hand, most likely reflects a complex and relatively enduring interaction between maladaptive cognitive schema (thought processes) or life scripts (enduring beliefs) and emotional experiences of the individual who engages in drug-seeking behaviour (Madden, 1987b).

Coping with stress (Madden, 1987b; Madden et al., 1990a, 1990b) and performance enhancement (Smith & Perry, 1992) are common reasons why athletes use drugs. Picou and Gill (1986) examined three situations in which athletes use drugs. These were situations in which drugs could be used to enhance performance; situations in which drugs were used as a response to injury; and recreational-use situations. College and professional basketball players were the subjects in the study. Interviews were examined for the periods 1939–1965 and 1971–1982. A modest overall increase in drug use over time was found for all three drug-use situations. Considering the attention given to the use in sport of performance-enhancing drugs such as steroids (LaBree, 1991; Freed, Banks, Longson, & Burley, 1975; Smith & Perry, 1992), it is interesting that a recreational setting was found to be the *primary-use situation* identified for contemporary basketball players.

The use of alcohol and drugs represents a problematic way of coping that is not likely to benefit the athlete's long-term development or well-being. Research with (non-athlete) persons who have chronic alcohol and drug problems reveals that these people have a coping profile characterised by wishful thinking, self-blame, and self-isolation on Folkman and Lazarus's Ways of Coping Checklist [WOCC] (Madden, Hinton, Holman, & Mountjouris, 1989, 1992). This profile indicates an approach to coping which is not considered to be helpful to the person. The individual relies on wishes to change aspects of their life. In the case of athletes using performance-enhancing drugs, guilt and shame (self-blame) may result from feeling that they have "cheated" in order to win at all costs. The self-isolating behaviour makes it very difficult for the athlete to be helped by other people such as coaches or team mates. Consequently, such an athlete has a diminished opportunity to use these people as a way of coping with the stress of competition and of life generally.

In view of the negative effects resulting from some athletes' overuse of alcohol and drugs as a way of coping, drug prevention programs for athletes are recommended. These programs are likely to be most effective if they are designed as follows. First, they should reflect a skills-based rather than a knowledge-based education approach. Second, they should be designed as primary and secondary prevention programs and not simply developed for use with those who already have a severe problem. Finally, they ought to consist of coping strategies derived from the area of tertiary prevention, which can be individually tailored to the needs of each athlete (Madden, 1991a; 1991b). Moreover, in view of the findings from the Picou and Gill (1986) study, such programs should have a focus that takes into account the fact that drugs are used by athletes predominantly in recreational settings.

CONSEQUENCES OF MALADAPTIVE COPING

Fatigue and under-performance may result from the continual stress of excessive training schedules. An *overtraining syndrome* has been identified which may be associated with depression and an increased susceptibility to infections (Budgett, 1990). While coping strategies, such as the setting of realistic and reasonable training schedules, appear to be the logical way of preventing the development of this syndrome, once it is present, Budgett (1990) recommends rest and a sustained stress management program (over three months) as the treatment of choice.

When an athlete withdraws from a sport it is increasingly common to attribute this withdrawal to *burn-out* (Smith, 1986; Nashman, 1987). The term burn-out implies that the individual has exhausted his or her coping resources. Smith (1986) proposes an athletic burn-out model in which knowledge about the nature, causes and consequences of burn-out are incorporated. Within this cognitive–affective model of stress, the role of situational, cognitive, physiologic and behavioural components of stress and burn-out are noted. This model has implications for preventing and coping with burn-out.

COPING QUESTIONNAIRES AND COPING SKILLS TRAINING PROGRAMS

The Ways of Coping with Sport [WOCS] (Madden, 1987a; Madden et al., 1990a, 1990b), is a sport-related checklist, adapted from Folkman and Lazarus's (1985) Ways of Coping Checklist [WOCC], which was later to become known as the Ways of Coping Questionnaire [WOCQ]. The WOCS is a process questionnaire consisting of various coping strategies utilised by competitors across a range of sports and performance situations. It consists of thoughts and actions used by competitors to cope with stressful situations in sport (e.g., "Just concentrate on what I have to do next — the next step"). The eight scales of the WOCS are described earlier in this chapter. The WOCS, which has been found to have good reliability and face validity, has many applications. Usually, subjects are asked to indicate on a Likert scale how often they used the WOCS strategies to cope with their last performance or competition. Alternatively, subjects may be asked to indicate on the WOCS how they coped when experiencing a slump in personal performance.

The basketball sample to which the WOCS was first administered revealed patterns of coping related to low, mid and high levels of perceived stress. Results showed that subjects reporting high levels of competitive stress used increased effort and resolve, problem-focused coping, and seeking social support coping strategies more frequently than subjects reporting low competitive stress. The relatively high frequency of these scales indicated a qualitatively positive coping set in which the typical basketball player uses problem-focused strategies to change his or her performance. It is consistent with the sport psychology literature showing that stratagems comprising the increased effort and resolve factor were utilised frequently by basketball players reporting high levels of stress. Effort and resolve (or commitment) are held to be important ingredients of success in sport. Indeed, effort is held to be one of four central attributions commonly put forward by competitors to explain success in sport (Roberts & Pascuzzi, 1979; Bukowski & Moore, 1980). Given that competitors strive for success in sport, as evidenced by competitive behaviour, it is not surprising that when the competitor experiences a slump in personal form, stratagems are employed which are widely held to contribute to successful performance in sport. As mentioned in a previous section of this chapter, additional scales have subsequently been identified from the application of the WOCS to sports other than basketball.

The Mental Attributes of Performance [MAPS] (Madden & Evans, 1993, June; 1993, October) is a process questionnaire consisting of 48 sport-relevant coping stratagems. It was designed as an instrument that could be used to monitor the mental aspects of performance (coping strategies) on a continuing basis, from performance to performance. It purports to provide information that can assist sport psychologists to devise a program of intervention that is individually tailored to the needs of the athlete or performer. The MAPS, which was initially administered to Australian Rules Football coaches and players, was developed from coping strategies generated from research and practice in sport psychology. The MAPS items refer to things an individual might do or feelings or experiences they might have in preparation for or during a performance. Players are asked to indicate, on a Likert scale, how often they did these things or had these experiences prior to or during a performance. The MAPS has been found to have good reliability and face validity. The nine MAPS scales were initially described in Madden and Evans (1993, June). Subsequent examination and re-appraisal of the items comprising the nine scales has led to the renaming of some of the scales. The revised MAPS scale nomenclature is described below.

Scale 1 comprises attributes that allow an athlete to be aware of or concentrate on relevant or important stimuli and play options, and consequently to perform well (e.g., item 15: "When I had possession of the ball I was able to be aware of many options for disposing of it effectively"). This factor is now termed "Attention". Scale 2 contains items describing mental preparation techniques and other proactive problem-focused coping strategies (e.g., item 29: "I mentally rehearsed my game in the week prior to the game, seeing myself performing well"). It is therefore termed "Proactive problem-focused coping". Scale 3 comprises items pertinent to or reflecting the arousal level of the athlete, including the way the athlete is oriented to others (e.g., item 6: "I was able to relax myself when necessary during the game"). It is therefore named "Arousal". Scale 4 consists of items referring to the communication initiated by the athlete and processes, such as perceptual abilities, that inform the communication process or increase the likelihood of communication (e.g., item 9: "I let other players know what they could do in order to help me to perform well"). This factor is now termed "Communication". Scale 5 comprises items tapping the ability of the athlete to control thoughts, feelings, or communications (e.g., item 28: "I was able to concentrate well during the game"). This factor is now termed "Self-control". Scale 6 is named "Effort". It contains items reflecting the effort expended by the athlete (e.g., item 32: "I felt as though I had pushed myself to the limit during the game"). Scale 7 is a "Task focus" factor. It comprises items relating to the focusing of thoughts and actions towards a task (e.g., item 36: "During the game I did not go over past plays or think about what the end result of the game would be; I was able to maintain my attention in the present"). Scale 8 includes items reflecting risk-taking behaviour and items depicting the way athletes commit themselves to such behaviour (e.g., item 42: "I took risks in the game"). It is now termed "Risk taking and commitment". Scale 9 comprises items that underlie or embody calmness and poise, even in pressure situations (e.g., item 26: "I was able to perform well in pressure situations"). It is now termed "Self-assurance".

Research findings (Madden & Evans, 1993, June; 1993, October) show that the MAPS questionnaire can successfully discriminate between groups of athletes, and is a useful assessment device (with individual, team, sport-specific and general versions) for determining coping strategies that are being used successfully or unsuccessfully by athletes.

TRAINING IN ADAPTIVE COPING SKILLS

Anshel, Gregory, and Kaczmarek (1990) examined the efficacy of the COPE model for coping with acute stress. Stress was induced by critical feedback given in a sport situation. The authors used an instructional program, on which the model is based, for teaching coping strategies to male baseball and female softball intercollegiate athletes. Included in the study were a group trained in the use of cognitive strategies for coping with unpleasant information feedback; a placebo group (watching sport-related video-tapes); and a no-treatment control group. Training focused on the *control of emotions, organising and filtering feedback information, planning responses,* and *executing responses* (or COPE). Athletes in the trained group demonstrated less fear of negative evaluation; maintained a sense of control over their baseball future; reported feeling less upset by negative feedback; and tended to attribute their performance to internal rather than external factors. The COPE model has both theoretical appeal and practical utility.

Madden (1991a; 1991b) developed an iterative Coping Skills Training [CST] model which involves training athletes in coping strategies. CST is a 12-stage program devised to address the need to promote adaptive coping responses for athletes in stressful situations. CST can be used with a range of coping questionnaires and lists of coping responses. Typically, it is used with the coping profiles of athletes on the WOCS or the MAPS. CST provides a method for assessing and reviewing a person's current cognitive appraisals and coping strategies, with a view to maximising adaptive coping responses. The 12 stages of CST are: initial questionnaire completion; education and induction; appraisal identification; emotions identification; coping strategies identification; relaxation training; mental rehearsal; appraisal evaluation and review; coping strategy evaluation and selection; emotion review; in-vivo application; and post-program questionnaire completion. The essence of the CST program is that it provides an opportunity for performers to identify and examine their coping profile. In doing so, the athlete becomes aware of the relative frequency with which he or she uses various coping strategies. Thus, the program is individually tailored to the needs of each athlete. For example, if an individual has the coping profile typical of basketball players experiencing a slump in performance, the athlete can be made aware that a WOCS coping profile dominated by increased effort and resolve may not put an end to the slump in personal form; that increased effort and resolve does not necessarily improve one's performance, and may in fact maintain the slump because of an accompanying increase in arousal level (Madden 1987a; Madden et al., 1990a, 1990b). The following section comprises a brief and limited explanation of CST, using the MAPS questionnaire.

AN EXAMPLE OF THE USE OF COPING SKILLS TRAINING (CST) WITH INDIVIDUAL ATHLETES

In stage 1 of CST (the initial questionnaire completion stage) the athlete is asked to recall the last competition he or she was in, and a measure of the athlete's performance is obtained. The athlete then rates his or her performance in the previous game on a scale from 0 (poor performance) to 100 (peak performance). Descriptions are elicited of what situations were *difficult or demanding,* what the player *did well* and what were the areas of the player's game where he or she *could have performed better.* The athlete is then asked to indicate *how often* they used the MAPS coping items in their last competition.

By way of explanation, in the previously reported study on football players (Madden & Evans, 1993, October), players completing the MAPS who reported performance levels in the previous game at below 60 were designated *low performance* players, and those reporting performance levels at or above 60 were designated *high performance* players. Profiles drawn from high and low performing players are presented in Figures 12.1 and 12.2, respectively. In interpreting the figures, the reader is referred to a description of the nine scales of the MAPS, as described on pages 300–301.

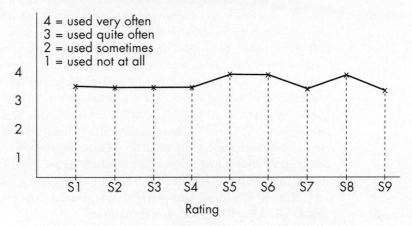

The nine scales of the MAPS: S1: Attention; S2: Proactive problem–focused coping; S3: Arousal; S4: Communication; S5: Self–control; S6: Effort; S7: Task focus; S8: Risk–taking and commitment; S9: Self–assurance.

Figure 12.1: Subject 1: The MAPS profile of a football player who has performed "very well" — "high" performance level (having a score of 80 on a scale from 0 to 100)

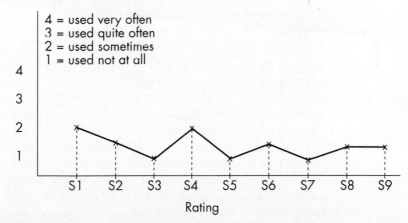

Figure 12.2: Subject 2: The MAPS formulation profile of a football player who has performed "poorly" — low performance level (having a score of 30 on a scale from 0 to 100)

The profile for Subject 2 (performance rating of 30) as presented in Figure 12.2 is of a player who reported that "being shifted in position" and receiving criticism from his coach were the difficult and stressful situations he identified in the previous game. In reporting on the area of his game in which he could have performed better, Subject 2 stated that when he was shifted from his normal position his "concentration faltered" because he was "angry" with his coach and himself, and that he "wanted to become aggressive".

From Figure 12.2 it can be seen that the *formulation profile* for a football player who reacts to criticism from a coach has a MAPS profile characterised by deficits in arousal, self-control, and task focus. In analysing this player's profile, the following formulation and intervention plan emerges:

The criticism this player (Subject 2) received from the coach led to a loss of control of his arousal level, with subsequent poor concentration, as evidenced by his relatively low score on Arousal (Scale 3); and a loss of personal control in the player, as evidenced by his relatively low score on Self-control (Scale 5). This emotional and cognitive disruption, in turn, led to his losing focus on what he was required to do in the game, as evidenced by his relatively low score on Task focus (Scale 7).

An intervention designed to inoculate the player (Subject 2) against distractions which affect the player's emotional responses and cognitions is thus called for. This plan would include

- a social perspective-taking exercise to put the coach's behaviour in a context which reflects the coach's needs rather than the player's perceived abilities
- relaxation training (to enhance arousal control)
- cognitive restructuring to include belief statements about the player's self-efficacy (to enhance self-control)
- mental rehearsal to enhance task-focus (This might involve practising task-focused behaviour while being distracted. Distraction could take the form of critical remarks from others.)
- selection of positive coping self-statements
- in-vivo application of these strategies.

Thus, in applying the MAPS to a football player who identifies that reacting to criticism in a particular situation is "difficult or demanding", an intervention approach is taken which includes specific elements of emotion regulation, cognitive restructuring and behavioural planning.

The content of each intervention is selected to meet each specific problem identified by the MAPS. The sequence of intervention also changes, so that the elements most important for that case are introduced first. Thus, the intervention that the sport psychologist develops is based on the interpretation of the MAPS. The intervention plan consists of a sequence of effective or adaptive ways of coping. In essence, the role of the applied sport psychologist is to assess the current coping strategies of the athlete, and to devise interventions that improve the ways the athlete copes with potential stressors.

FUTURE DIRECTIONS

The identification, promotion and training of adaptive or effective ways of coping in sport is a relatively new endeavour. Coping is a complex and changing process, and this underlines the importance of devising intervention programs that are based on appropriate assessment procedures that yield intervention recommendations specific to individuals and different sports. The emphasis is likely to continue to shift away from early — largely fruitless — attempts by sport psychologists to identify personality traits that are construed as important in various sports or elements of sport performance. Unlike the trait approach, which connotes stability of behaviour, the process approach is suggestive of change. As the emphasis on a process rather than trait approach to sport psychology develops, new research, assessment procedures, and interventions that are task-specific, situation-specific, domain-specific, and sport-specific will be devised and promoted.

This development promises to be useful in promoting flexibility in the way athletes respond to the complex and changing demands they face in sport. It calls for an approach which provides the athlete with a range of coping strategies, and shifts the locus of control to the athlete. Future athletes are more likely to be able to select appropriate strategies to modify or control their cognitions, emotions, and behaviours, rather than rely on external change agents to implement change. From the perspective of the applied sport psychologist, the intervention process will involve a role for them that is more catalytic than interventionist in orientation. Procedures and interventions will be such that the athlete will possess the means for change. The sport psychologist will be seen more as an expert who educates and trains the athlete. The athlete will be able to recognise the important elements in a given situation, will have a wide repertoire of coping strategies (skills) from which to select, and the knowledge of when it is appropriate to select and implement particular strategies. The effective sport psychologist will need to keep abreast of new coping strategies and shifts in knowledge related to the complex relationship between coping strategies, different situations, and different sports; and on the unique characteristics of the individual athlete.

There is still a need for new sport-specific coping assessment methods that are based on the task-specific elements in different sports. While there is a proliferation of trait and global questionnaires in the area of sport psychology, there are still relatively few process questionnaires to measure coping responses and coping strategies. One approach is to use qualitative methods, such as interviews and observation, to determine elements of coping in a particular sport. These elements can then be shaped into items in a questionnaire which elicits responses by a quantitative technique, such as a rating scale. Reliability and validity methods sensitive to the relative instability of responses on previous questionnaires can then be used to validate the questionnaire. However, the development of these instruments ought not to be indiscriminate; test construction would best be guided by the fundamental principle that the instrument is capable of generating specific formulations for intervention, based on the needs of individual athletes. The WOCS and the MAPS are examples of recently developed instruments that have been designed to be sensitive to the responses of individual athletes. These instruments provide the sport psychologist with information which, at once, structures the assessment stage of intervention and indicates the area of cognitive, emotional and behavioural functioning requiring input, as well as the type of intervention required to enhance performance.

CONCLUSIONS

Stress is a commonly occurring phenomenon in sport and in everyday life. It can be conceptualised as a consequence of the perception that current demands outweigh the individual's resources. Although stress and the anxiety that often accompanies it have long been recognised as factors that can impede performance, it is only recently that psychologists have begun to examine the ways that people attempt to cope with stress as a potential source of strategies for stress management. Certain coping strategies can buffer the individual against stress, but some strategies can be maladaptive; that is, they can lead to increased stress in the long term. The use of drugs and alcohol to cope with stress is a prime example discussed in this chapter. Nonetheless, it has been argued here that the study of ways of coping in various situations holds great potential for the management of stress in sport.

One area which is particularly susceptible to intervention is the development of ways of coping during childhood and adolescence. Often, coping develops during childhood in a purely arbitrary manner, so that maladaptive strategies might become the preferred ways of coping for many young athletes. Understanding the process of coping-strategy development may provide a means to teach children adaptive coping strategies before less effective strategies arise by chance. Teaching effective ways of coping in the formative years might also reduce the need to resolve maladaptive behaviours in adult performers.

This chapter has noted that a range of behaviours can be regarded as adaptive coping strategies. These include exercise, relaxation, association and dissociation, social support from coach and team mates, as well as from family and friends, various emotion-focused and problem-focused strategies. While emotion-focused strategies are sometimes maladaptive, it was pointed out that the nature of coping is complex and variable. Thus, the same strategy might be effective in one situation and at one specific time but of little value in another. Again, training in a range of ways of coping and experience of when each strategy is effective can give the athlete a means of enhancing his or her ability to cope in many situations.

The breadth of application of the ways of coping perspective was emphasised by the discussion of coping with injury, substance abuse, over-training and burn-out. These specific uses of coping strategies supplement the need to cope with the everyday stresses of training and competition. The research reported in this chapter suggests that it is possible to identify ways of coping using paper and pencil tests and that there is potential for training athletes in adaptive coping strategies, based on their personal preferences and the sport environment in which they choose to function. The area of coping in sport is still relatively new and there is a great need for further research on the nature of coping and the processes associated with coping responses to perceived stress. However, the progress achieved suggests that this is a most promising area in which sport psychology can help sport participants at all levels.

SUMMARY

This chapter outlined a context within which ways of coping can be construed. The way in which coping strategies develop in children and in adolescents through to adulthood was examined. The transactional model of Lazarus and his colleagues was outlined. The moderating variables or factors that buffer an individual against stress — and therefore represent ways of coping — were discussed, and their importance appraised. The nature and function of various coping strategies in relation to specific sports was discussed, and effective coping strategies were described. The consequences of maladaptive coping were outlined, and models for coping intervention were proffered. An iterative Coping Skills Training (CST) intervention model is advocated in which information is gathered through questionnaire administration (e.g., administration of the WOCS or the MAPS) and an individually tailored formulation is derived from the questionnaire profile (from the analysis of the questionnaire responses), which informs the rational process through which the sport psychologist arrives at an intervention plan. The intervention plan consists of training in a sequence of effective or adaptive ways of coping. Thus the role of the sport psychologist in an applied setting is to assess the current coping strategies of the athlete, and to devise interventions that improve the ways the athlete copes with stressors. An outline and example of this process was given in the chapter, after which directions for future research and practice were suggested.

REFERENCES

Adams, G. M. (1979). Running for your health. *NJEA Review, 53*(1), 23, 40.

Anshel, M., Gregory, W., & Kaczmarek, M. (1990). The effectiveness of a stress training program in coping with criticism in sport: A test of the COPE model. *Journal of Sport Behavior, 13*, 194–196.

Anthony, W. A., & Liberman, R. P. (1986). The practice of psychiatric rehabilitation: Historical, conceptual, and research base. *Schizophrenia Bulletin, 12*(4), 542–559.

Bandura, A. (1986). *Social foundations of thought and action.* Englewood Cliffs, NJ: Prentice-Hall.

Berger, B. G., & Owen, D. R. (1988). Stress reduction and mood enhancement in four exercise modes: Swimming, body conditioning, Hatha yoga, and fencing. *Research Quarterly for Exercise and Sport, 59*, 148–159.

Brown, J. D., & Siegel, J. M. (1988). Exercise as a buffer of life stress: A prospective study of adolescent health. *Health Psychology, 7*, 341–353.

Budgett, R. (1990). Overtraining syndrome. *British Journal of Sports Medicine, 24*, 231–236.

Bukowski, W., & Moore, D. (1980). Winners' and losers' attributions for success and failure in a series of athletic events. *Journal of Sport Psychology, 2*, 195–210.

Cohen, S., & Wills, T. A. (1985). Stress, social support, and the buffering hypothesis. *Psychological Bulletin, 98*, 310–357.

Crundall, I. (1988). *Survey of drug use among young people in Victorian Youth Training and Reception Centres.* Melbourne: Alcohol and Drug Services Unit, Health Department, Victoria.

DeBenedette, V. (1988). Getting fit for life: Can exercise reduce stress? *Physician and Sports Medicine, 16*, 185–186.

Feltz, D. L. (1992). Understanding motivation in sport: A self-efficacy perspective. In G. C. Roberts (Ed.), *Motivation in sport and exercise* (pp. 93–105). Champaign, IL: Human Kinetics.

Folkman, S., Bernstein, L., & Lazarus, R. (1987). Stress processes and the misuse of drugs in older adults. *Psychology and Aging, 2*, 366–374.

Folkman, S., & Lazarus, R. (1985). If it changes it must be a process: A study of emotion and coping during three stages of a college examination. *Journal of Personality and Social Psychology, 48*, 150–170.

Folkman, S., Lazarus, R., Gruen, R. J., & De Longis, A. (1986). Stress processes and depressive symptomatology. *Journal of Abnormal Psychology, 95*, 107–113.

Freed, D. L., Banks, A. J., Longson, D., & Burley, D. M. (1975). Anabolic steroids in athletics: Crossover double-blind trial on weightlifters. *British Medical Journal, 2*, 471–473.

Hobfoll, S. E. (1991). Gender differences in stress reactions: Women filling the gaps. *Psychology and Health, 5*, 95–109.

Kello, P., & Madden, C. (1993). *If it is a process it can be changed!* Unpublished manuscript, La Trobe University.

Khantzian, E. J. (1974). Opiate addiction: A critique of theory and some implications for treatment. *American Journal of Psychotherapy, 28*(1), 59–70.

Kirkby, R., Kolt, G., & Lindner, H. (1993). *Coping in gymnasts: Injury and gender factors.* Unpublished manuscript, La Trobe University.

Konopka, G. (1980). Coping with the stresses and strains of adolescence. *Social Development Issues, 4*, 1–17.

LaBree, M. (1991). A review of anabolic steroids: Uses and effects. *Journal of Sports Medicine and Physical Fitness, 31*, 618–626.

Lariviere, M., & Sydney, K. (1992). The relaxation effect of exercise: Implications for childhood fears and anxieties. *C.A.H.P.E.R. Journal, 58*, 16–21.

Madden, C. (1987a). *Coping with competitive stress.* Unpublished master's dissertation, University of Melbourne.

Madden, C. (1987b, May). *The therapeutic community and psychosocial rehabilitation.* Paper presented at the Australian Psychological Society Conference: Psychology and Social Responsibility, Gippsland Institute of Advanced Education, Victoria.

Madden, C. (1991a). Coping skills training: A training model based on the implementation of coping strategies. In C. Fraser & D. Harvey (Eds.), *Health, psychology and the community* (pp. 49–56). Gippsland: Monash University College.

Madden, C. (1991b, November). *Coping skills training in sport.* Paper presented at the First Asian South Pacific Association of Sports Psychology International Congress, Southern Cross Hotel, Melbourne, Australia.

Madden, C., & Evans, L. (1993, June). *Mental attributes of performance in sport (MAPS).* In S. Serpa, J. Alves, V. Ferriera, & A. Paula-Brito (Eds.), *Proceedings of the VIII World Congress of Sport Psychology* (pp. 463–466). Lisbon: International Society of Sport Psychology.

Madden, C., & Evans, L. (1993, October). *Applying the MAPS questionnaire to individual athletes.* Paper presented at Invited Speaker Session, Australian Sports Medicine Federation Conference, Melbourne, Australia.

Madden, C., Kirkby, R., & McDonald, D. (1989, August). Coping with competitive middle distance running. In C. K. Giam, K. K. Chook, & K. C. Teh (Eds.), *Proceedings of the VII World Congress in Sport Psychology* (pp. 88–89). Singapore: Singapore Sports Council.

Madden, C., Kirkby, R., & McDonald, D. (1989b). Coping styles of competitive middle distance runners. *International Journal of Sport Psychology, 20,* 287–296.

Madden, C., Hinton, E., Holman, C. P., & Mountjouris, S. (1989, May). Anxiety, depression and coping in alcohol and drug dependent persons undergoing rehabilitation. In R. Godding, D. Rankin, & G. Whelan (Eds.), *Proceedings of the Autumn School of Studies on Alcohol and Drugs.* Department of Community Medicine, St. Vincent's Hospital, Melbourne.

Madden, C., Hinton, E., Holman, C. P., & Mountjouris, S. (1992). Anxiety, depression and coping style in alcohol and drug dependent persons. *International Journal of Psychology, 27,* 347.

Madden, C., Summers, J., & Brown, D. (1990a). Coping with competitive sport. *Proceedings of the 9th Commonwealth and International Conference on Physical Education, Sport, Health, Dance, Recreation and Leisure* (pp. 148–153), Vol. 3, *Sport Science,* Part 1. Auckland, New Zealand.

Madden, C., Summers, J., & Brown, D. (1990b). The influence of perceived stress on coping with competitive basketball. *International Journal of Sport Psychology, 21,* 21–35.

McDonald, D., & Madden, C. (1991, November). *Ways of coping with injury.* Paper presented at the First Asian South Pacific Association of Sports Psychology International Congress. Melbourne, Australia.

Meyers, M. C., Bourgeois, A. E., Stewart, S., & LeUnes, A. (1992). Predicting pain response in athletes: Development and assessment of the Sports Inventory for Pain. *Journal of Sport and Exercise Psychology, 14,* 249–261.

Nashman, H. W. (1987). The burnout syndrome: A global concern. *Physical Education Review, 10,* 114–118.

Nieman, D. C. (1989). Exercise and the mind. *Women's Sports and Fitness, 11,* 54–57.

Patterson, J. M., & McCubbin, H. I. (1987). Adolescent coping style and behaviours: Conceptualisation and measurement. *Journal of Adolescence, 10,* 163–186.

Picou, J. S., & Gill, D. A. (1986). Drug use among basketball players: An historical analysis of use situations. *Journal of Applied Research in Coaching and Athletics, 1,* 226–238.

Powell, K. E. (1988). Habitual exercise and public health: An epidemiological view. In R. K. Dishman (Ed.), *Exercise adherence: Its impact on public health* (pp. 15–39). Champaign. IL: Human Kinetics.

Roberts, G., & Pascuzzi, D. (1979). Causal attributions in sport: Some theoretical considerations. *Journal of Sport Psychology, 1,* 203–211.

Rosenfeld, L. B., Richman, J. M., & Hardy, C. J. (1989). Examining social support networks among athletes: Description and relationship to stress. *The Sport Psychologist, 3*, 23–33.

Sachs, M. L. (1984). The mind of the runner: Cognitive strategies used during running. In M. L. Sachs & G. W. Buffone (Eds.), *Running as therapy: An integrated approach* (pp. 288–303). Lincoln, NE: University of Nebraska Press.

Smith, A., Scott, S., & Wiese, D. (1990). The psychological effects of sports injuries: Coping. *Sports Medicine, 9*, 352–369.

Smith, D. A., & Perry, P. J. (1992). The efficacy of ergogenic agents in athletic competition. Part I. Androgenic anabolic steroids. *Annals of Pharmacotherapy, 26*, 520–528.

Smith, R. E. (1986). Toward a cognitive–affective model of athletic burnout. *Journal of Sport Psychology, 8*, 36–50.

Terry, D., Nielsen, M., & Perchard, L. (1993). Effects of work stress on psychological well-being and job satisfaction: The stress-buffering role of social support. *Australian Journal of Psychology, 45*, 168–175.

Thomas, P. R., & Over, R. (1994). Psychological and psychomotor skills associated with performance in golf. *The Sport Psychologist, 8*, 73–86.

Tucker, L. A., Cole, G. E., & Friedman, G. M. (1986). Physical fitness: A buffer against stress. *Perceptual and Motor Skills, 63*, 955–96.

Turk, D., Meichenbaum, D., & Genest, M. (1983). *Pain and behavioural medicine: A cognitive–behavioural perspective.* New York: Guilford Press.

Valliant, G. (1977). *Adaptation to life.* Boston: Little Brown & Co.

Watson, G. G. (1984). Intrinsic motivation and competitive anxiety in sport: Some guidelines for coaches and administrators. *Australian Journal of Science and Medicine in Sport, 16*, 14–20.

Wilks, B. (1991). Stress management for athletes. *Sports Medicine, 11*, 289–299.

C H A P T E R

13

CONFIDENCE AND SPORTING PERFORMANCE

CHRIS HORSLEY

Confidence in sport is easy to recognise and difficult to change. Composure, timing, space and effortless rhythm are the performance hallmarks of confident athletes. They thrive on pressure. They look for challenges that extend their limits and display their skills. Highly confident athletes rarely question their capabilities or their right to be successful. They think and act differently from athletes who lack confidence.

Doubt, uncertainty and anxiety plague the thinking of athletes who lack confidence. Compared to highly confident athletes, the less confident are likely to be less persistent, more hesitant, make more unforced errors and lack the time and space to execute their skills.

In this chapter a brief introduction to the major concepts related to self-confidence will precede a description of intervention strategies used to develop the self-confidence of athletes. Intertwined within the chapter will be issues relating to the practical implementation of techniques and strategies. The success of an intervention program is dependent, in part, on the use of proven techniques and strategies and the skill of the practitioner to use the appropriate strategy at the appropriate time and in the appropriate situation. An appreciation of context is as important for effective intervention as is the understanding of techniques that work. Issues relating to the implementation of intervention strategies within the sporting context will be addressed.

APPLIED ISSUES

Self-confidence is a generic, and at times, complex phenomenon. Mainstream psychology researchers have devised a number of theoretical constructs — self-efficacy, self-concept, self-image — to explain self-confidence. Each construct is defined specifically and can be used to explain and predict specific behaviours. However, in an applied setting, consideration of too many specific concepts can serve to confuse. When working to develop the self-confidence of athletes, attempts to implement strategies that are specific to each and every concept may diffuse the effectiveness of intervention.

In this chapter a brief overview of a number of constructs related to self-confidence will be defined. The purpose is not to confuse. The objective is to clarify and provide a theoretical basis for intervention strategies that will be presented later in the chapter. Successful interventions will be enhanced by an understanding of the factors which contribute to the development and maintenance of self-confidence.

Juxtaposed throughout the chapter is the issue of general versus sport-specific self-confidence. For example, a woman rower presents with a loss of self-confidence specific to ergometer tests. Her belief in her ability to achieve international rowing success is strong, she is confident at university, socially and in her relationship. Her problem is specific to one task — ergometer tests. Intervention strategies will be directed to issues relating to ergometer testing.

A basketball coach phones, concerned about a young player who has all the physical attributes but lacks confidence. The confidence problem is not specific to basketball but seems to be affecting many areas of the player's life — at school, socially and coping with problems. At issue is not basketball confidence, per se, but the personal development of the athlete. In this case, the efficacy of intervention strategies will be reduced if focused solely on the "basketball player" while ignoring the "person".

While the same psychological processes may be at play for both the rower and the basketball player, intervention would be different. In this chapter the development of self-confidence will be presented as a multi-dimensional approach during which the general psychology of the individual (personal development) and the sport specific confidence of the athlete (performance enhancement) will be explored and addressed.

Another issue impacting upon the effectiveness of an intervention program is the way techniques and strategies for change are presented. Self-confidence is an abstract concept that coaches and athletes can find difficult to understand and develop. Many do not want to be sport psychologists but do want enhanced self-confidence. If intervention strategies are weighted heavily towards a theoretical education of what self-confidence is and how it is developed, the coach and athlete may not be around long enough to finish the program. Intervention strategies need to be appropriate for the individual coach and athlete. Interventions that are practical, concrete and address the needs of the coach and athlete, rather than the needs and methods of the sport psychologist, will be the most effective.

THEORIES OF SELF-CONFIDENCE

Self-confidence is closely related to a variety of other constructs such as self-concept, self-efficacy and self-image. While theoretically similar they differ in definition, the specific behaviours they attempt to explain, and robustness.

SELF-CONCEPT

Self-concept is a person's perception of him/herself (Shavelson, Hubner, & Stanton, 1976). "These perceptions are formed through experience with, and interpretations of, one's environment. They are especially influenced by evaluations by significant others, reinforcements, and attributions for one's own behaviour" (Marsh, 1990, p. 83).

A rower's self-concept is formed by comparing his or herself to other rowers; by the variety of reinforcements received from the coach, other rowers, selectors, and achievements in the boat; and, the manner in which the rower accepts, or minimises, responsibility for personal behaviour and performances.

Three aspects of the self-concept construct are relevant to sport and the process of changing self-confidence: the multidimensionality of self-concept, the importance of an individual's frame of reference in the formation and maintenance of self-concept, and changes that occur in self-concept as a function of human development and maturity (Marsh, 1990).

MULTIDIMENSIONALITY

Self-concept is multidimensional. According to Marsh (1990) athletes do not have just one global perception of themselves. They have a number of self-concepts, specific to situations. An athlete's physical self-concept may be different from his or her social self-concept which is different again from the academic self-concept. In other words, self-confidence is specific to the task.

The specificity of self-concept can be refined even further, differentiated within a particular pursuit. Marsh (1986) showed that there was no one global academic self-concept but that a student's self-concept in relation to verbal performance varied from the student's Maths self-concept. While an athlete may have a high physical self-concept, the athlete's perception of his or her capability to kick a football and throw a waterpolo ball may vary.

FRAME OF REFERENCE

The second feature to consider when working with athletes is the impact frame of reference has upon self-concept. Your self-concept will depend upon your perceptions of your own strengths and weaknesses and the frame of reference you use to evaluate these self-perceptions. Cricketers will form opinions of their cricketing capabilities not only by evaluating their batting, bowling and fielding strengths and weaknesses in relation to their own individual standards but also by comparing themselves to the cricketers they play with and against. Their team mates and the opposition are their frame of reference, a comparison group against which they can judge their individual capabilities.

Marsh (1990) proposed two mechanisms by which an athlete's self-concept is influenced by frame of reference: the Big Fish Little Pond Effect (BFLPE) and the Internal/External Model (I/E).

The *Big Fish Little Pond Effect* is at work when equally able athletes exhibit lower self-confidence when they *compare* themselves to more able athletes, and exhibit high self-confidence when they *compare* themselves with less able athletes (Marsh, 1990). The BFLPE demonstrates that the accomplishments of others in one's immediate environment provides an important frame of reference.

According to the *Internal/External Model*, the development of an athlete's self-concept will be a function of both *internal* comparisons — comparisons with themselves over time and in other athletic pursuits, and *external* comparisons — during which athletes will compare their self-perceptions of their athletic ability with athletes within their frame of reference (Marsh, 1990).

For example, a swimmer's self-confidence will be enhanced if an improvement can be observed in times, stroke or mental application over time. Or, if the swimmer perceives that successes when playing waterpolo will help with swimming. Accordingly, comparison with oneself over time and across skills will contribute to the development and maintenance of one's self-concept.

Marsh and Peart (1988) suggested that the enhancement of an athlete's skill levels may have a negative effect on self-concept if the gains in skills are more than offset by a change in the athlete's external frame of reference — the athlete's comparison group changes from one of lower ability to one that is of a higher standard.

Strategies to control and utilise the social versus self comparison process for the benefit of athletes will be discussed later in this chapter.

DEVELOPMENT OF SELF-CONCEPT WITH AGE

The third feature of self-concept relevant to sport psychologists, especially those working with youth sports, is the changes that occur in the self-concept of young people as they move from preadolescence to adulthood. During early preadolescence, children begin to develop situation-specific self-concepts.

During preadolescence and early adolescence, self-concept declines systematically with age as individuals strive to match "unrealistically high self-concepts" with realistic feedback from external sources. By late adolescence, self-other agreement — adjustment to external feedback — is markedly strong. "... the results suggest that as children grow older their self-concepts more accurately reflect information provided by external sources" (Marsh, 1990, p. 165).

Therefore, the self-confidence of an eight-year-old female gymnast may be unrealistically high even though she can differentiate her capability levels across situations. Four years later, as reality checks adjust self-perceptions, she may experience a crisis of confidence.

Maturity can be characterised by a balanced use of both internal and external comparison processes and a confluence of self-perceptions and reality. The work of the sport psychologist in developing an athlete's self-confidence centres on the athlete's flexible use of frame of reference processes and the development of realistic self-perceptions.

SELF-EFFICACY

The self-concept and self-efficacy constructs overlap substantially. Both are cognitively based attempts to explain a relationship between one's perceptions of oneself in relation to performance on a specific task.

Both constructs propose that self-confidence is specific to the task. An individual may have high self-confidence when playing basketball but not so when playing football. Even when playing basketball, the player may be confident to shoot but less confident when playing defence.

The similarities between the two are greater than the differences. Despite the emphasis on specificity, Bandura (1982) refers to the generality of self-efficacy and Marsh (1990) highlights global self-concept at the top of the self-concept hierarchy. It would appear that while the robustness of both constructs to explain behaviour is enhanced by specificity, more global measures of self-efficacy and self-concept should not be dismissed out of hand.

The differences between the two constructs revolve around the distinction between the roles of significant others (role modelling versus frames of reference) and assessment application (descriptive versus evaluative).

Research indicates that vicarious experiences provide individuals with information about effective strategies for specific tasks, thereby contributing to self-efficacy. Bandura places little emphasis on the social comparison processes or frames of reference that are used by athletes to evaluate their own capabilities (Marsh, 1990). In terms of devising techniques for the development of self-confidence both vicarious experiences and social comparison processes need to be included.

Tony Morris has written on the theoretical framework and research efforts in the area of self-efficacy in Chapter 6. He has detailed research support for a relationship between high levels of self-efficacy and superior athletic performances (e.g., Barling & Abel, 1983; Lee, 1982; McAuley & Gill, 1983).

Bandura (1977) proposed four categories of information that influence the level and strength of self-efficacy.

1. Successful performance accomplishments
2. Vicarious experiences
3. Persuasive techniques
4. Techniques to reduce and change one's perceptions of physiological arousal.

Feltz and Doyle (1981) defined the categories as "sources of information from which expectations of self-efficacy are derived" (p. 90).

In Chapter 6, Morris illustrated, with empirical studies, the positive impact performance accomplishments and vicarious experiences can have upon self-efficacy. Both categories are translated into applied strategies later in this chapter. The efficacy of persuasive techniques and arousal control is equivocal. However, the importance of internal persuasive techniques and physiological control strategies should not be dismissed when an athlete is striving to develop self-confidence.

 ## SELF-IMAGE

"Your self-image reflects the sum total of your experience, thoughts and emotions. It is something that deserves considerable attention and gentle development" (Syer & Connolly, 1984, p. 107).

Self-image is a construct that is written about in the sport psychology literature for coaches and athletes but, compared to self-concept and self-efficacy, has not attracted a great deal of research. This is so, in part, because one's self-identity is purely subjective. It is a set of beliefs about oneself and others, formed from past experiences and current perceptions.

One's self-image is developed at an early age based on one's self-talk, habits acquired from significant others and messages received from other people such as parents, brothers and sisters, coaches and friends.

Self-image is a popularly applied concept because it can be defined by the coach or athlete, free of abstract psychological theories, to which they can attach personal reference; it can be expressed in concrete terms and related directly to current thoughts, feelings and behaviours.

Self-image can have a positive impact and inhibiting effect upon behaviour and sporting performance. Judgmental overt verbal comments and self-talk athletes make about themselves are insights into their self-image: "I can never drive properly when the pressure is on", "I am a slow starter", "My backhand has always been weak", "I'm hopeless and inadequate".

Not all verbalisations are negative. "I thrive on pressure", "I am good at what I do", "I am quick to change and adapt to make the most of the situation" are indications of a positive self-image, so long as they are based on realistic assessments.

Image barriers abound in sport. Witness the golfer who, after six holes is five strokes below her handicap. Her self-talk: "When is this going to stop? I can't go on like this for long" — precedes a few bad holes. She drops a few strokes to conform to her self-image.

In 1984 Steve Cram, the British middle distance runner, was emerging from the shadows of world record-breaking compatriots Steve Ovett and Sebastian Coe. After one 1500-metre race, when Coe just held off Cram to win, Cram described how his self-image had caused him to lose the race. He claimed that as he came around the final bend, with Coe in front and accelerating, he surged, and within ten metres found himself on Coe's shoulder. At that moment the thought shot through his head "I shouldn't be here. Coe is my hero, the world record holder". Instead of continuing the surge past Coe and into the straight, Cram hesitated momentarily, allowing Coe to react and surge again. The opportunity was lost. Cram was astute enough to recognise, after the race, the limiting reins he had placed on himself and vowed never to let it happen again. Cram went on to break Coe's world records.

The Cram anecdote illustrates not only the limitations one's self-image can place on performance but also the important link between beliefs and self-talk. When trying to develop self-confidence, beliefs and self-talk need to be addressed simultaneously. The anecdote also highlights an issue confronting sport psychologists working at the elite end of the sporting spectrum. A magnificent opportunity would have been lost for Cram if the 1500-metre race in question had been an Olympic or World Championship final. When preparing for major events you cannot afford to wait for the issue to manifest itself or be exposed as a problem, as Cram did. The exploration of an athlete's self-image and identification of self-imposed barriers to performance need to occur well in advance of the competition so that they can be addressed and changed. Changing well-established belief systems and habits of self-talk takes time.

Athletes wanting to develop their self-confidence need to explore current attitudes about themselves and others. They need to identify attitudes that are productive and assist their self-confidence and performance. They need to identify attitudes that are counter-productive, attitudes that undermine their self-confidence and performance. Next, they must be willing to change, to remove the self-imposed limits to their potential and identify a new self-image, one that will enhance their self-confidence and improve their performance.

ATTRIBUTIONS

Constructs such as self-efficacy and self-concept that help to explain an athlete's confidence to perform a particular task have links to attribution theory (Heider, 1944; Russell, 1982; Weiner, 1979). Shavelson claimed that self-concept is formed by "one's attributions for one's own behavior"

(Shavelson & Bolus, 1982, p. 3). Marsh (1990) proposes that there is a mutual interaction between self-concept and self-attributions whereby changes in self-concept will lead to changes in self-attribution and that changes in self-attributions will lead to changes in self-concept. Bar-Tal (1978) and Marsh, Cairns, Relich, Barnes, and Debus (1984b) found that school performance, self-concept and academic behaviours were related to the children's attributions of their outcomes.

Attribution theory is a cognitive approach to motivation and self-confidence based on the assumption that "people strive to explain, understand and predict events based upon their cognitive perception of them" (Cox, 1985, p. 176). Stephanie Hanrahan provides a detailed theoretical and empirical overview of attribution theory in Chapter 5.

Weiner (1979) proposed that athletes will make evaluations along three dimensions: stability, locus of control and controllability. Cox (1985) reports that winning athletes attribute their success to internal, stable and controllable factors more than losing athletes do. Individuals with a high self-concept are more likely to attribute success to internal factors and to attribute failure externally (Marsh, 1990).

Anshel (1990) reports that athletes with a high internal locus of control exhibit higher self-confidence and self-esteem, set relatively higher performance goals, persist longer at tasks and react more adversely to continued failure than athletes with a high external locus of control. McAuley and Gross (1983) found that habitually successful athletes focus on internal causes (ability and effort) to explain their performances.

Research has generally indicated that an internal locus of control is better than an external locus of control. Rotter (1971) associated an internal locus of control with maturity while Bandura (1977) claimed that internalising success is of great value in developing self-efficacy. Chalip (1980) suggests that internals are less likely to be affected by performance stress and are better able to use task-centred coping behaviours.

Athletes develop habits of thinking that are manifested in their attribution style. They acquire their attribution style from their parents, coaches and team mates at a young age so that by the time they reach the age of twenty years their reasons for their successes and failures are well established.

When I first worked with the Australian waterpolo team prior to the Seoul Olympics, the attribution style of the players and coaches was mixed. They willingly claimed credit for a win not only because "we are the better team" (internal — ability) but also because the opposition was not very good (external). They tended to denigrate the opposition, in effect giving the opposition some credit for their victory. If they lost they tended to blame the cheating referees and/or bad luck (external and unstable) among other external causes. This style of attribution was conditioned in the older players and taught to new players as they joined the team. It became an integral part of the team's self-image. It was manifested in game situations (e.g., losing composure after the referee had made a few dubious calls) and after games.

Despite a re-education program, during which the logic behind appropriate attributions was explained, it took two years before a significant difference occurred in the content of the post-game post mortems. The players were consistently reminded to take responsibility for their own performance and that they could only "control the controllables" — we were not concerned with the uncontrollables. After games, the heretics would jokingly be reprimanded by team mates if they transgressed the party line.

The coach, in particular, played a significant role in changing the team's perceptions of the causes of a result. He came from the old school so had to be regularly reminded before post-game evaluations to focus on aspects of the game we could control. As a powerful agent of influence and change he reconditioned the attributional style of the team — in effect, it became part of a culture change.

The self-confidence, of an individual and team, is formed and maintained by the attributions one makes of one's own behaviour. A change in self-confidence requires a change of attributions.

INTERVENTION STRATEGIES

1. SUCCESSFUL EXPERIENCES

"Performance accomplishments provide the most dependable source of information upon which to base one's self-efficacy because they are based on one's own mastery expectations" (Feltz, 1984, p. 192).

Sport psychologists and coaches who wish to develop the self-confidence of athletes through performance accomplishments have two avenues — manipulate the training and competition environment and, influence the perceptions of the athlete so that challenging achievements are perceived as successful experiences.

Manipulate the environment

The first avenue, manipulating the environment, is the domain of the coach, usually not the sport psychologist. The coach organises and runs the training sessions and is a primary source of influence in relation to competitions.

Sport psychologists are not always involved in decisions about the content and structure of training drills, the periodisation of the competition program, the setting of performance goals and the coaching processes during competition. And yet most techniques for enhancing the self-efficacy of athletes via performance accomplishments require some degree of environmental control and manipulation.

The challenge for sport psychologists is to work closely with the coach to have drills incorporated in the training and competition situations that positively contribute to the self-efficacy of athletes. Coaching methods aimed at providing performance accomplishments for athletes should follow the basic principles of skill acquisition. The following are guidelines for enhancing self-efficacy during skill acquisition (Feltz & Doyle, 1981): introduce new skills at the level consummate with the capabilities of the athlete; ensure the athlete gains early successful experiences. In team sports, ensure all team members experience success. Challenge the athlete with new skills, but do it gradually — accomplishments achieved on difficult tasks contribute more to self-efficacy than the achievements of easier tasks. Concomitantly, allow enough time for the athlete to appreciate and internalise the success.

Ensure the goals for success are appropriate for the standards of the individual, not the standards of the coach, parent or peers; promote an acceptance of failure as a learning process and that failure, in and of itself, is not bad; ensure, as much as possible, that the athlete achieves success with the skill by him or herself. Performance accomplishments achieved independently carry greater efficacy than those achieved with assistance.

At the elite level it is more difficult to manipulate the environment to provide success for athletes. Imagine asking the Russian waterpolo team if they would mind playing dead for a game so that some of the younger players of the Australian team can experience success at the international level. Or, asking a professional basketball player to not play too aggressively on a team mate, who may be in a slump, but is also fighting for the starting position.

The culture of elite sport, especially in the professional arena, is outcome oriented. Although highly confident individuals would help the organisation achieve the required results, few compensations are made for experienced athletes who are in a slump or young athletes whose performances would improve if their self-confidence developed.

The sport psychologist, working at the elite level, who wants to manipulate the training or competition environment is faced with many challenges besides the development of the athlete's confidence. Very little, if anything, will be achieved unless the sport psychologist has a strong working relationship with the coach based on mutual professional respect.

The sport psychologist and coaching staff have to work as a team with common objectives. Regular communication is paramount. The sport psychologist has to be flexible and adaptive, respect the fact that the ideal program may not be implemented but at the same time be assertive enough to present a convincing argument. Creative thinking is required to produce opportunities for the development of self-efficacy within a structured, and sometimes, rigid system.

Changing the athlete's perception of success

The second avenue available for a sport psychologist when helping an athlete develop self-confidence is through the manipulation of the athlete's perceptions of performance accomplishments. Feltz (1984) states that if mastery experiences "have been repeatedly perceived as successes, they will raise efficacy expectations; if they have been perceived as failures, they will lower expectation" (p. 192).

Some athletes find it difficult to perceive their performance accomplishments as successes despite contradictory evidence. Those who engage in social comparison rather than self-comparison, athletes who set their goals and expectations unrealistically high, and athletes with a low self-image may objectively achieve success but subjectively perceive the result as a failure. The role of the sport psychologist in such cases is independent of the coach; the function is to assist the athlete to change belief systems, alter perceptual processes and self-talk and set more realistic goals.

2. EFFECTIVE GOAL SETTING

The confidence of athletes will be assisted if they conform to the normally accepted guidelines of goal setting, i.e., challenging, realistic and attainable, specific and concrete, process oriented and written.

A number of features associated with goal setting and expectations have the potential to undermine an athlete's self-confidence. Athletes who set unrealistic goals place unnecessary pressure on themselves when confronted with reality. The direction of causation is unsubstantiated. Do athletes with low self-confidence set unrealistically high goals in an attempt to boost their self-confidence or do the failures resulting from unrealistically high expectations undermine self-confidence? The direction of initial causation is probably not as important as the realisation of a circular maintenance system — unrealistic goal setting will negatively impact upon self-confidence which will in turn feed back to the type of goals set and so on.

Reminding athletes to set realistic goals is one way of helping them to develop their self-confidence. Another way is to ask athletes regularly to verbalise their goals and, if necessary, and in private, challenge the athletes' perceived ability to achieve their stated goal.

Short-term goals

Realistic and appropriate short-term goals should provide athletes with feedback of performance accomplishments. Short-term goals can be set for a week, a day, a training session or a particular training set. Athletes can always achieve a feeling of satisfaction and accomplishment if they are prepared to set many small achievable goals. Sometimes they need to be convinced that many small goals add up to a few large goals — that mountains are climbed with many small steps.

As an example, consider the case of a young basketball player from the Australian Institute of Sport, whose weights training had reached a plateau and yet, she still derived a feeling of accomplishment from each session. She used her weights session to work on one of her primary mental goals — to develop her ability to stay focused. Her aim was to reduce the number of times during each session she was distracted by other athletes in the weights room. She also worked on her ability to stay focused on a single point or cue during a game.

Injured athletes, denied the opportunity to gain positive feedback from training and competition, have to be particularly vigilant to set short-term goals in a range of areas that allow them to gain a feeling of accomplishment from small successes.

Multiple goals

Goals need not be limited to technical pursuits. The types of goals athletes can set that will contribute to self-confidence are limitless. Athletes can always achieve a feeling of satisfaction and accomplishment if they are creative enough. The important criterion is that the goals should be appropriate to the needs of the athlete at that particular time. An athlete who is trying to become more assertive may set a goal to, "keep shoulders back, head up and look people in the eye when I talk with them". An athlete who places negative labels on herself may want to, "Accept myself. Replace with a positive attribute". An athlete who gets emotional and negative after making a mistake may strive to, "stay relaxed and keep involved in the game — no emotion". Athletes can derive satisfaction by considering their personal and athletic development as a long-term and on-going process. Goals can be set in many areas that will contribute to this process.

As a general rule, the goals athletes set should be based on their own standards and own desires, not on the standards or expectations of significant others. The impact of significant others needs to be assessed by the sport psychologist. Parents, peers and coaches can undermine the confidence of athletes by being excessively influential in placing their expectations on the athlete.

An exception to the rule is the case of coaches providing young and immature athletes with direction and guidance. Hersey and Blanchard's (1969) model of situational leadership emphasises flexible, adaptive leadership that is responsive to the age and confidence of athletes. In many cases it may be appropriate for the coach to be more directive when athletes set goals. Sport psychologists can teach parents and coaches strategies to empower the athlete while simultaneously assisting the athlete to set challenging and realistic goals based on their own desires.

Process goals

One of the fundamental platforms for enhanced self-confidence is successful experiences. In its most simplistic form, successful experiences can be derived from the outcome — winning. If athletes win regularly they will develop confidence in their ability to perform at the required level. However, the vast majority of athletes who do not win regularly can still be self-confident if they set goals appropriate to their own level of performance, set process goals not just outcome goals and consider their long-term development not just short-term results. Athletes need to set goals that provide them with successful experiences, that allow them to derive satisfaction and provide feedback that they are worthwhile and capable individuals.

One role of a sport psychologist

Highly motivated athletes, who are striving to achieve at the highest level, can find it difficult to accept this holistic approach. Prior to the Barcelona Olympic Games, and as final selection came closer, a national waterpolo player experienced a crisis of confidence. Kevin (not his real name) not only wanted to make the team for the Olympics but also wanted to play as much time as the team's leading players. His self-confidence fluctuated each time the coach announced the starting line-up for the game and made substitution decisions during the game. Kevin set process goals based on what he wanted to do to play to the best of his ability. But these goals were overridden by an emotionally tied expectation that he should play more time and should be given a chance to prove himself in the starting line-up.

The coach did not hold the same opinion. The coach placed Kevin high on his list of players to be selected for the Olympics but to perform a specific role as a substitute. He wanted Kevin to play for short periods, perform his role in attack, but most significantly, make minimal errors in defence. Kevin, in his desperation to impress the coach and make the team, tended to overplay his role, make numerous unforced errors and, in the process, undermined his own self-confidence.

Given the coach's criteria, Kevin's goal of playing for long periods of time was unrealistic and placed him under unnecessary pressure. The solution, in this case, was for the coach to explain clearly to Kevin what he wanted of him in the water and for Kevin to accept this diminished, but significantly important role. My role was to facilitate the communication between coach and player and to assist Kevin to accept the new role.

In this case Kevin's goals were not entirely inappropriate but needed fine tuning, adjustments that could only be achieved with communication. Kevin's goals were adjusted to include psychological objectives such as "readiness to play from the bench", "maintain high self-confidence" and "derive something positive from each game irrespective of time in the water".

Using goal setting to help athletes develop confidence is not a simple matter of teaching athletes the principles of goal setting. The development of self-confidence is dynamic and fluid. Effective goal setting requires flexibility and adjustments.

3. COGNITIVE TECHNIQUES

One of the challenges facing young athletes is gaining control of seemingly involuntary and spontaneous thoughts. The challenge for sport psychologists is two fold: increasing athlete awareness of the important role that thoughts play in determining feelings and behaviour and assisting athletes to control their self-talk for positive benefit — self-confidence.

Positive self-talk and positive images are the hallmarks of confident athletes. They say positive things to themselves, imagine themselves being successful and in control, and keep their attention focused on achieving the task at hand rather than worrying about the possibility of failing or of possible negative consequences.

Negative and destructive self-talk are identifying features of athletes who are lacking confidence. Talking negatively to themselves, calling themselves unflattering names, thinking irrationally and focusing on failure and all the terrible consequences that will result in the future are the cognitive symptoms, and cause, of a lack of confidence.

The key to cognitive control is self-talk. It is important athletes understand how the mind works, appreciate how self-talk affects feelings and actions and, ultimately, how the mind can be disciplined (Bunker, Williams, & Zinsser, 1993). Self-talk is of benefit when it is positive, task related and enhances self-confidence. Mahoney (1979) found self-talk to be a useful method for building self-efficacy expectations of athletes. In an investigation involving elite college and national coaches Gould, Hodge, Peterson, and Giannini (1989) found that encouragement of self-talk was highly rated as a means of enhancing self-efficacy. Self-talk becomes a liability when it is negative, distracting from the task, or so frequent that it disrupts automatic performance.

Understanding the cognitive links — self-awareness

Athletes need to understand the link between their self-talk and their confidence to perform a task. This link is not difficult for most athletes to grasp. Athletes tend to remember the thoughts and feelings they had when full of confidence and performing to the best of their ability. By comparison, they are often aware of the negative thoughts and less satisfying feelings they had when performing badly.

The first step in gaining cognitive control is for athletes to monitor their self-talk, keeping a log of their thoughts and associated feelings and actions, in a range of situations. The format of the log should be appropriate to the age and introspective capability of the athlete. Complexity and comprehensiveness does not always equate with better.

Once athletes understand how their minds work they need to appreciate that their self-talk can be controlled: that they are not at the mercy of spontaneous and involuntary self-talk. Self-defeating thoughts can be replaced by positive, constructive thoughts. A mind crowded with random thoughts can be calmed and focused. Athletes can learn to think in a way that enhances their self-worth, confidence and performance (Bunker, Williams, & Zinsser, 1993).

Control techniques

There are a number of techniques used by athletes to control their self-talk and modify their feelings. *Thought-stopping* is particularly useful because it is simple and concrete. When using the "stop" techniques athletes recognise the negative thought, are motivated to initiate the "stop" and replace the unwanted thought with one that is more positive and task related (Meyers & Schleser, 1980). A click of the fingers or a snap of a rubber band around the wrist can be substituted for the word "stop".

Replacing negative thoughts with positive thoughts will not be effective if the athlete continues to accept the negative statement as valid, based on fact. *Countering* is a technique whereby the athlete argues a case against the negative statement to undermine its validity (Bunker, Williams, & Zinsser,

1993). For example, a heavy thunderstorm immediately before a hockey game stimulated the thought in the mind of one player, "I'm hopeless when there are puddles on the ground. I'm going to play badly". The player realised quickly that if he was to play to his potential he had to counter this negative belief, "No! I have played well on a heavy track before. Keep it simple and stay low to the ground". Bell (1983) states that athletes do not have to blindly accept negative thinking but can ask themselves, "Is this thinking in my best interest? Will thinking like this help me play well and enjoy myself?" If not, change it.

Reframing is a cognitive strategy used by individuals to change their perception of a specific situation. Athletes have the capability to reframe negative self-talk, "to transform what appears at first to be a weakness or difficulty into a strength or possibility, simply by looking at it from a different point of view" (Bunker, Williams, & Zinsser, 1992, p. 235). Members of the 1988 Australian men's Olympic hockey team reframed stifling and debilitating heat and humidity during a training camp in Cairns to an opportunity to be better prepared than their opposition for the conditions in Barcelona for the Olympic Games.

Athletes undermine their confidence when they engage in *irrational thinking* (Bunker et al., 1993). Common examples of irrational thinking include magnification, catastrophising, personalisation and perfectionist thinking. As with countering, athletes need to recognise the irrational thoughts and replace them with thoughts that are rational and more appropriate to high self-confidence and successful performance. For example, a female gymnast who regularly tells herself she must always be perfect and successful would be better served reminding herself to "strive to achieve the highest standards I possibly can". Her new, more rational, self-statements will not lower the quality of her training or performance standards but will relieve her of unrealistic expectations and unnecessary pressure.

4. ROUTINES

Terry Orlick (1986) emphasises the importance of mental plans in achieving control over aspects of sporting performance, control that solidifies self-confidence. Mental plans, or routines can be established for most aspects of performance. A tennis player may have a pre-competition routine, a routine between points and between games, a routine after the game and a refocusing plan for a range of potentially disruptive circumstances that may occur before, during or after the game. Incorporated in the routines will be actions, thoughts, images and feelings that help a player perform to the best of his or her ability.

Young athletes and athletes in a performance slump tend to experiment with a range of routines and activities trying to find the elusive secret to success. Instead of striving for control and consistency, the building blocks of self-confidence, they repeat what worked yesterday and change it if it does not work tomorrow.

A mental plan promotes a sense of control within athletes and, if implemented consistently, enhanced self-confidence. The confidence comes from knowing what thoughts, feelings and actions will help athletes perform to the best of their ability rather than allowing distracting and destructive thoughts, feelings and images to interfere. Orlick's (1986) book provides a detailed explanation of the process of establishing and refining competition plans and routines.

5. ROLE MODELS

As was outlined earlier in this chapter, researchers have found that, after performance accomplishments, vicarious learning is the next most effective source of information for the development of self-efficacy. Commonly used forms of vicarious learning include watching others perform, live or on video, symbolic learning and imagining others perform.

The efficacy of vicarious learning is enhanced if the characteristics of the role model are similar to the athlete; in particular skill level, age, gender and personal characteristics (Feltz, 1984). Although watching an Australian team player may be motivating for a young basketball player, skill relevance would not be high and the impact upon self-efficacy limited. The self-efficacy of a young player would be better enhanced by observing a player of similar or slightly higher standard — a standard to which the player can realistically aspire. A model from which the player can derive a belief that "I can do that".

Most of the self-efficacy research and literature in sport relating to vicarious learning has focused on the acquisition of physical skills. Athletes can watch their role model perform and develop a mental picture of the skill. They can also watch their role model on video followed by mental rehearsal of themselves performing the skill. Flotation tanks are used for the same process — watch a role model perform on video and then mentally rehearse.

Physical sporting skills are not the only behaviours athletes model. Athletes attempting to develop their self-confidence can model a range of behaviours unrelated to physical prowess. An athlete can observe the coping strategies of Alan Border; relaxed intensity of Linford Christie; composure under pressure from Nick Farr Jones; and controlled aggression from Andrew Vlahov.

An exercise performed with the Australian waterpolo team required the players to attend a game of hockey between the Australian women's team, who at that time were ranked number one in the world and the visiting Canadians. The waterpolo players were not trying to acquire hockey skills but were observing the professional and psychological practices of the Australian hockey team — practices such as pre-game focus, reactions after a mistake, reactions after a bad call from the umpire and communication between players.

Another example is of an Australian team track athlete who was experiencing a dramatic loss of self-confidence prior to a number of important international races. She worked on a range of mental skills that were specific to her racing — arousal control techniques, routines before the race, self-talk and coping strategies and post-race evaluation methods. They helped, to a degree. There appeared to be a number of personal characteristics, beyond mental sporting skills, that impacted upon her performance. They related to her self-image and the belief she had of her capabilities to perform. One of a number of methods used by her to develop greater self-confidence was to identify characteristics she admired in other people. A number of sporting and non-sporting role models were identified and their behaviour in specific situations observed. Assertiveness was identified as one characteristic she wanted to develop, believing it would help her self-confidence and capability to take charge in stressful situations. Role models gave her a point of reference. This case highlights the dual role of personal characteristics and sport-specific skills in the formation of self-confidence in sport.

Symbolic learning is used extensively in sport, without extensive empirical evidence, as a method of enhancing self-confidence. However, it has been found to be effective in a systematic desensitisation program with phobic subjects (Bandura, Adams, & Beyer, 1977; Kazdin, 1979). Having athletes imagine their role model performing a task may assist self-efficacy.

Kerry Saxby, race walker and holder of thirty-two world records over a variety of distances, revolutionised race walking technique. She developed an up-beat, high tempo technique replacing the traditional long stride, loping style. A number of young walkers used imagery to model Kerry's style. Firstly, they imagined themselves training with Kerry, along a familiar section of road, walking close to her and getting a feel for her technique. Picking up the technical feel is common for athletes when training together. Once they gained a vivid feel for Kerry's technique they imagined themselves in Kerry's body, feeling the tempo, bounce, strength and foot strike. After a short period of time they imagined themselves leaving Kerry's body and walking beside her again, maintaining the feel.

6. BODY LANGUAGE AND WALK

How you carry yourself, move and walk can affect what you think and how you feel. One can observe this phenomenon most poignantly during a tennis match. A few bad shots, one broken serve and the body language of a player can change. Gone is the body language of confidence — head held high, chin up, shoulders back, racquet head up, arms swinging and bounce in the step — replaced by negative body language — head down, shoulders down, head of the racquet down, feet dragging and flat step (Taylor, 1983).

Tony Pickard, coach of Stefan Edberg, claims that opposition players picked up on, and used to their advantage, the change in Edberg's body language when he fell behind in a match. Pickard's philosophy is: Fix the body language, and the mind stands tall.

There is not a direct correlation between body language and confidence. However, one's body language can influence one's thoughts, feelings and ultimately behaviour, especially if the loss of self-confidence is a short-term occurrence for an athlete who normally has a high self-belief. It is more effective if athletes combine appropriate body language with appropriate self-talk. Increasing awareness of different types of body language and the relationship to self-confidence can provide the athlete with a technique to overcome momentary challenges to their self-confidence.

7. IMAGERY

Mental imagery is a widely used technique for the enhancement of self-confidence, per se, despite a lack of empirical data to support such a contention. However, imagery should not be discarded as an intervention strategy while the anecdotal evidence continues to support its use.

Imagery is useful for a range of purposes that impact upon self-confidence.

- Skill acquisition. As a technique for the acquisition of new skills. Vivid imagery allows an athlete to develop a mental blueprint of a specific skill.
- Preparation for training and competition. As a method for preparing for training and competition. Sylvie Bernier, diver and Canadian Olympic gold medallist, described the impact of imagery before training as giving her the feeling that she had done the skill before.
- Automation of coping strategies. As a means of developing and automating coping strategies specific to sport. Athletes can image themselves dealing effectively with potential distractions during competition. Rowers use imagery to practise pain desensitisation — imagining themselves at the 1500-metre mark, feeling the lactic acid building but refocusing on relaxed shoulders, exhaling any pain and tension, talking encouragingly to themselves and staying focused on one technical cue.
- Personal development. Athletes who are working on their personal development may imagine themselves in a social situation displaying composure and maturity or channelling their anger when their expectations are not fulfilled.
- Changing self-image. Syer and Connolly (1984) suggest five creative imagery exercises aimed at changing self-image. The exercises utilise imagery in association with changing self-talk, use of affirmations and evocative words, role models and the exploration of polarities.
- Replaying the movie of life. After a successful performance or pleasing personal experience, mental rehearsal is an effective method of reinforcement. The behaviour as well as associated self-talk and feelings should be reinforced.
- Editing the movie of life. If the performance or experience was less than satisfying, it can be replaced, just like splicing a film, by a more positive experience so that the lasting memory is positive.
- Systematic desensitisation. A systematic desensitisation program will recondition anxiety responses which may be felt by a cricketer when facing a fast bowler, or a high diver who wants to overcome the fear associated with a previous experience when he hit his head on the board.

Many types of mental imagery aim to enhance athletes' confidence to perform a specific task. The other general area for which mental imagery is used is in the process of self-image change. Mental imagery appears to be an effective adjunct to other cognitive strategies and actual performance accomplishment in the development of self-confidence.

8. ATTRIBUTIONS

Self-confidence will be enhanced when athletes are willing to take control over events in their lives and are able to attribute their successes and failures to factors within their control.

The significant role attributions play in the development and maintenance of self-confidence was discussed in Chapter 5 and earlier in this chapter. Individuals vary in their attribution style and the attributions they make in different situations. The goal of the sport psychologist is to move athletes towards attributions that are most productive for self-confidence and future performances — attributions to factors that are internal, controllable and, depending on the situation, stable or unstable.

The attribution style of athletes can be assessed by using questionnaires; by observing the body language of the athlete after a competition or training session; by being involved in the athlete–coach evaluation post competition and by interviewing the athlete about their perceived cause of performance outcome.

Be wary of the effect emotions can have upon rational thought immediately after a competition. A 1500-metre runner who has just performed badly may be casting assertions immediately after a race but be able to evaluate the positives and negatives logically and rationally once the emotions have subsided.

As a sport psychologist, be sensitive to information immediately after a competition but be careful not to jump to conclusions too early or based upon a single observation. Detailed evaluations of a competition should be left until after the emotion has subsided. The Canberra Raiders Rugby League team do not evaluate the game until the first training session after the game and the players have had a chance to watch their personal videos. If the players' attributions are unproductive and unbalanced after 48 hours, the issue of attribution style needs to be addressed.

An example of a post-game evaluation sheet used by the Australian women's hockey team is shown in Figure 13.1 (page 330). The objectives of the exercise were for the players to:

- get into the habit of evaluating their goals and specific skills after a game
- move to a more balanced and productive attribution style
- attend to aspects of their performance under their control
- use the evaluation as a basis for future goal setting and as a symbolic mechanism for tuning out from hockey to assist their emotional recovery. The players are encouraged to identify positive aspects of their performance and identify areas they can improve upon — not negatives, but areas of improvement.

Aspect	Rating
Pre-game preparation	
Arousal control	1 2 3 4 5 6 7 8 9 10
Dealing with distractions	1 2 3 4 5 6 7 8 9 10
Interaction with team mates	1 2 3 4 5 6 7 8 9 10
Understanding coaching instructions	1 2 3 4 5 6 7 8 9 10
Skills	
Passing	1 2 3 4 5 6 7 8 9 10
Receiving	1 2 3 4 5 6 7 8 9 10
Intercepting	1 2 3 4 5 6 7 8 9 10
Trapping skills	1 2 3 4 5 6 7 8 9 10
Game skills	
Composure	1 2 3 4 5 6 7 8 9 10
Coping with distraction associated with	
• own errors	1 2 3 4 5 6 7 8 9 10
• team mate errors	1 2 3 4 5 6 7 8 9 10
• umpiring decisions	1 2 3 4 5 6 7 8 9 10
Mental toughness	1 2 3 4 5 6 7 8 9 10
Communication skills/emotional control	
Clarity of communication	1 2 3 4 5 6 7 8 9 10
Body language	1 2 3 4 5 6 7 8 9 10
Anger management	1 2 3 4 5 6 7 8 9 10

Figure 13.1: Post-game evaluation sheet used by the Australian women's hockey team

In terms of attribution style, the players were asked to pay particular attention to aspects of the game they could control. In one game, played in 40 degree heat in Spain, the officials delayed the start of the second half by ten minutes while they saturated the artificial turf. After the game the Australian team evaluated how effectively they dealt with the delay and aspects that were within their control.

Evaluation sheets should not be too detailed. Athletes vary in their capabilities for analysis and information processing. A highly detailed and complex evaluation sheet will repel some athletes and thereby negate the potential benefits of the exercise. Evaluation sheets should be appropriate to the individual and, if to be used for a team, be more simple than complex.

Athletes make causal attributions during competition as well as after the event. During a game of tennis, players make regular attributions to explain their success or failure on a specific point or game. Under pressure, with limited time, the players' habitual attributional style will dominate. Players can benefit from a between-point routine that incorporates control of arousal, focus and cognitions.

Tim Gallwey (1985) proposed that evaluations should not interfere with performance; that the mind should be quiet, operating on automatic, making subconscious adjustments — such a state occurs during peak performance, when in the flow.

However, there are times when balanced evaluations at the appropriate time are beneficial for performance. A Rugby player kicks for goal and pushes it wide — evaluation and refocus. A springboard diver executes the dive and scores well — evaluation and refocus. The capability to make simple, balanced and productive evaluations in a short period of time is an automatic process required for success at the elite level.

One of my roles with the Australian Institute of Sport men's basketball team is to remind players, during training, of this process. In effect, I am a specialist coach; a mental coach, picking players up if they are evaluating on the run, questioning players during breaks about their self-talk, reinforcing rejections of uncontrollables. One of my objectives is to assist the players replace inappropriate and unproductive habits of attributions with habits of attributions that will contribute to their self-confidence and are more appropriate for success.

An athlete's attributions, during and after competition, play a significant role in the athlete's self-confidence. Attributions are habits of thinking that, if inappropriate and unproductive, need to be changed if the athlete's level of self-confidence is to be developed.

9. COPING STRATEGIES

What happens to you is not nearly as important as how you react to what happens to you.

Jack Donohue, Canadian Olympic Basketball Coach

One of the characteristics of confident and successful athletes is their consummate belief that they will successfully cope with any difficulty or problem. One reason for their composure is that their thoughts tend to be positive, task-related and focused on what they want to do, not on the judgements of others. The second contributing reason is that experience has taught them to be confident in their capability to cope. Successful past experiences are one of the pillars of Bandura's self-efficacy concept.

Trevor Hendy, leading Australian ironman, is a case in point. Between races in the 1993/94 spring series at Portsea Beach, with three metre waves breaking on three sandbanks: one out the back, one particularly treacherous break in the middle, and a dangerous beach break, with broken surfcraft and paddles littering the beach, one of Hendy's competitors applauded Hendy's ability to cope with the conditions: "Trevor is just so confident. It doesn't matter what the situation: he has been there before. He is so experienced. He is the only ironman out there who is handling these waves and he does it with such ease. He can cope with anything."

Not all athletes have the confidence to cope with unexpected circumstances or adversity in sport and in life. Very little research has investigated the correlation between coping confidence in life and coping confidence in sport. It would appear that one's confidence to cope is situation specific, but there is also a strong indication that personality characteristics, belief systems and the thinking habits one brings to the sporting arena are generalised.

Two issues are relevant to the development of self-confidence in difficult and unusual situations. The first has to do with human development and maturity. Part of growing up is the acquisition of a range of coping strategies that helps one to deal with the stresses and demands of life. Mature individuals have a range of coping strategies at their disposal which they use at appropriate times.

Billings and Moos (1981) identified a range of cognitive and behavioural coping strategies that can be utilised by athletes. Figure 13.2 gives examples of these strategies.

Coping strategies	Method of coping	
	Active cognitive	Active behavioural
Avoidance	X	
Tried to see the positive side	X	
Took things one step at a time	X	
Considered several alternatives	X	
Took some positive action		X
Talked to friend		X
Prepared for the worst		X
Kept feelings to myself		X

Figure 13.2: Some behavioural coping strategies utilised by athletes

Dysfunctional individuals use coping strategies inappropriately or rely exclusively on one or two coping strategies, rather than utilising a range of strategies. For example, the excessive use of denial may be appropriate in some situations when dealing with pain and fatigue but, if used inappropriately, may lead to injury or burn-out.

There are always a number of alternative solutions to any problem, some better than others. Athletes will become frustrated and angry when locked into one method of dealing with a situation if they fail to recognise alternative ways of solving the problem.

The role of a sport psychologist and coach is to assist the personal development of athletes, to assist them to develop, and effectively use, a range of coping strategies.

The second issue relevant to the development of athlete self-confidence revolves around exposing athletes to a range of experiences from which they can gain coping confidence. Prior to the Barcelona Olympic Games, one dual Olympian described how uncertain and unsure he was at his first Olympics — not in his ability to play hockey, but in his lack of awareness about the Olympic experience. By his second Olympics he was more relaxed and composed because he knew what to expect and was confident in his ability to cope.

There is no substitute for experience. Even bad experiences can be reframed as opportunities to learn. Athletes learn from experience, learn how to deal with different situations and gain confidence from their successes. The challenge for sport psychologists and coaches is to prepare inexperienced athletes to deal confidently and successfully with new situations.

Prior to the Barcelona Olympics, elaborate efforts were made to prepare the Australian women's hockey team for the uniqueness of the "Olympic circus". All the players had visited Barcelona, the village and hockey pitch at least once in the two years prior to the games. A ten-day "simulation camp" was held in Darwin prior to leaving for the Olympics. Darwin was chosen because the temperature and humidity of Darwin was similar to Barcelona thus allowing for physiological and psychological adjustment. A mixed team of males and females competed against the Olympic team, playing in the style of opposition nations, in the colours of respective nations, under international rules and in the Olympic tournament format. Crowd noise, taped in Spain, was pumped from loud speakers; the games were interrupted for fictitious reasons; a mock bomb scare during the bus trip to a game was simulated by the local police. The objective of the exercise was to condition the players to the situations and conditions they were about to experience at the Olympics.

During the twelve months prior to the Barcelona Olympics, the Australian waterpolo team devised coping strategies for specific game and non-game situations. The strategies were devised in workshop situations, with the players identifying responses they did not want and responses they did want for each situation. Responses included self-talk, attentional focus, arousal levels, emotions and behaviours.

10. SOCIAL COMPARISONS

An axiom of the Shavelson et al. (1976) and Marsh (1990) self-concept construct is the influence an athlete's frame of reference will have on self-confidence. It would appear that individuals who engage in frequent and inappropriate social comparison produce negative self-perceptions. Regular comparisons of oneself with better athletes produces negative outcomes and the consequential lowering of self-confidence. However, if internal comparisons are utilised, whereby comparisons are made with one's own standards and achievements, positive evaluations are achievable irrespective of the level of competition. The process of internal comparisons is enhanced with realistic goal setting that incorporates developmental goals.

An enlightening exercise to conduct with athletes is to ask them to compare the thoughts, feelings and behaviours they experienced during the days and hours before a competition when they were very confident with those they experienced during a competition when their confidence was particularly low. The following is a list compiled by a leading Australian track athlete.

High confidence	Low confidence
• Relaxed and composed	• Tense and anxious
• Pumped and excited	• Too nervous
• "Knew what I had to do"	• Worried, lots of doubts, uncertain
• Focused on myself	• Worried about other competitors
• Focused on my job	• Thinking a lot about the outcome
• Calm and clear headed	• Thoughts got jumbled — too many
• Didn't think too much about the race	• Spent a lot of time thinking about the race

Note the differences between high and low confidence states of mind, in particular the comments about being "focused on myself" and "worried about other competitors". Highly confident and less confident athletes can be differentiated by the attention they direct to others. Anecdotal evidence indicates that highly confident athletes focus considerable attention towards themselves and the achievement of their goals. Less confident athletes tend to be aware of, and sensitive to, others.

The distinction between social- and self-comparison and the impact each can have upon self-confidence is an important realisation for athletes. Self-confidence will be developed when athletes learn to recognise, and change, beliefs and self-talk associated with social comparison; learn to set goals appropriate for themselves and not other people; engage more often in self-comparison; avoid irrational mind-reading; and accept that they, and not others, are the final judge of their own performances.

11. CHANGING SELF-IMAGE

The relationship between self-image, self-confidence and performance was explained earlier in this chapter. If performance is to change, there must be a change in the self-image. The following exercise can be used to stimulate a change in self-image.

Step 1: Ask the athlete to describe in detail his or her self-image, that is, the image portrayed to other people. There is no right or wrong, simply the individual's perception. Encourage the athlete to include non-sporting as well as sporting characteristics. Typical prompts may include: "How would people describe you at an official function?" "How do you react to adversity?" "What image do you portray at work?"

This is an exercise in self-awareness. Young athletes are relatively unaware of their own beliefs, thoughts, emotions and behaviours. They can fail to recognise a relationship between their self-image and self-confidence. Self-awareness is the first step in the process of change. At the same time, the sport psychologist needs to be sensitive to athletes who are excessively introspective, who spend an excessive amount of time analysing their own behaviour and emotions. Over-analysis, especially of perceived weaknesses and mistakes can undermine self-confidence.

Step 2: Ask the athlete to imagine the self-image he or she wants in the future — one, two or three years hence. A helpful technique is to create an image of a crystal ball, ask the athlete to look into the crystal ball and describe what he or she sees. Some athletes find it helpful to close their eyes and visualise themselves in two years' time. Other athletes prefer to draw a picture of themselves or create a collage of photographs of their role models.

When the Australian women's hockey team wanted to develop their team image they drew characteristics from hockey players as well as from people outside hockey and outside sport, including Debbie Flintoff-King, Daly Thompson, Bob Hawke and Kay Cottee.

The objective of this step is for athletes to develop a vision that provides direction for their development, a vision that can be translated into concrete goals.

Step 3: Ask the athlete to set goals and priorities from the list of characteristics of the new self-image. Characteristics in need of change are identified and a plan established to implement the change. The important role of beliefs and self-talk that maintain the old self-image need to be discussed.

Also worth discussing are potential barriers to change. For example, a female athlete who wants to become more confident by becoming more independent and in control of her life may find it difficult to achieve this while she continues to live at home with a controlling mother and still relies upon her family for financial support.

The process of changing self-image takes time. Beliefs about one's self are established early in one's life and are supported by a set of cognitive and behavioural habits. Change takes time and considerable attention.

FUTURE DIRECTIONS

Considerable research efforts have been devoted to the development of theories of self-confidence and associated constructs. Bandura (1977), Marsh (1990), and Weiner (1972) have each provided well-constructed theories that have been supported with empirical data.

Research into effective and efficient methods and strategies to change athletic self-confidence has been limited. Factors that relate to self-confidence such as cognitions and beliefs, and concepts that can assist with the development of self-concept such as goal setting and mental imagery, have been investigated. However, a systematic process that addresses the method of change rather than the components of self-confidence needs to be addressed.

The training and service style of sport psychologists needs to also be addressed if sport psychologists are to reliably develop the self-confidence of athletes. If the capabilities and methods of the sport psychologists are confined to mental skills and mental skill training, the potential for change is limited. Mental skills are important techniques to be utilised in the development of self-confidence. But, self-confidence is part of the athlete's psychology — childhood experiences, emotions, belief systems, the influence of significant others and cognitions. The role of the sport psychologist is to change the psychology of the athlete, to move the athlete from one set of perceptions and habits to a new set of perceptions and habits that augment self-confidence. Self-confidence will only be developed if the psychology of the athlete is changed. Therefore, attention in the future needs to be directed towards the psychology of the athlete and mechanisms for change.

The work of the sport psychologist in developing the self-confidence of an athlete can be undermined if not supported by the coaching staff. To achieve this end, sport psychologists have to consider, and operate within, the athlete's system. They need to consider the coach as a confederate in the process of change, not as an outsider. Coaches, as omnipotent influences, can undermine the confidence of athletes. They can also serve to assist the development of an athlete's self-confidence. Sport psychologists need to be skilled enough, and in many cases assertive enough, to change inappropriate coaching behaviours and to work with the coach towards a common goal.

CONCLUSIONS

The development of an athlete's self-confidence is dynamic and fluid. It requires consideration of antecedents, the system within which the athlete operates and the psychology of the athlete.

Confidence can be a complex, intangible concept. The role of the sport psychologist is to simplify and clarify; to identify the significant issues that are relevant to a particular individual's self-confidence; and to provide mechanisms for change.

In this chapter I have presented eleven intervention strategies. In practice, eleven is too many. The job of the sport psychologist is to identify only those intervention strategies that are most relevant and would be most effective in assisting a change in an athlete's self-confidence. But, the sport psychologist cannot rigidly stick with strategies that are no longer relevant. A flexible, adaptive approach is most effective. Intervention strategies need to be practical and concrete and address the needs of the athlete and coach, not serve the agenda of the sport psychologist.

SUMMARY

This chapter began with a discussion of four issues that are relevant to the development of an athlete's self-confidence — general versus specific self-confidence; the need for a practical, concrete approach; a needs-based orientation to service and a simplification of the numerous constructs that are used to explain self-confidence.

The next section addressed specific theoretical constructs that are supported with empirical data (self-efficacy and self-concept); confidence concepts that are used regularly in sport but have limited empirical backing (self-image) and attribution theory, which has been found to relate closely to self-confidence.

The tenor of the theoretical discussion was applied; in particular, how the theoretical constructs provided a framework for the development of sporting confidence.

The remainder of the chapter addressed eleven strategies that can be utilised by sport psychologists to change self-confidence. Issues of practical implementation were addressed and methods of change illustrated with examples taken from teams and athletes with whom I have worked.

REFERENCES

Anshel, M. H. (1990). *Sport psychology: From theory to practice*. Gorsuch Scarisbrick, Scottsdale, Arizona.

Bandura, A. (1977). Self-efficacy: Toward a unifying theory of behavior change. *Psychological Review, 84*, 191–215.

Bandura, A. (1982). Self-efficacy mechanism in human agency. *American Psychologist, 37*, 122–147.

Bandura, A., Adams, N. E., & Beyer, J. (1977). Cognitive processes mediating behavioral change. *Journal of Personality and Social Psychology. 35*, 125–139.

Barling, J., & Abel, M. (1983). Self-efficacy beliefs and tennis performance. *Cognitive Therapy and Research, 7*, 265–272.

Bar-Tal, D. (1978). Attributional analysis of achievement-related behavior. *Review of Educational Research, 48*, 259 271.

Bell, K. F. (1983). *Championship thinking: The athlete's guide to winning performance in all sports*. Englewood Cliffs, NJ: Prentice-Hall.

Billings, A. G., & Moos, R. H. (1981). The role of coping resources and social resources in attenuating the stress of life events. *Journal of Behavioural Medicine, 4*(2), 139–157.

Bunker, L. E., Williams, J. M., & Zinsser, N. (1993). Cognitive techniques for improving performance and building confidence. In J. M. Williams (Ed.), *Applied sport psychology: Personal growth to peak performance* (2nd ed.) (pp. 225–242). Mountain View, CA: Mayfield.

Chalip, L. (1980). Social learning theory and sport success: Evidence and implications. *Journal of Sport Behaviour, 3*, 76–85.

Cox, R. H. (1985). *Sport psychology: Concepts and applications* (1st ed.). Dubuque, IA: WmC. Brown.

Feltz, D. L. (1984). Self-efficacy as a cognitive mediator of athletic performance. In W. F. Straub & J. M. Williams (Eds.), *Cognitive sport psychology* (pp. 191–198). Lansing, NY: Sport Science Associates.

Feltz, D. L., & Doyle, L. A. (1981). Improving self-confidence in athletic performance. *Motor Skills: Theory into Practice, 5*(2), 89–95.

Gallwey, T. (1985). *The inner game of golf* (3rd ed.). London: Jonathan Cape.

Gould, D., Hodge, K., Peterson, K., & Giannini, J. (1989). An exploratory examination of strategies used by elite coaches to enhance self-efficacy in athletes. *Journal of Sport and Exercise Psychology, 11*, 128–140.

Heider, F. (1944). Social perception and phenomenal causality. *Psychological Review, 51*, 358–374.

Hersey, P., & Blanchard, K. H. (1969). Life cycle theory of leadership. *Training and Development Journal, 23*(2), 26–34.

Kazdin, A. E. (1979). Imagery elaboration and self-efficacy in the covert modeling treatment of unassertive behavior. *Journal of Consulting Clinical Psychology, 47*, 482–733.

Lee, C. (1982). Self-efficacy as a predictor of performance in competitive gymnastics. *Journal of Sport Psychology, 4*, 405–409.

Mahoney, M. J. (1979). Cognitive skills and athletic performance. In W. F. Straub & J. M. Williams (Eds.), *Cognitive sport psychology* (pp. 11–27). Lansing, NY: Sport Science Associates.

Marsh, H. W. (1986). Verbal and math self-concepts: An internal/external frame of reference model. *American Educational Research Journal, 23*, 129–149.

Marsh, H. W. (1990). A multidimensional, hierarchical model of self-concept: Theoretical and empirical justification. *Educational Psychology Review, 2*(2), 77–172.

Marsh, H. W., Cairns, L., Relich, J. D., Barnes, J., & Debus, R. (1984b). The relationship between dimensions of self-attribution and dimensions of self-concept. *Journal of Educational Psychology, 76*, 3–32.

Marsh, H. W., & Peart, N. (1988). Competitive and cooperative physical fitness training programs for girls: Effects on physical fitness and on multidimensional self-concepts. *Journal of Sport and Exercise Psychology, 10*, 390–407.

McAuley, E., & Gill, D. L. (1983). Reliability and validity of the physical self-efficacy scale in a competitive sport setting. *Journal of Sport Psychology, 5*, 410–418.

McAuley, E., & Gross, J. B. (1983). Perceptions of causality in sport: An application of the causal dimension scale. *Journal of Sport Psychology, 5*, 72–76.

Meyers, A. W., & Schleser, R. A. (1980). A cognitive behavioral intervention for improving basketball performance. *Journal of Sport Psychology, 2*, 69–73.

Orlick, T. (1986). *Psyching for sport — mental training for athletes.* Illinois: Leisure Press.

Rotter, J. B. (1971). External and internal control. *Psychology Today, 5*(1), 37–42.

Russell, D. (1982). The causal dimension scale: A measure of how individuals perceive causes. *Journal of Personality and Social Psychology, 42*, 1137–1145.

Shavelson, R. J., & Bolus, R. (1982). Self-concept: The interplay of theory and methods. *Journal of Educational Psychology, 74*, 3–17.

Shavelson, R. J., Hubner, J. J., & Stanton, G. C. (1976). Validation of construct interpretations. *Review of Educational Research, 46*, 407–441.

Syer, J., & Connolly, C. (1984). *Sporting body sporting mind: An athlete's guide to mental training.* New York: Cambridge University Press.

Taylor, J. (1983). *The mental edge for competitive sports.* Aspen: Jim Taylor.

Weiner, B. (1972). *Theories of motivation: From mechanism to cognition.* Chicago: Rand McNally.

Weiner, B. (1979). A theory of motivation for classroom experiences. *Journal of Educational Psychology, 71*, 3–25.

C H A P T E R

14

MENTAL IMAGERY IN SPORT

CLARK PERRY • TONY MORRIS

Imagery has long been a subject of research interest in psychology, motor learning and sport psychology. It has become a central pillar of applied sport psychology practice. Gould, Tammen, Murphy, and May (1989) found it to be the most widely used technique among United States Olympic sport psychology consultants; and Jowdy, Murphy, and Durtschi (1989) discovered that imagery techniques were used regularly by 100% of consultants they sampled, 90% of athletes and 94% of coaches. The popularity of imagery probably has a number of origins. It is certainly intuitively appealing, as many people daydream and mentally prepare themselves for future action, for example giving someone bad news, driving the best route to a particular location or playing a tune on the piano. It is readily accepted that greater success is likely if one rehearses an activity mentally before having to perform it. Anecdotal reports from elite sports performers provide another basis for the implementation of formal imagery programs, as does the research on mental practice and mental imagery in the psychological literature. Consistent with many other areas of psychological skills training, it could be claimed that the use of imagery techniques in applied sport psychology represents the systematic application of processes which most sports performers use in a "naive" form anyway. In a long history of theory and research, however, psychologists have clarified the processes which constitute imagery and determined the personal and situational factors which present problems in the imagery process.

Although this is a chapter about the use of imagery in practice, it is important to appreciate the underlying theory and research, so that imagery techniques can be applied effectively. As there is no corresponding theoretical chapter on imagery in Part 1 of this book, some time will be spent reflecting on major aspects of theory and research as a background to the discussion of practice. A number of theoretical issues will only be summarised, as there are several recent reviews of imagery in sport (e.g., Murphy & Jowdy, 1992; Suinn, 1993; Vealey & Walter, 1993). More attention will be paid to several issues which have direct bearing on the use of imagery. Having introduced the topic, the chapter will consider definitions of imagery, briefly commenting on operational issues and conceptual clarity. Under the general heading of research, a range of aspects of imagery will be discussed, including the different approaches of mental practice and imagery rehearsal in studying the imagery process and person and situation variables which have been linked to imagery processes. Measurement issues are addressed, acknowledging the concerns for research and practice. The measurement of imagery is an area of research where attention has not matched the examination of imagery moderators and outcomes. Theories which address the processes by which imagery influences behaviour and particularly sports performance are, thus, reviewed next. The chapter moves on to consider the application of imagery. A section discussing some of the more common uses of imagery is followed by some discussion of how the idea of imagery can be positively introduced, so that a sports performer is motivated to develop the skills through practice. It is then important to consider how imagery can be integrated into competition, so that it is effectively used to enhance performance. Several special techniques have been employed to facilitate the effective use of imagery. Discussion of these includes the use of video recordings of good performance as a means of enhancing the generation of positive images; and the use of flotation in order to reduce stimulation and possibly increase the efficacy of imagery. The role of relaxation in effective imagery is also discussed. To conclude, the chapter considers future directions in imagery research and practice.

NATURE OF MENTAL IMAGERY

Ancient philosophers the likes of Plato and Aristotle based their teachings on their images of the future. Christopher Columbus convinced the King and Queen of Spain that his image of a round earth was not mere fantasy and hence was funded for his exploration of the new world. Great visionaries of today, Mandela and Yeltsin have transformed their countries by following an image of change. Imagery is the crucial step in converting thoughts to reality. It is during the imagery phase that mental pictures are formed and some rational sequences of events are ordered within the brain. These images are also a powerful tool in enhancing sporting performances. Sports imagery can help game plans. During this chapter, we will discuss the practical application of imagery in a sporting context. In work with elite athletes, we have found imagery to be a valuable technique in optimising performance. If you watch and listen to many sporting stars of today you can see the effects that imagery has had on their career. A number of world class athletes are advocates of mental imagery (Suinn, 1983). The techniques are very popular among elite athletes and their success is documented in the sports literature.

Olympic gold medallist Linford Christie uses imagery as a way of preparing for his races. Mike Powell, world record holder in the long jump, gives seminars on the ways that imagery has enhanced his performances. Tim Forsyth, Australian Olympic high jumper, pauses, shuts his eyes and makes that imaginary jump just prior to approaching the bar. Jack Nicklaus, the professional golfer, has written books on the subject and attributes much of his success to mental practice (Nicklaus, 1974). Tennis stars Jim Courier, Andre Agassi and Pat Cash have all extolled the benefits of imagery in maximising performance. Olympic medallist and world record holders Kieren Perkins and Nicole Stevenson use imagery to "see" themselves at the pool, swimming at their best. Commonwealth champion Jane Flemming imagines herself running in a tunnel of light that illuminates only her lane, thus eliminating her competition and helping her to focus solely on herself. Anecdotally, the benefits of imagery are well documented, but what research do we have to substantiate these claims? This issue must be addressed, but first it is necessary to clarify what is meant by mental practice, visualisation, mental imagery and related terms.

DEFINITION OF MENTAL IMAGERY

Defining mental imagery remains one of the more contentious issues in sport psychology. Corbin (1972) defined *mental practice* as the "repetition of a task, without observable movement, with the specific intent of learning" (p. 94). Mental practice has long been a focus of study in psychology, although it fell out of favour in the heyday of behaviourism. Most reviewers of mental imagery refer to a substantial amount of mental practice research. An immediate problem with Corbin's definition is its all-encompassing nature. It excludes anything which involves actual movement, but this still leaves a very wide range of mental processes, including verbal repetition of a movement sequence, thinking one's way through a movement, mental problem-solving and singing a song in one's head. The reference to the intent of learning would not preclude these mental activities, but it would preclude several common uses of imagery, such as imagery for stress management, for the control of physiological functions, or for pre-game mental warm-up.

Richardson (1969) considered the term *mental imagery* to apply to "all those quasi-sensory and quasi-perceptual experiences of which we are self-consciously aware and which exist for us in the absence of those stimulus conditions that are known to produce their genuine sensory or perceptual counterparts" (pp. 2–3). This definition does not clearly distinguish imagery from a range of other mental phenomena. Murphy and Jowdy (1992) argue that the element of conscious awareness in the definition does distinguish mental imagery from dreaming and daydreaming, but daydreams are typically experienced in a fully conscious state. A more pertinent distinction might be that imagery is under volitional control, that is, the imager intends to generate the experience. It is this conscious control that appears to allow the individual to rehearse the needed movement skills. There are still problems here, as it is recognised that the degree of control over generated images can vary. This is exemplified in the case reported by Clark (1960) of the basketballer in an imagery study on foul shooting, who found that whenever he tried to image bouncing the ball, he had an image of it sticking to the floor instead. This image was not only out of the performer's control, it was also counterproductive.

A number of other terms have been used almost interchangeably with mental practice and mental imagery. These include *mental rehearsal, visualisation, imaginal practice, imagery rehearsal, symbolic rehearsal, ideomotor training,* and *visual motor behaviour rehearsal*. Popular among these terms is visualisation. It is commonly used in books for athletes, but it fosters the misapprehension that imagery is totally or largely visual in nature and for this reason we advise against its use. Imagery rehearsal and visual-motor or visuo-motor behaviour rehearsal (VMBR) are two terms proposed by Suinn (1983, 1984a, 1984b). VMBR actually refers to a specific imagery technique whereby the imagery process is preceded by a relaxation exercise. Suinn (1984b, 1993) makes a very clear distinction between imagery rehearsal and mental practice. Referring to the Corbin (1972) definition of mental practice, Suinn notes that "this broad definition considers the term as a generic one, covering a diverse set of activities" (1993, p. 498). In contrast, Suinn considers imagery rehearsal to be a covert activity whereby a person experiences sensory-motor sensations that reintegrate reality experiences, and which include neuromuscular, physiological, and emotional involvement (1993). Suinn (1984b) considers that the rich multimodal (involving all the sense-modalities) imagery rehearsal process can closely replicate the original experience, even arousing similar emotions to those associated with victory and defeat, success and failure.

Operationally, imagery rehearsal in research and applied work can be distinguished from mental practice research in a number of ways. Typically, protocols in mental practice research involve one session that often lasts half an hour or less. The most common design involves a pre-test on the task in question, a mental practice exercise of ten to twenty minutes' duration and a post-test of performance on the task. Instructions often emphasise "thinking about" the task or "picturing oneself" doing it. Even where they use the term "image", mental practice experiments often give no instructions that would help the subjects to generate images; that is, they give no training in imagery. Much of the literature involves laboratory studies using analogue tasks, which are artificial tasks constructed for use in the laboratory, usually with the intent that subjects will not be familiar with them. Because of the laboratory context and the use of tasks designed to give clear measurements and not to be interesting, subjects often do not have high levels of motivation. Moreover, because the tasks don't require real-world skills of any importance to the subjects, ego-involvement can often be low. Additionally, many studies have not employed elite or even competitive sports performers as subjects. Even when they do use elite performers, studies employing analogue tasks still raise concerns about level of motivation and ego-involvement. Additionally, research on expertise, reviewed by Abernethy (1993), indicates that ecological validity is still dubious, because experts develop cognitive architecture which is task specific, so their behaviour is unlikely to differ from typical laboratory subjects, such as undergraduate students or average sports performers, when performing analogue tasks which are new to them.

Conversely, imagery rehearsal, as used in preparation for sports performance, frequently involves weeks or months of practice, several times per week. As the practical part of this chapter describes, this practice, especially in the early stages, involves education and training in how to go about generating rich multimodal imagery and why it is a valuable skill to develop. Various aids are employed to help athletes develop their imagery skills. These might include heightening awareness by taking a footballer, for example, to the oval where the team practises or competes and having the individual visually inspect the area in detail, then close his or her eyes to hear, smell and feel the environment; or by having an athlete closely examine equipment used in the sport, like a netballer observing the look, feel, smell and handling of a netball; or by watching a video of his or her best performance of skills, moves or routines. In each case, the real sensory experience would be followed by recreation through multimodal imagery. This sort of application is typically done with skilled athletes in their own sport or a particularly important aspect of it. Thus, commitment and motivation are likely to be high and because their sport closely reflects many elite athletes' self-concept, the ego-involvement of these performers is also high for these tasks. This operational distinction between mental practice and imagery rehearsal not only reflects on the issue of defining imagery, but also presents a strong argument for the need to study skilled athletes using imagery rehearsal for actual practice of and competitive performance in their own sport.

The distinction between mental practice and imagery rehearsal should be kept in mind when reading the following sections, which consider research on mental practice and the more limited research literature on imagery rehearsal. In all following discussion of mental imagery (MI) in practice, the phenomenon under discussion closely approximates Suinn's (1993) conceptualisation of imagery rehearsal, so both terms are used, where appropriate, in this chapter.

BRIEF REVIEW OF RESEARCH

An overview of the literature suggests the following typical findings. First, it should be mentioned that it is unusual to find results showing that the mental imagery (MI) condition leads to performance identical to (or not significantly different from) the control (C) condition. In general, experiments produce results which may be of two types: (a) in comparison to the C condition, MI produces significantly higher gain scores, while physical practice (PP) produces greater gains than MI (e.g., Egstrom, 1964; McBride & Rothstein, 1979; Mendoza & Wichman, 1978; Twining, 1949); (b) in comparison to the C condition, both MI and PP produce significantly higher gain scorcs, but the MI and PP conditions do not differ from each other (e.g., Clark, 1960; Kohl & Roenker, 1983; Rawlings, Rawlings, Chen, & Yilk, 1972; Vandell, Davis, & Clugston, 1943; White, Ashton, & Lewis, 1979; Wrisberg & Ragsdale, 1979). Clearly, in both cases, MI of the skill under study is credited with influencing performance more than no practice at all. A further case is also illustrated in the MI literature by a condition where MI is combined in some way with PP. The experiments which have taken this combined condition into consideration demonstrated that it was at least as effective as PP alone (Egstrom, 1964; Oxendine, 1969; Stebbins, 1968), and in some cases could even produce significantly greater effects than PP alone (McBride & Rothstein, 1979; White, Ashton, & Lewis, 1979). One explanation for this is that a finite time is needed to consolidate the outcome of one attempt in memory and, whereas the PP alone condition did not allow sufficient time between trials, the MI component of the PP/MI condition provided this opportunity.

The research reported thus far has largely adopted the mental practice conceptualisation and research protocol. While the meta-analysis conducted by Feltz and Landers (1983; Feltz, Landers, & Becker, 1988) concluded that research supported the effectiveness of mental practice, especially with tasks involving large cognitive components, Suinn and his colleagues have specifically examined the imagery rehearsal research protocol, using, in most cases, Suinn's (1976) visual-motor or visuo-motor behaviour rehearsal technique (VMBR). This starts with a relaxation exercise and then has the subject complete the imagery work in a relaxed state. Using a case study approach, Suinn (1980) measured electromyographic (EMG) activity, indicative of muscle innervation, in the thigh muscles of an alpine skier. The skier then imaged skiing a downhill run, verbalising the terrain, so that the bends and jumps could be plotted on the EMG readout. Suinn reported observing spikes or bursts of EMG activity (denoting increases in muscle activity), which were concurrent with imagery of bends and jumps, when substantial movement of the leg would have been needed if the skier had been skiing in reality.

Suinn (1993) distinguishes between single case design studies and group or experimental studies. Single case designs have been proposed as a strategy to handle the real world study of psychological skills, where there are often small numbers of highly trained performers; where not every athlete needs precisely the same treatment; and where elite athletes and their coaches are not willing to act as control subjects in traditional group design studies (e.g., Bryan, 1987; Morris, 1991; Zaichkowsky, 1980). In such designs, each subject acts as his or her own control during a baseline period prior to treatment. Most studies on imagery use the multiple-baseline, across-subjects design, where each subject is moved from the baseline to the treatment condition at a different time, minimising the chance that an extraneous variable might account for any changes observed. Kirchenbaum and Bale (1980) examined the effects on the performance of three varsity golfers of a self-regulation package which used imagery along with relaxation, self-monitoring and positive self-instruction. Results were not conclusive and it was noted that it is extremely difficult to measure improvement in high-level golfers by number of strokes per round. It was argued that a one-stroke improvement might have little impact, but that it might also determine a tournament winner. The study also used a small number of practice sessions, which might explain the absence of clear improvement. A similar type of study investigated a defensive skill in female basketball players (Kendall, Hrycaiko, Martin, & Kendall, 1990). Over a season, Kendall et al. (1990) gave six players a package including relaxation, imagery and positive self-talk, using a multiple-baseline, single-case design. Results were very promising. Other researchers, using single-case designs, have found packages to be effective (e.g., Hall & Erffmeyer, 1983; Mumford & Hall, 1985; Wrisberg & Anshel, 1989). Single case studies using combination packages including VMBR have also produced positive results (Desiderato & Miller, 1979; Schleser, Meyers, & Montgomery, 1980). While it is encouraging for the practice of psychological skills training, one difficulty with this type of research is that it is not clear which element or elements of the package are responsible for the effect. Kirchenbaum and Bale (1980) found that imagery was rated highest by their subjects; and Kendall et al. (1990) considered imagery to be the major aspect of their package, but the performance data does not distinguish imagery from other elements.

The package approach, therefore, provides valuable information about the efficacy of applied techniques, but more information can usually be gleaned about the processes involved in imagery from research in which only that psychological skill is under examination. In this respect, it is not clear where to locate VMBR studies, as imagery rehearsal is preceded by relaxation. The relaxation–imagery combination is used so often, especially in applied work, that one might argue that this is a single technique. Nevertheless, there still exists the question of whether relaxation does facilitate imagery, and several studies have brought this assumption (which underlies the work of Suinn and many practitioners) into question. Gough (1989) used soft music as a means of promoting relaxation and then had three varsity baseball players image batting in a single-case design. Two of the three showed improvement. Callery and Morris (1993) gave ten Australian Football League (AFL) players an imagery training program on the skill of disposal of the ball by foot. Though they did not use VMBR, the imagery training was preceded by a brief relaxation skill. The players used this before the imagery exercise, which was presented three times a week for several weeks. In a single-case, multiple-baseline design, Callery and Morris measured performance by expert judges' ratings of match disposals. They found that four of the players showed a strong effect of the program, four showed trends in the predicted direction and one of the others suffered a dramatic loss of form, hardly touching the ball in the later matches. The tenth subject was injured for half the period of study. These studies may reflect more closely on imagery, but it could be that improved performance resulted from lower levels of game arousal caused by the relaxation skill, which is not only developed in the training, but is associated with performance of the skill during the imagery sessions, an association which could generalise to performance of the skill in the game.

Kolonay (1977), a student of Suinn, explored the relaxation–imagery issue in an early study on VMBR. She studied 72 male basketball players, assigned to either a VMBR (relaxation plus imagery) group, an imagery-only group, a relaxation-only group or a control group. Again, subjects had substantial training and practice of the technique in 15 sessions over six weeks. Results clearly favoured the VMBR group over all others, it being the only group to show a statistically significant improvement. It should be noted that experimental conditions were organised along team lines, but performance was measured by individual foul-shooting percentage. Weinberg, Seabourne, and Jackson (1981) replicated this study in karate, but their control group was given a placebo. Only one karate skill, sparring, showed the predicted effect at a significant level, although the VMBR group also improved most on skills combinations. Three more VMBR studies by Suinn's students, in basketball (Lane, 1978), baseball (Lane, 1980), and tennis (Noel, 1980), and all using multiple imagery training sessions, showed some indications of positive VMBR effects, but conventional statistical significance was not achieved. The exception here was in an analysis of covariance of Noel's tennis data, where high-ability subjects in the VMBR condition showed significant improvement, whereas low-ability players showed a drop in performance after training with VMBR. This appears to be consistent with the research which suggests that it is important to image correct performance of the task. Woolfolk, Parrish, and Murphy (1985) found that a negative image group performed significantly worse than either the positive image group or the control group. Imaging incorrect performance or outcome is thus likely to inhibit performance and players of lesser ability are more likely to image incorrect performance.

To summarise this section, the long history of research on mental practice has not produced a detailed description of the nature, mechanisms and processes of imagery, but it has indicated that mental practice can enhance performance on a range of motor tasks, including sports skills.

Research on the much more elaborate imagery rehearsal procedure has not been so substantial. What has been done in this area does support the process, but there are many questions yet to be addressed on imagery as practitioners use it. Researchers must have the confidence to employ the full range of research methodologies to explore the imagery process and factors which moderate it in the real competitive environment.

INFLUENCE OF INDIVIDUAL DIFFERENCES

In order to explain these results, researchers have explored the possibility of individual differences playing a part in performance enhancement. Clark (1960) investigated the effects of mental imagery and physical practice on the performance of basketball free-throw shooting. The three ability groups were (a) varsity basketball players, (b) junior varsity basketball players, and (c) novices. Subjects were rated on intelligence, arm strength and basketball-playing experience and were divided into mental practice and physical practice groups. After 14 days of practice, both groups showed significant gains in foul-shooting ability. In addition, Clark found that the novice and junior varsity groups exhibited greater percentage gains in performance in the mental practice condition than the varsity group. It would appear from these results that mental practice may be more effective for less skilled athletes.

Contrary to Clark's results, Start (1962) found that those rated high on games ability exhibited a significant improvement in their performance on a basketball task after five minutes of mental practice for nine days, whereas those rated as average or poor on games ability displayed no significant improvement. In support of these findings, Whitely (1962) found that performers of higher ability used mental practice more effectively than individuals who scored low in motor ability. A later study by Start and Richardson (1964), however, revealed non-significant correlations between percentage gains on a single gymnastic skill and motor ability. Although the literature appears equivocal on the issue of whether individuals of high or low sports ability benefit most from mental practice, some related research indicates that a minimum amount of experience on the task is necessary for mental practice to be effective (e.g., Corbin, 1972; Phipps & Morehouse, 1969; Schramm, 1967). Corbin (1967a) instructed subjects to perform a novel task in which they had no prior experience. Results produced no significant gains in performance for the mental practice group. In a follow-up study (Corbin, 1967b), subjects were given physical practice before receiving mental practice training and in this case the mental practice subjects displayed significant improvement. It appears that mental practice can improve performance in both the early and the later stages of learning, although subjects need to have a minimum amount of physical practice before mental practice can be effective, especially in a complex skill.

A variable that would seem important in the effective use of mental imagery is an individual's ability to image or conceptualise themselves performing the task. Individuals who can construct clear, vivid, controllable images would most benefit by the use of mental practice. Whitely (1962) conducted the first study designed to test imaging ability as a factor which mediates the effect of imagery on performance. His measure of imaging ability required subjects to view for two minutes a random arrangement of 12 objects on two square trays. Subjects then had to recall the objects and try to place them into the correct quadrant. The number of accurately recorded objects was taken as a measure of imaging ability. Results indicated a significant correlation between test scores and actual performance of a ball-throwing task for the mental imagery group. Start and Richardson (1964) investigated the hypothesis that the more controlled and vivid an image, the better the performance when using mental imagery for a simple gymnastic skill. Results revealed that subjects with vivid, controlled images displayed the greatest gain in performance, with subjects having controlled, non-vivid images next. Subjects with uncontrolled, non-vivid images were third and subjects having uncontrolled, vivid images produced least performance effect.

Further to the issue of imagery ability, White, Ashton, and Lewis (1979) found no significant correlation between performance improvement scores of subjects using mental imagery and the total scores on Sheehan's (1967) shortened adaptation of Betts's imagery scale, the Questionnaire on Mental Imagery (QMI), which measures vividness of images created. A study by Chevalier-Girard (1983) examined the imaging ability of swimmers. The subjects were divided into three groups based on proficiency of swimming ability: beginners, average and advanced. All groups answered a questionnaire that measured the general vividness of the individual's visual imaging ability. The three groups did not differ on this test. However, when they took another questionnaire about the vividness of imagery for several patterns of swimming, the group of advanced swimmers revealed a higher level of vividness than the other groups. It was concluded that skilled athletic ability may increase imagery vividness specifically for that task, which may assist in the effectiveness of mental imaging for athletic performances.

When considering individual differences, it is important to discuss the issue of locus of control. Wichman and Lizotte (1983) examined the effects of locus of control and mental practice on the performance of dart throwing. High school students were assessed by their scores on the Nowicki–Strickland Locus of Control (LOC) Scale. The 130 subjects were divided equally into an internal LOC mental practice group, an external LOC mental practice group, and a no-practice control group. The results showed that only the internal LOC mental practice group improved their dart throwing. The mental practice had no utility for external scorers. It appears, from these results, that mental practice can be effective in improving performance and individuals that take responsibility for their actions are more strongly affected by imagery techniques.

IMAGERY ORIENTATION OR PERSPECTIVE

Another parameter of imagery which has received increased attention is that of its "orientation" (Mahoney, 1979). A distinction has been made between what has been termed "internal" imagery and "external" imagery. Mahoney defines external imagery as occurring when a person views him or herself from the perspective of an external observer (much like a movie). Internal imagery requires an approximation of the real-life experience such that the person actually feels those sensations which might occur while participating in the real situation. In addition, internal imagery involves seeing or feeling something from the performer's own perspective. This type of imagery is similar to what has been called "kinaesthetic imagery", in that the kinaesthetic sense plays a major role. However, in internal imagery there is also visual involvement, but from the perspective of the performer. The idea that internal and external imagery are physiologically distinct was first supported by Jacobson (1930, 1931) and Shaw (1938, 1940), who found that greater muscular activity occurs during internal imagery than during external imagery. More recent evidence for this distinction comes from work on the muscular and occular concomitants of internal and external imagery by Hale (1982) and from Lang's (1977) demonstration that subjects trained in "response propositions" (similar to internal imagery) exhibited higher levels of physiological arousal during imaging than subjects instructed to respond perceptually. Furthermore, Davidson and Schwartz (1977) found that subjects who engaged in kinaesthetic imagery displayed greater somatic arousal and less visual activity than subjects who employed external imagery.

A study by Jowdy, Murphy, and Durtschi (1989) examined responses to a questionnaire from elite athletes and coaches. A majority of the respondents indicated a preference for internal imagery as compared to external imagery in assisting performance. If kinaesthetic feedback is important to the effectiveness of mental practice, then internal imagery should produce higher levels of performance than external imagery because it is accompanied by higher levels of muscular activity and somatic arousal. Experimentally, this hypothesis has not been proven conclusively. Burhans, Richman, and Bergey (1988) examined the effect of external imagery on outdoor-track running performances. They reported a significant decrease in times for the imaging group compared to controls, but it is important to note that they chose not to include an internal imagery group in their study.

Epstein (1980) examined the relationship of imagery perspective and performance using dart throwing as the dependent measure. Results indicated no significant differences in performance of subjects under internal versus external imagery instructions. In addition, only a slight relationship existed between natural imaginal style (the style subjects prefer to use) and motor performance, with internal imagers exhibiting a slight positive relationship and external imagers displaying a slight negative relationship.

Epstein states that it was difficult to classify individuals as either exclusively internal or external imagers, because an individual's images varied greatly both within and between images. There is a need to examine the relationship between internal and external perspective more closely and under greater experimental scrutiny. The results to date tend to indicate that internal imagery is associated with increased electrical activity in the muscles and greater somatic arousal, and there is some anecdotal evidence that internal imagery enhances performance.

WHAT MAKES IMAGERY WORK?

A number of theories have been proposed to explain why imagery enhances performance of physical skills, and affects self-perceptions and emotions.

PSYCHONEUROMUSCULAR THEORY

One suggested explanation is the psychoneuromuscular theory. In some of the earliest studies on the subject, Jacobson (1930, 1931), using electromyography, was able to find changes in muscle activity while subjects were imagining performance in a motor task. He found that these were the same muscles used during the actual physical performance. These studies examined mental activities as an aid in enhancing performance and they were the first to show a physiological relationship between imagery and motor skills. It has been proposed that the electrical stimulation of the muscles and central/peripheral nervous system that occurs when performing quality imagery, is similar to that which occurs during physical movements. The apparent difference between imagery and actual movement is the amplitude of the electrical stimulation to the muscles. Vealey and Walter (1993) recommend the use of the term "muscle memory" when explaining this theory to athletes. They emphasise that imagery strengthens the muscle memories by causing the muscles to fire in the correct sequence similar to the actual physical activity.

Research through the years has tested this theory by measuring the electrical activity in muscles needed to perform various skills. When experiencing vivid imagery without actually experiencing movement, sub-threshold electrical activity occurs in those muscles that are needed to perform the skills. It appears that the neural pathways used in performing skills are activated during the use of vivid imagery, especially from an internal perspective (e.g., Hale, 1982; Harris & Robinson, 1986; Jowdy & Harris, 1990). Shaw (1938, 1940) found low-level innervation of the arm muscles during imaging of a biceps curl, but he also found innervation in the left leg, which led him to suggest that the muscle activity was not task specific. He did not test for muscle activity in the leg when subjects performed the physical action, however, and there could, for example, be some postural activity. Another difficulty with this research is that all the studies which have measured low-level muscle innervation have chosen physical actions with no performance element. Because they do not measure performance of a skill, it is not possible to link the muscular activity to skill enhancement, so the muscular activity might only be a by-product.

SYMBOLIC LEARNING THEORY

A second possible explanation of how imagery works is the symbolic learning theory. Sackett (1934, 1935) proposed that imagery symbolises in the brain the movements needed to perform skills and, hence, to facilitate performance. Vealey and Walter (1993) have used the term "mental blue-print" and suggest that the use of imagery strengthens the blueprint that enables the skill to become automatic. When an athlete is learning a new skill, it helps to create a mental map of the movements required and, therefore, to store and recall the skills easily when needed. These mental maps are created through physical training and they explain how habits are formed. Research has shown that vivid imagery or mental practice also creates these maps and, therefore, accelerates and enhances the learning process. Ryan and Simons (1981) provided support for the cognitive or symbolic interpretation in a study where there was no difference between a mental practice group and a control group on a stabilometer (motor task), whereas on a dial-a-maze (cognitive task) there was a significant difference and the mental practice group improved as much as the physical practice group. Hird, Landers, Thomas, and Horan (1991) found, after imagery, greater gains on a pegboard task (defined as cognitive) than a pursuit rotor task (defined as motor). Other research also supports the symbolic/cognitive theory (Minas, 1980; Morrisett, 1956; Ryan & Simons, 1983; Wrisberg & Ragsdale, 1979), and the meta-analysis by Feltz and Landers (1983) concluded that effect size was much larger in studies which used cognitive rather than motor or strength tasks.

BIO-INFORMATIONAL THEORY

A third theory which has been applied to the explanation of imagery is the bio-informational theory. This theory, proposed by Lang (1977, 1979), adds the dimensions of "stimulus propositions" and "response propositions" to the cognitive domain of imagery. Propositions are representations of the stimuli and responses associated with an action. Lang argues that learning and performance involve the linking of appropriate stimulus and response propositions. Imagery, in Lang's view, is a process which permits these links to be strengthened. Prominent among the response propositions are the emotional and physiological responses associated with performance. Feelings such as fear, anxiety, anger and elation, as well as physical symptoms such as fatigue, perspiration and tension should all be a part of quality imagery because they are generally included in actual performance. It is believed that by modifying responses to given situations through imagery the athlete gains more control and hence improves performance. Vealey and Walter (1993) have recommended the term "response set" when explaining this approach to athletes. They emphasise the importance of including behavioural, psychological and physiological responses in the utilisation of imagery. At present there is little research that has tested this theory. One study which specifically used response propositions was carried out by Hecker and Kaczor (1988), using propositions for a familiar action scene, a familiar athletic anxiety scene and an unfamiliar fear scene. A neutral control scene had no response propositions attached to it. Heart-rate physiological data supported the effects of the response propositions on the familiar scenes, as bio-informational theory would predict. However, the effect on performance was not linked to the physiological data in this study.

ACTIVATION/AROUSAL THEORY

Schmidt (1982) proposed that imagery has a general rather than a specific effect and that the effect is on the athlete's preparation for task performance. Imagery provides a means of more closely approximating level of arousal or physiological activation to the optimal level for that task. Thus, the performer is "merely preparing for action" (p. 520) or "generally getting prepared for good performance" (p. 520). Vealey and Walter (1993) refer to this as a "mental set" perspective. While this suggestion has not been tested directly, a number of studies have looked at the role of general arousal in the effectiveness of imagery. Murphy, Woolfolk, and Budney (1988) used three types of imagery — anger, fear and relaxation — for 24 males trying to squeeze a hand-grip dynamometer as hard as they could. They found no evidence that emotional imagery increased strength performance, but the imagery did lead to increases in emotional arousal. Using track athletes as subjects, Machlus and O'Brien (1988) compared five conditions: one group received only relaxation and another group received imagery but no relaxation. A third group was given relaxation and imagery, a fourth received a relaxation, imagery and arousal treatment, while the fifth was an attention control group. Only the imagery group showed improvement in all events. Lee (1990) noted that Murphy et al. (1988) used negative emotional states. She compared positive mood with specific imagery content in 52 male student subjects doing bent-knee sit-ups. One group was instructed to image performing well on the task, that is, task-relevant imagery. The other group remembered experiences where positive mood states were experienced. The relevant image group produced performance significantly superior to the general positive mood group and a control group. Lee repeated the study with 142 male subjects and added the profile of mood states (POMS) as a measure of mood. Again, the relevant imagery group performed best, while POMS scores added nothing to the variance explained in a stepwise regression analysis. It was concluded that the content of the imagery rehearsal is important. Lee asserted that "imagery effects do not occur by affecting mood state" (p. 72). The role of arousal and attention in the imagery process is, thus, not yet clear.

MOTIVATIONAL EXPLANATION

When imagery is used by practitioners there is usually an introductory educational statement or session. The intention of this session is to ensure that the athletes believe that imagery will facilitate performance. Techniques used in this process are presented later in this chapter (see also Vealey & Walter, 1993). Creating the appropriate expectancy in those who are going to work on imagery is considered as simply a means of preparing them for the imagery experience. It is, however, likely to create an expectancy of superior performance, so that after doing imagery, performers try harder or are more motivated. In many pre-experimental presentations to prospective subjects or in imagery conditions within research projects, it is likely that some comments will be made about the usefulness of imagery. Even when this is not done, explicitly, the nature of the imagery training program often creates an expectancy in subjects that performance will be enhanced by the procedure. Johnston, Morris, and Shaw (1985) argue that research on mental practice has not adequately addressed the possibility that imagery is effective when the conditions motivate performers in this way to try harder after receiving the imagery treatment. Paivio (1985) has also proposed a motivational interpretation of imagery. Testing this issue in imagery rehearsal studies should be straightforward, as such studies are likely to include a strong statement, and even some demonstrations, indicating to athletes that the mind–body link is the basis for the influence of mental imagery on physical performance. An experimental condition where no such comments are made should be equally effective, if the motivational explanation is incorrect.

CONFIDENCE AS A MEDIATOR

In their study of the effect of an imagery program on the disposal skills of AFL footballers, Callery and Morris (1993) noted in informal comments from the players during the early stages of the treatment that they felt more confident about performing the skills. This impression was supported by the formal social validation procedure conducted at the end of the study. The relationship between imagery and confidence has been intimated in Bandura's (1977) conceptualisation of self-efficacy. Bandura (1977) proposed that there are four major antecedents of self-efficacy, three of which — performance accomplishments, vicarious experience and verbal persuasion — might be linked to imagery. Taking Suinn's (1984b) perspective on imagery rehearsal, the intention is to recreate, or create anew, successful performance, as if it were actually happening. As with some dreams, skilled imagers may later be unsure whether they imagined a successful performance or whether it really happened. Bandura (1969) prefaced the idea of imagery as vicarious experience when he noted that "virtually all learning phenomena resulting from direct experiences can occur on a vicarious basis..." (p. 118). He also pointed out that when an individual observes the behaviour of another (a model), "but otherwise performs no overt responses, he can acquire the modeled responses while they are occurring only in cognitive, representational forms" (p. 133), so that a major role is envisaged in modelling or vicarious experience involving the "utilization of symbolic representations of modeled patterns in the form of imaginal... contents to guide overt performances" (p. 141). Feltz (1992) modified Bandura's category of verbal persuasion, calling it simply "persuasion" and included imagery as a category of persuasion. (See Chapter 6 for further discussion of the antecedents of self-efficacy and its relationship to imagery.)

Following her study of the effects of mood, discussed earlier, Lee (1990) noted that imagery did not have a "general effect on mood or confidence" (p. 70). The self-efficacy approach suggests a task specific effect, however. This is supported by a study of imagery, self-efficacy and performance by Feltz and Riessinger (1990). Their 120 student subjects were performing an endurance task called the skiers' squat, in which one maintains a sitting position, with back straight against a wall and knees at right angles, for as long as possible. The task was done in competition with one opponent who was actually a confederate. Instructions for imagery included holding out longer than the opponent and generating feelings of competence. The results indicated that what Feltz and Riessinger (1990) called "*in vivo* emotive imagery*" (p. 132) did increase "sense of perceived self-efficacy... and, to a lesser extent, one's actual performance time" (p. 140). It should be noted that the imagery here consisted of one relatively brief session that included instructions about the desired content of the imagery, but no training to enhance its effectiveness with naive subjects. Thus, any improvement in performance is noteworthy, although it is difficult to control for motivational effects, especially with endurance tasks.

It appears that there are theoretical and limited empirical grounds for considering the proposition that confidence might be a mediating factor in the imagery–performance relationship. Particularly, but not exclusively, in the use of imagery rehearsal with athletes, it is possible that the direct effect of imagery is to increase self-confidence or self-efficacy. There is a substantial body of literature which indicates that increasing self-efficacy leads to enhanced performance (e.g., Feltz, 1982; Feltz & Mugno, 1983; McAuley, 1985). In the Feltz and Riessinger (1990) study and in the more tentative involvement of confidence in Callery and Morris's (1993) study with AFL players, an equally plausible explanation is that imagery independently facilitated both performance and confidence, the latter, perhaps, through the self-efficacy processes considered earlier, and the former through any of the other theories discussed in this section. Callery and Morris (1993) approached the application of imagery from Suinn's (1980) notion of transfer of skill from training to competition, based on experience that the players performed disposal drills very effectively on the training ground week after week, but did not reproduce that skill in matches at the weekend. To examine the possible role of confidence as a mediator between imagery and performance, it will be necessary to adopt a causal modelling methodology in the future. At the same time, there needs to be further evidence that confidence and performance are both enhanced by imagery, and this evidence must come from studies which include more formal, objective measures of self-confidence or self-efficacy.

This section has considered a number of attempts to explain the mechanisms through which imagery might facilitate performance and, to a lesser extent, confidence. Unfortunately, none of the large amount of research has managed to clarify the roles of low-level muscle innervation or symbolic representation, although the theories of Jacobson (1931) and Sackett (1934) have been considered for 60 years. The alternative propositions have not been subjected to rigorous study to date and, aside from Lang's (1977, 1979) bio-informational theory, they do not represent comprehensive theories based on underlying mechanisms. Clarification of some of the arousal-associated, attentional, motivational and confidence-related concomitants of imagery will be of value to its application. At the same time, research must continue to seek a well-substantiated theoretical basis for the imagery phenomenon.

The psychoneuromuscular theory and the symbolic learning theory were developed to explain skill learning. Imagery use in sport psychology encompasses a much wider range of applications than the acquisition of relatively simple movements. Often imagery is used with elite performers who have perfected the skills, at least to perform them in training. They do not need to enhance "muscle memory" or strengthen the "mental blueprint". The utility of these theories may be restricted to the acquisition of movement skills. Other explanations must be invoked to account for the effectiveness of imagery as used by elite performers.

MEASUREMENT OF IMAGERY

The measurement of imagery has been a problem for as long as imagery has been studied in psychology. Because imagery is a mental process, it is not directly observable. Assessing how well somebody images by measuring improvement on a task is not acceptable, as so many other factors might influence performance. One approach which has successfully made inferences about imagery processes from performance has been through the mental rotation of spatial figures (Shepard & Metzler, 1971). This task involves determining whether a test spatial figure is the same as an alternative comparison figure. It is assumed that, to carry out the task, the person must create an image, which is then mentally rotated to match the comparisons. Speed of performance, as well as accuracy is examined. While this approach is of interest, the task is the mental rotation itself rather than an external motor skill, and it would appear difficult to generalise performance to imagery beyond the rotation of mental figures.

The practical and conceptual problems associated with the area have meant that psychologists have largely ignored the issue of measuring imagery. Those who have addressed the question have primarily adopted self-report methods, that is, they have devised questionnaires that simply ask individuals to estimate how proficient they are at imagery, usually by selecting a number on a scale. The reliability and validity of such an approach are clearly of concern for interindividual research, that is, for testing whether those who score high on the imagery test actually improve more on the task as a result of imagery rehearsal. Since nobody can observe other people's quality of imagery to make a comparison, two people experiencing the same phenomenon may rate themselves high and low on the test based on other criteria than the image. The approach may have greater validity for intra-individual work, that is, looking at the change in rated imagery *within* the individual as a result of imagery rehearsal, provided test–retest reliability can be demonstrated. In other words, it may be possible to show that the same person produces the same score on different occasions, when nothing in the intervening time has occurred that might change the person's rating of imagery.

The measurement of imagery is further complicated by the question of which parameter or parameters of the experience to measure. Suinn's (1984b) conception of imagery is multimodal, but some researchers have been particularly interested in one sense-modality. Visual imagery has held primacy in this respect. Certainly, deciding which sense-modalities to measure is an issue in this field. Then there are the different aspects of imagery. Vividness has long been considered important and so has controllability. The role of these factors was supported in research conducted by Start and Richardson (1964), who found that vivid, controllable images were the most potent, while vivid, uncontrollable images were dysfunctional, that is, they hampered performance. Nonetheless, there are other aspects which might be noteworthy, such as the duration of the image or the ease with which images can be generated. Thus, it could be that images are very vivid, but do not last very long, making it impossible for a gymnast, for example, to image a whole routine. Similarly, it could be that when they are generated, images are clear and controllable but they do not come easily, so that both in research and in practice, time spent in an imagery session may not reflect accurately time spent imaging.

Despite these difficulties, a number of tests of imagery have been developed. It is not possible here to review the breadth of tests comprehensively or to examine their psychometric properties in detail. The main tests that have been applied to research on motor skills and sport will be referred to, and their nature and use in sport will be described. The tests assess some aspects of imagery ability. The main reason for their inclusion in research is that in a study in which the performance of subjects in the imagery condition did not differ significantly from that of control subjects, and with no measure of subjects' ability to generate appropriate images, it is possible that the conclusion would be that imagery does not enhance performance, whereas a poor imagery outcome might have been caused by the subjects' low imagery ability (Hall, 1985). In practice, it is important to determine the imagery strengths and weaknesses of athletes so that exercises can be assigned to develop any weak areas considered important to the particular imagery training program. For example, kinaesthetic imagery would be important to performers of body movement sports. As well as variations between the senses, vividness or controllability may need to be developed before specific sports-performance imagery rehearsal commences. The issue of measurement is important in research and in applied work, so the following review of tests should be informative.

Tests of imagery were published more than 80 years ago, when the Betts (1909) Questionnaire on Mental Imagery (QMI) appeared. A version which substantially reduced the 150 items of the original, the Shortened Questionnaire on Mental Imagery (SQMI), developed by Sheehan (1967), has been popular in recent research. It is a 35-item version, with self-report responses given on a Likert scale. The SQMI measures vividness of imagery across a range of sense-modalities. Juhasz (1972) found an acceptable internal consistency (r = 0.95) and Sheehan demonstrated sound stability over a seven month period (r = 0.78), as well as a homogeneous factor structure (Sheehan, 1967).

Another test that has been used for some years, but has also been adapted more recently, is Gordon's (1949) Test of Imagery Control (GTIC), which was modified by Richardson (1969). It is a rather short scale consisting of only 12 items, which are designed to measure controllability by requiring unusual mental manipulations of real objects, for example, imaging a car standing on its end. Although its test–retest reliability (r = 0.84) over a three-week period and its split half reliability (r = 0.76) are acceptable (McKelvie & Gingras, 1974), Moran (1993) notes that it has been shown to correlate significantly with the QMI (r = 0.47). As the QMI purportedly assesses vividness, the independence of these two imagery dimensions is therefore brought into question. Further study is therefore needed to test the claim that dimensions of imagery — at least those which have been the focus of measurement — are conceptually (or empirically) distinguishable (Moran, 1993).

While the QMI/SQMI and the GTIC have been used in research relevant to sport, two interesting measures that have not attracted much research are the Individual Differences Questionnaire (IDQ; Paivio, 1971) and the Group Test of Mental Rotations (GTMR; Vandenberg & Kuse, 1978). The IDQ test measures individual differences in verbalising and visualising, which are the two representational systems proposed in Paivio's (1971) Dual Code Theory. Because of the verbal scale not appearing relevant, Moran (1993) suggests that the scale has not been widely used in imagery research. It may be that further examination of this test, which has sound psychometric properties, is warranted, because low visualisers, who are high imagers, might benefit from a more verbally oriented approach. In contrast, perseverance with imagery may not bring rewards that match effort.

Moran (1993) includes the GMRT (Vandenberg & Kuse, 1978) in his review of measures of imagery, even though the GMRT is claimed to be an objective test of spatial visual ability, after the style of Shephard and Metzler (1971), where the orientations of three-dimensional drawings must be judged. There are 40 items, each containing a target and four alternatives, two of which are correct. The GMRT has good test–retest reliability (r = 0.83) and Kuder–Richardson reliability (r = 0.88) in the original work (Vandenberg & Kuse, 1978). It also has sound internal consistency (r = 0.90) in a study by Moran (1991). Additionally, and contrary to earlier comments on the lack of relevance of this type of test to sports performance, Moran (1991) found that the GMRT was significantly correlated (Spearman's *rho* = 0.44) with successful performance in World Cup canoe slalom racing.

Hall and Pongrac (1983) developed the Movement Imagery Questionnaire (MIQ) with much more of an orientation to motor skill and sport, as the name suggests. It consists of 18 items, which describe nine short movement sequences. Each sequence is executed physically twice, once followed by instructions to recreate the experience using visual imagery, and once with kinaesthetic imagery instructions. After each imagery episode, the person rates the quality of imagery on a Likert scale. The visual scores provide one total and the kinaesthetic items generate another total. Together these scores are claimed to reflect independent capacities to see and to feel movements through imagery, that is, both visual and kinaesthetic imagery may be high, moderate or low, as well as one being high while the other is moderate or low. Moran (1993) notes that although the MIQ has been used in research (e.g., Jowdy & Harris, 1990), it has not been adequately validated.

The test which has taken over as the most popular in research in recent times is the Vividness of Visual Imagery Questionnaire (VVIQ), which was developed by Marks (1973). More recently, Marks (1989) has published a bibliography of research using the scale. The VVIQ is a 16-item scale, which is derived from the visual sub-scale of Betts's (1909) QMI. It is scored on Likert type scales. Test–retest reliability estimates vary from adequate (r = 0.67) to good (r = 0.87) according to McKelvie (1990). Moran (1993) notes that construct validity of the test has been "debated vigorously" (p. 162).

Some time after the VVIQ was published, an equivalent with a kinaesthetic focus, the Vividness of Movement Imagery Questionnaire (VMIQ) was developed by Isaac, Marks, and Russell (1986). It claims to measure the visual imagery associated with movement itself, as well as the kinaesthetic sensations, suggesting that in the terminology of orientations dicussed earlier in the chapter, it requires subjects to adopt an internal imagery orientation. The VMIQ contains 24 items scored on Likert scales. Isaac et al. (1986) estimated a test–retest reliability of 0.86 over three weeks. Moran (1993) proposes that its convergent validity is supported by a significant correlation with the VVIQ (r = 0.81). It is not clear why it would be expected that visual and movement imagery should share over 60% common variance. It may be that part of the commonality relates to the format and response modes of the two tests.

One more test should be mentioned, because it is widely used in applied sport psychology. This is Martens' (1982) Sport Imagery Questionnaire (SIQ). The SIQ presents descriptions of four experiences common in sport. These are practising alone, practising with others, watching a team mate, and playing in a contest. For each of these scenes, after spending a minute imaging it, ratings are made on five-point Likert scales from no image to clear, vivid image for three sense-modalities — vision, hearing, and kinaesthesis — and for the degree to which emotions were stimulated. Vealey and Walter (1993) have recently added controllability to these four response dimensions. This is assessed on a five-point scale from no control to complete control, and an internal-imagery-perspective question asks, for each experience, whether it could be seen from inside the body, allowing a yes/no response choice. Although the SIQ, or some modification of it, has been widely used in practice, there has been no attempt to validate it. It is the only test discussed here which is sport specific, which is consistent with Martens' (1975) proposition that sport-specific tests are more sensitive, a proposal which is supported by Martens' own work in developing the Sport Competition Anxiety Test (SCAT) and the Competitive State Anxiety Inventory-2 (CSAI-2), as reported by Martens, Vealey, and Burton (1990).

Clearly, with no reliability and validity to support it, the SIQ cannot be used in research and even its use in applied work may carry ethical risks, should inappropriate prescriptions be based on results from it. However, Moran (1993) points out that none of the tests considered here has acceptable validity, even though some have satisfactory reliability. This means that while they might give the same result on different occasions and all their items may be measuring the same construct, there is no evidence that the construct being measured is imagery or, more precisely in most cases, vividness of imagery, or its controllability. It would seem that there is a need for somebody to develop a test which measures the involvement of all the senses in imagery and at the same time measures a number of dimensions, such as ease, quality and duration, as well as vividness and controllability. Substantial investigation of the factor structure would be necessary, using confirmatory factor analysis, to examine the possibility that these dimensions are not independent. As well as test–retest and split-half reliability and internal consistency, considerable demonstration of the construct validity of the test would be essential and this would call for a great deal of creativity. One other possibility should be explored. Likert scales have been used almost exclusively for responses in the tests developed to date. While they are simple for subjects to understand and for researchers to analyse, a more sophisticated method, such as multi-dimensional scaling, might reflect the nature of imagery more clearly. Murphy (1985) used a similar technique in a series of studies in mental imagery, but did not develop these ideas further. The development of a sound psychometric device is not generally considered a glamorous activity by many psychologists. It is a long, gruelling process, without the gratification that intervention research brings when performers develop as intended. Still, it is essential to the progress of many fields and imagery is certainly one area which is desperately in need of a valid, reliable, comprehensive and relevant test.

 **USES OF IMAGERY**

Probably one of the most appealing aspects of imagery rehearsal is that it is an extremely versatile technique that can be used in a wide range of situations in sport. This section introduces some of these ways of using imagery. It is by no means comprehensive; in fact the limits of uses of imagery are probably reflected in the limits of the imaginations of athletes, coaches and sport psychologists. Each use mentioned in this section is explained only briefly, in the context of the breadth of this chapter. Examples accompany each application.

Skill learning. Deriving, as it does, from mental practice, it is not surprising that one use of imagery rehearsal is in the learning of skills. For example, a tennis player who is shown a new service variation could speed up the process of integrating it into his or her game by doing a ten minute imagery rehearsal of the service every evening, as well as using that action to serve 50 balls in training each morning. In the imagery session, attention should be paid to the differences between this service action and those already in the player's repertoire. Imagery immediately after the physical practice or even interwoven with it might also be very effective.

Skill practice. At the elite level, learning new skills is not needed often, but there are many occasions when practising skills is valuable in keeping them well tuned. One example of this is during long overseas trips, when many hours might be spent on a plane or coach, where there is no opportunity to practise. Another example would be when a performer is injured and cannot practise physically.

Strategy learning. Teams develop new strategies to combat particular aspects of the play of specific opposition or just to keep opponents guessing. To familiarise themselves with the roles of all their team mates, as well as to fit their own part in with the others, both temporally and spatially, the members of a basketball team might each use imagery to enhance their performance of a new offensive strategy.

Strategy practice. A common situation in team games is that alternative strategies must be adopted against each opposing team, because they all play with different styles. Often, in football for instance, the B team is drafted to play like next week's opposition, but their speed and competence cannot match the real thing. Imaging strategy implementation against the actual players who will be confronting the team, playing up to form and at full speed can help players sharpen up that strategy during the week before the match.

Mental warm-up. All top-level athletes know that it is important to be physically warmed up when the match starts, not only to avoid soft-tissue injuries, which are more likely to affect cold, tight muscles, but also to ensure they are physically ready to give maximum effort in the vital first few minutes of the match. Athletes are less aware that the same sort of early game disaster can occur because the player or team is mentally cold.

In table tennis, for example, players hit to each other in the pre-game knock, going through a range of shots for a minute or two each. The skills involved use automatic rather than controlled processing and a player could be thinking of a film seen the night before. Imaging the end of the knock, the toss up, the start of play and the first ten rallies against an opponent who is playing well and stretching them, if done shortly before going to the table, should send the player into competition much more focused on what to expect in play.

Preview. Mental warm-up is a technique most applicable to open-skill sports, where the player does not know exactly what the opponent will do within the parameters of the game. In closed skills, such as gymnastics, figure skating or trampoline, the performer knows exactly what the performance involves. Imaging the whole routine can help to automatise the sequence, so that during performance focus can be on precision of movement, difficult transitions or even, in a task like women's gymnastics floor exercises, investing the performance with the "personality" which will win over judges and audience. This type of imagery can be done at any time, but when a final run-through of the routine is carried out using imagery just a few minutes before performance, it is called a preview.

Review. After performance, imagery can be used to "replay" the whole performance or a part of it. With practice it is possible to "fast forward" through uninteresting phases of a badminton game, 800-metre swim or lacrosse match and then to examine the critical parts in "slow motion", as if watching a video of the event. Review using imagery should emphasise positive aspects of performance, but should not neglect the negative. Detecting weaknesses and errors, which are then replaced by the correct response, should help future performance. Because positive and negative emotions are often aroused by performance and outcome, it is usually recommended that review be left until a few hours after the event, when a more objective assessment can be made. In long events with substantial breaks, such as cricket batting, tennis or golf, players often review each shot and immediately image corrections to it. This can involve physical correction, but imagery is often used here as well.

Problem-solving. Just as it is possible to use imagery to review performance, picking out the highs and lows, imagery can also be used to examine a routine or a skill to detect a problem and then to correct it in readiness for the next physical practice session or competitive performance. A gymnast who is an experienced imager can use internal and external perspectives to help identify the difficulty in a beam routine. Further, it is possible to employ a number of external orientations, such as viewing from the side, from the front, from the back and even from above if it might help. Running through the skill at normal pace in imagery to locate the portion where the problem occurs could be followed by a slow motion re-run for detailed examination of the precise difficulty. Having identified the problem as being associated with the smoothness of a particularly complex transition, the gymnast could employ a part-to-whole practice approach in imagery to mentally rehearse the specific transition several times until it is consistently performed correctly. The gymnast would then go through the previous move and the one which follows the transition a number of times without error and, finally, run through the whole routine using imagery rehearsal.

Stress management. Imagining a relaxing scene can generate feelings of relaxation. A pistol-shooter suffering somatic anxiety prior to and during competition will not perform well with trembling arms. The shooter can decide on a scene which he or she finds pleasant and relaxing, such as lying in soft, white sand on a beach, with the waves gently rolling in and the sun making him or her feel warm and comfortable (but not drowsy). Imagery of this scene would be practised at home first, then before training and, once the performer felt comfortable with it, before a competition. Where the anxiety is cognitive, not producing bodily reactions, but raising self-doubts about performance, imaging a scenario where the person is coping with the performance situation effectively might help reduce the anxiety.

Developing psychological skills. Whereas the imagery above was employed to directly cope with somatic or cognitive anxiety, it is also possible to use imagery to help develop psychological skills. An example here might be a cricket batter who finds it difficult to maintain a narrow external focus of attention, being prone to distraction during the bowler's run-up. In Chapter 15, Bond and Sargent describe an exercise where the player focuses on an object from the sport, maintaining that focus of attention for as long as possible. It is equally possible to maintain focus on an imaged object, so the cricketer in question could sit and relax and then image a ball on a table right in front of him or her, looking closely to check any emblem, read the manufacturer's name, or examine the seam. To include other senses, the player could image picking up the ball and running his or her fingers over the seam, smelling the leather, or appreciating the shape and weight of the ball. The cricketer should be instructed to develop passive concentration, where the concentration is not forced but occurs naturally, and any distraction is allowed to wash over the player, who remains focused on the ball.

Building confidence. As noted earlier in this chapter, imagery has been widely canvassed as a means of enhancing self-confidence. For example, a netball goal-shooter who has had a couple of consecutive poor shooting percentages might begin to doubt her ability. Imagery of being in shooting positions against the next opponents, being well defended, but still feeling relaxed and confident and netting the ball might bolster that flagging confidence, if done each evening of the week for ten minutes. Care should be taken that imagery for confidence building is realistic. The shooter in the example may not believe imagery of 19 out of 20 shots successful if she usually hits 60%. However, 17 out of 20 for a shooter who would typically expect 80% in matches should ring true and, thus, be more effective.

Recovering from injury or heavy training. Imagery can be employed to facilitate physical recovery from injury, especially to soft tissue. The same process can be applied to the soreness associated with heavy training. Physically, greater blood flow to an injured area, as well as warmth in the locality of damaged tissue promote recovery. It has been shown that imagery of increased blood flow and warmth can lead to measurable increases in an area as specific as a finger (Blakeslee, 1980). A long-jumper with a pulled hamstring could alleviate some of the frustration of being unable to practise by imaging the flow of warm, rich, bright-red blood to flood the whole of the muscle area at the back of the thigh. This might be done twice or three times a day. After heavy training, with weights or on the track, a sprinter might use the same imagery but would systematically image every major muscle group for one minute or focus on the sorest muscles. A more substantial example, which also uses the special properties of flotation, is presented in a later section of the chapter.

HOW DO WE BEGIN AN IMAGERY-TRAINING PROGRAM?

It was noted in the discussion of the motivational explanation of the effect of imagery on performance that many practitioners consider belief to be a prerequisite for effective imagery. More specifically, it seems important that an athlete believes that thoughts can influence behaviour, not so much to "make the imagery process work", but to persuade the performer to add yet another discipline to a largely dedicated life, especially when the level of commitment to practise imagery must be high if it is to be effective. In order to persuade athletes of the effectiveness of imagery training, a number of exercises have been devised to add to the explanations of theory, citations of research and anecdotes of successful athletes, because athletes are often doers, and talk does not impress them as much as action. In Chapter 15, Bond and Sargent describe one exercise that is sometimes used, namely the "Arm as Iron Bar", which they call "The Unbendable Arm". As a demonstration of imagery, the only modification needed is to ensure that in the second part of that exercise when giving the instruction to image the arm as an iron bar reaching out and fixed to the wall, the emphasis is on the involvement of the imagery process. Another two widely used techniques for the introduction of mind–body links are briefly described here. These are the string-and-bolt exercise and biofeedback of arousal.

String and bolt. Despite its name this exercise can be done with any type of thread, whether it be string, cord, wool, cotton or metal, and any small weight, such as a nut, bolt, paper clip, screw or the like. The weight is tied to the end of the piece of string, forming a pendulum about 20 centimetres long. The person is instructed to place his or her elbow on a solid surface, with forearm at an angle of around 45 degrees, keep their arm still and image the pendulum swinging to and fro. Soon it starts to swing. The amount varies between people, but very few get no movement. Once it is swinging, the instruction is to image the pendulum standing still. Soon this will happen for most people or at least it will slow down a lot. Then the person is instructed to image it swinging toward and away from them; then stopped again. Then they image it describing a clockwise circle, stop it, then an anticlockwise circle and stop again. The reactions of athletes as they watch the pendulum is akin to one's reaction to a magic trick. It is important that the psychologist then notes that the only trick being played is by the athlete's brain. Nothing moves without a force being applied to it, so small movements of the arm are being made, but many people feel they are holding their arm so rigid that it aches. The crucial point to make is that although the person is actively trying to stop the arm from moving, the imagery still gets the message through to the muscles to act. Another interesting point can be made by asking how one stops a swinging pendulum in two to three swings, as often happens here. Most people don't know — aside from using the free hand, of course! Thus, under imagery conditions, it is also possible to carry out actions or skills for which directions are not consciously accessible.

Biofeedback of arousal. Another exercise which is particularly pertinent to the use of imagery to manage arousal level, but which can be invoked to make a general point about the mind and the body, is to give heart rate, galvanic skin response or other feedback of physiological arousal level, while an athlete images emotive events. The events can be guided, for example by instructing the athlete to select a very close, tense game they played and the final few minutes of it, or to imagine an especially pleasant and relaxing experience. The athlete can then be shown how arousal changed as he or she imaged the two contrasting scenes. An alternative or follow-up is to simply instruct performers to image something which they believe will make their arousal level increase/decrease. In addition to making the point that they can control their arousal level by learning to use imagery, it is also possible to make the more general point that this is just one example of how the mind can control the body, thus linking the demonstration to imagery used for skill enhancement, concentration, confidence and other purposes. Once the point is made by any of these techniques, imagery training can commence with an enhanced likelihood of adherence.

When beginning imagery training with athletes, it is helpful to start with an assessment of their abilities in a number of areas. Firstly, it is important to ascertain a basic level of competence in the motor skill. If the athlete has no knowledge of the appropriate movements required to perform the task, chances are their imagery will not closely approximate the physical skills needed for enhanced performance. In this case, imagery may actually be detrimental to performance because the individual will be mentally rehearsing movements that may not be appropriate to the successful completion of the task. Imagery should be used as an adjunct to physical training. As the athlete's physical talents improve, the complexity of the imagery may also increase. That is not to say that the imagery must always be based on current performance levels. Imagery that is grounded on sound principles based on the requirements of the sport will help in the acquisition of the skill. For example, a swimmer may watch world record holder Phil Rogers' breaststroke in order to improve his or her kick under water. This swimmer may not be at the same level of performance as Rogers at the time, but by watching the film and internalising the image, improvement of the under water kick can occur.

Additionally, it is important to assess the imagery abilities of the athlete. Dimensions of imagery commonly mentioned in the literature are quality, vividness and controllability. The quality of the imagery involves the utilisation of the various senses. As mentioned earlier, there are six major senses that should be used in imagery training; visual (sight), olfactory (smell), auditory (hearing), gustatory (taste), tactile (touch), and kinaesthetic (body awareness). As more senses are used, the quality of the image improves and, hence, the effectiveness of imagery on performance also improves. Typically, we have found that athletes have a dominant or preferred sense — some are not able to "see" themselves competing, but are able to feel the leather of the football in their hands. The term "visualisation" has been used extensively in the literature, but it has been our experience that many athletes have difficulty creating a visual picture. At times, these athletes feel as if they have failed and quit on the idea of imagery, unless their ability to image in other sense modalities is quickly tapped. Despite vivid descriptions of the green of the rink and the tracks of the balls rolling across to the jack, a bowler could not generate a visual image of the bowling green at all. She reported a strong kinaesthetic image, so focus was kept on smooth delivery in kinaesthetic imagery. This worked very well for that performer. Thus, we must have a more balanced approach to the presentation of imagery training. The overall quality of the image may actually be greater even if the athlete can't visualise. For example, a basketball player may feel the bumps and seams on a ball, smell the odour of the ball or perspiration on the skin, hear the echoes of the gym as the ball bounces on the floor, feel the coolness of the air on his or her body, or feel as if his or her arms moved while imaging taking a shot. It is the goal of the person doing imagery training to acquire a rich experience in as many senses as possible.

The issue of vividness pertains to the "sharpness" of the image. It is the removal of all the "noise" that can be associated with mentally rehearsing skills, as if you have focused a fuzzy picture on the television, or quieted a room full of people to hear someone speak, or perhaps lifted the lid off a pot of homemade spaghetti sauce and taken in the delicious aroma. By eliminating all extraneous stimuli, you can concentrate more clearly on the important information. As athletes work on their concentration skills (see Chapter 15), they find that the vividness of their images improves. This improvement in vividness enhances the mental picture and creates a more accurate representation of life.

Finally, controllability allows the individual to be creative and manipulate the mental picture. Especially when creating images that have not actually taken place in reality, the individual has to take known events and manipulate them in the mind to represent the ideal condition. As athletes move items and themselves within their image they learn to have more control over outcomes. This not only enhances the effectiveness of the imagery, it also increases athletes' self-confidence as they see and feel that they are able to achieve success. Just as quality and vividness are learned skills, controllability may be improved through practice.

Once these abilities have been assessed, a personalised training program is designed. In group imagery sessions, it is important to allow for a wide variation in abilities. Be sure to include a gradation of skill levels, use all the senses, present a variety of vivid images, and allow the athlete an opportunity to control and change the image. Individually, be sure that the athlete practises and develops all phases of physical and mental skills to enhance his or her imagery effectiveness.

WHEN AND WHERE DO WE DO IT?

Imagery is a skill that can be utilised at any time and in any place for a wide variety of reasons. Imagery is extremely effective in the acquisition of skills. The "mental maps" set the groundwork for future physical acts. Depending on the physical and imagery-ability level of the athlete, we would prescribe different types of imagery, timing and locations.

In the early stages, incorporating imagery at the end of a quality relaxation session is advocated. This relaxation session removes unwanted distractions, such as thoughts, emotions, tension and so on, and allows the athlete to concentrate more effectively on the images. In these developmental stages, this can be done away from the training/competition venue, which again assists in minimising distractions. For beginners, it is common to start with images of well-known objects, such as the house they grew up in, a family pet, or a favourite location like the beach or mountain. These are recollections that are fairly easy for most people and, with practice, can be manipulated to enhance controllability of images.

Once the athletes show some proficiency in these skills, the focus is moved on to more sport-specific examples. Again the athletes can practise these at the end of a relaxation session away from the venue. They should be guided to use as many senses as possible when recreating themselves playing their sport. The images can be restricted to actions that have already taken place so as to tap into the memory portion of their minds. As they gain confidence in these skills, more self-directed imagery of possible changes to the mental picture can be introduced.

After achieving sport-specific imagery, athletes need to practise the imagery at the training site. It is important for the athletes to progress to the level of producing mental pictures without the need for total relaxation. They need to be able to block out all distractions at a moment's notice and to focus solely on the task at hand. In order to attain this level, they must begin to practise in distracting conditions. It is important for the athletes to practise imagery skills before, during and after physical training sessions. They can learn to internalise images by performing a task and by immediately noticing the feelings that were internally generated during the movement: for example, a swimmer doing butterfly, with eyes closed, focuses on the sounds below and above the water; feels the water as it rolls over the head and down the back; smells the chlorine as he or she comes up to take a breath; feels the movement of the arms and legs as they propel themselves through the water. By programming these images into the brain while they are actually being physically executed, there is an increased likelihood of retrieving them during imagery training away from the pool.

As mentioned earlier, imagery is a vital tool in preparing oneself just prior to competition. Therefore, it needs to be practised at all competitions, regardless of the importance of the outcome. Some athletes have been heard to say that it is only important to practise imagery before big competitions. It is argued here, however, that if it is not practised before all competitions, it won't be there when you need it before big competitions. Imagery is a skill that should be practised as often as the individual deems necessary. It can be used in very small doses many times a day or once a day for 20 to 30 minutes prior to going to bed. Once the performer is proficient, there is no particular time or place where athletes should practise imagery. It is a life skill that should be used to assist individuals to plan and achieve success.

HOW DO WE USE IMAGERY? EXAMPLES OF THE USE OF IMAGERY IN SPORT

In the previous section, a number of factors were discussed which are pertinent to the introduction of imagery to an athlete. Once these general and basic aspects of the imagery procedure have been addressed, the imagery program to be developed must be specific to the sport and the individual. It is not possible to describe every aspect of every program. Instead, a number of specific examples are now presented in order to illustrate the range of issues and the nature of the imagery rehearsal that might be used in each case.

Learning a new gymnastics routine. Julie, a developing gymnast, is learning a new floor routine. This routine will include movements from a previous program and some new pieces her coach has introduced.

1. In practising imagery of this routine, Julie will call upon her memory of her previous program to recollect those components that are familiar to her. If done properly, Julie will use as many of her senses as possible to recollect that image. She should see the colour of the mat, feel the mat under her feet and hands, hear the music being played, smell the aroma of the gym, be aware of her body position as she moves, perhaps even tasting dryness, moistness or flavours in her

mouth. Using as many senses as possible enhances the "picture" that is generated in the mind. As you add each of the senses, it is similar to taking a black and white photo and converting it to state-of-the-art virtual reality. Julie can "examine" a black and white photo but she can "relate" to virtual reality.

2. When imaging new movements, Julie must call upon her knowledge of gymnastics and how things move in order to create the appropriate picture. She has memories of the visual pictures and colours in the gym, what the mat feels like, the smells in the air, the various tastes that are possible, the feel of her body in space as she performs gymnastic movements. She must now take this knowledge of her sport and create images of these new, unperfected elements. By using multisensory imagery, Julie's new program will be learned more quickly and efficiently.

Improving imagery ability in free-style swimming. To improve the athlete's ability to use imagery, it is often effective to have them experience the real sensory input and then immediately recreate it. In some cases, such as swimming, this might actually happen in the pool, as the automatised strokes are done in the following example.

1. After a standard warm-up, the swimmer swims 50 metres of freestyle at a controllable speed that allows for maximal technique without undue fatigue.

2. The next 50 metres is swum four strokes with eyes open and a broad focus of attention, four strokes with eyes closed, practising imagery of the senses used for the four previous strokes.

3. This rotation is continued for 400 metres, alternating between awareness of internal and external conditions, and imaging those same conditions with eyes closed.

4. At the conclusion of 400 metres, 7 to 8 minutes is spent imaging the 400-metre freestyle in its entirety, without actually swimming.

5. Once out of the pool, the swimmer repeats the imagery of the full 400-metre swim several times a day.

This drill will enhance the swimmer's imagery ability in a number of areas. It will:

- assist the swimmer in acquiring an internal perspective of imagery in co-operation with the external (movie) perspective
- utilise more senses than just visualisation, through the internal perspective and the immediate feedback
- improve controllability by allowing the swimmer to change images and senses during an actual swim
- increase vividness by recreating sensory experiences currently in short-term memory
- assist in transfer of images from short-term memory for storage in long-term memory by immediate rehearsal and programming for future recall
- enhance the ability to create images instead of just recreating images.

Improving confidence of a road cyclist during and after rehabilitation from a crash on the bike, which involved no other riders or vehicles. Use of imagery during recovery from injury often has multiple value. Not only can it facilitate recovery, it can also relieve some of the stress of being injured by giving the athlete something constructive to do. In the example below, imagery not only occupies the cyclist and thus reduces the stress of being injured, but also rebuilds confidence.

1. During rehabilitation, the cyclist imagines the conditions surrounding the crash: thoughts, emotions, environment, situation, and so on. With this heightened awareness, the cyclist may understand personal responsibility for the outcome, leading to personal forgiveness. This process allows the cyclist to learn how the crash situation should be avoided in the future.

2. The cyclist uses this information to image being on the bike again in the same situation, but at a slower speed and under greater control. As the cyclist becomes comfortable with this step, the rate of speed is systematically increased and so is the degree of difficulty associated with the situation.

   The important point here is that the cyclist must always feel in control of the bike and situation, even though his or her abilities are being tested. If the cyclist starts to feel that control is being lost, it is simply a matter of leaving the scene for a moment, and gaining control of thoughts and emotions before returning to the bike.

3. Once the cyclist is physically ready to return to the bike, the risk level must be systematically increased in proportion to confidence level. The cyclist must continue to use imagery at a slightly increased level of risk than is actually being taken in physical training on the bike. This will expedite the recovery time, because the imagery will prepare the cyclist for the next level while reducing the amount of anxiety associated with the memory of the crash.

Accelerating the healing process of a soccer player after major knee surgery. As in the previous example, imagery in rehabilitation is of value in several ways. Here, the focus is on the recovery process itself.

1. Immediately after surgery, the player must undertake an imagery rehabilitation program as well as physical rehabilitation. These two programs work in conjunction with each other.

2. It is important for the player to have vivid internal imagery that utilises as many senses as possible. Therefore, the first step is to work on enhancing the athlete's internal multisensory imagery ability. Biofeedback is one way to enhance an individual's controllable, internal imagery. As the soccer player imagines the blood flowing to the injured knee, biofeedback equipment will detect physiological changes to that area, e.g., EMG and skin temperature.

3. Each day the player uses imagery training to perform the following tasks.
   - Imagine a team of construction workers rebuilding the area around the knee. Use as many senses as possible to see the well-orchestrated

movements of all the workers, hear the sound of machinery around the site, feel the activity in the injured location. The more senses used, the more powerful the imagery will be.

- Imagine a warm, softly glowing light radiating down the leg into the injured knee. See this light as a vibrant golden colour that illuminates and envelops the injured area, bathing it in healing energy. Feel the warmth in the knee as all the parts are mending, coming back together and becoming stronger by the moment.
- Imagine being on the pitch and playing really well, completely healed and stronger than ever. Focus on the positive emotions of confidence, competence and well-being that are associated with playing one's best.

These exercises must be practised every day, at least a couple of times per day.

4. As mentioned earlier, it is extremely beneficial to practise these skills in a flotation tank, as this is an environment that reduces distracting stimuli, but also promotes healing through the natural properties of the salinated solution.

Minimising muscle soreness in the heavy training phase of a middle distance runner. This exercise is undertaken in a flotation tank. This provides three advantages. First, there is a direct physical effect, whereby the removal of a large part of gravity allows more rapid healing. (This is in contrast to lying on a bed, where part of the body, including many important muscle groups, is still under pressure.) Second, flotation facilitates physical, as well as mental relaxation, and relaxing the muscles also enhances their recovery. Third, flotation reduces sensory stimulation, so that one can focus on the imagery-rehearsal process without distractions, which leads to more vivid, sustainable and controllable imagery.

1. The runner visits the flotation facility every day, not too long after training. At first, short floats are used to permit orientation as initially the tank and the experience can be distracting. Length of sessions increases, perhaps 15 minutes to start, then 25, 35, and 45 minutes may be used. Once the runner has been able to attain and maintain a relaxed state, imagery is introduced to sessions. (Time to achieve this will vary between athletes.)
2. Full 45 to 60 minute sessions are employed. For the first 20 minutes, the runner simply settles into a deeply relaxed state.
3. At around the 20-minute mark, the runner commences an imagery protocol based on the physiological processes involved in recovery of soft tissue:
   - A stream of bright-red, oxygenated blood is imaged flowing to a specific, major-muscle group, say in the lower legs.
   - As the blood flows through these muscles, its colour changes to dark-red, signifying that the impurities (such as lactic acid), which cause muscle soreness, are being taken up by the blood. This removes soreness and stiffness, while the oxygen in the blood is being supplied to the muscles to re-energise them.

- As the fresh, clean, bright-red blood flows in and the de-oxygenated blood carrying the impurities flows away, the runner feels the warmth of the cleansing, re-energising process in the muscles.

   The athlete must be introduced to this concept of blood cleaning muscles during imagery training, which takes place while phase 1, the non-imagery, orientation phase, is in progress. The athlete is also trained to become sensitive to signals from the body. Then, once the runner is skilled at the imagery, he or she can take responsibility for the focus of the imagery, spending more time on those muscle groups which are signalling more soreness on any occasion.

4. Imagery lasts 15 to 20 minutes, leaving 10 to 20 minutes to relax and enjoy the flotation experience at the end of the session. Auditory signals can be used to indicate approximate times to start and conclude imagery, but they should not be too intense or high pitched.

While this exercise may appear to be dependent on an expensive piece of technology, not accessible to many, in fact flotation facilities are to be found around most cities and towns in Australia. Access to flotation facilities is also possible at major sport psychology centres such as the AIS, SASI, and Victoria University.

Developing a pre-performance routine for golf. As psychological skills training has become more widely applied, it has become more systematic. There has also been recognition that it can be particularly effective when closely associated with actual performance, especially in competition (see Chapter 9). There are often opportunities to use imagery to great effect in or close to performance. In the build-up to an open-skill team game, such as basketball, a pre-competition routine can be developed; this would include imagery used for warming-up mentally against the style of the present opposition and for rehearsing set moves against them. A pre-performance routine could be developed, whereby imagery was used by a gymnast to preview her floor exercise. In games with breaks from play, a pre-shot or pre-point routine can be developed, whereby imagery of the intended shot is used on every occasion. This can be effective for service and return in racquet games, for each shot in archery, darts, pistol- and rifle-shooting and prior to each shot in golf. The following might be an appropriate pre-shot routine developed to improve consistency in a golfer's performance.

1. The golfer is trained in rapid muscular relaxation, using a technique such as centring or breathing. Whether relaxation enhances the effectiveness of imagery or not, it should be used prior to the performance of each golf shot to ensure that the player's muscles are loose for shot execution.

2. Imagery will vary depending on the shot required. To simulate this, a range of shots can be listed and the one used on each occasion is then selected at random. Practice of the relaxation and imagery combination can then take place on a daily basis off the course, until the player is comfortable with the procedure and reports effective imagery.

3. An individual's routine must incorporate psychological skills or they will be distracting. Examination of the current pre-shot routine leads to the identification of a way to introduce the relaxation and imagery with minimum disruption. For example, imagine that the player's current pre-shot routine is: to check location of the hole or a desired target on the fairway or green; decide on the best club to use and the type of shot; pick the club from the golf bag; walk behind the ball and check the shot down the fairway or across the green; address the ball; do a couple of practice swings; then adjust stance and play the stroke. Relaxation and imagery might fit best at the point where the player stands behind the ball, having decided on club and stroke. It might be decided that it is suitable to take two or three deep breaths, to image the feel of the shot, using an internal imagery perspective, then image the ball travelling to its desired destination. The rest of the routine is maintained.

4. The player then starts to use the relaxation and imagery in the full routine for every shot during practice. This continues until the revised routine becomes habitual.

5. Only at this point is the routine introduced to competition and it would only be used in less important events, such as club pennant tournaments. When the player reports being unaware of consciously executing the relaxation and imagery, but observation indicates that it was happening for every shot, then the new routine can be applied in major events.

Note that it might be best to introduce such a technique in a period where major competition is not regularly occurring. This is because there will be a transition period during which some confusion may arise, as the new routine is becoming habitual but is not yet ready to be introduced into big events.

VIDEO MODELLING AS AN AID TO IMAGERY

A technique which is commonly used in conjunction with imagery rehearsal is video modelling of performance. One argument which supports this practice is Bandura's (1977) social learning theory. He claims that vicarious experience (observation of a model performing a task successfully) enhances performance, as does performance accomplishment.

In video modelling associated with imagery, the individual watches an expert performer execute the movement or skill. For elite athletes, they are the expert performers and the videotape simply comprises edited examples of them performing at their best. The edited tape can repeat those few really excellent examples over and over again. The idea is to ensure that the ideal or near ideal performance of the skill becomes the image which is used in the mental rehearsal.

The Australian Institute of Sport has a video editing suite, where athletes are taught to edit video, so they can produce their own examples for imagery. Such video modelling is commonly used at the AIS in conjunction with flotation. Floating for 20 minutes or so induces a very relaxed state in many athletes, especially after a few sessions of becoming accustomed to the environment and to the sensations produced. After about 20 minutes in a float, the video modelling is introduced via a monitor mounted into the top of the tank, so the person can view the screen from the supine position. It plays the athlete's best performances of the skill, after which imagery rehearsal is used to recreate the images viewed on screen. Alternatively, blank spaces can be left in the edited video to allow the athlete to recreate the first example on the tape through imagery, then watch the second, recreate it and so on.

Another good reason for including video of best performance as a model for imagery is that viewing correct performance immediately prior to the imagery exercise may reduce the chance that incorrect imagery will be used. It was noted earlier that imagery of incorrect performance can lead to decreases in performance in competition (e.g., Woolfolk, Parrish, & Murphy, 1985).

The use of video modelling, athough based on substantial literature in the modelling field, is an applied technique which has yet to be investigated thoroughly by research in sport psychology. Hall and Erffmeyer (1983) included video modelling in a study of relaxation and imagery with 10 female college basketball players. The modelling group watched a player, on video, perform 10 consecutive successful foul shots and then imaged themselves performing the perfect 10. The video modelling group improved significantly more than the group which did imagery and relaxation without video modelling. Suinn (1993) notes that with the small sample and the absence of other evidence, the result is interesting but "can only be considered suggestive" (p. 495). Another study by Gray (1990) provides support for the findings, however. Out of a class of 24 novice racquetball players, significantly greater improvement was found in the performance of those subjects who received relaxation, imagery and modelling than those who received relaxation and imagery but no modelling. Suinn (1993) also cites a study by Gray and Fernandez (1990) which replicates the Hall and Erffmeyer result with varsity basketball players performing free throws. Should the early research be supported, future research might test the conditions under which video modelling is most effective and determine the basis for its influence.

FLOTATION AS AN AID TO IMAGERY

The idea of flotation in an enclosed tank containing a salt solution dense enough to support the body was developed by Lilly (1977) out of an area of research and practice termed restricted environmental stimulation therapy (REST). The whole area is based on the finding from early studies on sensory deprivation that although long periods of reduced sensory input were distressing, causing hallucinations, irrational fear and the like, subjects often reported very pleasant, relaxing experiences during the first one to two hours. REST attempts to utilise that early feeling of relaxation. Early work used REST chambers, which were rooms in which the sensory stimulation was kept to a minimum. Flotation was introduced because it permits all the usual sensory restriction, but also reduces the sensation of gravity by virtue of the float.

Research has suggested that flotation REST can facilitate a whole range of positive physical, behavioural and psychological changes. Among these, it appears to be a potent environment for imagery. Several studies have now been published, all providing support for the claim that imagery is very effective in the flotation environment. Lee and Hewitt (1987) compared visualisation in a flotation tank, imagery on a mat, and a no-practice control group. The 36 female gymnasts were also divided into high-anxiety and low-anxiety groups. Imagery groups had six 40-minute sessions over as many weeks. The flotation group had significantly higher meet scores than either of the other groups after the treatment. Wagaman, Barabasz, and Barabasz (1991) used 22 elite college basket-ballers in a study which compared imagery during flotation REST with an imagery "control" group. The float group showed significantly higher scores on the objective measure of performance after the training. McAleney, Barabasz, and Barabasz (1990) found similar results with 10 male and 10 female varsity tennis players on the service shot, while Sued-feld and Bruno (1990) showed a significant effect in basketball foul-shooting with 30 university students. This study compared flotation to imagery in an alpha chair (another high-technology, sensory-reduction environment), as well as measuring the effect of imagery in an armchair in an office. Most recently, Suedfeld, Collier, and Hartnett (1993) pro-vided further support for the use of flotation in a study of dart thowing with 40 student subjects.

It should be noted that all these studies supporting the use of imagery in flotation were executed by major figures in the flotation field. This is not surprising since they have the facilities to conduct such research. Still, it will be interesting to see similar work done by sport psychology groups. The Australian Institute of Sport, the South Australian Sports Institute and the Victoria University all have flotation facilities. To date, the AIS has developed substantial support from its athletes for use of the flotation tanks as an adjunct to sport science support services, but this success has not been reflected in published research as yet. One avenue for such research is to determine what aspect of flotation enhances imagery. Hutchison (1984) proposed a range of theories which might account for REST effects, especially in flotation. They were mainly predicated on altered states of consciousness, involving such processes as a shift to right-brain dominance. Two other possibilities involve relaxation and sensory deprivation. Briefly, the essence of the relaxation hypothesis is that flo-tation is deeply relaxing and relaxation facilitates imagery. This assumes, as many sport psychologists do, largely following Suinn (1983), that relax-ation does facilitate the production and transmission of images, a claim which is yet to be verified. The sensory deprivation proposition is that flotation REST, by definition, is intended to produce a substantial reduction in external stimulation. In these quieted circumstances for the central nervous system, it is argued, images can be produced much more vividly and with greater control, so they are more effective. Again, the research community has not started to examine these issues. The flotation environment does seem to offer a good laboratory for the examination of a number of issues in imagery research, and the development of research programs in these facilities is awaited with interest.

RELAXATION AND IMAGERY

There has been a tradition in mainstream psychology to employ relaxation as part of therapies. For example, Wolpe (1958) combined progressive relaxation with increasingly realistic and physically close experiences of an anxiety-provoking stimulus, a technique called systematic desensitisation. In the Behaviourist tradition, the concept underlying this approach was to decondition or disconnect the bond between the stimulus and the response of increased anxiety by ensuring that relaxation continued as the potency of the stimulus increased. Some of the stimuli could be images. Suinn (1976) proposed the combination of imagery with relaxation in his visual motor behaviour rehearsal (VMBR) technique. In VMBR, relaxation is seen as a base for the imagery, so it precedes imagery rehearsal. A number of studies using VMBR have shown it to be effective (e.g., Lane, 1978, 1980; Noel, 1980), but only Kolonay's (1977) study included a direct comparison of imagery with and without relaxation in basketball free-throw shooting. She found that a group that used only imagery and a group that used only relaxation did not differ from a control group, but the shooting of the VMBR group was significantly superior to all other groups. Weinberg, Seabourne, and Jackson (1981) replicated the design using 32 players performing several karate skills, but they also employed a placebo control group. Only sparring produced a result favouring relaxation plus imagery.

Murphy and Jowdy (1992) cite the last study as support for their contention that in research which has examined the role of relaxation in imagery "None of the studies conducted to date have found any significant benefits to using relaxation with imagery (Gray, Haring, & Banks, 1984; Hamberger & Lohr, 1980; Weinberg, Seabourne, & Jackson, 1981, 1987)" (p. 230). This conclusion seems premature. Without giving any justification, Murphy and Jowdy (1992) do not include Kolonay's study and, as was noted above, Suinn (1993) interprets the Weinberg et al. (1981) study as providing partial support for VMBR. Kremer, Morris, and Allen (1994) argue that while Kolonay's study may be methodologically weak, so are those of Gray et al. (1984) and Hamberger & Lohr (1980). Murphy and Jowdy (1992) do make the point that many studies of imagery have produced significant results without the inclusion of relaxation procedures (e.g., Clark, 1960; Corbin, 1967; Woolfolk, Parrish, & Murphy, 1985). They conclude that "while relaxation may interact with imagery, it is not a critical variable in producing imagery effects upon performance" (p. 230). This would seem a reasonable conclusion in the light of present evidence. It can be noted that Vealey's (1986) seminal chapter on the application of imagery included a section on relaxation, while the recent revision (Vealey & Walter, 1993) mentions relaxation only once when introducing a specific exercise on relaxation imagery. Despite these reactions, practitioners should be cautious before discarding relaxation. For example, it is possible that in some studies, subjects who were not instructed to relax did so naturally as a precursor to imaging; or that when this occurred, studies found significant results. There remains a need to examine the role relaxation plays and under what circumstances. To do this, it is necessary to monitor the level of physiological arousal in a range of imagery conditions in order to determine whether reductions in arousal level (that is, relaxation) are consistently associated with stronger imagery effects. Until the issue of the role of relaxation is empirically resolved it seems sensible to include relaxation in applied work in imagery.

FUTURE DIRECTIONS

Although imagery is the most widely practised psychological skill (Gould, Tammen, Murphy, & May, 1989; Jowdy, Murphy, & Durtschi, 1989) and has been the subject of a large amount of research in motor performance and sport (for a substantial list of references, see Murphy & Jowdy, 1992), there is still much that is not clearly understood about this ubiquitous mental process. Basic research is needed to clarify the mechanisms underlying the imagery process, to determine more precisely the concomitants of effective imagery, and to provide future research and practice with measures that are reliable, valid and which address the richness of the imagery phenomenon. Such research can lead to answers to questions which will facilitate applied work, while more practice-oriented research is also necessary. Issues include the most effective conditions for imagery; the usefulness of aids such as video modelling and flotation, which have entered practical work; and aspects of the nature of sessions, such as their optimal length and the most appropriate locations for imagery rehearsal sessions.

After 60 years, the psychoneuromuscular theory and the symbolic learning theory are still the major theoretical perspectives in the area, but little more is known about them. Well designed studies need to be conducted to clarify the role of muscular innervation and symbolic representation. For one thing, there has been no sound study that has measured muscle innervation in a range of muscle groups during imagery of a performance task and demonstrated equivalence to the innervation which occurs during the movement and then showed that performance was enhanced by that imagery (Hale, 1982; Harris & Robinson, 1986). Without such evidence, it is not clear that the low level innervation affects performance; it may simply be an epiphenomenon. Continuing with the electrophysiological approach, although they are still open to interpretation, electroencephalographic (EEG) techniques, especially sophisticated brain mapping technology, could be applied to study the functional location of imagery in the brain, and could compare the areas of the brain most involved in internal and external imagery orientations. More sytematic examination of Lang's (1977) bio-informational theory is also overdue. All studies should bear in mind the motivational explanation in their design and explore the role of confidence as a mediator of imagery. Understanding how imagery works is not a question of knowledge for its own sake. It is essential for the most effective use of imagery processes in applied work.

Thoughtful examination of those factors which appear to influence the operation of imagery is another direction for future research. Major concomitants of imagery include, again: the role of motivation; expectancy or belief in the imagery process; and the interaction between skill level and the nature of the imagery presented. For example, is video modelling particularly effective with athletes who are just learning a skill, because it increases the likelihood that they will image the correct execution of the skill? The precise role of imagery ability in successful imagery is another issue, along with benefit to the practitioner's capability to design effective programs based on the measurement of a range of parameters of imagery ability. The role of relaxation is still relevant, not as a necessary condition for imagery to take place, but as a factor which might enhance the experience greatly in some circumstances, while just adding time to the session in others.

Without a valid measure of imagery ability across a range of dimensions, it may still be that much research cannot be conclusive. The measurement of imagery ability remains an important issue and psychometricians should be encouraged to work with imagery theorists and practitioners to create such measures. Should valid multidimensional imagery tests be developed, then it is likely that they will permit much greater precision in the application of imagery in sports contexts. A range of aspects of imagery, such as ease of establishing images, vividness, quality and controllability of images, and duration for which images can be retained, needs to be measured. The involvement of all sense-modalities also needs to be assessed. Use of techniques such as multidimensional scaling would seem to be appropriate.

In addressing the issues above, much might also be learned about the best conditions in which to practise imagery. The value of the flotation REST environment is particularly pertinent here. The research evidence to date suggests that it is an effective location for imagery training and practice. It is not clear why this is the case. Perhaps it is merely an effect of expectancy or demand characteristics, where subjects believe that it must be very effective or the experts would not have gone to the trouble of setting up an elaborate environment. Certainly, one can understand subjects feeling that the space-age tank in its specially designed room is more potent than imaging on a mat or a massage table. To determine whether sensory deprivation or relaxation plays an important role, it is necessary to include high-tech controls for expectancy effects in flotation.

The practice of combining video modelling with imagery is widespread, but there is little direct research support, although the initial studies have been promising. Certainly there is a sound theoretical basis for this approach, coming from Bandura's (1977) social learning theory. The demonstration that the imaging of incorrect skills or outcomes can have a negative effect on performance (Woolfolk, Parrish, & Murphy, 1985), most likely with novices performing that skill, provides further support. Closer examination of the role of video modelling in imagery is warranted.

Imagery is such a rich and complex phenomenon that there are many directions for future research that have not been recorded here. Practitioners and many theorists clearly consider it is a premier psychological skill. The range of uses of imagery in stress management, confidence building, recovery from injury and the like, as well as in direct performance enhancement, should give students the assurance that well-designed research on aspects of imagery will be greatly appreciated and welcomed in the field.

CONCLUSIONS

There can be little doubt about the value of imagery as a resource in the practice of applied sport psychology. Imagery techniques have been used systematically in psychological skills training since the early peak performance research of Mahoney and Avener (1977), Ravizza (1977) and others, and were included in early, practically oriented texts, including Suinn (1980) and Orlick (1980). The amount of use and the range of applications of imagery has grown and continues to grow. Similarly, there appears to be little waning of interest in the study of imagery in order to provide knowledge that will optimise its use in sport psychology. To date, there has been more anecdotal and empirical evidence that imagery works, particularly in terms of enhancing performance, than there has been clarification of the underlying mechanisms that account for its efficacy, the concomitants that affect its action, or the ancillary techniques that aid in its operation.

Because imagery will clearly remain as a means of enhancing performance, solving problems, reviewing skills, building confidence, coping with stress, focusing attention, easing pain, facilitating recovery from injury or heavy exercise, and helping in other ways yet to be discovered, many of the questions raised by research and practice still urgently await answers. As the previous section on future directions intimated, the ideal approach is to solve theoretical and practical problems together. In fact, most of the theoretical issues have bearing on practical problems. Collaboration between practitioners working with elite and non-elite athletes and researchers who have access to the infrastructure, including equipment and facilities, will also facilitate progress in this field.

As in other areas of sport psychology, it is necessary for a range of research techniques to be used. One which has shown initial promise in imagery research is the single-case design. Another approach not yet used to its full potential in imagery research in sport is the electrophysiological approach. Yet, ironically, Jacobson (1931) pioneered this approach in the earliest days of modern research in the field. The advent of sophisticated brain mapping technology could stimulate such research. Technical difficulties with the measurement of low-level electrical signals from the brain or the nervous system still present an obstacle, but it is more easily surmountable in imagery research, where subjects are not required to move, than in most areas of sports research. Application of these techniques in a flotation REST environment might further enhance the clarity of results.

While research goes on, so must application of imagery in sport. It is intended that the underlying theory and research reviewed here and the guidance on the use of imagery should reflect current best practice. This "academic" experience can only be enhanced by working with athletes. By doing this, students will soon appreciate that while general principles are useful, what works with some doesn't necessarily prove effective with others. Sensitivity to the needs of the individual, and a creative imagination that matches those needs to the content of imagery training and practice, will continue to produce positive experiences for athletes using imagery.

SUMMARY

This chapter considered the theoretical base and the application of imagery in sport. After defining imagery and related terms, a general summary of research was presented. This was followed by closer examination of issues relating to individual differences and imagery orientations. The next section considered theories of imagery, including the psychoneuromuscular theory, the symbolic learning theory, the bioinformational theory, and arousal/attention, motivation and confidence perspectives on how imagery works. The issue of measuring imagery was then discussed, followed by a description of a number of uses for imagery in sport. Procedures for the introduction of imagery and its use were then presented and this section led on to a range of examples of imagery programs in different contexts and for different purposes. Related issues of the use of video modelling, the role of flotation REST and the relationship between relaxation and imagery were then covered. Finally, a number of future directions were suggested.

REFERENCES

Abernethy, B. (1993). The nature of expertise in sport. In S. Serpa, J. Alves, V. Ferreira, & A. Paula-Brito (Eds.), *Proceedings of VIIIth World Congress of Sport Psychology* (pp. 18–22). Lisbon, Portugal.

Bandura, A. (1969). *Principles of behavior modification.* New York: Holt, Rinehart & Winston.

Bandura, A. (1977). Self-efficacy: Toward a unifying theory of behavioral change. *Psychological Review, 84,* 191–215.

Betts, G. H. (1909). *The distribution and functions of mental imagery.* New York: Teacher's College, Columbia University.

Blakeslee, T. R. (1980). *The right brain.* New York: Anchor Press.

Bryan, A. J. (1987). Single-subject designs for evaluation of sport psychology interventions. *The Sport Psychologist, 1*, 283–292.

Burhans, III, R. S., Richman, C. L., & Bergey, D. B. (1988). Mental imagery training: Effects of running speed performance. *International Journal of Sport Psychology, 19*, 26–37.

Callery, P., & Morris, T. (1993). The effect of mental practice on the performance of an Australian Rules football skill. In S. Serpa, J. Alves, V. Ferreira, & A. Paula-Brito (Eds.), *Proceedings of VIIIth World Congress of Sport Psychology* (pp. 646–651). Lisbon: International Society of Sport Psychology.

Clark, L. V. (1960). The effect of mental practice on the development of a certain motor skill. *Research Quarterly, 31*, 560–569.

Corbin, C. B. (1967a). The effect of covert rehearsal on the development of a complex motor skill. *Journal of General Psychology, 76*, 143–150.

Corbin, C. B. (1967b). Effects of mental practice on skill development after controlled practice. *Research Quarterly, 38*, 534–538.

Corbin, C. B. (1972). Mental practice. In W. P. Morgan (Ed.), *Ergogenic aids and muscular performance* (pp. 94–116). New York: Academic Press.

Davidson, R. J., & Schwartz, G. E. (1977). Brain mechanisms subserving self-generated imagery: Electrophysiological specificity and patterning. *Psychophysiology, 14*, 598–602.

Desiderato, O., & Miller, I. B. (1979). Improving tennis performance by cognitive behavior modification techniques. *The Behavior Therapist, 2*, 19.

Egstrom, G. H. (1964). Effect of an emphasis on conceptualizing techniques during early learning of gross motor skill. *Research Quarterly, 35*, 472–481.

Epstein, M. L. (1980). The relationship of mental imagery and mental rehearsal to performance on a motor task. *Journal of Sport Psychology, 2*, 211–220.

Feltz, D. L. (1982). Path analysis of the causal elements of Bandura's theory of self-efficacy and an anxiety-based model of avoidance behavior. *Journal of Personality and Social Psychology, 42*, 764–781.

Feltz, D. L. (1992). Understanding motivation in sport: A self-efficacy perspective. In G. C. Roberts (Ed.), *Motivation in sport and exercise* (pp. 93–105). Champaign, IL: Human Kinetics.

Feltz D. L., & Landers D. M. (1983). The effect of mental practice on motor skill learning and performance: A meta-analysis. *Journal of Sport Psychology, 2*, 211–220.

Feltz D. L., Landers D. M., & Becker B. J. (1988). A revised meta-analysis of the mental practice literature on motor skill learning. In D. Druckman & J. Swets (Eds.), *Enhancing human performance: Issues, theories and techniques* (pp. 1–65). Washington DC: National Academy Press.

Feltz, D. L., & Mugno, D. A. (1983). A replication of the path analysis of the causal elements in Bandura's theory of self-efficacy and the influence of autonomic perception. *Journal of Sport Psychology, 5*, 263–277.

Feltz, D. L., & Riessinger, C. A. (1990). Effects of *in vivo* emotive imagery and performance feedback on self-efficacy and muscular endurance. *Journal of Sport and Exercise Psychology, 12*, 132–143.

Gordon, R. (1949). An investigation into some of the factors that favour the formation of stereotyped images. *British Journal of Psychology, 39*, 156–167.

Gough, D. (1989). Improving batting skills with small college baseball players through guided visual imagery. *Coaching Clinic, 27,* 1–6.

Gould, D., Tammen, V., Murphy, S. M., & May, J. (1989). An examination of the US Olympic sport psychology consultants and the services they provide. *The Sport Psychologist, 3,* 300–312.

Gray, J. J., Haring, M. J., & Banks, N. M. (1984). Mental rehearsal for sport performance: Exploring the relaxation imagery paradigm. *Journal of Sport Behavior, 7,* 68–78.

Gray, S. W. (1990). Effect of visuo-motor rehearsal with videotaped modeling on racquet ball performance of beginning players. *Perceptual and Motor Skills, 70,* 379–385.

Gray, S. W., & Fernandez, S. J. (1993). Effects of a visuo-motor behaviour rehearsal with videotaped modeling on basketball shooting performance. *Psychology: A Journal of Human Behavior, 26,* 41–47.

Hale, B. D. (1982). The effects of internal and external imagery on muscular and occular concomitants. *Journal of Sport Psychology, 4,* 379–387.

Hall, C. R. (1985). Individual differences in the mental practice and imagery of motor skill performance. *Canadian Journal of Applied Sport Sciences, 10,* 17s–21s.

Hall. C. R., & Pongrac, J. (1983). *Movement imagery questionnaire.* London, Ontario. University of Western Ontario.

Hall, E. G., & Erffmeyer, E. S. (1983). The effect of visuo-motor behavior rehearsal with video taped modeling on free throw accuracy of intercollegiate female basketball players. *Journal of Sport Psychology, 5,* 343–346.

Hamberger, K., & Lohr, J. (1980). Relationship of relaxation training to the controllability of imagery. *Perceptual and Motor Skills, 51,* 103–110.

Harris, D. V., & Robinson, W. J. (1986). The effects of skill level on EMG activity during internal and external imagery. *Journal of Sport Psychology, 8,* 105–111.

Hecker, J. E., & Kaczor, L. M.(1988). Application of imagery theory to sport psychology: Some preliminary findings. *Journal of Sport and Exercise Psychology, 10,* 363–373.

Hird, J. S., Landers, D. M., Thomas, J. R., & Horan, J. J. (1991). Physical practice is superior to mental practice in enhancing cognitive and motor task performance. *Journal of Sport and Exercise Psychology, 13,* 281–293.

Hutchison, M. (1984). *The book of floating.* New York: Morrow.

Isaac, A., Marks, D. F., & Russell, D. G. (1986). An instrument for assessing imagery of movement: The vividness of movement imagery questionnaire (VMIQ). *Journal of Mental Imagery, 10,* 23–30.

Jacobson, E. (1930). Electrical measurement of neuromuscular states during mental activities. *American Journal of Physiology, 94,* 24–34

Jacobson, E. (1931). Electrical measurement of neuromuscular states during mental activities. *American Journal of Physiology, 96,* 115–121.

Johnston, H., Morris, T., & Shaw, J. (1985). Mental practice: A review. In T. Hale, T. Morris, & N. Smith (Eds.), *Proceedings of the British Association of Sport Sciences Annual Conference.* Chichester, England.

Jowdy, D. P., & Harris, D. V. (1990). Muscular responses during mental imagery as a function of motor skill level. *Journal of Sport and Exercise Psychology, 12,* 191–201.

Jowdy, D. P., Murphy, S. M., & Durtschi, S. K. (1989). *Report on the United States Olympic Committee survey on imagery use in sport: 1989.* Colorado Springs, CO: U.S. Olympic Training Center.

Juhasz, J. B. (1972). On the reliability of two measures of imagery. *Perceptual and Motor Skills, 35,* 874.

Kendall, G., Hrycaiko, D., Martin, G. L., & Kendall, T. (1990). The effects of an imagery rehearsal, relaxation, and self talk package on basketball game performance. *Journal of Sport and Exercise Psychology, 12,* 157–166.

Kirchenbaum, D. S., & Bale, R. M. (1980). Cognitive-behavioral skills in golf: Brain power golf. In R. Suinn (Ed.), *Psychology in sports: Methods and applications* (pp. 334–343). Minneapolis, MN: Burgess.

Kohl, R. M., & Roenker, D. L. (1983). Mechanism involvement during skill imagery. *Journal of Motor Behavior, 15,* 179–190.

Kolonay, B. J. (1977). *The effects of visuo-motor behavior rehearsal on athletic performance.* Unpublished master's thesis, City University of New York, Hunter College.

Kremer, P., Morris, T., & Allen, N. (1994). *Mental imagery and mental relaxation in sport psychology.* Unpublished manuscript, University of Melbourne.

Lane, J. F. (1978). *Four studies of visuo-motor behavior rehearsal.* Unpublished manuscript.

Lane, J. F. (1980). Improving athletic performance through visuo-motor behavior rehearsal. In R. Suinn (Ed.), *Psychology in sports: Methods and applications* (pp. 316–320). Minneapolis, MN: Burgess.

Lang, P. J. (1977). Imagery in therapy: An informational processing analysis of fear. *Behavior Therapy, 8,* 862–886.

Lang, P. J. (1979). A bio-informational theory of emotional imagery. *Psychophysiology, 16,* 495–512.

Lee, A. B., & Hewitt, J. (1987). Using visual imagery in a flotation tank to improve gymnastic performance and reduce physical symptoms. *International Journal of Sport Psychology, 18,* 223–230.

Lee, C. (1990). Psyching up for a muscular endurance task: Effects of image content on performance and mood state. *Journal of Sport and Exercise Psychology, 12,* 66–73.

Lilly, J. C. (1977). *The deep self.* New York: Simon & Schuster.

Machlus, S. D., & O'Brien, R. M. (1988, August). *Visuo-motor behavior rehearsal and preparatory arousal in improving athletic speed.* Paper presented at the Annual Meeting of the American Psychological Association, Atlanta, GA.

Mahoney, M. J. (1979). Cognitive skills and athletic performance. In P. C. Kendall & S. D. Hollon (Eds.), *Cognitive-behavioral interventions: Theory, research, and procedure* (pp. 423–443). New York: Academic Press.

Mahoney, M. J., & Avener, M. (1977). Psychology of the elite athlete: An exploratory study. *Cognitive Therapy and Research, 3,* 361–366.

Marks, D. F. (1973). Visual imagery differences in recall of pictures. *British Journal of Psychology, 64,* 17–24.

Marks, D. F. (1989). Bibliography of research utilising the vividness of visual imagery questionnaire. *Perceptual and Motor Skills, 69,* 707–718.

Martens, R. (1975). The paradigmatic crisis in American sport personology. *Sportwissenschaft, 1,* 9–24.

Martens, R. (1982, September). *Imagery in sport.* Paper presented at the Medical and Scientific Aspects of Elitism in Sport Conference, Brisbane, Australia.

Martens, R., Vealey, R. S., & Burton, D. (Eds.). (1990). *Competitive anxiety in sport.* Champaign, IL: Human Kinetics.

McAleney, P. J., Barabasz, A., & Barabasz, M. (1990). Effects of flotation restricted environmental stimulation on intercollegiate tennis performance. *Perceptual and Motor Skills, 71,* 1023–1028.

McAuley, E. (1985). Modeling and self-efficacy: A test of Bandura's model. *Journal of Sport Psychology, 7,* 283–295.

McBride, E. R., & Rothstein, A. L. (1979). Mental and physical practice and the learning and retention of open and closed skills. *Perceptual and Motor Skills, 49*(2), 359–365.

McKelvie, S. J. (1990). The vividness of visual imagery questionnaire: Commentary on the Marks–Chara debate. *Perceptual and Motor Skills, 70*, 551–560.

McKelvie, S. J., & Gingras, P. P. (1974). Reliability of two measures of visual imagery. *Perceptual and Motor Skills, 39*, 417–418.

Mendoza, D., & Wichman, H. (1978). Inner darts: Effects of mental practice on performance of dart throwing. *Perceptual and Motor Skills, 47*(3), 1195–1199.

Minas, S. C. (1980). Mental practice of a complex perceptual-motor skill. *Journal of Human Movement Studies, 4*, 102–107.

Moran, A. (1991, September). *Measuring the mental imagery skills of athletes: A psychometric evaluation of available tests.* Paper presented at VIII European Congress of Sport Psychology, Deutsche Sporthochschule Köln, Köln, Germany.

Moran, A. (1993). Conceptual and methodological issues in the measurement of mental imagery skills in athletes. *Journal of Sport Behavior, 16*, 156–170.

Morris, T. (1991, October). *Single-case designs to study treatment effects in sport psychology.* Paper presented at the Annual Conference of the Australian Sports Medicine Federation, Canberra, Australia.

Morrisett, L. N. (1956). *The role of implicit practice in learning.* Unpublished doctoral dissertation, Yale University, New Haven, CT.

Mumford, P., & Hall, C. (1985). The effects of internal and external imagery on performing figures of figure skating. *Canadian Journal of Applied Sport Sciences, 10*, 171–177.

Murphy, S. M. (1985). *Emotional imagery and its effects on strength and fine motor skill performance.* Unpublished doctoral dissertation, Rutgers University, NJ.

Murphy, S. M., & Jowdy, D. P. (1992). Imagery and mental practice. In T. S. Horn (Ed.), *Advances in sport psychology* (pp. 221–250). Champaign, IL: Human Kinetics.

Murphy, S. M., Woolfolk, R. L., & Budney, A. J. (1988). The effects of emotive imagery on strength performance. *Journal of Sport and Exercise Psychology, 10*, 334–345.

Nicklaus, J. (1974). *Golf my way.* New York: Simon & Schuster.

Noel, R. C. (1980). The effect of visuo-motor behavior rehearsal on tennis performance. *Journal of Sport Psychology, 2*, 220–226.

Orlick, T. (1980). *In pursuit of excellence* (1st ed.). Champaign, IL: Human Kinetics.

Oxendine, J. B. (1969). Effect of mental and physical practice on the learning of three motor skills. *Research Quarterly, 40*, 755–763.

Paivio, A. (1971). *Imagery and verbal processes.* New York: Holt, Rinehart & Winston.

Paivio, A. (1985). Cognitive and motivational functions of imagery in human performance. *Canadian Journal of Applied Sport Sciences, 10*, 22–28.

Phipps, S. J., & Morehouse, C. A. (1969). Effect of mental practice on the acquisition of motor skills of varied difficulty. *Research Quarterly, 40*, 773–778.

Ravizza, K. (1977). Peak experiences in sport. *Journal of Humanistic Psychology, 17*, 35–40.

Rawlings, E. I., Rawlings, I. L., Chen, S. S., & Yilk, M. D. (1972). The facilitating effects of mental rehearsal in the acquisition of rotary pursuit tracking. *Psychonomic Science, 26*, 71–73.

Richardson, A. (1969). *Mental imagery.* New York: Springer.

Ryan, E. D., & Simons, J. (1981). Cognitive demand imagery and frequency of mental practice as factors influencing the acquisition of mental skills. *Journal of Sport Psychology, 4*, 35–45.

Ryan, E. D., & Simons, J. (1983). What is learned in mental practice of motor skills: A test of the cognitive motor hypothesis. *Journal of Sport Psychology*, *5*, 419–426.

Sackett, R. S. (1934). The influences of symbolic rehearsal upon the retention of a maze habit. *Journal of General Psychology*, *10*, 376–395.

Sackett, R. S. (1935). The relationship between amount of symbolic rehearsal and retention of a maze habit. *Journal of General Psychology*, *13*, 113–128.

Schleser, R., Meyers, A. W., & Montgomery, T. (1980, November). *A cognitive behavioral intervention for improving basketball performance.* Paper presented at the Association for the Advancement of Behavior Therapy 18th Annual Convention, New York.

Schmidt, R. A. (1982). *Motor control and learning: A behavioral emphasis.* Champaign, IL: Human Kinetics.

Schramm, V. (1967). *An investigation of the electromyographic responses obtained during mental practice.* Unpublished master's thesis, University of Wisconsin–Madison, WI.

Shaw, W. A. (1938). The distribution of muscular action-potentials during imaging. *Psychological Record*, *2*, 195–216.

Shaw, W. A. (1940). The relation of muscular action potentials to imaginal weight lifting. *Archives of Psychology*, *247*, 50.

Sheehan, P. (1967). A shortened form of Betts' Questionnaire Upon Mental Imagery. *Journal of Clinical Psychology*, *23*, 386–389.

Shepard, R. N., & Metzler, J. (1971). Mental rotation of three-dimensional objects. *Science*, *171*, 701–703.

Start, K. B. (1962). The influence of subjectively assessed "games ability" on gain in motor performance after mental practice. *Journal of General Psychology*, *67*, 159–173.

Start, K. B., & Richardson, A. (1964). Imagery and mental practice. *British Journal of Education Psychology*, *34*, 280–284.

Stebbins, R. J. (1968). A comparison of the effects of physical and mental practice in learning a motor skill. *Research Quarterly*, *39*, 728–734.

Suedfeld, P., & Bruno, T. (1990). Flotation REST and imagery in the improvement of athletic performance. *Journal of Sport and Exercise Psychology*, *12*, 82–85.

Suedfeld, P., Collier, D., & Hartnett, B. (1993). Enhancing perceptual-motor accuracy through flotation REST. *The Sport Psychologist*, *7*, 151–159.

Suinn, R. M. (1976). Visual motor behavior rehearsal for adaptive behavior. In J. Krumboltz & C. Thoresen (Eds.), *Counseling methods.* New York: Holt, Rinehart & Winston.

Suinn, R. M. (1980). Psychology and sports performance: Principles and applications. In R. Suinn (Ed.), *Psychology in sports: Methods and applications* (pp. 26–36). Minneapolis: Burgess.

Suinn, R. M. (1983). Imagery and sports. In A. Sheikh (Ed.), *Imagery: Current theory, research and application* (pp. 507–534). New York: John Wiley & Sons.

Suinn, R. M. (1984a). Visual motor behavior rehearsal: The basic technique. *Scandinavian Journal of Behavior Therapy*, *13*, 131–142.

Suinn, R. M. (1984b). Imagery and sports. In W. F. Straub & J. M. Williams (Eds.), *Cognitive sport psychology* (pp. 253–271). New York: Sport Science Associates.

Suinn, R. M. (1993). Imagery. In R. N. Singer, M. Murphey, & L. K. Tennant (Eds.), *Handbook of research on sport psychology* (pp. 492–510). New York: Macmillan.

Twining, W. E. (1949). Mental practice and physical practice in learning a motor skill. *Research Quarterly, 20,* 432–435.

Vandell, R. A., Davis, R. A., & Clugston, H. A. (1943). The function of mental practice in the acquisition of motor skills. *Journal of General Psychology, 29,* 243–250.

Vandenberg, S., & Kuse, A. R. (1978). Mental rotations: A group of three dimensional spatial visualisation. *Perceptual and Motor Skills, 47,* 599–604.

Vealey, R. E. (1986). Imagery training for performance enhancement. In J. M. Williams (Ed.), *Applied sport psychology: Personal growth to peak performance* (1st ed.) (pp. 209–231). Mountain View, CA: Mayfield.

Vealey, R. E., & Walter, S. M. (1993). Imagery training for performance enhancement and personal development. In J. M. Williams (Ed.), *Applied sport psychology: Personal growth to peak performance* (2nd ed.) (pp. 200–224). Mountain View, CA: Mayfield.

Wagaman, J. D., Barabasz, A. F., & Barabasz, M. (1991). Flotation REST and imagery in the improvement of collegiate basketball performance. *Perceptual and Motor Skills, 79,* 119–122.

Weinberg, R., Seabourne, T., & Jackson, A. (1981). Effects of visuo-motor behavior rehearsal, relaxation and imagery on karate performance. *Journal of Sport Psychology, 3,* 228–238.

Weinberg, R., Seabourne, T., & Jackson, A. (1987). Arousal and relaxation instructions prior to the use of imagery. *International Journal of Sport Psychology, 18,* 205–214.

White, K. D., Ashton, R., & Lewis, S. (1979). Learning a complex skill: Effects of mental practice, physical practice, and imagery ability. *International Journal of Sport Psychology, 10*(2), 71–78.

Whitely, G. (1962). *The effect of mental rehearsal on the acquisition of motor skill.* Unpublished doctoral dissertation, University of Manchester.

Wichman, H., & Lizotte, P. (1983). Effects of mental practice and locus of control on performance of dart throwing. *Perceptual and Motor Skills, 56*(3), 807–812.

Wolpe, J. (1958). *Psychotherapy by reciprocal inhibition.* Stanford, CA: Stanford University Press.

Woolfolk, R. L., Parrish, W., & Murphy, S. M. (1985). The effects of positive and negative imagery on motor skill performance. *Cognitive Therapy and Research, 9,* 335–341.

Wrisberg, C. A., & Anshel, M. H. (1989). The effect of cognitive strategies on the free throw shooting performance of young athletes. *The Sport Psychologist, 3,* 95–104.

Wrisberg, C. A., & Ragsdale, M. R. (1979). Cognitive demand and practice level: Factors in the mental rehearsal of motor skills. *Journal of Human Movement Studies, 5,* 201–208.

Zaichkowsky, L. D. (1980). Single case experimental designs and sport psychology research. In C. H. Nadeau, W. R. Halliwell, K. M. Newell, & G. C. Roberts (Eds.), *Psychology of motor behavior and sport: 1979* (pp. 171–179). Champaign, IL: Human Kinetics.

C H A P T E R

15

CONCENTRATION SKILLS IN SPORT: AN APPLIED PERSPECTIVE

JEFFREY BOND • GREGORY SARGENT

I could concentrate for long periods... if I could concentrate and play each ball the best way I could... I would score... the concentrating player plays each ball on its merits... I often hit good scores when Australia was in trouble... because I could concentrate...

Greg Chappell, Australian cricketer (*Writer*, 1990, p. 126)

Chapter 3 overviewed several theoretical aspects of attention in sport. The chapter included an examination of a number of issues resulting from a variety of research and theoretical approaches which have enhanced our understanding of the concept of attention or concentration in sport. The chapter examined the theoretical models and the research which has been conducted, and proposed that attention was comprised of a number of complementary dimensions by examining:

- the distinction between controlled and automatic processing of information
- the direction of attentional focus
- the width of attention or breadth of attended cues
- the intensity of attention
- the flexibility of attentional shifting.

Chapter 3 provided a number of definitions for the term "attention" and although the definitions reinforce the difficulties in understanding the concept, the present chapter focuses on an operational definition which most athletes, coaches and applied sport psychologists can relate to.

This chapter examines the area of attention in sport from an applied perspective. We acknowledge the importance of attention or concentration in sporting performances, both in training and competition. Coaches and athletes use the terms interchangeably and on a frequent basis. We hear about "lapses" in concentration, about the need to "concentrate harder" and so on. Most of us also believe that we generally concentrate far less than 100%, and that is true of elite athletes too. Our brains have an amazing capacity for the processing of information. The number of cues we focus on, the speed with which our focus can change and the number of irrelevant things we focus on seems almost limitless.

The essential interest in this chapter will be in discussing concentration as a skill which can be operationally defined relative to a specific sporting context, measured relative to individual differences in style, and then effectively changed.

In the first section of this chapter, we discuss the importance of concentration from the athlete's performance perspective and briefly review two studies which have looked at the components of peak sporting performances. We also describe several case studies which illustrate the central importance which concentration holds in high quality sporting performances.

The second section of this chapter examines an applied model of concentration which has demonstrated utility for the practising applied sport psychologist. We examine Nideffer's (1976a, 1993a, 1993b) approach to attention via his emphasis on the theoretical constructs underpinning his model and their application to high performance sport. The Nideffer attentional model has had immense impact on applied sport psychology around the world in terms of the general structure of attention, the concept of attentional style and the types of exercises which can be used to develop concentration.

The third section investigates Nideffer's (1976a) Test of Attentional and Interpersonal Style (TAIS). We look very briefly at the psychometric properties, but more importantly, examine the TAIS as a means of measuring attentional style, explaining some of the attentional factors which may be influencing a specific aspect of performance, and as a diagnostic tool for the development of attentional training exercises.

In the fourth section of this chapter we describe a number of useful concentration exercises that have been introduced to elite athletes in a variety of sports. We have attempted to illustrate a number of different ways in which athletes can be assisted in enhancing their attentional control skills. These drills and techniques are readily adaptable to a wide variety of sports and can be used by the athlete, coach or applied sport psychologist.

In the final section, future approaches to the area of concentration in applied sport psychology will be examined. This section looks at a number of possible developments in training exercises given proposed developments in computer and other applied technologies.

THE IMPORTANCE OF FOCUSING ON THE RIGHT THING AT THE RIGHT TIME

It is perhaps paradoxical that our performances on virtually all tasks depend so much on attentional capacities (to be focused on the right thing at the right time) and yet the efficient application of these very capacities is so volatile and at times fragile. It takes only the slightest distraction at times to bring a performance down from exceptional to substandard. The following three case studies clearly illustrate the central importance of concentration skills in high performance situations.

CASE STUDIES

CASE STUDY 1

An Olympic weightlifter competing in a major international competition missed out on a gold medal and personal best performance because a train rattled past the rear of the stadium as he prepared for his third and final clean and jerk. Examination of the weightlifter's attentional style assisted the athlete in understanding what had happened and helped the athlete and coach to design training exercises to prevent a recurrence in future competitions.

CASE STUDY 2

Top tennis professionals often lose matches worth millions of dollars because they inadvertently shift their focus from the return they are about to hit to the consequences of losing the point. Those who watched the 1993 women's Wimbledon final witnessed a classic psychological "choke" situation. The question is: Did Jana Novotna lose the final from what appeared to be a commanding position because she lacked the requisite technical and physical skills, or was it a clear case of an ineffective attentional focus? One can imagine the high levels of stress in that situation which may have led Novotna to shift her focus inwards to a point where she became overly analytical and unable to read and react to what was occurring on the court. The negative spiral initiated by the loss of a crucial point seemed to proceed unabated until the match ended with Novotna barely able to hit a ball over the net and into the court. It seems that all the technical and physical skills in the world cannot make up for the inefficient application of concentration, certainly not in high performance situations.

CASE STUDY 3

Kieren Perkins is a very well known and popular Olympic gold medallist and world record holder in the 1500 metres freestyle event. He is certainly one athlete who has consistently demonstrated an exceptionally high level of technical and physical skill. At the 1992 Barcelona Olympics he was the clear favourite for a gold medal and the object of a great deal of media and public attention. When asked how he coped with the potential distractions of the high stress Olympic environment he replied that when he was under such stress he always remembered what his coach had told him in their pre-race discussion and refocused onto his race plan and the task confronting him at that specific time. In this way he was able to block out the distractions, keep his focus on task and allow the countless hours of technical and physical training to come through.

We could have described many different examples of attentional factors affecting the outcome quality in elite sport situations. The above examples illustrate a need for athletes and coaches to enhance their understanding of the applied aspects of concentration or attention. They reinforce the need for these mental skills to be practised and developed by athletes in their quest for excellence. They also emphasise the central nature of attention in the production of superior quality athletic performances.

Whilst several practitioners have previously stressed the importance of attention as a vital aspect in performance (e.g., Boutcher, 1990, 1992; Nideffer, 1976b), much of the discussion has centred on theoretical and research notions. Whereas there is a need for this emphasis to continue to develop, there is a very strong case which argues for an applied approach which will produce useful outcomes for athletes and coaches.

This chapter presents information which has accumulated over many years of applied sport psychology experience with elite athletes across a variety of closed and open skill sports, from male and female sports, and from individual and team sports. We cannot hope to address all of the theoretical and research concepts discussed in Chapter 3, but we will attempt to present our experience with the issues which have an intuitive and experiential worth to the athlete and coach. We trust that this may assist in bridging the much-maligned gap between theory/research and applied practice.

The two terms "concentration" and "attention" are so often inter-changed with each other in the language of athletes and coaches that for the purposes of this chapter, we will refer to them as the same concept. Concentration is very often linked with exceptional athletic performances and there are many anecdotal examples which appear in post-performance interviews. There have been a number of attempts to investigate aspects of peak performance via qualitative methods.

Garfield and Bennett (1984) investigated the components of exceptional performances and suggested eight physical and mental capacities that elite athletes describe as associated with those moments when they perform extraordinarily well. Of these eight, three were particularly associated with high levels of concentration.

Firstly, athletes described themselves as mentally relaxed. This was explained as an inner calm, a sense of control and a high degree of concentration. Secondly, there was a sense of being focused in the present with a feeling of "harmony between the mental and physical". Athletes were absorbed in the present with no thoughts or feelings about the past or future. Thirdly, Garfield and Bennett reported that athletes were in a state of extraordinary awareness, being acutely aware of their bodies and of all around them. They suggested that this state was also described as one of heightened responsiveness with actions being effortless and automatic.

The importance of concentration and attention is further underlined in Garfield and Bennett's peak performance "compass" where the optimal attentional focus is a major contributor along with feelings of energy (see the work of Morgan (1980) for more information on emotion and performance).

Orlick and Partington (1988) conducted a more scientific analysis of the elements which make up success and mental readiness, using the 1984 Canadian Olympic squad. Again, the importance of concentration was reinforced with athletes stressing that it was "not until focusing skills were refined that their dreams became reality" (p. 119). Furthermore, concentration as an important variable was mentioned in the areas of:

1. *Quality training*: "When I'm training, I'm focused... By focusing all the time on what you're doing when you're training, focusing in a race becomes a by-product... Knowing how to focus gives you that little extra push..." "I'm concentrating, and I make a good run... You have to be continually aware." (p. 111)

2. *Mental preparation for competition*: "Most pre-competition plans included ... reminders to focus on what had previously worked well... All I had to think about was doing it, and doing the best we could... I was going to be good, I was feeling strong... all positive, trying to feel like I wanted to feel... I concentrated on that a lot." (p. 115)

3. *Competition focus plan*: The best athletes had time to discover what kind of focus worked for them in competition, the best focus being where the athlete connected with what he or she had to do without dwelling on factors over which he or she had no direct control. "My focus was very concentrated throughout the race. We have a short plan, and in it I concentrate only on the first few strokes. I've found that if I concentrate beyond that, those first strokes won't be strong enough. Then I concentrate on the next little bit of the race." (p. 116)

4. *Competition evaluation*: "If the performance was off,... I tried to assess why, paying particular attention to my mental state or focus before and during competition." (p. 116)

5. *Distraction control*: Athletes who performed at the highest level consistently were reported to have excellent strategies for getting back on track quickly when things didn't go well, or when faced with distractions. "I knew that I dove better if I concentrated on my diving instead of concentrating on everyone else... I decided to stop looking at everyone else, just be myself and focus on preparing for my next dive... At the Olympics I really focused on my diving instead of on other divers... I am focused on where I am at the time...." (pp. 117–118)

We know from the research, from reports from athletes and coaches and also intuitively and experientially that concentration on the right thing at the right time is a crucial component of a highly skilled sporting performance. Summers and Ford, in closing Chapter 3, state: "In ending the chapter we are forced to conclude that while everyone may think they know what attention is, no one really knows what it is."

From the applied sport psychologist's perspective and in the interests of performance enhancement, it is essential that we attempt to find something useful and capable of application from amongst the sometimes confusing theoretical and research literature. One critical issue for practitioners is the existence of a useful model of attention which can be applied in sporting situations, which can be readily understood and accepted by athletes and coaches, and which will lead to an enhanced understanding, prediction and control over attentional capacities in high performance situations.

THE NIDEFFER ATTENTION MODEL

Nideffer's background in competitive diving and martial arts led him to the development of a model of attention and a theory of attentional and interpersonal style which he proposed would aid in the understanding, prediction and control of behaviour (Nideffer, 1976a).

The Nideffer model of attention (Nideffer, 1981) is based on the existence of two dimensions of concentration: direction and width. It is proposed that we can direct our attention in one of two ways in order to attend to relevant performance cues. We can focus our attention on cues which are external to us (e.g., a target, ball, team mate or opponent) or we can focus on internal cues (e.g., thoughts, images, feelings, kinaesthetic sensations). In Chapter 3 it was suggested that this dimension of direction was not a continuum, as one's effective attentional focus could really be either external or internal, not somewhere between. Nideffer (1981) states that we can choose to attend to a large number of cues or a small number and that this dimension probably extends along a continuum. This provides us with a possible four types of attention (see Figure 15.1 below). It must be remembered that Nideffer's model is not simply a model of visual attention, even though a good deal of attention in some sports is predominantly visual. Attention involves the use of each of the human senses of sight, sound, feel, taste and smell.

EXTERNAL

Broad–External	**Narrow–External**
• Peripheral awareness	• Focused targeting
• Ability to read and react to the environment	• Ability to block out distractions and remain focused on specific ones
• Good at scanning, picking the open team mate	• Will stick at a task for long periods
• A requirement in open skill team sports	• Typical attentional focus for target sport athletes

BROAD ——————————————————————— **NARROW**

Broad–Internal	**Narrow–internal**
• Analysis, problem solving and creative thinking, planning	• Ability to focus on a single thought or idea and stay with it
• The strategists and "thinkers" in sport	• Enhanced kinaesthetic (body) awareness
• Good at competition planning, developing an alternative plan of attack, debriefing	• Often an indication of dedication and capacity to follow instructions, to stick to a game plan

INTERNAL

Figure 15.1: The Nideffer (1981) model of attention

An athlete who adopts a *broad–external* focus of attention in response to the demands of a performance situation will be attending to a large number of cues relating to the external environment. There are some sports (e.g., team and open skill sports) where one would intuitively expect such an attentional focus to be required for a significant part, but not exclusively for all of the time. In team sports involving fast ball activities, such as the various football codes, basketball, netball, field and ice hockey, one major attentional requirement is commonly referred to as "field or peripheral awareness". This type of awareness is not exclusively the realm of open skill sports, as there are readily identifiable times in static, target sports where the ability to read and react to the environment is essential for high level performance. When we observe that an athlete has above-average ability to be aware of what is occurring around him or her (where team mates are, where the ball is, where the opponents are), we are referring to what Nideffer (1981) calls a broad–external focus of attention. These athletes quickly read a situation, can find the best passing option and rarely get hit in contact sports. They seem to have an extra sense that makes them special athletes.

When an athlete adopts a *broad–internal* focus of attention in response to the demands of the performance, he or she is shifting the focus of concentration to internal thoughts, feelings, images and self-talk. There are many situations prior to, during and after a sporting performance where it is necessary for the athlete to take up a broad–internal focus. This would typically involve planning, problem-solving, reminding oneself of specific coaching instructions, imagining or visualising aspects of the performance, and debriefing after a performance. In short, Nideffer (1981) was referring to an analytical, thinking type of concentration. Most of us can probably identify an athlete we know who is a master strategist, a great problem-solver and extremely analytical. This same athlete was probably very good at planning and writing creative essays in school. These athletes are the thinkers in sport and perform exceptionally well in those areas of their sport which demand a high capacity for analysis and creativity.

Some sports demand that athletes adopt a *narrow–external* focus of attention at specific times. Target sports like archery and shooting require a good deal of narrowing in order to be successful. Even open skill team sports have clearly identifiable times when the athlete must narrow down and block out distractions in order to be successful (e.g., when shooting for goal, passing the ball). Athletes who have exceptional capacity to focus in a narrow–external way are very good at keeping the blinkers on, remaining focused amidst distractions and at targeting for extended periods of time. These athletes will often be oblivious to spectator noise and movements around them.

Nideffer's (1981) *narrow–internal* focus of attention is required on those occasions when an athlete must remember a single coaching point (e.g., "keep in front!"), must focus on a specific kinaesthetic feeling, or flash up an immediate image of part of the action. This type of attention is internal in that it involves an instant of thought, feeling, self-talk or image, and narrow because it is focused on very few attentional cues.

Nideffer (1981) draws attention to the relationship between attentional efficiency and level of arousal (see Chapters 2 and 3). Under conditions of ideal arousal (physiological and psychological), Nideffer postulates that an athlete will effectively match the attentional demands of the performance situation with an appropriate focus of attention. In these situations the athlete's attentional style may not have a major impact on the performance. When arousal levels are too low, the athlete typically experiences a lack of intensity or motivation and wandering or irrelevant thoughts, resulting in reduced levels of performance (the lazy and/or loose mistakes).

Too-high levels of arousal result in errors often brought about by focusing on the wrong cues or in an inappropriate way for the demands of the situation. Under conditions of critical or life-threatening stress, Nideffer (1981) predicts a tendency for the individual to involuntarily adopt a narrow–internal attentional focus which may contribute to errors because the athlete is not attending or reacting to the environment (see the cue utilisation theory proposed by Easterbrook, 1959).

Presumably, an athlete who has achieved an ideal arousal level is able to very quickly shift attention to match the rapidly changing demands of the performance situation without the need for conscious thought. This is confirmed in the reports of athletes who have experienced peak performances and describe being in an almost trance like state where there was little conscious thought. Intuitively, it would seem that prior experience in identical situations, a thorough knowledge of and control over the skill requirements, superior levels of physical conditioning and an appropriate level of achievement motivation might combine with an ideal arousal level and effective matching of the attentional demands to provide the antecedents for optimal performance.

ATTENTIONAL ERRORS

Nideffer (1976b, 1981, 1977) and Nideffer and Pratt (1981) suggest that athletes can make the following kinds of attentional errors.

Attentional mismatch

Nideffer (1976b, 1981) proposes that individuals possess a unique attentional style characterised by specific strengths and weaknesses in the various areas of attention. An individual's developmental background, including long-term involvement in specific activities requiring specific types of attentional focus, and specific personality traits may contribute to the development of a unique attentional style. This suggestion by Nideffer is in accord with those theorists who have developed trait personality theories (e.g., Cattell, 1957).

Because an athlete may have a dominant attentional style, for example, by a high level broad–external focus, it is feasible that under stressful conditions the athlete might subconsciously return to that style of attention in circumstances which require a different, more appropriate attentional focus. This involuntary return to an existing attentional strength may occur because the athlete has successfully used his or her attentional strength to advantage in previous high stress situations. The broad–external athlete may mismatch the attentional demands of the performance situation and become too influenced by the surrounding environment. Behaviourally, a coach would observe an athlete who was very distractible under stress. How often do we see a professional tennis player during a critical point in a major tournament, interrupt a service action because someone has moved in the back corner of the spectator area (nowhere near the line of sight for the serve)?

The broad–internal athlete is likely to mismatch the attentional requirements of a performance because he or she is focused on a range of internal cues at a time when other cues, perhaps external or more narrow, are more important. Under high stress conditions, this athlete will become very analytical and therefore slow to react to external cues. This athlete may not "read" the passing options or may overlook an appropriate cue. Some years ago, an AFL footballer who was within kicking distance and running towards goal during a particularly intense and important part of the game, was knocked unconscious by an opponent in a fair tackle on open ground. The 100 000 spectators in the stands could see the tackle coming, but the player was presumably reminding himself of the importance of this potentially match-winning goal (and perhaps on the consequences of a missed kick at goal). The player was unable to focus in a manner which would have detected the opponent running full speed, straight at him from a shallow angle. This was a clear example of an attentional mismatch which may have been related to the inappropriate return to an attentional strength (broad–internal) under pressure.

The athlete whose attentional style is characterised by a strength in either of the narrowing areas is likely to use that type of focus under high stress conditions and make mistakes because he or she misses important information by being too narrow, or by focusing narrowly on the wrong cue. During the 1988 Calgary Winter Olympics the team sport psychologist was discreetly approached by an alpine skier immediately prior to a race with a request to assist in blocking out a real fear of injury/accident. It was apparent that the skier had inappropriately narrowed onto a cue which was likely to increase the likelihood of a fall. The intensity of that particular cue was so strong that the athlete was unable to clear his mind and focus on more positive aspects of his performance. Another example would be an athlete who finds it impossible to shift his or her focus off an existing injury while performing.

Inability to adopt or maintain appropriate attentional focus

This inability may occur because the athlete has not sufficiently developed a particular type of attentional focus. For example, an athlete who has below average capacity to effectively narrow attention (perhaps the individual has a developmental background which enhanced other attentional capacities) may find it difficult to produce a narrow attentional focus when it is required during a performance. This type of athlete will very likely make a mistake because he or she is unable to narrow appropriately onto the cues important for the successful performance of a specific skill. Many athletes have trained for long periods of time in order to improve their ability to narrow onto appropriate cues. Coaches can of course be essential in assisting the athlete to identify the appropriate cue and then in designing specific drills to enhance the athlete's capacity in this type of attentional focus.

Internal and external overloads

In high stress situations, athletes can produce errors because their attentional capacity is exceeded by the overwhelming nature of the stimuli. Internal overloads occur because the athlete simply has too much internal information or noise clogging up the attentional system. There are too many coaching points, too many "what ifs" or too much self-talk. Examples of internal overload are common in sporting situations where the stakes are very high, where the consequences of failure are extremely significant or aversive or where the athlete feels externally controlled and dominated by a need to please others. External overloads occur under stressful circumstances where the athlete is bombarded with too much external information. This typically occurs in major competitions where large numbers of athletes compete, large crowds are watching and a significant media presence is obvious. Olympic Games are a trap for the uninitiated and inexperienced young athlete who is not used to such a wealth of potentially distracting information.

Involuntary internal narrowing

Under critical stress conditions, Nideffer (1976b, 1981) predicts that athletes will ultimately focus inwards in a very narrow way and make major mistakes because they are basically "paralysed" by the situational stresses. Athletes who find themselves in life-threatening situations, such as Greg Louganis's skull-splitting reverse two-and-a-half dive at the Olympics (which he had to follow up with another dive later in the competition program), often experience an involuntary narrowing which may be part of a final stage protective survival mechanism. In life-threatening "fire in the theatre" situations, people have sometimes been killed because they narrowed so much that they did not even contemplate an alternative and available exit.

In applied sport psychology settings we use the Nideffer attentional model (Bond, 1984) to enhance athletes' understanding of the nature of concentration and how it might explain what happens in sporting situations. There have been numerous occasions over the past decade or so, where our work with elite athletes has been enhanced by the use of the Nideffer model. It makes intuitive sense to coaches and athletes. They can relate the model directly to situations in their sporting experience, and the model provides a useful perspective for the post-performance analysis of the factors that may have influenced a performance outcome. For some athletes a clear and applied description of the Nideffer model is sufficient for them to develop their own self-help attentional strategies.

An example of the latter outcome involved a volleyball player who had sought assistance with a problem she was having with her spiking in games. She could spike well in practice, but under the stress of a competitive game she hit most of her spikes into the waiting arms/hands of the opposition blockers. Initially, this recurring error was analysed as an in-adequacy with spiking technique. After a considerable amount of spiking practice there was little change in the percentage of spikes which came back via the opposition blockers. It seemed that the harder she tried the worse things became. It transpired that the player described herself as having an attentional style dominated by a narrow–external focus. Following a detailed description of the Nideffer model the player decided to adjust her attentional focus in spiking situations. She believed that she had been focusing on the ball too narrowly (a legacy of the traditional coaching instruction to "keep your eye on the ball") and could probably improve her awareness of the position of the opposition blockers if she looked at a point between the ball as it approached the hitting zone and the position of the blockers' hands as they jumped to block the impending spike. Because she also understood the importance of a controlled level of arousal during spiking, she practised taking a preliminary centring breath before starting her run in and being a little more relaxed in her upper body as she jumped for the spike. This, combined with the shift in visual focus, produced a significant improvement in her spiking statistics.

THE TEST OF ATTENTIONAL AND INTERPERSONAL STYLE

The Test of Attentional and Interpersonal Style (TAIS) was developed by Nideffer as a means of measuring a number of attentional and interpersonal characteristics which might have applicability in a range of situations including high performance sport (Nideffer, 1976a, 1976b). The instrument was designed to look at behaviourally relevant characteristics and is multidimensional, looking at cognitive styles (attentional processes) as well as interpersonal characteristics. Nideffer (1990) postulates that both attentional and interpersonal characteristics have state and trait components and that these can be examined by manipulating arousal.

The TAIS has been used extensively in Australian sport over a 15-year period as a means of identifying a number of individual elite athlete characteristics which are related to high performance sport. The TAIS has demonstrated internal consistency and good test–retest reliability (Nideffer, 1976a). Construct validity has been confirmed in a number of studies (Antonelli, Caldarone, & Gatti, 1982; DePalma & Nideffer, 1977;

Feifel, Strack, & Nagy, 1987; Salmela & Ndoye, 1986; Wiens, Harper, & Matarazzo, 1980; Whitney & Pratt, 1987). Support for the predictive validity of the TAIS has been found in studies by Bond and Nideffer (1992), Kirschenbaum and Bale (1980), Landers and Richards (1981), Nideffer (1987), Nideffer and Bond (1989), Reis and Bird (1982) and Zuckerman, Larrance, Hall, DeFrank, and Rosenthal (1979).

There have been a number of studies which have questioned the validity of the TAIS factor structure and its predictive utility (see Chapter 3) and argued for the development of more sport-specific versions of the test. Interest in the model underlying the attentional subscales of the TAIS has prompted the development of a number of sport-specific versions, including a tennis version (Van Schoyck & Grasha, 1981), a baseball and softball batting version (Albrecht & Feltz, 1987) and a basketball version (Vallerand, 1983). For a rebuttal to the studies which have criticised various aspects of the TAIS refer to Nideffer (1990).

Applied sport psychologists use the TAIS as a means of assisting athletes to understand their attentional style and as a diagnostic tool for helping to explain performance-related phenomena which are affecting the athlete and/or coach. On the basis of further consensual validation of the TAIS subscale scores (from coach reports, athlete interview, structured observations and performance statistics), attentional training strategies are designed with the coach and athlete.

Figure 15.2 (page 398) provides an example from the attentional subscale portion of a full TAIS completed by an elite athlete with a response set that included answering as honestly and accurately as possible, knowledge that there were no right or wrong answers, that the results would not be used for selection purposes and that the results would remain confidential and be returned directly to the athlete as a means of enhancing performance. Athletes should always be directed to relate the behavioural descriptions in the TAIS questionnaire to their own training and competition situations in such a way that the "average" athlete in their group would respond "sometimes" to most of the questions.

This athlete's attentional profile shows a clear strength in the capacity to use a broad–external focus of attention (high BET). This was confirmed by the athlete via a number of examples from training and competition situations. There was discussion about a prediction which arose from this attentional strength, that during times of increased arousal the athlete might subconsciously revert to the use of this type of focus at the expense of a concentration focus which would be more appropriate to high quality performance. Further discussion centred on learning to control arousal levels prior to entering that type of situation in competitions. Also, the athlete was encouraged to focus on identifying appropriate attentional cues appropriate for that specific situation. The coach was advised to develop a specific drill that required that the athlete adopt a specific type of focus (NAR) and to progressively increase the competitive intensity as a way of "testing" the athlete's ability to maintain the appropriate focus.

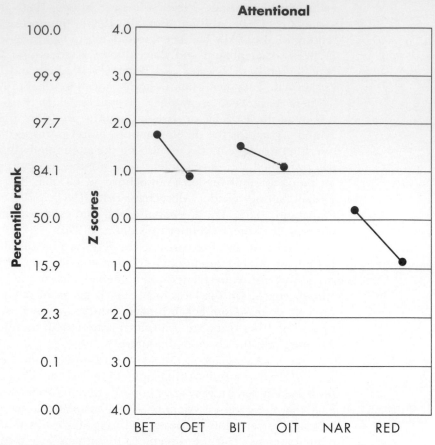

Note: For the purpose of discussion, only the six subscales from the complete TAIS are shown here – see below. A more complete TAIS diagnostic interpretation is obtained by using all of the 19 TAIS attentional and interpersonal subscales.

Attentional subscales – brief description

BET Broad External Focus – measures the ability to assess the environment, to read, react to and integrate multiple environmental cues at once.

OET Overloaded by External Stimuli – measures the tendency to become distracted and overloaded by too many environmental cues.

BIT Broad Internal Focus – measures the ability to analyse, plan, anticipate and to deal with multiple internal cues.

OIT Overloaded by Internal Stimuli – measures the tendency to make mistakes because of an overly analytical focus or thinking about too many things at once.

NAR Narrow Focus – measures the ability to narrow attention when required and to avoid distraction.

RED Reduced Attentional Focus – measures the tendency to make mistakes because of a failure to attend to all task relevant cues, a failure to shift from an external focus to an internal one, and vice versa.

Figure 15.2: Example of an effective attentional subscale portion of a TAIS for an elite athlete

Figure 15.3 shows an attentional style which demonstrates a tendency to experience external and internal overloads (high OET and OIT) under pressure and an inability to narrow attention (low NAR) when required. Following further validation of the examples which the athlete discussed during an individual TAIS feedback session, the athlete and sport psychologist discussed the need for improved arousal control strategies (centring breath), an investigation of some of the cognitive components contributing to the excessive anxiety the athlete typically experienced in this situation, and the identification of specific cues important in the efficient execution of the specific skill required. These strategies were further enhanced by the use of carefully structured imagery sessions and a transfer to training and low level competition situations.

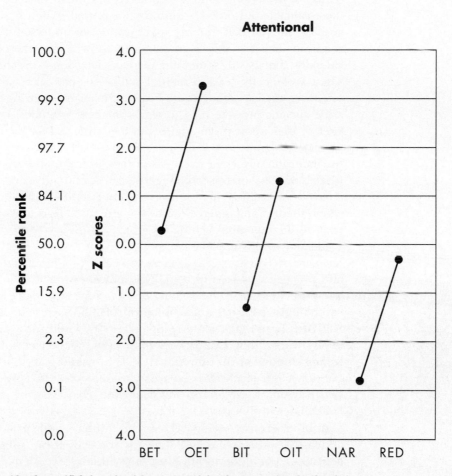

(*See figure 15.2 for a brief description of the above attentional subscales.*)

Figure 15.3: Example of overloaded attentional subscales on the TAIS for an elite athlete

SPECIFIC ATTENTIONAL TRAINING EXERCISES FOR ATHLETES

Within an applied chapter such as this one, we believe that a major emphasis should centre on appropriate exercises for the development of attentional skills. This section therefore deals with some of the exercises which have been described in the literature and some additional drills which we use on a regular basis with elite Australian athletes. Any list of training exercises can never be complete so we encourage readers to be creative in developing specific concentration exercises for inclusion within their own programs. This creativity is further required when preparing exercises which may have originally been developed for other sports and other circumstances.

Before presenting some of the exercises which have been found to be most valuable, a word of caution is warranted. When designing any program of mental skill training it is essential to understand that practice is required. This has long been an accepted principle when coaching physical skills, but is still somewhat neglected by some coaches and athletes when seeking to develop mental skills. An important antecedent of an effective practice regime could involve the coach ensuring that athletes set aside specific practice time to work on these exercises, before reporting back to their sport psychologist with feedback and for further fine-tuning. Of critical significance is the coach's support for this type of practice and the inclusion of specific exercises in regular training sessions where appropriate. Success in reinforcing athletes' continued work in the area of attentional training may well contribute significantly to the degree to which the training is perceived by the athlete to be a "normal" and regular part of the ongoing coaching program.

Related to this practice component is an assumption that athletes will have the necessary self-awareness to realise when concentration training and practice may be indicated. This awareness could result from the athlete's self-analysis, from coaching observations or those of an applied sport psychologist, or from a psychological profiling exercise (e.g., the TAIS). Athletes should take some responsibility by identifying the types of situations where they exhibit less than effective concentration, as well as testing out any of the attentional skills in training and ultimately in competition. The coach and sport psychologist can also give good feedback (verbally or via the use of video) of their own assessment of an athlete's capabilities in this area.

Another consideration which the athlete and professional should address is when is the best time for some of these attentional training activities to be undertaken. Most elite athletes experience the frustration of being injured and unable to join in regular training, and this may be an excellent time to enhance an important performance building block. Coaches should also be encouraged to include attentional training into their ongoing training program. Within current coaching philosophies and terminology, the idea of "periodisation" is extremely popular (Bompa, 1983). This concept assists coaches in deciding when certain skills and activities should be performed in relation to the global training and competition program. A full discussion of this concept is beyond the scope of this chapter, however it is a practical concern which deserves consideration by those responsible for program planning. A close working relationship with the coach and an understanding of the sequence of the total training program is essential for the applied sport psychologist to be able to make effective decisions with the coach about where mental training should be placed relative to other areas of the total program.

Within applied sport psychology, practitioners are often interested in testing out how athletes cope with different situations and use many simulations and tasks to examine responses. In order for athletes to gain the most from these activities, however, they must be properly trained in the techniques. One of these techniques is the ability to be in control and to relax or elevate arousal where appropriate. The reader is referred to Chapters 2, 11 and 12 for a more in-depth examination of these issues.

The different concentration activities can be crudely divided into those activities which are traditionally set in a non-sport context, and those which are specifically related to the sporting environment. Within this section, both types will be examined.

NON-SPORT ACTIVITIES

For most of these concentration activities it is assumed that the athlete has adopted a comfortable and relaxed position. As such, the description will describe the more important concentration aspects of the exercises without including the relaxation component.

Passive thinking (Albinson & Bull, 1988)

This particular exercise evaluates how ideas tend to flow freely in and out of the conscious mind. Initially, athletes are required to practise one minute of "free flow" thought (letting all and any ideas just flow in and out, without holding onto any of them) followed by one minute of rest. Athletes can then examine what sort of thoughts they have difficulty letting go of when thoughts lead to further associations and distraction. This can be a difficult exercise as it seems to run counter to our daily lives which seem to consist of rationalisation and serious concentration. However, it is important for athletes to understand how their thought processes operate. This is especially true for those who get distracted easily or who find that thoughts seem to keep intruding into their task-relevant focus, for example, the player who continues to participate yet is still thinking about the last umpiring decision or error. The task may be difficult to begin with, so the period of free flow will be originally set as quite small. Over time, athletes should be able to work from the initial one minute to up to five minutes of free flow thinking and control practice. In order to increase task difficulty, athletes may like to practise with their eyes open or in different environments (e.g., at training, in their own room, in a crowded place). This also ensures that athletes can make the connection to the sport setting in which they may need the skill.

Watching the clock face (adapted from Albinson & Bull, 1988)

This is another activity that athletes have found valuable. It is useful in developing an athlete's ability to maintain focus on a particular object. The idea is to focus attention on a clock face and to watch the second hand sweep. At prescribed times, the athlete is required to blink or tap their fingers. This requirement may involve a simple sequence to begin with, such as every five seconds, with more difficult demands made later on. Different sequence patterns can be adopted, such as changing from every five seconds to every ten seconds then back to five. Athletes are instructed to examine how their thoughts moved in and out of their mind during the exercise, with special interest for the longer time intervals between blinks/taps, as these are when distractions are most likely to occur. Again, the difficulty of the task can be increased by attempting it while listening to music (progressing to more irritating types of music), or to a television program or even while someone is talking loudly.

Focusing and refocusing in the present

Some athletes develop specific and extensive routines to refocus during an event (see pages 409–410 for more on routines). Other athletes, according to Landers, Boutcher, and Wang (1986), are unable to refocus and are constantly performing below their optimal level because of this problem. The key to resolving this concern is to ensure that athletes focus on the "now" rather than on the past or the future, while at the same time being able to move from negative thinking to a more constructive, positive approach. Some approaches which have been proposed to train this type of concentrational style include:

- Single-thought focus: This requires focusing on one single idea for as long as possible.
- Video and computer games: These are especially helpful in training athletes to remain in the present as much as possible while also being valuable for helping them get their minds off stressful events. Elite swimmers, for example, have used various electronic games, reporting that the games enhance their concentration by the immediate feedback they provide when an error is made.
- The concentration grid exercise (adapted from Weinberg, 1988): The grid exercise is another technique used to evaluate and train focusing and refocusing. The grid is typically a box of ten rows and ten columns drawn up into cells. Each cell has a random two-digit number placed in it, ranging from 00 to 99. The athlete is required to mark in ascending numerical sequence as many numbers as possible in a given time (usually

one minute). Scores in the high 20s and 30s have been suggested as being indicative of good concentration skills (Burke, 1992). Variations of this task include changing the numbers in each of the cells, using different orders and sequences, using letters instead of numbers or even using specific sport pictures as targets within each cell. In order to increase the difficulty of the task once mastered, distractions may be introduced. For example, the use of background noises such as loud talking, television programs and direct questioning of the performer will place the athlete's attention under considerable pressure. This grid has been used to successfully demonstrate the effects of distractions by requiring athletes to perform within a distracting environment before/ after attempting the same task when distraction-free.

Soft eyes–hard eyes

When we focus intently onto a specific external cue it is possible to feel a tightening of the muscles around our eyes and a "hardening" of the eye itself (a tightening of the muscles and eyelid may produce a feeling of increased pressure within the eye or hardening). When we attempt to focus on peripheral cues it is possible for some individuals to feel their eyes become "soft" as they relax the muscles around their eyes. Athletes can be shown how to practise narrowing by making their eyes slightly harder and to broaden their visual focus by relaxing the muscles around their eyes and allowing their eyes to become soft.

A further simple technique we have developed involves the athlete holding one thumbnail up at arm's length (a thumbs-up position) and practising a narrow focus on to a specific mark or part of the thumbnail, then shifting to a broad–external focus to bring into focus the background detail of the surrounding, then back to the narrow focus and so on. Athletes can be encouraged to practise this attentional switching technique in a variety of general situations outside their sport.

Awareness exercise (adapted from Schmid & Peper, 1993)

After obtaining a relaxed state, athletes are instructed to listen to the environment (scanning), first identifying any sound (targeting), then listening without identification and finally letting all of these sounds just blend together. The same process is then followed when listening to bodily sensations and then with thoughts and feelings, finally identifying specific aspects of bodily functioning or single thoughts or feelings .

In another variation, athletes may introduce a specific implement related to their sport which should be placed in front of them. The athlete is then instructed to focus on specific features of the object, then switch to the use of peripheral vision to be aware of other details within the room. This zooming of concentration is an effective technique for developing the ability to switch from one focus of attention to another as the situational demands change.

Expanding awareness (adapted from Schmid & Peper, 1993)

This is an excellent exercise for ensuring athletes experience the different attentional styles as discussed earlier in this chapter. It was originally developed by Gauron (1984) and has been adapted successfully with a range of athletes. The advantage of this exercise is that it ensures that the athlete moves from a narrow to a broad focus while also demonstrating the difference between external and internal concentration. It is also beneficial in helping athletes determine which style of concentration they are most comfortable with and which style may cause them some difficulty.

The first step is to focus on breathing alternating between normal breathing and a deeper, slower breath. It is important to assume a relaxed state during this breathing exercise; Gauron even suggests the use of biofeedback monitoring equipment to gauge physiological relaxation. The second step involves attending to specific sounds which may be present, identifying and labelling each sound. Then the athlete is required to simultaneously listen to all the sounds blending together without any attempt made at identification. Alternating between a specific (narrow) and broad awareness is then repeated for the athlete's bodily experiences and then for emotions and thoughts. Within this thought phase, the athlete is instructed not to force any feeling or thought and to remain calm throughout. The goal is to empty one's mind of all thoughts and feelings. The final stage of this exercise requires athletes to fixate on an object whilst using peripheral vision to be aware of other features in the environment. The athlete is then asked to imagine a narrow funnel centring on the chosen object before gradually widening the funnel to take in everything in the room. This type of task is another example of the "zooming" activity which athletes have found to be most valuable.

Object cueing

As with many of the attention exercises, athletes are required to assume a relaxed position in an environment free of obvious or potential distractions. Athletes are then required to hold an object in front of them while repeating a meaningful cue word which relates to that object. A slight variation is actually ensuring that the object is sport-related and that the cue word is relevant to that sport and chosen object. The object can then be taken away and the athlete instructed to use the cue word to "return" the object to consciousness.

One technique for assisting athletes to deal with any extraneous thoughts that may enter their mind emphasises the need to retain a passive attitude then focus on an appropriate cue word which can be applied to the actual sporting situation. The use of specific cue words during actual performance is often reported by elite athletes and can be used for the blocking out of irrelevant thoughts and also when concentration is waning.

Using biofeedback equipment

Athletes can also be helped to gain further control over their concentration by using a number of biofeedback devices which are available. These instruments can be used to demonstrate a number of things such as how thoughts can affect the body, how relaxation is reflected physiologically and which components of imagery might appear to be stressful. These instruments reveal alterations in autonomic arousal which are reflected in skin conductance changes, or, alternatively, functions such as heart rate, muscle tension or temperature may be used as indicators. The feedback device typically shows this alteration through a change in pitch (increased pitch showing when conductivity and arousal increase and vice versa) or through changes in a lighting display or click frequency. As emphasised by Schmid and Peper (1993), athletes seem to respond differently on a physiological level so the instrument may be required to measure cardiovascular or muscular changes instead. When trained with these biofeedback instruments, athletes have reported enhanced concentration.

These devices can also be used to show how thoughts affect performance by demonstrating a corresponding physiological effect. Even asking athletes to think of a stressful situation may change the feedback from the instrument. This type of demonstration is valuable in helping athletes identify and stop disturbing thoughts and self-talk by creating a connection to altered psychophysiological states. The subsequent challenge is to alter this self-talk to something more positive.

Athletes have also used these instruments to give valuable feedback about their mental rehearsal. With the aid of the instrument during mental rehearsal, athletes are better able to identify stressful cues when the pitch changes. This may reflect some psychophysiological change (possibly muscle tightening or increased anxiety) during a particularly stressful movement sequence. After subsequent intervention, athletes are able to approach these sequences in a more controlled way during their mental rehearsal as well as in real practice or performance situations.

The stork stand

This particularly novel task requires the athlete to stand on one leg with both arms outstretched to the sides while eyes are closed. The task involves maintaining balance for as long as possible, the trial finishing when balance is lost. This can be attempted a number of times and is a good task for developing concentration. The exercise can be varied somewhat by first concentrating on cues (physical or kinaesthetic) which assist with balance. Athletes are then required to discuss the value of the cueing exercise and its usefulness in assisting with balance.

A very successful and experienced Olympic class yachtsman has related how he managed to draw his focus of attention into his boat immediately prior to the start of a yachting race. When he noticed that his focus had broadened too much or he was feeling too anxious through thinking about the consequences of a poor performance, he stood up in his boat with one foot on each side of the hull. Naturally, the boat initially behaved in a very unstable way and he was able to bring the boat to a stable state by centring and consciously relaxing/centring himself until he felt at one with the boat. This had proven to be a very effective technique primarily because the exercise forced him to focus on himself and the movement of the boat (blocking out external factors and thoughts). The settling effect of the centring breathing combined with the attentional shift to bring about the desired result.

Leadership activities

A particularly good concentration exercise which has been used frequently with athletes is an activity which combines leadership qualities with communication, trust and concentration. This activity requires all participants to be blindfolded except for one person, the leader (the leader can be someone who has a need to develop leadership type qualities or it may be a captain or somebody who has a certain leadership role in the team). All participants in the team are then required to link up by holding hands with the leader who takes up a position at the front of the group. The leader is then required to lead the rest of the group around some obstacle course (comprised of chairs, hurdles, trees, etc.), warning them about impending danger. It is imperative that the leader is clear about the type of information that he or she supplies to the rest of the group and that each team member concentrates to accurately comprehend this communication. This activity has been particularly well accepted by athletes as it results in a compensatory shift in attentional focus when the blindfold is in place. It seems that when vision is impaired, other senses must come into play in order for us to make sense of our surroundings.

Another version of the above activity requiring the components of concentration, communication and leadership involves the formation of groups of five people. In each group, three are blindfolded. One of those not blindfolded becomes the patient and is then required to be carried by the blindfolded trio. The other sighted person then becomes the guide for the patient and his blinded carriers. However, the guide cannot communicate directly, only the patient can whisper to the blindfolded carriers. This is again a good activity conducted through an obstacle course which ensures that the patient supplies clear and unambiguous messages to the carriers. The carriers must concentrate on these messages while at the same time ensuring that the patient remains safe.

The unbendable arm

Athletes are asked to pair up, with one athlete seated on a chair holding one arm out in front at shoulder height. The partner stands beside the seated athlete and is instructed to place one hand around the wrist of the seated athlete's outstretched arm and the other hand on top of the outstretched elbow. The task is for the standing athlete to bend the seated athlete's arm by pressing down on the elbow and pulling up on the wrist of the outstretched arm. The seated athlete is instructed to tense up the arm muscles to prevent the outstretched arm from being bent. It is normal for the standing athlete to fairly easily bend the outstretched arm, presumably because the seated athlete typically tenses up antagonistic muscles (such as biceps and triceps) in an attempt to brace the elbow. In doing so the seated athlete is in fact making it more difficult to maintain a straight arm as the biceps, for example, work against the natural action of the triceps in locking the elbow.

The second stage of this exercise is to instruct the seated athlete to only tense the triceps by pointing the outstretched arm towards the wall of the room or some other immovable object and to imagine that there is a steel beam stretching from the shoulder of the outstretched arm to the immovable object, making it impossible for the arm to be bent. If this instruction is followed to the letter, and preceded by one or two centring breaths, it will be extremely difficult for the standing athlete to bend the outstretched arm. We use this exercise to demonstrate the strength of an appropriate attentional focus in tapping into physical functions.

It is important for coaches or applied sport psychologists who choose to use these types of activities to understand the need for a clear debriefing after each activity. It is essential that the message about the need for effective concentration is clear and that appropriate reference is made to specific types of attentional focus necessary for success in the activity. The activity presenter should also relate the attentional information to relevant aspects of the sport.

SPORT-RELATED ACTIVITIES

Sport object focusing

For this exercise, athletes need to have a specific object from their particular sport to concentrate on. The concept revolves around examining the object in as much detail as possible while at the same time ensuring that distractions from the immediate environment or from outside thoughts do not inhibit concentration. As with many of the above tasks, athletes may find this difficult to do initially, and it may be necessary to work in 30-second periods followed by rest. With practice, athletes should be able to improve up to a five-minute period. At this stage, the exercise can be extended so that the athlete alternates between narrow concentration on the object followed by broadening the focus to other objects in the field of vision. Difficulty can be increased by introducing other distractions to the environment.

Centring (Nideffer, 1981, 1989)

Many of the exercises which have been presented suffer from taking an inordinate amount of time. The attraction of the centring procedure (Nideffer, 1976b) is that it is specifically designed to be used at the sporting site. While also a relaxation technique (see Chapters 11 and 12 for more information on relaxation techniques), centring also doubles as a form of attentional shifting or refocusing. This one- or two-breath technique serves as a form of preparation for more effective and appropriate concentration.

One Australian tennis champion used centring techniques as a way of clearing his thoughts before serving and waiting to return service. Part of this player's pre-service routine involved a centring breath to bring the focus of attention in (narrow–internal) as a blocking out technique. In order to feel his centre of gravity sink down as he breathed out he could not be thinking about other details or attending to external cues. The centring breath also reduced his arousal level and reduced upper body muscle tension (appropriate for a fluid service action). Following the centring breath the player shifted his focus onto the service target (a specific mark on the service court) and from there to the position of the ball toss.

Using specific cues

Cues have been found to be most beneficial for athletes in regaining concentration when distracted or ensuring that it remains properly focused. For example, track athletes use cue words (self-talk instructions) like "relax", "see a tunnel", "stay in touch", "rhythmic movements", to assist in remaining optimally focused during competition performances. It is important to realise that these cues must be individualised as different athletes have very different approaches to their competition.

"Parking" thoughts

A very effective behavioural tool in dealing with intruding thoughts is to "park" them. This effectively means to put them aside for another time, typically by using a rational self-talk instruction or a form of visualisation which places the troublesome thought in a safe and non-distracting place until after the performance. This technique can be extremely effective for athletes who tend to bring outside issues into competition situations. Athletes are sometimes advised to record these ideas on a piece of paper (either actual or metaphorically in the imagination) and then to put this paper in some other place (this is the parking component). Upon completion of the performance, the athlete can go back and deal with the issue by "unparking" it. The benefit is that the athlete has been able to compete without the distracting thought continually intruding and after the performance to deal with the issue in an appropriate way.

Response to errors

Many athletes suggest that after they make a mistake they find it difficult to refocus and to "get back on track". A useful technique has been to use this error as an opportunity to learn, by very quickly analysing why the error was made and then mentally rehearsing the skill again, except this time ensuring that it is done perfectly. In this way, the athlete learns from the experience and also sees any errors as challenges (to be turned into a positive self-instruction) rather than as negative and emotion-disturbing mistakes. This rationalisation is also effective for retaining confidence and a high self-image.

Injured athletes can also use this thought switching approach by not concentrating on the negative aspects of the injury (that is, a description of why it happened) but rather using it as an opportunity to learn so that in the future the same situation is of little concern.

Group discussion (controlling the controllables/what ifs)

Athletes are required to list all the factors which are likely to affect their performance (one column for the positive factors and another for the negative). The activity may be facilitated by supplying them with typical areas such as tactical, psychological, technical. After collating the responses, athletes are invited to discuss which factors they have control over (e.g., execution of skills, maintaining an ideal level of arousal or concentrating effectively) and which ones they do not (e.g., weather conditions, the presence of spectators or the media or surrounding noise).

One of the common themes which seems to repeat itself when discussing concentration is the fact that athletes get distracted by such things as the score, the situation, other thoughts. In discussion, athletes should be encouraged to examine what factors distract them and coping strategies that can be used in dealing with those distractions. Whilst there will be vast individual differences reported, one of the main themes is emphasising the need to focus on the present as well as on the task at hand.

Another related discussion area is for athletes to consider all the "what ifs" which may be associated with a particular competition, or all the possible factors which may affect a situation, and then to devise coping strategies to deal with them. In this way, if (and when) these factors do happen, the athlete will not be distracted by them and will remain optimally focused.

A word of warning with this area. There are both appropriate and inappropriate times to consider "what ifs". Examine "what ifs" at those times when something can be done about them, when effective coping strategies can be put in place. It is important to ensure that "what ifs" are not considered on race/event day as this can seriously disrupt an optimal concentration mode for that competition.

Routines and segmenting before and during performance

One of the building blocks of consistently high quality performances is the development of high quality pre/during performance routines (Bond, 1985; Orlick, 1986a, 1986b; Rushall, 1979). Many athletes have been assisted towards successful competition outcomes by having them prepare specific performance plans which are in fact attentional cue sequences which are perceived by the athlete and coach to be a significant part of a successful performance. Once the routine is established, the athlete is assisted to learn the routine by mentally practising (visualisation), writing it down, by placing the point by point description in a visible place, by recording the routine on audiotape, by listening to the audiotape in a variety of situations (including during salt water flotation sessions) and by physically practising the routines in training sessions, competition simulations and low level competitions.

Cohn (1990) has examined some of the theoretical and empirical factors surrounding the creation of routines. These include an examination of the nature of the task such that the chosen routine reflects the tempo and feel of the activity in order to prepare the appropriate mind-set. The routine should also take into account some awareness of the learning stage of the performer which may imply more clearly defined cognitive steps or something more automatic. Chosen cue words could also reflect this difference and direct concentration to important aspects while retaining optimal arousal. Cohn also emphasises an awareness of the performer's specific individual characteristics to ensure that the routine reflects the dominant perceptual style as well as any coping difficulties.

Playing it in your head

Many players report the benefits of playing the game in their head prior to the actual game (for a longer discussion of imagery/visualisation refer to Chapter 14). Imagery is an effective tool in facilitating concentration and minimising distractions. Many athletes have reported that they have visualised their event in every way possible prior to the competition as a way of minimising distraction and improving concentration. It should be emphasised that salt water flotation provides an ideal environment for the enhancement of visualisation/imagery (Bond, 1987).

Schmid and Peper (1993) presented an interesting variation to mental rehearsal. They organised team members into pairs in which one member relaxes and mentally rehearses. The other person in the pair is required to cause distractions to the rehearsal by any method except touch. The roles are then switched. Upon completion of the activity, both members are required to evaluate their concentration on a rating scale. Over time, participants report an improved ability to concentrate by dissociating themselves from distractions and remaining focused on the mental rehearsal task. Part of this training could also include athletes being required to regain concentration after being distracted.

Goal setting

A useful exercise for developing concentration is to encourage athletes to set specific, measurable goals during training and competition (refer to Chapter 10 for a more detailed discussion on goal setting). For example, a basketballer may decide that her goal is 85% shooting accuracy during training or that she will not complete her shooting training until she has shot 20 in a row. To make this activity more realistic, the player should ensure that she includes some of the same movement patterns required in the game (e.g., dodging defenders, whose court positions may be substituted by appropriately placed chairs) and a number of shots taken from various positions on the court. These specific goals serve to keep the athlete focused on task, even in the event of distractions such as a build-up of fatigue or when other players leave the court having finished their training.

Game simulation activity

The concept behind developing game simulations is to minimise the negative effects of novelty and the pressure often associated with high level competition. The assumption is that if athletes have been able to practise in an environment close to the game situation, then they will have enhanced coping strategies for the actual game. Importantly, the closer that the simulation is to the "real thing", the better the effect.

Players are required to perform in a typical game set-up during a training session. It is vital to organise the scenario so that players approach it as if it were a "real" game. This may involve paying attention to as many details as possible, such as wearing the correct game uniform, ensuring the usual pre-game routine, warm-up and pre-match discussion, using appropriate announcements and music, setting up a typical change-room, inviting real referees to officiate and using a crowd noise tape or organising a crowd to attend.

Glencross (1993) presented another dimension of this simulation idea in the preparation undertaken for the Australian women's Olympic hockey team for the 1992 Barcelona Olympics. The aim of one of the pre-Olympic camps was to simulate the situation and conditions that the team was likely to confront, in an attempt to ensure enhanced coping strategies at the actual Olympic site. Glencross included the following in the simulation: climatic conditions, competition schedule, opponents and their styles of play, umpire rulings, playing conditions, tournament rules and regulations, spectators and crowd bias, transport conditions, accommodation and meals, and media exposure. Glencross also organised unexpected situations (such as a bomb scare) as a part of the camp.

To test athletes' abilities to cope, the distractions chosen may even be beyond the usual expectations. This extension of the simulation task has been used very successfully in the applied setting with a range of sports. In a tennis example, the distractions were chosen to be as extreme as possible. Players were required to play as well as possible whilst ignoring distorted radio sounds, taped crowd noise, clearly incorrect calls from line-judges and umpires, balls rolling onto court whilst playing and spectators speaking to players between and in the middle of points. Some players have been found to cope with this kind of extreme pressure whilst other players have been clearly unsettled. However, all athletes tend to gain from this attention "overtraining" practice.

Positive self-talk

A technique (borrowed from meditational ideas and the use of positive affirmations) which is used regularly within the applied setting is the creation of positive statements in a self-talk format (e.g., "I am feeling fit and ready to go" or "I feel relaxed and happy with my form"). These statements are often listed in a poster-style format and displayed in athletes' rooms for continual referral. This type of exercise ensures that athletes are in a focused frame of mind when preparing for training or competition. The poster style can also be adopted for the display of other reminders to athletes to stay in a correct concentrational mode. A list of daily mental goals, inspirational quotes and uplifting songs have all been presented in this way and have proved to be invaluable for athletes.

Designing individualised sport exercises

With some imagination, it is possible to design effective exercises which ensure that any athletes can practise moving from one attentional focus to another. Consideration might be given to specific circumstances which occur in a particular sport where athletes are required to use one attentional style and then shift to another. For example, it is common practice in team sports involving dribbling to require players to dribble the ball while wearing special blinker glasses which effectively force the athlete to look ahead. In another exercise, the basketball coach stands to one side of the court. As the players dribble the ball down the court, the coach calls out to the players, asking them how many fingers he or she has raised in the air.

FUTURE DIRECTIONS

The future direction in concentration training is indeed exciting. Given the central importance of concentration within sport performance, there remain a number of issues to be resolved in coming to terms with the construct from a number of different research domains. In spite of the lack of agreement about a number of key issues in the attention area, we believe that this chapter has demonstrated just how valuable work within the applied concentration area can be for the athlete, coach and applied sport psychologist.

There is great potential for the further development of attentional style testing, analysis and feedback procedures for the benefit of athletes and coaches. Our long-term use of the TAIS has proven to be valuable. The TAIS is currently undergoing further development as an interactive feedback system and the future appears to be full of interesting and creative opportunities.

Improved technology and further use of what is available should also ensure that the simulations designed for athletes will reflect the real environment even more accurately. Creative use of multiple camera video feedback should ensure that athletes are able to experience more closely the appropriate attentional demands of competition situations. Used in conjunction with controlled environments, such as salt water flotation tanks, the efficiency of this process will increase even further. Development of three-dimensional holograms may even allow the athlete to experience the concentration requirements of a game situation within the confines of a training venue or professional's office.

There has also been considerable interest in the planning of mental training programs to ensure that all skills are systematically treated. Some understanding of the physical training requirements of the individual is necessary when developing a program which aims to develop the mental components in line with physical training demands. This is the basis of the principle of periodisation which Bompa (1983) has popularised. As yet little attempt has been made in the literature to address the relationship of Bompa's approach with mental skill development, though Sargent (1991) attempted to address this issue.

Specific mental training programs have been presented which further reflect how concentration skills can be effectively addressed. Gordon (1990) presented a program based on the mental demands of cricket. Gordon adopted an educational approach using a workbook procedure in developing the mental skills of a high level representative team. For concentration, Gordon emphasised the importance of focusing on one thing at a time, selective attention to important cues, focusing in the present as well as developing the ability to maximise the quality of required periods of optimal concentration, and shifting attentional focus as a form of concentration "relaxation". This "switching off" is a requirement brought about by the immense time demands of the sport and was facilitated by the use of checklists, cue words and refocusing plans similar to the type presented by Orlick (1986a, 1986b). Gordon also described the use of commercially available tapes in developing concentration skills though it was felt that effectiveness could be improved by making the material more specific to cricket. A great deal more can be gained from attentional training programs where they are individualised. Intuitively, it seems naive for applied sport psychologists to be relying on commercially available tapes (audio or video) as a means of training an individual athlete's concentration skills.

Savoy (1993) presented a mental training program for a college basketball player. Of particular interest was the applied nature of her approach as well as the application of the TAIS as an evaluation tool along with anxiety questionnaires and stress scales. Savoy's applied intervention approach demonstrates the value of testing instruments as a part of the overall analysis of an athlete's attentional capacities. Savoy determined that the athlete had weaknesses in the areas of dealing with distractions and getting psyched up for practice. For the distraction–concentration area, Savoy describes a program to control the tendency to be overloaded by both external and internal information. This was presented in the form of an imagery worksheet and a mental checklist for game-like situations. This extremely practical approach again demonstrates how these procedures can be adopted in the actual sport setting through a blend of theory and practice.

A five-step model proposed by Singer (1988) includes:

- readying (positive thinking, segment the day according to what has worked well in the past, consistency in pre-competition preparation)
- imaging (visualise the skill from start to finish using the feel of the movement as well)
- focusing (intense concentration on one relevant cue at the expense of all else)
- executing (perform when ready and do not consider the outcome)
- evaluating (assess the routine and subsequent performance according to any feedback).

It is beyond the scope of this chapter to fully analyse the strategy though it offers an interesting approach to routine development.

Another challenging future direction is in the area of working with children. Orlick (1993) presents an approach which addresses important issues in the mental development of children. Under interesting titles such as "Leaf Connection", "Focus on Flakes" and "Animal Round-up", Orlick describes a number of activities and games specifically designed to enhance concentration as well as the ability to shift the focus of attention. This exciting development reflects an awareness that concentration skills can be developed from an early age.

There still exists a great deal of interest in further understanding the ideal performance state. Whilst Orlick and Partington (1988) and Garfield and Bennett (1984) have previously described attentional aspects of peak performance, applied sport psychologists remain interested in describing conditions which lead to this state along with the added challenge of educating and assisting athletes in creating those antecedent conditions. Csikszentmihalyi (1990) and others (Jackson, 1992; Jackson & Roberts, 1992; Kimiecik & Stein, 1992) have also been particularly interested in the flow experience sometimes reported by athletes when performing exceptionally well. Whilst there still appear to be methodological concerns regarding the assessment of flow, Csikszentmihalyi (1990) has indicated some basic elements which characterise the flow state. These include such things as:

- the merging of action and awareness (the activity is spontaneous and almost automatic)
- clear goals and unambiguous feedback (a direction must be set as well as some kind of feedback about progress)
- a loss of self-consciousness (complete immersion in a task without being forced, so that concentration can be directed completely to the task)
- a paradox of control (performers feel in control without being concerned about losing it)
- concentration on the task at hand (a complete focusing on the task, shutting out other distractions).

The importance of concentration in the flow state is reflected in these basic elements. While there has been some effort to describe those situations which ensure the highest likelihood of a flow experience (such as when task challenges match skill level) there needs to be more investigation of this experience before the applied professional can use the concepts in any practical way. Nevertheless, the concept of flow provides a particularly interesting area for future research and practice if only because of its interaction with such factors as apathy, boredom, anxiety and complete enjoyment "for it's own sake" (Kimiecik & Stein, 1992).

CONCLUSIONS

This chapter extends the theoretical bases of attention presented in Chapter 3 and endorses an applied model of concentration in work with athletes and coaches. We urge the reader to acknowledge, as many athletes and coaches have done, the significance of the concentration area to enhancement of athletic performance.

We emphasise the applied utility of the Nideffer model of attention in one to one work with athletes and in a broader educational sense, with teams and group work. The model is useful in understanding, predicting (in conjunction with psychometric profiles and other measures), strategies for change in the area of concentration and sport performances. Nideffer's Test of Attentional and Interpersonal Style (TAIS) has continued to prove useful in our applied work with athletes and coaches. We encourage applied sport psychologists to include this measure as part of their repertoire. The TAIS used in conjunction with other measures, is an excellent way to assess and educate athletes and coaches and an important precursor for attentional training programs. The attentional exercise section of the chapter should not be regarded as complete, but more as a starting point for use by applied sport psychologists, coaches and athletes in designing individualised training strategies for the enhancement of concentration in performance environments.

Readers are encouraged to closely examine our suggestions for the future development of resources, programs and strategies in the area of concentration. In particular we conclude that development of interactive software by Nideffer will increase further the effectiveness of education and athlete involvement in concentration training. We also acknowledge the importance of further work on flow states and the relationship between ideal arousal levels and effective concentration. Finally we encourage readers to be creative in exploring ways to approach the issues of concentration training for young athletes, the use of video simulations and holograms and in the application of phasing principles. Applied sport psychology will benefit from more quantitative and qualitative research on attention, which is the responsibility of both academic and applied sport psychologists in collaboration with coaches.

SUMMARY

This chapter addressed the importance of attention for the serious athlete and coach via a number of applied case studies. Despite the difficulties in accurately defining the concept there appear to be a number of areas which offer opportunities for the applied sport psychologist, coach and athlete. These have been provided primarily by the work of Nideffer through his attentional model and Test of Attentional and Interpersonal

Style. Nideffer has given the practitioner, athlete and coach a means of enhancing the understanding, explanation, prediction and control or change of attentional factors.

We have provided a reasonably extensive list and accompanying descriptions of a variety of generalised and sport-specific attentional exercises. These should prove to be a useful starting point for those with a creative mind intent on stimulating the further development of concentration training activities.

The final section of the chapter has examined a number of performance enhancement activities which may assist athletes in understanding, explaining, predicting and controlling their attentional responses. We can only stress that there is a need for a great deal of further research of an applied nature in the area of attention. Whilst there have been a number of studies which have criticised aspects of the Nideffer model and questionnaire, a number of those investigations have been flawed (Nideffer, 1990). To date no-one has proposed a more workable and more easily understood and applied diagnostic model and profile.

We close this chapter with a quotation to encourage others to develop knowledge in this vital area of applied performance psychology:

> The practical study of concentration opens us not only to the world of results, but also of causes, and this lifts us beyond the slavery of uncontrolled feelings and thoughts...
>
> (Sadhu, 1986, p. 20)

REFERENCES

Albinson, J. G., & Bull, S. J. (1988). *A mental game plan: A training program for all sports*. London, Ontario: Spodym.

Albrecht, R. R., & Feltz, D. L. (1987). Generality and specificity of attention related to competitive anxiety and sport performance. *Journal of Sport Psychology, 9*, 231–248.

Antonelli, F., Caldarone, L., & Gatti, M. (1982). Profile psychologique du gymnaste national Italien. In T Orlick, J. T. Partington, & J. H. Salmela (Eds.), *Mental training for coaches and athletes* (pp. 100–101). Ottowa: Coaching Association of Canada.

Bompa, T. (1983). *Theory and methodology of training: The key to athletic performance*. Iowa: Kendall/Hunt Publishing Co.

Bond, J. W. (1984). Concentration: Focusing on the right thing at the right time. Unpublished manuscript, Australian Institute of Sport.

Bond, J. W. (1985). Segmenting or performance planning for success in sport. Unpublished manuscript, Australian Institute of Sport.

Bond, J. W. (1987). Flotation therapy: Theoretical concepts. *Sports Science and Medicine Quarterly, 4*, 2–4.

Bond, J. W., & Nideffer, R. M. (1992). Attentional and interpersonal characteristics of elite Australian athletes. *Excel, 8*, 101–110.

Boutcher, S. H. (1990). The role of performance routines in sport. In G. Jones & L. Hardy (Eds.), *Stress and performance in sport* (pp. 231–245). London: John Wiley & Sons.

Boutcher, S. H. (1992). Attention and athletic performance: An integrated approach. In T. S. Horn (Ed.), *Advances in sport psychology* (pp. 251–265). Champaign, IL: Human Kinetics.

Burke, K. L. (1992). Concentration. *Sport Psychology Bulletin, 4*(1), 1–8.

Cattell, R. B. (1957). *Personality and motivation structure and measurement.* Yonkers-on-Hudson, NY: World Book Company.

Cohn, P. J. (1990). Preperformance routines in sport: Theoretical support and practical applications. *The Sport Psychologist, 4,* 301–312.

Csikszentmihalyi, M. (1990). *Flow: The psychology of experience.* New York: Harper & Row Publishers.

DePalma D. M., & Nideffer, R. M. (1977). Relationships between the Test of Attentional and Interpersonal Style and psychiatric subclassification. *Journal of Personality Assessment, 41,* 622–631.

Easterbrook, J. A. (1959). The effect of emotion on cue utilization and the organization of behaviour. *Psychological Review, 66,* 183–201.

Feifel, H., Strack, S., & Nagy, V. T. (1987). Degree of life-threat and differential use of coping modes. *Journal of Psychosomatic Research, 31*(1), 91–99.

Garfield, C. A., & Bennett, H. Z. (1984). *Peak performance: Mental training techniques of the world's greatest athletes.* Los Angeles, CA: Warner.

Gauron, E. F. (1984). *Mental training for peak performance.* Lansing, NY: Sport Science Associates.

Glencross, B. (1993). Simulation camp. *Sports Coach, 16*(1), 7–10.

Gordon, S. (1990). A mental skills training program for the Western Australia state cricket team. *The Sport Psychologist, 4,* 386–399.

Jackson, S. A. (1992). Athletes in flow: A qualitative investigation of flow states in elite figure skaters. *Journal of Applied Sport Psychology, 4,* 161–180.

Jackson, S. A., & Roberts, G. C. (1992). Positive performance states of athletes: Toward a conceptual understanding of peak performance. *The Sport Psychologist, 6,* 156–171.

Kimiecik, J. C., & Stein, G. L. (1992). Examining flow experiences in sport contexts: Conceptual issues and methodological concerns. *Journal of Applied Sport Psychology, 4,* 144–160.

Kirschenbaum, D. S., & Bale, R. M. (1980). Cognitive behavioral skills in golf: Brain power of golf. In R. M. Suinn (Ed.), *Psychology in sports: Methods and applications* (pp. 334-343). Minneapolis, MN: Burgess.

Landers, D. M., Boutcher, S. H., & Wang, M. Q. (1986). A psychobiological study of archery performance. *Research Quarterly for Exercise and Sport, 57,* 236–244.

Landers, D. M., & Richards D. E. (1980). Test of Attentional and Interpersonal Style scores of shooters. In G. C. Roberts & D. M. Landers (Eds.), *Psychology of motor behaviour and sport* (p. 94). Champaign, IL: Human Kinetics.

Morgan, W. P. (1980). Test of champions. *Psychology Today, 14,* 92–108.

Nideffer, R. M. (1976a). Test of Attentional and Interpersonal Style. *Journal of Personality and Social Psychology, 34,* 394–404.

Nideffer, R. M. (1976b). *The inner athlete.* New York: Thomas Crowell.

Nideffer, R. M. (1981). *Predicting human behaviour: A theory and test of attentional and interpersonal style.* San Diego, CA: Enhanced Performance Associates.

Nideffer, R. M. (1987). Issues in the use of psychological tests in applied settings. *The Sport Psychologist, 1,* 18–28.

Nideffer, R. M. (1989). *Attention control training for athletes.* Oakland, CA: Enhanced Performance Services.

Nideffer, R. M. (1990). Use of the Test of Attentional and Interpersonal Style (TAIS) in sport. *The Sport Psychologist, 4*, 285–300.

Nideffer, R. M. (1993a). Attention control training. In R. Singer, M. Murphey, & L. K. Tennant (Eds.), *Handbook of research on sport psychology* (pp. 542–556). New York: Macmillan.

Nideffer, R. M. (1993b). Concentration and attention control training. In J. M. Williams (Ed.), *Applied sport psychology: Personal growth to peak performance* (pp. 243–261). Palo Alto, CA: Mayfield.

Nideffer, R. M., & Bond, J. (1989). *Test of attentional and interpersonal style — cultural and sexual differences.* Paper presented at the XXI International Conference on Psychology, Sport and Health Promotion, Banff, Canada.

Nideffer, R. M., & Pratt, R. W. (1981). *Taking care of business: A manual to guide the refinement of attention control training.* San Diego, CA: Enhanced Performance Associates.

Orlick, T. (1986a). *Psyching for sport: Mental training for athletes.* Champaign, IL: Leisure Press.

Orlick, T. (1986b). *Coaches' training manual for psyching for sport.* Champaign, IL: Leisure Press.

Orlick, T. (1993). *Free to feel great — teaching children to excel at living.* Carp, Ontario: Creative Bound Inc.

Orlick, T., & Partington, J. (1988). Mental links to excellence. *The Sport Psychologist, 2*, 105–130.

Reis, J., & Bird, A. (1982). Cue processing as a function of breadth of attention. *Journal of Sport Psychology, 4*, 64–72.

Rushall, B. S. (1979). *Psyching in sport.* London: Pelham Books.

Sadhu, M. (1986). *Concentration.* London: Unwin Paperbacks.

Salmela, J. H., & Ndoye, O. D. (1986). Cognitive distortions during progressive excercise. *Perceptual and Motor Skills, 63*, 1067–1072.

Sargent, G. I. (1991). A model of psychological periodisation — including a presentation of training principles, intervention techniques and some of the mental training programs being used in Australia. Unpublished manuscript, Deakin University, Melbourne.

Savoy, C. (1993). A yearly mental training program for a college basketball player. *The Sport Psychologist, 7*, 173–190.

Schmid, A., & Peper, E. (1993). Training strategies for concentration. In J. M. Williams (Ed.), *Applied sport psychology: Personal growth to peak performance* (2nd ed.) (pp. 262–273). Mountain View, CA: Mayfield.

Singer, R. N. (1988). Strategies and meta strategies in learning and performing self-paced athletic skills. *The Sport Psychologist, 2*, 49–68.

Vallerand, R. J. (1983). Attention and decision making: A test of the predictive validity of the Test of Attentional and Interpersonal Style (TAIS) in a sport setting. *Journal of Sport Psychology, 5*, 449–459.

Van Schoyck, R. S., & Grasha, A. F. (1981). Attentional style variations and athletic ability: The advantages of a sport specific test. *Journal of Sport Psychology, 3*, 149–165.

Weinberg, R. S. (1988). *The mental advantage: Developing your psychological skills in tennis.* Champaign, IL: Leisure Press.

Whitney, D. L., & Pratt, R. W. (1987). Paying attention: A study of attentional and interpersonal styles of hotel and restaurant administration students. *Hospitality and Education Research Journal, 11*(3), 43–58.

Wiens, A. N., Harper, R., & Matarazzo, J. D. (1980). Personality correlates of non-verbal behaviour. *Journal of Clinical Psychology, 36*(1), 205–215.

Writer, L. (1990). *Winning: Face to face with Australian sporting legends.* Chatswood, NSW: Ironbark Press.

Zuckerman, M., Larrance, D., Hall, J., DeFrank, R., & Rosenthal, R. (1979). Posed and spontaneous communication of emotion via facial and vocal cues. *Journal of Personality, 47,* 712–733.

C H A P T E R

16

BUILDING AND MAINTAINING AN EFFECTIVE TEAM

N E I L   M c L E A N

Sporting teams provide a fascinating opportunity for naturalistic observation of groups and individual behaviour. Few groups receive the same public scrutiny as professional sporting teams; the interpersonal relationships of the team are played out in front of massive audiences with reactions of players to each other and to coaches under the microscope of action replays and multimedia inquiry.

Teams vary considerably in their degree of interdependence (see Chapter 8). Some teams are essentially groups of individual athletes who simply compete under the same national, State or club banner (e.g., an Olympic swim team) whereas other sports require a high degree of interdependence from team members (e.g., volleyball, basketball). Other sports such as cricket incorporate both individual performance and interactive activity, with each individual's effort contributing to the team's success.

The interaction patterns of teams have been variously referred to as team spirit, harmony, cohesion and morale, while the team dynamics are often referred to more colloquially as "the chemistry" of the team. Some coaches view this team chemistry as an indefinable process that describes the interaction of team members, and something that is outside the control of the coach. It is seen as an unpredictable result of the mixture of the personalities gathered together in the team. When the chemistry is not right, the team struggles to prosper.

However, this view is simplistic in several ways. Successful teams are not always harmonious and harmonious teams are not necessarily winners. Furthermore, the so-called chemistry of a team need not be seen as a chance process beyond the control of the coach. The creation of an effective team mix is very much the responsibility of the coach and it may even be argued that this is a central challenge for coaching staff. So-called team building exercises describe efforts to improve the functioning of a group, and this process is the focus of this chapter.

Unfortunately, it is extremely difficult to bring experimental rigour to the assessment of team functioning. At the top levels of professional sport, coaches are understandably reluctant to allow the level of manipulation and control required to rigorously assess team building procedures. As a consequence, much of our understanding of this area comes from descriptive research, and much of this research comes from the world of commerce and business. Successful businesses across the world have been identified, and the corporate strategies and styles that underpin this success provide useful guidelines for team building in the sporting environment.

In this chapter, the principles and practices of successful teams will be reviewed. It will be emphasised that successful team building is influenced more by a philosophy and a set of values than by a bag of team building tricks and strategies.

THE CHALLENGE OF TEAM SPORT

The National Basketball Association (NBA) in America is a high-profile competition where the athletes attract worldwide attention and hefty financial rewards. Basketballers are drafted by NBA clubs, with the American collegiate system providing the most common recruiting path. Basketballers attracting college scholarships are generally selected from American high schools. A promising high school basketballer is likely to be feted by college scouts and subject to all sorts of promises and flattery. A successful college basketballer is likely to be a hero on campus, and if his team is successful he will receive national television exposure and will be pursued by a host of NBA scouts. Any player recruited by an NBA franchise will have been a standout athlete at high school and college levels, and will have become accustomed to attention and adulation. He will have invariably been a member of the starting lineups for each team he has represented, and will have received court time commensurate with this star status. Yet in his first season with an NBA team, this standout college athlete may hardly get to play. Consider the adjustment needed to come to terms with playing a minor, almost invisible, support role, when this player has been used to star status!

This very real example highlights the complexity of team sport and the challenges facing a coach. Elite athletes by nature are likely to be high achievers, but the demands of a team sport not infrequently mean that an individual may be asked to put aside individual or personal needs for the benefit of the team. Even the superstars may be asked to make compromises; the Chicago Bulls won an NBA title only after a year of turmoil as the team struggled to come to terms with the dominant presence of superstar Michael Jordan, and Jordan wrestled with how to play with his less talented team mates.

The challenge facing Bulls coach Phil Jackson was to maximise the talents of Jordan, but to do so in a way that allowed the remainder of the team to contribute effectively to the team output. In essence this represents a classic situation facing the coach of a team, where the challenge is to meet the individual needs of team members at the same time as maximising the team output. Give Jordan a free rein with the ball and he would probably score 50 points or more per game, but other team members are then starved of scoring chances and the team offence becomes predictable and less than maximally efficient. For several seasons, this scenario characterised the Chicago Bulls. Jordan became the game's superstar but the Bulls failed to win the championship. The Bulls became a championship team when Jordan was able to adjust to a role that allowed more room for his team mates to contribute (Smith, 1992).

The Chicago Bulls provide a fascinating example of a team that eventually succeeded despite a season wracked with internal conflict and turmoil. There are numerous other examples of teams succeeding despite significant interpersonal conflict, so it is apparent that the relationship between success and team dynamics is by no means straightforward. It has been suggested that internal conflict can at times work to promote success, but alternatively it might be argued that teams in conflict have managed to succeed despite the conflict, but not because of it. However, it is important to keep these examples in perspective, as it is also possible to cite examples of highly talented teams who have performed poorly, perhaps because of internal conflict and a lack of team spirit or cohesion. While it is impossible to draw clear cause–effect linkages, it is not unreasonable to suggest that most coaches would choose for their players to relate harmoniously, working from the assumption that a team which relates effectively is more likely to win than a team of similar or even superior talent which is in conflict. This belief is reflected in the old adage: "a champion team will beat a team of champions".

Chapter 8 outlines the different ways of viewing team dynamics. It is important to recognise that this is not as simple as interpersonal attraction. Syer (1986) cites numerous examples of teams where players worked effectively together as team mates but did not pursue or develop close friendships within the team. In fact, Syer (1986) went on to note that friendships within a team can impede performance if cliques and jealousies are allowed to form and fracture the group unity.

It has often been assumed that team chemistry is an uncontrollable interpersonal cocktail determined by the ingredients (i.e., the players), and beyond the control of coaches and/or other management staff. Following this line, if the chemistry is not right then the ingredients need to be changed, a philosophy which leads to players being regularly traded until the right mix is attained. Alternatively, it is argued that creating chemistry is the task of the coaching staff, so that individuals and the group (the ingredients) are moulded in ways that create a positive team climate. This latter view is at the basis of processes and procedures described as team building.

It would be naive to assume that the coach is all-powerful in this regard. Some players find it extraordinarily difficult to fit into the constraints of a team; they are not good team players and may be resistant to whatever efforts are made to harness their abilities within a team context. In these cases the best option may be to release the player and seek a replacement more in tune with the team demands. Successful teams frequently consider the team orientation of a recruit as well as athletic ability and are reluctant to choose talented athletes who appear to have difficulty meeting team needs. Maddux (1986) suggests that selecting people who work well with others is a cornerstone of effective team building. However, there is a point where a coach is faced with a squad that he or she must manage and cannot trade, and at this point the challenge is to maximise the individual and team potential of that squad.

DEFINITIONS OF TEAM BUILDING

At one level, a definition of team building is relatively straightforward. Buller (1986) suggests that "The primary purpose of team building is to improve the effectiveness of work teams within organisations" (p. 147). Bettenhausen (1991) describes the processes of team building as attempts to "improve group performance by improving communication, reducing conflict, and generating cohesion and commitment among work group members" (p. 369). Vogt and Griffith (1988) add another level of complexity in their definition, arguing that team building recognises the importance of satisfying individual needs as well as facilitating group effectiveness: "Team building is defined as the process by which a work group becomes more effective in accomplishing its tasks and in satisfying the needs of group members" (pp. 83–84).

This is clearly a complex process as there is no guarantee that individual and group needs will always be mutually compatible. On the contrary, as discussed earlier in this chapter, individual needs may frequently need to be subordinated in the interests of the group.

PHILOSOPHY OR BAG OF TRICKS?

It is a commonly held misconception that sport psychology essentially incorporates a set of techniques designed to maximise performance. This "bag of tricks" approach suggests that there is a range of discrete strategies, techniques and exercises which form the basis of mental skills training. The coach who holds this view will be inclined to hand the squad over to the sport psychologist for mental skills training sessions which are frequently carried out in isolation from the broader training program. This is akin to the company which sends senior executives on an adventure training weekend where they go abseiling, orienteering or even fire-walking, with the aim of building teamwork and cooperation. This "quick-fix" approach is likely to have ephemeral effects at best, unless more durable and long-lasting principles and practices are incorporated into the everyday working environment. Similarly, the coach who sees team building exercises as something that can be split off from the everyday activities of the team is unlikely to grasp or understand the complexity, consistency and depth of effort that is required to develop effective interactions within a team.

An alternative view is to see team building as the very essence of working with any group or team and as part of the philosophy of managing the human resources within that team. From this perspective, team building is not a set of exercises that get wheeled out from time to time, but it is a way of thinking which pervades every interpersonal interaction within that group. The coaches and teams who view team building from this perspective recognise that building an effective team is about understanding and respecting the individual components that make up that team and endeavouring to find a mode of operating that allows the individual to develop and prosper within the structure of an effective team.

The parallels with successful corporations are fascinating. In reviewing a series of business success stories Peters and Waterman (1982) identified "a plethora of structural devices, systems, styles and rules, all monitoring one another so that the companies are truly unusual in their ability to achieve extraordinary results through ordinary people" (pp. 238–239). This commitment to achieving group or team output comes from an orientation described by Peters and Austin (1985) as "bone-deep beliefs" (p. 203), which contrasts with companies which pay lip service to team development, or resort to gimmicks to achieve that end. The central message is that a characteristic of successful companies is that they are committed to enhancing output by developing people, in contrast to companies which may claim a similar orientation but fall well short of the everyday commitment to this ideal. This is succinctly and forcefully summarised by Peters and Austin (1985):

> Make no mistake about it. "Techniques" don't produce quality products, educate children, or pick up the garbage on time: people do, people who care, people who are treated as creatively contributing adults. (p. 201)

So what does this all mean in practical terms? There is a danger in somewhat lofty discussions of philosophy, values and bone-deep beliefs that the translation of these values into everyday actions can remain unclear. It is clear what we want to achieve but how do we get there? The following sections will attempt to explore how effective principles of team development can be operationalised.

EFFECTIVE PRINCIPLES OF TEAM DEVELOPMENT

TEAM PHILOSOPHY

As noted, team building is best seen as a commitment which is evident in all aspects of a team's functioning and interaction. It is not something to be left to chance, and as such, successful teams often work from a clearly stated and explicit philosophy or set of values.

It is unlikely that a team will work effectively towards a goal unless there is consensus as to the nature of that goal, and a good level of agreement on how that goal is to be achieved. Without this shared agenda, there is the danger that individuals will pursue personal agenda which may not coincide with, or may even be at odds with, the team goals.

In some instances these value systems will have evolved over time and are tied up with the history and traditions of the club or organisation. In other circumstances, more explicit effort is directed towards establishing and defining team values or team philosophy via discussion and meetings. In this latter case, it is desirable that all members of a team have some input to the discussion and establishment of the team philosophy.

Peters and Waterman (1982) noted the central importance of clear value systems in the successful companies they observed:

> Every excellent company we studied is clear on what it stands for, and takes the process of value shaping seriously. In fact, we wonder whether it is possible to be an excellent company without clarity on values and without having the right sorts of values. (p. 280)

Team philosophy should be articulated as clearly as possible; some teams develop a written manifesto of team ethics that guides their activity. Sessions should be held from time to time to allow team members to modify these principles if necessary, although it would be generally expected that basic principles and values would remain important over time and would provide a consistent core for a team's way of operating.

ATTENDING TO THE INDIVIDUAL

It may seem a paradox to highlight individual needs within a discussion of team building. Traditional coaches have often promoted a view that puts the team before the individual, and adopt a quasi-military discipline or philosophy of "good for one ... good for all". Within this approach, communication is generally at a group level, individuals' doubts, grievances and needs receive little or no attention, and team members are expected to submissively toe the line. Team members are foot soldiers, doing the bidding of their officer (coach) superiors.

It is true that for teams to work efficiently individual needs may sometimes become of secondary importance. However, this does not mean that the needs of the individual should be ignored. In fact, if team members are being asked to sacrifice personal goals for team benefit, this is something that is best discussed and negotiated with them, so that they retain a sense of their personal worth and value to the team.

It is one thing to be a member of a team; it is an altogether different thing to feel like a valued contributor to the success of that team. How does the cricket team's opening batsman feel when he is dismissed cheaply and then watches while his team mates amass a match-winning score? He is a member of a winning team, but how does he view his contribution? How does the bench player in basketball feel when her brief appearance on the court is submerged by the public recognition of her more prominent team mates?

A useful premise to start with is that team members want to contribute and be seen to be contributors to team success. It is imperative that an individual's role within a team is recognised and valued, ideally by the player, the coach and team mates. In some sports (e.g., rowing) the contribution of team members is largely indistinguishable, but in other sports the nature of a player's role varies considerably.

Coaches should talk with players about their role. Ultimately it is ideal if player and coach can agree on the broad parameters of an individual's role within the team. It is a recipe for disaster when a player believes he or she should be playing a certain role but the coach has quite different ideas. The gap between these two positions needs to be narrowed as much as possible. Meetings at the start of a season should be arranged to discuss the projected role for the individual, and this needs to be repeated at regular intervals through a season, especially if a player's role changes at any point. Players who expect to play a certain role but suddenly find themselves being used differently, will speculate about the reasons behind this change. It is preferable if changes in role are discussed openly rather than being left to speculation.

The stars in a team get considerable kudos and reinforcement because of their ability and prominence. It is the so-called lesser lights within a team who require more attention and feedback. This should come from coaches, but team mates should also be encouraged to recognise the efforts of their team mates. Sometimes this can be done by attending to the more subtle contributions such as screens set in basketball, tackles or shepherds in Australian Rules Football and running off the ball in sports like hockey and soccer. It is an ultimate team contribution for a player to run to create space for a team mate to get the ball, but this relatively anonymous activity will often go unnoticed by all but those very close to the game. This makes it all the more important that such efforts are recognised by team mates and coaching staff. The goal scorer in hockey or soccer frequently gets the bulk of congratulations, but a sensitive and unified team will also recognise the efforts of the full back who got the ball rolling quickly at the start of the play that led to the goal.

As is evident, recognition of the individual should occur formally through discussion and negotiation of individual goals, aims and aspirations, but recognition should also be inherent in everyday interaction, at training, after games and during competition. It is based around an ethos that team success rests on a variety of individual contributions which are likely to differ from person to person. Dr Sandy Ferguson, who presided over the Hawthorn Australian Rules Football club as they moved from a team that had rarely experienced success to a team that set the standards, espoused a philosophy that he felt was at the core of the Hawthorn dynasty. He said that he wanted to ensure that the great players in the team remained humble, so that the more humble contributors could feel great. This philosophy recognises that individuals will vary in their contributions, but the degree to which these contributions are respected and valued does not vary.

OWNERSHIP AND EMPOWERMENT

Individuals who feel they have a stake in an activity are likely to be much more committed to that task than individuals who are simply following the orders of somebody else's grand plan. As noted earlier, team members generally want to be active contributors to success and this happens ideally at all levels of planning and implementation.

There is considerable evidence to suggest that when people feel more in control of an activity they are likely to be more effective. Patients given control over their pain relief use less analgesic and do better post-operatively than conventionally treated patients not given this control (Peters & Austin, 1985).

It is valuable to give players the opportunity to be involved in as many aspects of planning and team policy as possible. Players are at the coal face of the team activities and frequently have ideas that can increase team effectiveness. Where players are not given the opportunity to voice opinions, the sense of frustration that is carried with them can have a significant negative effect.

The military style was referred to earlier to characterise structured authoritarian team interactions. However, even within the military there is a growing recognition that greater efficiency will come from informed participation. An American naval chief revolutionised Navy practice by working to involve the men on his ship in all aspects of operation:

> ... I tried... to... ensure that every officer and man on the ship not only knew what we were about, not only why we were doing each tactical evolution, however onerous, but also managed to understand enough about how it all fitted together that he could begin to experience some of the fun and challenge that those of us in the top slots were having. (Peters & Waterman, 1982, p. 236)

Apparently, within eighteen months, this radical departure from conventional military thinking had led to this ship moving from last to first in efficiency within the fleet. The process underlying these changes appears to rest on the extra commitment gained from people who are made to feel they are an integral part of the group's operation.

In sporting teams, empowerment comes both formally and informally. By organising regular review meetings, brainstorming sessions and debriefing discussions, players have the opportunity to become immersed in the efforts of the team, but again it is important to warn that this process must be genuine. If players are encouraged to offer opinions, but these are never acted upon, then the exercise will be counterproductive. This is not to say that all suggestions must be acted upon; team members must accept that final decisions lie with coaches and management.

The principle of ownership can be effectively used in setting team rules, with players given the responsibility of setting up, in consultation with coaching staff, a code of behaviour. This is much more likely to be adhered to if developed by players, than if the same set of rules were to be simply imposed upon them.

ACCOUNTABILITY

The team that is given responsibility must also be prepared to carry responsibility. It is well established that one negative artefact of group dynamics is a tendency for individual effort and contribution to diminish as group size increases. This concept of social loafing seems to occur when individuals lose a sense of individual responsibility in the relative anonymity of the group effort. In a discussion of the effect, Latane, Williams, and Harkins (1979) argued that social loafing would be neutralised when ways are found to channel social forces in a way that intensifies individual responsibility within a group, rather than diffusing it.

Some of the procedures designed to recognise individual contributions can be used to this end. Appropriate use of statistics can be used to measure individual effort, although care must be taken to measure as many aspects of team behaviour as possible if the breadth of individual contributions is to be effectively captured. Video sessions can be used to highlight both positive and negative behaviours. Players can be asked to set written objectives prior to games and then review these with coaching staff after the game, and pre-game meetings can call for players to state their objectives in front of their team mates. All of these strategies underline the importance of individual contributions, but also bring these to the awareness of the group, thus increasing individual accountability at the same time as enhancing player awareness of the roles of team mates.

In large teams, subgroups organised around specialist roles can meet together to facilitate accountability by the identification and recognition of teams within teams. For example, the defenders in an Australian Rules Football team may meet together to discuss individual and subgroup aims and responsibilities. This helps to enhance the importance of individual and subunit efforts within the larger group.

RESPECT, TRUST AND HONESTY

The "sergeant-major" style of coaching appears to pay little respect to the individual's sensibilities. It appears naive to believe that players will remain positive and respectful of coaching and management staff if they are not treated with similar levels of respect. As American footballer Dave

Casper noted: "If you treat players like dogs, they turn into dogs" (Peters & Austin, 1985, p. 223).

Sporting teams are intense environments where high achieving players are often competing with each other for places on the team, court time or even contracts. Coaches carry an enormous responsibility in this environment as they have the power to cast a major influence over the direction of an athlete's career. Team cohesion is threatened when players feel they are not being dealt with honestly.

A lack of trust occurs when communications get distorted, often as a consequence of a reluctance to confront difficult issues. The coach that gives messages to the players via the media will soon find he or she is working with a mistrustful group and this consequence will often be more difficult to manage than if the original issue had been dealt with openly and honestly.

Given the nature of team sports, a coach will frequently be called upon to give players negative messages, such as critical comment on performance or news of non-selection. There is no way to get around these situations, and any attempt to "sugar coat" the message will be recognised and will sow seeds of mistrust which in turn can permeate future interactions.

A team that feels it is constantly chasing hidden agendas will become cynical about every message, and effective communication within the team is then destroyed. In contrast, a commitment to open and honest communication which extends to management of the difficult issues will be much more likely to foster trust and openness in interactions.

SECURITY AND CHALLENGE

There is considerable debate as to the levels of security within teams and organisations associated with maximum performance. One argument suggests that athletes or employees work best when secure in their positions, while the alternative line suggests that internal competition for positions can bring out the best in individuals and teams.

George (1987) argues that team building and player attrition are not mutually compatible and suggests that individuals should be given the view that they will be together as a team for the foreseeable future. He describes this as the "promise of permanence" (p. 129) and argues that this builds a greater degree of commitment to the interpersonal relationships with the team.

This situation is exemplified by team selection policy which guarantees players tenure in the team for a specified period of time irrespective of their form during this period. The argument is that, freed of the doubts and insecurities associated with selection, the player will feel more confident and will thus perform more effectively in this psychological environment. While this approach has some obvious appeal for the athletes, coaches tend to be less comfortable with a policy that guarantees selection irrespective of performance! There is also a broader school of thought that suggests that players with a security of tenure can enter a "comfort zone" that is not conducive to peak performance. Tottenham Hotspurs manager Peter Shreeve described as "healthy competition" the battle for selection waged by his senior squad members (Syer, 1986). Basketball coaches frequently argue that the major benefit of a "strong bench" is that pressure from within the squad improves the quality of training and ensures that front line players are kept on their mettle to protect their court time. Hence, high standards of performance are maintained within the squad which in turn serve the team well in competition.

Once again, it is impossible to say that either position is the correct one. Some players may perform better when feeling secure in their team status, while others may become careless if they become comfortable.

When competition for team places exists it is important that players are aware of what is required of them to succeed or be selected. Without this awareness, the insecurity associated with competition is confounded by an uncertainty as to what is required to succeed.

STRUCTURAL PROCESSES

Much of what has been discussed draws on experience with professional sporting teams or successful businesses. Professional sporting teams take things like team uniforms, songs and social clubs for granted but these factors can certainly shape team identification and pride. The awarding of the county cap in cricket or the guernsey presentations in football have major symbolic value in inducting new members into "membership" of the team or organisation. Similarly, professional teams frequently travel together and spend considerable time together in airports, hotels, planes and restaurants, which can all work to consolidate relationships and increase the bonding within a team.

However, uniforms, songs and other team trappings are best seen as symbols of team unity rather than factors central to the promotion of unity. These are surface representations of a team, but as Syer (1986) pointed out, "team uniforms, mascots and anthems only help to inspire unity if the unity has been developed already" (p. 56).

On a different note, it is important to recognise that athletes are also family members who often benefit from the considerable support provided by their families. Spouses, partners, parents and siblings frequently make sacrifices to sponsor and support an athlete's career. Conversely, the athlete who attempts to perform from a family milieu that is hostile to these efforts is unlikely to fulfil potential. Families are more likely to remain supportive if they feel that their efforts are recognised and, hence, sporting organisations are wise to acknowledge the support provided by families. This can be done in various ways ranging from provision of game tickets through to social functions organised for team members and families.

COMMUNICATION

This is probably the thread that ties all the above sections together, as without effective communication there is little chance of addressing these various processes and values.

The essence of good coaching and team building is effective communication across a range of levels: coaches talking with players, listening to players, players talking with each other. Communication can occur in group set pieces such as game preparation talks, team philosophy sessions and match debriefing meetings; in formal individual settings (e.g., reviewing a player's season); in informal settings across the meal table or in an airplane; and in day-to-day interactions at training.

Traditional authoritarian styles of coaching centred on group talks where the coach addressed the players. There was little room for discussion and little consideration of the need to communicate with individuals within the group. This is analogous to a parent addressing his or her children as a group at the breakfast table, and then communicating with them no further during the day! This is hardly likely to lead to a close family!

Effective businesses and successful sporting teams now promote open communication as a cornerstone of success. In sporting teams, players and coaches often make several common communication errors. There is often an expectation of high standards of performance to the degree that this level of performance is taken for granted and often not acknowledged. Conversely, errors are focused upon, so that a negative communication style can quickly develop. No matter how skilled or experienced, most athletes want recognition of their efforts, especially from coaches and team mates. It has been shown that teams show a liking and commitment to coaches who are generally positive in their interactions and sparing in their use of punitive methods (Smith, Smoll, & Curtis, 1979). Teams that neglect individuals' needs for praise and recognition are likely to develop into groups that play without involvement or enthusiasm.

However, communication is not all about good news and positive reinforcement. As noted, coaches frequently face difficult communication situations such as informing a player of non-selection, or outlining the shortcomings or weaknesses in a player's game. In these settings players can become upset, angry, defensive or critical in return, and the communication and conflict resolution skills of the coach are sorely tested. Some coaches shy away from such situations and/or deal with them indirectly (e.g., announcing a team in a group, thus avoiding discussion with a non-selected player), but effective coaches are able to deal with such communications constructively. This does not happen easily, and should start with recognition across the team that such communications are designed to improve team and individual performances and should not be taken as personal criticisms. In this light, feedback is seen as a necessary and acceptable (albeit at times difficult) component of maximising performance. It is also the case that athletes are more likely to accept negative feedback if there is a general tone of respect in the interactions within the team, and if they believe that their positive characteristics and input will also be acknowledged.

It is also important to engender open and frequent discussion between team mates. This adds to both accountability and ownership of team strategy and efforts. In 1983, when the Australia II syndicate wrested the

America's Cup from the New York Yacht Club, the crew in Newport lived together in a relatively cramped crew house, but the effect of this was that they were thrown together in a way that facilitated valuable discussions between crew members. When the syndicate attempted the defence of the cup in Fremantle in 1986–87, many of the senior members of the crew rented apartments while the younger crew lived in the crew house. In the review sessions of this ultimately unsuccessful campaign, it was felt that the accommodation arrangements had a negative effect on crew cohesion and, more particularly, impeded the crew house communication and discussion that had characterised the 1983 campaign.

John Madden, long-term successful coach of the Los Angeles Raiders, succinctly summarises the nature of successful communication in a team sport context:

> ... Communication between a coach and his players was being able to say good things, bad things and average things. Conversely, it's being able to listen to good, bad and average things... I tried to talk to each (player)... Sometimes it was merely a quick "How ya doin'?" Sometimes it was a conversation. But by talking to them every day, they didn't feel something was up when I would stop to talk to them.... (Syer, 1986, pp. 99–100)

FUTURE DIRECTIONS

As noted, much of our knowledge of team building is based on anecdotal evidence. There is a paucity of experimental study of what makes an effective team. This is understandable given the difficulties in imposing experimental control in real-life settings.

It is likely that these gaps in research can be best filled in two different ways. Firstly, by careful examination of the team functioning of the more successful sporting teams, it may become possible to glean common themes that represent the essence of effective team interactions. Peters and Waterman (1982) have reported a similar exercise with successful companies, isolating and describing common themes observed in successful corporations as diverse as McDonalds, Delta Air, Hewlett Packard and Caterpillar. This fine-grained descriptive research requires considerable attention to the detail of the group's functioning, to a degree that has been rarely reported from a sporting context.

Once these key success themes are identified from such descriptive research, attempts can then be made to develop and evaluate team building strategies. This may entail the assessment of team building "packages", as well as evaluation of the individual components that form these packages. It is likely that research of this nature would be carried out initially with sub-elite teams, as top level teams are often reluctant to "try out" untested strategies.

As coach education becomes more professional and, more particularly, as instruction in the psychology of coaching becomes more sophisticated and central to coach education, it can be expected that there will be a greater awareness of how to manage athletes effectively on a day-to-day basis to maximise individual and team performance. This has already happened in some sports, but others are more conservative and still cling to practices that are dramatically out of step with effective management of interpersonal relationships within a team.

CONCLUSIONS

Sporting teams represent an intriguing social laboratory for the study of individual and group achievement. Much of our understanding of building effective teams rests on folklore and anecdote. This is understandable given the difficulties in setting up rigorous experimental studies of group functioning.

By drawing together knowledge and wisdom from areas as diverse as corporate philosophies and functioning, family and childrearing practices, social psychology laboratories and sporting locker rooms, it becomes possible to identify themes that recur and appear to be associated with individual and group success.

It is perhaps of critical importance to recognise that building and maintaining an effective team requires consistent attention and commitment and it is not something that can be achieved simply as an adjunct. Honest and open communication is at the basis of attempts to deal simultaneously with the development and achievement needs of the individual, and the ultimate success of the group or team.

It is a great challenge to guide the energies and aspirations of a group of high achieving individuals towards a team goal. To do so effectively, a coach must have the capacity to relate to and understand the needs of the individual while retaining a clear focus on the aims and needs of the group.

SUMMARY

Team sports pose a challenge to both coach and sport psychologist. To maximise group efficiency, an environment must be created within which individual team members understand, accept and feel challenged by their team role. This can be tricky, especially when team members are asked to subordinate individual needs for the good of the team. Team dynamics can have a significant impact on team performance, although this relationship is not straightforward; happy teams are not necessarily successful and successful teams are not necessarily happy. However, it is reasonable to suggest that a degree of team harmony is likely to facilitate team success.

Much of our knowledge of successful teams comes from analysis of successful business practices. It is apparent that many successful corporations are characterised by a "people emphasis". In these companies, attention to the aspirations and needs of individual employees is at the hub of the corporate philosophy. In contrast, some groups prefer to see team building as an adjunct to everyday activities rather than a central focus. It is argued that the bag of tricks approach to team building will be unlikely to establish a strong group ethos. On the contrary, successful teams are generally built around a philosophy that emphasises development of the individual, involvement and empowerment of team members, and accountability of individuals for their actions within the team. Communication is seen as the cornerstone of successful teams; open and regular discussions, a preparedness to grapple with the hard issues, and free flow of feedback between coach and players allow an atmosphere of trust and honesty to be developed.

Our understanding of the psychology of team sports will be enhanced by fine-grained analysis of the ethos and practices of successful teams and by experimental study of the impact of differing styles of team interaction.

REFERENCES

Bettenhausen, K. L. (1991). Five years of group research: What we have learned and what needs to be addressed. *Journal of Management, 17,* 345–381.

Buller, P. F. (1986). The team building–task performance relation: Some conceptual and methodological refinements. *Group and Organization Studies, 11,* 147–168.

George, P. S. (1987). Team building without tears. *Personnel Journal,* November, 122–129.

Latane, B., Williams, K., & Harkins, S. (1979). Many hands make light the work: The causes and consequences of social loafing. *Journal of Personality and Social Psychology, 37,* 823–832.

Maddux, R. B. (1986). *Team building: An exercise in leadership* (rev. ed.). Menlo Park, CA: Crisp Publications.

Peters, T. J., & Austin, N. K. (1985). *A passion for excellence.* Glasgow: Fontana/Collins.

Peters, T. J., & Waterman, R. H. (1982). *In search of excellence.* Sydney: Harper & Row.

Smith, S. (1992). *The Jordan rules.* New York: Simon & Schuster.

Smith, R. E., Smoll, F. L., & Curtis, B. (1979). Coach effectiveness training: A cognitive behavioural approach to enhancing relationship skills in youth sport coaches. *Journal of Sport Psychology, 1,* 59–75.

Syer, J. (1986). *Team spirit.* London: Simon & Schuster.

Vogt, J. F., & Griffith, S. J. (1988). Team development and proactive change: Theory and training implications. *Organization Development Journal,* Winter, 81–87.

PART

3

ISSUES IN SPORT PSYCHOLOGY

Part 3 of this book examines areas of sport and exercise psychology in which exciting new developments are taking place! Many psychologists now recognise the wide implications of the application of psychological principles to sport. Physical activity involves more than competitive sport; exercise is important for health and well-being every day. The area of exercise psychology has expanded rapidly. In Chapter 17, Grove provides a substantial summary of this rich area of development.

Sport psychologists' involvement in performance enhancement has sensitiscd them to issues beyond psychological skills training. Often, long-term athlete growth and well-being, including PST, depends on these issues being resolved. Such issues include psychological aspects of injury and overtraining and burn-out problems created by heavy training schedules. They also include the pressures of transitions in sport, such as preparing for life and a career and adjusting to retirement from high level sport. In Chapter 18, Kirkby reviews the area of sport injuries. Gordon, in Chapter 19, considers the topic of transitions in sport. He reports on active programs in careers and lifeskills education, as well as the underpinning theory and research in this field.

Again, awareness has been raised in issues associated with sports for special groups, such as women, children and the disabled. In Chapter 20, Hanrahan discusses major issues of working with disabled athletes and reports on Australian research. Tremayne addresses issues related to sport psychology and children, in Chapter 21. Plaisted proposes a shift from the conception of women as a "special group", symbolised by the title and focus of Chapter 22, *gender* in sport. The chapter considers ways in which gender does influence sport behaviour.

Along with the recent expansion of the domain, it has been recognised that there are many different ways to study sport and that a richer, more complete view will result from the judicious application of the breadth of research methods. In Chapter 23, Jackson contrasts the quantitative and qualitative approaches and reviews a range of qualitative research methods which are currently gaining popularity in sport psychology research. This book covers a wide variety of fields, depicting the main themes of sport and exercise psychology as it blossoms into a rich and varied discipline. In Chapter 24, Morris and Summers reflect on major issues facing theoretical sport psychology, future roles of sport psychologists and issues to be resolved by the profession. They conclude that the current situation reflects the positive challenges facing a healthy and vibrant discipline, which new generations of sport psychologists should address with enthusiasm.

CHAPTER

17

AN INTRODUCTION
TO EXERCISE
PSYCHOLOGY

J. ROBERT GROVE

Sport psychology established an identity during the 1970s and developed into a legitimate academic specialty during the 1980s. The period of identity formation began with the publication of the *International Journal of Sport Psychology* in 1970 and culminated with the publication of the *Journal of Sport Psychology* in 1979. As the discipline matured during the 1980s, its persona changed in a number of ways, and it became more diversified.

The early 1980s was a period when theoretical models and research paradigms from other areas of psychology were employed to examine sport-related phenomena. This "academic" emphasis was apparent in texts published at that time, such as Carron's (1980) *Social Psychology of Sport* and Straub's (1980) *Sport Psychology: An Analysis of Athlete Behavior*. In the mid-1980s, there was a decided shift toward a "professional" emphasis which, once again, was reflected in the nature of sport psychology publications. Books such as *Applied Sport Psychology: Personal Growth to Peak Performance* (Williams, 1986) and *Psyching for Sport: Mental Training for Athletes* (Orlick, 1986) focused on performance enhancement issues, and this applied orientation received formal endorsement when the journal *The Sport Psychologist* was first published in 1987.

During the late 1980s and early 1990s, sport psychologists began to look beyond sport in pursuit of their academic and professional interests. By doing so, they became involved in issues that, although related to sport, were also being addressed by colleagues in other psychological domains. Figure 17.1 illustrates how the interests of sport psychologists overlapped with those of exercise psychologists, health psychologists and medical psychologists (Rejeski & Brawley, 1988). The overlap of sport and exercise psychology is particularly noteworthy. A close relationship between these areas of study was implicitly acknowledged in 1988 when the *Journal of Sport Psychology* became the *Journal of Sport and Exercise Psychology*.

Since that time, exercise psychology has gained momentum and become a popular and important area of study at both the undergraduate and postgraduate level. The appearance of books such as *Exercise Adherence: Its Impact on Public Health* (Dishman, 1988), *Psychology of Physical Activity and Exercise* (Biddle & Mutrie, 1991), and *Exercise Psychology: The Influence of Physical Exercise on Psychological Processes* (Seraganian, 1993) provides evidence of this recent trend.

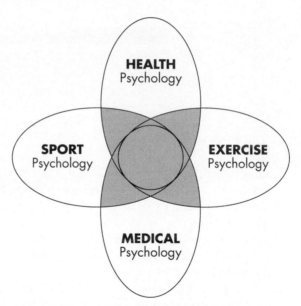

Figure 17.1: Interrelationships between sport psychology, exercise psychology, health psychology and medical psychology

A DEFINITION OF EXERCISE PSYCHOLOGY

Rejeski and colleagues suggested that definitional ambiguity could stifle the growth of sport and exercise psychology in a number of ways (Rejeski & Brawley, 1988; Rejeski & Thompson, 1993). In an attempt to clarify the boundaries of these fields, they defined *sport psychology* as "the educational, scientific, and professional contributions of psychology to the promotion, maintenance, and enhancement of sport-related behavior" (Rejeski &

Brawley, 1988, p. 239). *Exercise psychology*, on the other hand, was defined as "the educational, scientific, and professional contributions of psychology to promoting, explaining, maintaining, and enhancing the parameters of physical fitness" (Rejeski & Thompson, 1993, p. 5). Although similar issues might be addressed by sport and exercise psychologists, the dependent variable under investigation was viewed as the primary criterion for classification of specific topics. Thus, the effects of team cohesion on participation in an off-season weight training program was considered an exercise psychology study, but the effects of participation in an off-season weight training program on subsequent team cohesion was considered a sport psychology study.

Defining exercise psychology on the basis of its outcome variables encourages systematic research and provides a focus for curriculum development as well as professional training (Rejeski & Brawley, 1988). At the same time, however, this approach could lead to an overly narrow view of the field. It would relegate, for example, studies on the psychological consequences of exercise to the realm of health psychology despite an explicit focus on both exercise and psychology. Rejeski and Thompson (1993, pp. 5–6) obviously recognise this limitation, because they state that "the interface of exercise and health psychology is essential to the future development of both fields" and that "a general exercise psychology course... would probably include investigations in which exercise is considered both as an independent and dependent variable".

From the standpoint of curriculum development and professional training, then, a broad view of exercise psychology may be preferable to a more narrow one. Thus, I believe it is appropriate to define exercise psychology as contributions of psychology to the description, explanation and prediction of the antecedents, correlates and/or consequences of exercise behaviour. Consistent with the definition provided by Rejeski and Thompson (1993), it is assumed that:

(1) contributions can be made from educational, scientific and professional perspectives
(2) antecedents, correlates, and consequences can be cognitive, emotional or behavioural in nature
(3) exercise behaviour includes a variety of movement forms related to strength/endurance, cardiopulmonary fitness, flexibility and body composition.

This broad definition of exercise psychology provides a framework for organising areas of interest within the field. Some of these specific areas are shown in Figure 17.2. The list of topics in Figure 17.2 is far from comprehensive, and there may be some disagreement as to the placement of a given topic (especially within the correlates and consequences categories). However, the diagram does give a reasonable overview of the kinds of research conducted by exercise psychologists. In an effort to familiarise the reader with some of this work, research findings in a few of these areas are summarised below.

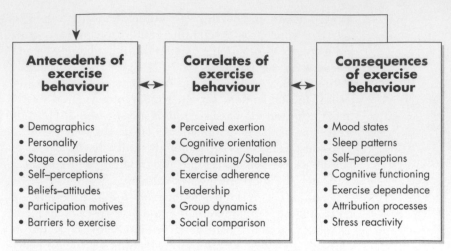

Antecedents of exercise behaviour	Correlates of exercise behaviour	Consequences of exercise behaviour
• Demographics • Personality • Stage considerations • Self–perceptions • Beliefs–attitudes • Participation motives • Barriers to exercise	• Perceived exertion • Cognitive orientation • Overtraining/Staleness • Exercise adherence • Leadership • Group dynamics • Social comparison	• Mood states • Sleep patterns • Self–perceptions • Cognitive functioning • Exercise dependence • Attribution processes • Stress reactivity

Figure 17.2: A conceptual framework for areas of interest within exercise psychology

AREAS OF INTEREST WITHIN EXERCISE PSYCHOLOGY

ANTECEDENTS OF EXERCISE BEHAVIOUR

Demographics

Epidemiological studies provide a descriptive profile of exercise behaviours within the general population. Although definitions of exercise vary considerably from one study to the next, some consistent patterns have emerged. In North America, for example, there appears to have been a general increase in the amount of vigorous leisure-time activity between 1967 and 1987 (Powell, 1988). At the same time, however, some segments of the population have remained less active than others. Physical activity levels are lower among women than among men, and they are also lower for older persons than for younger ones. In addition, persons with relatively low socioeconomic status are less active than those with higher socioeconomic status (Stephens, Jacobs, & White, 1985).

Results of national surveys conducted between 1984 and 1987 indicate that the physical activity patterns of Australians are very similar to those of North Americans (Bauman, Owen, & Rushworth, 1990; Owen & Bauman, 1992). Pooled data from these surveys (N = 17 053) revealed that a greater proportion of women than men were inactive, and women were less likely than men to engage in a level of physical activity sufficient for aerobic conditioning and cardiovascular protection. Inactivity also increased steadily from age 14 to age 50, while the number of people engaged in moderate to high levels of physical activity decreased steadily with age. Levels of activity were also low among young married people with children.

Findings related to various indices of socioeconomic status were somewhat mixed, but involvement in exercise did show a consistent connection to education level. Respondents with a tertiary education were almost twice as likely to be active as respondents with only a primary education.

Personality

Some studies also implicate personality as an important antecedent of exercise behaviour. Vingerhoets, Croon, Jeninga, and Menges (1990) examined a number of health habits, including exercise, among 978 Dutch men and women. Several personality variables differed significantly between respondents who exercised at least twice a week and those who did not exercise regularly. Specifically, the regular exercisers had higher levels of self-esteem and lower levels of neuroticism, hostility and social inadequacy, as measured by the Dutch Personality Inventory.

In addition, Hogan (1989) found evidence of a connection between personality and performance on a variety of physical fitness tests. Men who performed well on the tests (presumably because they maintained a high level of fitness) were more optimistic, energetic, perfectionistic and competitive than men who performed poorly. There is also some evidence that exercise adherence is affected by personality factors such as self-motivation, depression, anxiety and introversion/extraversion (Dishman, 1980; Martin & Dubbert, 1985).

The individual difference variable of social physique anxiety may play a role in various aspects of exercise behaviour. Social physique anxiety is defined as excessive concern about the evaluation of one's physique by other people (Hart, Leary, & Rejeski, 1989). Although little research has been published on this construct, there is evidence that it is related to various dimensions of self-concept (McInman & Berger, 1993). There is also speculation that social physique anxiety could influence the types of exercise activities people take part in, whether they exercise alone or in a group, the nature of their thought processes during exercise, and how much pleasure they derive from their involvement (Hart, Leary, & Rejeski, 1989; Rejeski & Thompson, 1993). Some of these hypotheses were supported in a study by Lantz, Hardy, and Ainsworth (1991). These investigators found a significant negative relationship between exercise behaviour and social physique anxiety, and this relationship was especially strong for older females with depressive tendencies.

Stage considerations

Behaviour change is a dynamic process that occurs in a series of stages. Prochaska and colleagues have shown that similar stages of change characterise a range of health-related behaviours including smoking cessation, weight control, sun exposure, safe sex and exercise adoption (Prochaska & Marcus, in press). With respect to exercise, pre-contemplators are those individuals who have no intention of changing their physical activity levels. At some point, however, they may progress to the contemplation stage where change is seriously considered but no new exercise behaviours are adopted. If a plan of action is subsequently developed and preliminary attempts are made to alter activity levels, then these individuals enter the preparation stage. When exercise behaviour reaches a suitable criterion (e.g., three times per week for 20 minutes at a moderate intensity), the action stage has been achieved. Progression to the maintenance stage requires exercise behaviour to remain at the criterion level for at least six months.

The proportion of people classified into each of these stages is very similar in Australia and the United States, and stage classifications are significantly correlated with self-reports of moderate and/or vigorous physical activity (Marcus & Owen, 1992; Marcus & Simkin, 1993).

Research has demonstrated that exercise-related cognitions and behaviours differ across the various stages of change. Marcus, Selby, Niaura, and Rossi (1992), for example, found that exercise self-efficacy increased steadily from pre-contemplation to maintenance. The extent to which people rely on various experiential and behavioural change processes also appears to be stage-related (Marcus, Rossi, Selby, Niaura, & Abrams, 1992). Use of experiential processes (e.g., dramatic relief, environmental re-evaluation, self re-evaluation) tends to rise during the contemplation stage, level off during preparation, and then peak in the action stage. On the other hand, use of behavioural processes (e.g., counterconditioning, reinforcement management, stimulus control) shows a more consistent, step-like increase across the contemplation, preparation and action stages.

When decisional balance measures are examined in relation to stage of change, there is an increase in both positive and negative perceptions of exercise from pre-contemplation to contemplation. Thereafter, positive perceptions increase across stages, while negative perceptions decrease (Marcus, Rakowski, & Rossi, 1992). These findings suggest that exercise interventions may need to be stage-matched for maximum impact, and that movement to a subsequent stage (rather than maintenance of criterion-related exercise behaviour) is an appropriate goal for some individuals (Prochaska & Marcus, in press; Marcus & Owen, 1992).

CORRELATES OF EXERCISE BEHAVIOUR

Perceived exertion

Subjective estimates of effort expenditure during exercise are influenced by a variety of physiological and psychosocial factors (Morgan, 1981; Pandolf, 1983). Physiological influences include "central" factors related to sensations from the cardiopulmonary system (e.g., heart rate, respiration rate, oxygen consumption) and "local" factors related to sensations from the exercising muscles/joints (e.g., blood lactate, catecholamine levels, golgi tendon activity). Literature reviews on the physiological determinants of perceived exertion generally conclude that local factors predominate over central factors, but there is evidence that central factors may increase in importance when aerobic demands are high (Watt & Grove, 1992).

With respect to psychosocial factors, high scores on measures of depression, neuroticism, anxiety and femininity are associated with exaggerated ratings of perceived exertion (RPE) (Hochstetler, Rejeski, & Best, 1985; Morgan, 1973), but the type A behaviour pattern is associated with suppressed RPE (Anshel, Anshel, & Gregory, 1991; Carver, Coleman, & Glass, 1976). In addition, expected task duration and the behaviour of models have been shown to affect perceived exertion. The expectation that one will be exercising for a relatively long time tends to lower RPE at moderate workloads (Rejeski & Ribisl, 1980), and a similar effect occurs if one observes other people exercising without difficulty (Hardy, Hall, & Prestholdt, 1986; Rejeski & Sanford, 1984). There is also evidence that music and hypnotic suggestion can influence RPE without corresponding changes in physiological indices of exertion (Boutcher & Trenske, 1990; Morgan, Hirota, Weitz, & Balke, 1976). Although psychological factors are often presumed to be most influential at moderate workloads, Boutcher, Fleisher-Curtain, and Gines (1988) found that men lowered RPE at heavy workloads when a female experimenter was present. They suggested that self-presentational concerns may have been responsible for this effect.

Cognitive orientation

Thought processes and state-of-mind during exercise have been examined by a number of investigators. One aspect of this research has been a focus on associative and dissociative cognitive strategies. Associative strategies involve either a self-monitoring of body sensations such as muscle tension/fatigue and respiration during exercise or a focus on the technical aspects of task performance (Morgan, 1978; Rushall, 1984; Schomer, 1986). Dissociative strategies are based on distraction principles, and they include a variety of techniques that divert attention away from the technical aspects of the task or the physical sensations that accompany its performance (Morgan, 1978; Rushall, 1984; Schomer, 1986).

Studies on the cognitive orientations of distance runners indicate a general preference for associative strategies (Masters & Lambert, 1989; Schomer, 1986; Summers, Sargent, Levey, & Murray, 1982; Ungerleider, Golding, Porter, & Foster, 1989). Dissociative strategies are also employed, however, and the frequency of their use may depend on the athlete's physical condition, competitive experience, ability level and/or motives for running as well as the nature of the run (training versus competition) and the stage of the run (Masters & Lambert, 1989; Morgan & Pollock, 1977; Okwumabua, 1985; Okwumabua, Meyers, Schleser, & Cooke, 1983; Summers et al., 1982).

Further, it appears that both association and dissociation can have positive effects on exercise-related behaviour. Associative strategies have been positively correlated with performance in several studies (Masters & Lambert, 1989; Morgan & Pollock, 1977; Rushall, 1984; Schomer, 1987; Spink & Longhurst, 1986), but dissociative strategies have been shown to decrease perceptions of effort and improve performance in other studies

(Gill & Strom, 1985; Morgan, Horstman, Cymerman, & Stokes, 1983; Pennebaker & Lightner, 1980; Rejeski & Kenney, 1987; Weinberg, Smith, Jackson, & Gould, 1984). Martin and colleagues (1984) have also found that instruction in the use of dissociative strategies improves adherence in the early stages of exercise.

The potential for exercise to induce a meditative, trance-like state-of-mind has also been examined. Such "alterations in consciousness" are most likely to occur after 30–60 minutes of steady-state exercise (Mandell, 1979; Solomon & Bumpus, 1981) and this "spin-out" quality has been identified as one aspect of commitment to regular running (Carmack & Martens, 1979). Extreme instances of exercise-induced states of altered consciousness have been labelled "the runner's high".

There are large discrepancies in estimates of how frequently this phenomenon occurs (Morgan, 1978; Sachs, 1984; Summers, Machin, & Sargent, 1983), and differences of opinion about the nature of the experience may be responsible for these discrepant findings (Acevedo, Dzewaltowski, Gill, & Noble, 1992). However, it is generally acknowledged that less intense alterations in consciousness occur quite often among exercisers (Acevedo et al., 1992; Sachs, 1984; Summers et al., 1983). These experiences are similar to flow states as described by Csikszentmihalyi (1990), and a recent study by Grove and Lewis (1993) indicates that personal and situational factors may influence the degree to which they occur during exercise. Specifically, these investigators found that hypnotic susceptibility and familiarity with the task increased the incidence of flow-like states for circuit trainers.

Overtraining and staleness

Involvement in a very heavy exercise schedule (i.e., overtraining) is sometimes accompanied by negative physiological and psychological changes. These changes include muscle soreness/damage, neuroendocrinological imbalance, suppressed immunity, lethargy, loss of appetite/weight, mood disturbance, insomnia, alteration of movement biomechanics, and decreased performance (Fry, Morton, & Keast, 1991; Kuipers & Keizer, 1988; Raglin, 1993). Although individual differences are apparent in susceptibility to this "overtraining syndrome" (Costill, Flynn, Kirwan, Houmard, Mitchell, Thomas, & Park, 1988; Morgan, Costill, Flynn, Raglin, & O'Connor, 1988; Raglin & Morgan, 1989), insufficient recovery time between exercise sessions is the primary predisposing factor for both acute and chronic episodes (Fry et al., 1991; Mackinnon & Hooper, 1991; Raglin, 1993). Additional stresses related to diet/sleep, travel, and competition may exacerbate the effects of insufficient recovery time (Costill et al., 1988; Nideffer, 1988; O'Connor & Morgan, 1990).

Because endurance athletes often undertake planned overtraining in an attempt to produce "superadaptation" effects, they may be especially prone to the overtraining syndrome. In studies of long distance runners and swimmers, Morgan and colleagues found a yearly incidence rate of 5–10%

and a career incidence rate of approximately 60% (Morgan, Brown, Raglin, O'Connor, & Ellickson, 1987; Morgan, O'Connor, Ellickson, & Bradley, 1988; Morgan, O'Connor, Sparling, & Pate, 1987).

Raglin (1993) notes that psychological variables are typically more consistent indices of "staleness" (i.e., the overtraining syndrome) than physiological variables, and the Profile of Mood States (POMS) (McNair, Lorr, & Droppleman, 1971) has provided reliable findings in this regard. Increases in POMS total mood disturbance (TMD) have been linked to corresponding increases in training workloads for periods ranging from three days (O'Connor, Raglin, & Morgan, 1991) to several weeks (Fry, Grove, Morton, Zeroni, Gaudieri, & Keast, in press; Raglin, in press) to full competitive seasons (Morgan, Brown, Raglin, O'Connor, & Ellickson, 1987; O'Connor, Morgan, Raglin, Barksdale, & Kalin, 1989). These changes in TMD have been observed in a variety of sport groups including swimmers, runners, speed skaters, rowers and basketball players (Raglin, in press; Raglin, 1993).

When individual POMS subscales are examined, increases in fatigue and decreases in vigour seem to account for much of the change in TMD among athletes who are exposed to training stress but who are not stale (Raglin, Morgan, & O'Connor, 1991). For stale athletes, however, substantial increases in depression also occur (Raglin, 1993). Most POMS subscales return to baseline levels when exercise workloads are decreased to "normal" training levels, but residual elevations during recovery have been found for tension and fatigue (Fry et al., in press; Raglin et al., 1991).

CONSEQUENCES OF EXERCISE BEHAVIOUR

Mood states

Mood states have also been examined as a consequence of involvement in exercise outside of sport at a level below that necessary to produce overtraining effects. Although some investigators have failed to find changes in mood from this type of exercise (e.g., Hughes, 1984), the bulk of the evidence favours a positive relationship (Plante & Rodin, 1990). Measures taken immediately after exercise have documented decreases in state anxiety, depression, tension and mental confusion as well as increases in vigour and exhilaration (Berger & Owen, 1988; LaFontaine, DiLorenzo, Frensch, Studk-Ropp, Bargman, & McDonald, 1992; McDonald & Hodgdon, 1991; McInman & Berger, 1993; Morgan, 1985; Steptoe & Cox, 1989). The nature of these acute mood changes may depend, however, on the previous fitness status of the individual, the type of exercise undertaken, the intensity of exercise, and/or the time lag between exercise and assessment of mood (Boutcher & Landers, 1988; Raglin, Turner, & Eksten, 1993; Raglin, Wilson, & Morris, 1993; Steptoe & Cox, 1989).

The long-term benefits of exercise on mood are not as well-documented as the short-term benefits (Plante & Rodin, 1990), but several studies have obtained positive findings. Correlational research by Hayden and Allen (1984) and Lobstein, Mosbacher, and Ismail (1983), for example, found that regular exercisers were less anxious and depressed than non-exercisers. Experimental studies have also shown positive mood effects from exercise interventions ranging in length from six weeks to 12 months (Blumenthal, Williams, Needels, & Wallace, 1982; Goldwater & Collis, 1985; King, Taylor, & Haskell, 1993).

Mood enhancement may be related to characteristics of the exercise activity itself and may occur for a number of reasons. Berger and Owen (1988) suggest that positive psychological outcomes are most likely to occur when exercise is pleasant/enjoyable, non-competitive, repetitive/rhythmical and temporally/spatially certain. Regular participation (three or four times per week) at a moderate intensity (60–75% of estimated maximum heart rate) for 20–60 minutes also contributes to positive mood effects. Although much of the research on exercise and mood deals with aerobic activities, there is some question as to the necessity for an aerobic component (Berger & Owen, 1992). Potential mechanisms for exercise-related mood enhancement include expectancy effects, distraction, increases in neurotransmitters, release of endorphins, and temperature changes (Morgan, 1985; Hatfield, 1991). A recent study by Petruzello, Landers, and Salazar (1993) examined the temperature hypothesis and found a strong positive correlation between core temperature and state anxiety during the first 30 minutes after exercise.

Sleep patterns

Several stages of sleep can be identified on the basis of physiological and perceptual processes. As a person begins to fall asleep, their heart rate, respiration rate and body temperature decrease, and alpha waves (8–13 cycles per second) appear on their electroencephalogram (EEG) profiles. The first stage of sleep (stage 1) is a semi-conscious state characterised by further reductions in heart rate, some irregularity in respiration, and muscle relaxation that may trigger involuntary twitching (hypnic jerks). As body temperature continues to decrease, the person enters stage 2 where the EEG profile exhibits short bursts of rhythmical activity in the 13–16 cycles per second range known as sleep spindles. These spindles mark the boundary between perceptions of semi-consciousness and sleep, because most people awakened after the appearance of spindles report that they have been asleep. With further loss of consciousness and the initial appearance of very slow brain waves (delta waves; .5–3 cycles per second), the person enters stage 3 sleep. In deep sleep (stage 4), there is no conscious awareness, and the EEG profile contains more than 50% delta waves.

Stages 3 and 4 are often combined when analysing sleep patterns and referred to as slow-wave sleep (SWS). Similarly, stages 2, 3 and 4 are collectively called non-REM sleep because rapid eye movements (REMs) and dreams rarely occur at these times. SWS and non-REM sleep are believed to facilitate body restoration processes, and a number of studies have examined the effects of exercise on these sleep phases.

Studies of sleep patterns in fit and unfit individuals have shown that fitness is positively correlated with both SWS and non-REM sleep (Griffin & Trinder, 1978; Montgomery, Trinder, Fraser, & Paxton, 1987; Walker, Floyd, Fein, Cavness, Lualhati, & Feinberg, 1978). In addition, a longitudinal study of army recruits by Shapiro, Warren, Trinder, Paxton, Oswald, Flenley, and Catterall (1984) found that increases in fitness and lean body mass were associated with increases in the duration of SWS.

Despite these findings, the more immediate effects of exercise on sleep patterns remain unclear. Some studies have found that SWS increases following exercise (Baekeland & Lasky, 1966; Horne & Staff, 1983; Shapiro, Bortz, Mitchell, Bartel, & Jooste, 1981), but other studies have found either no effects or disruptive effects from exercise (Montgomery, Trinder, Paxton, Fraser, Meaney, & Koerbin, 1985; Montgomery et al., 1987; Paxton, Montgomery, Trinder, Newman, & Bowling, 1982). Horne (1981) has suggested that exercise may increase SWS only for already-trained individuals, and there is also evidence that time of day and type of exercise are important moderators of the relationship between exercise and sleep patterns. Dynamic/aerobic exercise appears to increase the time taken to fall asleep and may result in less SWS if undertaken late in the day rather than early in the day (Baekeland & Lasky, 1966; Browman & Tepas, 1976). On the other hand, static exercise performed close to bedtime appears to decrease sleep latency and may increase SWS (Browman, 1980; Moorcroft, 1989).

Two recent studies examined the effects of exercise on sleep disturbance among individuals who were attempting to stop smoking. Grove, Wilkinson, and Dawson (1993) asked female smokers to substantially reduce their cigarette consumption for one week, and then compared self-reports of sleep disturbance in matched groups of exercisers and controls. The exercise intervention consisted of daily 15-minute sessions on a bicycle ergometer at 75% of estimated maximum heart rate. Sleep disturbances were above-baseline for both groups following cessation, but they were significantly higher in the exercise group than in the control group.

In a longer-term investigation, Wilkinson and Grove (1993) monitored sleep disturbances in exercisers and controls for several weeks before and after smoking cessation. The exercise intervention in this study was less intense than the one used in the previous study, but it began a month prior to cessation, continued during the post-quit period, and produced a tendency toward increased fitness levels in the exercise group. Once again, total sleep disturbance scores increased during initial withdrawal for all subjects. However, these increases were significantly larger in the *control* group than in the exercise group. Inspection of individual components of the total sleep disturbance score suggested that substantial increases in the time taken to fall asleep by control subjects was primarily responsible for this effect.

Self-perceptions

Self-concept and self-esteem are multidimensional constructs that include perceptions of intellectual, social, emotional and physical aspects of the self (Shavelson, Hubner, & Stanton, 1976). The physical domain is typically believed to consist of subdomains related to physical ability and physical appearance (see, for example, Marsh & Shavelson, 1985; Ryckman, Robbins, Thornton, & Cantrell, 1982), but Fox and Corbin (1989) suggest that a more complex structure could characterise this domain. Specifically, these investigators found evidence that the physical self-worth of young adults was influenced by perceptions of sport/athletic ability, physical condition/stamina/fitness, body attractiveness and physical strength. Fox (1990) further suggested that the perceived importance of each subdomain determined its impact on higher-order constructs, and that the relative importance of specific subdomains could change across the lifespan. Despite reservations that some of his subdomains might be relevant only for young adults, recent evidence suggests that they are capable of discriminating exercisers from non-exercisers and predicting exercise involvement among middle-aged and older adults (Sonstroem, Speliotis, & Fava, 1992).

Sonstroem and Morgan (1989) presented a model that predicted positive effects of exercise on self-concept and/or self-esteem. In this model, exercise-induced changes in measurable physical attributes (e.g., aerobic capacity, flexibility, muscular strength/endurance, body composition) give rise to task-specific judgements of physical self-efficacy. Improvements in task-specific competencies then produce broader feelings of mastery/control and a perception of general physical competence. Feelings of physical acceptance (i.e., satisfaction or dissatisfaction with the physical self) may also be influenced by task-specific physical self-efficacies and/or perceptions of physical competence. The effects of exercise on global self-concept or self-esteem are hypothesised to depend on the amount of change in physical self-efficacies, physical competence and physical acceptance as well as the perceived importance of these constructs for the individual (Fox, 1990).

The Sonstroem and Morgan (1989) model was tested in a study by Sonstroem, Harlow, Gemma, and Osborne (1991), and the results were generally favourable. Although physical acceptance was not included in this investigation, exercise-related self-efficacy was positively correlated with perceptions of physical competence, and physical competence was, in turn, positively correlated with global self-esteem. The direct path between physical self-efficacy and global self-esteem was not significant. In addition to supporting the Sonstroem and Morgan (1989) model, these findings imply that the development of specific and general physical competencies through exercise should lead to improvements in self-esteem. McDonald and Hodgdon (1991) conducted a meta-analytic review of 37 studies dealing with the relationship between exercise and self-esteem, and they concluded that such an effect does indeed occur. Moreover, their data indicated that exercise-related improvements in self-esteem were independent of gender, age classification (young, middle-aged, elderly) and form of exercise.

FUTURE DIRECTIONS

Exercise psychology has a relatively brief history, but popular and academic interest in this field is increasing rapidly. Over the next decade, there will undoubtedly be more exercise psychology content in certification courses for exercise professionals and in tertiary degree courses. There will also be considerably more scientific research conducted in this area. It is expected that this research will: provide more precise operational definitions for the constructs being studied; utilise both experimental and phenomenological methods; strive for ecological validity; extend the scope of inquiry beyond the present focus on aerobic exercise; and determine whether certain individuals are more likely to experience psychological benefits from exercise than others (Rejeski & Thompson, 1993; Seraganian, 1993). If input is derived from social, psychological, and biological perspectives, this research should lead to the development of more sophisticated theories about exercise behaviour (Rejeski & Thompson, 1993).

SUMMARY

The interests of exercise psychologists overlap to some extent with those of sport psychologists, health psychologists and medical psychologists. At the same time, it is possible to distinguish exercise psychology from these other areas of study. Exercise psychology was defined as *contributions of psychology to the description, explanation, and prediction of the antecedents, correlates and/or consequences of exercise behaviour.* On the basis of this definition, a conceptual framework was proposed, and the literature related to specific antecedents, correlates and consequences of exercise behaviour was briefly examined. This overview of topics was necessarily selective and brief, but it does illustrate the kinds of issues that have been and will continue to be addressed by researchers and practitioners in exercise psychology.

REFERENCES

Acevedo, E. O., Dzewaltowski, D. A., Gill, D. L., & Noble, J. M. (1992). Cognitive orientations of ultramarathoners. *The Sport Psychologist, 6,* 242–252.

Anshel, S. L., Anshel, M. H., & Gregory, W. L. (1991). The effect of Type A and Type B and fitness level on ratings of perceived exertion and physical fatigue by females. *Australian Journal of Science and Medicine in Sport, 23,* 106–110.

Baekeland, F., & Lasky, R. (1966). Exercise and sleep patterns in college athletes. *Perceptual and Motor Skills, 23,* 1203–1207.

Bauman, A., Owen, N., & Rushworth, L. (1990). Recent trends and socio-demographic determinants of exercise participation in Australia. *Community Health Studies, 14,* 19–26.

Berger, B. G., & Owen, D. R. (1988). Stress reduction and mood enhancement in four exercise modes: Swimming, body conditioning, hatha yoga, and fencing. *Research Quarterly for Exercise and Sport, 59,* 148–159.

Berger, B. G., & Owen, D. R. (1992). Mood alteration with yoga and swimming: Aerobic exercise may not be necessary. *Perceptual and Motor Skills, 75,* 1331–1343.

Biddle, S., & Mutrie, N. (1991). *Psychology of physical activity and exercise.* London: Springer-Verlag.

Blumenthal, J. A., Williams, S., Needels, T. L., & Wallace, A. G. (1982). Psychological changes accompany aerobic exercise in healthy middle-aged adults. *Psychosomatic Medicine, 44,* 529–535.

Boutcher, S. H., Fleisher-Curtain, L. A., & Gines, S. D. (1988). The effects of self-presentation on perceived exertion. *Journal of Sport and Exercise Psychology, 10,* 270–280.

Boutcher, S. H., & Landers, D. L. (1988). The effects of vigorous exercise on anxiety, heart rate, and alpha activity of runners and nonrunners. *Psychophysiology, 25,* 696–702.

Boutcher, S. H., & Trenske, M. (1990). The effects of sensory deprivation and music on perceived exertion and affect during exercise. *Journal of Sport and Exercise Psychology, 12,* 167–176.

Browman, C. P. (1980). Sleep following sustained exercise. *Psychophysiology, 17,* 577–579.

Browman, C. R., & Tepas, D. I. (1976). The effects of presleep activity on all-night sleep. *Psychophysiology, 13,* 536–540.

Carmack, M., & Martens, R. (1979). Measuring commitment to running: A survey of runners' attitudes and mental states. *Journal of Sport Psychology, 1,* 25–42.

Carron, A. V. (1980). *Social psychology of sport.* Ithaca, NY: Mouvement.

Carver, C. S., Coleman, A. E., & Glass, D. C. (1976). The coronary prone behavior pattern and the suppression of fatigue on a treadmill test. *Journal of Personality and Social Psychology, 33,* 460–466.

Costill, D. L., Flynn, M. G., Kirwan, J. P., Houmard, J. A., Mitchell, J. B., Thomas, R., & Park, S. H. (1988). Effects of repeated days of intensified training on muscle glycogen and swimming performance. *Medicine and Science in Sports and Exercise, 20,* 249–254.

Csikszentmihalyi, M. (1990). *Flow: The psychology of optimal experience.* New York: Harper & Row.

Dishman, R. K. (1980). Self-motivation and adherence to habitual physical activity. *Journal of Applied Social Psychology, 10,* 115–132.

Dishman, R. K. (1988). *Exercise adherence: Its impact on public health.* Champaign, IL: Human Kinetics.

Fox, K. R. (1990). *The physical self-perception profile manual.* Northern Illinois University: Office for Health Promotion.

Fox, K. R., & Corbin, C. B. (1989). The physical self-perception profile: Development and preliminary validation. *Journal of Sport and Exercise Psychology, 11,* 408–430.

Fry, R. W., Grove, J. R., Morton, A. R., Zeroni, P., Gaudieri, S., & Keast, D. (in press). Psychological and immunological correlates of acute overtraining. *British Journal of Sports Medicine.*

Fry, R. W., Morton, A. R., & Keast, D. (1991). Overtraining in athletes: An update. *Sports Medicine, 12,* 32–65.

Gill, D. L., & Strom, E. H. (1985). The effect of attentional focus on performance of an endurance task. *International Journal of Sport Psychology, 16,* 217–223.

Goldwater, B. C., & Collis, M. L. (1985). Psychologic effects of cardiovascular conditioning: A controlled experiment. *Psychosomatic Medicine, 47,* 174–181.

Griffin, S. J., & Trinder, J. (1978). Physical fitness, exercise and human sleep. *Psychophysiology, 15,* 447–449.

Grove, J. R., & Lewis, M. A. E. (1993). Flow experiences during circuit training. In S. Serpa, J. Alves, V. Ferreira, & A. Paula-Brito (Eds.), *Proceedings of the VIIIth World Congress of Sport Psychology* (pp. 836–839). Lisbon: International Society of Sport Psychology.

Grove, J. R., Wilkinson, A. W., & Dawson, B. T. (1993). Effects of exercise on selected correlates of smoking withdrawal. *International Journal of Sport Psychology, 24,* 217–236.

Hardy, C. J., Hall, E. G., & Prestholdt, P. H. (1986). The mediational role of social influence in the perception of exertion. *Journal of Sport Psychology, 8,* 88–104.

Hart, E. A., Leary, M. R., & Rejeski, W. J. (1989). The measurement of social physique anxiety. *Journal of Sport and Exercise Psychology, 11,* 94–104.

Hatfield, B. D. (1991). Exercise and mental health: The mechanisms of exercise-induced psychological states. In L. Diamant (Ed.), *Psychology of sports, exercise, and fitness: Social and personal issues* (pp. 17–49). New York: Hemisphere.

Hayden, R. M., & Allen, G. J. (1984). Relationship between aerobic exercise, anxiety, and depression: Convergent validation by knowledgeable informants. *Journal of Sports Medicine, 24,* 69–74.

Hochstetler, S. A., Rejeski, W. J., & Best, D. L. (1985). The influence of sex role orientation on ratings of perceived exertion. *Sex Roles, 12,* 825–835.

Hogan, J. (1989). Personality correlates of physical fitness. *Journal of Personality and Social Psychology, 56,* 284–288.

Horne, J. A. (1981). The effects of exercise upon sleep: A critical review. *Biological Psychology, 12,* 241–290.

Horne, J. A., & Staff, L. H. E. (1983). Exercise and sleep: Body-heating effects. *Sleep, 6,* 36–46.

Hughes, J. R. (1984). Psychological effects of habitual aerobic exercise: A critical review. *Preventive Medicine, 13,* 66–78.

King, A. C., Taylor, C. B., & Haskell, W. L. (1993). Effects of differing intensities and formats of 12 months of exercise training on psychological outcomes in older adults. *Health Psychology, 12,* 292–300.

Kuipers, H., & Keizer, H. A. (1988). Overtraining in elite athletes: Review and directions for the future. *Sports Medicine, 6,* 79–92.

LaFontaine, T. P., DiLorenzo, T. M., Frensch, P. A., Studk-Ropp, R. C., Bargman, E. P., & McDonald, D. G. (1992). Aerobic exercise and mood: A brief review, 1985–1990. *Sports Medicine, 13,* 160–170.

Lantz, C., Hardy, C., & Ainsworth, B. (1991, October). *The effects of social physique anxiety, gender, age, and depression on exercise behavior.* Paper presented at the annual meeting of the Association for the Advancement of Applied Sport Psychology, Savannah, GA.

Lobstein, D. D., Mosbacher, B. J., & Ismail, A. H. (1983). Depression as a powerful discriminator between physically active and sedentary middle-aged men. *Journal of Psychosomatic Research, 27,* 69–76.

Mackinnon, L. T., & Hooper, S. (1991). *State of the art review no. 26: Overtraining.* Canberra: Australian Sports Commission.

Mandell, A. J. (1979). The second second wind. *Psychiatric Annals, 9,* 57–69.

Marcus, B. H., & Owen, N. (1992). Motivational readiness, self-efficacy and decision-making for exercise. *Journal of Applied Social Psychology, 22,* 3–16.

Marcus, B. H., Rakowski, W., & Rossi, J. S. (1992). Assessing motivational readiness and decision making for exercise. *Health Psychology, 11,* 257–261.

Marcus, B. H., Rossi, J. S., Selby, V. C., Niaura, R. S., & Abrams, D. B. (1992). The stages and processes of exercise adoption and maintenance in a worksite sample. *Health Psychology, 11*, 386–395.

Marcus, B. H., Selby, V. C., Niaura, R. S., & Rossi, J. S. (1992). Self-efficacy and the stages of exercise behavior change. *Research Quarterly for Exercise and Sport, 63*, 60–66.

Marcus, B. H., & Simkin, L. R. (1993). The stages of exercise behavior. *The Journal of Sports Medicine and Physical Fitness, 33*, 83–88.

Marsh, H. W., & Shavelson, R. J. (1985). Self-concept: Its multifaceted, hierarchical structure. *Educational Psychologist, 20*, 107–125.

Martin, J. E., & Dubbert, P. M. (1985). Adherence to exercise. In R. L. Terjung (Ed.), *Exercise and sport sciences reviews — Volume 13* (pp. 137–167). New York: Macmillan.

Martin, J. E., Dubbert, P. M., Katell, A. D., Thompson, J. K., Raczynski, J. R., Lake, M., Smith, P. O., Webster, J. S., Sikora, T., & Cohen, R. E. (1984). Behavioral control of exercise in sedentary adults: Studies 1 through 6. *Journal of Consulting and Clinical Psychology, 52*, 795–811.

Masters, K. S., & Lambert, M. J. (1989). The relations between cognitive coping strategies, reasons for running,, injury, and performance of marathon runners. *Journal of Sport and Exercise Psychology, 11*, 161–170.

McDonald, D. G., & Hodgdon, J. A. (1991). *Psychological effects of aerobic fitness training: Research and theory.* London: Springer-Verlag.

McInman, A. D., & Berger, B. G. (1993). Self-concept and mood changes associated with aerobic dance. *Australian Journal of Psychology, 45*, 134–140.

McNair, D. M., Lorr, M., & Droppleman, L. F. (1971). *Profile of Mood States manual.* San Diego: Educational and Industrial Testing Service.

Montgomery, I., Trinder, J., Fraser, G., & Paxton, S. J. (1987). Aerobic fitness and exercise: Effect on the sleep of young and older adults. *Australian Journal of Psychology, 39*, 259–272.

Montgomery, I., Trinder, J., Paxton, S. J., Fraser, G., Meaney, M., & Koerbin, G. (1985). Sleep disruption following a marathon. *Journal of Sports Medicine and Physical Fitness, 25*, 69–74.

Moorcroft, W. H. (1989). *Sleep, dreaming, and sleep disorders.* Lanham, MD: University Press of America.

Morgan, W. P. (1973). Pscyhological factors influencing perceived exertion. *Medicine and Science in Sports, 5*, 97–103.

Morgan, W. P. (1978, April). The mind of the marathoner. *Psychology Today, 11*, 38–49.

Morgan, W. P. (1981). Psychophysiology of self-awareness during vigorous physical activity. *Research Quarterly for Exercise and Sport, 52*, 385–427.

Morgan, W. P. (1985). Affective beneficence of vigorous physical activity. *Medicine and Science in Sports and Exercise, 17*, 94–100.

Morgan, W. P., Brown, D. R., Raglin, J. S., O'Connor, P. J., & Ellickson, K. A. (1987). Psychological monitoring of overtraining and staleness. *British Journal of Sports Medicine, 21*, 107–114.

Morgan, W. P., Costill, D. L., Flynn, M. G., Raglin, J. S., & O'Connor, P. J. (1988). Mood disturbance following increased training in swimmers. *Medicine and Science in Sports and Exercise, 20*, 408–414.

Morgan, W. P., Hirota, K., Weitz, G. A., & Balke, B. (1976). Hypnotic perturbation of perceived exertion: Ventilatory consequences. *American Journal of Clinical Hypnosis, 189*, 182–190.

Morgan, W. P., Horstman, D. H., Cymerman, A., & Stokes, J. (1983). Facilitation of physical performance by means of a cognitive strategy. *Cognitive Therapy and Research, 7,* 251–264.

Morgan, W. P., O'Connor, P. J., Ellickson, K. A., & Bradley, P. W. (1988). Personality structure, mood states, and performance in elite male distance runners. *International Journal of Sport Psychology, 19,* 247–263.

Morgan, W. P., O'Connor, P. J., Sparling, P. B., & Pate, R. R. (1987). Psychologic characterization of the elite female distance runner. *International Journal of Sports Medicine, 8,* 124–131.

Morgan, W. P., & Pollock, M. L. (1977). Psychologic characterization of the elite distance runner. *Annals of the New York Academy of Sciences, 301,* 382–403.

Nideffer, R. M. (1988, December). *Psychological factors associated with overtraining.* Paper presented at the Second Elite Coaches Seminar, Canberra.

O'Connor, P. J., & Morgan, W. P. (1990). Athletic performance following rapid traversal of multiple time zones: A review. *Sports Medicine, 10,* 20–30.

O'Connor, P. J., Morgan, W. P., Raglin, J. S., Barksdale, C. N., & Kalin, N. H. (1989). Mood state and salivary cortisol levels following overtraining in female swimmers. *Psychoneuroendocrinology, 14,* 303–310.

O'Connor, P. J., Raglin, J. S., & Morgan, W. P. (1991). Psychobiologic effects of 3 days of increased training in female and male swimmers. *Medicine and Science in Sports and Exercise, 23,* 1055–1061.

Okwumabua, T. M. (1985). Psychological and physical contributions to marathon performance: An exploratory investigation. *Journal of Sport Behavior, 8,* 163–171.

Okwumabua, T. M., Meyers, A. W., Schleser, R., & Cooke, C. J. (1983). Cognitive strategies and running performance: An exploratory study. *Cognitive Therapy and Research, 7,* 363–370.

Orlick, T. (1986). *Psyching for sport: Mental training for athletes.* Champaign, IL: Leisure Press.

Owen, N., & Bauman, A. (1992). The descriptive epidemiology of a sedentary lifestyle in adult Australians. *International Journal of Epidemiology, 21,* 305–310.

Pandolf, K. B. (1983). Advances in the study and application of perceived exertion. In R. L. Terjung (Ed.), *Exercise and sport sciences reveiws — Volume 11* (pp. 118–158). Philadelphia, MS: Franklin Institute.

Paxton, S. J., Montgomery, I., Trinder, J., Newman, D. J., & Bowling, A. (1982). Sleep after exercise of variable intensity in fit and unfit subjects. *Australian Journal of Psychology, 34,* 289–296.

Pennebaker, J. W., & Lightner, J. M. (1980). Competition of internal and external information in an exercise setting. *Journal of Personality and Social Psychology, 39,* 165–174.

Petruzello, S. J., Landers, D. M., & Salazar, W. (1993). Exercise and anxiety reduction: Examination of temperature as an explanation for affective change. *Journal of Sport and Exercise Psychology, 15,* 63–76.

Powell, K. E. (1988). Habitual exercise and public health: An epidemiological view. In R. K. Dishman (Ed.), *Exercise adherence: Its impact on public health* (pp. 15–40). Champaign, IL: Human Kinetics.

Plante, T. G., & Rodin, J. (1990). Physical fitness and enhanced psychological health. *Current Psychology: Research and Reviews, 9,* 3–24.

Prochaska, J. O., & Marcus, B. H. (in press). The transtheoretical model: Applications to exercise. In R. K. Dishman (Ed.), *Exercise adherence II.* Champaign, IL: Human Kinetics.

Raglin, J. S. (in press). Mood state responses to a pre-season conditioning program in male collegiate basketball players. *International Journal of Sport Psychology.*

Raglin, J. S. (1993). Overtraining and staleness: Psychometric monitoring of endurance athletes. In R. N. Singer, M. Murphey, & L. K. Tennant (Eds.), *Handbook of research on sport psychology* (pp. 840–850). New York: Macmillan.

Raglin, J. S., & Morgan, W. P. (1989). Development of a scale to measure training-induced distress. *Medicine and Science in Sports and Exercise, 21* (Suppl.), S60 (abstract).

Raglin, J. S., Morgan, W. P., & O'Connor, P. J. (1991). Changes in mood states during training in female and male college swimmers. *International Journal of Sports Medicine, 12,* 585–589.

Raglin, J. S., Turner, P. E., & Eksten, F. (1993). State anxiety and blood pressure following 30 minutes of leg ergometry or weight training. *Medicine and Science in Sports and Exercise, 25,* 1044–1048.

Raglin, J. S., Wilson, M. W., & Morris, M. J. (1993). State anxiety and blood pressure following 20 minutes of leg ergometry at differing intensities. *Medicine and Science in Sports and Exercise, 25* (Suppl.), S46 (abstract).

Rejeski, W. J., & Brawley, L. R. (1988). Defining the boundaries of sport psychology. *The Sport Psychologist, 2,* 231–242.

Rejeski, W. J., & Kenney, E. (1987). Distracting attentional focus from fatigue: Does task complexity make a difference? *Journal of Sport Psychology, 9,* 66–73.

Rejeski, W. J., & Ribisl, P. M. (1980). Expected task duration and perceived effort: An attributional analysis. *Journal of Sport Psychology, 2,* 227–236.

Rejeski, W. J., & Sanford, B. (1984). Feminine-typed females: The role of affective schema in the perception of exercise intensity. *Journal of Sport Psychology, 6,* 197–207.

Rejeski, W. J., & Thompson, A. (1993). Historical and conceptual roots of exercise psychology. In P. Seraganian (Ed.), *Exercise psychology: The influence of physical exercise on psychological processes* (pp. 3–38). New York: John Wiley & Sons.

Rushall, B. S. (1984). The content of competition thinkings. In W. F. Straub & J. M. Williams (Eds.), *Cognitive sport psychology* (pp. 51–62). Ithaca, NY: Sport Science Associates.

Ryckman, R. M., Robbins, M. A., Thornton, B., & Cantrell, P. (1982). Development and validation of a physical self-efficacy scale. *Journal of Personality and Social Psychology, 42,* 891–900.

Sachs, M. L. (1984). The runner's high. In M. L. Sachs & G. W. Buffone (Eds.), *Running as therapy: An integrated approach* (pp. 273–287). Lincoln: University of Nebraska Press.

Schomer, H. (1986). Mental strategies and the perception of effort of marathon runners. *International Journal of Sport Psychology, 17,* 41–59.

Schomer, H. H. (1987). Mental strategies training program for marathon runners. *International Journal of Sport Psychology, 18,* 133–151.

Seraganian, P. (Ed.). (1993). *Exercise psychology: The influence of physical exercise on psychological processes.* New York: John Wiley & Sons.

Shapiro, C. M., Bortz, R., Mitchell, D., Bartel, P., & Jooste, P. (1981). Slow-wave sleep: A recovery period after exercise. *Science, 214,* 1253–1254.

Shapiro, C. M., Warren, P. M., Trinder, J., Paxton, S. J., Oswald, I., Flenley, D. C., & Catterall, J. R. (1984). Fitness facilitates sleep. *European Journal of Applied Physiology, 53,* 1–4.

Shavelson, R. J., Hubner, J. J., & Stanton, G. C. (1976). Self-concept: Validation of construct interpretations. *Review of Educational Research, 46,* 407–441.

Solomon, E. G., & Bumpus, A. K. (1981). The running meditation response: An adjunct to psychotherapy. In M. A. Sacks & M. L. Sachs (Eds.), *Psychology of running* (pp. 40–49). Champaign, IL: Human Kinetics.

Sonstroem, R. J., Harlow, L. L., Gemma, L. M., & Osborne, S. (1991). Test of structural relationships within a proposed exercise and self-esteem model. *Journal of Personality Assessment, 56*, 348–364.

Sonstroem, R. J., & Morgan, W. P. (1989). Exercise and self-esteem: Rationale and model. *Medicine and Science in Sports and Exercise, 21*, 329–337.

Sonstroem, R. J., Speliotis, E. D., & Fava, J. L. (1992). Perceived physical competence in adults: An examination of the Physical Self-perception Profile. *Journal of Sport and Exercise Psychology, 14*, 207–221.

Spink, K. S., & Longhurst, K. (1986). Cognitive strategies and swimming performances: An exploratory study. *Australian Journal of Science and Medicine in Sport, 18*, 9–13.

Stephens, T., Jacobs, D. R., & White, C. C. (1985). A descriptive epidemiology of leisure-time physical activity. *Public Health Reports, 100*, 147–158.

Steptoe, A., & Cox, S. (1989). Acute effects of aerobic exercise on mood. *Health Psychology, 7*, 329–340.

Straub, W. F. (Ed.). (1980). *Sport psychology: An analysis of athlete behavior* (2nd ed.). Ithaca, NY: Mouvement.

Summers, J. J., Machin, V. J., & Sargent, G. I. (1983). Psychosocial factors related to marathon running. *Journal of Sport Psychology, 5*, 314–331.

Summers, J. J., Sargent, G. I., Levey, A. J., & Murray, K. D. (1982). Middle-aged, non-elite marathon runners: A profile. *Perceptual and Motor Skills, 54*, 963–969.

Ungerleider, S., Golding, J. M., Porter, K., & Foster, J. (1989). An exploratory examination of cognitive strategies used by masters track and field athletes (research note). *The Sport Psychologist, 3*, 245–253.

Vingerhoets, A. J. J. M., Croon, M., Jeninga, A. J., & Menges, L. J. (1990). Personality and health habits. *Psychology and Health, 4*, 333–342.

Walker, J. M., Floyd, T. C., Fein, G., Cavness, C., Lualhati, R., & Feinberg, I. (1978). Effects of exercise on sleep. *Journal of Applied Physiology, 44*, 945–951.

Watt, B., & Grove, R. (1992). Perceived exertion: Antecedents and applications. *Sports Medicine, 15*, 225–241.

Weinberg, R. S., Smith, J., Jackson, A., & Gould, D. (1984). Effect of association, dissociation, and positive self-talk strategies on endurance performance. *Canadian Journal of Applied Sport Science, 9*, 25–32.

Wilkinson, A. W., & Grove, J. R. (1993). *Sleep disturbance in relation to exercise during smoking cessation.* Manuscript submitted for publication.

Williams, J. M. (Ed.). (1986). *Applied sport psychology: Personal growth to peak performance.* Palo Alto, CA: Mayfield.

C H A P T E R

18

PSYCHOLOGICAL FACTORS IN SPORT INJURIES

ROB KIRKBY

During the last decade, participation in sports activities has increased at every age level, in all Western countries (Backx, Erich, Kemper, & Verbeek, 1989). Parallel with this has been a growth in sport injuries to the point where they have been described as a "major public health problem" (de Loes & Goldie, 1988). This certainly appears to be the case for Australia and other Western societies where health costs associated with sport injuries far exceed those arising from motor vehicle accidents (van Mechelen, Hlobil, & Kemper, 1992). A recent report to the National Better Health Program estimated that in 1987–88 the medical treatment of sport injuries in Australia cost an estimated $333–400 million, with a further $400 million being lost through absenteeism from work. A total of $1 billion in injury costs was predicted for future years (Centre for Health Promotion and Research, 1990). The situation appears to be no better in other countries. For example, it has been estimated that sport injuries cost West Germany more than $US 2500 million per year (van Mechelen et al., 1992). Kvidera and Frankel (1983) calculated that in the United States, the yearly cost to the economy of roller skating accidents alone was $100 million!

Traditionally, inadequate conditioning, improper use of sporting equipment, poor coaching, environmental factors and the aggressive nature of some sports have been seen as the major causes of sport injuries (May & Sieb, 1987; Yaffe, 1983). Yet, as Nideffer (1989) has pointed out, despite alterations to rules and improvements in safety equipment, coaching techniques, training practices and medical care, the number of injuries incurred by athletes has risen. Thus, external causes alone do not explain the occurrence of sport injuries and it seems that other influences, including psychological factors, play a role in injury vulnerability. How extensive the influence of these variables might be is unknown, but estimates of the contribution of psychological causes to sport injuries have ranged as high as 30% (Ryde, 1965).

This chapter reviews the literature on psychological antecedents of sport injuries and psychological factors in recovery from injury. The first section considers the research into personality. Life events is the research area addressed next. Stress and coping is then discussed. Finally, future directions are proposed for research on psychological aspects of sport injuries.

PERSONALITY RESEARCH

Investigators have studied vulnerability to injury from the viewpoint of a range of psychological factors, including variables such as anxiety, attention, locus of control, mood, risk acceptance and self-concept (see reviews by May & Sieb, 1987; Nideffer, 1989; van Mechelen et al., 1992). Unfortunately, many of the findings from these investigations have been contradictory. For example, while some investigators have reported a significant relationship between external locus of control and increased injury (Dalhauser & Thomas, 1979; Pargman & Lunt, 1989), other studies have failed to show significant relationships between locus of control and athletic injuries (Kerr & Minden, 1988; Passer & Seese, 1983). Similarly, Bond, Miller, and Chrisfield (1988) found that contrary to their prediction, and to previous findings, the injured elite swimmers in their study were *more* attentionally effective than non-injured swimmers.

Much of the earlier work in this area (e.g., Ogilvie & Tutko, 1966) focused on specific components of personality and suggested that athletes' sport injuries resulted from personal characteristics such as: masochistic tendencies, determination to punish others, desire to escape from competition, fear of success, need for sympathy, wish to avoid training, attempt to evade the pressures of "demanding" parents, and specifically for male athletes, their resolve to prove their manhood (Burckes, 1981; Noakes & Schomer, 1983; Sanderson, 1977). These conceptualisations, interesting though they might be, have been based on subjective interpretations and, as they lack any empirical support, are at best speculative.

More objective research on personality and injury has involved the assessment of personality by validated psychometric instruments such as the 16 Personality Factor Questionnaire (16 PF) and the Californian Psychological Inventory (CPI). An example of this was the study by Valliant (1981) who tested competitors at the conclusion of a 10-mile road race. Valliant reported that runners who said that they had been injured in preparation for or during the race scored as less "toughminded" and less "forthright" on the 16 PF. Notwithstanding that this study involved a relatively small group of subjects and a poor response rate (which raises questions about the representativeness of the sample), the major fault with the Valliant investigation related to the retrospective nature of the research. As Kolt and Kirkby (1991) pointed out, such a design does not allow the determination of cause: were athletes more likely to be injured because of their particular personality characteristics, or did they display such characteristics because they had suffered injury? Differing outcomes from retrospective and prospective inquiry were demonstrated in a study of Finnish soccer players (Taimela, Österman, Kujala, Lehto, Korhonen, & Alaranta, 1990). Although retrospective investigation indicated that players who had been injured during the previous three years scored higher on factor N (astute) and lower on factor H (shy) of the 16 PF, prospective analysis, based on injuries sustained during the 12 months following the psychological assessments, revealed no significant differences in personality between injured and non-injured players.

Another study that used the 16 PF prospectively was that of Jackson, Jarrett, Bailey, Kausek, Swanson, and Powell (1978). These investigators assessed 110 high school gridiron players at the commencement of the football season, then collected injury data over the subsequent weeks. The investigators' findings that players who scored as tenderminded on the psychometric test were more likely to be injured, should be interpreted cautiously. Unfortunately, the investigators did not report precise statistical outcomes to support their conclusions and, as well, their statistical analyses involved a large number of univariate tests carried out without adjustments to alpha rates to protect against type 1 errors.

In another prospective study, Brown (1971) administered the CPI to 186 high school gridiron players at the beginning of the competition year and collected injury data over the following season. Brown reported that there were no differences in measures of personality between injured and non-injured players. Similar findings of no link between injury and psychometrically-assessed personality have been reported by other investigators (e.g., Abadie, 1976; Govern & Koppenhaver, 1965; Kraus & Gullen, 1969). Taken together, these findings indicate that general personality tests have little predictive value in sport injuries.

An interesting line of research, pursued by several investigators, has implicated motivation in sport injuries. McClay, Appleby, and Plascak (1989) assessed 28 high school cross-country runners on their "self-motivation" at the beginning of the competition season. When injuries were collated across the season it was found that those who sustained severe injuries had scored as significantly more self-motivated. This effect was particularly strong for the female competitors. McClay et al. (1989) interpreted these findings to indicate that high self-motivation could influence athletes to push themselves to physical limits, thus increasing the likelihood of injury. In his review of running injuries, van Mechelen (1992) cited several other findings indicating that highly motivated runners were more likely to sustain injuries. Consistent with this finding is the report that runners with Type A characteristics are more likely to incur injuries (Fields, Delaney, & Hinkle, 1990).

EXPLANATIONS OF THE LINK BETWEEN PSYCHOLOGICAL FACTORS AND SPORT INJURIES

Most attempts to explain how psychological variables could influence an athlete's predisposition to injury have been based on anxiety concepts. For example, as Nideffer (1983) pointed out, stress and anxiety can lead to widespread muscle tension, which in turn can reduce motor coordination and flexibility, making the athlete more vulnerable to injury. As well, a relationship has been suggested between stress and anxiety and perceptual processes. May and Sieb (1987) applied the principle of the inverted U-curve to illustrate how either relatively low or relatively high levels of arousal result in impaired concentration and lessened perceptual effectiveness. Thus, when the athlete is too relaxed or too stressed, his or her perceptual field will be overly broadened or excessively narrowed which can prevent the athlete picking up the action (e.g., a tackler charging in from the side) or environmental cues (e.g., a slippery section of the court) necessary to avoid potential injury situations (Landers, 1980).

Vulnerability to injury can be mediated through factors other than stress and anxiety. For example, physical fatigue can result in reduced motor coordination. As well, attention can be impaired through distraction. Take the case of a netballer who during the game focuses not on what she or he should be doing but, rather, is thinking about the successful play executed a few minutes before! While players are so distracted they are more at risk of injuring themselves by landing awkwardly or colliding with another competitor.

Injury as a result of reduced flexibility through stress-related muscle-tension or fatigue, or as a result of a lowering of the athlete's attentional capacity has been incorporated into the theoretical model of sports injury proposed by Andersen and Williams (1988). This model was derived from the literature linking stress and the likelihood of increased accidents, illness and injury. Andersen and Williams hypothesised that injury resulted from the interaction between personality factors (e.g., hardiness, locus of control, sense of coherence, anxiety, achievement motivation), history of stressors (e.g., life events, daily hassles, previous injuries), coping resources (e.g., social support, stress management skills) and potentially stressful situations.

The role of some components of this model has yet to be confirmed. For example, several investigators have questioned the contribution of locus of control to sport injury (Fawkner, 1993; Kerr & Minden, 1988; Passer & Seese, 1983). Nevertheless, as discussed later in this chapter, the Andersen and Williams model has provided a stimulus for research into psychological factors and sport injury.

LIFE EVENT RESEARCH

The most promising avenue of research into psychological factors and sport injury has involved the investigation of stressful life events. This approach has stemmed from the early work of Holmes and Rahe (1967) suggesting that illness could be precipitated by an increase in the number of life changes requiring adaptive or coping behaviour. It should be noted that such life events are not necessarily negative: as Holmes and Rahe pointed out, a positive life event such as being promoted could require as much adjustment as being fired and moving to a new job. Support for the association between adaptation and morbidity has come from findings that individuals who experienced a high incidence of life events were more susceptible to a variety of illnesses, including tuberculosis, multiple sclerosis, cancer and psychiatric disorders such as depression (see Brown, 1981). Although there is a substantial literature supporting a link between life stress and illness, this area of research has attracted serious criticism, related largely to the retrospective nature of the majority of investigations (see Miller, Vaughn, & Miller, 1990).

The most popular instrument used to assess life stress has been the Social Re-adjustment Rating Scale (SRRS: Holmes & Rahe, 1967). Holmes (1970) used the SRRS to measure life stress in 100 gridiron players. He reported that players with high life stress were more likely to incur injury than were players with low life stress. On the basis of these findings, Bramwell, Masuda, Wagner, and Holmes (1975) modified the SRRS to be more appropriate for use with an athletic population. The new instrument, named the Social and Athletic Re-adjustment Rating Scale (SARRS), was administered to another sample of college gridiron players. It was found that players who had suffered major injuries had scored significantly higher on the SARRS preseason assessment than had non-injured players. In fact, almost three-quarters of the subjects from the high-risk group (that is, those with high SARRS scores) suffered injuries versus less than a third from the low-risk group. On this basis, Bramwell et al. concluded that the risk of injury to football players increased in direct relationship to the accumulation of perceived stressful life events.

Cryan and Alles (1983) also investigated stress and injury in football players. The sample ($N = 151$), larger than in previous studies, was made up of players drawn from three squads. The results indicated that players who experienced a high level of life change, as measured by the SARRS, were at greater risk of being injured than those who experienced a low level of change. Specifically, 38.5% of the players with scores below the median life stress score were injured, while 68% of the players with life stress scores above the median were injured.

Coddington and Troxell (1980) modified the SARRS to develop the Life Events Scale for Adolescents (LESA). This instrument separately assessed undesirable and desirable life events, and "object loss" (that is, actual or threatened loss of a person close to the player). The sample consisted of 114 American high school gridiron players. Coddington and Troxell reported that players who experienced high object loss were up to five times more likely to be injured than those who experienced no such loss. Although these findings appear to indirectly support the argument that injury was related to negative life events, in fact, no statistical relationship was evident between injury and either the negative or positive life events assessed by the LESA.

Passer and Seese (1983) carried out a similar study with a sample of 104 football players drawn from two American colleges. These investigators used the Athletic Life Experiences Survey (ALES) which had been modified from the Life Experiences Survey (Sarason, Johnson, & Sarason, 1978) for use with sports participants. The ALES allowed the subjects to indicate the valence (good or bad), as well as the degree of life change produced by each event. The data for subjects from one of the colleges suggested that injured players had experienced a greater number of negative (but not positive) life changes during the previous year. Furthermore, the injured players in this sample had higher object loss scores than the non-injured. No relationship between injury and any of the life change measures was observed for the sample from the other college.

To summarise, of the five studies that have investigated American footballers, three (Bramwell et al., 1975; Cryan & Alles, 1983; Holmes, 1970) reported a link between life events and injury. Another study (Passer & Seese, 1983) suggested that negative, but not positive, life events were associated with injury, but in only one of the two samples investigated. The final study (Coddington & Troxell, 1980) reported no significant relationships between injury and either positive or negative events.

The situation with non-contact sports is no less complex. Of the seven studies that have investigated injury as a direct product of life stress, four have reported that injury was associated with life stress, two have reported negative findings, and one reported positive effects for competitors from one sport but not for those from three other sports.

Williams, Haggert, Tonyman, and Wadsworth (1986) investigated the stress–injury paradigm in volleyball players, basketball players and cross-country runners. No significant relationship between life stress scores and injury occurrence was found. This led the researchers to speculate that the stress–injury relationship could vary between contact and non-contact sports. However, as Andersen and Williams (1988) pointed out, the small sample sizes and relatively low levels of stress reported by the subjects in the Williams, Haggert, Tonyman, and Wadsworth study could have limited the opportunity to find significant results.

A similar study by Williams, Tonyman, and Wadsworth (1986) investigated the role of life stress in injury occurrence in 179 male and female elite volleyball players from 15 universities. Both the SARRS and the ALES were used to measure life stress. No relationship was found between life stress and injury, regardless of how the data were analysed, and no gender differences were found. It should be noted that the volleyball players reported much lower levels of stress than the football players in earlier studies.

May, Veach, Southard, and Herring (1985) used the SARRS to measure the effect of life stress on injury, illness and performance in 97 elite male and female athletes from five different sports (biathalon, race walking, figure skating, gymnastics and basketball). It was found that the higher the life stress score, the more likely a person was to become ill or injured during the season. The basketball players reported the highest life stress mean score (773), whereas the figure skaters had the lowest (371). These findings must be treated cautiously because of the small samples involved (as low as nine subjects in the figure skating group). Unfortunately, although both male and female athletes were included in the study, the effect of gender differences on the stress–injury relationship was not reported.

In another study, involving 73 male and female members of the US Alpine Ski Team, May, Veach, Southard, Reed, and Griffey (1985) reported that those with high scores on the SARRS and the LESA were more likely to suffer musculoskeletal leg injuries and ear and throat problems of a greater duration. Although the investigators concluded that life changes, along with depression, uncontrolled emotions, increased tension, and lower life satisfaction could influence injury, illness and performance potential in athletes, they emphasised that these variables accounted for only a small part of the variance. As with the earlier May et al. (1985) study, the investigators failed to consider possible gender effects.

The results of an investigation by Kerr and Minden (1988) of 41 elite female gymnasts also supported the relationship between life stress and injury. It was found that stressful life events, measured by the LESA, were related significantly to both the number and severity of injuries. Gymnasts with the highest life event scores not only had four times as many injuries, but the severity of the injuries was substantially greater. While the relatively small number of subjects and the limiting of the sample to females restricted the generalisability of the conclusions, the major problem with this study related to the retrospective collection of injury data.

This was not a problem in the study by Hardy and Riehl (1988). Injury data from the 86 college athletes participating in baseball, softball, tennis and track were collected as the season progressed. Life stress, as measured by "total life change" on the ALES, appeared to be related to injury (at least for female subjects). However, separate regression analyses revealed that only in one sport (track) was there a significant relationship between life change and frequency of injury. It was noteworthy that for track athletes there was also a direct relationship between injury and reported object loss (actual or threatened loss of someone close to the respondent).

Lysens, van den Auweele, and Ostyn (1986) assessed 99 physical education students with a battery of tests including the "Life Events Questionnaire" which was adapted from the SARRS. Measurement over the following year revealed no differences in life event scores between those reporting overuse injuries sustained during sports practice sessions and those who were not injured, and only a trend ($p = .09$) toward differences in life event scores for acute injuries. A limiting factor in this study was the restrictive definition of injury (resulting in at least three days of no practice activities) which did not allow consideration of more minor injuries. As well, the investigators did not take into account sports injuries that might have occurred outside of practice classes.

As with the football studies, all of the investigations concerning non-contact sports were vulnerable to criticisms of research design or data interpretation. Problems with these studies included retrospective collection of data, a reliance on small samples, the inadequacy of instruments used to assess life events, inappropriate data analyses, problems of injury definition, lack of information on age, exposure time, and injury severity, and failure to account for possible gender differences.

STRESS, COPING AND INJURY

The lack of consistent findings in the area of stress and injury could reflect the fact that the majority of the studies have focused exclusively on the impact of life events, per se. Simply quantifying the stressful events in a competitor's life ignores the possible effects of moderating variables. According to Folkman and Lazarus (1985) stress is best viewed as a transactional process between the organism and the environment. That is, individuals experience stress when they appraise a potential threat as likely to exceed the resources available to combat it. This suggests that the impact of life stressors is likely to be a function of the extent of the stressor, the processes the individual uses to cope, and the resources they have to manage the stressor. This hypothesis has been supported by reports of an interaction between stress and coping variables in relation to disease and accidents (Brown & Lawton, 1986; Folkman & Lazarus, 1985).

Consistent with this interaction was the Andersen and Williams (1988) model of stress and athletic injury described earlier in this chapter. A search of the literature has revealed only two attempts to test the Andersen and Williams (1988) model. In the first of these, Blackwell and McCullagh (1990) tested 105 college gridiron players on life stress, as measured by the ALES, trait competition anxiety, and coping. They reported that the injured players could be differentiated from non-injured players by total scores on life-stress and that severely injured players could be identified by their scores on the ALES Positive Scale and the measure of competition anxiety. Not supporting the prediction of the Andersen and Williams model, the investigators found no relationship between injury and scores on coping resources.

A contrary finding was reported by Hanson, McCullagh, and Tonyman (1992) who investigated psychological factors affecting injury in 181 college track and field athletes. The subjects were assessed at preseason on six variables including life stress as measured by the ALES, social support, and coping. Data on injuries were collected during the 18-week competition season. The results showed that coping was the major factor in predicting injury. As well, the quantity of "positive" life stress was associated with frequency of injury while "negative" life stress was linked to severity of injury.

A serious problem with the Blackwell and McCullagh (1990) and Hanson et al. (1992) studies was their measure of coping. This test was based on a scale adapted from a larger instrument developed for non-sporting populations and, thus, had no established validity or reliability. Furthermore, the measure failed to differentiate between coping resources and coping processes (Folkman & Lazarus, 1985).

One study that did separate coping resources and processes was that of Smith, Smoll, and Ptacek (1990) which investigated 451 high school male and female competitors in basketball, wrestling and gymnastics. Prior to the sports season, life events (measured by the Adolescents Perceived Events Scale), social support, and psychological coping skills were assessed. When these were analysed with injury data collected over the season, no significant correlations were found between injury and any of the variables. However, when the scores of subjects who were low on both social support and psychological skills were analysed separately it was found that these factors accounted for 22% of the variance in injury. Smith et al. pointed out that for subjects with moderate or high levels of social support or coping skills, there was no relationship between life stress and injury. Although this study is vulnerable to criticisms relating to the lack of established validity of the instruments used to measure social support and coping, it does indicate an important role for these factors in the prevention of sports injury.

This indication has been supported by two recent studies by Australian researchers. Summers, Fawkner, and McMurray (1993), from the University of Melbourne, reported that injury was related to general coping skills in a sample of athletes from four different sports. Similarly, in a study of NBL basketball players, Kirkby and McLeod (1992), from La Trobe University, found that injury could be predicted by coping variables. A particular value of these findings was that, unlike those of previous investigations, they were based on data collected from professional athletes.

The University of Melbourne group (see Fawkner, 1993) were among the first to report on the role of "daily hassles" in sports injury. (Note, Blackwell and McCullagh (1990) assessed daily hassles, but not during the playing season.) Daily hassles relates to the minor chronic stressors of life, rather than major events as measured by life-crises scales (Kanner, Coyne, Schaefer, & Lazarus, 1981). Although daily hassles was included in the model of Andersen and Williams (1988), it has remained ignored by most researchers, probably because of the difficulties in motivating athletes to continually provide information on a day-to-day basis. Notwithstanding some design problems in her study (e.g., daily hassles and uplifts were assessed only on a weekly basis), Fawkner (1993) found that injury in her sample of triathletes and hockey and volleyball players was often preceded by an increase in reported daily hassles.

Psychological coping and rehabilitation after sport injury

Unlike the study of psychological factors in the aetiology of sport injuries, the effects of psychological variables in recovery from sport injuries have received relatively little empirical research. This is understandable. It is relatively easy for an investigator to prospectively assess the psychological characteristics of athletes prior to a season of competition and to analyse these data according to subsequent sports injuries; but it is much more difficult to recruit a statistically adequate sample of subjects with comparable backgrounds and relatively equivalent injuries in order to study psychological interventions in recovery. Thus, it is not surprising that many of the investigations in this area have relied on anecdotal information, or data collected from small samples, or case studies.

While for most athletes preparation for competition and competition itself is stressful, injury brings an added set of pressures. The injured athlete not only undergoes the psychological traumas associated with the pain of injury and sometimes stressful treatments but is vulnerable to the frustration of not being able to compete and, in some cases, not being able to participate even in their usual life activities. Studies using a variety of measures have shown a connection between injury and negative psychological states in athletes. For example, Kolt and Kirkby (1994) reported that gymnasts who had been previously injured were more likely to report fatigue and anxiety. In a study of middle distance runners, Madden, Kirkby, and McDonald (1989) found that the prevalence of injuries was correlated with an increased tendency to use emotional-focused coping styles and that the severity of injuries was correlated with the increased use of denial as a coping strategy. Similarly, Kirkby, Kolt, and Lindner (in press) reported that more-injured gymnasts could be differentiated from less-injured competitors by their increased use of denial and their lessened use of strategies such as increased effort and resolve to cope. The instrument used in these studies was the Ways of Coping with Sport. (This test is described by Madden in Chapter 12 of this text.)

Several investigators have likened an athlete's reaction to injury to the grief response experienced by terminally-ill individuals (e.g., Rotella & Heyman, 1986). According to Kubler-Ross (1969) this grief response involves five stages: denial, anger, bargaining, depression and acceptance. That is, individuals in these circumstances might initially deny that this has happened (or is happening) to them, they become angry with themselves and the world for allowing it to happen, they "bargain", promising that if the situation could be reversed or halted they would change their life, their risk-taking behaviours, etc., they become depressed, and finally move to accepting their circumstances. A description of how these stages could apply specifically to injured athletes has been outlined by Silva and Hardy (1991, pp. 122-124). However, Smith, Scott, and Weise (1990) have cautioned against too readily accepting grief–response theories based on the experiences of terminally-ill and other health-loss populations. They point out that these groups differ in many ways from injured athletes, and that approaches to the rehabilitation of sportspeople should focus on the special characteristics of this population.

An important factor in rehabilitation is adherence. The injured athlete who is uncooperative and does not follow the prescriptions of his or her rehabilitation adviser is likely to have a slower and ultimately more uncomfortable recovery. Duda, Smart, and Tappe (1989) assessed 40 injured college athletes undertaking rehabilitation. Adherence was rated for each athlete on the basis of appointments attended, exercises completed, and intensity of effort put into the rehabilitation exercises (as judged by the supervising trainer). Greater adherence was found in athletes who reported more belief in the efficacy of the treatment, perceived themselves as receiving more social support, and who were more self-motivated. A criticism of this study concerned the relatively low level of injury: on average, the athletes missed only three weeks of competition and training. In another study, Fisher, Damm, and Wuest (1988) investigated adherence in athletes with more extensive injuries requiring rehabilitation for at least six weeks. It is noteworthy that although these investigators used a different research design to that of Duda et al. (1989), their findings were similar. Fisher et al. (1988) reported that compared to "non-adherers", those athletes rated as adhering to their programs were more self-motivated, tolerated pain better, and worked harder to repair their injuries. Overall, support from significant others was the most important factor associated with adherence. The findings of both of these studies underscore the important roles of motivation and social support in recovery from sports injuries.

Ievleva and Orlick (1991) have listed factors important in recovery from illness and injury under seven headings: attitude and outlook; stress control; social support; goal setting; positive self-talk; mental imagery; and beliefs of the individual in the effectiveness of the treatments he or she is undertaking. To investigate these factors, Ievleva and Orlick assessed 32 athletes who had attended a sports medicine clinic for treatment of ankle or knee injuries. Notwithstanding some problems in the investigators' interpretation of statistical significance, their findings indicated a relationship between the rate of recovery and the injured athlete's use of goal setting, positive self-talk, and healing imagery strategies. Ievleva and Orlick's findings confirmed the earlier recommendations of Weiss and Troxel (1986) concerning an approach to the rehabilitation of athletes which included: setting appropriate goals; using affirmations to counter the effects of negative self-talk; and practising mental rehearsal to review the emotional and physical experiences of returning to competition. Suggestions as to how goal setting, self-talk and mental rehearsal can be used with injured athletes are shown in Box 1 (see page 467).

Box 1 Techniques to facilitate recovery from sport injuries

Goal setting

The goals set by injured athletes should be progressive, realistic and readily achievable. The injured athlete should be encouraged to concentrate on short-term targets (e.g., increasing rehabilitation exercise sessions from once to twice daily). The focus should be on "personal bests": that is, increasing effort and consequential achievements (e.g., from five minutes exercise yesterday to six minutes today) should be the aim rather than the distant and sometimes seemingly impossible "return to competition". Goals that are quickly achieved are likely to increase the athlete's sense of efficacy and will enhance his or her motivation to continue with the often stressful rehabilitation process. In the light of findings emphasising the value of social support, it is important that the athlete is encouraged and rewarded for efforts put into rehabilitation.

Positive self-talk

It is common for anxious and depressed individuals to view their environment negatively (Burns, 1980). It appears that this is mediated by a process of self-talk: the silent messages we give ourselves. The effects of negative self-talk can be challenged by Rational Emotive Therapy (Walen, DiGiuseppe, & Wessler, 1992). This involves identifying irrational responses (e.g., "this is hopeless, there's no point, I'll never get better!") and disputing them with more rational self-talk (e.g., "this injury is not what I want, but I can overcome it just as I have overcome other obstacles in my life"). These techniques can be learnt with little difficulty, by children and adults (Bernard, 1991) and are valuable skills for all athletes, injured or not.

Mental rehearsal

Mental training or "cognitive rehearsal" describes the process of imagining or carrying out an activity in one's head rather than practising it overtly. Mental training allows the athlete to rehearse a skill or behaviour at a level of competence higher than that usually attained in physical practice. As such, this technique has two clear benefits for injured athletes. First, according to Ievleva and Orlick (1991), imagery exercises oriented towards the healing process (e.g., visualising fibres mending and tissue being restored) can facilitate recovery. Second, by mentally rehearsing the techniques and strategies associated with their sports, injured athletes can keep their competition skills fresh until they are able to resume physical practice.

FUTURE DIRECTIONS

Most of the more recent research on psychological factors in injury has involved the measurement of life-stress. Although many findings in this area have been inconsistent and sometimes contradictory, the results of more recent studies have suggested that vulnerability to sport injuries could be predicted by the interaction of coping measures (particularly those related to social support) with life-stress. Future research on preventive approaches to sport injuries is likely to focus not only on techniques of stress management but also on appropriate strategies to reinforce the individual athlete's coping skills as well as increasing the coping resources available to him or her. This could lead to sportspeople undergoing a psychological screening procedure at the same time that they are being checked physically for the approaching season. Such a screening could be used to detect psychologically vulnerable athletes. Just as sportspeople who are perceived as at-risk undergo preventive physical treatments (e.g., preseason strengthening of weak muscle systems) or are provided with protective devices (e.g., special padding or splinting), in the future, sport psychologists could be training athletes with higher potential for injury in stress-reduction methods, coping skills, and techniques to develop increased coping resources.

In comparison to the study of predisposing factors, the role of psychological factors in recovery from sport injuries has been less well researched. Although many investigators have likened the consequences of sport injury to the experiences of the terminally ill, there has been no empirical investigation to verify this concept. Further research work in this area is likely to be aimed at confirming the effectiveness of goal setting, positive self-talk, and cognitive rehearsal as strategies for the athlete undergoing rehabilitation. Recent investigations have supported the positive influence of self-efficacy, self-motivation, and social support in facilitating an injured athlete's adherence to their recovery program. This suggests that the future will see an increased role for sport psychologists in helping injured (or even at-risk) athletes to strengthen these variables and so enhance their prospects of successful rehabilitation.

Regardless of where in this area sport psychologists orient their applied skills or their research endeavours, how psychological factors affect the vulnerability to and recovery from sport injuries is an intriguing question that is being researched by an increasing number of sport psychologists. The incidence of sport injuries is increasing. Given the high financial cost of these injuries to the community and the emotional, physical and psychological costs to the athlete, the potential payoff for this line of research is huge.

CONCLUSIONS

Sport injury is frequently highly disruptive for injured individuals and those around them. It is also a financial burden to people who are injured and to society. It is not surprising that a major focus of research in this area has been the prevention of sport injuries. Research on psychological factors which influence sport injury is not easy to execute, particularly with respect to demonstration of cause and effect. This chapter has recorded the methodological problems associated with much of the existing research. Nonetheless, it should be concluded that there does appear to be promise in the combination of life events, coping and social support for the prevention of sport injuries. Although it may present even greater methodological hurdles, research on psychological interventions involving these factors should now be a priority.

Whatever the future success of the prevention research, sport injuries will still occur. The study of psychological influences on the rehabilitation process also has much to offer. Research is currently limited, but there are suggestions that sport psychologists might play a role in ameliorating the personal distress often caused by sport injury. There is also promise in the use of psychological techniques to increase rate of recovery. Some potentially effective methods are exemplified in Box 1 (see page 467). Much more research is needed in the rehabilitation area before the place of psychological processes is established. This is another exciting area which is ripe for research. An increase in published work is anticipated.

Whether it is viewed from the perspective of the financial cost of sport injuries to society, the personal and social distress and disruption caused by sport injuries at all levels of competition, or their effects on domestic and international success in elite sport, there is no doubting the importance of the prevention of sport injuries and rehabilitation to sport. Sport injuries has been designated one of only four priority research areas by the Australian Sports Commission. Sport psychology is poised to play a major role in this work and, thus, in international research on sport injuries.

SUMMARY

This chapter considered psychological factors in sport injuries. It noted that sport injuries place large financial burdens on individuals and the state, but that changes in rules and protective equipment, as well as increased physical preparation have not halted the increase in the incidence of sport injuries.

The chapter considered a number of psychological approaches to sport injuries. First, it was noted that research into personality factors which might influence the probability of getting injured had not produced any clear-cut or consistent patterns. Next it was reported that the examination of life events has been a popular topic, with several studies supporting the life event–injury relationship. These investigations were also found to contain methodological weaknesses.

Focusing next on a coping skills and resources approach, the chapter suggested that research was limited and equivocal, but some indications have emerged that coping with stress might play a role in the incidence of sport injuries. More likely, it was suggested that a combination of life events and coping factors, including social support, perhaps with selected personality variables included, might explain a substantial percentage of the variance in sport injuries. In addition to emphasising the need for research to focus on the usefulness of interventions to prevent sport injuries, it was also proposed that more research is necessary on interventions to facilitate rehabilitation from injury.

The chapter concluded with some future directions in sport injury research and a section on major applied techniques.

REFERENCES

Abadie, D. A. (1976). Comparison of personalities of non-injured and injured female athletes in intercollegiate competition. *Dissertation Abstracts, 15*(2), 82.

Andersen, M. B., & Williams, J. M. (1988). A model of stress and athletic injury: Prediction and prevention. *Journal of Sport and Exercise Psychology, 10,* 294–306.

Backx, F. J. G., Erich, W. B. M., Kemper, A. B. A., & Verbeek, A. L. M. (1989). Sports injuries in school-aged children: An epidemiologic study. *American Journal of Sports Medicine, 17,* 234–239.

Bernard, M. (1991). *Using rational-emotive therapy effectively. A practitioner's guide.* New York: Plenum Press.

Blackwell, B., & McCullagh, P. (1990). The relationship of athletic injury to life stress, competitive anxiety and coping resources. *Athletic Training, 25,* 23–27.

Bond, J. W., Miller, B. P., & Chrisfield, P. M. (1988). Psychological prediction of injury in elite swimmers. *International Journal of Sports Medicine, 9,* 345–348.

Bramwell, S. T., Masuda, M., Wagner, N. N., & Holmes, T. H. (1975). Psychosocial factors in athletic injuries: Development and application of the Social and Athletic Readjustment Rating Scale (SARRS). *Journal of Human Stress, 1,* 6–20.

Brown, G. W. (1981). Life events, psychiatric disorder and physical illness. *Journal of Psychosomatic Research, 25,* 461–473.

Brown, J. D., & Lawton, M. (1986). Stress and well-being in adolescence: The moderating role of physical exercise. *Journal of Human Stress, 12,* 125–131.

Brown, R. B. (1971). Personality characteristics related to injury in football. *Research Quarterly, 42,* 133–138.

Burckes, M. E. (1981). The injury prone athlete. *Scholastic Coach, 6*(3), 47–48.

Burns, D. D. (1980). *Feeling good.* New York: Pergamon Press.

Centre for Health Promotion and Research. (1990). *Sports injuries in Australia: Causes, costs, and prevention.* A Report to the National Better Health Program. Sydney: National Better Health Program.

Coddington, D., & Troxell, J. R. (1980). The effect of emotional factors on football injury rates: A pilot study. *Journal of Human Stress, 6,* 3–5.

Cryan, P., & Alles, W. (1983). The relationship between stress and college football injuries. *Sports Medicine, 23,* 52–58.

Dalhauser, M., & Thomas, M. (1979). Visual disembedding and locus of control as variables associated with high school football injuries. *Perceptual and Motor Skills, 49,* 254.

de Loes, M., & Goldie, I. (1988). Incidence rates of injuries during sport activity and physical exercise in a rural Swedish municipality: Incidence rates in 17 sports. *International Journal of Sports Medicine, 9,* 461–467.

Duda, J. L., Smart, A. E., & Tappe, M. K. (1989). Predictors of adherence in the rehabilitation of athletic injuries: An application of personal investment theory. *Journal of Sport and Exercise Psychology, 11,* 367–381.

Fawkner, H. J. (1993). *Predisposition to injury in athletes: A role for psychosocial factors.* Unpublished master's thesis, University of Melbourne, Victoria.

Fields, K. B., Delaney, M., & Hinkle, J. S. (1990). A prospective study of Type A behavior and running injuries. *Journal of Family Practice, 30,* 425–429.

Fisher, A. C., Damm, M. A., & Wuest, D. A. (1988). Adherence to sports-injury rehabilitation programs. *The Physician and Sportsmedicine, 16,* 47–51.

Folkman, S., & Lazarus, R. S. (1985). If it changes it must be a process: Study of emotion and coping during three stages of a college examination. *Journal of Personality and Social Psychology, 48,* 150–170.

Govern, J. W., & Koppenhaver, R. (1965). Attempt to predict athletic injuries. *Medical Times, 93,* 421–422.

Hanson, S. J., McCullagh, P., & Tonyman, P. (1992). The relationship of personality characteristics, life stress, and coping resources to athletic injury. *Journal of Sport and Exercise Psychology, 14,* 262–272.

Hardy, C. J., & Riehl, R. E. (1988). An examination of the life stress–injury relationship among noncontact sports participants. *Behavioral Medicine, 14,* 113–118.

Holmes, T. H. (1970). Psychological screening. In *Football injuries: Papers presented at a workshop* (pp. 211–214). Subcommittee on Athletic Injuries, Committee on the Skeletal System, Division of Medical Sciences, National Research Council, Feb. 1969. Washington, DC: National Academy of Sciences.

Holmes, T. H., & Rahe, R. H. (1967). The Social Readjustment Rating Scale (SRRS). *Journal of Psychosomatic Research, 6,* 213–217.

Ievleva, L., & Orlick, T. (1991). Mental links to enhanced healing: An exploratory study. *The Sport Psychologist, 5,* 25–40.

Jackson, D. W., Jarrett, H., Bailey, D., Kausek, J., Swanson, J., & Powell, J. W. (1978). Injury prediction in the young athlete: A preliminary report. *American Journal of Sports Medicine, 6,* 6–14.

Kanner, A. D., Coyne, J. C., Schaefer, C., & Lazarus, R. S. (1981). Comparison of two models of stress measurement: Daily hassles and uplifts versus major life events. *Journal of Behavioral Medicine, 4,* 1–39.

Kerr, G., & Minden, H. (1988). Psychological factors related to the occurrence of athletic injuries. *Journal of Sport and Exercise Psychology, 10,* 167–173.

Kirkby, R. J., Kolt, G. S., & Lindner, H. (in press). Coping in gymnasts: Injury and gender factors. *Sports Medicine, Training and Rehabilitation.*

Kirkby, R. J., & McLeod, S. (1992, September). *The psychological antecedents of injury in national-level basketball players.* Paper presented at the 27th Annual Conference of the Australian Psychological Society, Armidale.

Kolt, G. S., & Kirkby, R. J. (1991, November). Injury, anxiety and mood in competitive gymnasts. Paper presented at the *First Asian South Pacific Association of Sport Psychology Congress,* Melbourne, Australia.

Kolt, G. S., & Kirkby, R. J. (1994). Injury, anxiety, and mood in competitive gymnasts. *Perceptual and Motor Skills, 78,* 955–962.

Kraus, J. F., & Gullen, W. H. (1969). An epidemiological investigation of predictor variables associated with intramural touch football injury. *American Journal of Public Health, 59,* 2144–2156.

Kubler-Ross, E. (1969). *On death and dying.* London: Macmillan.

Kvidera, D., & Frankel, V. H. (1983). Trauma on eight wheels: A study of roller skating injuries in Seattle. *American Journal of Sports Medicine, 11,* 38–41.

Landers, D. M. (1980). Cue utilization and the arousal-performance relationship. *Research Quarterly for Exercise and Sport, 51,* 77–90.

Lysens, R., van den Auweele, Y., & Ostyn, M. (1986). The relationship between psychosocial factors and sports injuries. *Journal of Sports Medicine, 26,* 77–84.

Madden, C. C., Kirkby, R. J., & McDonald, D. (1989). Coping styles of competitive distance runners. *International Journal of Sport Psychology, 2,* 287–296.

May, J. R., & Sieb, G. E. (1987). Athletic injuries: Psychological onset, sequelae, rehabilitation, and prevention. In J. R. May & M. J. Asken (Eds.), *Sports psychology: The psychological health of the athlete* (pp. 157–185). New York: PMA Publishing.

May, J. R., Veach, T. L., Southard, S. W., & Herring, M. W. (1985). The effects of life change on injuries illness and performance in elite athletes. In N. K. Butts, T. T. Gushikin, & B. Zarins (Eds.), *The elite athlete* (pp. 171–179). Jamaica & New York: Spectrum Publishing.

May, J. R., Veach, T. L., Southard, S. W., Reed, M. W., & Griffey, M. S. (1985). A psychological study of health, injury, and performance in athletes on the U.S. Alpine Ski Team. *The Physician and Sportsmedicine, 13,* 111–115.

McClay, M. H., Appleby, D. C., & Plascak, F. D. (1989). Predicting injury in young cross-country runners with the Self-motivation Inventory. *Sports Training, Medicine, and Rehabilitation, 1,* 191–195.

Miller, T. W., Vaughn, M. P., & Miller, J. M. (1990). Clinical issues and treatment strategies in stress-oriented athletes. *Sports Medicine, 9,* 370–379.

Nideffer, R. M. (1983). The injured athlete: Psychological factors in treatment. *Orthopedic Clinics of North America, 14,* 373–385.

Nideffer, R. M. (1989). Psychological aspects of sports injuries: Issues in prevention and treatment. *International Journal of Sport Psychology, 20,* 241–255.

Noakes, T. D., & Schomer, H. (1983). The "eager parent syndrome" and schoolboy injuries. *South African Medical Journal, 63,* 956.

Ogilvie, B. C., & Tutko, T. A. (1966). *Problem athletes and how to handle them.* London: Pelham.

Pargman, D., & Lunt, S. D. (1989). The relationship of self-concept and locus of control to the severity of injury in freshman collegiate football players. *Sports Medicine, Training and Rehabilitation, 1,* 203–208.

Passer, M. W., & Seese, M. D. (1983). Life stress and athletic injury: Examination of positive versus negative events and three moderator variables. *Journal of Human Stress, 9,* 11–16.

Rotella, R. J., & Heyman, S. R. (1986). Stress, injury, and the psychological rehabilitation of athletes. In J. M. Williams (Ed.), *Applied sport psychology: Personal growth to peak performance* (pp. 343–364). Palo Alto, CA: Mayfield.

Ryde, D. (1965). The role of the physician in sports injury prevention. *Journal of Sports Medicine, 5,* 152–155.

Sanderson, F. H. (1977). The psychology of the injury-prone athlete. *British Journal of Sports Medicine, 11*(1), 56–57.

Sarason, I. G., Johnson, J. H., & Sarason, J. M. (1978). Assessing the impact of life changes: Development of the Life Experiences Survey. *Journal of Consulting and Clinical Psychology, 46,* 932–946.

Seward, H. G., & Patrick, J. (1992). A three year survey of Victorian Football League injuries. *Australian Journal of Science and Medicine in Sport, 21,* 51–54.

Silva, J. M., & Hardy, C. J. (1991). The sport psychologist. In F. O. Mueller & A. J. Ryan (Eds.), *The sports medicine team and athletic prevention* (pp. 114–132). Philadephia, MS: F. A. Davis.

Smith, A. M., Scott, S. G., & Weise, D. M. (1990). Psychological effects of sports injuries: Coping. *Sports Medicine, 9,* 352–369.

Smith, R. E., Smoll, F. L., & Ptacek, J. T. (1990). Conjunctive moderator variables in vulnerability and resiliency research: Life stress, social support and coping skills, and adolescent sport injuries. *Journal of Personality and Social Psychology, 58,* 360–370.

Summers, J. J., Fawkner, H., & McMurray, N. (1993, July). *Predisposition to athletic injury: The role of psycho-social factors.* Paper presented at the VIII World Congress of Sport Psychology, Lisbon.

Taimela, S., Österman, L., Kujala, U., Lehto, M., Korhonen, T., & Alaranta, H. (1990). Motor ability and personality with reference to soccer injuries. *Journal of Sports Medicine and Physical Fitness, 30,* 194–201.

Valliant, P. M. (1981). Personality and injury in competitive runners. *Perceptual and Motor Skills, 53,* 251–253.

van Mechelen, W. (1992). Running injuries: A review of the epidemiological literature. *Sports Medicine, 14,* 320–335.

van Mechelen, W., Hlobil, H., & Kemper, H. C. (1992). Incidence, severity, aetiology and prevention of sports injuries. *Sports Medicine, 14,* 82–99.

Walen, S. R., DiGiuseppe, R., & Wessler, R. L. (1992). *A practitioner's guide to Rational Emotive Therapy* (2nd ed.). New York: Oxford University Press.

Weiss, M. R., & Troxel, R. K. (1986). Psychology of the injured athlete. *Athletic Trainer, 21*(2), 104–109.

Williams, J. M., Haggert, J., Tonyman, P., & Wadsworth, W. A. (1986). Life stress and prediction of athletic injuries in volleyball, basketball, and cross-country running. In L. E. Unestahl (Ed.), *Sport psychology in theory and practice.* Orebro, Sweden: Veje Publishers.

Williams, J. M., Tonyman, P., & Wadsworth, W. A. (1986). Relationship of life stress to injury in intercollegiate volleyball. *Journal of Human Stress, 12,* 38–43.

Yaffe, M. (1983). Sports injuries: Psychological aspects. *British Journal of Hospital Medicine,* March, 224–232.

C H A P T E R

19

CAREER TRANSITIONS IN COMPETITIVE SPORT

SANDY GORDON*

The trouble with making a game a profession is that you're at the top too young. The rest of the way's a gentle slide down. Not so gentle sometimes. It makes one feel so ruddy useless and old.

Sam Palmer, Test veteran (cited in Frith, 1990, p. 3)

It is 19 years since I was competing... a long time since the end of my swimming career, a long transition during which I was confused and bewildered by my range of emotions in relation to my career and its ending. I am getting to the coping stage only by becoming informed and educating myself about the normal athletic retirement process.

Shane Innes (née Gould), winner of three gold medals (three world records), one silver, one bronze, 1972 Olympics, at age 15 years
(*Sportsview*, WA Sports Federation, 1992, p. 6)

---

* The author gratefully acknowledges the assistance of the following individuals in the preparation of this chapter: Deidre Anderson (Victorian Institute of Sport), Ken Hawkins (Ballarat University), Craig McLatchey (Australian Olympic Committee, Director of Sport), Tony Morris and Vanda Fortunato (Victoria University of Technology), and SportsLEAP staff John Purnell (National Manager), Paul Austen (Tas.), Jenni Dewar (NSW), Jenny Everson (ACT), Ruth Gillies (SA), Lydia Najlepszy (Qld) and Annette Walker (WA).

Post-career is like losing someone close to you and grieving over them. I did it hard. I still do it hard. I still miss my running very much. It's just like you've lost a leg when you retire. You still think its there, even though its not.

Raelene Boyle (Davis, 1993, p. 6)

I am very solid with my decision not to play any more basketball in the NBA. I have always stressed that when I lose the sense of motivation and the sense to prove something as a basketball player, it's time to leave. I've been on this roller coaster for nine years. It's time to ride something else. If I get a pot belly, then I start exercising. Do I need a job? No. I've never had a job. I don't want one now. I'm gonna watch the grass grow, and I'm gonna have to cut it.

Michael Jordan (on the timing of his retirement on 7 October, 1993) (Smith, 1993, p. 78)

The above quotes from elite athletes provide some indication of the inevitable adjustments required following retirement from competitive sport. However, are these representative of the emotions and adaptations of all athletes? Do adjustments warrant closer scrutiny by the sport industry? Are all career transitions essentially negative experiences? Answers to these questions, and others, are the focus of this chapter.

Career transition is a subject that has been generally overlooked as an area of research by sport scientists in Australia, until very recently. Both career transition and career retirement issues have also received haphazard attention from sport administrators, coaches, athletes and those closely associated with athletes (e.g., family), who are nevertheless keenly aware of the complex personal adjustments and socio-psychological phenomena involved. This chapter is an attempt to provide an overview of certain theoretical approaches, the extant research, and existing intervention programs on career assistance, with the intention of encouraging more research interest in the general area. The first section introduces theoretical models from the social gerontological, thanatological and transitions literature that have been applied, more or less appropriately, to sport. The second section attempts to summarise the extant research conducted by sociologists and psychologists, including recent Australian research, and will be followed by brief descriptions of career assistance programs in different countries, but with a special focus on provisions for elite amateur Australian athletes. The fourth and fifth sections describe prevention and treatment interventions, and suggestions for further research, respectively.

However, to begin with, some major terms must be defined, and a statement of the problem — if that is possible — must be provided.

LEAVING COMPETITIVE SPORT: RETIREMENT OR REBIRTH? (COAKLEY, 1983)

Coakley's (1983) examination of the sociological ramifications of leaving competitive sport in America is perhaps an appropriate starting point for similar investigations in Australia. Coakley and others (e.g., Blinde &

Greendorfer, 1985; Greendorfer & Blinde, 1985; Lerch, 1981) have found that retirement does not necessarily signal trauma, identity crises or serious adjustment problems; however, without any substantive evidence either supporting or refuting such claims, can we assume this is also the case in Australia?

The major terms used in this chapter are borrowed from Coakley (1983), who defined competitive sport as "any organized sport activity in which training and participation are time-consuming and in which the level of performance meets relatively high standards of expectation" (p. 1); and retirement as "the process of transition from participation in competitive sport to another activity or set of activities" (p. 10). In Australia, therefore, we are referring to all boys and girls, men and women who participate in professional sports of all types, and in competitive amateur sports that often demand similar levels of commitment. In other words, the attention is on all individuals who allow their desire for competence in sport to dominate all other forms of human expression and especially those who allow sport to become the total focus of their lives. Coakley's definition of "retirement" differs from popular connotations of the term which suggest a "withdrawal from" or "an end to" an involvement. Such descriptions depict the experience as final and negative, while Coakley conceptualises retirement more positively and more accurately as a series of graduations of withdrawal that lead to commencements or beginnings in other spheres of activity or other relationships.

We will return to the question of whether or not career transitions or retirement are negative experiences in Australia later in the chapter, but answers will only emerge from systematic explorations of the phenomena involved. More specifically, explanatory models and theories that are grounded in the social structural context in which retirement takes place are required, so that transitions and retirement experiences and concerns can be both understood and researched thoroughly. In turn, these concerns can be anticipated and effectively planned for. The next section summarises several theoretical approaches that have been used or referred to in the study of career transitions and retirement in sport, and discusses their applied utility.

THEORETICAL MODELS

SOCIAL GERONTOLOGY THEORIES

McPherson (1980), in his discussion of occupational and psychological adjustment problems in athletic retirement, suggested that certain theories associated with social gerontology (the study of ageing) might have applicable orientations. Rosenberg (1981) discussed the merits and shortcomings of six such approaches, namely activity, disengagement, subculture, continuity, social breakdown and reconstruction, and exchange theories.

Activity (or substitution) theory (Burgess, 1960; Havighurst & Albrecht, 1953) maintains that lost roles are to be substituted for so that total activity continues, and the basic proposition is that high activity and maintenance of roles are positively related to self-concept and life satisfaction. Most older people, however, seem content to decrease their activity and do not retain patterns of activity associated with middle age, which is an anomaly activity theory fails to explain.

Disengagement theory (Cumming, Dean, Newell, & McCaffrey, 1960; Cumming & Henry, 1961) is a structural–functional theory which suggests that society and the ageing individual withdraw from one another to the mutual benefit and satisfaction of both. After retirement, society gets younger workers into the workforce and the elderly can enjoy their remaining years in leisure. While disengagement theory was developed to attack activity theory, neither theory provides mechanisms to predict whether activity or disengagement will result, and is, therefore, limited in its applied utility.

Building on activity theory, *subculture theory* (Rose, 1965) adds the possibility of subcultural norms, in which some elderly people may enjoy less activity but be well adjusted; this may be different from social norms. Rosenberg (1981) sees some merit in this approach since competitive athletes have fairly obvious and distinguishable subcultural characteristics.

Unlike activity theory, *continuity or consolidation theory* (Atchley, 1981) suggests that substitution is not necessary for lost roles. Time and energy can be redirected or redistributed among remaining roles or towards new roles. However, if the lost role was an important role, consolidation of other activities may not provide the same basis for a meaningful existence, and therefore may not provide a satisfactory solution.

Social breakdown theory (Kuypers & Bengston, 1973) proposes that with any role loss (e.g., retirement or widowhood), individuals become susceptible to external labelling (e.g., "hero to zero", Orlick, 1990) and if the social evaluation of status is unfavourable, there is a tendency to withdraw or to reduce certain activities. To combat this negative activity downward spiral, a "social reconstruction" cycle is proposed to restore and maintain positive self-image through counselling and engagement in alternative activities that enhance self-reliance.

Finally, *exchange theory* (Dowd, 1975) can be adapted to illustrate how successful ageing can be achieved, through rearrangement of social networks and activities to maximise return.

While all of the above theories have relevance for sport retirement, and warrant closer scrutiny than offered here, Rosenberg (1981) suggests that the latter two theories — social breakdown/reconstruction and exchange theories — are most salient. He believes that anecdotal evidence alone suggests that voluntary disengagement from sport is unlikely (Frith, 1990; Howe, Howe, & Wilkins, 1989; Smith, 1987) and that, contrary to disengagement theory, athletes typically try to hang on to sport sometimes long after their skills have begun to deteriorate. Also, the main messages of activity, subculture and continuity are, arguably, largely incorporated into social breakdown/reconstruction. For example, activity theory proposes concepts like role replacement and activity level maintenance, subculture theory acknowledges and identifies norms that are dysfunctional to retirement planning, and continuity theory is applicable in that commitment, sacrifice and self-concept from the competitive athlete role can be reallocated to remaining or new roles. Athletes who receive counselling on these issues can learn to minimise the potential for social breakdowns and take steps, through social reconstruction, to smooth out the transition period.

Exchange theory can help athletes understand their relationship with sport over time, and provide a perspective on what will happen to that relationship over time. For example, the athlete's resource — physical talent — is exchanged for meaningful rewards from the sport system, but that resource is finite and the inevitable deterioration in skill will affect the degree of control over the athlete/sport relationship. Rosenberg (1981) believes an exchange theory perspective "would, in pre-retirement counselling, make a fitting prelude to a discussion of social breakdown" (p. 123).

SOCIAL DEATH: THANATOLOGY

Both Rosenberg (1982) and Lerch (1982) have employed the concept of social death as a model for explaining the social and psychological changes involved in retirement from sport. Social death refers to the condition of being treated as if one were dead although still physiologically and intellectually alive. It derives from the science of thanatology (the study of death and dying), and although the concept of death is only an analogy, and there is a considerable difference between actual death and retirement from sport, the concept of social death is perceived as quite useful, particularly for designing career assistance/counselling programs. Lerch (1982), for example, discussed two thanatological models that reveal interesting parallels between the socially dying retiring athlete and the physically dying hospital patient: the "awareness context" notion of Glaser and Strauss (1965) and the "stages of dying" of Kubler-Ross (1969).

Glaser and Strauss (1965) suggest four different types of awareness context: closed, suspicion, mutual pretence and open. Applied to sport, *closed awareness* could apply in situations where an athlete is unaware of plans to cut, release or trade him or her from the team. Team mates may have seen "the axe" approaching but, because failure or deterioration in form is rarely discussed in competitive sport, the athlete concerned is often surprised and shocked. *Suspicion awareness* is more complicated in that athletes may suspect a demotion is forthcoming by subtle changes in personal interactions with coaches and administrators. For example, less verbal and non-verbal (body language) communication is perceived by the athlete when in the presence of coaches and administrators. The next context, *mutual pretence*, is analogous to make-believe, where all people concerned with the athlete — managers, coaches, trainers — know that no matter how well the athlete performs, his or her career is nearing its conclusion. If this is not sustained, mutual pretence can only change to the final context, *open awareness*, where both the athlete and others know that career end is inevitable and openly acknowledge the fact.

From interviews, Kubler-Ross (1969) identified certain reactions or coping mechanisms terminal patients use to deal with impending death that Lerch (1982) suggests draw interesting parallels with athletes coping with social death. Similar reactions by athletes responding to and rehabilitating from sport injury have been reported by sport physiotherapists (Gordon, Milios, & Grove, 1991). The first stage is denial (e.g., "No, it's not true"), followed by anger (e.g., "Why me? Why now?"), bargaining (e.g., "I'll do anything to stay in the game"), depression (e.g., "This loss is unbearably sad") and, finally, acceptance or resignation (e.g., "It's happened, my competitive sport career is over, now what?"). At the final stage, social death obviously differs from real death in that the athlete continues to live. Recovery from social death is, therefore, possible although athletes themselves will likely mourn the loss of their careers, either publicly or privately, in a cyclical fashion, drifting in and out of different stages of reaction. Regarded in this light, Rosenberg (1982) and Lerch (1982) maintain that the concept of social death, as an analogy, can be useful, particularly to involuntary rather than voluntary retirement. The consequences of voluntary retirement are less severe because the athlete retains control of his or her fate.

While models from social gerontology and thanatology dominate the literature, several researchers (e.g., Blinde & Greendorfer, 1985; Greendorfer & Blinde, 1985) have questioned the ability of those models to comprehensively capture the process of leaving sport. Crook and Robertson (1991) also criticise social gerontological models and specifically the analogy between athletic (functional) retirement and old age (chronological) retirement, and the inability of gerontological models to explain variations in athletes' responses to retirement. The thanatological model is also criticised for stereotyping athletes' reactions, and for portraying retirement in an overly negative light. Both models seem to assume that all retirement experiences require serious adjustment when, in reality, this does not appear to be the case. Crook and Robertson (1991), therefore, propose models of transition which they believe provide an alternative perspective to retirement and which can account for the many factors influencing athletes' responses to retirement more adequately, and explain both positive and negative experiences.

TRANSITION MODELS

Models of transition, used most often in counselling, usually define transition as "discontinuity in a person's life space" (Crook & Robertson, 1991, p. 122), where the person is aware of the discontinuity and requires new behaviour as a result of the newness of the situation. All transitions involve both obvious and subtle, positive and negative, anticipated and unexpected, and voluntary or forced, changes, and result in different degrees of loss and stress depending on the demands of the individual's behavioural repertoire (Brammer & Abrego, 1981).

Schlossberg's (1981, 1984) transition model theorises that three interacting factors affect adaptation:

(a) characteristics of the transition, e.g., the trigger, timing, source and duration of the transition, role changes, current stress involved, and the individual's previous experience with transition

(b) characteristics of the individual, e.g., personal and demographic characteristics, socioeconomic status, sex role, age and stage of life, state of health, as well as psychological characteristics such as ego development, personality, outlook, commitment and values, and coping skills

(c) characteristics of the environment, e.g., social support networks and options available for the athlete outside sport.

All three interacting factors are viewed as potential assets or liabilities depending upon the individual's appraisal of the situation (the transition), self, and personal environment, and may provide a clear, flexible and multidimensional approach to the understanding of factors related to successful adjustment (Crook & Robertson, 1991).

The tenets of transition models are supported by both Pearson and Petitpas (1990) and Ogilvie and Taylor (1993b) who suggest that experiences and responses to transition may be differentiated on the basis of whether or not athletes "retire" because of deselection, age or injury. Figure 19.1 is a conceptual model adapted from Crook and Robertson (1991), Pearson and Petitpas (1990), Ogilvie and Taylor (1993b) and Schlossberg (1981, 1984), illustrating causal factors that initiate career transition, factors that may differentiate responses to transitions, tertiary factors that might mediate the trauma associated with transitions, and interventions or treatment modalities for career transition and career assistance. This model will be referred to later in connection with both prevention and treatment strategies and recommendations for further research.

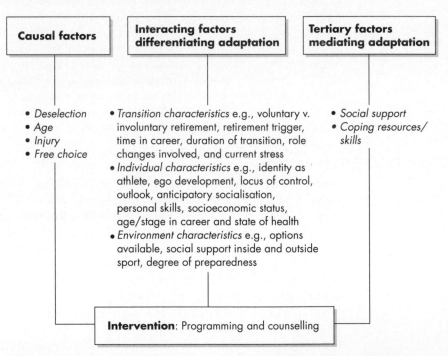

Figure 19.1: Conceptual model of the career transition process in competitive sport

CAREER TRANSITION RESEARCH

Several studies of the effects of sport participation or the processes of transitions, from four different decades, will be mentioned in this brief review of the extant literature. However, exploratory research on the potential rewards and risks of identifying strongly and exclusively with the athlete role are examined first.

Brewer and his colleagues (Brewer, Van Raalte, & Linder, 1993; Good, Brewer, Petitpas, Van Raalte, & Mahar, 1993) discuss athletic identity within the framework of a multidimensional construct, and describe a person with strong athletic identity as "more likely to interpret a given event (e.g., an injury) in terms of its implications for that individual's athletic functioning than a person only weakly identified to the athlete role" (Brewer et al., 1993, p. 238). They also describe athletic identity as a social role, one that is heavily socialised by the influences of family, friends, coaches, teachers and the media. While the benefits of strong athletic identity include adherence to and involvement in sport, exercise and health behaviours, development of athletic skills, sense of self, and confidence, the potential risks relate to difficulties athletes may experience during career transitions and specifically problems associated with deselection, injury and athletic career termination (Baillie & Danish, 1992; McPherson, 1980; Ogilvie & Howe, 1982; Pearson & Petitpas, 1990). The reason a strong, exclusive athletic identity is thought to be a risk factor for emotional problems following career end is that "Individuals who strongly commit themselves to the athlete role may be less likely to explore other career, education and lifestyle options due to their intensive involvement in sport" (Brewer et al., 1993, p. 241).

Three recent studies may have provided indirect support for the hypothesis that strong exclusive athletic identity creates potential for emotional difficulties upon career end. Werthner and Orlick (1986) found that former Canadian Olympians, who had pre-arranged alternative career options and commitments, adjusted to transition out of the athlete role more effectively than those without pre-arranged alternatives. Kleiber, Greendorfer, Blinde, and Samdahl (1987) demonstrated that intercollegiate athletes whose careers were terminated prematurely by injury reported lower postcollegiate life satisfaction than their student/athlete peers whose careers were not terminated by injury. Kleiber and Malik (1989), in their study of former Big 10 male football and basketball players, reported a significant relationship between academic involvement, as a college student, and postcollegiate life satisfaction and self-esteem, which suggests that a strong but not exclusive athletic identity affords more psychological benefits to competitive student/athletes. There would, therefore, appear to be considerable merit in exploring further the relationship of the exclusive athlete identity construct and career transitions, using the Athletic Identity Measurement Scale (AIMS; Brewer et al., 1993), among competitive athletes in different age and gender groups.

While studies of the process of transition are rare (McPherson, 1980), two earlier investigations by Mihovilovic (1968) and Haerle (1975) and two recent studies by Werthner and Orlick (1986) and Allison and Meyer (1988) are most commonly cited.

Mihovilovic (1968), using questionnaires and interviews, surveyed the reasons for career termination, and how the effects of retirement could be eased, among 44 male Yugoslavian soccer players. He found that only 5% retired voluntarily and the remainder retired as a result of injury, age, club contract arrangements or deselection. Over one-half (52%) reported retirement as a shock or sudden event which was closely related to illness, family factors or age. Only one-third (34%) retired at their peak while the remainder hung on until after their skills had begun to decline. Smoother transitions, it was suggested, could be facilitated by clubs maintaining contact with players, including players in tournaments and public announcements, and using players' experience and expertise in coaching or training.

Haerle (1975) surveyed 312 former baseball players, focusing on their pre-retirement planning or preparations for retirement, and responses and attitudes when the event occurred. He reported that 75% of the respondents did not consider retirement until their early thirties or the last quarter of their playing career, and 50% were more psychologically oriented toward their past sporting career than to their future. At the time of retirement only 25% were making plans for the future and had accepted their career end. In addition, Haerle found that while fame helped in securing the first postplaying job, educational attainment was more significant in predicting later careers. Interestingly, Haerle also reported that those who chose to stay in baseball experienced less stable career paths than those who quit the sport completely.

Werthner and Orlick (1986) studied the transitions of 28 Canadian Olympians using open-ended interview questions. Their results suggested that "seven major factors appeared to have an important role in determining the nature of the transition out of sport for a great number of athletes" (p. 351). These were:

1. A new focus: Alternatives or options to sports participation allowed for a redirection of attention and energy.
2. A sense of accomplishment: Achieving goals in their sport (e.g., medals) facilitated transition.
3. Coaches: "Lack of good coaches and conflicts with coaches or with coaching decisions... often made the actual transition quite difficult" (Werthner & Orlick, 1986, p. 354).
4. Injuries/health problems: Negative transition experiences were frequently precipitated by premature career termination due to injury.
5. Politics/sport association problems: Canada's boycott of the 1980 Summer Olympics had a negative impact on the transition of many of the athletes, however, a number also reported problems with their sport association. For example, several felt their sport association was responsible for their coaching problems. Some athletes were also concerned with the politics surrounding team selection procedures and

"carding" of athletes. The Sport Canada carding system classifies amateur athletes into A, B and C categories as a basis for providing the athletes with financial assistance. "Athletes were cut from teams or from carded status in what was, to them, extremely unfair circumstances and it resulted in a few very bitter athletes" (Werthner & Orlick, 1986, p. 355).

6. Finances: The cost of continued training and preparation and the lack of funding, which together contributed to the decision to retire, often resulted in negative consequences for the athlete and a sense of bitterness.

7. The support of family and friends: Many athletes reported that the social support of family and friends was a positive factor in their transition. Athletes who did not receive such support reported more difficulties in the transition process.

Allison and Meyer (1988) used open-ended items in a mailed questionnaire to survey 28 retired female tennis professionals regarding the experiences and perceptions of their competitive years and subsequent retirement. Results from 20 of the respondents indicated that most subjects did not find disengagement from competitive sport traumatic and in fact found it as an opportunity to re-establish more traditional social roles and lifestyles. This is perhaps not surprising since almost two-thirds (60%) commented that they had not intended to become professionals in the first place and had continued playing much longer than they had planned, and, after experiencing significant levels of frustration touring, 50% expressed relief upon retirement. One third (30%), however, did report initial adjustment problems (e.g., loss of identity, isolation) immediately following retirement.

In addition to the four studies previously described, data from surveys conducted by Blann and Zaichkowski (1986, 1988, 1989) among American professional hockey and major league baseball players, and Wylleman, de Knop, Menkehorst, Theeboom, and Annerel (1993) with former Belgian Olympic athletes, highlight the perceived need of athletes for post-sport career planning programs. Using Blann's (1984) Professional Athletes Career Transition Inventory (PACTI), Blann and Zaichkowsky (1989) surveyed 117 National Hockey League (NHL) and 214 Major League Baseball (MLB) players. A summary of their respective responses to both career awareness and career transition needs is illustrated in Figure 19.2.

The two most helpful career planning programs perceived by both NHL and MLB players were seminars and individual counselling to help players understand their personal strengths, interests and skills related to careers; and assistance to help players develop and carry out education/training programs and career action plans. The two least helpful types of services were arranging for jobs during the off-season, and help in developing and carrying out job search campaigns. Interestingly, these professional athletes believed that players' associations, and not management, were primarily responsible for the provision of such services. Wylleman et al. (1993), on the other hand, in their survey of 44 Belgian ex-Olympic athletes (M = 41.7 years; range 26–61 years), found that 45.5% reported "lack of pre-retirement planning and the failing of official organisations such as the sport federations, the Olympic Committee, and the Flemish Bureau for Top-Level Sport, had the most influence on the way in which their career termination and the following phase of adaptation and social integration evolved (mostly problematically)" (p. 904).

Career awareness	NHL (N = 117)	MLB (N = 214)	Career transition needs	NHL (N = 117)	MLB (N = 214)
• Delay planning for post-sport career	53%	70%	• Have a post-sport career plan	37%	25%
• Know resources to use to obtain a job	46%	27%	• Want help with post-sport career planning	85%	97%
• Know personal background related to best suited job/career options	23%	28%	• Adequate financing for two-year start-up for new career/ retirement	54%	19%
• Engage in off-season career/work	43%	36%	• Believe post-sport career critical to life satisfaction after sport	68%	67%

NHL = National Hockey League; MLB = Major League Baseball

Figure 19.2: Summary of NHL and MLB players' survey (Blann & Zaichkowski, 1989)

Taken together, Baillie and Danish (1992) believe that these and other studies (e.g., Lerch, 1981; Reynolds, 1981; Rosenberg, 1981) provide patterns of evidence that are useful in developing both career transition programs and directions for further research. For example, recurring themes include athletes being unprepared for retirement (financially or emotionally) while at the same time indicating a desire for more support; and, secondly, a need for a gradual resocialisation out of athlete identities and sport, into non-sport participatory roles either through education or second careers or both. These themes had previously been foremost in the development of the Career Assistance Program for Athletes (CAPA) in America, which Petitpas, Danish, McKelvain, and Murphy (in press) deliberately formulated within a life-span development framework.

The development of CAPA became possible in 1988 with funding from the United States Olympic Foundation to the Olympic Job Opportunities Program. Following a needs assessment survey among approximately 1800 Olympic and Pan-American Games team members who had participated from 1980–88, a small group of counsellors, sport psychologists, sociologists, elite athletes, Olympic Training Center personnel, and career development specialists met to design the program. The group decided that a life-span developmental model (Danish & D'Augelli, 1980), focusing on "preparation for transition" and "enhancement of personal skills" would be the framework, which is closely tied to the idea that athletes can increase their sense of personal competence through understanding and identifying the transferable skills they acquire through sports participation (Danish, Petitpas, & Hale, 1990). In a life-span developmental approach three types of interventions are provided: enhancement of coping skills to deal with future transitions; social support, which takes place during a transition; and counselling, which allows athletes to share their feelings after, as well as before, a transition (e.g., retirement) takes place. These interventions are reflected in the philosophy of the CAPA workshop, seminar and workbook content and material, which athletes are introduced to in lectures and through small group discussions. Workshops focus on three main topics: "1) managing the emotional and social impact of transitions; 2) increasing understanding and awareness of personal qualities relevant to coping with transitions and career development; and 3) introducing information about the world of work" (Petitpas et al., in press).

The initial responses of 142 athletes (77 males; 65 females) who participated in a formal evaluation of the first CAPA workshop were very positive. Seventy-two per cent were very satisfied with the workshop, 84% felt it met or exceeded their expectations, and 98% indicated they would recommend it to other athletes. Small group discussions, sharing feelings with other athletes, and presentations on transferable skills were rated most valuable and useful workshop activities, although some participants felt that there was too much information given in one day. Subsequent to this positive feedback, CAPA staff developed additional resources such as a revised CAPA Workbook and a CAPA Workshop Presenter's Guide and Group Facilitator's Guide, only to learn later, in 1993, that funding for the program had been suspended. Hopefully CAPA can re-emerge soon as one example of a career assistance program that is driven by athletes' needs and concerns, and that focuses on life-span development and planning.

Perhaps a major problem inhibiting athlete motives to develop career plans, however, and a variable researchers have not yet acknowledged, is the effectiveness of institutions of competitive sport (and commerce) that protect (or distract) athletes from longer term issues and problems. Elite sport can socialise a psychological focus on "the body" and performance, thus extending the adolescence of athletes and inhibiting their social and cultural lives. Also, as Connell (1990) suggests, coaches and administrators often function as "organic intellectuals (Gramsci's (1971) phrase) of commercial sport, articulating a meaning for, and a public defence of, the practices in which the whole industry is engaged" (p. 92). So coaches and administrators are more prone to operate as ideologists perpetuating a focus on "winning" and "the present" rather than as educators promoting "mastery or the process of competing" and discussions on "post sport career" issues. The influence of coaches on athlete career planning programs may be the most significant determinant of the effectiveness of such programs and, therefore, would appear to warrant closer examination.

RESEARCH IN AUSTRALIA

In Australia, Hawkins and Blann (1993) completed a survey of the career transition needs of a sample of elite male and female athletes and coaches, supported by a grant funded by the Australian Sports Commission's National Sports Research Program. Following pilot work to establish "cross cultural equivalency" in items from the Professional Athletes Career Transitions Inventory (PACTI; Blann & Zaichkowsky, 1986) adapted to suit Australian subjects, both the Australian Athletes Career Transition Inventory (AACTI) and Australian Coaches Career Transition Inventory (ACCTI) instruments were administered separately to 124 (69 males; 55 females) elite amateur athletes and 29 (22 males; 7 females) coaches from the Australian Institute of Sport (AIS) and Victorian Institute of Sport (VIS). The athlete (AIS 50; VIS 74) and coach (AIS 18; VIS 11) samples represented 19 and 15 sports respectively, including a broad range of individual and team sports. The main purposes of the survey were: to develop an instrument to assess Australian athletes' and coaches' career development and awareness needs, and to assess athletes' and coaches' levels of career awareness, post-sport career planning involvement and career transition needs, types of programs most useful in meeting career transition needs, and perceptions of life satisfaction after sport (projected in the future).

A full list of results from this pioneering work is available but in their Executive Summary Report Hawkins and Blann (1993) reported that:
1. Athletes in general had a higher awareness of the need for career development than did the coaches, although there were gender differences in this awareness.
2. Male athletes generally expected a prolonged athletic career, which was often unrealistically long for the majority of athletes, but they also had more specific career goals than did the female athletes.
3. Male athletes were more interested in internship programs and specific job experiences than the female athletes.
4. Female athletes were more interested in assistance in identifying their personal qualities, and the career that best matched those qualities, compared to males.
5. Both males and females agreed that programs using individual counselling or small group counselling would be most effective and that such programs would be most helpful if delivered both during and after their sport careers. (Hawkins & Blann, 1993, p. 3)

Coaches, on the other hand, were reportedly less aware of transition issues than athletes and seemed more reluctant to consider careers outside coaching despite an expression of job insecurity. In general, coaches believed:

1. The coaching profession is not greatly valued and that they (coaches) have limited opportunities for advancement in Australia.
2. Their profession left them limited time for relationships or personal development. (Hawkins & Blann, 1993, p. 3)

Being the first attempt to present an overview of the opinions of athletes and coaches on career transition issues in Australia, the recommendations from the study for athlete and coach career development and transitions, and future research in the area, are presented in full. The following recommendations for athlete career transition needs were:

1. Career education programs that help athletes become aware of the importance of engaging in career planning during their playing careers should be maintained (e.g., SportsLEAP, Olympic Job Opportunity Program) so that the current level of athlete career awareness is ensured and enhanced.
2. Career education programs should place increased emphasis on developing and initiating programs that will actually involve athletes, especially female athletes, in career planning strategies and activities in order to improve their current levels of career planning and involvement (e.g., formulating and carrying out actual career/education plans, making personal contacts with individuals in order to develop career networks during their playing careers, engaging in job searches and job interviews, preparing and continually updating résumés, practising personal presentation skills, practising communication skills, and working in job/internships related to desired careers).
3. Career education programs should be designed and delivered:
   (a) on an individualised and personalised basis and via small group counselling settings
   (b) both during and after athlete playing careers
   (c) in ways that appropriately involve former athletes as "mentors" for active players
   (d) in ways that appropriately involve athletes' spouses, significant others and families. (Hawkins & Blann, 1993, pp. vii–viii)

Similar recommendations were made for coaches, including types of services that should be provided to both coaches and their spouses. Specifically:

1. Sports administrators should work with coaches to identify their concerns and needs.
2. Sports administrators should work with coaches to determine appropriate ways of providing them with an "official" representative voice within the governing structures of their organisation.
3. Sports administrators should work with coaches to establish programs which coaches believe are needed and would help them most. Some program areas that might be considered include:
   (a) job stress and burn-out
   (b) relationships with spouses, significant others and/or families

(c) lifestyle management for coaches

(d) lifestyle management for coaches' spouses, significant others and/or families

(e) financial planning.

4. Coaches' personal and career development transition programs should be developed and designed and delivered:

(a) on a personalised/individualised basis or via small group counselling settings

(b) both during and after their coaching careers

(c) in ways that appropriately involve former coaches as "mentors" for active coaches

(d) in ways that appropriately involve coaches' spouses, significant others and/or families. (Hawkins & Blann, 1993 pp. viii–ix)

Finally, Hawkins and Blann (1993) believe that further research should be conducted:

1. Into the career education/transition needs of female athletes, with a specific focus on the role of coaches regarding female athletes' career education/transition process.

2. To identify and establish "mentoring programs" as an integral part of delivering career education/transition programs for athletes. It is strongly urged that former athletes who have adequate backgrounds and competencies and who are interested, willing, and committed to helping active athletes with their career development and transition, be involved in program delivery.

3. To identify and establish program strategies/activities that would most appropriately involve athletes' spouses, significant others and families in helping them make successful career transitions after their playing careers end (e.g., by developing family and social support networks for athletes).

Recommendations for research on coaches' career development and transition needs included:

1. Research on former elite/professional coaches' career transitions.

2. Career education/transition needs of female coaches.

3. Research to identify and establish mentoring programs as an integral part of delivering career education/transition programs for coaches. It is strongly urged that former elite/professional coaches who have adequate backgrounds and competencies, and who are interested, willing, and committed to helping active coaches with their career development and transition, be involved in program delivery.

4. Finally, to identify and establish program strategies/activities that would help coaches and their spouses, significant others, and/or families with "lifestyle management". (Hawkins & Blann, 1993 pp. ix–x)

Comments on this research and other directions for specifically Australian projects are made later in this chapter, however, Hawkins and Blann (1993) have clearly made several important observations from this exploratory investigation that require both replication and follow-up.

✎ CAREER ASSISTANCE PROGRAMS

Figure 19.3 illustrates brief details of known career assistance programs in Canada, the USA, the United Kingdom and Australia. While Hawkins and Blann (1993) report similar interest and sport-specific programs operating among professional sports in the USA (e.g., American football, baseball, basketball and ice hockey), in all cases the target group is amateur athletes. One Australian initiative not featured is the Sports Development Officers Scheme (SDOS), run by the Australian Sports Commission (ASC) and the Department of Sport and Recreation. Compared to others, SDOS is perhaps a peripheral program, but "its main objective is to enhance junior sports development by employing elite athletes as Development Officers. To be eligible the athlete must be ranked in the top five nationally, and as part of their employment, special leave arrangements are provided for the purpose of official representation in competition" (Anderson, 1993, p. 5).

In Australia, following the 1988 Seoul Olympics, feedback and concerns relating to careers outside sport, primarily from athletes, prompted the introduction of the Lifeskills for Elite Athletes Program (LEAP). In 1990, the Victorian Institute of Sport's (VIS) Athlete Career and Education (ACE) program was established and, two years later, the Olympic Job Opportunity Program (OJOP) was initiated.

LEAP was launched by the Australian Institute of Sport (AIS) in 1989 and was developed as a result of a needs-based survey conducted among 1200 elite Australian athletes by the Australian Sports Commission. LEAP programs (renamed SportsLEAP in 1993) now exist in institutes and academies of sport in the Australian Capital Territory, New South Wales, Queensland, South Australia, Tasmania and Western Australia, funded jointly by the AIS and respective host institutes and academies.

While the scope and exact content of each SportsLEAP program may vary according to athlete demand, coordinators in each State endeavour to offer at least three forms of career assistance. First, there is direct assistance in finding employment through career advice, training paths and vocational training; second, there is secondary and tertiary education support through networking with individuals in secondary schools, TAFE and universities who can offer unit or course selection advice, assistance in negotiating deferment or extension or credit, and provide general campus information; and third, there are personal development seminars and programs on goal setting, media training, personal presentation and grooming, preparation of résumés, techniques for approaching sponsors, and job applications skills.

A survey (SportsLEAP coordinator meeting, personal communication, 25 November, 1993) of six SportsLEAP coordinators (five female, one male) conducted at their annual meeting (November, 1993) indicated that all had backgrounds and experience in the "people industry" (e.g., human resources, sales/retail, psychology, PE teaching, coaching), had contracts ranging from 20–35 hours per week, and worked mostly alone (assistants only employed in WA and ACT).

Program	Country	Year	Administration	Target group	Goal	Services
Making the Jump Program (MJP)	USA	1989	Advisory Resource Centre for Athletes (Springfield College, Massachusetts)	High school	Assist in making transition from high school to college athletics.	Seminars/information/counselling; academic study/injuries colleges
Whole-istic (W-istic)	USA	1990	American College Athletic Association	Elite college	Life development for meaningful planning of college athletes.	Career counselling, academic support, GS
Olympic Job Opportunity Program (OJOP)	USA	1977	United States Olympic Committee	Olympic	"Resolving conflict" for Olympic athletes.	Career guidance, goal setting, job skills
Career Assistance Program for Athletes (CAPA; not operating 1993)	USA	1988	Grants from Olympic Job Opportunity Program	1992 Olympians Transition athletes	Assist elite athletes in transition out of sport.	Enhancement, support, counselling
Women's Sports Foundation New York (WSF)	USA	mid-1994	WSF Athlete Services	All girls/women particularly African-American athletes	Education opportunity, advocacy recognition.	Travel funding, media training, public speaking, player/agent selection programs
Olympic Athletic Career Centre (OACC)	Canada	1985	Canadian Olympic Association	Olympic	Career services that ease transition to life after sport for Olympic and elite athletes.	Career plan, aptitude testing, résumé preparation, etc.
Goldstart	UK	1989	British Olympic Association	Olympic	Non-sporting problems as a result of sporting commitment faced by Olympic athletes.	Job finding, employer lobby, résumé preparation, etc.
Lifeskills for Elite Athletes Program (SportsLEAP)	Australia	1989	Australian Institute of Sport (with State-based Institutes of Sport)	Elite criteria	Balanced lifestyle: • career, sport, PD of elite athletes • top 20 individual; top 10 team member • national representative • State representative, special other.	Career advice, PD seminars, education network, job skilling, employer contact
Athlete Career and Education Program (ACE)	Australia	1990	Victorian Institute of Sport (VIS)	Elite criteria	"Athlete driven" long-term developmental perspective; to enhance PD of athletes.	Presentation skills, career planning, PD, education
Olympic Job Opportunity Program (OJOP)	Australia	1992	Australian Olympic Committee	Olympic	"Resolving conflict" for Olympic athletes.	Career guidance, goal setting, job skills

GS = Goal Setting   PD = Personal Development

Figure 19.3: Brief summary of athlete career programs, goals and services

Each coordinator is responsible for a range of two to ten AIS programs, five to 20 State programs and potentially 80 to 600 athletes. While their data on initial patterns of inquiries from younger or older, male or female athletes were inconclusive, it was apparent that résumé preparation, media or public speaking, goal setting (for careers) and further education advice and support, seemed to be the services most requested. There was general agreement that relationships with coaches and administrators in each State were positive; however, most coordinators hoped for more integration of SportsLEAP services by both national and State programs, and more formal incorporation of the program's philosophy in a national and holistic approach to athlete development, in the future. While the majority of the coordinators reported that they liked both the flexibility of their working conditions and the career assistance package they were marketing, three mentioned some difficulty selling SportsLEAP to the few non-focused and complacent athletes who seemed overly obsessed with their sport. Priority recommendations for improving SportsLEAP were: more funding to allow a closer focus on each sport; more corporate marketing of the program; and closer working relationships with all institutes and academies of sport, national sport organisations, schools, TAFE colleges and universities.

The Athlete Career and Education (ACE) Program, coordinated through the Victorian Institute of Sport (VIS), was established in 1990 and offers over 25 workshops in four modules (see Figure 19.4). Each workshop lasts about two hours and is structured on a two-tier basis. The first tier is designed to assist the needs of athletes of all ages and educational backgrounds, while the second tier provides specialist assistance to senior athletes.

In addition to workshops, ACE provides individual career counselling, vocational assessment programs, and computerised programs of information on all tertiary, TAFE and community courses in Victoria, Austudy information, and Courscan which assists Year 11 and 12 students to match secondary school subjects to tertiary and TAFE courses. Other educational sources include tapes, videos and books on different personal (e.g., relaxation) and professional (e.g., interview techniques) skills. The ACE Program is currently under consideration for accreditation by the Department of Education, Employment and Training (DEET) but, while Anderson, the ACE manager (1993), is generally encouraged by the development of lifeskills programs in Australia, "future developments must ensure that the sole motive for introducing any support program is the athlete, and that they are constantly involved in the process. Just as importantly, such programs must be integrated into the main objectives of an athlete's (athletic) development" (p. 6; parenthesis added). One final important recommendation by Anderson, which has considerable merit, is "to develop a cooperative program between the National and State Institutes and the Australian Olympic Committee which would enable the best of each program to be utilised and long term solid commitments ... made to this vitally important area" (p. 6).

Module 1: Presentation	**Module 2: Career planning**
Public speaking	Maximising the résumé
Television training	Making the right career choice
Understanding the print media	Getting the job you want
Radio training	"The interview"
Effective vocal skills	
Deportment and grooming	
Effective listening skills	
Module 3: Personal development	**Module 4: Education**
Effective time management	VCE study skills
Goal setting, "The key to success"	Tertiary study skills
Financial planning	Effective listening
Leisure: How to balance your time	Returning to study
Increasing your confidence through assertiveness	Selecting courses
	Career planning for graduates
Self-confidence through relaxation	English as a second language
Overseas travel: What's the problem?	
Injury prevention	
Being an elite athlete	

Figure 19.4: Victorian Institute of Sport Athlete Career and Education (ACE) Program (Deidre Anderson, ACE manager, personal communication, 30 November 1993)

The Olympic Job Opportunity Program (OJOP) is an Australian Olympic Committee (AOC) project, and was initiated in 1992. It mirrors the American OJOP program and is also sponsored by the international chartered accountancy firm of Ernst and Young. According to Craig McLatchey (AOC Director of Sport, personal communication, 7 April 1994), the principle goal of OJOP is to develop and source career opportunities for Olympians and potential Olympians. The program does not attempt to find short-term employment or "fill in" job opportunities, nor focus on athlete education and development, nor similar career planning opportunities which, it is assumed, would normally be provided by the employer as part of the athlete's conditions of employment. Eligible athletes, screened by both the AOC and Ernst and Young, are either current Olympians or Olympic calibre athletes and must be certified as such by their respective National Federations. AOC and Ernst and Young state coordinators help eligible athletes identify future career goals and, subsequently, contact companies who can provide them a career opportunity and, at the same time, allow athletes time off for training and competition without loss of either pay or career advancement. In addition to providing direct employer contact and identifying job positions, OJOP provides career analysis services, personality aptitude testing, interview skills training and resumé preparation advice.

While SportsLEAP, ACE and OJOP, and their sport-specific adaptations (e.g., Volleyball Olympic Job Opportunity Program — VOJOP) are helping to address the concerns of elite amateur athletes who, as "soldiers of the state", are also supported with scholarships at different levels of funding, what about semi-professional and professional athletes? Do we in Australia assume that because these athletes can, theoretically at least, "earn a living" from their art that they do not require similar levels of interest and support? There is an apparent need to look more closely at semi-professional and professional sport in Australia and the potential for career assistance program interventions. Assuming the concerns regarding post-sport careers of professional Australian athletes are similar to their American peers, there is much to be done on the players' behalf by both sport management (e.g., Australian Baseball League, Australian Cricket Board, Australian Football League, National Basketball League, National Soccer League and New South Wales Rugby League) and respective players' associations.

Prior to addressing some proposed intervention strategies in the next section, this is perhaps an appropriate place to return to Coakley's (1983) "retirement or rebirth?" concept, and discuss its validity and utility. In his discourse on retirement from competitive sport, Coakley suggested that neither athletes, coaches, administrators nor researchers should assume that the experience is inherently negative. Rather, he suggests that the transition experience may result in a positive and favourable perspective leading to benefits previously not considered by those involved in the process. In reality and in practice, however, Coakley's view appears to be neither valid nor useful. The literature seems to be replete with ecologically valid evidence that retirees, in general, do experience problems both prior to and upon career end, and that concerns about retirement and lack of career planning, which may affect performance, would most likely be allayed by career assistance programming. Therefore, while the rebirth/ challenge view may accurately describe the retirement experience of certain individuals, it seems to be an unrepresentative view and, in the context of career assistance program planning and development, lacks utility.

PREVENTION AND TREATMENT STRATEGIES

It is evident that prevention of crises associated with adjustments to career transitions and career retirement can be facilitated by the various career assistance programs described in the previous section. However, Ogilvie and colleagues (Ogilvie, 1987; Ogilvie & Howe, 1982; Ogilvie & Taylor, 1993a, 1993b) stress the importance of targeting athletes as early as possible in their athletic development. They also emphasise the benefits of using a "primary prevention model" — preventing problems prior to their occurrence. Pearson and Petitpas (1990) claim primary prevention approaches will work in sport because: "(a) the presence of widespread organisational structures that organise and implement sports programs make preventive programs a possibility, and (b) an ample literature supports the position that, in the long run, primary prevention-focused approaches offer the most efficient way of using limited human service resources" (p. 7).

These authors are recommending that parents, coaches and youth sport administrators promote a holistic approach to youth participation in sport, an approach that de-emphasises success and winning (outcome orientation) and emphasises instead personal growth and social development (mastery and a process orientation). The intention, therefore, is for young athletes to experience psychological and social phenomena in sport that promote, and not inhibit, the development of coping behaviours that become necessary in non-sport aspects of their lives. In adopting a primary prevention model, long-term personal and social development hold precedence over short-term athletic success, allowing sports participation to become the vehicle through which young athletes attain general lifeskills that enable them to grow personally and socially and function in diverse situations. The adult manifestations associated with the single-minded pursuit of excellence and winning, and the socialisation of "uni-dimensional" younger athletes, can be avoided using "primary prevention" in youth sports.

Pearson and Petitpas (1990) also believe that prevention-oriented programs can help identify individuals who are likely to experience transition difficulties. These "at risk" individuals, who can immediately be referred to preventive programs such as SportsLEAP, characteristically have strong sport identities and define their "self" exclusively as "athlete", have a considerable gap between their level of aspiration and level of ability, have little or no experience with sport transitions, are limited in general ability to adapt to change because of emotional or behavioural deficits, are limited in their ability to form and maintain support networks, and must make the transitions with meagre emotional and material resources that could be helpful (Pearson & Petitpas, 1990).

For those athletes who already experience "existential moments" ("Who am I?" "Where am I heading?") and who become increasingly preoccupied with the spectre of career retirement or termination, the aforementioned career assistance programs can also help. Ogilvie and Taylor (1993b), however, further recommend the therapeutic assistance of sport psychologists who can help athletes clarify and modify their changing values, priorities, interests and goals. Broadening the athlete's social identity and role repertoire while maintaining or enhancing feelings of self- confidence and self-worth will also be helpful. Finally, and still within sport, Ogilvie and Taylor refer to the significance of social systems for athletes leading up to and immediately following career termination. They refer to the findings of Svoboda and Vanek (1982) who reported the significance of different methods of coping with career termination among 163 elite former athletes in Czechoslovakia. Social support was the most important factor, with the family (37%) perceived to be most important, followed by colleagues in the new profession (13%), friends (8%), and the coach (4%). In that study it was interesting to note that even in a socialist society, in which elite athletes need not worry too much about finding a job, only 35% reported that they coped immediately with the psychological adjustments associated with retirement, while 15% coped in half a year, 8% in a year, 17% up to 3 years, 4% more than 3 years, and 18% not at all.

Athletes either in the midst of, approaching, or at the end of their athletic careers, are likely to experience crises that will adversely affect them cognitively, emotionally, behaviourally and socially (Ogilvie & Taylor, 1993a). Subsequently, traditional therapeutic strategies such as cognitive restructuring (Beck, 1979; Burns, 1980; Ellis & Harper, 1975), stress management (Meichenbaum, 1979), talking through stages of loss (Kubler-Ross, 1969) and emotional expression (Yalom, 1980) may be considered in this process. Consistent with this multi-site approach, Brammer and Abrego (1981) outside of sport, and Wolff and Lester (1989) inside sport, utilised an interactive coping model for dealing with transitions consisting of listening and confrontation, cognitive therapy (appraisal processes), and vocational guidance (planning for implementing change). In regard to the latter issue, long-term financial planning and money management, part of some but not all career assistance programs, would provide financial stability at the conclusion of careers which might bolster, at least temporarily, the negative effects of "social death".

FUTURE DIRECTIONS

Based on the research conducted on both career transition and career termination in Australia, but primarily Europe and North America, the following recommendations for Australian researchers and sport administrators are stated in general terms.

1. While Hawkins and Blann (1993) have made an important start to scholarly inquiry in this area in Australia, and such efforts must be commended, their conclusions and recommendations for athletes, coaches and administrators can only be accepted as "preliminary". For more generalisable results to be obtained and subsequently applied with total confidence in Australia, tighter experimental controls are necessary. For example, their instruments (AACTI and ACCTI) would need to be psychometrically refined and then administered among truly representative and more clearly defined groups of male and female athletes. Hawkins and Blann, however, appropriately used quantitative and qualitative approaches during both data collection and data analysis and made several significant observations and several recommendations for further study among athletes that merit investigation. For example, consistent with approaches by Kane (cited in Hawkins & Blann, 1993), Howe, Howe, and Wilkins (1989) and Wylleman et al. (1993), they recommend sport-specific examinations of career transitions that include spouses and family members. Also, they advise investigating the utility of gender-specific assistance, and programs that include "mentoring services" involving former athletes.

2. Hawkins and Blann (1993) also make several recommendations for research among coaches, however, the first step must involve an occupational analysis of sport and particularly coaching in Australia. For example, a formal investigation of "coaching as a profession" and the relevance and utility of this concept might clarify the best means of assisting coaches with both career development and career transition.

3. Related to the previous recommendation, a survey of how different sport associations deselect players and where these players go (e.g., first job post-playing career, second job, etc.) would be useful. Are there differences and similarities across different sports, male and female organisations, and between semi/full-time professional sports (e.g., Australian Rules Football, baseball, basketball, cricket, Rugby League, soccer) and elite amateur sports (including Olympic sports) organised through institutes of sport and major clubs? Given that only selected elite amateur athletes seem to be eligible for career assistance programs at present, what are the implications for "professional" sports? Furthermore, are there gender and/or race qualitative differences in adjustment success following voluntary and involuntary retirement (Lerch, 1982) from professional sport?

4. As in some other areas of sport psychology, there is a noticeable lack of career assistance research and programs (cross-sectional or longitudinal) based on sound theoretical concepts or models. Therefore, as Fortunato (1994), Ogilvie and Taylor (1993b) and Svoboda and Vanek (1982) suggest, more effort must be made generally to devise a systematic program of research, and this is particularly relevant in Australia. Conceptual models, as illustrated in Figure 19.1, that would drive pertinent empirical questions, would also help identify various causal factors that trigger both career transition and career retirement effects, specify personal factors that differentiate traumatic and healthy responses, identify coping resources and factors that might mediate adverse effects, and recommend prevention and treatment modalities for extreme and negative reactions (Ogilvie & Taylor, 1993b).

5. An amalgamation of existing programs (e.g., SportsLEAP, ACE and OJOP) is strongly recommended. As the Sydney 2000 Olympic Games approach, such an arrangement would not only provide elite amateur athletes and coaches with a nationally coordinated and accredited curriculum of skills and services, it would also provide expert leadership and a framework for professional athlete associations to consult. Amalgamation would also facilitate collaborative and cooperative efforts among researchers and program developers and help secure full commitment to, and integration of, life-span career planning within existing elite athlete programs.

6. Existing career assistance programs might also benefit from research on "career orientation" being conducted by Chisholm (1994). Career orientation describes the awareness, priority and readiness of athletes for career assistance, and follows Prochaska and Diclemente's (1986) research on the Transtheoretical Model of Behaviour Change (TM).

The TM, in this case, would theorise that athletes and coaches may be individually located at different stages of career orientation and therefore are more or less "ready" for the services SportsLEAP, ACE and OJOP offer. As Prochaska (1986) observed with other health benefit programs, "We must quit pretending that all we have to do is deliver state-of-the-art action programs to the people and they will take advantage of them" (p. 32). TM provides both cognitive and behavioural processes (techniques) for athletes at different "stages of change" which theoretically results in a gradual shift in attitude from, for example, "I should attend career assistance programs", to "I want to attend career assistance programs".

7. Finally, as discussed by Ogilvie and Taylor (1993b) and Snyder (1981), Australian sport institutions must consider what can be done in early sport participation to not only promote commitment to sport as a life-long activity but also to promote positive influences on career transition and career retirement. Regardless of intensity of involvement in sport (recreational or professional) what issues in childhood and adulthood development in sport promote and sustain a balanced perspective and, most importantly, fun and enjoyment? Replication and extension of the studies conducted on fun and enjoyment (e.g., Scanlan, Ravizza, & Stein, 1989) and in particular those focused on adults in specific sports (e.g., squash; Gorely & Gordon, 1994) are recommended to not only enhance balanced perspectives in sport but also sustain participation in physical activity.

CONCLUSIONS

This chapter has been about the process of desocialisation from competitive sport and career retirement or termination and has addressed the relevant research that has tried to understand, explain and predict both negative and positive consequences. Evidently the answer to whether career transitions or retirement are stressful is likely to be "sometimes yes, sometimes no". Much more Australian-based research, therefore, is recommended, both quantitative and qualitative, to explicate culturally determined causal factors of transitions and how these affect responses to and, in turn, the consequences of transitions at all levels of competitive sport. Leading up to and beyond the Sydney 2000 Olympics, will sport, as one of Australia's dominant social institutions, become more or less interested in preparing athletes for post-sport careers? Can commercialism in elite amateur and professional sport incorporate and enhance the prevention-oriented programs recommended by career assistance program coordinators in both Australia and overseas? Time will tell. However, if recent efforts on behalf of elite amateur athletes and coaches in Australia are any indication, trends toward the provision of Federally-based holistic programs will hopefully continue. Semi-professional and professional sports will likely follow this lead and perhaps the examples set in North America and the United Kingdom.

SUMMARY

The content of this chapter included references to both the extant theoretical and applied literature on an important and topical area of sport psychology and sport sociology research in Australia — career transitions in competitive sport. First, social gerontological, thanatological and transitions theoretical models were described and, in terms of driving both future research and program development, their applied utility was discussed. Next, the research on career retirement or career termination from Australia and overseas, was reviewed, followed by a section summarising the current career assistance programs available primarily for elite amateur athletes and some professional athletes. Finally, some approaches and proposals for prevention and treatment interventions were described, and the concluding section listed recommendations for both research and practice, specifically for Australia.

REFERENCES

Allison, M. T., & Meyer, C. (1988). Career problems and retirement among elite athletes: The female tennis professional. *Sociology of Sport Journal*, *5*, 212–222.

Anderson, D. (1993). *Research tour — Elite Athlete Education Programs*. Melbourne: Victorian Institute of Sport.

Atchley, R. C. (1981). *The social forces in later life*. Belmont, CA: Wadsworth.

Baillie, P. H. F., & Danish, S. J. (1992). Understanding the career transition of athletes. *The Sport Psychologist*, *6*, 77–98.

Beck, A. T. (1979). *Cognitive therapy and emotional disorders*. New York: New American Library.

Blann, W., & Zaichkowsky, L. (1986). *Career/life transition needs of National Hockey League Players*. Report prepared for the National Hockey League Players' Association.

Blann, W., & Zaichkowsky, L. (1988). *Major League Baseball Players' post-sport career transition needs*. Report prepared for the Major League Baseball Players' Association.

Blann, W., & Zaichkowsky, L. (1989). *National Hockey League and Major League Baseball Players' post-sport career transition surveys*. Final report for the National Hockey League Players' Association.

Blinde, E. M., & Greendorfer, S. L. (1985). A reconceptualization of the process of leaving the role of competitive athlete. *International Review for Sociology of Sport*, *20*, 87–93.

Brammer, L. M., & Abrego, P. J. (1981). Intervention strategies for coping with transitions. *The Counselling Psychologist*, *9*(2), 19–36.

Brewer, B. W., Van Raalte, J. L., & Linder, D. E. (1993). Athletic identity: Hercules' muscles or Achilles' heel? *International Journal of Sport Psychology*, *24*, 237–254.

Burgess, E. (Ed.) (1960). *Aging in Western societies*. Chicago: University of Chicago Press.

Burns, D. D. (1980). *Feeling good: The new mood therapy*. New York: Nal Penguin.

Chisholm, K. (1994). Career orientation of elite amateur athletes. Unpublished honours research proposal, the University of Western Australia.

Coakley, J. J. (1983). Leaving competitive sport: Retirement or rebirth? *Quest*, *35*(1), 1–11.

Connell, R. W. (1990). An iron man: The body and some contradictions of hegemonic masculinity. In M. A. Messner & D. F. Sabo (Eds.), *Sport, men, and the gender order: Critical feminist perspectives* (pp. 83–95). Kingswood, SA: Human Kinetics.

Crook J. M., & Robertson, S. E. (1991). Transitions out of elite sport. *International Journal of Sport Psychology, 22*, 115–127.

Cumming, E., Dean, L. R., Newell, D. S., & McCaffrey, I. (1960). Disengagement — A tentative theory of ageing. *Sociometry, 13*, 23.

Cumming, E., & Henry, W. E. (1961). *Growing old and the process of disengagement.* New York: Basic Books.

Danish, S., & D'Augelli, A. R. (1980). Promoting competence and enhancing development through life development intervention. In R. R. Turner & H. N. Reese (Eds.), *Life-span developmental psychology: Intervention* (pp. 49–78). New York: Academic Press.

Danish, S. J., Petitpas, A. J., & Hale, B. D. (1990). Sport as a context for developing competence. In T. Gullotta, G. Adams, & R. Montemayor (Eds.), *Developing social competence in adolescence* (Vol. 3) (pp. 169–194). Newberry Park, CA: Sage.

Davis, M. (1993). Why a super athlete can turn problem child. The *Weekend Australian,* 7–8 August 1993, p. 6.

Dowd, J. J. (1975). Ageing as exchange: A preface to theory. *Journal of Gerontology, 30*, 584–594.

Ellis, A., & Harper, R. A. (1975). *A new guide to rational living.* New York: Prentice-Hall, Inc.

Fortunato, V. (1994). *Role transitions in elite sports.* Doctoral project in progress, Victoria University of Technology.

Frith, D. (1990). *By his own hand: A study of cricket's suicides.* Crows Nest, NSW: Australian Broadcasting Corporation.

Glaser, B., & Strauss, A. (1965). *Awareness of dying.* New York: Aldine.

Good, A. J., Brewer, B. W., Petitpas, A. J., Van Raalte, J. L., & Mahar, M. T. (Spring 1993). Identity foreclosure, athletic identity and college sport participation. *The Academic Athletic Journal,* 1–12.

Gorely, T., & Gordon, S. (1994). *Development of the Squash Enjoyment Inventory (SEI) for adults.* Manuscript submitted for publication.

Gordon, S., Milios, D., & Grove, J. R. (1991, December). Psychological aspects of the recovery process from sport injury: The perspective of sport physiotherapists. *Australian Journal of Science and Medicine in Sport, 23*(2), 53–60.

Greendorfer, S. L., & Blinde, E. M. (1985). Retirement from intercollegiate sports: Theoretical and empirical considerations. *Sociology of Sport Journal, 2*, 101–110.

Haerle, R. (1975). Career patterns and career contingencies of professional baseball players: An occupational analysis. In D. W. Ball & J. W. Loy (Eds.), *Sport and social order* (pp. 457–579). Reading, MA: Addison-Wesley.

Havighurst, R. J., & Albrecht, R. (1953). *Older people.* New York: Longmans Green.

Hawkins, K., & Blann, F. W. (1993). *Athlete/coach career development and transition.* Australian Sports Commission Applied Sports Research Program Report.

Howe, C., Howe, G., & Wilkins, C. (1989). *After the applause.* Toronto: McClelland & Stewart.

Kleiber, D., Greendorfer, S., Blinde, E., & Samdahl, D. (1987). Quality of exit from university sports and life satisfaction in early adulthood. *Sociology of Sport Journal, 4*, 28–36.

Kleiber, D., & Malik, P. B. (1989). Educational involvement of college athletes and subsequent well-being in early adulthood. *Journal of Sport Behaviour, 12*, 203–211.

Kubler-Ross, E. (1969). *On death and dying.* New York: Macmillan.

Kuypers, J. A., & Bengston, V. L. (1973). Social breakdown and competence: A model of normal aging. *Human Development, 16,* 181–220.

Lerch, S. H. (1981). The adjustment to retirement of professional baseball players. In S. L. Greendorfer & A. Yiannakis (Eds.), *Sociology of sport: Diverse perspectives* (pp. 138–148). West Point, NY: Leisure Press.

Lerch, S. H. (1982). Athlete retirement as social death. In N. Theberge & P. Donnelly (Eds.), *Sport and the sociological imagination* (pp. 259–272). Fort Worth, TX: Texas Christian University Press.

McPherson, B. D. (1980). Retirement from professional sport: The process and problems of occupational and psychological adjustment. *Sociological Symposium, 30,* 126–143.

Meichenbaum, D. (1977). *Cognitive-behaviour modification: An integrative approach.* New York: Plenum.

Mihovilovic, M. (1968). The status of former sportsmen. *International Review of Sport Sociology, 3,* 73–93.

Ogilvie, B. (1987). Counselling for sports career termination. In J. R. May & M. J. Asken (Eds.), *Sport psychology: The psychological health of the athlete* (pp. 213–230). New York: PMA Publishing Corp.

Ogilvie, B., & Howe, M. (1982). Career crisis in sport. In T. Orlick, J. Partington, & J. Salmela (Eds.), *Mental training for coaches and athletes.* Ottawa: Fitness and Amateur Sport.

Ogilvie, B., & Taylor, J. (1993a). Career termination in sports: When the dream dies. In J. M. Williams (Ed.), *Applied sport psychology: Personal growth to peak performance* (pp. 356–365). London: Mayfield.

Ogilvie, B., & Taylor, J. (1993b). Career termination issues among elite athletes. In R. N. Singer, M. Murphey, & L. K. Tennant (Eds.), *Handbook of research on sport psychology* (pp. 761–775). Sydney: Macmillan.

Orlick, T. (1990). *In pursuit of excellence: How to win in sport and life through mental training.* Kingswood: Human Kinetics.

Pearson, R. E., & Petitpas, A. J. (1990). Transitions of athletes: Developmental and preventive perspectives. *Journal of Counselling and Development, 69,* 7–10.

Petitpas, A., Danish, S., McKelvain, R., & Murphy, S. (in press). A career assistance program for elite athletes. *Journal of Counselling and Development.*

Prochaska, J. (1986). *What causes people to change from unhealthy to health enhancing behaviour?* Invited paper in the *Proceedings of the American Cancer Society: Consensus Conference on the Current Unmet Research Need for Cancer Prevention,* Denver, CO.

Prochaska, J., & Diclemente, C. (1986). Toward a comprehensive model of change. In W. E. Miller & N. Heather (Eds.), *Treating addictive behaviours* (pp. 3–27). London: Plenum Press.

Reynolds, M. J. (1981). The effects of sports retirement on the job satisfaction of the former football player. In S. L. Greendorfer & A. Yiannakis (Eds.), *Sociology of sport: Diverse perspectives* (pp. 127–137). West Point, NY: Leisure Press.

Rose, A. (1965). The subculture of the ageing: A framework in social gerontology. In A. Rose & I. Peterson (Eds.), *Older people and their social world.* Philadelphia, MS: F. A. Davis Company.

Rosenberg, E. (1981). Gerontological theory and athletic retirement. In S. L. Greendorfer & A. Yiannakis (Eds.), *Sociology of sport: Diverse perspectives* (pp. 119–126). West Point, NY: Leisure Press.

Rosenberg, E. (1982). Athletic retirement as social death: Concepts and perspectives. In N. Theberge & P. Donnelly (Eds.), *Sport and the sociological imagination* (pp. 245–258). Fort Worth, TX: Texas Christian University Press.

Scanlan, T. K., Ravizza, K., & Stein, G. L. (1989). An in-depth study of former figure skaters: I. Introduction to the project. *Journal of Sport and Exercise Psychology, 11*, 54–64.

Schlossberg, N. K. (1981). A model for analysing human adaptation to transition. *The Counselling Psychologist, 9*(2), 2–18.

Schlossberg, N. K. (1984). *Counselling adults in transition*. New York: Springer.

Smith, M. A. (1987). *Life after hockey: When the lights are dimmed*. St Paul, MN: Codner Books.

Smith, S. (1993). Those elusive titles kept Jordan going. The *West Australian*, 8 October 1993, p. 78.

Snyder, E. E. (1981). A reflection on commitment and patterns of disengagement from recreational physical activity. In S. L. Greendorfer & A. Yiannakis (Eds.), *Sociology of sport: Diverse perspectives* (pp. 108–117). West Point, NY: Leisure Press.

Svoboda, B., & Vanek, M. (1982). Retirement from high level competition. In T. Orlick, J. T. Partington, & J. H. Salmela (Eds.), *Mental training for coaches and athletes* (pp. 166–175). Ottawa. Fitness and Amateur Sport.

Werthner, P., & Orlick, T. (1986). Retirement experiences of successful Olympic athletes. *International Journal of Sport Psychology, 17*, 337–363.

Wolff, R., & Lester, D. (1989). A theoretical basis for counselling the retired professional athlete. *Psychological Reports, 64*(3), 1043–1046.

Wylleman, P., de Knop, P., Menkehorst, H., Theeboom, M., & Annerel, J. (1993). Career termination and social integration among elite athletes. In S. Serpa, J. Alves, V. Ferreira, & A. Paula-Brito (Eds.), *Proceedings: VIII World Congress of Sport Psychology* (pp. 902–906). Lisbon, Portugal.

Yalom, I. D. (1980). *Existential psychotherapy*. New York: Harper/Collins.

C H A P T E R

20

SPORT PSYCHOLOGY FOR ATHLETES WITH DISABILITIES

STEPHANIE HANRAHAN

In the last few years there has been a large increase worldwide in the number of mental skills training programs available to athletes. This has been accompanied by an influx of applied sport psychology journals and books as well as the development of professional organisations in sport psychology. This rapid growth has also been apparent in Australia. In November 1991, the Australian Psychological Society officially recognised sport psychology with the formation of the Board of Sport Psychologists. This development of sport psychology has been marked by increased teaching, research and practice within the field. At the same time, there has been considerable growth in the area of sport for people with disabilities. Opportunities and facilities continue to improve for athletes with disabilities. As an example, in 1992, 17 athletes with disabilities were recommended for scholarships at the Australian Institute of Sport. Additionally, researchers are beginning to extend the knowledge of various sport sciences including physiology, biomechanics, neuroanatomy, sociology, biochemistry, motor control and psychology in regard to athletes with disabilities.

Given the expansion of both applied psychological skills training programs and programs for athletes with disabilities, there is a surprising dearth of information on adapting methods of mental skills training to special populations. It is incorrect to assume that a psychological skills training program designed for able-bodied athletes is ideal for athletes with disabilities. Although the content of any mental skills training program should be designed on the basis of the needs of the athletes involved, the techniques and skills taught in these programs tend to be similar across sports and across athletes. It may be that athletes with disabilities will best be served by comparable programs, but it is conceivable that modifications to some skills will enhance the effectiveness of a psychological skills training program.

Considering the expansion of both sport psychology and disabled sport, it is astonishing how little research has been accomplished in the adaptation of mental skills training for athletes with disabilities. This absence of research into how mental training programs can be developed and implemented for athletes with disabilities has been noted by several investigators (Asken, 1987; Goodling & Asken, 1987; Henschen, 1988; Sachs, 1988).

DESCRIPTIVE PROFILES/ASSESSMENT

The bulk of existing research in the area of sport psychology and disability has focused on descriptive profiles of athletes with disabilities and/or the reliability of specific assessment tools which might be used with these athletes. Henschen, Horvat, and French (1984), for example, found that wheelchair athletes were psychologically similar to able-bodied athletes, and Ewing, Dummer, Habeck, and Overton (1987) presented an overview of selected psychological characteristics of athletes with cerebral palsy. Mastro, French, Henschen, and Horvat (1985) reported that the State-Trait Anxiety Inventory is as suitably reliable for oral use with visually impaired athletes as it is for written use with sighted athletes. Elite male visually impaired athletes were found to have state and trait anxiety levels similar to the university norms for sighted individuals (Mastro & French, 1985). In a similar study, however, blind male golfers were found to have higher levels of state and trait anxiety when compared to published norms for sighted university students (Mastro, French, Henschen, & Horvat, 1986). Higher levels of anxiety during competition have also been found for basketball players with intellectual disabilities when compared to basketball players who are not classified as intellectually disabled (Levine & Langness, 1983).

Mastro et al. (1986) also studied mood states of blind golfers and found their mood profiles to be similar to the published norms of the general population. It should be noted, however, that this investigation only involved six subjects. A similar study contrasted 48 elite visually impaired athletes with reported findings of sighted athletes on the Profile of Mood States (POMS) (Mastro, Sherrill, Gench, & French, 1987). Male visually impaired athletes demonstrated similar mood profiles as elite sighted athletes. The female visually impaired athletes, however, were below average in tension, depression, anger, fatigue, and confusion, and above average in vigour when compared to sighted athletes. Comparisons have also been made on the POMS between sighted and unsighted beep baseball players (Mastro, Canabal, & French, 1988). Unsighted players were significantly higher on tension and depression than sighted players, with no significant differences on the other moods measured by the POMS. Obviously there is some discrepancy in the literature. An additional mood state comparison, this time between college able-bodied and wheelchair basketball players, in fact found that the athletes with disabilities felt more vigour and less tension, depression, anger, fatigue and confusion than their able-bodied counterparts (Paulsen, French, & Sherrill, 1991).

Henschen, Horvat, and Roswal (1992) have completed an additional investigation into the mood states of athletes with disabilities. This time, however, comparisons were made between individuals who made the US Wheelchair Basketball Paralympic team, and those who tried out for the team but were not selected. All of the participants completed the POMS prior to the beginning of tryouts. It was found that subjects who made the team were significantly less tense and less angry than those who did not make the team. The same authors have also compared the POMS profiles of male wheelchair athletes prior to and after a major competition (Horvat, Roswal, & Henschen, 1991). They concluded that male competitors with disabilities demonstrate stable emotional states throughout and after an entire competition with the exception that fatigue increases significantly after a performance.

Although questionnaires about mood states and anxiety provide information about an individual's psychological well-being, they fail to indicate what psychological skills the athlete may use to enhance performance or enjoyment of participation. Cox and Davis (1992) administered the Psychological Skills Inventory for Sports (PSIS) to 31 international wheelchair competitors and 50 intercollegiate track athletes. The PSIS assesses an individual's psychological skills of anxiety control, concentration, confidence, mental preparation, motivation and emphasis on team goals. The wheelchair athletes were found to score significantly better than the able-bodied athletes for the skills of anxiety control, confidence and motivation. These differences, however, may have been due to the differences in relative skill level (international versus intercollegiate) rather than to the presence or absence of disability.

APPLICATION OF MENTAL SKILLS TRAINING

Only recently has any introductory work been completed in the application of mental skills training to athletes with disabilities. Hanrahan (1990a) conducted a series of six sport psychology seminars for State, national and international competitors associated with the Western Australian Disabled Sports Association. The group of athletes involved in the seminars consisted of blind, hearing impaired, intellectually disabled, head injured, cerebral palsied, and amputee athletes from a variety of sports. The content of the seminars was based on able-bodied programs and was not geared for any particular disability group (although style and manner of communication was at times altered).

Although the effectiveness of the skills included in the seminars was not evaluated, observations made during the course of the seminars stimulated a variety of questions. It should be noted that ideas and observations also originated from four sport psychology presentations made at Paralympic Training Camps in 1988 which included a variety of athletes with disabilities. The observations and questions arising from the seminar series and the camp presentations are listed below by skill area:

- relaxation/centring
- body awareness/imagery
- goal setting
- pre-competition preparation.

RELAXATION/CENTRING

- Athletes with little or no use of their abdominal muscles found the physical mechanics of abdominal breathing very difficult. Even so, the athletes may have benefited from the concentration aspects of the exercise.
- When practising centring in a standing position, blind athletes had a tendency to feel they were falling forward because of their reliance on vestibular feedback. Therefore, instead of allowing their necks to relax and their heads to fall slightly forward, they had erect postures. They still seemed to be able to use the exercise to refocus their attention on the task at hand, suggesting that the slight difference in head angles between sighted and blind athletes is of little importance.
- During progressive muscular relaxation exercises athletes with missing limbs or limbs with no muscular control were inadvertently requested to tense and relax those muscles. Individually prepared tapes which take these circumstances into account may be more effective.
- Individuals with intellectual disabilities could follow guided progressive muscular relaxation sessions. Using the technique independently, however, was very difficult for some.

BODY AWARENESS/IMAGERY

- Some amputee athletes said that increasing body awareness resulted in them being more aware (and concerned) about muscle imbalances. This could have potentially positive or negative effects.
- One amputee found the body awareness exercise frustrating as she found it difficult to be aware of where her stump ended without actually looking at it. This leads to potentially interesting research in the area of phantom limbs and body awareness.

- Cerebral palsied and wheelchair athletes commented that the body awareness exercise was helpful in determining exactly what muscles they could use. In one instance this increased awareness led to ideas for technique modifications in training.
- Some athletes with physical disabilities imaged themselves participating in their respective sports with full use of their bodies. One amputee swimmer got very angry because she vividly imaged herself swimming with good technique with two arms. When she returned to the water she found it incredibly upsetting that she only had one arm. As with able-bodied athletes, unless imagery skills are highly controlled, mental practice may be potentially harmful for athletes. Other athletes with physical disabilities found imagery to be a very useful skill. It may be that the problems encountered were due solely to poor control of images rather than anything inherent in having a physical disability.
- Although senses other than sight seemed better developed, it was interesting to note that blind athletes (even those totally blind from birth) stated they were able to create visual images. One blind athlete pointed out that his visual images were based on what sighted people had described to him, and in fact may be very different from what would actually be seen in a particular situation. It would be interesting to investigate the vividness and controllability of imagery across various sensory modalities in blind and sighted athletes.

GOAL SETTING

- Individuals with poor writing skills (such as severe cerebral palsied, blind, and intellectually disabled athletes) were encouraged to record their goals on tape rather than in writing.
- Some individuals felt that their physical dependence on others required them to rely on others when it came to setting goals for their sport. The idea of setting goals which they have personal control over was emphasised.

PRE-COMPETITION PREPARATION

- Some athletes expressed concern about feeling in control of their own pre-competition preparation. They felt that their partial dependence on others led to a feeling of not being in control. Some realised that many of the tasks that they rely on others to do could be done by themselves. In some instances athletes are dependent on others. In these situations it was suggested that the athletes take a bit more control of the situation by having things that require help from others done as far in advance of competition as possible, by setting up alternate plans in case someone fails to do what has been promised, and finalising all plans with other people well in advance so that the athlete is not just waiting for others to realise what needs to be done. Being in control of one's own mental preparation was emphasised.

DISABILITY-SPECIFIC STUDIES ON MENTAL SKILLS TRAINING

Although this introductory project illustrated how specific psychological skills may be used by athletes with disabilities, it may be that these considerations may differ depending on the specific disability. What follows is a review of disability-specific studies on psychological skills training.

BLIND/VISUALLY IMPAIRED

A pilot psychological skills training program for blind athletes was developed and implemented at the request of the Western Australian Blind Olympic Sports Association (Hanrahan, Grove, & Lockwood, 1990). Five athletes representing four different sports and all three classes of the International Blind Sports Association Eye Classification System were involved in the program which met once a week for five weeks. The three classifications as stipulated by the International Blind Sports Association Eye Classification System are B3 (visual acuity above 2/60 up to a visual acuity of 6/60 and/or a visual field of more than five degrees and less than 20 degrees), B2 (ability to recognise the shape of a hand up to a visual acuity of 2/60 and/or a visual field of less than five degrees), and B1 (no light perception in either eye).

The content of the program was designed to be a general introduction into psychological skills training and therefore did not address any individual needs of the participants. The program briefly covered goal setting, relaxation, imagery, thought stopping and pre-competition preparation.

The participants gave an overall positive evaluation of the program. Different athletes preferred different aspects of the program, but everyone felt that something useful had been learned.

A number of recommendations became apparent as a result of the pilot program. These recommendations include the following:

- Ensure that the consultant has practical experience with blind individuals.
- 60–90 minutes appears to be the ideal length for group sessions.
- More than five group sessions are required.
- The program should take place several months before an important competition or a final evaluation of the program to allow the participants time to practise and implement the various skills.
- If holding the sessions at a venue which is not familiar to the athletes, allow time for the room to be explored and avoid major changes in furniture arrangement.
- Ensure that all participants have access to information. This may require a variety of communication methods (e.g., large type, cassette recordings, Braille).
- When administering questionnaires either translate them to Braille, read them aloud and devise an answer sheet for the blind, or schedule

times for athletes to complete the questionnaires with the consultant on an individual basis. (In the pilot study inventories were completed with the aid of coaches, other athletes, or family members.)

- Provision should be made for athletes to record their goals.
- Athletes should have individual access to personal cassette players. None of the participants in the pilot program owned them, however, personal cassette players were found to be immensely successful when borrowed for the use of listening to music to create a desired mood prior to training or competition.

A major drawback of this particular report is the lack of systematic assessment. Although feedback regarding the entire psychological skills training program was requested at the completion of the program, no attempt was made to evaluate the relative effectiveness of the specific techniques (Hanrahan et al., 1990).

DEAF   Considerations for sport psychologists working with deaf athletes have been reported by Clark and Sachs (1991). These authors stated that working with deaf individuals is not very different from working with individuals with no hearing impairment. The only real difference may be in communication methods.

It is important to have eye contact and attention of deaf athletes when communicating. The method of communication will vary with the athlete. Deaf athletes may communicate through sign language (which is not a single universal language), gestures, lipreading, speech, writing or a combination of methods. When speaking to deaf individuals use facial expressions, body language and other visual means of communication such as videotape, slides or demonstrations. When verbalising, speak clearly and slowly, but avoid overenunciating or exaggerating words. Lastly, keep in mind that even athletes who have lived in an English speaking country their entire lives may not have English as a native language. Pencil and paper tests and inventories are not appropriate for use with deaf athletes whose native language may be American Sign Language (ASL) or another version of signing. If a great deal of work with deaf athletes is foreseen, learning the suitable sign language would be appropriate (Clark & Sachs, 1991).

INTELLECTUALLY DISABLED

A case study of sport psychology intervention with an athlete with a mild intellectual disability was reported by Travis and Sachs (1991). The study concluded that the development of trust and rapport was critical, the sport psychologist must work at the individual's level of understanding, and that solicitation of help from relatives, case managers or residential staff was important.

Specific considerations to aid a sport psychologist's ability to communicate with athletes with intellectual disabilities are based on awareness and commonsense. Individuals should be aware that an athlete with an intellectual disability may be unable to think in abstract terms, lack the ability to make decisions, have poor short-term memory, have limited literacy or numeracy skills, and have inconsistent concentration spans (Hanrahan, 1990b). With these possibilities in mind, instructions should be kept simple, skills should be broken down into smaller teaching components, sessions should be fun and enjoyable with practice times on specific activities kept short.

PHYSICALLY DISABLED

In 1989 an interview with an elite wheelchair athlete was reported in *The Sport Psychologist* (Asken, 1989). The use of sport psychology techniques by this individual as well as potential contributions of sport psychology and suggested methods of integrating sport psychology with disabled sport were discussed. The article nevertheless ended with a plea for research to be conducted in the area. Asken followed up this entreaty with an article of his own on the challenge of delivering sport psychology services to athletes with physical disabilities (Asken, 1991). Some of the unique issues noted by Asken (1991) include the psychological response to becoming disabled, altered physical responses and considerations such as problems with temperature regulation, and performance problems unique to specific disabilities.

The 1990s have gradually seen the introduction of articles aimed at improving the mental skills of physically disabled athletes. Although focusing on environmental stressors, Banks (1992) provided recommendations for maximising athletic performance of Australians at the Barcelona Paralympics. Specific recommendations for minimising environmental stress and maximising performance were divided into pre-departure aspects such as athletes familiarising themselves with aspects of the Games environment, on-route aspects such as increasing fluid intake and decreasing caffeine and alcohol intake, and post-arrival aspects such as maintaining a routine as similar as possible to that followed at home. Similarly, Hedrick and Morse (1991) have supplied step-by-step instructions on how wheelchair basketball players can effectively set goals.

Despite the above, very little research has been done on the implementation and evaluation of mental skills training programs for athletes with physical disabilities. Asken's (1991) plea has largely been ignored. Although fairly exploratory in nature, an Australian study, however, has initiated research in this area (Hanrahan, 1992). The purpose of this study was to determine the effectiveness of various components of a psychological skills training program for amputee and wheelchair athletes.

Hanrahan's (1992) project involved the creation, implementation and evaluation of a psychological skills training program for competitive wheelchair and amputee athletes. Although the content of the program was dependent on the needs and wants of the individuals involved, the general conclusion was that an effective mental skills training program can be developed for athletes with physical disabilities.

The creation of the program, or determining what skills to include in what order, was not influenced by the disabilities. The identical questions and forms which have been used with able-bodied athletes successfully determined the basis for the content of the program.

A group of six internationally competitive wheelchair and amputee athletes participated in the mental skills training program which was developed on the basis of their self-reported psychological skills. The program lasted for three months and primarily consisted of eight group sessions. In addition, some athletes chose to have themselves videotaped at training or competition. A couple of the subjects also attended individual sessions for further clarification of some of the mental skills.

The program included goal setting, controlling arousal levels, concentration and attention skills, imagery, self-talk, self-confidence, competition preparation, and controlling problem situations.

Minor changes were required for the implementation of some aspects of the program. For example, personalised progressive muscular relaxation (PMR) tapes which omitted unusable body parts were created for the subjects. Balancing exercises were individually devised during the concentration session. Instead of a balance task which ordinarily requires participants to complete a variety of movements while standing on one leg, athletes created their own balancing exercises such as balancing on the rear wheels of the wheelchair. Additionally, amputee athletes experimented with body awareness exercises and imagery both with and without their prostheses.

Most of the program did not require any modifications to account for physical disabilities. For example, the skills of goal setting and positive self-talk were presented in exactly the same manner as for able-bodied athletes. Even some exercises where one would expect that changes would be necessary were found to be effective as they were. For example, it was found that abdominal breathing exercises provided concentration and relaxation benefits for athletes with no use of abdominal muscles.

Five of the six athletes completed and returned post-tests rating their knowledge of, use of, and importance placed on eight mental skills on five-point Likert-type scales. The subjects completed the post-tests between nine and 26 weeks after the last group session (mean time lapse = 15.6 weeks).

Even with a small sample of five, there were statistically significant increases in reported knowledge of attention/concentration, positive self-talk, controlling problem situations, and imagery. Increases in knowledge of arousal regulation and competition preparation approached but failed to achieve statistical significance.

There were no significant changes in the subjects' ratings of the importance of the various mental skills, although the increase in perceived importance of positive self-talk approached significance. This general lack of change in importance ratings may be due to a ceiling effect as the overall mean of the initial ratings was 4.4 out of a possible 5.

The athletes' reported use of imagery, positive self-talk, and controlling problem situations was significantly greater after the program than before. Taking into account changes in knowledge, importance and use of the various skills, the mental skills sessions on imagery, positive self-talk and controlling problem situations had the greatest impact on the subjects from a purely quantitative point of view.

On a subjective basis, there were strong individual differences in judging the aspects of the program with the greatest impact. Goal setting, imagery and self-confidence development all received special mention by various athletes. When comparing standard PMR tapes to personalised PMR tapes which take into account muscle or limb losses, individual differences were again apparent. Two of the athletes preferred the standard tape which included all body parts. One athlete stated that the tailor-made tape was too short because of the limited number of usable muscle groups he had. Future research may investigate the benefits of altering the content of personalised tapes while maintaining the length of the standard version. Three of the participants preferred the personalised tapes, and the sixth subject asserted that there was not much difference between the tapes and, therefore, had no preference.

Other subjective observations were made regarding increasing the pre-competition arousal level for a quadriplegic and the use of prostheses during imagery for amputees. The challenge for a quadriplegic was to raise arousal levels prior to competition. Instead of working on relaxing prior to competition, the desired goal was to raise the heart rate or become more aroused. This problem of lack of arousal may be associated with the tendency for quadriplegics to have lower levels of blood pressure.

Regarding amputees and imagery it was determined that if an amputee performs in competition without a prosthesis then imagery should be done when the prosthesis is off. Similarly, if an athlete competes with a prosthesis then imagery sessions should be completed with the prosthesis in place.

An important note is that all of the athletes voluntarily remained in the program for the duration of the sessions. This persistence indicates that the program was providing all of them with useful, or at least interesting, information. The apparent success of this program suggests that similar programs should be made available to other elite competitive wheelchair and amputee athletes.

 # GENERAL CONSIDERATIONS FOR ATHLETES WITH DISABILITIES

Regardless of the type or degree of disability, any training program, whether psychological or physical, should focus on the abilities of the athlete. Unfortunately, chapters such as this one which focus on disability may have the tendency to centre readers' attention on the disabilities of specific individuals. Whether playing the role of coach, training partner, manager or sport psychologist, one should approach the individual as an athlete rather than as a disabled person. The reason a coach or sport psychologist is working with any individual is because that person is an athlete, not because that person has a sensory, intellectual or physical disability.

Although every athlete should be treated as an individual, there are three important principles that may be applied in any situation. These principles hold true for disabled as well as able-bodied athletes. However, these considerations are often overlooked when working with athletes with disabilities.

First of all, ascertain the nature and extent of the athlete's abilities. Just as people often assume that all Rugby players are naturally aggressive or that short people cannot play basketball, it is also often believed that those who compete in blind competitions are totally without sight, or that those in wheelchairs have the same amount of functional ability. Instead of making these generalisations or assumptions, determine the specific characteristics of each individual athlete.

Second, use the athletes as an information resource on themselves. They have been living with themselves all their lives. Instead of starting from scratch to ascertain what particular techniques or methods may be effective, ask the people involved.

Third, assist when and where requested but do not offer sympathy when athletes experience temporary failure, frustration or confusion when learning new skills or increasing intensity levels. If an individual has chosen to be a competitive athlete, the person needs to develop the capacity to handle both success and failure. It is not the role of the sport psychologist or coach to protect the individual from failure.

FUTURE DIRECTIONS

Providing applied sport psychology services for athletes with disabilities is a relatively new undertaking. Future gains in this area of research could be made by focusing on specific areas. For example, future projects could seek to determine the ideal progressive muscular relaxation tape in terms of length and content for athletes with physical disabilities. Additionally, longitudinal studies with precise methods of measuring body awareness could ascertain the usefulness and success of becoming more aware of exactly which muscles can be controlled and used to improve performance in sport for amputee, wheelchair or cerebral palsied individuals.

Obviously, many more questions than answers exist. A small list of additional questions follows which beg for active consideration by researchers.

- What method of communication is best when using questionnaires for assessing mental skills and evaluating programs when working with sensory impaired athletes?
- With limited or no visual distractions, are disruptive or distracting thoughts of major concern to blind athletes? If so, is thought stopping an effective technique for dealing with this concern?

- Is the general kinaesthetic awareness of blind and visually impaired athletes greater than that of sighted athletes?
- What modalities of imagery are used by athletes with different disabilities? For example, is external imagery ever used by blind athletes?
- Is the use of pre-competition audio tapes effective for everyone? With the reliance of blind individuals on sound, does listening to pre-competition cassettes help prepare athletes for competition or does it have a negative effect such as increasing feelings of isolation? What alternatives can be found for deaf individuals?
- Do body awareness exercises influence phantom limb experiences in amputee athletes and/or increase their awareness of muscle imbalances?
- What changes or additions could be made to the content or presentation of mental skills training programs which would make them more effective for athletes with intellectual disabilities?

CONCLUSIONS

At a time when sport psychology is expanding in terms of practice, recognition and research, it would be remiss to limit this growth to able-bodied athletes. Understanding the structure, use and potential benefits of mental skills training as applied to athletes with disabilities will allow these athletes to enhance their performance and enjoyment of sport. The dissemination of this information is as important as the gathering of this information.

In addition to evaluating the overall effectiveness of a given program, different techniques or skills should be independently evaluated (Gould, Petlichkoff, Hodge, & Simons, 1990), particularly when modifications have been made. Research is needed which clearly outlines the effectiveness of various psychological skills in enhancing the performance and enjoyment of athletes with disabilities. These programs should cater to athletes with physical or sensory disabilities as well as to those with intellectual disabilities.

SUMMARY

This chapter has provided a review of the existing research in the area of sport psychology and disability. A large percentage of studies in the area have focused on the descriptive profiles of athletes with disabilities, with the most heavily investigated domain being that of mood states.

Observations and questions arising from applied sport psychology education programs involving athletes from a variety of disability groups have been presented by skill area. Disability-specific studies on mental skills training followed. A prevalent finding in these studies is that psychological skills training programs can be structured to cater for athletes with different disabilities. Although this finding is encouraging, much more research is needed to determine the best format and content of these programs.

REFERENCES

Asken, M. J. (1987, March). *Sport psychology: Psychological effects of sport participation in physically disabled individuals.* Paper presented at the Conference on Sports Medicine and Science for Disabled Athletes, Bartlett, New Hampshire.

Asken, M. J. (1989). Sport psychology and the physically disabled athlete: Interview with Michael D. Goodling, OTR/L. *The Sport Psychologist, 3,* 166–176.

Asken, M. J. (1991). The challenge of the physically challenged: Delivering sport psychology services to physically disabled athletes. *The Sport Psychologist, 5,* 370–381.

Banks, J. (1992, July-December). Maximising athletic performance at the 1992 Paralympics. *Sports Coach, 15,* 18–24.

Clark, R. A., & Sachs, M. L. (1991). Challenges and opportunities in psychological skills training in deaf athletes. *The Sport Psychologist, 5,* 392–398.

Cox, R., & Davis, R. (1992). Psychological skills of elite wheelchair athletes. *Palaestra, 8*(3), 16–21.

Ewing, M. E., Dummer, G. M., Habeck, R. V., & Overton, S. R. (1987, September). *Psychological characteristics of cognitions of athletes with cerebral palsy.* Paper presented at the Association for the Advancement of Applied Sport Psychology, Newport Beach, CA.

Goodling, M. D., & Asken, M. J. (1987). Sport psychology and the physically disabled athlete. In J. R. May & M. J. Asken (Eds.), *Sport psychology: The psychological health of the athlete* (pp. 117–133). New York: PMA Publishing.

Gould, D., Petlichkoff, L., Hodge, K., & Simons, J. (1990). Evaluating the effectiveness of a psychological skills educational workshop. *The Sport Psychologist, 4,* 249–260.

Hanrahan, S. J. (1990a, January). *Psychological skills training for the disabled.* Paper presented at the Commonwealth and International Conference on Physical Education, Sport, Health, Dance, Recreation, and Leisure, Auckland, New Zealand.

Hanrahan, S. J. (1990b, January). *Coaching disabled individuals: Some practical considerations.* Paper presented at the Commonwealth and International Conference on Physical Education, Sport, Health, Dance, Recreation, and Leisure, Auckland, New Zealand.

Hanrahan, S. J. (1992). *Psychological skills training for competitive wheelchair and amputee athletes* (Contract No. AUST SC — 18). Canberra, Australian Sports Commission.

Hanrahan, S. J., Grove, J. R., & Lockwood, R. J. (1990). Psychological skills training for the blind athlete: A pilot program. *Adapted Physical Activity Quarterly, 7,* 143–155.

Hedrick, B., & Morse, M. (1991, November/December). Setting goals in wheelchair basketball. *Sports 'N Spokes, 17,* 64–67.

Henschen, K. P. (1988). More on sport psychology's neglected population. *Association for the Advancement of Applied Sport Psychology Newsletter, 3*(2), 8.

Henschen, K. P., Horvat, M., & French, R. (1984). A visual comparison of psychological profiles between able-bodied and wheelchair athletes. *Adapted Physical Activity Quarterly, 1*(2), 118–124.

Henschen, K. L., Horvat, M., & Roswal, G. (1992). Psychological profiles of the United States wheelchair basketball team. *International Journal of Sport Psychology, 23*(2), 128–137.

Horvat, M., Roswal, G., & Henschen, K. (1991). Psychological profiles of disabled male athletes before and after competition. *Clinical Kinesiology, 45,* 14–18.

Levine, H. G., & Langness, L. L. (1983). Context, ability, and performance: Comparison of competitive athletics among mildly mentally retarded and non-retarded adults. *American Journal of Mental Deficiency, 87*(5), 528–538.

Mastro, J. R., Canabal, M. Y., & French, R. (1988). Psychological mood profiles of sighted and unsighted beep baseball players. *Research Quarterly for Exercise and Sport, 59*(3), 262–264.

Mastro, J., & French, R. (1985). Sport anxiety and blind athletes. In C. Sherrill (Ed.), *Sport and disabled athletes.* Champaign, IL: Human Kinetics.

Mastro, J., French, R., Henschen, K., & Horvat, M. (1985). Use of the state-trait anxiety inventory for visually impaired athletes. *Perceptual and Motor Skills, 61,* 775–778.

Mastro, J., French, R., Henschen, K., & Horvat, M. (1986). Selected psychological characteristics of blind golfers and their coaches. *American Corrective Therapy Journal, 40*(5), 111–114.

Mastro, J.V., Sherrill, C., Gench, B., & French, R. (1987). Psychological characteristics of elite visually impaired athletes: The iceberg profile. *Journal of Sport Behavior, 10*(1), 39–46.

Paulsen, P., French, R., & Sherrill, C. (1991). Comparison of mood states of college able-bodied and wheelchair basketball players. *Perceptual and Motor Skills, 73,* 396–398.

Sachs, M. L. (1988). Sport psychology's neglected population: Persons with disabilities. *Association for the Advancement of Applied Sport Psychology Newsletter, 3*(2), 8.

Travis, C. A., & Sachs, M. L. (1991). Applied sport psychology and persons with mental retardation. *The Sport Psychologist, 5,* 382–391.

CHAPTER

21

CHILDREN AND
SPORT PSYCHOLOGY

PATSY TREMAYNE

The children of today may well be the athletes of tomorrow. Their sporting and physical education experiences now will have a major impact on their participation, values, and attitudes towards physical activity and well-being, not only as young adults, but throughout life. However, children's physical education experiences are often limited, and involvement in competitive sport before the development of a wide range of physical skills can lead to a high dropout rate in sport. For Australia to maintain its sporting successes there should be a greater depth of participation in children's sport. This can be attained if children spend their early years building a general repertoire of movement experiences and sporting skills and developing a healthy self-concept through activities that cater for the "total" child. The use of psychological principles in children's sport and physical education classes enables children to develop and utilise their own natural ability at their own pace; it also fosters an appreciation of sport skills as a continuing developing process in which achievement results in satisfaction and self-fulfilment.

The chapter will propose that there are many factors in sport and physical education which may discourage the continuation of healthy physical activity; that children's actual sporting experiences do not always equate with their psychological and sociological needs; that enjoyment may be a main reason for continued participation in sport; that the foundation skills of sport psychology, which influence motor skill acquisition, should be emphasised in primary school and utilised in children's sport in the wider community.

CHILDREN'S DEVELOPMENT

Physical growth slows substantially after early childhood and the stage from 6 to 12 years is a period of fairly steady growth and fundamental motor skill refinement (Gabbard, 1992; Kirchner, 1992). Two of the most influential developmental factors in motor skill development and refinement during this period are sport and physical education programs, as children's participation in physical activity normally occurs through the primary school curriculum, in spontaneous play activities, and in community sport programs.

FACTORS INFLUENCING MOTOR SKILL ACQUISITION

A number of factors influence the acquisition of motor skills and a child's readiness to learn is affected by such components as maturity level (attention span and developmental age); previous practice; prerequisite skills; body management skills; and the state of physical fitness (Kirchner, 1992; Magill, 1993; Seefeldt, 1988).

Motivation is another important element. Wankel and Kreisel (1985a) found that motivation to participate in sport was enhanced by using the skills, feeling excitement about the sport and feeling a sense of competence. For children, this sense of competence is vital to intrinsically motivated behaviour and it is suggested that there may be a higher dropout rate in sport if children do not feel competent (Klint & Weiss, 1987; Roberts, 1984; Watson, 1984).

Other factors influencing motor learning include goal setting, which a study by Weinberg, Bruya, Longino, and Jackson (1988) indicates is more satisfactory for perceived competence than a "do-your-best" approach; feedback (that is, the impressions, feelings or concepts that a child derives from his or her learning experience) (Corbin, Stewart, & Blair, 1981; Magill, 1993; Salmoni, Schmidt, & Walter, 1984) and positive reinforcement (which strengthens, consolidates and stores up learned experiences as a result of feedback) (Kirchner, 1992; Weiss, 1991).

The transfer of movement learning (where skills in one sport are transferred to another) and progression (Kirchner, 1992), the part versus whole method of teaching (Knapp & Dixon, 1952; Magill, 1993) and perceived stress and anxiety (Ommundsen & Vaglum, 1991), are also concepts that must be considered as influencing skill acquisition.

These factors may either hinder, facilitate, or have no effect on the learning of a new skill, and these variations in learning also enhance or detrimentally affect children's perceptions of themselves in relation to their sporting environment.

PSYCHOLOGICAL AND SOCIOLOGICAL CONSIDERATIONS

Children between 7 and 12 years are emerging from early childhood where parents were the dominant factor, and children's peers become increasingly significant (Kirchner, 1992; Spink, 1990). At this age, social play and games provide situations that are crucially important to the child's sense of identity and his or her ability to socialise (Harter, 1978). This period may also be a time that is important for moral development, and games are particularly effective in providing social interaction and "fair play". Team games, in particular, provide an opportunity for children to share power and to experience collective achievement. In fact, part of the appeal and security of games that are organised by children lies in the fact that there is no fear or loss of love due to performance — they are fun (Orlick, 1978; Spink & Longhurst, 1990).

For children, in their games "getting along" and "making the game work" are important, because this gives children information about themselves and their abilities (Passer, 1988). Unlike parents, who accept their children on the basis of love, peers relate to other children on the basis of what they offer the group. This interpersonal dependence develops quite naturally in spontaneous games and free play. Children readily accept rules from each other and make their own agreements for "the greater good" and they rarely require standards imposed by adults (Polgar, 1976). So it would seem that much of the psychological development and socialisation that occurs during this stage is as a result of the child's entrance into the culture of the peer group.

WHY DO CHILDREN PLAY SPORT?

Children play sport for a variety of reasons and it is somewhat naive to believe that children will be restricted from participating in highly structured competitive sport. But with awareness of the sociological and psychological factors that contribute to a child's well-being and through the application of these factors to sporting situations, some of the detrimental effects of competitive sport may be minimised.

The research literature indicates that the important aspects of children's sport include opportunity, satisfaction, appreciation and enjoyment. It is suggested that if children truly enjoy what they are doing, it may well become the main reason for continuous participation in the activity, as well as the motivation for them to seek higher levels of performance (Brustad, 1988; Scanlan & Lewthwaite, 1986; Wankel & Sefton, 1989). A recent study by Clough, McCormack, and Traill (1993) on junior sports participation in the Australian Capital Territory, indicated that 98% of participants chose "It's fun" from a list of 25 possible reasons for playing sport.

Alderman and Wood (1976), in an early study of incentive motivation in youngsters involved in competitive sport, found that children enjoyed their sport if three conditions were met: affiliation (having friends in the same sport, or being a useful member of the group); excellence (just being able to do the skills for personal satisfaction); and stress (the excitement, novelty and complexity of performing certain tasks).

More recent studies concur with Alderman and Wood (1976). For instance, Wankel and Kreisel (1985b) explored the factors underlying enjoyment of children's sport and found that components related to the process of the sports activity (such as improving one's skills, testing skills against others, performing the skills, and the excitement of the sport) were rated as being most important, whereas outcome-related components of the sport (such as winning the game, pleasing others and obtaining rewards) were rated as being least important. Of intermediate importance were social factors (such as being on a team or being with friends). It was also found, in a study of youth basketball, that the strongest predictor of high levels of enjoyment was an intrinsic motivational orientation (Brustad, 1988). A later investigation of fun in youth sport indicated that fun could be interpreted as a positive mood state determined primarily by children's perceptions of personal achievement and their matching of skills against realistic challenges (Wankel & Sefton, 1989).

Perceptions of ability and parental and coach satisfaction affected children's enjoyment of sport. Scanlan and Lewthwaite (1986) found that children involved in competitive wrestling who perceived that there was more positive adult sport involvement and interactions, and less maternal pressure and negativity regarding performance, experienced greater enjoyment when compared with their counterparts.

EFFECTS OF ORGANISED SPORT

Sport plays an important part in the lives of many children, with children as young as 4 and 5 years being exposed to organised competitive sport (Walsh & Snyder, 1982). In fact, the Australian study by Clough, McCormack, and Traill (1993) found that boys chose sport, from a list of seven leisure time activities, as being the most preferred leisure activity, while for girls it was ranked equal first with "being with friends". Involvement in children's sport has been found to contribute significantly to children's physical, social, emotional and psychomotor development and there are many positive outcomes associated with children's sports participation. These include opportunities to affiliate with others, to develop skills, to enjoy increased status associated with sporting success and to enjoy enhanced levels of physical fitness (Passer, 1981). However, questions have been raised relating to potential psychological and physical damage. These questions include the physical risks of high-contact sports, lack of expertise by teachers and/or coaches, the effects of competitive anxiety and stress and the psycho-social effects of intense early participation (Evans, 1986; Martens, 1978; Scanlan, 1984; Weiss & Gould, 1986).

Community sport programs often rely on parents and former players to volunteer as coaches, because of the difficulties in obtaining interested and qualified coaches to volunteer their time. Teachers and coaches involved with children's sport need to understand children's growth and development stages in order to choose appropriate skill practices. Not only are there physiological changes, but also there are psychological changes involving self-image and attention span, as well as sociological changes relating to peer group importance, which have significant implications for sport. Coaches inexperienced in children's sport do not always have the expertise to plan and implement skill practice sessions that fulfil children's needs and capacities. They may well deter children from further sport participation because of their lack of knowledge and insensitivity to problems (Evans, 1986; 1990).

Highly structured, competitive sports in our society place tremendous importance on winning. This emphasis carries over to competitive sports for children, with excessive emotional pressures applied by teachers, parents and coaches. At increasingly early ages children have been exposed to the reward systems that operate in sport and they have experienced the various emotions that accompany success and failure. According to Alexander (1991), children often receive contradictory messages about sport. While watching team sports they may see skilled or sturdy players control and intimidate opposing players while receiving encouragement from parents or coaches on the sidelines. Teachers and coaches may present high-profile athletes as winners and ideal role models, despite the fact that these athletes have been observed regularly flouting the rules of fair play in order to increase their chances of winning. Brustad (1988) observes that many parents place undue emphasis on winning, as this is seen to equate with success. Although the spirit of competition is acknowledged as being of value and competition is promoted as being normal and healthy, the reality is that children's sport has become a victim of a situation in which competition and winning are primary values in our society.

Adult-organised sports, often evaluated by parents, take away the security children have when they organise their own games. Most children under 10 years rely on objective outcomes, such as winning or losing, or adult feedback, in order to gain information regarding their personal ability (Horn & Hasbrook, 1987). Unless this feedback from parents, teachers and coaches is encouraging and children perceive that their sport experiences are positive, motivation and self-esteem may suffer. Duda (1987) implied that when children are affected by parents' negative evaluation, there is an increased probability of developing an ego-involved orientation towards their sport participation.

Studies indicate that moral development may be affected by organised sport. According to Weiss (1991), moral development is heavily influenced by the coach, and a study by Bredemeier, Weiss, Shields, and Cooper (1986) suggested that the types of social interactions fostered by relatively high contact sports may impede moral growth.

Some youngsters may excel in sport in a particular age group due to the fact that they are more physically mature than other children of the same age (Pang, 1973) and may be encouraged to focus on developing excellence at one or two sports. Pushing children into one or two sports at an early age can actually restrict them from reaching their full potential and cause them to develop inappropriate motor patterns (Gabbard, 1992).

Differences in the process of play in peer group sport and in adult-organised sport are quite marked (Eitzen & Sage, 1986). In the former, the game usually begins quickly, whereas in adult-organised sport children tend to wait to be told what to do. There are usually no spectators or time limitations in peer-organised sport, the game is self-paced, there is immediate feedback and the activity is intrinsically rewarding. In adult-organised sport, there are spectators and time limitations, a high priority on winning and skill development, behaviour is governed by adult-generated norms and rules, and success is viewed in terms of material rewards. According to Coakley (1978), "the emphasis in the organised setting is on the development of sport skills, not on the development of interpersonal skills" (p. 98).

SPORTING MYTHS

The following arguments are offered in support of highly competitive sports for children.

1. *Better athletes result from children's competitive sporting programs.*
Kemp (1985) stated that, in some sports, international performances were achieved in childhood or early youth and therefore basic training at an early age was necessary. Certainly, in sports such as swimming, gymnastics, skating and tennis, participation at an early age would seem to have a positive effect on later performance. However, in many sports, such as cricket, basketball, netball and football, one may ask if there is any positive relationship between competition at an early age and future success, as children can readily learn these sporting skills in the local playground or park and do not require specialised equipment and/or facilities.

Another factor is that children may not persist in their sport. If they have been exposed to rigid authoritarian training from an early age (for example, in swimming or gymnastics), by the time they reach adolescence they may well have reached saturation point for a particular sport. Clough, McCormack, and Traill (1993) reported that youngsters overwhelmingly selected negative factors associated with the coach as being reasons for being discouraged from playing sport. An earlier study indicated that one of the reasons for children dropping out of football was because they perceived the coach as being an autocrat (Robinson & Carron, 1982). Other reports indicate that by the time children reach early adolescence there is a high drop-out rate from sport and physical activity (Robertson, 1982; Sport for Young Australians, 1991).

2. *Sports provide additional play opportunities for children.*
First, it is speculated that television and the enormous importance placed on competitive sports has led children in their free time away from spontaneous games towards more structured sport (Polgar, 1976). Organised sport can take up a considerable amount of leisure time and may actually reduce play opportunities for children.

Second, it is well known that allowing children to feel a sense of accomplishment is the best way to promote continued behaviour in that activity (Brustad, 1988; Wankel & Kreisel, 1985b). Yet, the very nature of highly competitive sport means that children are exposed to an environment where success, which is based on winning, is possible for only a few children.

The child who needs physical activity the most is shunted away from exercise by the competitive nature of sport and the unavailability of suitable alternatives. This can have a detrimental effect on the child's level of aspiration and physical self-concept and, according to Alexander (1991), a number of children learn to become competent bystanders.

3. *Organised sports are safer and healthier as they are well supervised.*
Highly competitive sports are potentially harmful to both physiological and psychological growth and development (Evans, 1986; Graham, 1992; Martens, 1978; Scanlan, 1984). The psychological damage is difficult to measure, but it has been noted that, while normal game playing allows the child to experiment with social interaction and movement in a "safe", non-judgemental environment, the child who fails in front of a large group of people may bear the scars of humiliation for some time. Some children can easily be placed in situations where they experience a series of losses leading to lowered self-esteem. For instance, Scanlan and Passer (1979) found that low self-esteem children displayed higher pre-competition state anxiety levels than did high self-esteem children, whereas Ommundsen and Vaglum (1991) found that lower soccer-related self-esteem was related to soccer competition anxiety among young players. Thus, it is understandable why many children find physical activity neither relaxing nor enjoyable and observers often note that children's soccer or Rugby competitions have an emotionally charged atmosphere created largely by the parents' and coaches' aspirations. Studies with young wrestlers and gymnasts confirm this by finding that children worry about meeting the expectations of their parents and coaches (Scanlan & Lewthwaite, 1984; Weiss, Weise, & Klint, 1989).

Sports that have a high degree of physical contact, such as Rugby, may also be developmentally counterproductive. The study by Bredemeier, Weiss, Shields, and Cooper (1986), investigating the relationship between children's sports involvement and aspects of children's morality, found that participation and interest in high contact sports positively correlated with less mature moral reasoning and greater tendencies towards aggression.

4. *Children are going to have to learn how to compete when they are adults. Better now than later.*
Eitzen and Sage (1986) pointed out that there was no documentation to the effect that children were worse off in their occupational careers for not participating in competitive, organised sports. It is probably not the experience of competition alone which is detrimental to children, but the intensity of that experience — the feeling of "competing against" or competing aggressively, rather than "competing with", either with oneself or with others. In children's sports, cognitive, developmental and skill levels vary dramatically, and participation, although representing an important source of fun and excitement for some children, may lead to stress and anxiety for others. The intensity and social evaluation involved in competitive sport is particularly stressful and anxiety-provoking for those children

high in trait anxiety and can be detrimental to performance and participation (Martens, 1977; Scanlan & Lewthwaite, 1984; Scanlan & Passer, 1979). If anxiety results in too many negative consequences and attitudes, there is the likelihood that these children will avoid future competitive situations.

Highly competitive, adult-controlled sports programs for children may, for other reasons, actually discourage the continuation of healthy physical activities later in life. First, coaches in highly structured sport are often untrained, well-meaning volunteers, not always sensitive to the developmental needs of the obese, uncoordinated, or frail child who may have had virtually no experience in the motor skills needed for success. Second, when adults direct the competition, children are not exercising control of the experience. This may not necessarily parallel their later competitive experiences in adulthood, where they will probably have more control of any competitive challenges that they choose to take on. Therefore, some children are positively reinforced by their physical education and sporting experiences, while other children may be alienated from wanting to participate in any form of physical activity (Bunker, 1981, Tinning, 1987).

PHYSICAL EDUCATION VERSUS SPORT

Sport and physical education are, by their very nature, activities that can provide fun and enjoyment — key elements associated with successful learning (Passer, 1981). However, they do have very different purposes. Sporting programs are basically for children who are keen to specialise in one or more sports and refine their talents in order to compete with others of similar abilities and interests. Developmentally appropriate physical education programs, however, are designed for every child, with the intent of providing children of all abilities and interests with a foundation of movement experiences that will eventually lead to active and healthy lifestyles. If children experience enjoyment in their physical activities, the desire to participate in physical activity in the future is increased. However, it is doubtful if the element of enjoyment is given more than token acknowledgement in the training of those people who usually provide children with their earliest experiences of organised sport and physical activity — the generalist teachers who teach physical education in primary school.

Detailed lesson planning, maximum pupil participation and firm class control are considered to be characteristic of effective teaching (Graham, 1992). These teaching practices may be satisfactory for the class as a whole, but ignore the needs of individual children. Tinning (1987) points out that the individuality of physically competent children in most physical education lessons is heightened through activities that recognise their strengths, whereas the individuality of children whose perceptions of physical activity are threatening and alienating is seldom recognised.

PROBLEMS IN PHYSICAL EDUCATION

In 1975 Stirrat observed that the primary school teacher tended to neglect the physical education lesson for a variety of reasons ranging from "not enough time" to feelings of personal inadequacy. Nearly two decades later, children's physical education has not changed much. Although educational growth is now acknowledged by many as taking place not only in the classroom but also in the gymnasium or on the playing field, the experience of teaching physical education by generalist teachers is not always fulfilling. Many primary school teachers still believe that physical education is not as valid a learning experience as classroom lessons. A study carried out in Victorian schools indicated that 40% of generalist teachers value physical education as "a break from formal education" (Hickey, 1992, p. 20).

In Australia children have the opportunity to commence competitive sport before they even start school (Walsh & Snyder, 1982). This can create problems for primary teachers in their physical education classes, as many children may be in organised sporting teams before they have experienced school physical education lessons. These children may have a better awareness of the rules of the game and have experienced a wider variety of skill practices than the teacher and this may well shape their expectations of any future physical activity.

Thus, as Bunker (1981) pointed out, primary teachers may have to contend with classes where the range of skill and knowledge about a particular game is extremely diverse. They are teaching children who, on the one hand, might have thrived on the community sport program and find the physical education lesson less than challenging, and, who on the other hand, have had unpleasant experiences in community sporting programs and who are apprehensive about physical education activities. This can be threatening to the primary teacher without expertise and there is a disinclination to do much more than supervise and "keep control" in physical education classes. As Tinning (1992, p. 25) reports, teachers "are only too pleased to hand responsibility for the subject over to such outside agencies as Aussie Sports".

The Australian Sports Commission's "Aussie Sports" program was first implemented in Australian primary schools in 1986. This program has had a significant impact on children's sports as it has encouraged many sporting organisations to evaluate and modify the way sport is presented to children aged 7 to 12 years. "Aussie Sports" was designed to complement the existing school physical education programs and has been adopted by many primary schools as a ready-made source of physical education lessons. Yet, this has created problems, which have included the inappropriateness of program content for the lower primary grades, lack of teacher expertise and lack of equipment (Dry, 1991). More disturbing is the fact that, in some cases, the Aussie Sports program has replaced regular physical education activities (Tinning, 1992).

The generalist teacher does not usually have enough training in physical education or sport in order to teach competently in this area. A recent study, to determine the quantity and quality of physical and sport education offered to pre-service primary education teachers in New South Wales universities, found that hours devoted to compulsory physical education courses in the various institutions varied between 48 hours and 126 hours. It was considered alarming that not one institution had made the attainment of coaching qualifications a mandatory part of its course, since all primary teachers are required to teach physical education and sport (Webb, Moore, Gray, & Jessup, 1993).

This leads to situations in school where, not only is the physical education program ad hoc, with little planning, but the program may also be unbalanced in terms of content. In many cases, the types of experiences in the school physical education program are inappropriate for the developmental level of the child. For instance, the playing of Rugby, soccer and other team sports by 6 and 7-year-old children may encroach on lesson time better spent on basic movement experiences.

It is less stressful for the generalist teacher to give children activities that keep the class under control, rather than to facilitate the learning of appropriate motor skills. Competitive relays and elimination games are frequently used, yet these are activities that promote feelings of inferiority in some children. Invariably it is the poorly skilled or overweight children who are eliminated or run last in the relays. At the same time, children may be learning double standards. They mirror the attitudes of their teacher if winning is emphasised and cheating or flouting the rules of the game in order to win is not discouraged (Graham, 1992).

Physical education is not perceived by teachers as being an important subject in the school curriculum (Hickey, 1992) and, when teachers are not dressed appropriately for physical activity, this may provide poor role modelling. Children are not always appropriately dressed for physical activity either and often are not encouraged to change because of lack of time and facilities. This may lead to perceptions that physical activity is not an important part of the school curriculum.

WHY CHILDREN FAIL

A recent video on the status of children's sport and physical education, filmed by the Australian Broadcasting Commission and shown on the "Four Corners" program ("Fool's Gold", 1992), raised several issues of interest. Several reasons were given as to why many children failed to thrive in physical education and sport. One important point was that children were not able to exhibit the fundamental motor skills necessary for sporting involvement and other physical activities. This was due to inadequate school physical education programs that were affecting children as early as Year Two.

It was also pointed out that physical education in primary schools had been reduced to the extent that many children had less than one hour of programmed physical activity per week. Often this programmed physical activity was organised sport, which did not provide a balanced repertoire of movement experiences necessary for the developing child. In addition, because children, on average, were watching four hours of television each day either before or after school, this meant that unless children had school programs that required and promoted a variety of physical activities, increasingly, they would have none ("Fool's Gold", 1992).

There are many factors, physical, mental and environmental, which cause children to feel alienated and threatened by sporting activities at school. The physical factors include actual physical disabilities (many children formerly in special schools are now integrated into State primary schools); low fitness levels (poor coordination, balance or flexibility, lack of stamina, strength or agility); obesity or inadequate body build; temporary sickness (due to lack of energy after illness and needing more time to recuperate); and fatigue (due to lack of sleep) (Gabbard, 1992; Kirchner, 1992; Magill, 1993).

The child's psychological condition may also affect perceptions about participating in physical activities. Children develop feelings about their popularity among peers, their perceived ability to perform physical activities, or their intellectual abilities. Feelings of inadequacy may be heightened because of disinterest in the activity; conflicting interests; fear (either of failure or injury); shame (of performing in front of their peer group or the teacher); or an overriding problem (psychological, family-related, or within the classroom). Other factors may include mental exhaustion (due to lack of readiness or maturation); poor self-image (due to frame of reference effects with other children); dislike of subject or teacher; lack of challenge (task too easy); no enjoyment or fun; no sense of achievement (task too hard); or poor self-concept (Graham, 1992; Marsh, 1993; Robertson, 1989; Tinning, 1992).

Children often have to contend with a poor external environment that affects their success or failure. These environmental factors include poor facilities; poor equipment; bad weather (with no provision for wet weather areas); a teacher who is uninspired, or unable to coach; lack of individual attention; excess numbers of students; inadequately planned sport programs; poorly prepared lessons; tasks at wrong levels; an over-emphasis on winning; an incompatible group; an unsafe situation; or a poor image of physical education in school (with lack of support) (Coakley, 1978; Eitzen & Sage, 1986; Robertson, 1989; Tinning, 1992).

 ## PSYCHOLOGICAL SKILLS TRAINING FOR CHILDREN

Most psychological skills training (PST) has been targeted towards elite athletes. Their physical skills are well developed and coaches perceive that the use of psychological skills is applicable to elite athletes to enhance or fine tune performance (Weinberg & Williams, 1993).

In recent years, however, other researchers have also proposed that mental skills training should be introduced for children (Vealey, 1988; Weinberg & Williams, 1993; Weiss, 1991). Weiss (1991) also suggested that many young athletes participating in organised, competitive sport are in need of specific techniques that will enhance their physical and psychosocial development. Orlick (1982) observed that if children were to be exposed to stressful situations such as competitive, adult-organised sport, coaches and teachers had a responsibility to teach them strategies to deal effectively with that stress. He declared that "games themselves have become rigid, judgmental, highly organised, and excessively goal-oriented. There is no freedom from the pressure of evaluation and the psychological distress of disapproval" (Orlick, 1978, p. 5).

The performance and personal development of young athletes who are taught PST techniques may progress faster than the performance and personal development of youngsters who do not receive PST. As Vealey (1988) states, PST may be particularly effective with younger athletes as they are developing physically and psychologically and can learn appropriate skills to cope with the stresses of sporting competition. Weinberg and Williams (1993) also point out that it may be easier to teach PST to beginners. They use the analogy that experienced teachers and coaches know it is easier to teach the proper physical technique to a beginner than to correct a poor physical technique in a more experienced athlete.

ENVIRONMENTAL FACTORS

If a mental training program is to be effective with children, the interaction that takes place between the individual and the environment needs to be taken into account (Danish & Hale, 1981; Weiss, 1991). It is important that the significant adults in the child's sporting environment, that is, teachers, coaches and parents, project a positive belief in each child's strengths and capacity to surmount obstacles and maintain personal goals. These adults would need to be encouraged to focus on the desirable qualities or behaviours to be attained by children through sport, rather than on the outcomes of the sport. According to Horn and Hasbrook (1987), young children rely primarily on feedback and reinforcement from significant adults in order to judge their competency at sport and it is important that this means of communication to children be evaluated regularly. Children enjoy learning new skills, they appreciate any hints that will help them improve and they want praise that is appropriate to the difficulty of the skill performed. So it makes sense that children's psychological, physical and sociological needs in a specific situation be taken into account by their parents, coaches and teachers. Weiss (1991) suggests emphasis should be placed on the following environmental factors in order to enhance the development of youngsters' psychological skills:

1. Decrease the emphasis on peer comparison.
2. Give appropriate and contingent feedback.
3. Emphasise self-improvement.
4. Provide enjoyable sport experiences.
5. Enhance perception of competence by prudent structuring of the sporting activity.

6. Organise intrinsically motivating physical activities.
7. Structure the environment to enhance the teaching of moral development.
8. Develop a variety of positive communication skills, including effective listening and body language skills.
9. Involve children in the decision-making process.
10. Choose effective role models.
11. Identify and take advantage of "readiness to learn" moments.
12. Carefully consider the ability levels of each child and construct appropriate skill progression.

ROLE MODELLING

Modelling is an environmental factor that can have a profound effect upon the development of motor skills, especially during childhood and adolescence. Children respond well to the use of role models and, if chosen wisely, these models can have a marked psychological effect on children's self-perceptions. These role models can be other children, athletes, coaches, teachers or parents (Gabbard, 1992). As Orlick and McCaffrey (1991, p. 332) point out, "If well chosen, a role model can set a positive example to emulate with respect to mental skills, physical skills, a healthy perspective, persistence, or anything else one might want to pursue".

The use of mastery models is an effective method of increasing physical proficiency and enhancing psychological skills. The models are used by enthusiastic instructors, sensitive to the needs of children, to demonstrate technically correct skill patterns, or to emphasise appropriate strategies or interactions. Weiss (1991) suggests the use of coping models as a way to target the learning of both psychological and physical skills. She indicates that this type of model is one who starts out by displaying, both verbally and behaviourally, similar fears and uncertainties to those of the observing children. With instruction this model gradually exhibits the ability to overcome these negative feelings and perform the skill effectively. This conveys to the children watching that, with practice, a skill can be learnt; at the same time they are provided with motivating and confidence enhancing skills.

INDIVIDUAL PSYCHOLOGICAL STRATEGIES

Vealey (1988) describes a useful model that differentiates between skills, which are the desired qualities or behaviours, and the methods that are used to attain these skills. In her model she divides the skills into:
(a) foundation skills (volition, self-awareness, self-esteem, self-confidence)
(b) performance skills (optimal physical and mental arousal, optimal attention)
(c) facilitative skills (interpersonal skills, lifestyle management).

The methods consist of foundation methods (physical practice, education); and PST methods (goal setting, imagery, physical relaxation, thought control). Using a structured model, such as the one described, would enable a trained coach or teacher implementing PST to focus on the skill to be acquired and to choose a method or methods by which this skill could be achieved.

Aspects of mental training that may be useful for the young athlete include the development of a positive attitude to competition. By teaching youngsters to understand which aspects of competition are and are not in their control, and then helping them to focus on personally controllable goals, competition may be more enjoyable and less intense. Children can also be taught to visualise success and to react to situations constructively. Other easily taught strategies include simple attentional skills such as verbal cues and positive imagery. Verbal cues are concrete strategies frequently used by teachers and coaches to focus attention to the task (e.g., a child may be encouraged to say aloud the words "step-hit" when practising a forehand in tennis).

All these skills can be of benefit to young athletes provided they remain interested in learning (Vealey, 1988; Weinberg & Williams, 1993). A recent study investigated the appropriateness of mental training for 7- to 10-year-old children playing table tennis and found that children who used mental imagery experienced significantly greater improvement in the accuracy and technical quality of their shots than children in comparison groups (Zhang, Ma, Orlick, & Zitzelsberger, 1992).

There may need to be an adjustment in the way the above strategies are taught to children, such as simpler verbal instructions, fewer goals and shorter training sessions to allow for developmental differences. However, if mental training includes an element of fun, appropriate role models, positive and individualised approaches and the cooperation of parents, the successful learning of the above strategies would very likely lead to an increase in intrinsic motivation, self-esteem, self-awareness and self-confidence, which Vealey (1988) describes as foundation skills.

PSYCHOLOGICAL SKILLS TRAINING IN SCHOOLS

Most sport psychologists have full-time jobs in universities or are involved in private practice and, according to Vealey (1988), a need has been created for people other than sport psychologists to implement PST. She advocates that, in North America, coaches are the most appropriate people to implement PST with athletes. Williams (1986) has noted that almost all coaches of elite athletes in Eastern European countries have been trained in the use of PST, as they have long been seen as key people in the PST process. By the same token, coaches and physical educators, if trained in psychological techniques and strategies, would be the most appropriate people to teach PST in schools. Educating coaches and physical educators in various aspects of PST may be an effective way to develop mental skills in children, as these people work in positions where they advise and counsel youngsters in sport.

In 1976, the South Australian Education Department began a major review of its physical education curriculum to assess the health of students and the effectiveness of current programs and practices in schools. The development of this Lifestyle Education Program occurred in two phases. The first phase, from 1977 to 1983, experimented with methods for achieving lifestyle modification through the school curriculum for children from 10 to 14 years. It was found that the incorporation of self-awareness, goal setting, and self-monitoring through the use of a specially developed booklet, *The body owner's manual*, produced significant improvements in lifestyle modification (Maynard, Coonan, Worsley, Dwyer, & Baghurst, 1987). The results led to the second phase, involving the establishment of a 5-year, school-based, demonstration program incorporating the above mental skills. According to Wooller (1993), the program incorporating *The body owner's manual* is now replaced by a newer, more child-based program called "Action Pact", which started in South Australian primary schools in January, 1994. This program is designed to improve physical fitness, self-esteem and self-confidence in relation to physical activity. It includes the self-awareness, goal setting and self-monitoring strategies of the previous program and also incorporates relaxation strategies using guided imagery.

The school system in Orebro, Sweden, incorporated use of *The body owner's manual* after visits to Australia by Lars-Eric Unesthal (Wooller, 1993). Further mental skills training for children has been added as part of the normal primary school curriculum, where the emphasis is on teaching relaxation, stress management and imagery (Solin, 1991).

Orlick (1990) and Orlick and McCaffrey (1991) have expounded on the potential benefits of mental skills training for young children. They reported that mental training had been in effect in selected sport settings for approximately 20 years in Canada and, that using games and play, a mental skills program had been recently introduced to primary school children. The key elements of this program include the use of simple, concrete strategies, individualised and positive approaches, involvement of parents, the use of role models and an element of fun.

The use of these strategies may have important implications for curricular policy in physical education. If inner mental training programs were to be introduced in schools in Australia, there would need to be a systematic approach that facilitated their implementation. There would also need to be some structured evaluation of the efficacy of inner mental training to enhance enjoyment, improve intrinsic motivation and persistence in sport, and increase self-confidence, self-awareness, self-esteem and physical self-concept. According to Fox (1992, p. 52) "an approach that emphasizes a mastery orientation to competence and that also encourages self-acceptance of worth is most likely to succeed".

FOCUS ON PERSONAL DEVELOPMENT

There is an increasing emphasis on integrating personal development and health into physical education programs in Australian schools. In these programs the focus is on personal growth and change and gaining control over lifestyle, rather than just skill development and performance enhancement. This integration of personal development and physical education is seen by many physical education teachers as weakening the position of their subject within the school curriculum (Tinning, 1992). Yet, this could be seen as an opportunity to introduce mental skills training whereby children learn to develop positive attitudes towards competition in sport and other lifestyle activities. The National Health and Physical Education curriculum, which provides a framework upon which existing or new subjects could be developed, is still under consideration. It would not be difficult to include a mental skills training program within a personal development program. A well-structured program may ultimately improve intrinsic motivation, positive self-perceptions and self-awareness, strategies to cope with stress and the development of positive values towards leading a healthy and physically active lifestyle.

Universities that have teacher education and sports science programs would be the most appropriate settings in which to incorporate mental skills training, because of the trend towards integration of personal development with physical education. Vealey (1988) reports that there is support for this type of delivery system in North America to be available for college athletes and coaches.

FUTURE DIRECTIONS

If sport and physical education work together, some of the problems that have arisen in children's sport may be alleviated. "A quality physical education program on a regular basis is a critical first step in schools before sport can be played" (Pettit, 1991, p. 12). Children need the basic movement skills, which enable them not only to enjoy physical activity, but also to improve their self-esteem through succeeding at a rudimentary level. The teaching of movement skills to children by specialist teachers in primary schools and the teaching of psychological skills to youngsters involved in competitive sport, would ensure that there is sufficient junior talent to make up future elite sporting programs. As Evans (1991, p. 14) suggests, "while we continue to neglect the physical education of the younger children then we will continue to see some children entering sport... deficient in the essential skills". According to Turnbull (1992, p. 14), "sufficient documentation already exists which clearly identifies and supports the need for a comprehensive program of physical education in Australian primary schools".

Basic mental skills training could be taught to teacher trainees within a university personal development and physical education program. Another type of delivery system is through the use of a standardised training program with approved and formatted materials and techniques (Vealey, 1988). This package could be presented, with modifications to allow for the specific demands and characteristics of particular sports, to various State sporting associations for the training of coaches in junior sport. There is already an awareness that sport psychology should be included in coaches' qualifications, but these programs are presented on an ad hoc basis by the various sporting associations and the concerns of children in sport are not always addressed in a systematic fashion using a holistic approach.

If children are given the opportunity to participate in a structured mental skills training program adjusted to their developmental level, it is likely they will have more effective, enjoyable and successful experiences in sport.

CONCLUSIONS

Children have very different needs, interests and abilities from those of adults. It is not enough to simply tone down adult sporting programs and assume that they will be beneficial for children (Graham, Holt/Hale, & Parker, 1993).

The factors leading to attrition in children's sport need to be studied further (Gould, 1982). Youth sport psychology research has not adequately taken into account the significant social interactions that affect children's psychological processes. This has led to a restricted understanding of children's perspectives towards their sport participation. The psychological, sociological and behavioural variations among children caused by differing developmental levels are certain to influence their socialisation experiences and sport motivation (Brustad, 1992; Weiss & Bredemeier, 1983). Consequently, it would appear that adult intervention in children's games has very disparate social consequences for the children. It is probable that adult intervention into children's games socialises youngsters into the adult world and this appears to have varying effects on their growth. There is a distinct possibility that, if the interference in these activities is negative, the natural process of growing up may be impaired.

SUMMARY

Sporting and physical education experiences during childhood have a major impact on future participation in sport. The number of children who maintain their interest in sport may well affect Australia's future international sporting successes. There are a number of factors that need to be considered when children learn motor skills, as their cognitive, developmental and skill levels vary greatly. These factors may either hinder, facilitate or have no effect on learning. Children's perceptions of themselves in relation to their sporting environment may also be affected by these variations in learning. Between the ages of 7 and 12 years, social play and games provide situations and interaction with peers that are important for developing the ability to socialise and a sense of identity.

Although involvement in competitive sport has many positive aspects, there are also problems because of the negative effects of intense, early competitive participation. There are a number of arguments endorsing highly competitive sports for children, which are not supported by the research. So often in competitive sport there is little acknowledgement of well-established theoretical guidelines relating to the principles of learning, physical development, intellectual development and emotional development.

School physical education is not without its problems. The generalist teacher does not usually have enough training in physical education in order to teach competently. This leads to inadequate school physical education programs in which children are not able to exhibit the fundamental motor skills necessary for later sporting involvement. Any programmed physical activity is often organised sport where the range of skill and knowledge is extremely diverse, causing problems for the inexperienced teacher.

Children are failing to thrive in physical education and sport because of a variety of physical, mental and environmental conditions. Many of the detrimental effects of competitive sport could be minimised if the sociological and psychological factors that contribute to a child's well-being are taken into account. Children's enjoyment of their sports is a factor that contributes towards an understanding of children's involvement in sport and the research literature indicates that there are a number of elements that affect children's enjoyment of sport.

Psychological skills training adapted for use by children would provide an opportunity for children to maintain their interest and enjoyment of sport. If PST is to be effective with children, environmental factors and developmental differences would need to be taken into account. It is suggested that a PST program, integrated into a personal development program, could be implemented in schools and teacher training institutions. A better understanding of the significant social interactions in competitive sport that affect children's perceptions and the effective use of a program that can enhance their experiences in competitive sport, may encourage greater participation in healthy physical activity throughout life.

REFERENCES

Alderman, R., & Wood, N. (1976). An analysis of incentive motivation in young Canadian athletes. *Canadian Journal of Applied Sport Sciences, 1,* 169–176.

Alexander, K. (1991). Seeking change in school physical education: Learning from a negative result. *The ACHPER National Journal,* Summer.

Bredemeier, B., Weiss, M., Shields, D., & Cooper, B. (1986). The relationship of sport involvement with children's moral reasoning and aggression tendencies. *Journal of Sport Psychology, 8,* 304–318.

Brustad, R. (1988). Affective outcomes in competitive youth sport: The influence of intrapersonal and socialization factors. *Journal of Sport and Exercise Psychology, 10,* 307–321.

Brustad, R. (1992). Integrating socialization influences into the study of children's motivation in sport. *Journal of Sport and Exercise Psychology, 14,* 59–77.

Bunker, L. (1981). Elementary physical education and youth sport. *Journal of Physical Education and Recreation,* Feb., 26–28.

Bunker, D., & Thorpe, R. (1982). A model for teaching of games in secondary schools. *Bulletin of Physical Education, 18,* 5–8.

Clough, J., McCormack, C., & Traill, R. (1993). A mapping of participation rates in junior sport. *The ACHPER National Journal*, Winter, 4–7.

Coakley, J. J. (1978). *Sport in Society*. St. Louis: C. V. Mosby.

Corbin, C., Stewart, M., & Blair, W. (1981). Self-confidence and motor performance of preadolescent boys and girls studied in different feedback situations. *Journal of Sport Psychology, 3*, 30–34.

Danish, S. J., & Hale, B. D. (1981). Toward an understanding of the practice of sport psychology. *Journal of Sport Psychology*, *3*, 90–99.

Duda, J. (1987). Toward a developmental theory of children's motivation in sport. *Journal of Sport Psychology, 9*, 130–145.

Dry, J. (1991). P.E. and sport. *Aussie Sports Action, 2*, 6–7.

Eitzen, D. S., & Sage, G. H. (1986). *Sociology of American sport* (2nd ed.). Dubuque, IA: Wm C. Brown.

Evans, J. (1986). Physical education and the challenge of youth sport. *The ACHPER National Journal*, December, 13–16.

Evans, J. (1990). Sport in schools threatened by lack of teacher training. *The ACHPER National Journal*, Summer, 8–22.

Evans, J. (1991). A reaction. In A. Pettit, Cinderella and the two uglies: Physical education, sport and fitness in primary schools. *The ACHPER National Journal*, Summer, 13–14.

Fool's Gold. (1992). Video distributed by ACHPER on behalf of the Australian Broadcasting Corporation.

Fox, K. R. (1992). Physical education and the development of self-esteem in children. In N. Armstrong (Ed.), *New directions in physical education: II. Toward a national curriculum*. Champaign, IL: Human Kinetics.

Gabbard, C. (1992). *Lifelong motor development*. Dubuque, IA: Wm C. Brown.

Gould, D. (1982). Sport psychology in the 1980s: Status, direction, and challenge in youth sports research. *Journal of Sport Psychology, 4*, 203–218.

Graham, G. (1992). *Teaching children physical education: Becoming a master teacher*. Champaign, IL: Human Kinetics.

Graham, G., Holt/Hale, S., & Parker, M. (1993). *Children moving: A reflective approach to teaching physical education*. (3rd ed.). Mountain View, CA: Mayfield.

Harter, S. (1978). Effectance motivation reconsidered. *Human Development, 21*, 34–64.

Hickey, C. (1992). Physical education in Victorian primary schools: A review of current provision. *The ACHPER National Journal*, Summer, 18–23.

Horn, T., & Hasbrook, C. (1987). Psychological characteristics and the criteria children use for self-evaluation. *Journal of Sport Psychology, 9*, 208–221.

Kemp, N. G. (1985). Ready or not: The real winners in children's sport aren't necessarily the medallists. *Sports Science Periodical on Research and Technology in Sport*, April, 1–5.

Kirchner, G. (1992). *Physical education for elementary school children* (8th ed.). Dubuque, IA: Wm C. Brown.

Klint, K. A., & Weiss, M. R. (1987). Perceived competence and motives for participating in youth sports: A test of Harter's Competence Motivation Theory. *Journal of Sport Psychology, 9*, 55–65.

Knapp, C. G., & Dixon, W. R. (1952). Learning to juggle: A study of whole and part methods. *Research Quarterly, 23*, 389–401.

Magill, R. (1993). *Motor learning: Concepts and applications* (4th ed.). Dubuque, IA: Wm C. Brown.

Marsh, H. (1993). Physical fitness self-concept: Relations to field and technical indicators of physical fitness for boys and girls aged 9–15. *Journal of Sport and Exercise Psychology, 15*, 184–206.

Martens, R. (1977). *Sport competition anxiety test.* Champaign, IL: Human Kinetics.

Martens, R. (Ed.). (1978). *Joy and sadness in children's sports.* Champaign, IL: Human Kinetics.

Maynard, E. J., Coonan, W. E., Worsley, A., Dwyer, T., & Baghurst, P. A. (1987). The development of the lifestyle education program in Australia. In B. S. Hetzel & G. S. Berenson (Eds.), *Cardiovascular risk factors in childhood: Epidemiology and prevention.* Amsterdam: Elsevier.

Ommundsen, Y., & Vaglum, P. (1991). Soccer competition anxiety and enjoyment in young boy players. The influence of perceived competence and significant others' emotional involvement. *International Journal of Sport Psychology, 22*, 35–49.

Orlick, T. (1978). *The cooperative sports and games book: Challenge without competition.* New York: Pantheon.

Orlick, T. (1982). Beyond excellence. In T. Orlick, J. T. Partington, & J. H. Salmela (Eds.), *Mental training for coaches and athletes.* Ottawa: Coaching Association of Canada.

Orlick, T. (1990). *In pursuit of excellence.* Champaign, IL: Leisure Press.

Orlick T., & McCaffrey, N. (1991). Mental training with children for sport and life. *The Sport Psychologist, 5*, 322–334.

Pang, H. (1973). The biology of competitive school sports. *Australian Journal of Physical Education, 60*, 10–15.

Passer, M. W. (1981). Children in sport: Participation motives and psychological stress. *Quest, 33*, 231–244.

Passer, M. W. (1988). Psychological issues in determining children's age-readiness for competition. In F. L. Smoll, R. A. Magill, & M. J. Ash (Eds.), *Children in Sport* (3rd ed.), (pp. 67–78). Champaign, IL: Human Kinetics.

Pettit, A. (1991). Cinderella and the two uglies: Physical education, sport and fitness in primary schools. *The ACHPER National Journal*, Summer, 11–14.

Polgar, S. K. (1976). The social context of games: Or when is play not play. *Sociology of Education, 49*, 265–71.

Roberts, G. (1984). Achievement motivation in children's sport. In J. Nicholls (Ed.), *The development of achievement motivation.* Greenwich, CT: JAI Press.

Robertson, I. (1982). Sport in the lives of South Australian children. In T. Orlick, J. T. Partington, & J. H. Salmela, (Eds.), *Mental training for coaches and athletes.* Ottawa: Sport in Perspective Inc. and The Coaching Association of Canada, 61–63.

Robertson, I. (1989). The coach and the drop out. *Sports Coach*, April–June, 8–14.

Robinson, T., & Carron, A. (1982). Personal and situational factors associated with dropping out versus maintaining participation in competitive sport. *Journal of Sport Psychology, 4*, 364–378.

Salmoni, A. W., Schmidt, R. A., & Walter, C. B. (1984). Knowledge of results and motor learning: A review and critical reappraisal. *Psychological Bulletin, 95*, 355–386.

Scanlan, T. (1984). Competitive stress and the child athlete. In J. M. Silva & R. S. Weinberg (Eds.), *Psychological foundations of sport.* Champaign, IL: Human Kinetics.

Scanlan, T., & Lewthwaite, R. (1984). Social psychological aspects of competition for male youth sport participants: I: Predictors of competitive stress. *Journal of Sport Psychology, 6*, 208–226.

Scanlan, T., & Lewthwaite, R. (1986). Social psychological aspects of competition for male youth sport participants: IV: Predictors of enjoyment. *Journal of Sport Psychology*, *8*, 25–35.

Scanlan, T., & Passer, M. W. (1979). Sources of competitive stress in young female athletes. *Journal of Sport Psychology*, *1*, 151–159.

Seefeldt, V. (1988). The concept of readiness applied to motor skill acquisition. In F. L. Smoll, R. A. Magill, & M. J. Ash (Eds.), *Children in sport*. Champaign, IL: Human Kinetics.

Solin, E. (1991). Mental training in the Swedish school systems. Presented at the First World Congress on Mental Training, University of Orebro, Sweden. In T. Orlick & N. McCaffrey (Eds.), Mental training with children for sport and life, (1991). *Sport Psychologist*, *5*, 322–334.

Spink, K. S. (1990). *Give your kids a sporting chance: A guide for parents*. Melbourne: Sun Books.

Spink, K. S., & Longhurst, K. (1990). Participation motives of Australian boys involved in traditional and modified cricket. *Australian Journal of Science and Medicine in Sport*, *21*(1), 28–31.

Sport for Young Australians. *Widening the gateways to participation*. (1991). Australian Sports Commission, Canberra.

Stirrat, M. (1975). *Introducing educational gymnastics in the primary school*. Sydney: Physical Education Publications.

Tinning, R. (1987). *Improving teaching in physical education*. Melbourne: Deakin University.

Tinning, R. (1992). On speeches, dreams, and realities: Physical education in the year 2001. *The ACHPER National Journal*, Summer.

Turnbull, J. (1992). Daily PE and specialist teachers of PE in Australian primary school: Rhetoric and actuality. *The ACHPER National Journal*, Winter, 14–19.

Vealey, R. (1988). Future directions in psychological skills training. *The Sport Psychologist*, *2*, 318–336.

Walsh, W. D., & Snyder, C. W. (1982). Young participants' perception of Australian football. *The Australian Journal of Sport Sciences*, Spring, 22–25.

Wankel, L., & Kreisel, P. (1985a). Methodological considerations in youth sport motivation research: A comparison of open-ended and paired comparison approaches. *Journal of Sport Psychology*, *7*, 65–74.

Wankel, L., & Kreisel, P. (1985b). Factors underlying enjoyment of youth sports: Sport and age group comparisons. *Journal of Sport Psychology*, *7*, 51–64.

Wankel, L., & Sefton, J. (1989). A season-long investigation of fun in youth sports. *Journal of Sport and Exercise Psychology*, *11*, 355–366.

Watson, G. G. (1984). Intrinsic motivation and competitive anxiety in sport: Some guidelines for coaches and administrators. *The Australian Journal of Science and Medicine in Sport*, December, 14–20.

Webb, P., Moore, D., Gray, T., & Jessup, S. (1993). *Analysis and evaluation of primary physical education courses in tertiary institutions*. Paper presented at the 19th ACHPER National/International Biennial Conference, Darwin, 1993 and abstracted in the Conference Proceedings, p. 48.

Weinberg, R., Bruya, L., Longino J., & Jackson, A. (1988). Effect of goal proximity and specificity on endurance performance of primary-grade children. *Journal of Sport and Exercise Psychology*, *10*, 81–91.

Weinberg, R. S., & Williams, J. M. (1993). Integrating and implementing a psychological skills training program. In J. M. Williams (Ed.), *Applied sport psychology* (2nd ed.). Mountain View, CA: Mayfield.

Weiss, M. (1991). Psychological skill development in children and adolescents. *The Sport Psychologist, 5*, 335–354.

Weiss, M., & Bredemeier, B. (1983). Developmental sport psychology: A theoretical perspective for studying children in sport. *Journal of Sport Psychology, 5*, 216–230.

Weiss, M., & Gould, D. (Eds.). (1986). *Sport for children and youths.* Champaign, IL: Human Kinetics.

Weiss, M., Weise, D. M., & Klint, K. A. (1989). Head over heels with success: The relationship between self-efficacy and performance in competitive youth gymnastics. *Journal of Sport and Exercise Psychology, 11*, 444–451.

Williams, J. M. (1986). *Applied sport psychology: Personal growth and peak performance.* Palo Alto, CA: Mayfield.

Wooller, P. (1993). Personal communication.

Zhang, L., Ma, Q., Orlick, T., & Zitzelsberger, L. (1992). The effect of mental-imagery training on performance enhancement with 7–10 year-old children. *The Sport Psychologist, 6*, 230–241.

CHAPTER

22

GENDER AND SPORT

VICKI PLAISTED

Whether one looks at football players having a few beers with their mates after the game or netballers who put on their make-up before the televised match, it is clear that gender influences sport and exercise behaviour in pervasive ways. However, the concept of gender relations has been conspicuously absent from most sport psychology scholarship. Indeed, only a few years ago the title of this chapter would have been "women in sport", thus attesting to the fact that historically sport has been seen as a male preserve. It is therefore an enormous challenge for researchers and practitioners to treat gender as a complex, socially dynamic and multifaceted phenomenon which has a profound influence on both male and female sport and exercise behaviour.

Virtually all the research in this area has focused on how the sport and exercise performance and experience of women differs from that of men. The assumption underlying this approach is that the behaviour of men — specifically white, middle-class men — is the standard or norm against which all other behaviour is measured (Dewar & Horn, 1992). This is not surprising given that more than two-thirds of research from the larger discipline of psychology has been based on males and generalised to all humans (Wine, 1982). Recent critiques of the psychology research on gender (Hare-Mustin & Maracek, 1988) have pointed to the biases which occur when gender differences are exaggerated or maximised, as, for example, when only statistically significant differences are regarded as worthy of discussion and publication. This "alpha" bias pervades sport psychology as well as the sport sciences (Oglesby & Hill, 1993). The emphasis on individual differences obscures the similarities between men and women, despite the fact that we know that "within-sex variations on any psychological variable are much larger than the mean between-sex differences" (Eccles, 1987, p. 166).

It might be useful at this point to clarify the terms "sex", "gender" and "gender relations" by tracing their history. "Sex", as used in the psychology literature, traditionally referred to dichotomous distinctions between females and males based on physiological characteristics that are genetically determined (Hall, 1990). Some 25 years ago, authors began to use the term "gender" to designate the psychological, cultural and social dimensions of maleness and femaleness. The distinction, therefore, between sex and gender was meant to clarify the biological versus the cultural. However, there is now evidence to suggest that division between sex and gender is not so clear. "We really do not know where biology ends and culture starts" (Fasting, 1993, p. 1).

For example, the meaning of biological sex difference may vary according to the culture through which it is mediated (Eichler, 1980). Butler (1990) has posited that sex is not a totally objective, value-free binary phenomenon, but rather that each individual is a mosaic of male and female biological components. The gender verification tests given to all international athletes who wish to compete as females illustrate how what we once thought of as simple — the difference between male and female — is actually complex. These "sex tests" are sensitive to the presence of the Y chromosome. Individuals who have body builds and muscularities culturally defined as female have been disqualified from competition because their cell chromosome structure was XOY or XXY. As Hall (1985) writes: "As social beings we have constructed a world in which there are two, and only two, sexes. In fact, it is extremely difficult to imagine any other kind of world. We often forget that sexual dualism is socially constructed in such a way that it appears as an immutable fact" (p. 26).

Current theorising now recognises gender as a social construct, thus a new term, "gender relations", has emerged. The gender relations approach has largely been a product of feminist and post-modernist critiques of positivism. Dewar and Horn (1992) have recently suggested that these epistemological and methodological critiques be applied to all sport psychology research. They show how traditional research paradigms have not adequately represented the behavioural diversity that exists among sport and exercise participants (e.g., women, people of colour, gays, lesbians and working-class men). "Put simply, we need to abandon the belief that there is only one legitimate way of knowing in sport psychology and begin to understand that it is both possible and desirable to examine behaviour in different ways" (Dewar & Horn, 1992, p. 17).

A plethora of terms has been used to describe this process by which the social construction of gender occurs, including gendering, gender belief system and gender order. Connell (1987) utilises the latter and defines the construct as an "historically constructed pattern of power relations between men and women and definitions of masculinity and femininity" (pp. 98–99). From this perspective, gender is a powerful psychosocial mediator influencing the sport experiences of men and women in complex patterns. For example, there is evidence to show that sport is used to celebrate particular forms of masculinity (those that stress strength, speed and power) as natural rather than socially developed (e.g., Messner & Sabo, 1990). This will influence the manner in which participants respond to their sport and exercise experiences in ways that the individual differences approach fails to capture. The gender relations concept builds upon the difference data, but recognises that it is only one potential source of theorising and analysis (Oglesby & Hill, 1993).

The evolution of research in gender and sport has progressed from early individual sex differences research through to more current complex, social contextual and systems analysis approaches. This chapter will trace this development in five particular topic areas showing the limitations in the early work and pointing to promising future directions which may advance our knowledge of the implications for gender relations. The biologically based sex differences, social role and achievement motivation topic areas are representative of the scope of past research on sport psychology and gender, while aspects of sexuality and gender study and men are burgeoning areas likely to make a greater impact on gender relations scholarship in the future.

STATUS OF THE GENDERS IN SPORT

In order to understand the significance of the gender relations construct, the patterns of power relations that exist between men and women in Australian sport must be established. This is important because, as Darlison (1993) has pointed out, a broad-based feminist consciousness has not yet emerged in Australia. In her history of Australian women in sport, Stell (1991) notes that sportswomen have often lacked a political analysis of their own oppression. Sportsmen, on the other hand, are often the ones who have benefited from the institution of sport without an awareness of their own dominance, compared to men who have had less positive experiences (e.g., Aboriginal, gay, less competent participants). Research has found that some boys perceived sport as being owned by males and have problems in coming to terms with girls participating in "male" sports (Australian Sports Commission, 1991a). Similarly, a major survey of youth attitudes conducted by the Australian Sports Commission (ASC) showed that girls still perceive sport as a "boys'" game (Australian Sports Commission, 1991b). A cursory examination of the jargon used in sports and physical activity contributes to this situation in that language structures our experience of reality (e.g., Hare-Mustin & Marecek, 1985). Phrases like "sportsmanship", "on your man", "man to man defence", "man up" and "playing like a girl" or "an old woman", as well as the desirability of being a "tomboy" rather than a "sissy", may well serve to constrain women's sport and exercise experiences. Thus it may be difficult for some readers to acknowledge that men as a social group have more power over women than women have over men and that this is socially constructed, not biologically given (Hall, 1990).

For example, in 1992, reportage of women's sports occupied approximately 4.2% of total sports reportage and this reportage has increased by only 2.2% in 12 years. The situation is even more bleak with respect to television coverage. In 1988, coverage of women's sport occupied approximately 1.3% of the total sport time and this showed no improvement four years later on in 1992 (Stoddart, 1992). Female athletes experience fewer opportunities to compete, especially at the national and international levels. For instance, only 24% of the total number of events at the Olympic Games from 1948 to 1992 were available to women and women comprised only 21% of the total participants in Australian teams. Despite this, they have won 25 of the 64 gold medals (i.e., 39%) won by Australians (Australian Sports Commission, 1993). In 1992, women held 39% of Australian Institute of Sport (AIS) scholarships and they received 24% of the Sports Talent Encouragement Plan Grants (Australian Sports Commission, 1993).

Despite these disincentives, Australian women in the last 20 years have been world champions in netball, hockey, cricket, softball, lacrosse and waterpolo. They have won Wimbledon, the USA Open Golf Championships and the British Squash Championships. Stell's (1991) book is an enlightening history of successful, but largely unrecognised, Australian women athletes. It documents the attitude of prejudice towards female athletes including allegations through the ages that women are not physically or psychologically equipped to compete successfully in sports. As late as 1980, the International Olympic Committee (IOC) refused to allow women to compete in long-distance running events because it was believed that women could not endure the strain, despite the fact that they had been competing successfully in these events at other levels for years.

Even below the elite level, participation rates of males and females remain unequal. Among registered sports participants nationally, men outnumber women by more than three to one (Australian Sports Commission, 1992). At both primary and high school levels, there is a lower involvement by females than males in school and community organised sport (South Australian Sports Institute, 1992). A government inquiry into physical and sport education found a range of institutional and structural impediments confront girls in schools. These factors include more sports available to boys than girls; fewer female physical education teachers and coaches; teacher training programs not adequately preparing teachers to address gender issues; greater access to facilities, finances and scheduling for male sports; differences in learning opportunities between boys and girls; gender-based harassment; and emphasis on body shape and femininity (Senate Standing Committee on Environment, Recreation and the Arts, 1992).

Women are also vastly under-represented in administrative positions, particularly at the executive and senior management levels, and this restricts their influence in decision-making processes in sport. For example, in the ASC in 1992 100% of executive level staff were male and 83% of senior management and professionals were male. It is not until the middle management levels that women appear in larger numbers: 55% were male and 45% were female. Similarly, within the national sporting organisations (NSOs), males were over-represented with 90% as presidents, 82% as national executive directors, 78% as national coaching directors and 73% as national development officers. Similar male/female distributions exist within the Australian Olympic Committee, the Australian Commonwealth Games Association and the Confederation of Australian Sport, although in all these organisations there was a general trend toward greater female representation in 1992 compared to 1988 levels (Australian Sports Commission, 1993).

An Australian study by McKay (1992) explored the reasons why there is such a significant gender difference in Australian sports administration. In this qualitative research, middle and senior managers were interviewed about the perceived barriers to women in sports administration. Both men and women perceived similar internal barriers, mostly relating to insufficient experience. However, most women and very few men believed that there was an array of external barriers that disheartened even the most determined and talented female administrators. Major external obstacles included masculine recruitment biases; old boys' networks; myths and stereotypes about gender abilities; sexual harassment and physical intimidation; the masculine ambience of sport; and feelings of exclusion and isolation in organisations.

In coaching, too, women are significantly under-represented, especially at the higher levels of accreditation. In 1992, 10% of all Level 3 accredited coaches, 15% of national team coaches and 9% of AIS coaches were women (Australian Sports Commission, 1993). These levels are similar to those in 1988 and there is some fear that Australia will follow North American trends which showed the numbers and percentages of female coaches dropping during the 1980s (e.g., Acosta & Carpenter, 1990). Recent Australian research has attempted to explore reasons for this dearth of female coaches by comparing patterns of involvement and withdrawal of male and female coaches in netball, hockey and basketball (Reynolds, Otago, Plaisted, & Randell, 1992). Findings included that having family members and close friends in the same sport and perceiving that personal coaching and playing records were successful were important factors in preventing female coaches from dropping out.

Knoppers (1992) has explained the male dominance and sex segregation which exists in coaching using a gender relations approach. She argues that coaching is gendered through the meanings assigned to it and these meanings are strongly associated with hegemonic masculinity. However, Staurowsky (1990) surveyed women who coach boys and found that, in these interactions, patriarchal notions of maleness as being the key prerequisite for coaching and leadership, were challenged. Her findings showed that boys did not reject women coaches, and they demonstrated little difficulty in accepting women as leaders, although male coaches and officials and parents were initially resistant. Research needs to clarify whether women are adopting primarily male models in their coaching.

Two recent articles in *The Sport Psychologist* have described the issues which arise from cross-sex sport psychology consulting (Henschen, 1991; Yambor & Connelly, 1991). Yambor and Connelly (1991) acknowledge that it is a disadvantage being a female consultant of male athletes in sport, although not an insurmountable one: "... it may in some instances be harder for a woman to be considered competent, accepted, trustworthy or effective in these settings" (p. 311). Although not analysed in this way, there is, in the female consultant article, an inference of sport being a male preserve, and this is also evident from a reading of the male consultant's description of cross-sex sport psychology practice (Henschen, 1991). Henschen (1991) writes that young girls "... can tug at the heart-strings of a mature male if he is not vigilant about his professional responsibilities" (p. 316). Here, masculinity is linked with sexuality in a way which is considered normal. It is unlikely that the sexuality link would emerge in female sport psychologists' descriptions of issues that arise from consulting young boys. The article seems to indirectly suggest evidence of hegemonic masculinity in applied sport psychology.

Although these statistics and research findings go some way in illuminating the unequal relationships among males and females in sport and exercise, it is often difficult to accept these messages. According to a gender relations approach, this is because hegemony ensures that the dominant group (in sport this typically means white, heterosexual, middle-class males) has more power and has the ability to make its meanings or interpretations of social phenomena "stick" (Knoppers, 1992). In short, we have been socialised to see the current situation relating to gender and sport as normal, even natural. The gender relations approach does not place its main focus on these individual differences between and amongst males and females, instead it attempts to show how these socially constructed power relations impact on the sport and exercise experiences of all participants — all types of men and all types of women — in dramatic ways. The outcome of the difference approach has been that the cultural norms for masculinity have become the norms for humans. Thus, "... by not including analysis of power relations between women and men, psychological analysis may easily end up by repeating cultural interpretations" (Fasting, 1993, p. 5).

BIOLOGICALLY BASED SEX DIFFERENCES

As mentioned, most of the early work in this context area assumed dichotomous performance and psychological differences that stemmed from biological male and female differences. As we shall see, this sex differences approach is comparative, normative and static in that it fails to consider the multidimensional influences on gender-related behaviour.

PERFORMANCE

Studies in exercise physiology have long shown that sex differences in performance exist. Among Western adults, for example, men are around 50% stronger in most muscle groups than women (McArdle, Katch, & Katch, 1981). While we know that these sex-related differences exist, we do not know to what extent these differences are due to physiological factors and to what extent they are due to social or cultural factors. For example, the average woman has not been encouraged to participate in activities that would develop the potential in her muscles in the same way men are encouraged. Indeed from birth, women have been socialised in activities and roles that differ from those of men. Douglas and Miller's (1977) survey on research in strength differences between males and females concludes "that the social influences [on strength] are so great that inherent physiological differences in strength cannot yet be estimated" (p. 172). Thus, the physical performance differences between men and women have been hopelessly confounded with the differences in physical activity experience and expectations influenced by sex role stereotypes.

Australian researcher Ken Dyer (1976) has compared the difference between male and female athletic performance in different countries. In track events, he found that there was a large disparity between countries in the percentage of difference between male and female performance. That is, in some countries the difference was large and in others the difference was small. He concluded that social, psychological and cultural factors must account for the relative parity or disparity of female and male track performance. Current research shows that athletic training offers women the same physiological advantages it provides for men, although not always via the same biological mechanisms or to the same degree. Improved performances in athletic records for women attest to the fact that many of the differences in male and female performances that were considered "natural" just a few years ago were actually the result of lack of physical training for women (Dyer, 1982).

The socialisation process not only confounds studies on sex differences in performance to the extent that we cannot accurately measure them, but it also makes a judgement about these differences. Due to the patriarchal bias of sociocultural institutions, the result is often the arbitrary assignment of male advantage valued over female advantage (Duquin, 1978). For example, attention to strength is in discrete areas. We tend not to consider strength in terms of susceptibility to disease, child mortality or life expectancy, where women have the advantage (Butt, 1987).

Oglesby and Hill (1993) have recently argued that the tendency to conceptualise gender as two independent sets, one for males and one for females, has coloured past research on gender and sport and has limited the sporting experience of both males and females. They contend that a union-of-sets conceptualisation of gender more accurately reflects the relationship between males and females in every culture, "since all humans share, in varying proportions, the same male and female sex hormones, and [since] overlapping distributions exist for virtually all human characteristics, both physical and psychological" (Oglesby & Hill, 1993, p. 719). Certainly, this emphasis on similarities puts performances like Lisa Martin's time in the 1990 Commonwealth Games marathon, where she ran faster than Australia's third-fastest male marathoner, and Bev Francis's win in a men's middleweight weightlifting competition, where she set a woman's world record, into some perspective.

INTELLECTUAL ACCOMPLISHMENTS

This emphasis on the common elements in both males and females is also consistent with Maccoby and Jacklin's (1974) classic survey on the vast existing literature on psychological sex differences. Their main finding was that few conclusions concerning sex differences could be drawn from the diverse literature on this topic. They did note, however, that the literature suggested the possibility of sex differences in four specific areas: maths ability, visual–spatial ability, verbal ability and aggressive behaviour. Nevertheless, subsequent work casts doubt on even these differences. Meta-analyses consistently indicate that less than 5% of the behavioural variance in these areas is accounted for by sex. Moreover, sex differences are inconsistent, and interactions are common (e.g., Eagley, 1987; Hyde & Linn, 1986). In general, then, and consistent with Oglesby and Hill's (1993) reconceptualisation, overlap and similarities are much more apparent than differences when comparing males and females.

Clearly the main problem with research that has utilised a sex difference approach is that it assumes an underlying, unidimensional cause (i.e., biology). It has been shown both with performance and intelligence research that biological, psychological, social and cultural factors influence gender-related behaviour in complex interactive and dynamic ways. As Jacklin (1989) has pointed out, gender changes as society changes.

SOCIAL ROLE

The focus on individual differences evident in the biologically based sex differences research was carried through to subsequent research on social roles. In this line of work, socialisation practices were posited as the singular rationale for the position of women in sport. Socialisation is the process through which individuals are taught how to behave and what is expected of them, and this process begins at birth. Two of the most influential topics of the 1970s and early 1980s were role conflict and gender role orientations (masculinity, femininity and androgyny). Both of these traditions had an impact on our understanding of the relationship between women and men and sport that is still felt today.

ROLE CONFLICT

Role conflict research in this early period represented one of the first attempts to find a "theory" that would explain why women are less involved in sport than men. Sex roles identify certain activities and qualities as being appropriate for males and/or females. Qualities such as passivity, submissiveness, grace and beauty became associated with and define the less powerful group, usually females, while strength, toughness, aggressiveness and achievement became associated with and define the empowered group, usually males (Oglesby & Hill, 1993). Sport activities themselves are categorised with respect to the presumed gender appropriateness of the activity. Sports which are considered most "masculine" include team sports, boxing and power lifting while those which are considered most "feminine" are those such as gymnastics, ballet and other dance. Role conflict occurs when individuals choose to engage in activities or express qualities that have been reserved for the opposite sex.

A number of sport theorists suggested that women could experience role conflict when they choose to engage in sport, as do men who choose to become accomplished in activities such as dance (Duquin, 1978; Felshin, 1974; Harris, 1979). Theorists, notably Del Rey (1978), speculated that women in sport feel this role conflict profoundly as evidenced in their tendency to over-emphasise femininity in their appearance, for example, by wearing make-up, jewellery and pastel colours, and through exaggeration of their heterosexuality.

Research proceeded to look for evidence of role conflict and its relationship to masculine and feminine personality traits and masculine and feminine sports. Indeed, data have accrued to suggest that athleticism and femininity are not perceived as consistent with one another. Studies conducted with pre-adolescent children (Selby & Lewko, 1976), high school male and female athletes and non-athletes (Sheriff, 1971) and college-age athletes and non-athletes (Fisher, Genovese, Morris, & Morris, 1977; Freeman, 1988; Snyder & Spreitzer, 1976; Watson, 1987) have demonstrated that negative stereotypes of female athletes exist. Moreover, these stereotypes vary with the gender appropriateness of the activity. For example, Kane (1988), in work on the status system of adolescents in high school, found that while being an athlete was the greatest source of status attainment for the male, it was the least valued role for the female adolescent. More importantly she found that female athletes who participated in team sports had significantly less status with their peers (both male and female) than their female counterparts who participated in tennis and golf.

However, instead of focusing on the prevalence of stereotyping and the social problems which elicited stereotypes (e.g., prejudice, power relations between men and women) (Birrell, 1988; Hall, 1988), research focused on the female athlete's apparent struggles with role conflict. Sage and Loudermilk (1979) were among the first to empirically assess the nature and degree of role conflict among female athletes. Their questionnaire distinguished between two types of conflict — perceived role conflict among female athletes in general and personally experienced conflict — and this methodological parameter was used in the subsequent research. Sage and Loudermilk (1979) found that only 20% of their college athlete sample perceived role conflict and only 20% experienced role conflict to a great or very great extent. A review of the subsequent literature reveals a similar picture of relatively low levels of perceived and experienced role conflict amongst female athletes including power lifters (e.g., Allison & Butler, 1984; Jackson & Marsh, 1986) and high school athletes (e.g., Anthrop & Allison, 1983; Desertrain & Weiss, 1988).

In an article entitled "Role conflict and the female athlete: Preoccupations with little grounding", Allison (1991) summarises the criticisms of this line of research which centre on the way in which researchers have blindly accepted the concept of role conflict without questioning the nature of the construct. Perhaps it is because of a lack of willingness to give up traditional images of the female athlete that researchers/scholars have "clung on to a phenomenon which the athletes suggest is not a problem. Moreover, by clinging to the construct, researchers reinforce and continually re-establish the very stereotypes many wish to eradicate" (Allison, 1991, p. 56). As with the sex differences approach, the role conflict research simplifies or masks the very complex nature of gender and sport behaviour. There are so many roles which are "played" simultaneously, it is impossible to isolate which of the multiple roles have an impact on an individual. Hall (1981), for instance, questions whether or not two roles, such as athlete and woman, can be separated in the mind of the athlete.

GENDER ROLE ORIENTATIONS

Reinforcement of stereotypes and oversimplification are also evident in the gender role orientation research. Nevertheless, this type of research approach has been the basis from which most of the existing sport psychology research on gender has developed.

Traditionally, the concepts of masculinity and femininity in early personality scales were conceived as bipolar so that if men are high in a particular trait, such as independence, women are the direct opposite, i.e., dependent. Bem (1974, 1978), however, theorised that masculinity and femininity are separate clusters of desirable personality characteristics, and that there is no reason why males should possess only masculine characteristics or females only feminine characteristics. Androgyny refers to the combination in one individual of both feminine and masculine behavioural qualities. Indeed, Bem (1974, 1978) argues that androgynous people are more flexible, adaptable and generally better off. She developed an inventory, the Bem Sex Role Inventory (BSRI), to measure individual differences in gender role orientation, which included stereotypically feminine items (e.g., affectionate, sensitive to others' needs) and stereotypically masculine items (e.g., independent, willing to take risks).

Around the same time, Spence and Helmreich (1978) developed their own gender role orientation inventory, the Personality Attributes Questionnaire (PAQ). This similarly assesses separate clusters of desirable feminine and masculine characteristics, although the authors now suggest that the personality clusters are more appropriately labelled instrumental (masculine) and expressive (feminine).

Numerous studies used the BSRI and the PAQ to investigate the gender role orientation of sport participants. Generally, the results of these studies suggest that athletes and sport/recreation participants are more likely to be masculine or androgynous than are non-participants (e.g., Colker & Widom, 1980; Del Rey & Sheppard, 1981; Helmreich & Spence, 1977; Henderson, Stalnaker, & Taylor, 1988; Myers & Lips, 1978; Wrisberg, Draper, & Everett, 1988). For example, Jackson and Marsh (1986), as part of the study cited previously, used a scale based on the BSRI and the PAQ to assess the sex role identification of Australian female power lifters and high school students (both athletes and non-athletes). They found that the female athletes, both those of high school age and those involved in power lifting, were more masculine than the non-athlete group and that feminine scores for all three groups were higher than the corresponding masculine scores. They concluded that the results provide support for the androgyny construct, that is, female athletes can be more masculine without being less feminine.

As with the role conflict research, this line of research has been widely criticised because it reifies sex roles and perpetuates gender stereotypes, thus reproducing the gender relations which it purports only to describe or measure. Further, Birrell (1983) has argued that while the theory purports to ascribe equal value to traditional male and female behaviour patterns, in practice androgyny subverts female qualities to male qualities.

There are not just conceptual drawbacks, but methodological inadequacies as well. Firstly, while the scales on the BSRI and the PAQ seem to measure self-assertion and nurturance and are good predictors of specific assertive and nurturant behaviours respectively, they show a weak relationship to actual gender role behaviours associated with the broader concepts of masculinity and femininity (Deaux, 1985). Secondly, the research suggests that female athletes possess more masculine/instrumental personality characteristics than female non-athletes. However, this is not particularly enlightening given that sport demands instrumental, assertive behaviour. Both inventories include "competitive" as one of the masculine/instrumental items. Thus, the higher scores of female athletes probably reflect an overlap with competitiveness, and this can be measured more directly using other scales (e.g., Gill & Deeter, 1988). Overall, trait research isolates the individual from any social context by assuming that internal, stable traits control behaviour. Sport personality theorists have been aware for some time that personality characteristics are typically weak predictors of behaviour, but we have not progressed beyond this approach with gender role behaviour. For example, individuals may have expressive or feminine dispositions but behave in instrumental ways because of the specific situation in which they find themselves.

In summary, then, the sport psychology scholarship on gender role orientation has all the limitations of early personality research along with potentially destructive gender stereotypes and biases. Yet, as Fasting (1993) points out, "people still use these tests uncritically, and get their articles published in sport psychology journals" (p. 10).

GENDER BELIEF SYSTEMS

More recent attempts to understand interactions between social roles, gender and sport have moved away from individual difference approaches characterised by univariate relationships and simple research designs, as these are clearly inadequate. What is beginning to emerge is a recognition that gender belief systems are influenced by and influence interacting variables in complex and dynamic ways. Gender is beginning to be recognised as a social category and is likely to be best understood when the focus is on specific contexts. There is a hint of recognition that the meanings of gender identity are constructed socially and individually and that these become mechanisms by which we organise our perceptions and experiences.

Even Bem, who spurred so much of the research on gender role orientation, has begun to emphasise social stereotypes and social processes (Bem 1981, 1983). In this gender schema theory, persons who are sex-typed (high masculine males and high-feminine females) perceive situations in gender stereotyped ways and are labelled gender-schematic, whereas non-sex-typed persons are gender-aschematic in that they tend to avoid seeing situations in gender terms and using stereotypes on themselves or others. Research has shown that gender-schematic people are more likely to classify sports as gender-appropriate and to restrict their participation to what they perceive as gender-appropriate sport and exercise activities than gender-aschematic individuals (Csizma, Wittig, & Schurr, 1988; Matteo, 1986, 1988). Interestingly, there is evidence outside of sport to suggest that gender-schematic people indicate that sex should not influence their attitudes and behaviours, even though they see the world in gendered terms and behave in line with those perceptions (Frable, 1989). However, the work still relies on the BSRI measure and an individual difference classification and is, therefore, still subject to many of the criticisms that marked the earlier work on gender role orientation.

Research by Deaux (1984; Deaux & Kite, 1987; Deaux & Lewis, 1984) on gender belief systems focuses not only on the gender constructs of the individual, but also on the gender beliefs of others and the gender context of the situation. Gender stereotypes are posited as having multiple components, that is, we hold gender stereotypes or gender beliefs about role behaviours, occupations, physical appearance, sexuality and traits. Deaux (1984) suggests that these multiple components are interrelated and that the relationships and implications for gender-related behaviour may vary with the social context. For example, Deaux and Lewis (1984) found that people weigh physical appearance heavily and infer other gender-related traits and behaviours (e.g., personality, sexuality) from physical characteristics. The centrality of physicality in the gender stereotyping of sports has also been shown (Kane & Snyder, 1989).

A more complex influence on the formation and consequences of gender stereotypes is evidenced in research which builds on the general finding that there is a gender bias in the evaluation of male and female performance and achievement. For instance, a series of studies on male and female attitudes toward hypothetical male and female coaches (Parkhouse & Williams, 1986; Weinberg, Reveles, & Jackson, 1984; Williams & Parkhouse, 1988) found a bias favouring male coaches. However, Williams and Parkhouse (1988) reported that female basketball players who were coached by a successful female did not exhibit the male bias when rating hypothetical male coaches but actually exhibited a female bias. This work is only beginning and clearly we have a long way to go before we fully understand the detail and dynamic complexity of gender belief systems.

In summary, although we know that actual differences between males and females on psychological and behavioural measures are small and inconsistent, we maintain our beliefs in gender differences. Often we may not consciously recognise the influence of gender stereotypes in ourselves or others, yet these gender belief systems are likely to restrict both males and females from fulfilling their potential. As Oglesby and Hill (1993) write, rigid gender role socialisation may inhibit growth in order to promote social mandated power distribution. If we only visualise role-appropriate behaviours, then we will never actualise other unapproved, but potentially gratifying, behaviours. It is not possible to move beyond the influence of gender stereotypes, unless we become fully conscious of their existence in ourselves and others and realise that their meanings are socially invented. Awareness is, in and of itself, curative.

ACHIEVEMENT

It has been shown how research relating to gender and social roles in sport has progressed from early individual difference research through to more complex, multifaceted and social approaches. A similar evolution is evident in the achievement area, which represents one way of understanding motivation, specifically by exploring what factors influence individuals when they decide to enter competitive situations and to excel in these situations.

ACHIEVEMENT ORIENTATIONS

Early achievement research noted that women did not respond to achievement instructions as did men (McClelland, Atkinson, Clark, & Lowell, 1953). However, gender differences were not pursued, and the theories and findings on achievement motivation became theories and findings on men's motivation to achieve.

One of the first researchers to focus on the role of gender in achievement behaviour was Horner (1972) who proposed a fear of success (FOS) factor to explain women's scarcity in sport. In this individual difference approach, Horner suggested that success has negative consequences for women because success requires competitive, achievement behaviours that conflict with traditional feminine images. However, the research contains serious flaws. First, FOS is not found predominantly in women, and therefore is not significantly related to gender (e.g., reviews by Condry & Dryer, 1976; Zuckerman & Wheeler, 1975). Secondly, the inventory does not measure a stable and enduring personality disposition (e.g., review by Tresemer, 1974). Finally, it has been argued that the approach, like most of the individual difference approaches relating to gender, falsely implies that women's lower rates of participation are their own fault (Birrell, 1988).

As with the FOS motive and measure, more recent research on sport achievement has failed to endorse a unique gender-related personality construct. Instead, gender may play a role in specific aspects of achievement behaviour such as the emphasis an individual places on social comparison and winning in sport. McNally and Orlick (1975) introduced a cooperative broomball game to urban North American children and found that the girls were more receptive than the boys. Male Anglo children were the most win-oriented and placed the most emphasis on athletic ability. In a similar vein, Gill (1988), using a general, as well as a multidimensional sport-specific measure of achievement orientation, found that males consistently scored higher than females on sport competitiveness and win orientation. However, females were just as high as males, and sometimes higher, on sport goal orientation and on all general achievement scores except competitiveness. In sum, there is some evidence to suggest a gender influence on competitive sport behaviours. However, searching for a unique gender-related personality construct as an explanation does not seem particularly fruitful, as was previously argued in terms of the gender role orientation work. Most investigators are now looking beyond trait approaches to consider perceptions and broader socialisation and societal influences on achievement behaviour.

ACHIEVEMENT PERCEPTIONS

Most cognitive approaches to motivation focus on expectations for success. Although popular theories vary in specific constructs (e.g., self-efficacy, perceived ability, confidence) and proposed relationships, the vast majority of them highlight expectations as key predictors of behaviour. Research consistently indicates that expectations are good predictors of achievement behaviour and performance (e.g., Bandura, 1977, 1986; Feltz, 1988; Roberts, 1984). Further, researchers have asserted that females tend to demonstrate lower expectations of success than males in achievement situations (e.g., Sherman & Fennema, 1977).

However, gender differences in expectations are not completely consistent and are likely to vary with the situation or context. Lenney (1977) suggested that females may display less self-confidence than males in three situations: (a) when the task is perceived as masculine, (b) when the situation emphasises social comparison, and (c) when feedback or ability information is ambiguous. The achievement literature provides some evidence that these task characteristics mediate gender differences (e.g., Deaux & Farris, 1977; Lenney, Browning, & Mitchell, 1980).

Several studies specifically in motor performance have also been conducted to test these hypotheses (e.g., Corbin & Nix, 1979; Gill, Gross, Huddleston, & Shiflett, 1984; Stewart & Corbin, 1988). A recent meta-analysis conducted by Lirgg (1991) provided a synthesis of this line of research. Results showed that females displayed, on average, less confidence than males. However, the gender differences were not as large as expected, amounting to less than one-half of a standard deviation. In addition, Lirgg (1991) noted the possible biases in the research which may be contributing to the appearance of these gender differences, that is, ignoring feminine tasks and using sex-typing practices that may be questionable. Further, these are experimental studies in controlled settings so their relevance to the real world of sport and exercise is limited. As we have seen with other topic areas within this chapter, socialisation and social contextual factors must be considered.

There are a variety of current motivational theories but one model which incorporates both sociocultural factors and gender interactions throughout to explain achievement is that of Eccles (1984, 1987; Eccles, Adler, Futterman, Goff, Kaczala, Meece, & Midgley, 1983). Eccles recognises that expectations of success are key determinants of achievement choices and behaviours, as is the importance or value an individual attaches to a specific activity. Both of these factors are subjective interpretations and both are seen as developing over time from gender role socialisation, stereotyped expectations of others, sociocultural norms as well as individual characteristics and experiences. Thus, to understand gender and achievement, early socialisation and the social context are critical.

The model was first tested using academic achievement, although Eccles and Harold (1991) have shown that the model holds for sport equally well. In this research, both adolescents and primary school children were administered measures over time. With respect to gender differences with adolescents, it was found that boys, more than girls, saw value in sport and perceived their ability as higher, and that these gender differences were stronger than those for expectations and value in English and maths. It was shown, through path analysis, that the gender difference in free time spent on sport was mediated by gender differences in adolescents' ability self-concepts and in the value they attach to sport competence.

These researchers found similar gender differences on expectations of success and perceived sport value in the younger children, and that this was evident by the end of grade one. Further, although girls actually scored only 2% lower than boys on a battery of motor skill tests, they rated their skills as 14% lower than the boys. A number of sociocultural and socialisation factors were found to contribute to these gender differences. For instance, teachers rated boys' sport ability higher than girls' sport ability; sport was rated as much more sex-typed than maths or reading and these ratings correlated with children's self-confidence; and boys felt that it was more important to their parents that they did well in sports than did girls. Clearly, both Eccles's theoretical model and empirical data suggest that sociocultural factors make a substantial contribution to gender differences in achievement in sport. Although much more research is needed in the achievement area, Eccles's work is significant in that it goes some way in dispelling the notion that "natural" aptitude accounts for the gender differences in achievement in sport and instead points to broader social experience factors, which are potentially modifiable.

Certainly Eccles's work indicates that social norms do not work towards encouraging females into high levels of academic achievement. One wonders then what does motivate those girls and women who do persist in athletic endeavours? Oglesby and Hill (1993) have posited that it is significant relationships in the sport setting which motivate female athletes and influence their performances. Certainly there is much written in the general psychological literature about the importance of relationships to women in terms of their general psychological development (e.g., Surrey, 1991); ways of knowing (e.g., Belenky, Clinchy, Goldberger, & Tarule, 1986); moral development (e.g., Gilligan, 1982); and conversational style (e.g., Tannen, 1990), and it is likely that "relationship" infuses a female's sporting life as well.

This idea is consistent with recent qualitative research which explored elite female netballers' perceptions of confidence (Plaisted, 1993). By inductively content analysing a series of interviews, Plaisted showed how participants outlined the meaning of confidence to them as well as factors which they perceived as enhancing and inhibiting their confidence. The most frequently endorsed conceptualisation of confidence was communication skills, i.e., relating effectively to others, an idea which does not feature in other sport achievement research. The most common factors perceived as enhancing confidence also related to relationships, namely positive coaching and team cohesion, while negative coaching and lack of team cohesion were the first and third most common themes endorsed by the netballers as inhibiting their confidence.

Traditionally, sport has been seen as an achievement arena and this assumption has remained unquestioned. Perhaps there is a need to examine the way in which achievement and relationship become fused in sport to influence the performance of both males and females alike. As we have seen in the fear of success and androgyny line of work, constructs which start out being identified among women typically have predictive value among men as well. As Oglesby and Hill (1993) note, relationship and endeavour have been acknowledged as intimately intertwined in parent–child rearing, in the therapeutic model and in concepts of role modelling and mentoring, so sport and exercise is not likely to be the exception.

ATTRIBUTIONS

The topic area of attribution provides another example of the way in which research has progressed through to more complex, contextual and systems analysis approaches. Social role stereotyping initially provided an explanation for male/female differences in attribution. Studies done in the late 1960s and early 1970s indicated that males tend to make internal attributions for positive performance outcomes (this was referred to as a self-appreciating bias) while females tend to adopt external attributions for success and internal attributions for failure (a self-depreciating bias) (e.g., Bar-Tal & Frieze, 1976; Deaux & Emswiller, 1974; Feather, 1969; McHugh, Duquin, & Frieze, 1978). The underlying rationale was that females explain their successes by looking to luck or other external factors because they internalise societal norms which tell them that females are unsuited to success in sport and have limited potential (Neal & Tutko, 1975). Males, it was thought, have their ego invested in sport and other achievement areas and, thus, adopt a self-enhancing bias.

Attribution research in the 1980s became more sophisticated and moved beyond male/female individual difference explanations to incorporate dynamic interactions of individuals and perceptions in particular social contexts. It is now recognised that gender stereotypes have some role in influencing attributions (e.g., Deaux, 1984) but so too do a wide range of other variables including perceived ability (Roberts & Duda, 1984); sport confidence and competitive orientation (Vealey, 1988); recent performance (Valle & Frieze, 1976); social comparison (Darley & Goethals, 1980); gender schematic or aschematic orientation (Markus, Crane, Bernstein, & Siladi, 1982); and skill level (Vealey, 1988). Once again, it is not productive to see gender as a static independent variable when attempting to understand psychological phenomena.

ASPECTS OF SEXUALITY

Two topic areas that are only beginning to receive research attention in relation to the broad study of gender and sport are the relationship between body image and disordered eating, and sexual harassment. In order to stimulate research in the future, these areas will be briefly reviewed as they clearly have important psychosocial dimensions and are likely to influence the experiences of those involved in sport and exercise.

BODY IMAGE AND DISORDERED EATING

Recent research has indicated that Australian female adolescents report greater body image disturbances and dissatisfaction than males (Maude, Wertheim, Paxton, Gibbons, & Szmukler, 1993). Indeed, one Australian study found that 95% of female high school and university students want to be slimmer (Abraham, Mira, Beaumont, Sowerbutts, & Llewellyn-Jones, 1983). There is evidence that exercise can enhance a woman's self-esteem and body image and that active women are more positive about themselves and their bodies (e.g., Brown, Morrow, & Livingston, 1982; Penny & Rust, 1980; Prakasa-Rao & Overman, 1986; Snyder & Kivlin, 1975; Trujillo, 1983). However, the sociocultural stereotype of the female physique and desire for slenderness can have a deep effect even on the active woman and may counteract this and even cause body image distortion (Campbell, 1986).

For instance, Davis (1990) investigated the influence of exercise participation on the relationship between subjective and objective measures of body size and weight preoccupation. It was found that subjective assessments of body size, and not actual size (i.e., body mass index, BMI), influenced the degree to which regular exercising women were preoccupied with their weight and dissatisfied with their appearance. However, in non-exercising women, the relationship was reversed in that only BMI was significantly related to weight preoccupation. An Australian study of participants in recreational aerobics classes suggested that for some, participation may intensify body shape concern. Warrick and Tinning (1989) used naturalistic methods of inquiry and identified six types of participants. While participation in aerobics seemed to liberate some women from the pressures of body shape and weight concerns, the "compulsive", "cheated" and "resigned" groups saw their involvement as a reinforcement, or at least a constant reminder, of such values.

Tinning (1985) has noted that physical educators often condone a unidimensional cultural concept of physique acceptability, even though they are the very professionals who should be sensitive towards different body types and help everyone develop positive body images based on their natural physiques. Similarly, several feminist authors have noted that the fitness industry may detract from the way women feel about their bodies (e.g., Hall, 1985; Theberge, 1985).

Sport participants, in particular, seem to be excessively body and weight preoccupied. For instance, Davis (1992) found that a greater number of high-performance female athletes who were underweight by objective standards (i.e., BMI), wanted to lose weight and were frequently dieting compared to female non-athlete university students. Indeed, it has been suggested that athletes are a "high risk" group for developing eating disorders (e.g., Thompson, 1987) for a number of reasons. Some sports require certain weights to be maintained in order to participate, such as lightweight rowing, boxing and horse racing. In other sports, like running and swimming, low body fat is encouraged to increase performance. The aesthetic appeal of a lean figure is crucial in sports like gymnastics, diving, ballet and body building, if the athlete is to be competitive (Black & Held, 1991). Moreover, the athlete's performance, in which the body is central, provides much of the individual's sense of identity (Thompson, 1987). Given the current prevalence ratio of eating disorders of 10–12 women to one man (Black & Held, 1991), the most distinctive gender difference of all psychiatric disorders, it is likely that the female athlete will be particularly susceptible.

It is difficult to ascertain the prevalence of eating disorders and eating disorder symptoms due to inconsistencies in the way in which these conditions are defined and measured in the research. Anorexia nervosa and bulimia nervosa are typically diagnosed using the American Psychiatric Association's Diagnostic and Statistical Manual of Mental Disorders (DSM-III), but the revised version, DSM-III-R utilises more strict criteria to classify these disorders, making comparisons across studies difficult. Sundgot-Borgen (1993) utilised the more recent version in a study of 522 elite female athletes from 35 sports and found that a significantly higher number of athletes (18%) than non-athlete controls (5%) suffered from eating disorders, particularly athletes competing in sports in which leanness or a specific weight were considered important. This study also found evidence to suggest that when questionnaires alone are used to estimate the prevalence of eating disorders, as is common practice in the vast majority of studies, there is a significant under-reporting of eating disorders amongst athletes. The researcher suggests that surveys should be considered merely as a screening instrument for further investigation by personal interview and clinical evaluation.

Individuals with eating disorder symptoms, sometimes referred to as anorexia athletica (Pugliese, Lifshitz, Grad, Fort, & Marks-Katz, 1983), have serious eating problems but do not meet the psychiatric criteria for true eating disorders. These individuals have an intense fear of gaining weight even though they are underweight, often exercise intensely, and frequently report bingeing, self-induced vomiting, or the use of laxatives or diuretics. Rosen and Hough (1988) found that 62% of the female college gymnasts in their sample were using at least one form of pathogenic weight control. A study of 182 female collegiate athletes from a variety of sports indicated that 32% practised at least one pathogenic weight control behaviour (Rosen, McKeag, Hough, & Curley, 1986) and these included sports where extreme thinness is not the ideal somatotype (e.g., field hockey, volleyball, track and tennis). However, in the Sundgot-Borgen (1993) study cited previously, only 8.2% of athletes exhibited eating disorder symptoms.

The dramatic inconsistencies in these percentages are likely to be due to different data collection methods, different study populations (e.g., different sport groups and levels of performance) and differences in how frequently pathogenic weight control methods are practised to be classified as an eating disorder symptom case. Certainly it is clear, as Black and Held (1991) note, that there are far more athletes who engage in behaviours and attitudes and use weight loss methods that are unhealthy than there are athletes with true eating disorders. There is a need for more methodological clarity in this line of research and for data on prevalence rates using Australian athletic samples.

Of course, excessive concerns about weight and diet in athletes do not just develop because of competition pressures to minimise body fat to very low levels. Social pressures on females to conform to standards of slenderness are likely to play a role in athletes, as well as recreational exercise participants. Unhealthy family dynamics, peer and team mate modelling and acceptance, and pressure from coaches are also thought to be influential factors. With respect to the latter, it has been suggested that practices like conducting group weigh-ins and posting "fat lists" of offenders on notice-boards are likely to cause anxiety and shame (Lenskyj, 1992; Thompson, 1987). A study by Harris and Greco (1990) found that 56% of competitive female gymnasts felt pressure from their coaches to lose weight. Harris (1987) has written: "... many coaches are unmerciful with demands to attain an ideal weight for sport performance. Attitudes of 'I don't care how you get it off, just get it off!' create anxieties among athletes leading to poor eating habits and eating disorders" (p. 113). Personality characteristics also tend to be associated with eating pathologies. For instance, Davis (1992) in the study cited earlier, found that emotional reactivity (measured by the Neuroticism scale of the Eysenck Personality Inventory) was a significant predictor of weight and diet concerns amongst elite female athletes from a variety of sports.

A pattern of poor nutrition and inadequate calorie intake may lead to serious eating disorders which, for the female athlete, may also contribute to bone loss and menstrual irregularities. Drinkwater (1993) has termed eating disorders, osteoporosis and amenorrhoea "the female athlete triad". Although research on body image and disordered eating in athletes is still in its infancy, and the methodology somewhat crude, there is evidence to suggest that sport and exercise participation may intensify body image concerns and increase the risk that individuals will develop eating disorder symptoms. Girls and women in sport and exercise appear to be particularly susceptible to these problems, although in much of the research, male athletes have not been studied. Future research should target both male and female athletes and should utilise a gender relations approach in understanding the issue.

SEXUAL HARASSMENT

The growing body of literature on eating disorders among female athletes has heightened awareness of a broader issue affecting athletes, that of sexual harassment in sport. Sexual harassment in sport does not just occur in relation to diet and weight. It consists of any unwanted, unwelcome, unreciprocated and repeated sexual attention and involves an abuse of power. Although little has been documented about the level of harassment experienced by women and girls in sport and physical education, and certainly no Australian studies have been conducted, anecdotal reports indicate that it does occur. As Baker-Finch (1993) notes, given that aggression, dominance and exertion of power over others are emphasised in sport, and that sport has traditions of male domination, sport can be a fertile breeding ground for the demonstration of male power over women, especially given the high levels of trust involved in coach–athlete relationships. Sexual harassment in sport may range from common forms such as flicking dresses or bra straps, "dacking" and ridiculing physical competence and appearance, to threats of exclusion from the team by male coaches unless female athletes agree to sexual liaison.

Another form of sexual harassment is homophobia, or the irrational fear and/or intolerance of homosexuality. In sport, the norm of heterosexuality is so strong that: "... the sexual relationship between a male coach and his female athletes is often known and visible, while the sexual preference of competent, assertive, and strong-willed women is the subject of gossip and innuendo. In these organisations, visible heterosexuality, whether positive or negative, is implicitly condoned, while homosexuality or lesbianism, whether real or imagined, is explicitly condemned" (Hall, Cullen, & Slack, 1989, p. 41). Regardless of sexual preference, people who reject traditional sex roles in their sporting careers pose a threat to existing power relations between the sexes. For this reason, their successes are devalued: women are given labels such as "dykes", "tomboys" or "butch" and men are stigmatised as "fags", "poofs" or "fairies" (Griffin & Genasci, 1990; Lenskyj, 1991).

A recent article in *The Sport Psychologist* listed some of the possible ramifications of homophobia (Rotella & Murray, 1991). Parents, for instance, may discourage their child's participation in a sport due to a concern that involvement will influence their child's sexual preferences or that a homosexual coach will "hit upon" their child. Homosexuals may feel they don't belong on predominantly heterosexual teams, and certainly homophobia has been a factor in the recent growth of gay and lesbian teams in particular sports. Other studies have reported that lesbians are often the target of discriminatory hiring and firing practices (see Lenskyj, 1992) and anecdotal reports suggest that the Australian scene is no different. Clearly, homophobia needs to be discussed in sport and physical education settings and presented as simply another issue of discrimination (like racism and ageism) that must be overcome in order to maximise performance and increase the attractiveness and enjoyment of sport for everyone. As Griffin and Genasci (1990) note, we also need much more research relating to homophobia in physical education and sport.

Although in Australia the *Federal Sex Discrimination Act* 1984 outlaws sexual harassment in the workplace and in educational institutions, it does not specifically cover sport (Human Rights and Equal Opportunity Commission, 1992). Thus the Act could not aid Michelle Baumgartner when she complained of sexual harassment by team members at the 1990 Commonwealth Games in Auckland (Baker-Finch, 1993). However, sport is considered under some sections of the Act including employment, providing goods, services and facilities, and the activities of certain clubs (basically those that sell or supply liquor). The fact that few complaints relating to sport have been lodged since the Act was enacted nearly a decade ago, and that many of those who do complain do not proceed with the complaint (personal communication, Human Rights and Equal Opportunity Commission, 1993) is evidence of the anxiety associated with women receiving a fair go in Australian sport.

Interactions between men and women in sport and exercise are clearly mediated by sexuality. Lenskyj (1987) coherently demonstrates this in her provocative analysis of sexuality and gender in sport. Lenskyj (1987) emphasises the historical and sociocultural pressures towards compulsory heterosexuality that impact upon women's experiences in sport and exercise. This brief review points to the need for much more research to be conducted to explore the ways in which issues such as body image and sexual harassment are used to negotiate and construct power and to ultimately have a major impact on the experiences of men and women in sport and exercise.

GENDER STUDY AND MEN

If gender is best treated as a relational process, as current scholars of gender advocate, then it is critical to study the patterns and practices of men's involvement in sport. Feminist studies have focused almost exclusively on women in order to illuminate the experiences, thoughts and actions of the oppressed group. An irony of this focus is that the dominant groups are posited as the norm. "Only the working class are analysed within a class framework, only ethnic minorities appear to have racial and ethnic identities, and only women appear to be gendered beings" (Messner & Sabo, 1990, p. 13). A relatively small band of scholars/ researchers have begun to use the feminist scholarship on gender to analyse men and their special relationships to sport.

The publication of *Sport, men, and the gender order* (Messner & Sabo, 1990) brings together a number of important themes and analyses relating to the study of gender and men. The radical critics of traditional sport write of the parallels between the hegemonic masculine orientation and various psychosocial ills including militarism, authoritarianism and violence toward women. Sociologist Connell (1990) makes a contribution to the text by using the life history of an Australian champion iron man to illustrate the main patterns of hegemonic masculinity including the subordination of women, the marginalisation of gay men, and the connecting of masculinity to toughness and competitiveness. Connell (1990) highlights the cost of this life for the iron man. His world is centred on the care and maintenance of his body to the point where his social world is constricted, his cultural world impoverished and he is prey to the vagaries of commercialised sport with its superficial interest in him as a recognisable "personality", and only as long as he remains a champion.

Other work focuses on the potential the area has for liberating men as well as women. Messner and Sabo (1990) point out that existing gender arrangements entail various costs for men, including low life expectancy, emotional inexpressivity and relational problems. Forsey (1990), writing about the Australian male, notes that it is often only the "super-masculine" sports heroes, whose masculinity is unquestionable, who are permitted displays of physical affection or grief. Messner (1987) argues that "... since the sports world is an important arena that serves partly to socialise boys and young men to hierarchical, competitive, and aggressive values, it is also an important context within which to confront the need for a humanisation of men" (pp. 65–66).

Further, Connell (1987) has argued for much more detail and dynamic complexity in our understanding of the masculinity concept. Across different periods and societies there are many masculinities from the hegemonic to the marginalised and stigmatised (e.g., gay men, Aboriginal men, working-class men). From such a perspective it is clear that sex role stereotyping impoverishes men as well as women in that neither sex has a wide range of movement experiences — those that are energetic, powerful and exciting are typically distinct from those that are more expressive and sensuous where the body is used with delicacy and flexibility (Hargreaves, 1990). In his recent book, Messner (1992) shows, through analysis of qualitative interviews with former top-level male athletes, how masculinity is not a monolithic category. Clearly, there is a need for much more research on gender relations and men's behaviours and experiences in sport and exercise settings.

FUTURE DIRECTIONS

The field of gender relations is a controversial one. Strong emotions are involved and this is no more clearly evident than in the sport and exercise domain. Historically, it seems that we are approaching a turning point in the way we think about gender and in the way we relate to each other as men and women involved in sport and exercise. Feminist and postmodernist movements have helped us realise that there is the opportunity for a dramatic change in consciousness, but there are also strong forces acting to prevent such a transformation in gender relations. This section will first consider the possible future scenarios for women and men in sport. It will then suggest directions research might take to spur a change in consciousness about gender that is enriching, not just for all future sport and exercise participants, but for society at large as we enter the 21st century.

One scenario is the exaggeration of traditional male-dominated sport with its emphasis on elitism, ceremonial violence and a "winning is the only thing" philosophy. Here, women in sport try to emulate men and, in the process, take on individualistic and competitive attributes and values. Indeed, Bredemeier (1984) has noted that the greater inclusion of females in sport has not led to a greater valuing of expressive qualities in sport. She argues that as women's sport has received more government, media, professional and business attention, it has been co-opted by the androcentric sports establishment, and has been encouraged to adopt male standards. Certainly, it would be interesting to explore whether Australian female coaches, for instance, are adopting male models and values in their coaching.

A second scenario is that law or social pressure dictate that males and females participate in sport equally, but that this is a pretense and no substantial changes in sport structure occur. The McKay (1992) study on gender in Australian sports administration, cited previously, is an example. Despite the existence of equal opportunity in employment policy, the gender distribution has not changed dramatically and major external obstacles for women remain. The same argument can be used to describe the expansion of commercialised exercise and fitness programs targeted at women. Some feminists have argued that these programs, particularly the television and video versions, are directed to the development of sexual attractiveness and appeal, rather than the development of physical capacities. Thus "the feminization of the fitness movement represents, not the liberation of women in sport, but their continued oppression through the sexualization of physical activity" (Theberge, 1987, p. 389). Similarly, the increased coverage of netball on Australian television might be seen as a progressive step. However, netballers' marketability still seems dependent on short skirts, make-up and ribbons. It is, therefore, not surprising that the introduction of tight-fitting lycra outfits for some superleague teams coincided with this greater media attention. Are we really making significant advances in changing the sport structure, if we still feel the need to focus on sexuality and femininity of sportswomen, rather than their athletic prowess?

A third option is the "sport-for-women" model which developed from feminists' attempts to transform sport to better serve the needs of women and eliminate concepts of domination and submission. Birrell and Richter (1987) present an example of such a sport structure in their analysis of a number of softball teams participating in a summer softball league. The women participants made a conscious effort to overcome the flaws they felt were inherent in male-structured sport. What emerged was a form of softball which was process oriented, collective, inclusive, supportive and infused with an ethic of care. This kind of model is now promoted as "cooperative" sport for all, with its focus on cooperative games and participation by everyone.

A fourth possibility is what Oglesby and Hill (1993) coin transformed sport. This model emerged from the notion that the significance of expressive ("feminine") aspects to sports has been overlooked. Oglesby (1984, 1990) has presented a number of expressive qualities that are already an aspect of participation in sport and have positive application to the sport experience. For example, passivity is evident when athletes have to curtail training following an injury or when they use quieting or "psych down" techniques as part of their psychological skills training programs. Subordination is necessary to change old habits and strategies and to accept assigned roles, such as sitting on the bench, when they may have negative consequences for personal achievement. Dependency is often required when an athlete has to give up personal control to a team mate or coach. Nurturance involves athletes showing care and honouring the challenger by acknowledging that an athlete's level of play only increases as the challenge presented by opponents increases. Oglesby (1984, 1990) has argued that if the value of expressiveness was emphasised in sport, both male and female athletes would have an opportunity to develop their expressive qualities in an atmosphere that promotes the overall growth of the athlete.

Oglesby and Hill (1993) recognise that the pure form of either this expressive model or the male-dominated model of sport is toxic. A transformed sport experience is one in which each individual strives to find her or his own internal balance of each pole of the qualities once seen as the dichotomous polarities of traditional sexuality. For example, athletes must balance independence with dependence/interdependence, activity with passivity/quiet, and seeing the opponent as the challenge with love/care for the challenger, in their own unique way. It is suggested that research and informed professional practice in physical education and sport psychology should move towards establishing such a model, the goal of which is to dispense with the need for gender as a social structure. As Oglesby and Hill (1993) suggest, sport programs could be assessed — even graded — for the emotional/cognitive impact on participants, thus increasing accountability for the immense personal and national expenditures on sport. By stressing recreation, health, a full range of physical skills and sensuous pleasure in movement, we can create values in sport and exercise that enrich not just the lives of individuals, but the fabric of society.

So what are likely to be positive future directions for gender and sport scholarship? Firstly, there is a pressing need for an increase in knowledge about males and females and their patterns of relations in sport. Researchers must be careful to avoid treating the structure and categories of men and women as universal, so that the implication is not that *all* women suffer from the omnipresent enemy, *all* men. Hegemonic masculinity is not necessarily what powerful men are, but what sustains their power and what a large number of men are motivated to support. Women may feel oppressed by non-hegemonic masculinities and may even find the hegemonic pattern more familiar and manageable (Connell, 1987). Thus, what is required is a focus on the way in which sport and exercise practices that institutionalise men's dominance over women are maintained, with a recognition that there are multiple femininities and masculinities.

Secondly, we need to acquire a greater understanding of female and male experiences, feelings, wants, attitudes and needs towards sport and in sport from a wide variety of conceptual frameworks, methods and interpretive strategies. The majority of studies published on gender and sport are quantitative analyses conducted with the intent of uncovering generalisations which can be applied to a large defined population. Applied sport psychologists' goal, however, is very different in that they aim to assist the unique individual athlete in exploring individualistic, interpersonal and intrapersonal phenomena which impact on performance (Oglesby & Hill, 1993). This creates a gap between the academic researcher and the practitioner. Bridging the gap involves acknowledging that it is both possible and desirable to examine behaviour in different ways.

One way to do this is to begin to contextualise the knowledge that is produced. As Dewar and Horn (1992) explain, we must make explicit the positions that we are adopting in our work by locating ourselves and our own values in the research process, rather than searching for universal statements of fact about behaviour. For example, this chapter has illustrated the dangers of research which reinforces gender stereotypes. This occurs when researchers fail to self-reflect about the value system on which they base their work. We must utilise more inclusive research methodologies which capture the complexities and multifaceted nature of human behaviour, but we must be wary of assuming that these methods will produce a better grand theory. Some alternative ways of knowing will be complementary, others will be oppositional, but we must learn to accept the ambiguity. As Dewar and Horn (1992) write: "If we can begin to understand how these [alternative narratives] come together so as to reflect that behaviour is dynamic and develops within the structures and contexts that themselves give meaning to behaviour, we can then celebrate both the similarity and the diversity that characterizes behaviour in sport" (p. 22).

Clearly, the traditional approach of exploring psychological differences between females and males in sport is hopelessly confounded with policies and practices of female exclusion and limitation, to the point where it could be reasonably argued that the past data would be best "thrown away" (Oglesby & Hill, 1993). What can be done is to use a method developed from the interpretation of literary texts, called deconstruction, to supply new and alternative meanings to existing research. This method focuses on what is *not* said as well as what is said and utilises gaps, inconsistencies and contradictions in the text to reveal meanings present in the work, but outside our everyday level of awareness (Hare-Mustin & Maracek, 1988). So rather than having to re-invent the wheel, it is possible to deconstruct our existing knowledge base in gender and sport to analyse it from an entirely different perspective.

The development of theories in sport and exercise psychology based on research with a gender perspective has already raised questions about epistemology and methodology. Many social scientists are sceptical about the positivist tradition and have argued that positivism is not particularly enlightening, although this is not yet a popular view within sport psychology. Nevertheless, it is contradictory, or at least extremely difficult, to conduct research with a gender relations perspective based on positivistic conceptualisations and methods, primarily because of the tendency for this approach to reinforce cultural myths. Deconstruction provides one way out of the darkness. Another post-modernist movement, hinted at early in this chapter when discussing the jargon used in sport, is constructivism. This approach acknowledges that scientific knowledge cannot be disinterested or politically neutral. Rather than passively observing reality, we actively construct the meanings that frame and organise our perceptions and experience (Hare-Mustin & Maracek, 1988). Representations of reality are shared meanings that derive from language, history and culture. From a constructivist standpoint, for instance, the "real" nature of male and female cannot be determined. What can be explored is our representation of gender. Gender and sport scholarship would be advanced if there was much greater acknowledgement of this viewpoint.

Thirdly, researchers need to expand the range of issues and behaviours examined. The inclusion of the role of gender in influencing body image, disordered eating and sexual harrassment in this chapter represents an attempt to promote further research on aspects of sexuality as they relate to sport and exercise involvement. For example, there is a dearth of literature on the psychological impact of menstruation and pregnancy on female athletes' performances, despite the folklore surrounding the issue. More generally, there is a need to look beyond elite and male-dominated sport systems to examine gender issues in youth sport, disabled sport, exercise settings and physical education classes. Concerning the latter, there is some alarming research beginning to emerge concerning the way in which physical education teacher education perpetuates hegemonic masculinity and lacks reflectiveness and self-criticism (Bennett, 1991; Dewar, 1987, 1990; Macdonald, 1993; Leahy & Plaisted, 1993). Research on racial, ethnic and cultural influences is virtually non-existent in sport psychology and this is particularly important in Australia's multicultural society. Finally, our understanding of the role of gender in sport will be enhanced by multi-disciplinary approaches. As has been shown in this chapter, psychological insights can benefit from knowledge acquired in fields as diverse as physiology, sociology, philosophy and literature.

CONCLUSIONS

There exists today a popular belief that things have improved for women since "the old days" and that men and women now stand on an equal footing in society. This is clearly a myth in terms of the relations between men and women in Australian sport. As we have seen in this chapter, there remain vast differences between females and males in areas such as participation rates of athletes, status of coaches, sport administrators and sport psychologists and in media representations of sport and exercise. Moreover, the individual difference approach used in most of the early research relating to gender and sport merely served to perpetuate gender stereotypes and maintain these power differentials between women and men. Women in sport appeared as an exception, a deviation from the unquestioned assumption of sport as a male preserve. The difference approach also tended to ignore the fact that humans share overlapping distributions in virtually all psychological characteristics (and physical characteristics, for that matter) and that the similarities between males and females far outweigh the differences. This approach, with its focus on unidimensional causes also dramatically oversimplifies what is, quite clearly, highly complex, namely human behaviour and experiences in sport and exercise settings.

Fortunately, what is beginning to emerge in the research on gender and sport is a recognition that gender impacts upon male and female sport and exercise experiences in multifaceted, interactive and dynamic ways. It has been shown that doctrines of natural difference are fundamentally mistaken and that biological, psychological and sociocultural factors interact in complex and changing ways to influence men's and women's physical performance and intellectual accomplishments. Concepts such as role conflict, masculinity, femininity and androgyny, and fear of success have been shown to be far too simplistic and to reinforce traditional stereotypes in ways which place limits on human potentialities in sport and exercise. Research in the areas of gender belief systems, expectations for success and attributions have begun to move away from individual difference approaches characterised by univariate relationships and simple research designs, to more complex and systems analysis approaches which recognise the importance of contexts, as well as the role played by factors such as gender role socialisation, stereotyped expectations of others and sociocultural norms. Although psychosocial work in the area of body image, disordered eating and sexual harassment is still in its infancy, its development is likely to follow a similar course to the more established topic areas in the gender and sport theme.

Overall, however, sport and exercise psychology research on gender is, at present, limited and lacking in sophistication. There are many challenges for the future. Research must move beyond the persistent assumption that natural patterns — biology — cause sport and exercise behaviour, so that gender can be treated as a social relational process. As sport psychologists, we must explore alternative ways of understanding and explaining behaviour in sport and physical activity and treat these as credible and useful contributions to the field. We must be clear about contextualising our findings to ensure that our work does not invoke white middle-class male standards as universal and normative. We should expand our research to include varied activities and settings, as well as focusing on participants from diverse racial and cultural backgrounds. We must learn from, and share our understandings with, scholarship from other fields, particularly feminist and post-modernist contributions. Most importantly, we need to see sport as a cultural product, created by humans and therefore able to be reconstructed to allow for a humanisation of sport and exercise so it is more attractive, enjoyable and positive for us all.

SUMMARY

The vast majority of studies relating to gender and sport have utilised sex as the independent variable to explore how women differ from men on various dependent variables. Research on athletic performance and intellectual accomplishments was used to demonstrate the inherent dangers in assuming that there is one underlying cause, namely biology, of any differences observed. Such an approach tends to obscure the similarities between men and women and to set up men — specifically, white middle-class men — as being the standard against which all other behaviour is measured. These problems are also evident in the early work conducted on social roles and achievement motivation. Moreover, the use of role conflict, masculine and feminine role orientations and fear of success to help explain why women are less involved in sport than men, tends to reify these psychological constructs and perpetuate potentially destructive gender stereotypes.

More progressive research on gender belief systems, attributions and Eccles' (1984, 1987) theory and research on achievement has moved beyond individual sex difference explanations, to incorporate more multi-faceted, interactive and dynamic models. This more recent work places greater emphasis on the importance of particular social contexts to the understanding of human behaviour in sport and exercise settings. Current theories, particularly those working from feminist and post-modernist perspectives, advocate the need for research to treat gender as a relational process, if we are to truly come to terms with the social/historical nature of gender. This recommendation is also relevant to less established topic areas such as studies which examine the role gender plays in influencing body image, disordered eating, sexual harassment and men's sport and exercise behaviour.

Four future scenarios illustrating the impact gender can make on the structure of sport were presented, ranging from the exaggeration of traditional male-dominated sport to the promotion of a more balanced, transformed sport experience for men and women. The chapter posits main wishes for future gender scholarship including an increased usage of a gender relations approach, the incorporation of a wider variety of conceptual frameworks, methods and interpretive strategies in the research, and an expansion of the range of issues and behaviours examined within the field. The chapter concludes with a plea for both researchers and practitioners involved in sport psychology to work fiercely in sport and exercise for values and outcomes that enrich, not just the lives of participants, but society as a whole.

REFERENCES

Abraham, S. F., Mira, H., Beaumont, P. J. V., Sowerbutts, T. D., & Llewellyn-Jones, D. (1983). Eating behaviours among young women, *Medical Journal of Australia*, *2*, 225–228.

Acosta, R., & Carpenter, L. (1990). *Women in sport: A longitudinal study — Thirteen year update*. Unpublished manuscript, Brooklyn College, New York.

Allison, M. (1991). Role conflict and the female athlete: Preoccupations with little grounding. *Journal of Applied Sport Psychology*, *3*, 49–60.

Allison, M., & Butler, B. (1984). Role conflict and the elite female athlete: Empirical findings and conceptual dilemmas. *International Review for Sociology of Sport*, *19*, 157–167.

Anthrop, J., & Allison, M. (1983). Role conflict and the high school female athlete. *Research Quarterly*, *54*, 104–111.

Australian Sports Commission (1991a, April). *Sport for young Australians: Widening the gateways to participation.* A summary of market research findings. Canberra: Australian Sports Commission.

Australian Sports Commission (1991b, May). *Strategies for change: Active girls campaign.* A summary of market research findings. Canberra: Australian Sports Commission.

Australian Sports Commission (1992). *Australian sports directory.* Canberra: Australian Sports Commission.

Australian Sports Commission (1993). *Women and sport: Active info facts.* Canberra: Women and Sport Unit.

Baker-Finch, S. (1993). Don't stand for sexual harassment. *Active: Quarterly newsletter of the Women in Sport Unit, A.S.C.,* Winter, 6–7.

Bandura, A. (1977). Self-efficacy: Toward a unifying theory of behavioral change. *Psychological Review, 84,* 191–215.

Bandura, A. (1986). *Social foundations of thought and action.* Englewood Cliffs, NJ: Prentice-Hall.

Bar-Tal, D., & Frieze, I. (1976). Attribution of success and failure for actors and observers. *Journal of Research in Personality, 10,* 256–265.

Belenky, M. F., Clinchy, B. M., Goldberger, N. R., & Tarule, J. M. (1986). *Women's ways of knowing: The development of self, voice and mind.* New York: Basic Books.

Bem, S. L. (1974). The measurement of psychological androgyny. *Journal of Consulting and Clinical Psychology, 42,* 155–162.

Bem, S. L. (1978). Beyond androgyny: Some presumptuous prescriptions for a liberated sexual identity. In J. Sherman & F. Denmark (Eds.), *Psychology of women: Future directions for research* (pp. 1–23). New York: Psychological Dimensions.

Bem, S. L. (1981). Gender schema theory: A cognitive account of sex typing. *Psychological Review, 88,* 354–364.

Bem, S. L. (1983). Gender schema theory and its implications for child development: Raising gender-aschematic children in a gender-schematic society. *Signs: Journal of Women in Culture and Society, 8,* 598–616.

Bennett, R. S. (1991). Empowerment = Work over time: Can there be a feminist pedagogy in the sport sciences? *JOPERD,* August, 62–67, 75.

Birrell, S. (1983). The psychological dimensions of female athletic participation. In M. A. Boutilier & L. San Giovanni (Eds.), *The sporting woman* (pp. 49–92). Champaign, IL: Human Kinetics.

Birrell, S. (1988). Discourses on the gender/sport relationship: From women in sport to gender relations. In K. Pandolph (Ed.), *Exercise and sport science reviews* (Vol. 16) (pp. 459–502). New York: MacMillan.

Birrell, S., & Richter, D. M. (1987). Is a diamond forever? Feminist transformations of sport. *Women's Studies International Forum, 10,* 395–409.

Black, D. R., & Held, S. E. (1991). Eating disorders and athletes: Current issues and future research. In D. R. Black (Ed.), *Eating disorders among athletes: Theory, issues and research* (pp. 27–41). Reston, VA: American Alliance for Health, Physical Education, Recreation and Dance.

Bredemeier, B. J. (1984). Sport, gender and moral growth. In J. M. Silva & R. S. Weinberg (Eds.), *Psychological foundations of sport* (pp. 400–414). Champaign, IL: Human Kinetics.

Brown, E. Y., Morrow, J. R., & Livingston, S. M. (1982). Self-concept changes in women as a result of physical training. *Journal of Sport Psychology, 4,* 354–363.

Butler, J. (1990). *Gender trouble: Feminism and the subversion of identity.* New York: Routledge.

Butt, D. S. (1987). *Psychology of sport: The behavior, motivation, personality, and performance of athletes.* (2nd ed.). New York: Van Nostrand Reinhold.

Campbell, J. (1986). Anorexia nervosa: Body dissatisfaction in a high risk population, *CAHPER Journal,* July/August, 36–42.

Colker, R., & Widom, C. S. (1980). Correlates of female athletic participation. *Sex Roles, 6,* 47–53.

Condry, J., & Dryer, S. (1976). Fear of success: Attribution of cause to the victim. *Journal of Social Issues, 32,* 63–83.

Connell, R. W. (1987). *Gender and power: Society, the person and sexual politics.* Stanford, CA: Stanford University Press.

Connell, R. W. (1990). An iron man: The body and some contradictions of hegemonic masculinity. In M. Messner & D. Sabo (Eds.), *Sport, men and the gender order* (pp. 83–96). Champaign, IL: Human Kinetics.

Corbin, C., & Nix, C. (1979). Sex-typing of physical activities and success predictions of children before and after cross-sex competition. *Journal of Sport Psychology, 1,* 43–52.

Csizma, K. A., Wittig, A. F., & Schurr, K. T. (1988). Sport stereotypes and gender. *Journal of Sport and Exercise Psychology, 10,* 62–74.

Darley, J., & Goethals, G. (1980). People's analyses of the causes of ability linked performances. *Advances in Experimental Social Psychology, 13,* 2–37.

Darlison, L. (1993). *Women moving ahead in changing times.* Paper presented at the XIIth Congress International Association of Physical Education and Sport for Girls and Women, Melbourne.

Davis, C. (1990). Body image and weight preoccupation: A comparison between exercising and non-exercising women. *Appetite, 15,* 13–21.

Davis, C. (1992). Body image, dieting behaviours, and personality factors: A study of high-performance female athletes. *International Journal of Sport Psychology, 23,* 179–192.

Deaux, K. (1984). From individual differences to social categories: Analysis of a decade's research on gender. *American Psychologist, 39,* 105–116.

Deaux, K. (1985). Sex and gender. *Annual Review of Psychology, 36,* 49–81.

Deaux, K., & Emswiller, T. (1974). Explanation for successful performance on sex-linked tasks: What is skill for the male is luck for the female. *Journal of Personality and Social Psychology, 29,* 80–95.

Deaux, K., & Farris, E. (1977). Attributing causes for one's own performance: The effects of sex, norms and outcome. *Journal of Research in Personality, 11,* 59–72.

Deaux, K., & Kite, M. E. (1987). Thinking about gender. In B. B. Hess & M. M. Ferree (Eds.), *Analyzing gender* (pp. 92–117). Beverly Hills, CA: Sage.

Deaux, K., & Lewis, L. L. (1984). The structure of gender stereotypes: Interrelationships among components and gender label. *Journal of Personality and Social Psychology, 46,* 991–1004.

Del Rey, P. (1978). The apologetic and women in sport. In C. A. Oglesby (Ed.), *Women and sport: From myth to reality* (pp. 107–111). Philadelphia, MS: Lea & Febiger.

Del Rey, P., & Sheppard, S. (1981). Relationship of psychological androgyny in female athletes to self-esteem. *International Journal of Sport Psychology, 12,* 165–175.

Desertrain, G., & Weiss, M. (1988). Being female and athletic: A course for conflict? *Sex Roles, 18,* 567–582.

Dewar, A. (1987). The social construction of gender in Physical Education. *Women's Studies International Forum, 10,* 453–465.

Dewar, A. (1990). Oppression and privilege in Physical Education: Struggles in the negotiation of gender in a university programme. In D. Kirk. & R. Tinning (Eds.), *Physical Education, curriculum and culture: Critical issues in the contemporary crisis* (pp. 67–99). Basingstoke, Hampshire: Falmer.

Dewar, A., & Horn, T. (1992). A critical analysis of knowledge construction in sport psychology. In T. Horn (Ed.), *Advances in sport psychology* (pp. 13–22). Champaign, IL: Human Kinetics.

Douglas, J., & Miller, J. (1977). Record breaking women. *Science News, 112*, 172–174.

Drinkwater, B. (1993). *Changing times in women's sports: The sports medicine perspective.* Paper presented at the XIIth Congress International Association of Physical Education and Sport for Girls and Women, Melbourne.

Duquin, M. (1978). The androgynous advantage. In C. Oglesby (Ed.), *Women and sport: Myth to reality* (pp. 89–106). Philadelphia, MS: Lea & Febiger.

Dyer, K. (1976). Social influences on female athletic performance. *Journal of Biosocial Science 8*, 123–136.

Dyer, K. (1982). *Challenging the men: The social biology of female sporting achievement.* St Lucia: University of Queensland Press.

Eagley, A. H. (1987). *Sex differences in social behavior: A social-role interpretation.* Hillsdale, NJ: Erlbaum.

Eccles, J. S. (1984). Sex differences in achievement patterns. In T. Sonderegger (Ed.), *Nebraska symposium on motivation* (Vol. 32) (pp. 97–132). Lincoln, NB: University of Nebraska Press.

Eccles, J. (1987). Gender roles and women's achievement-related decisions. *Psychology of Women Quarterly, 11*, 135–172.

Eccles, J. S., Adler, T. F., Futterman, R., Goff, S. B., Kaczala, C. M., Meece, J. L., & Midgley, C. (1983). Expectations, values and academic behaviors. In J. T. Spence (Ed.), *Achievement and achievement motivation* (pp. 75–146). San Francisco, CA: W. H. Freeman.

Eccles, J. S., & Harold, R. D. (1991). Gender differences in sport involvement: Applying the Eccles expectancy-value model. *Journal of Applied Sport Psychology, 3*, 7–35.

Eichler, M. (1980). *The double standard: A feminist critique of feminist social science.* London: Croom Helm.

Fasting, K. (1993). The development of gender as a socio-cultural perspective: Implications for sport psychology. *Proceedings of the VIII World Congress of the International Society of Sports Psychology, Lisbon* (pp. 81–91).

Feather, M. (1969). Attribution of responsibility and valence of success and failure in relation to initial confidence and task performance. *Journal of Personality and Social Psychology, 13*, 129–144.

Felshin, J. (1974). The triple option... for women in sport. *Quest, 21*, 36–40.

Feltz, D. L. (1988). Self confidence and sports performance. In K. Pandolf (Ed.), *Exercise and sport science reviews.* (Vol. 16) (pp. 423–457). New York: Macmillan.

Fisher, A., Genovese, P., Morris, K., & Morris, K. (1977). Perceptions of women in sport. In D. Landers & B. Christina (Eds.), *Psychology of motor behavior and sport* (pp. 448–461). Champaign, IL: Human Kinetics.

Forsey, C. (1990). *The making of men: Guidelines for working with boys to counter male sex role.* Footscray, Melbourne: West Education Centre.

Frable, D. E. S. (1989). Sex typing and gender ideology: Two facets of an individual's gender psychology that go together. *Journal of Personality and Social Psychology, 56*, 95–108.

Freeman, H. (1988). Social perception of body builders. *Journal of Sport and Exercise Psychology, 10*, 281–293.

Gill, D. L. (1988). Gender differences in competitive orientation and sport participation. *International Journal of Sport Psychology, 19*, 145–159.

Gill, D. L., & Deeter, T. E. (1988). Development of the Sport Orientation Questionnaire. *Research Quarterly for Exercise and Sport, 59*, 191–202.

Gill, D., Gross, J., Huddleston, S., & Shiflett, B. (1984). Sex differences in achievement cognitions and performance in competition. *Research Quarterly for Exercise and Sport, 55*, 340–346.

Gilligan, C. (1982). *In a different voice.* Cambridge, MA: Harvard University Press.

Griffin, P., & Genasci, J. (1990). Addressing homophobia in physical education: Responsibilities for teachers and researchers. In M. A. Messner & D. F. Sabo (Eds.), *Sport, men, and the gender order* (pp. 211–222). Champaign, IL: Human Kinetics.

Hall, M. A. (1981). *Sport, sex roles and sex identity.* (The CRIAW Papers). Ottawa: The Canadian Research Institute of the Advancement of Women.

Hall, M. A. (1985). Knowledge and gender: Epistemological questions in the social analysis of sport. *Sociology of Sport Journal, 2*, 25–42.

Hall, M. A. (1988). The discourse of gender and sport: From femininity to feminism. *Sociology of Sport Journal, 5*, 330–340.

Hall, M. A. (1990). How should we theorize gender in the context of sport? In M. Messner & D. Sabo (Eds.), *Sport, men, and the gender order* (pp. 223–240). Champaign, IL: Human Kinetics.

Hall, M. A., Cullen, D., & Slack, T. (1989). Organizational elites recreating themselves: The gender structure of national sport organizations. *Quest, 41*, 28–45.

Hare-Mustin, R., & Maracek, J. (1988). The meaning of difference: Gender theory, postmodernism, and psychology. *American Psychologist, 43*, 455–464.

Hargreaves, J. A. (1990). Gender on the sports agenda. *International Review for Sociology of Sport, 25*, 287–305.

Harris, D. V. (1979). Female sport today: Psychological considerations. *International Journal of Sport Psychology, 10*, 168–172.

Harris, D.V. (1987). The female athlete. In J. R. May & M. J. Asken (Eds.), *Sport psychology: The psychological health of the athlete* (pp. 99–116). New York: PMA Publishing Corp.

Harris, M. B., & Greco, D. (1990). Weight control and weight concern in competitive female gymnasts. *Journal of Sport and Exercise Psychology, 12*, 427–433.

Helmreich, R. L., & Spence, J. T. (1977). Sex roles and achievement. In R. W. Christina & D. M. Landers (Eds.), *Psychology of motor behavior and sport — 1976* (Vol. 2) (pp. 33–46). Champaign, IL: Human Kinetics.

Henderson, K. A., Stalnaker, D., & Taylor, G. (1988). The relationship between barriers to recreation and gender-role personality traits for women. *Journal of Leisure Research, 20*, 69–80.

Henschen, K. (1991). Critical issues involving male consultants and female athletes. *The Sport Psychologist, 5*, 313–321.

Horner, M. S. (1972). Toward an understanding of achievement-related conflicts in women. *Journal of Social Issues, 28*, 157–176.

Human Rights and Equal Opportunity Commission. (1992). *Women, sport and sex discrimination.* Sydney: Human Rights and Equal Opportunity Commission.

Hyde, J. S., & Linn, M. C. (Eds.). (1986). *The psychology of gender: Advances through meta-analysis.* Baltimore: Johns Hopkins University Press.

Jacklin, C. (1989). Female and male: Issues of gender. *American Psychologist, 44,* 127–133.

Jackson, S., & Marsh, H. (1986). Athletic or antisocial?: The female sport experience. *Journal of Sport Psychology, 8,* 198–211.

Kane, M. J. (1988). The female athletic roles as a status determinant within the social systems of high school adolescents. *Adolescence, 23,* 252–264.

Kane, M. J., & Snyder, K. E. (1989). Sport typing: The social "containment" of women. *Arena Review, 13,* 77–96.

Knoppers, A. (1992). Explaining male dominance and sex segregation in coaching: Three approaches. *Quest, 44,* 210–227.

Leahy, D., & Plaisted, V. (1993). *Developing a gender consciousness in physical education teacher training.* Unpublished preliminary masters manuscript, University of Ballarat, Victoria.

Lenney, E. (1977). Women's self-confidence in achievement settings. *Psychological Bulletin, 84,* 1–13.

Lenney, E., Browning, C., & Mitchell, L. (1980). What you don't know can hurt you: The effects of performance criteria ambiguity on sex differences in self-confidence. *Journal of Personality, 48,* 306–322.

Lenskyj, H. (1987). *Out of bounds: Women, sport and sexuality.* Toronto: Women's Press.

Lenskyj, H. (1991). *Women, sport and physical activity: Research and bibliography* (2nd ed.). Ottawa: Canada Communication Group.

Lenskyj, H. (1992). Sexual harassment: Female athletes' experiences and coaches' responsibilities. *Science Periodical on Research and Technology in Sport, 12,* 6.

Lirgg, C. (1991). Gender differences in self-confidence in physical activity: A meta-analysis of recent studies. *Journal of Sport and Exercise Psychology, 8,* 294–310.

Maccoby, E., & Jacklin, C. (1974). *The psychology of sex differences.* Stanford, CA: Stanford University Press.

Macdonald, D. (1993). Knowledge, gender and power in Physical Education teacher education. *Australian Journal of Education, 37,* 259–278.

Markus, H., Crane, M., Bernstein, S., & Siladi, M. (1982). Self-schemas and gender. *Journal of Personality and Social Psychology, 42,* 38–50.

Matteo, S. (1986). The effect of sex and gender-schematic processing on sport participation. *Sex Roles, 15,* 417–432.

Matteo, S. (1988). The effect of gender-schematic processing on decisions about sex-inappropriate sport behaviour. *Sex Roles, 18,* 41–58.

Maude, D., Wertheim, E. H., Paxton, S., Gibbons, K., & Szmukler, G. (1993). Body dissatisfaction, weight loss behaviours, and bulimic tendencies in Australian adolescents with an estimate of female data representativeness. *Australian Psychologist, 28,* 128–132.

McArdle, W. D., Katch, F. I., & Katch, V. L. (1981). *Exercise physiology: Energy, nutrition and human performance.* Philadelphia, MS: Lea & Febiger.

McClelland, D. C., Atkinson, J. W., Clark, R. A., & Lowell, E. C. (1953). *The achievement motive.* New York: Appleton-Century-Crofts.

McHugh, M., Duquin, M., & Frieze, I. (1978). Beliefs about success and failure: Attribution and the female athlete. In C. Oglesby (Ed.), *Women and sport: From myth to reality* (pp. 143–173). Philadelphia, MS: Lea & Febiger.

McKay, J. (1992). *Why so few? Women executives in Australian sport.* A report presented to the Applied Sports Research Program, Australian Sports Commission.

McNally, J., & Orlick, T. (1975). Cooperative sport structures: A preliminary analysis. *Mouvement, 7,* 267–271.

Messner, M. (1987). The life of a man's seasons: Male identity in the life course of the jock. In M. Kimmel (Ed.), *Changing men: New directions in research on men and masculinity* (pp. 53–67). London: Sage Publications.

Messner, M. A. (1992). *Power at play: Sports and the problem of masculinity.* Boston: Beacon Press.

Messner, M. A., & Sabo, D. F. (1990). *Sport, men, and the gender order.* Champaign, IL: Human Kinetics.

Myers, A. E., & Lips, H. M. (1978). Participation in competitive amateur sports as a function of psychological androgyny. *Sex Roles, 4*, 571–578.

Neal, P., & Tutko, T. (1975). *Coaching girls and women: Psychological perspectives.* Boston: Allyn & Bacon.

Oglesby, C. (1984). Interactions between gender identity and sport. In J. M. Silva & R. S. Weinberg (Eds.), *Psychological foundations of sport* (pp. 387–399). Champaign, IL: Human Kinetics.

Oglesby, C. (1990). Epilogue. In M. Messner & D. Sabo (Eds.), *Sport, men and the gender order* (pp. 241–247). Champaign IL: Human Kinetics.

Oglesby, C., & Hill, K. (1993). Gender and sport. In R. Singer (Ed.), *Handbook of research on sport psychology* (pp. 718–728). New York: Macmillan.

Parkhouse, B. L., & Williams, J. M. (1986). Differential effects of sex and status on evaluation of coaching ability. *Research Quarterly for Exercise and Sport, 57*, 53–59.

Penny, G. D., & Rust, J. O. (1980). Effect of a walking–jogging program on personality characteristics of middle-aged females. *Journal of Sports Medicine and Physical Fitness, 20*, 221–226.

Plaisted, V. (1993). *A qualitative study exploring elite netballers' perceptions of confidence.* Paper presented at 8th International Society of Sport Psychology World Congress, Lisbon.

Prakasa-Rao, W., & Overman, S. J. (1986). Psychological well-being and body image: A comparison of black women athletes and non-athletes. *Journal of Sporting Behaviour, 9*, 79.

Pugliese, M. T., Lifshitz, F., Grad, G., Fort, P., & Marks-Katz, M. (1983). Fear of obesity: A cause of short stature and delayed puberty. *New England Journal of Medicine, 309*, 513–518.

Reynolds, M. J., Otago, L., Plaisted, V., & Randell, S. (1992). *Patterns of involvement and withdrawal of coaches in basketball, hockey and netball: Comparisons between males and females.* Report submitted to the Australian Sports Commission, Applied Sport Research Program, Canberra.

Roberts, G. C. (1984). Toward a new theory of motivation in sport: The role of perceived ability. In J. M. Silva & R. S. Weinberg (Eds.), *Psychological foundations of sport* (pp. 214–228). Champaign, IL: Human Kinetics.

Roberts, G., & Duda, J. (1984). Motivation in sport: The mediating role of perceived ability. *Journal of Sport Psychology, 6*, 312–324.

Rosen, L. W., & Hough, D. O. (1988). Pathogenic weight-control behaviors of female college gymnasts. *The Physician and Sportsmedicine, 16*, 141–144.

Rosen, L. W., McKeag, D. B., Hough, D. O., & Curley, V. (1986). Pathogenic weight-control behavior in female athletes. *The Physician and Sportsmedicine, 14*, 79–86.

Rotella, R. J., & Murray, M. (1991). Homophobia, the world of sport, and sport psychology consulting. *The Sport Psychologist, 5*, 355–364.

Sage, G., & Loudermilk, S. (1979). The female athlete and role conflict. *Research Quarterly, 50*, 88–96.

Selby, R., & Lewko, J. (1976). Children's attitudes toward females in sport: Their relationship with sex, grade and sports participation. *Research Quarterly, 47*, 453–463.

Senate Standing Committee on Environment, Recreation and the Arts. (1992). *Physical and sport education: A report.* Canberra.

Sheriff, M. (1971). Girls compete. In D. Harris (Ed.), *DGWS Research Reports: Women in sports.* Washington, DC: AAHPER Publications.

Sherman, J., & Fennema, E. (1977). The study of mathematics by high school girls and boys: Related variables. *American Educational Research Journal, 14*, 159–168.

Snyder, E., & Kivlin, J. (1975). Women athletes and aspects of psychological well-being and body image. *Research Quarterly, 46*, 191–199.

Snyder, E., & Spreitzer, E. (1976). Correlates of sport participation among adolescent girls. *Research Quarterly, 47*, 804–809.

South Australian Sports Institute. (1992). *Junior sport in South Australia.* A summary of research findings commissioned by the Junior Sports Unit of the South Australian Sports Institute, Adelaide.

Spence, J. T., & Helmreich, R. L. (1978). *Masculinity and femininity.* Austin, TX: University of Texas Press.

Staurowsky, E. (1990). Women coaching male athletes. In M. Messner & D. Sabo (Eds.), *Sport, men, and the gender order* (pp. 163–171). Champaign, IL: Human Kinetics.

Stell, M. K. (1991). *Half the race: A history of Australian women in sport.* North Ryde, NSW: Angus & Robertson.

Stewart, M., & Corbin, C. (1988). Feedback dependence among low confidence, preadolescent girls and boys. *Research Quarterly for Exercise and Sport, 59*, 160–164.

Stoddart, B. (1992). *Women, sport and the media: 1992.* A report commissioned by the Australian Sports Commission, Canberra.

Sundgot-Borgen, J. (1993). Prevalence of eating disorders in elite female athletes. *International Journal of Sport Nutrition, 3*, 29–40.

Surrey, J. L. (1991). The "Self-in-Relation": A theory of women's development. In J. V. Jordan, A. G. Kaplan, J. B. Miller, I. P. Stiver, & J. L. Surrey (Eds.), *Women's growth in connection: Writings from the Stone Centre* (pp. 51–66). New York: Guilford Press.

Tannen, D. (1990). *You just don't understand: Women and men in conversation.* Milson's Point, N.S.W.: Random House.

Theberge, N. (1985). Toward a feminist alternative to sport as a male preserve. *Quest, 37*, 193–202.

Theberge, N. (1987). Sport and women's empowerment. *Women's Studies International Forum, 10*, 387–393.

Thompson, R. A. (1987). Management of the athlete with an eating disorder: Implications for the sport management team. *The Sport Psychologist, 1*, 114–126.

Tinning, R. (1985). Physical education and the cult of slenderness: A critique. *ACHPER Journal, 107*, 10–13.

Tresemer, D. (1974). Fear of success: Popular but unproven. *Psychology Today, 7*, 82–85.

Trujillo, C. M. (1983). The effect of weight training and running exercise intervention programs on the self-esteem of college women. *International Journal of Sport Psychology, 14*, 162–173.

Valle, V., & Frieze, I. (1976). The stability of causal attributions as a mediator in changing expectations for success. *Journal of Personality and Social Psychology, 33*, 579–587.

Vealey, R. (1988). Sport-confidence and competitive orientation: An addendum on scoring procedures and gender differences. *Journal of Sport and Exercise Psychology, 10*, 471–478.

Warrick, R., & Tinning, R. (1989). Women's bodies, self-perception and physical activity: A naturalistic study of women's participation in aerobics classes, Part 2. *The ACHPER National Journal*, December, 19–23.

Watson, T. (1987). Women athletes and athletic women: The dilemmas and contradictions of managing incongruent identities. *Sociological Inquiry, 57*, 431–446.

Weinberg, R. S., Reveles, M., & Jackson, A. (1984). Attitudes of male and female athletes toward male and female coaches. *Journal of Sport Psychology, 16*, 448–453.

Williams, J. M., & Parkhouse, B. L. (1988). Social learning theory as a foundation for examining sex bias in evaluation of coaches. *Journal of Sport and Exercise Psychology, 10*, 322–333.

Wine, J. (1982). Gynocentric values and feminist psychology. In A. Miles & G. Finn (Eds.), *Feminism in Canada: From pressure to politics* (pp. 67–87). Montreal: Black Rose Books.

Wrisberg, C. A., Draper, M. V., & Everett, J. J. (1988). Sex role orientations of male and female collegiate athletes from selected individual and team sports. *Sex Roles, 19*, 81–90.

Yambor, J., & Connelly, D. (1991). Issues confronting female sport psychology consultants working with male student-athletes. *The Sport Psychologist, 5*, 304–312.

Zuckerman, M., & Wheeler, L. (1975). To dispel fantasies about the fantasy-based measure of fear of success. *Psychological Bulletin, 82*, 932–946.

C H A P T E R

23

THE GROWTH OF QUALITATIVE RESEARCH IN SPORT PSYCHOLOGY

SUSAN A. JACKSON

In attempting to understand sport behaviour, early sport psychology researchers relied primarily on traditional scientific approaches, conducting controlled experiments in laboratory settings and trying to measure and quantify the behaviours of interest. Although substantial knowledge has been gained by following the traditional scientific method, there remains a need to better understand the behaviours *and experiences* of people in sport and physical activity settings. It may be necessary, in order to meet this need, to adopt alternative scientific approaches that are well-suited to providing in-depth understanding of people in real-world settings.

The purpose of this chapter is to discuss how qualitative research can and has been used in sport psychology as a method of generating knowledge about people's behaviour and experience in sport and exercise settings. The chapter will begin with an overview of the development of qualitative research in sport psychology, showing that the ability of qualitative research to bridge the gap between scientist and practitioner is a major reason for its growing popularity. The key to the growing role qualitative approaches have in sport psychology research is the potential they have to provide in-depth understanding of experiential and real-world issues in sport and physical activity. This will be illustrated with examples of sport psychological qualitative research. Suggestions will be made for future directions incorporating qualitative methods in this relatively new and exciting field of sport psychology research.

THE GROWTH OF QUALITATIVE RESEARCH

THE SCIENTIST–PRACTITIONER GAP

As the field of sport psychology grows, we face the challenge of overcoming the potentially destructive forces of divisiveness from formation of subgroups with agendas that emphasise perceived inability to integrate with the "other side". One of these schisms is between the researcher or scientist and practitioner in the field. Research in sport psychology in Australia has lagged behind the service delivery side and, understandably, practitioners often greet the development of research with scepticism, questioning the relevance of the research process and product to their work with athletes.

Rainer Martens, a leading US scholar and practitioner in sport psychology, recognised the schism between scientist and practitioner in the 1970s. His insightful 1979 article, entitled "About Smocks and Jocks", highlighted the gap between the research being done in the laboratories and what was happening out on the playing fields. Martens criticised the reliance on laboratory research in sport psychology and called for the development of sport-specific theories from field-based research, where the behaviour of athletes and coaches could be studied in authentic settings. (Hence the title — Martens believed sport psychology researchers should trade in their "laboratory smocks" for "athletic jocks" in order to conduct more meaningful research.)

Martens further developed his argument in the 1987 article, "Science, Knowledge, and Sport Psychology". Here Martens argued that there are in fact two sport psychologies: academic sport psychology and practising sport psychology. He argued that the reason for this separation is the belief among many researchers that positivistic, or orthodox, science is the only way to do science and that positivism cannot adequately answer all questions of interest and importance to practising sport psychologists. Martens called for the development not just of another type of method or methods as he did in his earlier article; now, an entirely new way of thinking about and doing research was advocated, in a paradigm he labelled heuristic research.

MOVING BEYOND POSITIVISM: ALTERNATIVE APPROACHES TO CONDUCTING RESEARCH

Within qualitative approaches, there is a plethora of terminology to describe what we commonly call qualitative research, heuristic research (Martens, 1987) being just one of these terms. All have slightly different philosophical assumptions and emphases but are joined together in their common departure from *positivism*, or the traditional scientific method. Positivism, or logical positivism, as it is more formally known, is a theory of knowledge about what constitutes appropriate methods for generating and discovering scientific knowledge (Dewar & Horn, 1992). But more than that, it is a way of defining and constructing reality and contains ideas about how scientific knowledge should be produced.

Critics of positivist research argue that the assumptions about how knowledge should be generated do not allow for the study of the richness and complexity of human behaviour. What constitutes knowledge when looked at from a broader framework, involving social context and implicating the researcher as an integral part of the knowledge production process, allows for understanding of complex human behaviours in context-specific settings. Alternative approaches to scientific inquiry can broadly be categorised as having a phenomenological, or interpretive, basis. That is, they seek to holistically understand human experience in context-specific settings (Patton, 1990). There are several ways of conducting "non-positivistic" research, each with its own terminology and methodological emphases. It is beyond the scope of this chapter to discuss the varying approaches that utilise qualitative methods — rather, an overview of common themes of qualitative inquiry that have been used to date in sport psychology will be presented. It will be shown how qualitative approaches have attempted to bridge the gap between scientist and practitioner, and possible future directions for qualitative research attempts in sport psychology will be identified.

THE INTERPRETIVE RESEARCH PARADIGM

I prefer the term, "interpretive inquiry" to describe my qualitative research approach since it puts emphasis on the interpretive processes of the researcher when conducting research. When comparing positivism with interpretive research, it is important to recognise that we are dealing with comparisons at two levels: the level of method and, perhaps more importantly, but often overlooked, the level of paradigm. These two levels are briefly compared below:

Level of method: how you go about actually doing research. These are the more easily identifiable characteristics with which we usually associate a particular method.

Level of paradigm: the philosophical assumptions behind doing a particular type of research. Deals with philosophy of science issues.

To illustrate the difference, Martens' 1979 article was a methodological critique, whereas his 1987 article was an epistemological critique. Figure 23.1 illustrates the two levels of analysis.

You can see from this diagram that it is possible to use qualitative or quantitative methods within either paradigm although, traditionally, quantitative methods have been aligned with the positivist paradigm and qualitative methods with the interpretive paradigm. Although it is possible to mix methods, the underlying philosophical differences between the approaches mean that we do not always get congruence between quantitative and qualitative data. Often, very different questions are asked by the interpretive and positivist paradigms because each involves a different way of looking at the world.

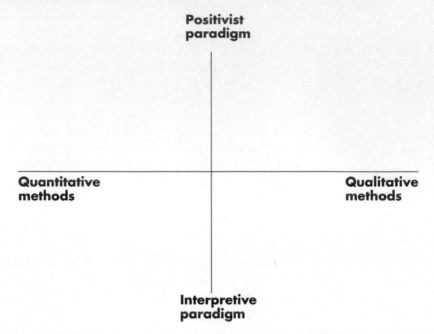

Figure 23.1: Qualitative and quantitative research: the two levels of analysis and decision making

To truly understand the distinction between positivistic and interpretive research paradigms, the relationship between the underlying philosophical assumptions of both approaches to science needs to be understood. A paradigm can be thought of as the scientist's spectacles — different paradigms represent different ways of looking at an issue. Interpretive and positivistic paradigms are two very different ways of viewing the scientific process, and encompass the assumptions and rules or viewpoints about how research should be conducted.

RESEARCH ASSUMPTIONS

I am going to address some of the fundamental differences in the axioms, or assumptions, of *positivist research* and one qualitative research approach that has been used quite widely in sport psychology research. Lincoln and Guba (1985) discuss in detail fundamental differences between positivism and their approach to qualitative research, *naturalistic inquiry*. The ideas presented below have been drawn from Lincoln and Guba's analysis, to illustrate how positivist and non-positivist paradigms differ markedly in their philosophies.

REALITY

Positivism rests on the assumption of there being one single reality, waiting to be "discovered" by the scientist. The notion that there may *not* be one single reality "out there" is critical to qualitative approaches. Reality is seen as being a social construction, that is, a perceived experience that differs according to the perceiver, and the information he or she has been exposed to.

RELATIONSHIP OF RESEARCHER TO PARTICIPANTS

If there are in fact multiple, constructed realities, then in order to understand each individual's reality, the researcher must get close to the person or persons being studied. In qualitative research, the researcher is expected to get close to the data, close to the study participants. This stands in contrast to the very distant, objective stance of the traditional researcher.

GENERALISABILITY

Following on again from the idea of subjective realities, qualitative research recognises the importance of context, thereby limiting the extent of generalisations that can be made about any one particular finding. Traditional research judges the quality of the research product on the extent of generalisability of the findings. Often, however, it is inappropriate to generalise from one situation to another. For example, the motivations of a professional golfer are likely to be very different to a young netball player, and probably need to be addressed in independent research that explores the sources of motivation for each participant, rather than attempting to generalise the findings from research with one group of athletes to another, very different group.

CAUSALITY

The idea of causality is another point of difference between positivistic and interpretive approaches. According to the former, showing causality is an advanced stage of the research process. However, the possibility of separating "causes" from often mutually shaping "effects" is questioned by qualitative researchers, who argue that events are mutually influencing, and therefore separating cause from effect can become difficult and somwhat arbitrary. For example, are some football players aggressive because they play football, or was it because they had aggressive tendencies that they were drawn to a sport like football? Probably the answer is wrapped up in complex interactions between the player and the sport, and aggressive acts on the football field may be best understood through using a variety of research approaches.

OBJECTIVITY

A final point of difference between traditional and more contemporary research is in relation to the role of values in research. Traditionally, research is supposed to be value-free; something supposedly attained through the objective stance taken by the researcher. More recent approaches stress the guiding role of values at all stages of the research process, from questions asked to methods chosen, to interpretation of the data.

WHY QUALITATIVE RESEARCH?

The axioms just presented raise many important issues about research, including the following:

1. *Truth v. perspective*: Is there such a thing as one truth, which the completely objective researcher "discovers" out in the "real world"? Or, are there multiple, constructed realities, making the researcher's role one of investigating perspectives of those he or she is interested in understanding?

2. *Beyond the numbers game*: Positivistic research gives numbers and statistics a reverence that can lead to inappropriate use of number-crunching to support a hypothesis that may not be fully addressed through quantitative methods. Often, through a misguided reverence for numbers, we sacrifice meaning for the sake of generating simple statements of supposed fact.

Qualitative research is embedded in the idea that there are multiple, holistic perspectives which can only be understood through asking people about their perceptions, behaviours, and experiences. In the asking, effort is made to keep the respondent's perceptions foremost; usually this requires using the respondent's words as the data, rather than assigning a number to a particular response and assuming this number captures the meaning of the response.

QUALITATIVE RESEARCH

The following section outlines some principles of conducting qualitative research. Qualitative research is not simply a matter of following a set of steps from "a" to "z". There is a great deal of flexibility and decisions to be made by the researcher based on the purposes of the study and the questions being asked. The following principles, therefore, are offered as a guiding framework only, and not an exhaustive list of qualitative research principles.

1. *Decide on the question(s) of interest*

The first step in any research endeavour, qualitative or quantitative, is to decide on the research question(s). It is important that the research questions drive the method, rather than vice versa. Open research questions are generally favoured over direct hypothesis testing for several reasons. First, the qualitative researcher does not assume to know how the study participants are likely to respond and thus takes an open stance to the research question. Second, most qualitative designs are not set out to "test" predictions but to investigate an issue, making the hypothesis inappropriate.

2. *Decide on the method(s) to be used*

   Interviews are probably the most popular method of inquiry within sport psychological qualitative research. However, other data collection methods not yet widely used, offer promise for generating understanding, including various forms of observation (e.g., participant and onlooker), video-taping, case-studies, and a life-history approach.

3. *Decide who you wish to study*

   In qualitative research, the value of researching particular respondents who have special insights into, or experience with, the area of investigation is recognised. One of the tenets of a positivistic approach is random sampling, where a sample is randomly selected from the population of interest to avoid any biases from conducting the research on a particular group. However, when the aim is to obtain an in-depth understanding of an issue, it makes sense to ask the people who have the most knowledge of the area. Therefore, the sample is purposefully chosen rather than randomly selected. Patton (1990) uses the terms, "purposeful sampling" and "information-rich cases" to describe sample selection in qualitative inquiry.

4. *Develop any instruments to be used in the inquiry*

   Instruments typically used in qualitative inquiry include interview guides, structured open-ended questionnaires, and observation data sheets. In addition, data from other sources may be collected to help support (or call into question) the study findings. This is known as triangulation of the data (Patton, 1990), and may come from various sources, including program documents and records, biographies, autobiographies, journal and newspaper clippings.

5. *Collect data*

   Depending on the method of inquiry, this may involve conducting interviews, observations, supplementary questionnaire data, or collecting archival data.

6. *Analyse data*

   The analysis methods used will depend on the methods of data collection and it is beyond the scope of this chapter to detail the various forms of analysis that may be used. An overview of one way of managing interview data will be presented because of its frequent use by qualitative researchers in sport psychology.

   The novice qualitative researcher may easily be overwhelmed by the amount of data that arises from a qualitative investigation. Interviews should usually be transcribed verbatim and this can result in several hundreds of pages of text, depending on the number of interviews conducted. Managing this amount of data requires systematic and carefully planned analyses that should be developed from the research questions. One method that has been frequently used by sport psychology qualitative researchers is an inductive content analysis theme-building procedure. The process (to be illustrated in the next section) involves a series of steps designed to create a hierarchy of themes. The first level of analysis is the actual words of the interviewee; these become the "raw data themes" and are usually either direct or paraphrased quotes. Similar ideas are grouped together into a "higher-order theme". The number of levels of higher-order themes depends on the number of similar ideas expressed and the level of generality to which the researcher wants to take the data. The final level of analysis, which may be three or four steps removed from the raw data theme, is often called a "general dimension". An example of the theme-building process taken from the author's research is illustrated in Figure 23.2.

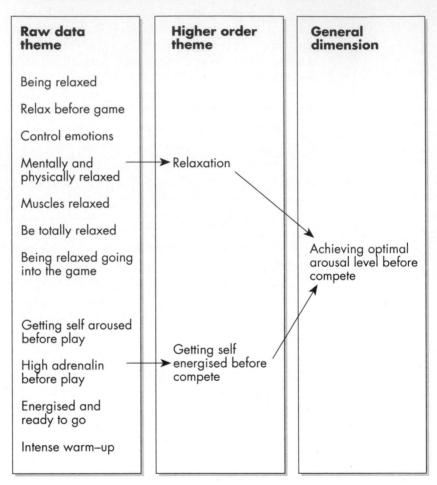

Figure 23.2: An example of the theme-building process in qualitative inductive data analysis: factors helping flow state in elite athletes (Jackson, 1994)

In Figure 23.2, the far left column represents raw data themes, that is, direct replies made by the athletes interviewed to the question about what factors help them to achieve a flow state. The middle column has grouped together like ideas from the raw data column about arousal level into two higher-order themes, Relaxation and Getting Self Energised Before Compete. In the far right column, these two higher order themes are grouped together under the general dimension, Achieving Optimal Arousal Level Before Compete. This is just one of the ten different general dimensions representing over 130 ideas put forward by elite athletes regarding the factors they perceive help them to achieve flow (Jackson, 1994). The content analysis process previously described helps to organise and synthesise a large amount of information into a more usable form and has been one of the more popular methods of analysing and presenting qualitative data within sport psychology.

7. *Employ "Trustworthiness" procedures to establish the credibility of the data*
Patton (1990) and Lincoln and Guba (1985) discuss the need to establish the credibility or trustworthiness of findings generated from qualitative analyses. The basic issue, as described by Lincoln and Guba is:
"How can an inquirer (researcher) persuade his or her audiences [including self] that the findings of an inquiry are worth paying attention to, worth taking account of?" (p. 290). Criteria that have been developed in positivistic approaches usually revolve around four main issues: internal validity, external validity, reliability, and objectivity. Similar criteria to these have been developed by qualitative researchers. However, different terms defining different criteria are used in qualitative research and it is important to remember that the criteria by which research is judged are going to be different, depending on the philosophical paradigm from which the research has evolved. Lincoln and Guba (1985) use the terms "credibility", "transferability", "dependability" and "confirmability" as their equivalents to the four positivistic criteria expressed above.

There are many methods that can be employed to help establish trustworthiness of the data. These are described in depth by Patton (1990) and Lincoln and Guba (1985). Some of the more widely-used procedures are briefly described below.

(a) Triangulation: The idea behind triangulation is to gather evidence in more than one way in order to provide support for generated findings. This may be done by involving more than one person in the data analysis process, and striving for consensual validation; or it may involve collecting data via more than one method, for example, interviews and questionnaires, or interviews and observation.

(b) Thick description: Patton (1990) reports that the qualitative researcher has an obligation to be methodical in reporting sufficient details of data collection and the process of analysis to permit others to judge the quality of the resulting product. Writing skills are an important skill for the qualitative researcher, whose task at the write-up stage is to attempt to convey the richness and detail provided by qualitative data collection procedures.

(c) Reflexive journal: A reflexive journal, as described by Lincoln and Guba (1985), is a type of diary in which the researcher regularly records information about self (hence the term "reflexive") and methods. This information can be used to assess the credibility of the researcher (an integral part of the research process) and the methodological decisions made. This form of record-keeping also helps the researcher reflect on past decisions made throughout the research process, especially helpful when decisions about future research directions need to be made.

(d) Design checks: Keeping the methods and data in context is important when writing up the results and attempting to extrapolate from the findings of the study. When making conclusions, the researcher must remember to limit them to the persons, contexts and purposes for which the data are applicable (Patton, 1990).

(e) Peer debriefer: Lincoln and Guba (1985) describe the role of peer debriefing as "a process of exposing oneself to a disinterested peer in a manner paralleling an analytic session and for the purpose of exploring aspects of the inquiry that might otherwise remain only implicit within the inquirer's mind" (p. 308). The peer debriefer provides an external check on the inquiry process. This may involve clarifying interpretations and decisions made by the researcher, exploring any biases held by the researcher, and generally acting in the role of "devil's advocate". A disinterested peer is someone knowledgeable about the methodological issues and topical area of the study but who is otherwise not involved in the study. Hanson (1992) and Jackson (1993) provide examples of peer debriefers in the research process.

(f) Audit check: Similar to the fiscal audit, and detailed by Lincoln and Guba (1985), an auditor carries out a thorough check of the total research process and product and makes a statement about the acceptability of the inquiry and its interpretations. A person not otherwise associated with the study, who should be an approximate peer (Lincoln & Guba, 1985) and knowledgeable both about the content and methods of the study, carries out a formal evaluation of all written aspects of the research process, including transcripts, journals, and the final written report or thesis. Jackson (1993) provides an illustrative example from sport psychology research of the steps involved in the audit check process.

EXAMPLES OF SPORT PSYCHOLOGICAL QUALITATIVE RESEARCH

To illustrate how qualitative research has been used in sport psychology to answer questions of interest and importance to practising sport psychologists, this section gives examples of qualitative studies conducted by sport psychology researchers. The aim is not to provide a description of how these studies were conducted but to give an overview of what they set out to accomplish and the main findings obtained. This is not an exhaustive but an illustrative list.

- Scanlan, Stein, and Ravizza (1989, 1991) and Scanlan, Ravizza, and Stein (1989): "Sources of Enjoyment in Elite Figure Skaters" and "Sources of Stress in Elite Figure Skaters". Often viewed as the groundbreaking and model approach in qualitative sport psychology research, Scanlan and colleagues set a fine early example of how to carry out a qualitatively based study. The aim of their research was to investigate the sources of enjoyment and stress in elite figure skaters. They interviewed 26 skaters and inductively content-analysed the interview transcripts.

  Four major sources of enjoyment were derived from the theme-building process described earlier: social and life opportunities, perceived competence, social recognition of competence, and the act of skating. Five major sources of stress included: negative aspects of competition, negative significant-other relationships, demands or costs of skating, personal struggles, and traumatic experiences.

- Cohn (1990; 1991): "An Exploratory Study of Sources of Stress and Athlete Burnout in Youth Golf" (1990). The aim of this first study was to examine sources of stress among 10 high school and competitive golfers. Major findings included the following stress sources: playing a particularly difficult shot, playing up to personal standards, and striving to meet parental expectations. All players said they had experienced a short period of burn-out. In a second study, "An Exploratory Study of Peak Performance in Golf", Cohn explored perceptions of peak performance in competitive golfers. During peak performance, golfers were highly focused and immersed in the task at hand, performed effortlessly and automatically, felt physically relaxed and mentally calm, and felt in control of themselves and their performance.

- Gould, Eklund, and Jackson (1992a, b; 1993): Commissioned by USA Wrestling, Gould, Eklund, and Jackson carried out an in-depth study of "Mental Preparation, Competitive Cognitions, Affect, and Coping Strategies in United States Olympic Team Wrestlers". The aim of the study was to investigate psychological factors associated with sporting excellence. The United States wrestling team entered the Seoul Olympics with expectations from outside of bringing home at least ten gold medals. While some team members performed extremely well at the Games and won medals, other wrestlers appeared to be negatively affected by the intense competitive stress associated with the Olympic tournament and failed to perform to expected potential. Considerable consistency was found across wrestlers' responses regarding all-time best and worst Olympic matches, whereas striking differences were found between the best and worst matches. For example, before best matches, wrestlers followed mental preparation plans and routines and were extremely confident, totally focused, and optimally aroused. They also focused on clear tactical strategies. Before worst matches, wrestlers were not confident, had inappropriate feeling states and experienced many task-irrelevant and negative thoughts, and deviated from preparation plans. Similarly, during performance, confidence, focus, and optimal arousal characterised best matches, whereas low confidence, inappropriate feeling states, task-irrelevant and negative thinking, plus deviations from strategic plans or poor strategy choices characterised worst matches. A number of coping strategies were employed to help cope with the Olympic experience, including thought-control strategies, task-focus strategies, behavioural based strategies and emotional-control strategies. Medal winners differed from non-medal winning wrestlers mainly in the degree to which coping strategies were well-learned or automatised.

- Gould, Jackson, and Finch (1993a, b) and Gould, Finch, and Jackson (1993): "The Experiences, Sources of Stress, and Coping Strategies of U.S. National Champion Figure Skaters". This series of articles describes the results of another in-depth investigation with elite athletes, this time with United States national champion figure skaters. The goals of the overall project were to determine the levels of stress, sources of stress, and stress-coping strategies experienced by these athletes at the top of their sport. The first article focuses on the experience of being a national champion and the skaters' views on the costs and benefits of holding a national title. Results revealed that none of the skaters regretted being a national champion, and a number of positive aspects of the experience were identified. However, a number of negative experiences, such as excessive obligations/responsibilities and pressure to prove their ability as national champions, were also identified. Skaters' recommendations for obtaining and retaining a national title were also examined. The second article focuses on the specific sources of stress experienced in being a national champion. Stress source dimensions were identified and included: relationship issues, expectations and pressure to perform, psychological demands on skater resources, life direction concerns, and a number of individual-specific uncategorisable sources. The amount of stress experienced prior to and after winning a national title was compared and most of the skaters reported experiencing more stress after winning their title than before. The third article, entitled "Coping strategies of national champion figure skaters", focuses on the coping strategies used by the skaters to deal with the stressors they faced. Major coping strategy dimensions included: rational thinking and self-talk, positive focus and orientation, social support, time management and prioritisation, pre-competition mental preparation and anxiety management, a "train hard and smart" attitude, isolation and deflection, and ignoring the stressor.
- Hanson (1992): "Mental Aspects of Hitting in Baseball — A Case-Study". Hanson followed a naturalistic approach (Lincoln & Guba, 1985) in his research into the mental aspects of hitting in baseball. He interviewed five of baseball's greatest hitters; this article presents the results of interviewing one of these men, Hank Aaron. Aaron's case study revealed how he placed considerable emphasis on mental preparation for hitting. This preparation was primarily through visualising himself hitting against the

pitcher he would next face. He stated that his visualisation helped him to be more focused during a game and consistent throughout his career. Other related topics, including studying the pitcher, visual focus, and at-the-plate orientation, were also discussed.

- Jackson (1992, 1993): "Elite Athletes in Flow: In-depth Investigations into the Flow Experiences of Athletes". The first study conducted with elite athletes on flow experiences (Jackson, 1992a) was part of a larger research project examining the experience of being a national champion figure skater (Gould, Jackson, & Finch, 1993a). The skaters were interviewed on their perceptions of, and experience with, flow state during their performances (Csikszentmihalyi, 1990). Rich accounts of flow experiences were gathered, and information about perceived controllable flow state characteristics, as well as factors that help, prevent or disrupt flow, was collected. Factors perceived as most important for getting into flow included a positive mental attitude, positive pre-competitive and competitive affect, maintaining an appropriate focus, physical readiness, and for some pairs/dance skaters, unity with the partner. Those factors which were perceived to prevent or disrupt flow included physical problems and mistakes, an inability to maintain focus, a negative mental attitude, and lack of audience response. The skaters placed very high value on flow-like states, and their descriptions of what was happening during optimal skating experiences paralleled many of the characteristics of flow described by the theorist behind the concept, Csikszentmihalyi.

A large scale extension of the first investigation was carried out (1993), involving in-depth interviews with 28 elite athletes from seven sports, all of whom were national-calibre athletes from Australia and New Zealand. Characteristics of flow were identified and compared with Csikszentmihalyi's (1990) model of flow. Considerable support was found for Csikszentmihalyi's flow dimensions through inductive content analysis of the athletes' descriptions of a flow state experience. Antecedent flow factors were identified and included components such as having optimal physical preparation, following a mental routine and event plan, confidence, and optimal arousal. Factors perceived as preventing flow included non-optimal preparation, poor environmental or situational conditions, lacking motivation and problems with confidence. Similar factors were found to disrupt flow, and environmental conditions played a major role in this respect. Also important to the disruption of flow was inappropriate focus, and feeling poorly or feeling that the performance was progressing poorly. The perceived controllability of flow was also examined, and the majority of these athletes felt that flow state was controllable, or more correctly, that the conditions impacting on flow were largely controllable and thus the potential to achieve flow was within their control. Finally, the relationship of flow to peak performance and peak experience was examined. Support was found for the interdependence of these constructs rather than for them being independent experientially-defined events, as has been found in previous research with non-athlete populations.

- Ripol (1993): "The Psychology of the Swimming Taper". Interviews with members of the US national team were conducted, with the purpose of identifying and understanding the psychological methods of preparation used during the tapers of some elite swimmers. The swimmers were asked to describe what they had thought about and focused on the most during tapers that had helped them to accomplish fast swims, as well as the things they avoided thinking about during tapers. Eight major themes emerged and became the organisational structure of the write-up: mind and body working in unison during the taper, confidence, general thoughts during the taper, visualisation and imagery, feel in the water, coaches' action, pressure and nervousness, and race thoughts.

FUTURE DIRECTIONS

The above review of qualitative studies was provided to show the breadth of topics that have thus far been addressed through a qualitative approach, as well as to stimulate your thinking about future avenues that could be followed in the sport psychologist's quest for further understanding of the behaviours and experiences of people in sport contexts.

Qualitative research is particularly suited to developing understanding of the experiences of people in various contexts. Experience has tended to be neglected in favour of overt behaviours, particularly outcome behaviours, in sport psychology research. Thus, studying the sport experience of participants from recreational tennis player to Olympic cyclist should help sport psychologists understand better what is being experienced and thus be in a better position to intervene to help improve the quality of the sport experience for all levels of sport participants.

In addition to the neglect of experience in favour of behaviour evident in sport psychology research, the area of *positive* experiencing has also been neglected in favour of *negative* experiences such as anxiety and burnout. Sport begins as an enjoyable activity which offers many benefits both of a physical and a psychological nature. Examining these positive experiences as well as the negative influences and stresses experienced by athletes will further understanding of the various dimensions of the sport experience and may also help in the promotion of sport and physical activity in society. Of course, there are many areas within sport and exercise psychology that could be addressed qualitatively. Qualitative and quantitative methods offer different strengths, and a multi-method approach to data collection and analysis may provide more information and understanding than reliance on one method alone. Examples of areas that could be profitably addressed through qualitative and/or quantitative methods include the following:

Participation and achievement motivation: An area that has received a lot of research attention in sport psychology, motivation studies have attempted to apply numerous theories from educational and social psychology to understanding sport motivation. Tapping into sources of motivation held by individuals and groups in various sport and exercise situations via qualitative approaches, may help understanding of this important area.

Mental skills and strategies of elite performers: Experts within a field can provide a wealth of information about the skills necessary for success; exploring the mental skills and strategies of elite performers not only in sport, but also in other performance-based professions (e.g., music, art, dance) could help build the performance enhancement knowledge base that sport psychology currently rests on.

Health beliefs and behaviours: As the field of exercise and health psychology grows, invstigating the health beliefs and behaviours of a number of groups will add valuable insights. Examples of possible groups that could be studied include various exercise populations, the elderly, the terminally or chronically ill/injured, cardiac rehabilitation patients, and athletes with eating disorders or substance-abuse problems.

The above examples are given as an illustration of the types of issues that could be addressed using qualitative (or a combination of qualitative and quantitative) research methods. The field is wide open and only limited by the researcher's imagination.

As the number of researchers in sport psychology doing qualitatively-based studies grows, the need for journals for transmission of knowledge is also growing. Recently, a new journal has been developed by a group of sport psychologists, that is designed to be a forum for publication of qualitatively-based research in performance enhancement. Called *Contemporary Thought in Performance Enhancement*, this journal is illustrative of the growth of interest and output of qualitative research in applied sport psychology.

Action Research — incorporating change in the research process: This chapter began with a discussion of how qualitative research offers the potential to help bridge the gap between scientist and practitioner in sport psychology. One type of research that has not to date been widely discussed or used within sport psychology research circles is *action research*. As suggested by the name, action research is a methodology which has the dual aims of action and research (Dick, 1993). Action research has been used in a number of disciplines, including education, psychology, sociology, and it is often the method of choice for those who like to combine the roles of researcher and practitioner. Generally, action research is qualitative, due to the greater potential of responsiveness to the situation provided by qualitative methods. For practising sport psychologists, who like to view themselves as agents of change, action research provides a method of combining intervention and research into one package, and growing use of this method within applied sport psychology is predicted. There are several forms of action research, and the interested reader is referred to Dick (1993) for an excellent discussion on the rationale and selection of an action research methodology, as well as an insightful comparison of the advantages and disadvantages of this research approach.

CONCLUSIONS

Qualitative research offers a number of advantages which make it a useful tool of inquiry in sport and exercise psychology. Some of the main strengths of qualitative research include: depth and richness of findings, the potential to understand individual experience, the holistic nature of findings, power in identifying new directions, and an ability to identify individual differences as well as examine between-case consistencies.

When making research decisions, one should:

(a) understand the paradigm assumptions one is operating from
(b) identify one's own research philosophy
(c) choose a method that will best address the question.

Qualitative research may be the method of choice when the interest is in understanding subjective experience, when the individual matters, when depth and richness of data is a priority, and when understanding the total picture counts.

SUMMARY

This chapter has focused on a rapidly growing, relatively new approach to research in sport psychology: the use of qualitative methods. A background to research assumptions was given to show the reader that research is guided by underlying philosophies about the nature of the research process. It was argued that the schism between scientist and practitioner apparent in many fields, including sport psychology, was an outcome of reliance on an orthodox rigid definition of scientific method, known as positivism. Alternative approaches, embracing qualitative approaches to research, offer the potential to bridge the gap between scientist and practitioner, and the assumptions behind one such alternative approach, naturalistic inquiry, were contrasted with the assumptions of positivism. Practical guidelines on conducting qualitative research were presented, and examples from the sport psychology literature presented to illustrate the breadth of topics thus far addressed, and the potential for future developments in qualitative research in sport psychology.

REFERENCES

Cohn, P. J. (1990). An exploratory study of sources of stress and athlete burnout in youth golf. *The Sport Psychologist, 4,* 95–106.

Cohn, P. J. (1991). An exploratory study of peak performance in golf. *The Sport Psychologist, 5,* 1–14.

Csikszentmihalyi, M. (1990). *Flow: The psychology of optimal experience.* New York: Harper & Row.

Dewar, A., & Horn, T. S. (1992). A critical analysis of knowledge construction in sport psychology. In T. S. Horn (Ed.), *Advances in sport psychology* (pp. 13–22). Champaign, IL: Human Kinetics.

Dick, B. (1993). *You want to do an action research thesis?* Chapel Hill, Queensland: Interchange.

Gould, D., Eklund, R. C., & Jackson, S. A. (1992a). 1988 USA Olympic wrestling excellence I: Mental preparation, precompetitive cognition, and affect. *The Sport Psychologist, 6*(4), 358–382.

Gould, D., Eklund, R. C., & Jackson, S. A. (1992b). 1988 USA Olympic wrestling excellence II: Competitive cognition and affect. *The Sport Psychologist, 6*(4), 383–402.

Gould, D., Eklund, R. C., & Jackson, S. A. (1993). Coping strategies used by U.S. Olympic wrestlers. *Research Quarterly for Sport and Exercise, 64*(1), 83–93.

Gould, D., Jackson, S. A., & Finch, L. M. (1993a). Life at the top: The experiences of U.S. national champion figure skaters. *The Sport Psychologist, 7*(4), 354–374.

Gould, D., Jackson, S. A. & Finch, L. M., (1993b). Sources of stress in national champion figure skaters. *Journal of Sport and Exercise Psychology, 15*(2), 134–159.

Gould, D., Finch, L. M, & Jackson, S. A. (1993). Coping strategies of national champion figure skaters. *Research Quarterly for Exercise and Sport, 64*(4), 453–468.

Hanson, T. (1992). The mental aspects of hitting in baseball: A case study. *Contemporary Thought on Performance Enhancement, 1*(1), 49–70.

Jackson, S. A. (1992). Athletes in flow: A qualitative investigation of flow states in elite figure skaters. *Journal of Applied Sport Psychology, 4*(2), 161–180.

Jackson, S. A. (1993). *Elite athletes in flow: The psychology of optimal sport experience.* (Doctoral dissertation, University of North Carolina at Greensboro, 1992) Dissertation Abstracts International, *54*(i), 124–A.

Jackson, S. A. (1994). Athletes in flow: Factors influencing the occurrence of flow state in elite athletes. Manuscript under review.

Lincoln, Y. S., & Guba, E. G. (1985). *Naturalistic inquiry.* Newbury Park, CA: Sage.

Martens, R (1987). Science, knowledge, and sport psychology. *The Sport Psychologist, 1*, 29–55.

Martens, R. (1979). About smocks and jocks. *Journal of Sport Psychology, 1*, 94–99.

Patton, M. Q. (1990). *Qualitative evaluation and research methods* (2nd ed.). Newbury Park, CA: Sage.

Ripol, B. (1993). The psychology of the swimming taper. *Contemporary Thought in Performance Enhancement, 2*(1), 22–64.

Scanlan, T. K., Ravizza, K., & Stein, G. L. (1989). Sources of enjoyment in elite figure skaters. *Journal of Sport and Exercise Psychology, 11*, 65–83.

Scanlan, T. K., Stein, G. L., & Ravizza, K. (1989). An in-depth study of former elite skaters: Introduction to the project. *Journal of Sport and Exercise Psychology, 11*, 54–65.

Scanlan, T. K., Stein, G. L., & Ravizza, K. (1991). Sources of stress in elite figure skaters. *Journal of Sport and Exercise Psychology, 13*, 103–120.

24

FUTURE DIRECTIONS IN SPORT AND EXERCISE PSYCHOLOGY

TONY MORRIS • JEFF SUMMERS

Sport and exercise psychology is a relatively new field of research and practice. Its theoretical base and use of research methods are still in the process of development. Practice in sport and exercise psychology often borrows from more established fields, while new methods and techniques typically emerge from the needs of particular consulting situations, rather than from theory and research, for example. Reflection on the development of the field during the last twenty years or so indicates that the paths down which sport and exercise psychology has travelled have not been easy to predict. At the same time, the rate of development, while slow to start with, has increased and there is now so much work in progress across so many aspects of the field that it is difficult for one person to keep fully abreast of all areas of sport and exercise psychology.

This "mushrooming" of theoretical and applied sport psychology is exciting to observe from the perspective of the profession, but it signals caution to anyone trying to predict the future. Precognition is not yet part of the training for sport psychologists, so this chapter does not present predictions about what the future of the field will be. Rather, by reflecting on what has been written in the present book, the following issues represent concerns about the way we do sport and exercise psychology, accompanied by some observations on general directions which seem to be important for the future of the profession. The authors of chapters have given their expert views on the directions which sport psychology should take, specific to their topics. It is not intended to repeat those topic–specific ideas, but, rather, to address issues which are consistently reflected in those discussions. The chapter will not enter into in-depth considerations of issues. That is not appropriate for the conclusion to such a wide-ranging text. It is important, however, that future issues are raised and it is critical that they be debated at length in more specialised forums.

This chapter addresses issues which relate to the way that theory and research are developing in the field. Concerns with the general focus of theory and research are introduced, as are methodological issues. Also issues of importance to practice are raised. These particularly apply to professional training and applied work. The artificial dichotomy of theory and practice, which is also reflected in the structure of the book, raises a number of issues which are then considered.

FUTURE DIRECTIONS IN THEORY AND RESEARCH

A scan of the field of sport and exercise psychology indicates that there are few theories and models which have been developed within the discipline. Many of the major directions taken in sport psychology have been signposted by its parent discipline, psychology. Broad, paradigmatic shifts from the person-centred focus of early theory and research to interactional and then cognitive phenomenological approaches reflect earlier developments in psychology. More importantly perhaps, theories on specific topics have often involved the application of a mainstream theory to sport and exercise, for example, Zajonc (1965) in social facilitation, Weiner (1974) in attribution theory, Deci (1975) in intrinsic motivation, Bandura (1977, 1986) in self-efficacy, and Spielberger (1966) in anxiety. While sport and exercise psychology should always be alert to developments in the general discipline, there is a need for theories and models to be generated in the field of sport.

Perhaps this sport-specific, theoretical approach is best exemplified in sport and exercise psychology by the work of Martens and his colleagues, culminating in the book *Competitive anxiety in sport* (Martens, Vealey, & Burton, 1990). That work originated in the application of Spielberger's state-trait theory and measures of anxiety in sport competition. It progressed through the development of sport-specific measures to permit a more sensitive examination of anxiety in sport. This has culminated in the statement of a theoretical model of competitive anxiety, which can be used to generate many hypotheses that should further develop our understanding of sport competition anxiety. The Martens et al. (1990) theoretical model of competitive anxiety in sport reflects another point which is crucial to the future development of theories and models in sport and exercise psychology. It is also a point which comes up repeatedly in the chapters in the present text. To reflect the complexities of human behaviour, theories and models must be multifaceted; we need to develop multifactor theories, because the single factor theories of the past have not produced a high level of understanding and prediction of behaviour. Theories need to consider a range of dimensions and to operate on a number of levels. For example, psychophysiological and psychosocial factors should be considered alongside purely psychological dimensions. Martens et al. (1990) include a personal factor (trait anxiety), a situational factor (the objective situation), and cognitive phenomenological factors (perceived uncertainty and perceived importance) in their theory. Andersen and Williams' (1988) model of stress and injury is another example of a multifactor theory which includes environmental, psychosocial and cognitive components, with the potential also for psychophysiological factors to be considered.

Generation of a viable theory or model is not very useful if there are no structured research programs which address its propositions. Consideration of the sport and exercise psychology literature reveals very few examples like that of Martens, where a particular issue has been systematically addressed through a long-term research program. The direction of such a program will inevitably shift as new knowledge leads to greater insight, as in the case of the original attempt, logical at the time, of Martens and his colleagues to develop a unitary measure of state anxiety, the Competitive State Anxiety Inventory (CSAI). When this proved to be unsuccessful (Martens, Burton, Rivkin, & Simons, 1980), Martens and colleagues went back to theoretical perspectives on anxiety. Through the application of work by Liebert and Morris (1967) on worry and emotionality and that of Davidson and Schwartz (1976) on cognitive and somatic anxiety, they produced the CSAI-2 (Martens, Burton, Vealey, Bump, & Smith, 1983). This distinguished between cognitive and somatic state anxiety applied specifically to sport competition and produced probably the most widely researched conceptualisation of the last fifteen years in sport psychology. Further, as Martens et al. (1990) acknowledge "perhaps the 'golden egg' of the CSAI-2 development was the fortuitous discovery of the state self-confidence component" (p. 213). It might be said that such "good fortune" is much more likely to arise in the context of clear, structured, systematic research programs than in the one-off study of psychological processes or techniques that litter the sport and exercise psychology journals.

The measurement and description of variables is an essential first stage in this process, but it should lead to the generation of theories and models, which give rise to testable hypotheses or research questions. A range of research designs can be used to examine these questions, increasing our understanding of the concepts and processes involved. Practice often functions in the absence of substantial testing of techniques in the sport context. Examination of the efficacy of applied interventions is an urgent need. Thus, research involving interventions is an important future direction, but it should do more than test whether the intervention works or is superior to another. It must help us to understand the underlying psychological mechanisms, so that the theory or model can be refined and will apply to a whole range of potential interventions, thus advancing practice as well as theory.

One approach to research which can focus and clarify thinking in this respect is causal modelling. The proposition of models is a favourite activity of sport psychologists, as exemplified by their generation at the conclusion of most contributions to Horn's (1992) text, *Advances in sport psychology*. The testing of those models using causal modelling procedures is, conversely, infrequent, as noted by Schutz (1993). An example of the way it can be done is McAuley's (1985) comparison of anxiety and self-efficacy as mediators between the situation and behaviour. More recently, Carpenter, Scanlan, Simons, and Lobel (1993) pioneered the use of structural equation modelling in sport and exercise psychology. The use of causal modelling techniques to generate and modify conceptions of the relationships between variables in a particular area of sport psychology is especially useful in examining the role of mediating and moderating variables. Gould and Krane (1992) note the need in the study of anxiety and performance to move from correlational to causal research. This suggestion applies much more widely in sport and exercise psychology and the new causal modelling techniques which are just starting to be used will be of great value in facilitating this shift.

Gould and Krane (1992) also make the point that much research in sport and exercise psychology limits its theoretical value by testing only one theory in a particular study. Where two or more theories are tested in the same study, more information is gleaned. McAuley's (1985) study again exemplifies this point. It has been argued by anxiety theorists that it is not necessary to employ self-efficacy as an explanatory concept mediating between the stimulus components of the environment and the subjects' reactions. This theoretical perspective contends that anxiety explains such relationships and self-efficacy is simply a by-product of the process, so that as anxiety increases, confidence (self-efficacy) in the situation decreases. This accounts for any covariation of self-efficacy with performance. Self-efficacy theory, on the other hand, suggests that self-efficacy is the important mediating variable and anxiety is simply a by-product of low self-efficacy for the task. McAuley was able to test both models using causal modelling. His results provided support for the latter contention, with stronger paths emerging when self-efficacy was the mediator in the causal model. This type of multitheory research design is to be commended and should become more frequent in sport and exercise psychology research in the future.

Sport psychology has been typified by the execution of cross-sectional research. There are few examples of studies which have considered the same group of subjects over an extended period of time to understand development and change processes. Longitudinal research of this nature could answer many questions which remain outstanding from the cross-sectional work. An example of an area where this would be the case is in the study of participation and drop-out from sport. Research on involvement in sport during the teenage years has indicated that the large drop-out observed in American sport is largely based on lack of time and failure to achieve desired goals (Weiss & Petlichkoff, 1989). Studies often asked subjects to consider their sport involvement retrospectively, with the associated problems of memory and reconstruction. Studies also commonly asked superficial questions about reasons for dropping out. Weiss and Petlichkoff (1989) note that deeper investigation by follow-up interviews has indicated that lack of time was often caused by the increasing demands of other sports in which the subjects were involved, while their limited goal achievement was also relative rather than absolute, that is, comparatively greater success was being achieved in their other sports activities. Longitudinal study of the sports activities of American and Australian teenagers, as well as those in other cultures, could substantiate the pattern implied in previous research, that many children try out lots of activities and often enjoy most of them, but as success increases, the demands of each expand, until some enjoyable activities must be given up to gain the greater perceived satisfaction from another sport or sports. If this was found to be the case, then in-depth longitudinal research, by interviewing adolescents about their motives as they drop out of one sport to give more time to another, would be able to explore the processes underlying the decisions made by young athletes much more effectively than cross-sectional or retrospective research are able to do.

Discussion of the changes in motives and sport behaviour which occur in a very short time during adolescence, bring into sharp relief the need for lifespan research in sport and exercise psychology. As individuals move through life, their needs and priorities change and they perceive situations differently. It is important for sport psychology to be aware of the shifting background to sport and exercise behaviour and for researchers not to simply assume that values and processes operating in adolescents and/or college students, who commonly act as subjects, apply to all people. A simple example of this comes from research we have completed, again in the area of participation motivation. Two studies were carried out using the Participation Motivation Questionnaire (PMQ) (Gill, Gross, & Huddleston, 1983), one on motives for initiation of tai chi (Morris & Jin-Song, 1991) and the other on motives for continuation in table tennis (Morris, Power, & Pappalardo, 1993). They looked across the lifespan from ten-year-olds to over sixties, following the original work of Brodkin and Weiss (1990). One finding was that adolescents and young adults rated a medical motive very low, presumably because most of them had no medical problems, especially problems of a chronic nature. For adults in their middle years, the ranking of this medical item moved up to a moderate position and, for older adults, it became one of the most important reasons for doing the activity. It may seem obvious now that older adults suffer more frequently than others from chronic illnesses and other medical conditions which may be alleviated by exercise and that this is likely to influence their motives for participation. Research on participation motivation before Brodkin and Weiss (1990) used adolescent samples and, while the researchers themselves were undoubtedly aware of the restrictions in generality of their findings, others may have assumed they applied to all participants in that sport or exercise activity.

It has long been noted that longitudinal research is relatively unattractive. This is largely because both the organisations interested in the practical outcomes of research and the academics who judge each other's work by published reports, anticipate a rapid outcome, admittedly for different reasons. Regnier, Salmela, and Russell (1993) report on an alternative approach which permits a longitudinal view to be inferred, but abbreviates the timescale, producing a technique which combines cross-sectional and longitudinal research designs. This is called the sliding populations approach. It involves measuring variables in what is called the "pool population". This refers to the younger age group of interest, for example, 13 year olds. A measuring instrument is devised to detect those athletes who will be successful at an older age, say, 16 years, which is termed the "target population". The pool population is then followed to target population age to test the predictive power of the instrument. By chaining together pool and target ages, for example, following the 13 to 16 year old phase, a 16 year old pool population may be examined (using a different instrument) with an 18 year old target population, and based on statistical checks across these groups, inferences can then be made about "longitudinal effects". The target population for a younger pool population should not be used as the pool population for an older target population. This approach may not remove the need for longitudinal studies, but it permits the reporting of much more rapid provisional conclusions to bodies, such as national sports organisations, which need to make decisions on talent identification and development, for example, with longitudinal research continuing, hopefully, to confirm these conclusions in due course.

The issue of generality of the results obtained from research also underlies one of the most important issues for sport psychology to address. The vast majority of research in sport and exercise psychology has used adolescent and college student samples. Typically these individuals were competitive athletes. This presents little problem in research concerned with mass participation processes. In a proportion of this research, however, inferences have been drawn from the results, for other groups, particularly elite performers. It is only relatively recently that it has been recognised that major differences exist in skills, motives, ego-involvement, and other psychological processes which make generalising from competitive to elite performers invalid. Even when elite performers are used as subjects in laboratory-based studies using analogue tasks, they are not using their skills and may not be highly motivated to do the task or do not feel personally threatened by possible failure at something they have never done before and which they might view as a trivial task.

Trite as it seems, it still must be stressed that to understand the psychological processes underlying the behaviour of elite performers in their chosen sports it is essential for research to observe the elite performers in that environment. In a recent study, Callery and Morris (1993) used a multiple-baseline, single-case design to examine the effects of an imagery program on the skill of disposal of the ball by foot, using as subjects ten Australian Football League players over most of a season. Performance was judged by three independent experts and inter-rater reliabilities exceeded 0.9. Eight of the ten subjects showed trends in the predicted direction, four revealing very clear positive effects of the imagery. Social validation questions at the end of the study indicated that the players felt more confident about the skill from an early stage of the study. This finding has led us to study the role of confidence as a mediator between imagery and performance in a causal modelling study. Perhaps without studying elite performers it would not have emerged that confidence is a critical factor for that group.

One reason why much research has not been done with elite performers in competitive situations is that it is not ethically or practically acceptable to use such individuals in a control group. Recognition that an understanding of elite performers, in practice as well as in competition, depends on studying elite performers in these contexts is an important step for sport psychology. The problems associated with the traditional experimental design, where an experimental group, which receives some sort of treatment, is compared with a control group, which does not, will not go away. It is, thus, essential that sport psychology recognises the value of alternative methods to the traditional experiment. The Callery and Morris (1993) study employed one method which avoids most of the ethical and practical difficulties. In single-case designs, all subjects receive the treatment, but they all spend time initially in a baseline condition, which means that in essence they act as their own controls. The multiple-baseline design has the added advantage that each subject starts to receive the intervention at a different time, say after four, five, six and seven weeks of baseline. The result of this is that any effects which arise for each subject shortly after starting the treatment are not attributable to the same extraneous event, such as a stirring team talk, as only one subject would have started the treatment at that time. Even so, the method has problems in practice. In our study, subjects assigned randomly to longer baselines became impatient to start the treatment when they perceived their colleagues to be benefiting from it. The single-case design still has a great deal of potential for research in real sport competition contexts.

Other research methods also offer the opportunity to conduct research in the field with elite performers. Observational methods have not been widely used in sport psychology to date, but they can permit the researcher to participate in the competition environment. They are particularly effective for investigating interpersonal aspects of sport. Observational methods are often used in conjunction with other approaches to provide validation through the process of triangulation, whereby several methods are used independently and their correspondence is indicative of validity. Better established are interview techniques, perhaps because the interview has long been part of psychological practice. Recently different methods have been established to analyse the transcripts generated by in-depth interviews and these inductive methods are starting to prove informative, as illustrated by the work of Gould and his colleagues (e.g., Gould, Eklund, & Jackson, 1992a, 1992b; Gould, Jackson, & Finch, 1993a, 1993b). Another approach to the interview is that of grounded theory (Glaser & Strauss, 1967). This approach intentionally avoids theory leading to testable hypotheses, typically permitting the theory to emerge from the data gathered. Choice of methods should be appropriate to the question being asked. Use of a range of methods can provide different sorts of information and insights, while the picture created can have increased validity because of the reciprocal support of several independent research methods. Whatever the methods used it is important for sport psychologists to be reflexive in their research processes. This means that they must be aware of and acknowledge their own perspectives when they execute research and interpret data.

The emphasis in the previous section was on the need to study elite performers in the competitive environment. This was not meant to suggest that sport psychology should focus entirely on the elite. On the contrary, sport and exercise psychology must research with a wide range of groups. Understanding human behaviour in sport and exercise cannot come from watching only those at the elite level. There are many other groups that sport psychologists must consider, if they are to convince the community that they can offer a service to everyone. Theory and research must address the needs of groups like older adults, young children, people with disabilities, people with chronic diseases and people at risk for whom prevention or primary care is possible. A variety of racial, ethnic and cultural factors should also be taken into account. The opportunities for this sort of research are legion, with so many diverse groups to study. Also, the nurturing of sport psychology around the world offers great potential for cross-cultural research collaboration. Research programs that demonstrate that a particular psychological process is universal or that show how a process is influenced by cultural factors will surely be more convincing than narrowly based research in one culture.

A final concern for theory and research, and also for practice, is the role of measurement in sport and exercise psychology. The comments of contributors to the 1989 Olympic sports issue of *The Sport Psychologist* suggested that tests were not used very much in applied work. It is of some concern to note that practitioners have little faith in the tests their colleagues have developed, preferring to use their own judgement. The measures which are generally available, with the exception of the SCAT and the CSAI-2, have not been substantially validated for research in the field. Validating tests is not the most attractive exercise to many researchers, but there is still a substantial way to go in this area before we can look at the results of tests and predict in which sport the athlete competes, let alone whether an individual will do well under pressure. These goals might never be attained, but sport psychology has hardly left the starting gate in sport-specific, test development. At the same time, it is essential in many studies that we measure factors which could influence the variable of particular interest. Without reliable and valid tests this becomes problematic. It is important for researchers to be prepared to spend some of their valuable time on the crucial activity of test validation.

FUTURE DIRECTIONS FOR THE SPORT PSYCHOLOGY PROFESSION

Research does not proceed in a vacuum. The development of theories and their investigation through controlled research have a purpose beyond the better understanding of human behaviour in sport. It is to provide more knowledge and skills for the professional sport psychologist to use to enhance the experience of people in sport and exercise contexts. Research is carried out in the service of the profession, so it is the responsibility of practitioners to identify and develop the range of practice situations in which research is needed. It should be the aim of sport psychologists to make sport and exercise psychology accessible to everyone in the community. In doing this they will also expand the work for the profession. Strategies to involve more of the community in sport psychology need to be generated. Sport psychologists must be proactive in promoting their profession in all spheres of life. Research should then be directed at a much wider range of applications of sport psychology.

Students in professional training need to be prepared for this process of creating sport psychology anew in areas of the community which have not previously had access to the field. Professional training is an area in itself which has received little formal attention. There is a standing joke about the tendency of psychologists to spend a lot of their time analysing themselves, the suggestion being that there are better things for them to do. While this overly reflexive attititude may be the case in general, the argument is strong for sport psychologists to study the way they practice, in an effort to facilitate training in practice of their professional students in the future. Fortunately, the largest single group of sport psychologists, the Association for the Advancement of Applied Sport Psychology (AAASP), has begun to do this. Australasian sport psychologists must also consider carefully the ways in which they do their job and then communicate their functional behaviours to those in training.

An important element of the kind of sport psychologist we aim to develop through training programs, concerns perceptions about the sport psychologist's role in relation to clients. An issue in the practice of psychology in general has long been the potential for the client/practitioner relationship to become one of dependency. This frequently refers to clients becoming dependent on the psychologist, but it can also involve a need felt by the practitioner to maintain the professional relationship with the client. The message from this book is clear: the aim of applied work in sport psychology should be to create a self-regulating athlete or exerciser, a person who possesses the skills, techniques and self-understanding to cope with the stress of competition or the demands to adhere to exercise when pressures of family, work, weather and more attractive alternatives encourage the person not to exercise. Sport psychologists must feel their job has been well done when clients do not need to see them any more.

Another part of the educational question concerns the actual mode of instruction. The didactic approach is only one method and others must be considered. Workbooks, audios and videos are beginning to emerge from a number of groups, but their advent has been slow. Multimedia technology is developing very rapidly, however, and it is important for sport psychology to be part of the technological revolution. Much of the subject matter of the field is particularly suited to the interactive, computer-based, educational tools currently being used by students at school and at play. Multimedia technology can also make sport psychology more accessible to those in rural communities and those with little money to spend on the frequent use of consultants.

Discussion of the broad range of teaching methods which can be used in sport psychology, introduces the issue of evaluation of outcomes. It was noted that many of the experts writing in the 1989 and 1990 issues of *The Sport Psychologist* reported that they carried out evaluation of their interventions. At the same time, those assessment procedures tended to be untested and, typically, they were ad hoc. Training in the formal procedures of evaluation is essential, but it should be illuminated by a literature on the effectiveness of the evaluation procedures in the sport and exercise psychology context. Evaluation is an important part of the learning process. Sports performers understand that feedback is a crucial component of learning. In the future, formative and summative evaluation of programs should be an integral part of the sport psychologist's approach to practice. The feedback gleaned from them should be used to enhance practice.

✐ THE THEORY–PRACTICE NEXUS

In the past, the degree to which theory and practice in sport psychology have been coordinated was limited. Whether this is a consequence of lack of communication between practitioners and researchers, the inapplicability of the orthodox research methods of sport psychology to real world settings, a focus on issues of traditional concern in physical education, the parent discipline, or any one or combination of a number of other factors, it must not be permitted to continue, for the future success of the applied field. Theories which do not apply to real world issues tend to be lifeless, while comparisons of interventions against each other with no systematic theory testing must ultimately consider every intervention, as no underlying principles can be deduced from ad hoc comparisons.

Models and theories must be generated to describe processes in real athletes involved in real sports competitions. For example, a theme in this text is that a shift is occurring in many areas from an obsession with outcomes in sport to a focus on the psychological processes which lead to those outcomes. As more process-oriented applied work is undertaken, there is a great opportunity to develop theory and research in concert with practice. These theories and models need to be tested using a range of paradigms in a systematic manner so that the theory can progress to the stage where it can be used to generate predictions about the best techniques to employ in a particular situation. Theory and practice can grow together in this way, where research is carried out on the application of sport psychology and practice is guided by existing research. It is to be hoped that future editions of this book can adopt a thematic approach, where the topic, whether it be anxiety, imagery or confidence, can be addressed in terms of theory and practice together.

CONCLUSIONS

The field of sport and exercise psychology has developed rapidly over the last two decades and is now expanding faster than ever. There are so many interesting areas of research in sport psychology that it is difficult to choose the most rewarding in which to work. Collaboration and teamwork seem to be practical ways of trying to keep up with as much as possible. As if this is not enough, it is becoming clear that few real world issues will be resolved by a single discipline approach. There is a need to collaborate also with colleagues in the other sports sciences in addressing some of the most important practical issues. It is to be hoped that we will soon see multidisciplinary and multidimensional research programs launched across Australasia and linking up with colleagues all over the world, perhaps most notably with colleagues in Asia. Collaborations which address major practical issues in a range of cultures will surely provide an exciting profession for the twenty-first century.

SUMMARY

This chapter has reviewed some of the major themes for the future which have arisen from the thinking of contributors to this text. A major thread in this review was the need for practice and research to move closer together. The first main section considered theory and research. It proposed that there is a need for more sport-specific theories and structured research programs to test them. Research on interventions is a particular need which was noted. New research designs, paradigms and statistical techniques should be used, including causal modelling, naturalistic and qualitative paradigms, and longitudinal and lifespan research designs. It was argued that research needs to examine a wide range of groups within the community, that it should attempt to test two or more theories against each other in single studies, and that it should locate research in real competition contexts. The next section was concerned with professional directions. It was suggested that there is a need to relate theory and practice more closely and to train new practitioners to a high standard, which requires research to be carried out on supervision of practice. It was also proposed that a range of alternative instructional methods and media should be used and that more attention should be given to researching program evaluation. Finally, the theory and practice section called for greater communication between professionals in the field and more research directly on the psychological processes of real athletes. Communication and collaboration between all professional sport psychologists in Australasia is the most important theme in this book. We hope that the book itself is a testimony that this can happen between a large group of sport psychologists when there is a common will.

REFERENCES

Andersen, M. B., & Williams, J. M. (1988). A model of stress and athletic injury: Prediction and prevention. *Journal of Sport and Exercise Psychology, 10*, 294–306.

Bandura, A. (1977). Self-efficacy: Toward a unifying theory of behavior change. *Psychological Review, 84*, 191–215.

Bandura, A. (1986). *Social foundations of thought and action*. Englewood Cliffs, NJ: Prentice-Hall.

Brodkin, P., & Weiss, M. R. (1990). Developmental differences in motivation for participating in competitive swimming. *Journal of Sport and Exercise Psychology, 12*, 248–263.

Callery, P., & Morris, T. (1993, June). Imagery Training and the Performance of a Skill in Elite Sport. In S. Serpa, J. Alves, V. Ferreira, & A. Paulo-Brito (Eds.), *Proceedings of the VIIIth World Congress of Sport Psychology* (pp. 648–651). Lisbon: International Society of Sports Psychology.

Carpenter, P. J., Scanlan, T. K., Simons, J. P., & Lobel, M. (1993). A test of the sport commitment model using structural equation modeling. *Journal of Sport and Exercise Psychology, 15*, 119–133.

Davidson, R. J., & Schwartz, G. E. (1976). The psychobiology of relaxation and related states: A multi-process theory. In D. I. Mostofsky (Ed.), *Behavior control and modification of physiological activity* (pp. 399–442). Englewood Cliffs, NJ: Prentice-Hall.

Deci, E. L. (1975). *Intrinsic motivation*. New York: Plenum.

Gill, D. L., Gross, J. B., & Huddleston, S. (1983). Participation motivation in youth sports. *International Journal of Sport Psychology, 14*, 1–14.

Glaser, B., & Strauss, A. (1967). *The discovery of grounded theory*. Chicago: Aldine.

Gould, D., Eklund, R. C., & Jackson, S. A. (1992a). 1988 USA Olympic wrestling excellence II: Mental preparation, precompetitive cognition, and affect. *The Sport Psychologist, 6*(4), 358–382.

Gould, D., Eklund, R. C., & Jackson, S. A. (1992b). 1988 USA Olympic wrestling excellence I: Competitive cognition, and affect. *The Sport Psychologist, 6*(4), 383–402.

Gould, D., Jackson, S. A., & Finch, L. M. (1993a). Life at the top: The experiences of U.S. national figure skaters. *The Sport Psychologist, 7*(4), 354–374.

Gould, D., Jackson, S. A., & Finch, L. M. (1993b). Sources of stress in national champion figure skaters. *Journal of Sport and Exercise Psychology, 15*(2), 134–159.

Gould, D., & Krane, V. (1992). The arousal-athletic performance relationship: Current status and future directions. In T. S. Horn (Ed.), *Advances in sport psychology* (pp. 119–142). Champaign, IL: Human Kinetics.

Horn, T. S. (Ed.). (1992). *Advances in sport psychology.* Champaign, IL: Human Kinetics.

Liebert, R. M., & Morris, L. W. (1967). Cognitive and emotional components of test anxiety: A distinction and some initial data. *Psychological Reports, 20,* 975–978.

Martens, R., Burton, D., Rivkin, F., & Simons, J. (1980). Reliability and validity of the Competitive State Anxiety Inventory (CSAI). In C. H. Nadeau, W. R. Halliwell, K. M. Newell, & G. C. Roberts (Eds.), *Psychology of motor behavior and sport — 1979.* Champaign, IL: Human Kinetics.

Martens, R., Burton, D., Vealey, R. S., Bump, L. A., & Smith, D. E. (1983). *The Competitive State Anxiety Inventory-2.* Unpublished manuscript, University of Illinois at Urbana-Champaign.

Martens, R., Vealey, R. S., & Burton, D. (Eds.). (1990). *Competitive anxiety in sport.* Champaign, IL: Human Kinetics.

McAuley, E. (1985). Modeling and self-efficacy: A test of Bandura's model. *Journal of Sport Psychology, 7,* 283–295.

Morris, T., & Han Jin-Song. (1991, November). Motives for taking up Tai Chi. *Proceedings of First Asian South Pacific Association of Sport Psychology International Congress,* Melbourne: ASPASP.

Morris, T., Power, H., & Pappalardo, B. (1993, June). Motivation for Participation in Table Tennis. Paper presented at the *VIIIth World Congress in Sport Psychology,* Lisbon.

Regnier, G., Salmela, J., & Russell, S. J. (1993). Talent detection and development in sport. In R. N. Singer, M. Murphey, & L. K. Tennant (Eds.), *Handbook of research on sport psychology* (pp. 290–313). New York: Macmillan Publishing Company.

Schutz, R. W. (1993, June). Methodological issues and measurement problems in sport psychology. In S. Serpa, J. Alves, V. Ferreira, & A. Paulo-Brito (Eds.), *Proceedings of the VIIIth World Congress of Sport Psychology* (pp. 119–131). Lisbon: International Society of Sport Psychology.

Spielberger, C. D. (1966). *Anxiety and behavior.* New York: Academic.

Weiner, B. (1974). *Achievement motivation and attribution theory.* Morristown, NJ: General Learning Press.

Weiss, M. R., & Petlichkoff, L. M. (1989). Children's motivation for participation in and withdrawal from sport: Identifying the missing links. *Pediatric Exercise Science, 1,* 195–211.

Zajonc, R. B. (1965). Social facilitation. *Science, 149,* 269–274.

AUTHOR INDEX

AAASP Newsletter 215
Abadie, D. A. 458
Abel, M. 146, 147, 156, 316
Abernethy, B. 43, 44, 65, 66, 68, 71, 72, 75, 82, 343
Abraham, S. F. 554
Abrams, D. B. 442
Abramson, L. Y. 129, 133, 135
Abrego, P. J. 479, 495
Acevedo, E. O. 444
Acosta, R. 542
Adams, G. M. 290
Adams, N. E. 327
Adler, A. 103
Adler, T. F. 97, 552
Ainsworth, B. 441
Alaranta, H. 457
Albinson, J. G. 401, 402
Albrecht, R. R. 17, 80, 204, 397, 476
Albright, A. 158
Alderman, R. 518
Alexander, K. 520, 522
Allard, F. 74
Allen, G. J. 157, 220, 446
Allen, N. 375
Alles, W. 460, 461
Allison, M. T. 482, 483, 547
Allport, D. A. 66
Allport, F. 173, 176
Alves, J. xxv
Ames, C. 165, 191
Andersen, M. B. 43, 217, 459, 461, 463, 464, 595
Anderson, C. A. 133
Anderson, D. 20, 489, 491, 492
Anderson, K. 133
Andrews, G. R. 135
Annerel, J. 483
Anshel, M. H. 30, 31, 33, 35, 45, 46, 48, 55, 57, 190, 199, 207, 239, 273, 277, 301, 318, 345, 443
Anshel, S. L. 443
Anthony, W. A. 289
Anthrop, J. 547

Antonelli, F. 396
Appleby, D. C. 458
Archer, J. 165
Arnoult, L. H. 133
Ary, D. V. 159
Ascough, J. C. 277
Ashley, M. A. 6
Ashton, R. 344, 348
Asken, M. J. 503, 509
Atchley, R. C. 477
Atkinson, J. W. 103, 104, 105, 107, 108, 196, 550
Austin, N. K. 424, 427, 429
Australian Sports Commission 106, 540, 541, 542
Avener, M. 48, 217, 222, 378

Backx, F. J. G. 456
Bacon, S. J. 76
Baekeland, F. 447
Baghurst, P. A. 530
Bahrke, M. 19
Bailey, D. 458
Bailey, S. 133
Baillie, P. H. F. 481, 484
Bain, J. D. 248
Baker-Finch, S. 557, 558
Bale, R. M. 345, 397
Balke, B. 443
Ball, J. 198
Bandura, A. 144, 145, 146, 147, 148, 149, 150, 151, 152, 154, 155, 156, 158, 159, 161, 162, 163, 166, 167, 204, 261, 294, 315, 316, 318, 327, 335, 353, 372, 378, 551, 593
Banks, A. J. 298
Banks, J. 509
Banks, N. M. 375
Barabasz, A. F. 374
Barabasz, M. 374
Barber, P. 68
Bard, C. 72
Bargman, E. P. 445
Barksdale, C. N. 445

Barling, J. 146, 147, 156, 316
Barnes, J. 318
Barrell, G. V. 113
Bar-Tel, D. 554
Bartel, P. 447
Bartis, S. 98
Bauman, A. 440
Baumeister, R. F. 22, 40, 45, 46, 184
Beaumont, P. J. V. 554
Beck, A. T. 224, 495
Becker, B. J. 344
Beeney, L. J. 165
Belenky, M. F. 553
Belgrave, F. Z. 133
Bell, G. J. 19
Bell, K. F. 325
Bem, S. L. 547, 549
Bengston, V. L. 477
Ben-Ishai, R. 78
Bennett, B. B. 217, 222
Bennett, H. Z. 222, 248, 389, 414
Bennett, R. S. 564
Benson, H. 224, 277
Berger, B. G. 34, 35, 290, 441, 445, 446
Berger, M. 158
Bergey, D. B. 349
Berliner, D. C. 246, 247, 251
Bernard, M. 467
Bernardo, P. 49
Bernstein, L. 289
Bernstein, S. 554
Best, D. L. 443
Best, J. B. 65
Bettenhausen, K. L. 423
Betts, G. H. 357, 358
Beuter, A. 149
Beyer, J. 327
Biddle, S. J. H. 129, 130, 220, 438
Biglan, A. 159
Billings, A. G. 332
Birch, D. 93
Bird, A. M. 30, 42, 135, 136, 397

Birrell, S.   546, 548, 551, 561
Black, D. R.   555, 556
Blackwell, B.   463, 464
Blair, W.   517
Blakeslee, T. R.   363
Blanchard, E. B.   151
Blanchard, K. H.   322
Blanksby, B. A.   101, 112
Blann, F. W.   486, 487, 488, 489, 495, 496
Blann, W.   218, 483, 486
Blinde, E. M.   475, 476, 479, 481
Bloomfield, J.   101, 113
Bloomgarten, Z. T.   164
Blumenthal, J. A.   34, 446
Boies, S. J.   75, 81
Bolus, R.   318
Bompa, T.   401, 413
Bond, C. F. Jr.   177, 179, 180, 181, 182, 187
Bond, J.   215, 217
Bond, J. W.   395, 397, 409, 410, 447
Bonnel, A. M.   67, 79
Bookman, J.   164
Bootsma, R. J.   73
Borden, R. J.   174, 182, 186, 188
Borkovec, T. D.   31, 274
Bortz, R.   447
Botterill, C.   225, 229, 230, 232, 276
Bouchard, C.   271
Bourgeois, A. E.   296
Boutcher, S. H.   65, 82, 225, 236, 237, 238, 241, 389, 402, 443, 445
Bowers, K. S.   16
Bowling, A.   447
Boys, J. H.   224
Bradley, P. W.   19, 445
Brammer, L. M.   479, 495
Bramwell, S. T.   460, 461
Brawley, L. R.   98, 191, 197, 198, 199, 202, 203, 204, 205, 206, 207, 216, 251, 438, 439
Bredemeier, B. J.   520, 522, 532, 560
Breslow, I.   278
Brewer, B. W.   481
Broadbent, D. A.   65, 68, 76
Brodkin, P.   116, 117, 596
Brody, E. B.   149, 152

Broen, J. E.   159
Brooks, D. R.   132
Brothers, M.   164
Browman, C. P.   447
Browman, C. R.   447
Brown, D.   292
Brown, D. F.   31, 45
Brown, D. R.   19, 445
Brown, E. Y.   555
Brown, G. W.   460
Brown, J. D.   290, 463
Brown, J. M.   31, 45
Brown, L.   228, 232
Brown, R. B.   458
Brown, V. R.   79
Brown, W. V.   165
Browning, C.   552
Brustad, R.   518, 519, 520, 521, 532
Bruun, S. E.   98
Bruya, L.   517
Bryan, A. J.   240, 345
Bryan, J. F.   260
Budgett, R.   299
Budney, A. J.   352
Bukowski, W. M.   126, 135, 136, 300
Bull, S. J.   401, 402
Buller, P. F.   423
Bump, L. A.   16, 76, 144, 156, 165, 230, 233, 234, 594
Bumpus, A. K.   444
Bunker, L. E.   151, 324, 325, 523, 524
Burchstead, G. N.   156
Burckes, M. E.   457
Burgess, E.   476
Burhans, R. S. , III   349
Burke, K. L.   403
Burley, D. M.   298
Burnett, N.   74
Burns, D. D.   467, 495
Burton, D.   16, 29, 76, 144, 156, 165, 186, 230, 259, 260, 266, 274, 359, 593, 594
Burwitz, L.   72
Butler, B.   547
Butler, J.   539
Butler, R. J.   243
Butt, D. S.   544

Cairns, L.   318
Caldarone, L.   396
Cale, A.   36

Callery, P.   345, 353, 354, 598
Camaione, D. N.   157, 220
Campbell, D. R.   159
Campbell, J.   555
Campbell, L. F.   220
Canabal, M. Y.   504
Cannon, W. B.   273
Cantrell, P.   149, 163, 448
Cantu, R. C.   158
Carey, C.   133
Carmack, M.   444
Carpenter, L.   542
Carpenter, P. J.   595
Carron, A. V.   6, 38, 98, 126, 129, 174, 184, 185, 186, 187, 191, 192, 193, 196, 197, 198, 199, 200, 201, 202, 203, 204, 205, 206, 207, 437, 521
Cartwright, D.   192
Carver, C. S.   13, 47, 443
Castiello, I.   73
Cattell, R. B.   5, 8, 393
Catterall, J. R.   447
Cauraugh, J. H.   69, 72
Cavness, C.   447
Cervone, D.   149, 166, 167, 204, 261
Chalip, L.   318
Chalip, P.   95, 96, 109
Chase, M. A.   144, 151, 153
Chase, W. G.   74
Chaumeton, N.   92, 95, 116
Chelladurai, P.   193, 198
Chemers, M.   198
Chen, D.   72
Chen, S. S.   344
Chevalier-Girard, N.   348
Chi, L.   191
Chisholm, K.   496
Chrisfield, P. M.   217, 457
Christiansen, G.   199, 202
Chu, D.   39
Church, R. M.   176
Clark, L. V.   342, 344, 347, 375
Clark, R. A.   103, 508, 550
Clews, G. J.   113
Clinchy, B. M.   553
Clough, J.   518, 519, 521
Clugston, H. A.   344
Coakley, J. J.   475, 476, 493, 521, 526
Coddington, D.   460, 461
Cohen, F.   37
Cohen, S.   293

Cohn, P. J.   248, 410, 585
Colavecchio, P. G.   80, 206
Cole, G. E.   290
Coleman, A. E.   443
Colker, R.   548
Collier, D. E.   279, 374
Collis, M. L.   446
Condry, J.   551
Connell, R. W.   485, 539, 559, 560, 562
Connelly, D.   543
Connolly, C.   316, 328
Cook, B.   100
Cook, R. E.   134
Cooke, C. J.   222, 443
Coonan, W. E.   530
Cooper, B.   520, 522
Cooper, L.   5
Corbin, C. B.   341, 342, 347, 375, 448, 517, 552
Corcoran, J.   204
Costill, D. L.   444
Cottrell, N. B.   174, 179, 182, 186
Courneya, K. S.   149, 174, 184, 185, 186, 187
Courtet, P.   76
Cox, R.   504
Cox, R. H.   4, 5, 6, 8, 14, 15, 16, 17, 18, 20, 116, 182, 318
Cox, S.   445
Cox, T.   47, 48
Coyne, J. C.   464
Crace, R. K.   195
Crane, M.   554
Cratty, B. J.   xxv, 39, 55
Crawford, S. A. G. M.   276
Crews, D. J.   81
Cripe, B. K.   30
Crook, J. M.   479, 480
Croon, M.   441
Crouch, J. G.   157
Crundall, I.   298
Cryan, P.   460, 461
Csikszentmihalyi, I. S.   206
Csikszentmihalyi, M.   206, 248, 249, 414, 444, 587
Csizma, K. A.   549
Cullen, D.   558
Cullen, J.   222
Cumming, E.   477
Curley, V.   556
Curtis, B.   431
Curtis, J.   236
Cymerman, A.   444

Daiss, S.   20
Dalhauser, M.   457
Daltroy, L. H.   137
Damm, M. A.   466
Danish, S. J.   97, 99, 114, 218, 481, 484, 485, 527
Darley, J.   554
Darlison, L.   540
Dashiell, J. F.   176
D'Augelli, A. R.   114, 484
Davids, K.   72, 198, 201
Davidson, R. J.   274, 277, 349, 594
Davis, C.   555, 557
Davis, K. E.   123, 124, 125
Davis, M.   475
Davis, R.   504
Davis, R. A.   344
Dawson, B. T.   447
de Castella, F. R.   113
de Groot, A. D.   74
de Knop, P.   483
de Loes, M.   456
De Longis, A.   289
Deakin, J.   72, 74
Dean, L. R.   477
Deaux, K.   126, 548, 549, 552, 554
DeBenedette, V.   290
Debus, R. L.   135, 318
DeBusk, R. F.   158
Deci, E. L.   xxx, 13, 94, 593
Deeter, T. E.   548
DeFrank, R.   397
Dehaene, S.   82
Del Rey, P.   546, 548
Delaney, M.   459
DePalma, D. M.   396
Desertrain, G.   547
Desharnais, R. B.   147
Desiderato, O.   345
Deutsch, D.   66
Deutsch, J. A.   66
Dewar, A.   538, 539, 563, 564, 577
Dick, B.   589
Diclemente, C.   496
Diener, C. I.   133
DiGiuseppe, R.   467
DiLorenzo, T. M.   445
Dishman, R. K.   157, 438, 441
Divers, P.   133
Dixon, W. R.   517
Djarova, T.   178
Donchin, E.   82

Donnelly, J.   159
Dorfman, H. A.   229, 232
Douglas, J.   544
Dowd, E. T.   133
Dowd, J. J.   477
Doyle, L. A.   316, 320
Draper, M. V.   548
Dreyfus, H. L.   246
Dreyfus, S. E.   246
Drinkwater, B.   557
Droppleman, L. F.   18, 230, 445
Dry, J.   524
Dryer, S.   551
Dubbert, P. M.   441
Duda, J. L.   xxx, 105, 149, 165, 191, 466, 520, 554
Dummer, G. M.   503
Dunn, S. M.   165
Duquin, M. E.   133, 544, 546, 554
Durtschi, S. K.   339, 349, 376
Dweck, C. S.   134
Dwyer, T.   530
Dyer, J. B.   157
Dyer, K.   544
Dzewaltowski, D. A.   19, 146, 147, 149, 158, 163, 444

Eagley, A. H.   545
Earle, W. B.   135
Easterbrook, J. A.   76, 77, 393
Eccles (Parsons), J.   97
Eccles, J. S.   97, 105, 539, 552, 566
Egstrom, G. H.   344
Eichler, M.   539
Eitzen, D. S.   517, 520, 522, 525
Eklund, R. C.   xxxii, 585, 599
Eksten, F.   445
Elig, T.   129
Elko, P. K.   228
Ellickson, K. A.   19, 445
Ellis, A.   224, 228, 273, 495
Emswiller, T.   554
Endler, N. S.   16, 35
Epstein, N. L.   349
Erffmeyer, E. S.   345, 373
Erich, W. B. M.   456
Ericsson, K. A.   63, 81
Eriksen, B.   79
Erikson, E. H.   91, 112
Estrada, A. M.   191
Etzel, E. F.   77

Evans, J. 519, 520, 522, 531
Evans, L. 300, 301, 303
Everett, J. J. 548
Ewart, C. K. 157, 158
Ewing, M. E. 503
Eysenck, H. J. 8, 9, 18, 156
Eysenck, M. W. 30, 32, 35, 41, 42
Eysenck, S. B. G. 8, 18

Faierman, D. 165
Farris, E. 552
Fasting, K. 539, 543, 549
Fava, J. L. 448
Fawkner, H. J. 459, 464, 465
Fazey, J. 234
Feather, M. 554
Feather, N. T. 133, 135, 136
Feifel, H. 397
Feigley, D. E. 274
Fein, G. 447
Feinberg, I. 447
Felshin, J. 546
Feltz, D. L. 17, 80, 116, 144, 146, 150, 151, 152, 153, 154, 155, 156, 157, 161, 162, 164, 165, 166, 204, 240, 250, 294, 316, 319, 320, 326, 344, 351, 354, 397, 551
Fender, L. K. 274
Fennema, E. 551
Fernandez, S. J. 373
Ferrante, A. P. 228, 232
Ferreira, V. xxv
Festinger, L. A. 13
Fields, K. B. 459
Fielstein, E. 135
Fillingim, R. B. 34
Finch, L. M. xxxii, 232, 586, 587, 599
Fincham, F. D. 133
Fine, A. 236
Fiorito, P. 72
Fischer, M. 135
Fisher, A. 546
Fisher, A. C. xxv, 4, 466
Fisher, C. F. 134
Fisk, A. D. 68
Fiske, S. T. 124
Fitzsimmons, P. A. 146, 153, 154
Fleisher-Curtain, L. A. 443
Flenley, D. C. 447

Flett, G. L. 38
Fleury, M. 72
Floyd, T. C. 447
Flynn, M. G. 444
Folkins, C. H. 34
Folkman, S. 37, 289, 292, 293, 299, 463, 464
Fontaine, G. 135
Fool's Gold 525, 526
Ford, S. K. 17, 81, 230
Forsey, C. 559
Fort, P. 556
Fortnam, S. P. 158
Fortunato, V. 496
Foster, C. D. 135, 136, 199, 204
Foster, J. 443
Fox, K. R. 448, 530
Frable, D. E. S. 549
Frankel, V. H. 456
Fraser, G. 447
Frazier, S. E. 157
Freed, D. L. 298
Freedson, P. 30
Freeman, H. 546
French, R. 19, 503, 504
Frensch, P. A. 445
Freud, S. 91
Freudenberger, H. 275
Fridhandler, B. M. 11, 32
Friedman, A. 68
Friedman, G. M. 290
Frieze, I. H. 129, 133, 554
Frith, D. 474, 477
Frost, R. O. 38
Fry, R. W. 444, 445
Fuchs, C. Z. 19
Fuoss, D. E. 55
Furst, D. M. 19, 132, 135, 136
Futterman, C. A. 97
Futterman, R. 552
Fyans, L. J. 135

Gabbard, C. 517, 520, 526, 528
Gabriel, T. J. 230
Gallwey, G. T. 279
Gallwey, T 331
Gange, J. J. 180
Garfield, C. A. 222, 248, 389, 414
Gatti, M. 396
Gaudieri, S. 445
Gauron, E. F. 225, 226, 404

Gauvin, L. 157
Gayton, W. F. 156, 184
Geen, R. G. 180
Gelfand, D. M. 191
Gemma, L. M. 448
Genasci, J. 558
Gench, B. 503
Genest, M. 298
Genovese, P. 546
Gentry, W. D. 14
George, P. S. 429
George, T. R. 144, 151, 153
Giannini, J. 204, 324
Gibbons, K. 554
Gill, D. A. 298, 299
Gill, D. L. 39, 40, 116, 117, 127, 130, 132, 136, 150, 153, 156, 192, 193, 194, 201, 316, 444, 548, 551, 552, 596
Gillian, R. E. 157
Gilligan, C. 553
Gines, S. D. 443
Gingras, P. P. 357
Ginsberg-Fellner, F. 165
Gipson, M. 228, 230, 231, 232
Glaser, B. 478, 599
Glasgow, R. E. 147, 149, 158, 159, 163, 164
Glass, D. C. 443
Glencross, B. xxv, 411
Glencross, D. J. 72
Godding, P. R. 147
Godin, G. 147
Goethals, G. 554
Goff, S. B. 97, 552
Goldberger, N. R. 553
Goldie, I. 456
Golding, J. M. 443
Goldstein, S. R. 184, 187
Goldston, S. E. 220
Goldwater, B. C. 446
Gollwitzer, P. M. 135
Good, A. J. 481
Goodling, M. D. 503
Gopher, D. 67, 68, 78
Gordin, R. D. 228, 230, 232
Gordon, N. F. 158
Gordon, R. 357
Gordon, S. 217, 225, 229, 230, 231, 232, 240, 413, 479, 497
Gorely, T. 497
Gorschuch, R. 31

Gough, D. 345
Gould, D. xxxii, 30, 31, 48, 49, 51, 57, 101, 102, 116, 146, 151, 153, 186, 204, 215, 217, 223, 225, 227, 228, 229, 230, 232, 240, 259, 274, 324, 339, 376, 444, 513, 519, 532, 585, 586, 587, 595, 599
Goulet, C. 72
Govern, J. W. 458
Grad, G. 556
Graham, G. 522, 523, 525, 526, 532
Graham, S. 74
Granito, V. J. 197
Grasha, A. F. 17, 80, 81, 397
Graves, J. 194
Gray, J. J. 375
Gray, S. W. 373
Gray, T. 525
Greco, D. 557
Green, L. B. 217
Greendorfer, S. L. 191, 476, 479, 481
Greene, D. 92, 99
Greenspan, M. J. 240, 250
Greenwood, C. M. 19
Gregory, W. L. 301, 443
Griffey, M. S. 462
Griffin, P. 558
Griffin, S. J. 447
Griffith, C. R. xxiv
Griffith, S. J. 423
Gross, J. B. 116, 127, 130, 132, 136, 318, 552, 596
Grove, J. R. 132, 134, 136, 137, 205, 444, 445, 447, 479, 507
Grove, R. 217, 442
Gruen, R. J. 289
Guba, E. G. 578, 583, 584, 586
Gullen, W. H. 458

Habeck, R. V. 503
Hacker, C. 198, 202
Hackfort, D. 31, 33, 34, 178
Haerle, R. 482
Hagberg, J. 19
Haggert, J. 461
Hale, B. D. 349, 350, 376, 485, 527
Hall, C. 345
Hall, C. R. 345, 356, 358
Hall, E. G. 345, 373, 443

Hall, H. K. 97
Hall, J. 397
Hall, J. R. 133
Hall, M. A. 539, 541, 546, 547, 555, 558
Halliwell, W. 225, 228, 229, 231, 232, 241
Haman, C. 135
Hamberger, K. 375
Hamill, J. 30
Hampson, S. E. 159
Han, M. W. 81
Han Jin-Song 596
Hanin, Y. L. 49, 50, 57
Hanrahan, S. J. 132, 134, 136, 504, 507, 508, 509
Hanson, S. J. 463, 464
Hanson, T. W. 57, 584, 586
Hardman, J. S. 19
Hardman, K. 5
Hardy, C. J. 98, 195, 200, 206, 293, 441, 443, 462, 466
Hardy, L. 48, 49, 50, 51, 76, 186, 234, 243, 245, 249, 276, 277
Hare-Mustin, R. 538, 540, 563
Hargreaves, J. A. 560
Haring, M. J. 375
Harkins, S. G. 98, 194, 195, 428
Harlow, L. L. 448
Harold, R. D. 97, 105, 552
Harper, R. A. 397, 495
Harris, B. L. 37, 225, 226
Harris, D. V. 37, 132, 225, 226, 350, 358, 376, 546, 557
Harris, M. B. 557
Hart, E. A. 441
Harter, S. 518
Hartmann, D. P. 191
Hartnett, D. G. 279, 374
Hasbrook, C. A. 91, 520, 527
Haskell, W. L. 157, 158, 446
Haslam, R. W. 18
Hatfield, B. D. 30, 31, 45, 46, 81, 149, 152, 174, 183, 184, 187, 446
Hathaway, S. R. 8
Hattie, J. A. 136
Hausfield, S. 155
Havighurst, R. J. 476
Hawkins, H. L. 78
Hawkins, K. 486, 487, 488, 489, 495, 496

Hayden, R. M. 157, 220, 446
Hayes, D. 157
Hayward, S. A. 20
Haywood, K. 30
Hecker, J. E. 352
Heckhausen, H. 134
Hedrick, B. 509
Heider, F. 13, 123, 125, 129, 131, 317
Heil, J. 217, 218
Held, S. E. 555, 556
Helmreich, R. L. 548
Henderson, K. A. 548
Henderson, K. J. 38
Henry, W. E. 477
Henschen, K. P. 19, 218, 228, 230, 232, 503, 504, 543
Herring, M. W. 462
Hersey, P. 322
Hewitt, J. 374
Hewitt, P. L. 38
Heyman, S. R. 207, 218, 465
Hickey, C. 524, 525
Highlen, P. S. 217, 222
Hill, K. 538, 540, 544, 545, 546, 550, 553, 561, 562, 563
Hindel, C. 44
Hinkle, J. S. 459
Hinton, E. 298
Hird, J. S. 351
Hirota, K. 443
Hlobil, H. 456
Hobfoll, S. E. 293
Hochstetler, S. A. 443
Hockey, G. R. 76
Hodapp, V. 39
Hodgdon, J. A. 445, 448
Hodge, K. 204, 240, 324, 513
Hodge, K. P. 215
Hogan, C. 236
Hogan, J. 441
Hogan, P. I. 152
Hokada, A. 133
Holloway, J. B. 149
Holman, C. P. 298
Holmes, T. H. 460, 461
Holt, D. 113
Holt/Hale, S. 532
Hooper, S. 19, 218, 444
Horan, J. J. 351
Horn, M. A. 42
Horn, T. S. 91, 101, 102, 192, 274, 520, 527, 538, 539, 563, 577, 595

Horne, J. A.   447
Horner, M. S.   551
Horstman, D. H.   444
Horvat, M.   19, 30, 503, 504
Hoskins, P. L.   165
Hough, D. O.   556
Houmard, J. A.   444
Howe, B. L.   15, 17, 19, 80
Howe, C.   477, 495
Howe, G.   477, 495
Howe, M.   481, 493
Hrycaiko, D.   xxix, 345
Hubner, J. J.   313, 448
Huddleston, S.   116, 552, 596
Hughes, J. R.   445
Hull, C. L.   174, 177, 179, 180, 187
Human Rights and Equal Opportunity Commission   558
Hunt, V. V.   45
Hutchison, M.   279, 374
Hyde, J. S.   545
Hyde, R. T.   278

Ickes, W.   133, 136
Ievleve, L.   217, 466
Ilkov, A.   178
Ingham, A.   194, 195
Irving, P. G.   184, 187
Irwin, I.   243
Isaac, A.   358
Ismail, A. H.   446
Iso-Ahola, S. E.   30, 31, 126, 132, 135, 174, 183, 184, 187

Jacklin, C.   545
Jackson, A.   146, 152, 153, 154, 157, 346, 375, 444, 517, 550
Jackson, D. W.   458
Jackson, J. M.   98
Jackson, S. A.   xxxii, 206, 248, 414, 547, 548, 582, 583, 584, 585, 586, 587, 599
Jacobs, A.   236
Jacobs, D. R.   440
Jacobson, E.   224, 277, 349, 350, 355, 379
Jacobson, L. B.   158
Jacoby, L. L.   68
James, W.   63, 64, 65, 83
Jamieson, K. J.   130

Jarrett, H.   458
Jeninga, A. J.   441
Jessup, S.   525
Jin-Song, H.   596
Johnson, J.   229, 231, 242
Johnson, J. H.   461
Johnson, R. S.   133
Johnson, R. W.   18
Johnston, H.   353
Jones, E. E.   123, 124, 125
Jones, G.   243
Jones, J. G.   36, 48, 276, 277
Jooste, P.   447
Jowdy, D. P.   339, 340, 342, 349, 350, 358, 375, 376
Joy, K. L.   6

Kaczala, C. M.   97, 552
Kaczmarek, M.   301
Kaczor, L. M.   352
Kahneman, D.   66, 68, 75, 78
Kaleman, M. D.   157
Kalin, N.   445
Kane, J. E.   6, 9
Kane, M. J.   546, 550
Kanner, A. D.   464
Karle, H. W. A.   224
Karmally, W.   164
Katch, F. I.   544
Katch, V. L.   544
Kausek, J.   458
Kavanagh, D.   155
Kazdin, A. E.   327
Keast, D.   444, 445
Keele, S. W.   66, 78
Keizer, H. A.   444
Keleman, M. H.   157
Kelley, H. H.   123, 124, 125, 131
Kello, P.   295, 296
Kelly, G.   4, 13
Kelso, J. A.   83
Kemmer, F. W.   158
Kemp, N. G.   521
Kemper, A. B. A.   456
Kemper, H. C.   456
Kendall, G.   xxix, 345
Kendall, T.   xxix, 345
Kenney, E.   444
Kerr, G.   457, 459, 462
Kerr, J. H.   47, 48, 49, 51, 52, 76, 186
Kerr, N. L.   98
Khantzian, E. J.   289

Kimiecik, J. C.   414, 415
King, A. C.   446
Kingery, P. M.   147, 149, 159, 163, 164, 165
Kirchenbaum, D. S.   345, 397
Kirchner, G.   517, 526
Kirkby, R. J.   297, 458, 464, 465
Kirwin, J. P   444
Kite, M. E.   549
Kivlin, J.   555
Kleiber, D. A.   97, 481
Klein, M. S.   135, 136, 199, 202
Klint, K. A.   156, 157, 517, 522
Knapp, C. G.   517
Knoppers, A.   542, 543
Kobasa, S. C.   13, 14
Koburger, P.   135
Koerbin, G.   447
Kohl, R. M.   344
Kolodny, K.   157
Kolonay, B. J.   346, 375
Kolt, G. S.   297, 458, 465
Konopka, G.   289
Konttinen, N.   82
Koppenhaver, R.   458
Korhonen, T.   457
Kraemer, W. J.   178
Krampe, R. T.   63
Krane, V.   30, 31, 48, 49, 51, 186, 222, 227, 274, 595
Kraus, J. F.   458
Kreiner-Phillips, K.   66
Kreisel, P.   175, 177, 179, 517, 518, 521
Kremer, P.   375
Kriegel, B.   279
Krohne, H.   44
Kroll, W.   10
Kruglanski, A. W.   130
Kubitz, K.   81
Kubler-Ross, E.   465, 478, 495
Kugler, P. N.   83
Kuipers, H.   444
Kujala, U.   457
Kukla, A.   134
Kuse, A. R.   357, 358
Kuypers, J. A.   477
Kvidera, D.   456

LaBerge, D. L.   79
LaBree, M.   298
Lacey, J. I.   82
LaFontaine, T. P.   445

Lambert, M. J.   443
Landers, D. L.   445
Landers, D. M.   45, 46, 76, 81,
    144, 146, 152, 153, 165,
    179, 198, 240, 344, 351,
    397, 402, 446, 459
Lane, J. F.   346, 375
Lang, P. J.   255, 349, 351, 377
Langness, L. L.   503
Lantz, C.   441
Lariviere, M.   290
Larrance, D.   397
Lasky, R.   447
Latane, B.   428
Latene, B.   98, 194, 195
Latham, G. P.   259, 261
Lawson, G. W.   133
Lawton, M.   463
Lazarus, R. S.   37, 273, 289,
    292, 293, 299, 463, 464
Leahy, D.   564
Leary, M. R.   441
Lee, A. B.   374
Lee, C.   156, 316, 352, 354
Lehrer, P. M.   58
Lehto, M.   457
Leigh, M. H.   91
Leitenberg, H.   135
Leith, L. M.   135
Lenk, H.   198, 201
Lenney, E.   551, 552
Lenskyj, H.   557, 558, 559
Lepper, M. R.   92, 99
Lerch, S. H.   476, 478, 479,
    484, 496
Lester, D.   495
Lettunich, J.   149
LeUnes, A. D.   19, 296
Leventhal, H.   137
Levey, A. J.   80, 443
Levine, H. G.   503
Levinger, G.   194
Lewinsohn, P. M.   159
Lewis, F. M.   137
Lewis, L. L.   549
Lewis, M. A. E.   444
Lewis, S.   344, 348
Lewko, J.   546
Lewthwaite, R.   518, 519, 522,
    523
Liberman, R. P.   289
Lidor, R.   69
Liebert, R. M.   594
Lifshitz, F.   556

Lightner, J. M.   444
Liles, L.   222
Lilly, J. C.   373
Limburg, J.   19
Lincoln, Y. S.   578, 583, 584,
    586
Linder, D. E.   481
Lindner, H.   297, 465
Linn, M. C.   545
Lips, H. M.   548
Lirgg, C. D.   153, 156, 204,
    552
Livingston, S. M.   555
Lizotte, P.   348
Llewellyn-Jones, D.   554
Lobel, M.   595
Lobstein, D. D.   446
Locke, E. A.   259, 260, 261
Lockwood, R. J.   507
Loehr, J. E.   222, 223, 225,
    229, 230, 231, 232, 236,
    241
Logan, G. D.   68, 74
Lohr, J.   375
Longhurst, K.   92, 101, 443,
    518
Longino, J.   517
Longson, D.   298
Lorr, M.   18, 230, 445
Lotan, M.   78
Loudermilk, S.   546, 547
Lowe, S.   228
Lowell, E. W.   103, 550
Lualhati, R.   447
Lucschen, G.   198
Lunt, S. D.   457
Lysens, R.   462
Lyytinen, H.   82

Ma, Q.   529
McArdle, W. D.   544
McAuley, E.   132, 144, 146,
    149, 150, 152, 153, 156,
    157, 158, 163, 164, 165,
    167, 316, 318, 354, 595
McBride, E. R.   344
McCaffrey, I.   477
McCaffrey, N.   528, 530
McClay, M. H.   458
McClelland, D. C.   103, 550
McClure, B. A.   199, 204
Maccoby, E.   545
McCormack, C.   518, 519, 521
McCormick, R. A.   133

McCubbin, H. I.   289, 290
McCullagh, P. D.   179, 220,
    463, 464
Macdonald, D.   564
McDonald, D. G.   297, 445,
    448, 465
McGill, J. C.   133
McGrath, J. E.   192, 273
Machin, V. J.   80, 444
Machlus, S. D.   352
McHugh, M. C.   133, 554
McInman, A. D.   34, 35, 132,
    441, 445
Mackay, D.   280
McKay, J.   542, 561
McKeag, D. B.   556
MacKean, J. M.   113
McKelvain, R.   218, 484
McKelvie, S. J.   357, 358
McKenzie, T.   228
McKinley, J. C.   8
Mackinnon, L. T.   19, 218, 444
McLean, N.   207
McLeod, S.   464
McMahan, I.   135
McMurray, N.   464
McNair, D. M.   18, 230, 445
McNally, J.   551
McPherson, B. D.   271, 476,
    481, 482
Madden, C. C.   292, 295, 296,
    297, 298, 299, 300, 301,
    302, 303, 465
Maddocks, D.   80
Maddux, R. B.   423
Maehr, M. L.   93, 106, 135
Magill, R.   517, 526
Mahar, M. T.   481
Maharashi Mahesh Yogi   278
Mahoney, M. J.   31, 48, 217,
    222, 230, 279, 324, 349,
    378
Malik, P. B.   481
Mandell, A. J.   444
Manley, J. D.   157
Mann, B.   192
Manning, M. M.   147
Maracek, J.   538, 540, 563
Marcus, B. H.   441, 442
Mark, M. M.   132
Marks, D. F.   358
Marsh, H. W.   313, 314, 315,
    318, 333, 335, 448, 526,
    547, 548

Martens, R.   xxv, xxvii, 5, 8, 11, 16, 24, 29, 33, 37, 40, 42, 75, 76, 77, 78, 80, 106, 144, 156, 165, 186, 225, 230, 233, 236, 237, 239, 274, 358, 359, 444, 519, 522, 523, 576, 577, 593, 594
Martin, C.   235
Martin, D. J.   129, 135
Martin, G.   236
Martin, G. L.   xxix, 345
Martin, J. E.   441, 444
Martin, J. J.   39
Martin, T. P.   18
Martinek, T. J.   207
Maruyama, G.   135, 136
Maslow, A. H.   13
Masters, K. S.   443
Mastro, J.   503, 504
Masuda, M.   460
Matarazzo, J. D.   397
Mateev, G.   178
Matteo, S.   549
Matthews, G. R.   156, 184
Maude, D.   554
May, J. R.   215, 217, 223, 225, 227, 228, 232, 339, 376, 456, 457, 459, 462
Maynard, E. J.   530
Maynard, I. W.   15, 17, 80
Meaney, M.   447
Meece, J. L.   97, 552
Meichenbaum, D.   54, 277, 279, 298, 495
Melnick, M.   198
Mendoza, D.   344
Menges, L. J.   441
Menkerhorst, H.   483
Messner, M. A.   540, 559, 560
Metalsky, G. I.   135
Metzger, J.   164
Metzler, J.   355, 357
Meyer, C.   482, 483
Meyer, W. N.   134
Meyers, A. W.   31, 48, 222, 324, 345, 443
Meyers, M. B.   296
Meyers, M. C.   19
Michela, J. L.   125
Midgley, C.   97, 552
Mihovilovic, M.   482
Mikulincer, M.   133
Milios, D.   217, 479
Miller, B.   193
Miller, B. P.   217, 447

Miller, D. T.   131, 132
Miller, F. D.   130, 131
Miller, I. B.   345
Miller, J.   544
Miller, J. M.   460
Miller, K.   17, 80, 230
Miller, N.   279
Miller, N. H.   158
Miller, T. W.   460
Minas, S. C.   351
Minden, H.   457, 459, 462
Mira, H.   554
Mischel, W.   11
Mitchell, D.   447
Mitchell, J. B.   444
Mitchell, L.   552
Moates, D. R.   66
Moller, L.   96
Montgomery, I.   447
Montgomery, T.   345
Mood, D.   220
Moorcroft, W. H.   447
Moore, D.   126, 136, 300, 525
Moos, R. H.   332
Moran, A.   357, 358, 359
Morehouse, C. A.   347
Morgan, W. P.   5, 6, 8, 9, 14, 15, 18, 19, 24, 80, 220, 389, 442, 443, 444, 445, 446, 448
Morris, K.   546
Morris, L. W.   594
Morris, M. J.   445
Morris, T.   10, 20, 216, 225, 240, 345, 353, 354, 375, 596, 598
Morrisett, L. N.   351
Morrow, J. R.   555
Morse, M.   509
Morton, A. R.   445
Mosbacher, B. J.   446
Mosher, R.   92, 99
Moss, R. F.   133
Mountjouris, S.   298
Mueller, L. M.   150, 163
Mugno, D. A.   144, 154, 155, 354
Mullin, J.   19
Mumford, P.   345
Murphy, S. M.   215, 217, 218, 223, 225, 227, 228, 232, 339, 340, 342, 346, 349, 352, 359, 373, 375, 376, 378, 484
Murray, D.   18

Murray, H. A.   103
Murray, K. D.   80, 443
Murray, M.   192, 558
Mustari, E. L.   98
Mutrie, N.   132, 220, 438
Myers, A. E.   548

Nagy, V. T.   397
Nashman, H. W.   299
National Heart Foundation   157
Navon, D.   67
Ndoye, O. D.   397
Neal, P.   554
Nechemias, C.   164
Needels, T. L.   446
Neff, F.   229, 230, 242
Neugarten, B.   22
Neumann, O.   68
Newell, D. S.   477
Newman, D. J.   447
Niaura, R. S.   442
Nicholls, J. G.   xxx, 105, 106
Nicklaus, J.   341
Nickless, C. J.   184
Nideffer, R. M.   16, 17, 43, 44, 70, 76, 77, 80, 84, 224, 225, 228, 229, 230, 232, 278, 280, 387, 389, 391, 392, 393, 395, 396, 397, 407, 416, 444, 456, 457, 459
Nielsen, M.   293
Nieman, D. C.   290
Nikiforova, A.   178
Nisbet, J.   15
Nisbett, R. E.   92
Nissen, M.   73
Nix, C.   552
Noakes, T. D.   457
Noble, J. M.   158, 444
Noel, R. C.   346, 375
Norman, D. A.   66
North, T. C.   220
Nougier, V.   67, 79
Nutter, A.   198, 201

O'Brien, R. M.   352
O'Connor, P. J.   19, 444, 445
Ogden, W.   73
Ogilvie, B. C.   5, 447, 480, 481, 493, 494, 495, 496, 497
Oglesby, C.   538, 540, 544, 545, 546, 550, 553, 561, 562, 563
Okwumabua, T. M.   443

Ommundsen, Y. 517, 522
Orlick, T. D. 29, 40, 54, 66, 92, 99, 217, 225, 226, 228, 231, 232, 233, 325, 326, 378, 390, 409, 413, 414, 437, 466, 467, 477, 481, 482, 483, 518, 527, 528, 529, 530, 551
Osborne, S. 448
Osborne, T. 228
Ostell, A. 133
Österman, L. 457
Ostrow, A. C. 228, 239
Ostyn, M. 462
Oswald, I. 447
Otago, L. 542
Over, R. 295
Overman, S. J. 555
Overton, S. R. 503
Owen, D. R. 290, 445, 446
Owen, N. 158, 440, 442
Oxendine, J. B. 31

Paarsalu, M. E. 74
Paffenbarger, R. S. 278
Paivio, A. 353, 357
Panagis, D. M. 137
Pandolf, K. B. 442
Pang, H. 520
Pappalardo, B. 596
Parfitt, C. G. 48
Parfitt, G. 51, 245, 249
Pargman, D. 134, 217, 218, 457
Park, S. H. 444
Parker, J. D. A. 35
Parker, M. 532
Parkhouse, B. L. 550
Parrish, W. 346, 373, 375, 378
Parry-Billings, M. 178
Partington, J. 390, 414
Pascuzzi, D. 127, 130, 300
Passer, M. N. 103
Passer, M. W. 135, 457, 459, 461, 518, 519, 522, 523
Pate, R. R. 19, 445
Patterson, J. M. 289, 290
Patton, M. Q. 557, 581, 583, 584
Paull, G. 72
Paulo-Brito, A. xxv
Paulsen, P. 504
Paxton, S. J. 447, 554
Pearson, R. E. 480, 481, 493, 494

Peart, N. 314
Peckham, V. 194
Pelletier, L. G. 80, 206
Pennebaker, J. W. 444
Penny, G. D. 555
Peper, E. 403, 404, 405, 410
Perchard, L. 293
Perkins, T. S. 230
Perry, P. J. 298
Peters, M. 68, 79
Peters, T. J. 424, 425, 427, 429, 432
Peterson, C. 135, 137
Peterson, K. 204, 324
Petitpas, A. J. 218, 480, 481, 484, 485, 493, 494
Petlichkoff, L. M. 240, 513, 596
Petosa, R. 133
Petrie, T. A. 206
Petruzzello, S. J. 81, 446
Pettit, A. 531
Petty, R. E. 98
Phares, E. J. 91
Phillips, D. H. 91
Phipps, S. J. 347
Picou, J. S. 298, 299
Pijpers, J. R. 70
Pinheiro, V. E. D. 74
Plaisted, V. 542, 553, 564
Plante, T. G. 445, 446
Plascak, F. D. 458
Plowman, S. A. 30
Polgar, S. K. 518, 521
Pollock, M. L. 80, 443
Polson, C. M. 68
Pongrac, J. 358
Porter, K. 443
Posner, M. I. 73, 75, 81, 82
Powell, J. W. 458
Powell, K. E. 290, 440
Power, H. 596
Prakasa-Rao, W. 555
Prapavessis, H. 129, 132, 136
Pratt, R. W. 393, 397
Prestholdt, P. H. 443
Prochaska, J. O. 441, 442, 496, 497
Ptacek, J. T. 464
Pugliese, M. T. 556

Raeder, U. 144, 152, 165
Raglin, J. S. 19, 444, 445
Ragsdale, M. R. 344, 351
Rahe, R. H. 460

Rainey, D. W. 197, 201
Rakowski, W. 442
Randell, S. 542
Ratliff, W. R. 133
Ravizza, K. xxxii, 217, 222, 227, 228, 229, 231, 239, 240, 242, 248, 378, 497, 585
Rawlings, E. I. 344
Rawlings, I. L. 344
Ray, W. J. 45, 71
Rayfield, E. 165
Reason, J. T. 68
Reed, M. W. 462
Reese, L. B. 158
Reeves, L. H. 35
Regnier, G. 597
Reis, J. 397
Rejeski, W. J. 216, 251, 438, 439, 441, 443, 444, 449
Relich, J. D. 318
Reppert, S. 179
Repucci, N. D. 134
Reveles, M. 550
Reynolds, M. J. 484, 542
Ribisl, P. M. 443
Richards, D. E. 397
Richardson, A. 341, 347, 348, 356, 357
Richman, C. L. 349
Richman, J. M. 206, 293
Richter, D. M. 561
Riehl, R. E. 462
Riessinger, C. A. 144, 146, 154, 354
Ripol, B. 588
Ripoll, H. 72, 73
Ritter, B. 151
Rivkin, F. 156, 594
Robbins, M. A. 149, 163, 448
Roberts, G. C. 90, 103, 107, 116, 126, 127, 130, 134, 135, 206, 300, 414, 517, 551, 554
Robertson, I. 94, 101, 110, 115, 521, 526
Robertson, S. E. 479, 480
Robinson, T. 521
Robinson, W. J. 350, 376
Rodin, J. 445, 446
Roenker, D. L. 344
Roepke, N. 44
Rogers, C. R. 4, 13, 91, 92
Rohsenow, D. J. 277
Rose, A. 477

Rosen, L. W.   556
Rosenberg, E.   476, 477, 478, 479, 484
Rosenfeld, L. B.   206, 293
Rosenthal, R.   397
Ross, C. E.   157
Ross, D.   151
Ross, L.   109, 151
Ross, M.   131, 132
Rossi, B.   82
Rossi, J. S.   442
Roswal, G.   504
Rotella, R. J.   207, 218, 225, 229, 230, 231, 232, 236, 237, 238, 241, 242, 465, 558
Rothstein, A. L.   344
Rotter, J. B.   318
Rowney, T.   158
Ruble, V. E.   15
Ruder, M. K.   127, 130, 132, 136
Ruffer, W. A.   4
Rushall, B. S.   234, 409, 443
Rushworth, L.   440
Russell, D.   130, 135, 136, 317
Russell, D. G.   71, 72, 358
Russell, S. J.   597
Rust, J. R.   555
Ryan, E. D.   102, 351
Ryan, R. M.   94
Ryckman, R. M.   149, 163, 448
Ryde, D.   457

Sabo, D. F.   540, 559
Sachs, M. L.   54, 226, 291, 444, 503, 508
Sackett, R. S.   351, 355
Sadhu, M.   416
Safer, M. A.   137
Saffer, D.   274
Sage, G. H.   517, 520, 522, 526, 546, 547
Salazar, W.   81, 446
Sallis, J. F.   158
Salmela, J. H.   72, 215, 228, 231, 232, 397, 597
Salmoni, A. W.   517
Samdahl, D.   481
Sanders, A. F.   68
Sanderson, F. H.   457
Sanford, B.   443
Santomier, J. P.   152
Sarason, I. G.   43, 461
Sarason, J. M.   461

Sargent, G. I.   80, 413, 443, 444
Savelsbergh, G. J. P.   70
Savoy, C.   413
Scanlan, T. K.   xxxii, 135, 497, 518, 519, 522, 523, 585, 595
Schaefer, C.   464
Scheier, M. F.   13, 47
Schellenberger, H.   190, 191, 207
Schleser, R. A.   324, 345, 443
Schlossberg, N. K.   479, 480
Schmid, A.   403, 404, 405, 410
Schmidt, R. A.   42, 352, 517
Schneider, M. J.   135
Schneider, W.   68, 75
Schomer, H.   80, 443, 457
Schoner, G.   83
Schramm, V.   347
Schumacher, G. M.   66
Schurr, K. T.   6, 7, 8, 15, 549
Schutz, R. W.   32, 595
Schwartz, G. E.   274, 277, 349, 594
Schweickert, G. J.   201
Schwenkmezger, P.   31, 33, 34, 178
Scott, S.   297
Scott, S. G.   466
Seabourne, T.   346, 375
Seese, M. D.   457, 459, 461
Sefton, J.   518, 519
Selby, R.   546
Selby, V. C.   442
Seligman, M. E. P.   129, 133, 135, 137
Scmmel, A.   129, 133, 135
Senate Standing Committee on Environment, Recreation and the Arts   541
Seraganian, P.   220, 438, 449
Serpa, S.   xxv
Seyle, H.   273
Shangi, G.   198
Shapiro, C. M.   447
Sharp, C.   178
Sharpe, R.   280
Shavelson, R. J.   313, 318, 333, 448
Shaw, J. M.   158, 353
Shaw, W. A.   349, 350
Sheehan, P.   357
Shepard, R. N.   355

Shephard, R. J.   271
Sheppard, S.   548
Sheriff, M.   546
Sherman, J.   551
Sherman, W. M.   158
Sherrill, C.   503, 504
Shields, D.   520, 522
Shiffrin, R. M.   68, 75
Shiflett, B.   552
Shivers, J. S.   207
Shultz, B. B.   18
Sieb, G. E.   456, 457, 459
Siegel, J. M.   290
Siladi, M.   554
Silva, J. M., III   18, 190, 259, 260, 466
Sime, W. E.   34
Simkin, L. R.   442
Simmons, M. W.   158
Simon, H. A.   74
Simon, J.   156
Simons, J. P.   240, 351, 513, 594, 595
Sinardi, M.   152, 153
Singer, R. N.   69, 72, 414
Skinner, B. F.   91, 92
Slack, T.   558
Smart, A. E.   105, 466
Smith, A.   297
Smith, A. M.   466
Smith, D. A.   298
Smith, D. E.   16, 76, 144, 156, 165, 230, 594
Smith, E. R.   130, 131
Smith, J.   444
Smith, M.   243
Smith, M. A.   477
Smith, R. E.   32, 54, 56, 229, 231, 240, 242, 277, 299, 431, 464
Smith, S.   422, 475
Smoll, F. L.   32, 431, 464
Snodgrass, M. A.   133
Snyder, C. W.   519, 524
Snyder, E. E.   497, 546, 555
Snyder, K. E.   550
Solin, E.   530
Solomon, D. S.   158
Solomon, E. G.   444
Solomon, Z.   133
Sonstroem, R. J.   33, 49, 448
South Australian Sports Institute   541
Southard, S. W.   462
Sowerbutts, T. D.   554

Spalding, T. W.   149, 152
Sparling, P. B.   19, 445
Speliotis, E. D.   448
Spence, J. T.   548
Spence, K. W.   174, 177, 179,
    180, 187
Spielberger, C. D.   12, 16, 18,
    31, 33, 50, 273, 274, 593
Spink, K. S.   92, 101, 204, 205,
    207, 443, 517, 518
Spreitzer, E.   546
Staff, L. H. E.   447
Stalnaker, D.   548
Stanley, J.   279
Stanton, G. C.   313, 448
Starkes, J. L.   72, 74
Start, K. B.   347, 348, 356
Staurowsky, E.   542
Stein, G. L.   xxxii, 414, 415,
    497, 585
Stein, J. F.   67, 79
Steiner, I.   193, 194
Steinhilber, A.   184
Stell, M. K.   540, 541
Ste-Marie, D.   68
Stepanus, T. V.   158
Stephan, W. G.   135
Stephens, T.   271, 440
Steptoe, A.   445
Sterling, J. C.   19
Stewart, A.   236
Stewart, K. J.   157
Stewart, M.   517, 552
Stewart, S.   296
Stirrat, M.   524
Stoddart, B.   541
Stokes, J.   444
Strack, S.   397
Straub, W. F.   xxvi, xxx, 216,
    437
Strauss, A.   478, 599
Strom, E. H.   444
Studk-Ropp, R. C.   445
Suedfeld, P.   279, 374
Suinn, R. M.   54, 151, 233,
    280, 340, 342, 343, 344,
    353, 354, 356, 373, 374,
    375, 378
Sullivan, J.   215
Summers, J. J.   17, 68, 80, 81,
    153, 230, 291, 292, 443,
    444, 464
Sundgot-Borgen, J.   556
Surrey, J. L.   553

Sutton, J. R.   271
Svoboda, B.   113, 494, 496
Swain, A.   36
Swanson, J.   458
Sweeney, P. D.   133
Sydney, K.   290
Syer, J.   316, 328, 422, 430, 432
Szmukler, G.   554
Szymanski, K.   98, 195

Taber, J. I.   133
Taimela, S.   458
Tammen, V.   215, 217, 223,
    225, 227, 228, 339, 376
Tannen, D.   553
Tappe, M. K.   105, 466
Tarule, J. M.   553
Taylor, C. B.   158, 446
Taylor, G.   548
Taylor, J.   480, 493, 494, 495,
    496, 497
Taylor, J. A.   33
Taylor, S. E.   124
Tenenbaum, G.   132, 135, 136
Tepas, D. I.   447
Terry, D.   293
Tesch Romer, C.   63
Theberge, N.   555, 561
Theeboom, M.   483
Thomas, J. R.   92, 133, 146,
    153, 351
Thomas, M.   457
Thomas, P. R.   225, 238, 248,
    295
Thomas, R.   444
Thompson, A.   438, 439, 441,
    449
Thompson, R. A.   555, 557
Thornton, B.   149, 163, 448
Tice, D. M.   22
Tiggeman, M.   135, 136
Timsit-Berthier, M.   82
Tinning, R.   523, 524, 526,
    531, 555
Titus, L. J.   177, 179, 180, 181,
    187
Tonyman, P.   461, 463
Tonymon, P.   43
Toobert, D.   159
Toth, J. P.   68
Traill, R.   518, 519, 521
Travis, C. A.   508
Treisman, A.   68
Trenske, M.   443

Trinder, J.   447
Triplett, N.   xxiii,   174, 175,
    176
Troppmann, R. J.   55
Troxel, R. K.   466
Troxell, J. R.   460, 461
Trujillo, C. M.   555
Tucker, L. A.   290
Turk, D.   298
Turnbull, J.   531
Turner, P. E.   445
Turtle, J. R.   165
Turvey, M. T.   83
Tutko, T. A.   457, 554
Twining, W. E.   344

Uleman, J.   130, 131
Ulich, E.   280
Umilta, C.   73
Underwood, G. L.   186
Unestahl, L.   277, 278
Ungerleider, S.   443

Vaglum, P.   517, 522
Valenti, S. A.   157
Valle, V.   554
Vallerand, R. J.   80, 206, 397
Valliant, G.   289
Valliant, P. M.   457
van den Auweele, Y.   462
van der Mars, H.   146, 153
van Mechelen, W.   456, 457,
    458
Van Raalte, J. L.   481
Van Schoyck, S. R.   17, 80, 81,
    397
Vandell, R. A.   344
Vandenberg, S.   357, 358
Vanek, M.   113, 494, 496
Varbanova, A.   178
Vaughn, M. P.   460
Veach, T. L.   462
Vealey, R.   526, 527, 529, 531,
    554
Vealey, R. E.   340, 350, 351,
    352, 353, 359, 376
Vealey, R. S.   1, 4, 5, 6, 11, 12,
    13, 14, 15, 16, 18, 20, 21,
    22, 24, 29, 30, 39, 76, 144,
    156, 163, 165, 186, 225,
    230, 236, 237, 239, 274,
    359, 593, 594
Verbeek, A. L. M.   456
Veroff, J.   93

Vingerhoets, A. J. J. M.   441
Vogt, J. F.   423
von Baeyer, C.   129, 133, 135
Vranisan, M. S.   158

Wachtel, P.   70, 77
Wadsworth, W. A.   461
Wagaman, J. D.   374
Wagner, N. M.   460
Walen, S. R.   467
Walker, J. M.   447
Wallace, A. G.   446
Wallace, D.   15
Walling, M.   191
Walsh, W. D.   519, 524
Walter, C. B.   517
Walter, S. M.   340, 350, 351, 352, 353, 359, 376
Wang, M. Q.   76, 402
Wankel, L.   175, 177, 179, 517, 518, 519, 521
Warren, P. M.   447
Warrick, R.   555
Waterman, R. H.   424, 425, 427, 432
Watkin, B.   101, 102
Watson, G. G.   93, 101, 104, 110, 112, 289, 517
Watson, T.   546
Watt, B.   442
Waxman, D.   224
Webb, P.   525
Webb, S.   205
Weinberg, R. S.   30, 45, 49, 50, 146, 152, 153, 154, 157, 190, 221, 225, 226, 240, 259, 260, 346, 375, 402, 444, 517, 526, 527, 529, 550
Weiner, B.   xxx, 13, 122, 125, 126, 127, 128, 129, 134, 136, 317, 318, 335, 593
Weingarten, G.   135, 136

Weise, D. M.   156, 157, 217, 297, 466, 522
Weiss, M. R.   91, 92, 95, 116, 117, 151, 153, 156, 157, 196, 198, 204, 217, 466, 517, 519, 520, 522, 526, 527, 528, 532, 547, 596
Weitz, G. A.   443
Weldon, E.   98
Wertheim, E. H.   554
Werthner, P.   481, 482, 483
Wessler, R. L.   467
Westre, K. R.   196, 198, 204
Wheeler, L.   551
White, C. C.   440
White, K. D.   344, 348
Whitely, G.   347, 348
Whiting, H. T. A.   70
Whitney, D. L.   397
Wichman, H.   344, 348
Wickens, C. D.   68, 71
Widmeyer, W. N.   98, 191, 197, 199, 201, 202, 203, 205, 206, 207
Widom, C. S.   548
Wiens, A. N.   397
Wilkes, R. L.   153
Wilkins, C.   477, 495
Wilkinson, J. W.   447
Wilks, B.   291, 296
Williams, J.   72, 198, 202
Williams, J. M.   xxvi, xxx, 43, 44, 151, 201, 216, 217, 218, 222, 225, 226, 227, 324, 325, 437, 459, 461, 463, 464, 526, 527, 529, 550, 594
Williams, K.   428
Williams, K. D.   98, 194, 195
Williams, M.   72
Williams, S.   446
Willis, J. D.   220
Wills, T. A.   293
Wilson, M. W.   445

Wilson, W.   159
Wine, J.   538
Wing, A. L.   278
Winter, G.   235
Wittig, A. F.   549
Wolff, R.   495
Wolpe, J.   224, 274, 375
Wood, N.   518
Woolfolk, R. L.   58, 346, 352, 373, 375, 378
Wooller, P.   530
Worlsey, A.   530
Wright, T. L.   147
Wrisberg, C. A.   344, 345, 351, 548
Writer, L.   386
Wuest, D. A.   466
Wylleman, P.   483, 484, 495

Yaffe, M.   456
Yalom, I. D.   495
Yamamoto, Y.   127, 130, 136
Yambor, J.   543
Yan Lan, L.   153
Yeh, Y. Y.   79
Yilk, M. D.   344
Youngen, L.   101, 102
Yukelson, D.   196, 198, 200, 201, 217

Zaccaro, S. J.   98
Zaichkowsky, L. D.   19, 218, 345, 483, 486
Zajonc, R. B.   174, 176, 177, 179, 180, 181, 182, 184, 187, 593
Zander, A.   192, 193, 196, 201
Zani, A.   82
Zeroni, P.   445
Zhang, L.   529
Ziegler, S. G.   179
Zinsser, N.   82, 151, 324, 325
Zitzelsberger, L   529
Zuckerman, M.   397, 551

SUBJECT INDEX

A-state 33, 35, 39
  factors affecting 36–9
A-trait 33, 35, 38, 41
AAASP, *see* Association for the
    Advancement of Applied
    Sport Psychology (AAASP)
ability (attribution) 126
ability-oriented behaviour 106
academic self-concept 313
academic sport
    psychology 576
acceptance 296, 479
accomplishment, and career
    transition 482
accountability
  and performance 98
  of coaches 98
  of individuals in team
    success 197
  of individuals in teams 428
accreditation xxvi, xxx–xxxi
ACE, *see* Athlete Career and
    Education (ACE) Program
achievable goals 262
achievement 550–4
achievement
    behaviour 104–7, 551
  and attributions 127–9
achievement motivation xxix,
    103, 550, 566
  and participation in
    sport 588–9
achievement
    orientation 103–9, 550–1
achievement
    perceptions 551–3
Action Pact 530
action plans, in goal
    setting 265
action research 589
activation/arousal theory 352
activity theory 476–7
actual productivity 193
adaptive coping 289
adherence, during
    rehabilitation 466

adolescents
  coping strategies 289
  drop-out from sport 521,
    596
  gender views on sport 540
  holistic approach to
    participation in sport 494
  life stresses and
    injury 460–1, 462
  motivation to participate in
    sport 101–2, 107–9, 115,
    596–7
  self-concept levels 314–15
Adolescents Perceived Events
    Scale 464
adult-organised sport 520,
    521, 523
advanced beginner
    practitioners 246
aerobic fitness, and anxiety 34
age, and development of
    self-concept 314–15
aggression xxvii, 182, 184,
    290, 292, 545, 560, 579
AIS, *see* Australian Institute of
    Sport (AIS)
alcohol 298, 299
alertness 176, 274
  and arousal 75
  and attention 69, 75
ALES, *see* Athletic Life
    Experiences Survey
    (ALES)
alpha bias 538
amenorrhoea 557
American Coaching
    Effectiveness
    Program 233–4
American Psychological
    Association xxvi
  Division 47 xxvi
Americans, motivation to
    participate in sport 101–2
amputee athletes, *see* physically
    disabled athletes
androgyny 548, 565

anger 351, 479
anorexia athletica 556
anorexia nervosa 556
anticipation, by experts/
    novices 72
anxiety 16, 29–59, 273–4, 351,
    352, 593
  and performance 173–4,
    595
  and poorer
    performance 44
  and sport injury 459
  behavioural measures 34–5
  cognitive measures 33
  comparison with
    self-efficacy 595
  definitions 30–1
  effect on motor
    performance 41–7
  future research 56–8
  in elite/non-elite
    athletes 47–8
  management
    coaching
      techniques 54–6, 57
    cognitive-behavioural
      strategies for 52–4
    value of relaxation
      training 57–8
  measurement 32–5
  physiological
    indicators 178–9
  physiological
    measures 33–4
  reduction, through
    Rational–Emotive
    Therapy 228
  see also cognitive anxiety;
    competitive state anxiety;
    state anxiety; trait anxiety
Anxiety Management Training
    (AMT) 54
applied goal setting, *see* goal
    setting
applied sport and exercise
    psychology 216

applied sport
   psychologists   215, 216
   commitment to
      athletes   232–3
   effectiveness of   245–6
   expertise
      development   247–8
   flow within work   248–9
   models used in
      training   231–2
   performance enhancement
      process phases   238–40
   preference for one-to-one
      programs   230–1
   problems
      encountered   232
   professional development
      stages   246–9, 251
   professional literature
      issues   227–9
   role limitations   244–6
   use of mental skills
      training   231–2
   use of psychological
      tests   229–30
applied sport
   psychology   xxviii, xxx,
      215–52
   and psychological skills
      training   220–43
   future directions   249–51
   nature of   216–20
APS, see Australian
      Psychological Society
"Arm as Iron Bar"
      exercise   363
arousal   17, 274, 301, 302, 304
   and alertness   75
   and anxiety   30–1
   and attention   75–6, 393
   and self-efficacy   154–5, 162
   and stress   185–6
   as measure of drive   177–80,
      182
   biofeedback of   364
   theories   48–52
arousal-stress continuum, of
      reversal theory   51–2
assessment phase
   and performance-profiling
      approach   243–4
   psychological skills training
      (Morris model)   240–1

Association for the
   Advancement of Applied
   Sport Psychology
   (AAASP)   xxvi, 227, 600
associative coping   291
associative thinking   443–4
Athlete Career and Education
   (ACE) Program   117, 219,
      489, 491–2
athletes, national support
   structure for   92–3
athletes with
   disabilities   502–13
   AIS scholarships   502
   anxiety profiles   503
   application of mental skills
      training   504–6
   future research   512–13
   general
      considerations   511–12
   mood states   503–4
   psychological support
      for   219
athletic identity   481
Athletic Identity Measurement
   Scale (AIMS)   481
Athletic Life Experiences
   Survey (ALES)   461, 462,
      463
athletic personality   15
athletic scholarships
   in American colleges and
      universities   102
   in Australia   102
Athletics Australia   100
attention   63–85, 301, 386–7
   and arousal   75–6, 393
   and performance   388–9
   basketball example   67
   capacity limits   73–5
   definitions   64, 65
   dimensions of   70–8, 84
   direction of   70–3, 84
   future directions   81–3
   intensive aspects   73–5, 84
   models   78–81, 84–5, 387,
      391–3, 395–6
   psychophysiological
      mechanisms   65
   shifting of   78
   terminology problems   69
   theoretical perspectives   17,
      65–70, 80–1

what is it?   64–5
   see also concentration
attention control training   280
attentional capacities   388–90
attentional errors   393–6
attentional flexibility   76–8, 84
attentional focus   64, 388, 393
   inability to adopt or
      maintain   394–5
attentional functioning   81
attentional mismatch   393–6
attentional narrowing   76
   and anxiety   43
   and likelihood of injury   44
attentional shifting   408
attentional skills   233
attentional style   17–18, 70,
      77–8, 80–1, 387, 388,
      404
   and personality traits   393
attentional switching
      technique   403
attentional training exercises
   cautionary note   400
   for athletes   400–12
   non-sport activities   401–7
   sport-related
      activities   407–12
   timing of   400–1
attribution theories   13,
      123–7, 317, 318, 593
attributional bias   131–3
attributional
   dimensions   125–7,
      129–31
attributional style   133, 318,
      329, 330
   and intrinsic
      motivation   133–4
Attributional Style
   Questionnaire
   (ASQ)   135
attributions   122–3, 317–19
   and achievement
      behaviour   127–9
   and gender
      differences   554, 565
   and self-confidence   329–31
   four causal elements
      (Weiner)   125–7
   future directions   137
   general measurement
      considerations   136–7

measures 134–7
non-sport measures 134–5
sport measures 135–6
attrition, *see* drop out
audience, influence on
performance 173,
179–85
audio tapes
for pre-competition
use 513
for psychological skills
training 235–6
for stress management 281
audit check 584
auditory attention 78
augmentation of dominant
responses 177
Aussie Sports program 106,
524
Australian Athletes Career
Transition Inventory
(AACTI) 486, 495
Australian Baseball
League 493
Australian Coaches Career
Transition Inventory
(ACCTI) 486, 495
Australian Coaching
Council xxxi, 103
Australian Commonwealth
Games Association 542
Australian Cricket Board 493
Australian Football
League 493
Australian Institute of Sport
(AIS) 486
amalgamation with
Australian Sports
Commission 102
establishment 97
flotation facilities 374
professional staff recruitment
factors 97, 98
program to minimise drop
out 111–12
scholarships for athletes with
disabilities 502
scholarships held by
women 541
sport psychologists at xxv
Sport Psychology Bulletin 236
(SPORTS)LEAP
program 489, 491

stress control
training 185–6
video editing
facilities 372–3
Australian Olympic
Committee xxxi, 215,
491–2, 542
Australian Psychological
Society xxv, xxvi, xxx,
502
Australian Sports
Commission xxv, xxxi,
102, 106, 107, 111, 486,
489, 524, 540, 541
autogenic training 278
automatic processing 66, 67,
68
automaticity 68–9, 74–5, 83–4
automation of coping
strategies 328
autonomic arousal 405
autopilot state 66
avoidance behaviour 104, 296
awareness context 478
awareness exercise 403,
513

balance tasks 405–6, 510
Balanced Attributional Style
Questionnaire
(BASQ) 135
basic skills training phase,
psychological skills
training (Morris
model) 241
be realistic, in coaching 55
behavioural anxiety
management 34–5
behavioural coping
strategies 332
behavioural measures, of
anxiety 34–5
Bem Sex Role Inventory
(BSRI) 547, 548, 549
benchmarks 261
Benson's Relaxation
Response 277
better athletes, from children's
competitive sporting
programs 521
Betts' imagery scale 348, 357
Big Fish Little Pond
Effect 314

bio-informational
theory 351–2, 377
biofeedback 279, 369
biofeedback equipment
use 405
biofeedback monitoring 404
biofeedback of arousal 364
biologically-based sex
differences 539, 543–5
blind athletes, *see* visually
impaired athletes
blood pressure 45
Board of Sport
Psychologists xxv, xxvi,
xxx, 502
body awareness 296, 505–6
body image 554–5, 564, 565
body language 327–8
The body owners manual 530
body size/weight 555, 556
books xxiv, xxv, 226, 437, 438
bottleneck theories, of
attention 65–6
Boutcher and Rotella model,
performance
enhancement
process 237–8
breathing exercise 404
British Amateur Gymnastics
Association 249
broad-external focus of
attention 391, 392
and attentional
mismatches 393–4
broad-internal focus of
attention 391, 392
and attentional
mismatches 394
BSRI, *see* Bem Sex Role
Inventory (BSRI)
buffering effects, of social
support 293
bulimia nervosa 556
burn-out 275–6, 284, 299
in youth golf 585

Californian Psychological
Inventory 457, 458
Canadian Society for
Psychomotor Learning
and Sport Psychology
(CSPLSP) xxiv
cancer 460

capability, and
self-efficacy 145
capacity limits on
attention 73–5
cardiac rehabilitation, and
exercise 143–4, 157–8,
161
Career Assistance Program for
Athletes (CAPA) 484, 485
career assistance
programs 484–5, 487,
489–93, 496–7
by country 489, 490
career awareness 483–4, 486
career orientation 496–7
career planning 484–6, 486
problems 485–6
career termination, coping
methods 494–5
career training 218–19
career transition 113–14,
474–98
conceptual models 479–80
future directions 495–7
prevention and treatment
strategies 493–5
primary prevention
models 493–4
reasons for 482–3
research 481–6
in Australia 486–8
social death concept 478–9
social gerontology
theories 476–8
theoretical models 476–80
career transition
needs 483–5, 486–8
catastrophe theory 50–1
catastrophising 296, 325
Causal Dimension Scale
(CDS) 135, 136
causal modelling 125–7, 595,
598
causality 579
centring 407–8
for athletes with
disabilities 505
techniques 234, 235
cerebral palsied athletes 503,
506
ceremonial violence, in
male-dominated
sport 560

certification xxvi
challenge for places, within
teams 430
challenging goals 262
changing self-image 334–5
child development 517–18
factors influencing motor
skill acquisition 517
psychological and
sociological
considerations 517–18
children
and sport
psychology 516–33
competitive sport and
production of better
athletes 521
coping strategies 289
development of
concentration strategies
with 414
encouragement to play
sport 100, 106
failure to thrive in physical
education and
sport 525–6
future psychological research
areas 531–2
individual psychological
strategies 528–9
intrinsic motivation of 100
learning how to
compete 522–3
motivation to participate in
sport 101, 112
organised sport 519–21
participation in sport,
factors 518–23
perception of sport 529
physical education
programs 523–6, 530–1
play opportunities through
sport 521–2
psychological skills
training 526–30
self-concept levels 314–15
teaching of movement skills
to 531
worry about meeting
parents' and coaches'
expectations 522
choice, in achievement
behaviour 105

choking 45–7, 51, 184, 275,
388
definition 45
strategies for
overcoming 46–7
chosen/not chosen
dimension 130–1
chunking 73–5
closed awareness 478
coaches
and athletes process
goals 322–3
career development and
awareness needs 486–7
career development
transition programs 488
communication with team
members 429, 430–2
development of athletes'
self-confidence 319–20,
322–3, 336
discussion of individual's role
in a team 426
effect on career
transition 482
in competitive children's
sport 520, 522, 523
influence on career planning
programs 486
manipulating the
environment 319–20
responsibility and
accountability of 98
stress on 272, 284
under-representation of
women as 542
coaching techniques
and player confidence 553
for anxiety
management 54–6
inappropriate 54–5
coaction effects xxiii, 173,
176, 177–9
coactive dependent
tasks 201
cognitive-affective model, of
stress 299
cognitive anxiety 30–1, 32,
42–4, 274, 594
determination 177–9
cognitive appraisal 273
and anxiety 37
cognitive coping 296

cognitive evaluation
theory 94–5
cognitive explanation, of
attributional bias 132
cognitive measures, of trait
anxiety 33
cognitive orientation, and
exercise behaviour 443–4
cognitive phenomenological
approach xxx, 13, 594
cognitive
psychophysiology 81–2
cognitive rehearsal 467
cognitive restructuring 304,
495
cognitive strategies, for anxiety
management 54
cognitive techniques, as
intervention
strategies 323–5
cohesion, see team cohesion
collaborative research 602
collective efficacy 204–5
college athletic
scholarships 102
commercialised exercise and
fitness programs 561
common-sense
psychology 123
communication
in MAPS questionnaire 301
see also effective
communication
community involvement, in
sport psychology 600
community sport programs, for
children 519–20
competence, and motivational
behaviour 517
competent practitioners 246
competition, definition 40
competition diaries 262, 265
competition evaluation 390
competition focus plan 390
competition goals 266–7, 269,
270
competition stress 275
competitive cognitions, used by
wrestlers 585–6
competitive
performance xxviii
competitive sport

and achievement
motivation 106
definition 476
for children 519–21
myths 521–3
competitive state anxiety 40,
274
cognitive effects 42–4
effect on motor
performance 41–7
physiological effects 45
theoretical model 593
Competitive State Anxiety
Inventory (CSAI) 156,
594
Competitive State Anxiety
Inventory-2 (CSAI-2) 16,
33, 156, 230, 239, 359, 594
competitive stress 300
competitiveness 548, 559, 560
concentration 223, 386–416
and attention 69
and exceptional
performance 389
and performance, case
studies 388
applications 390
see also attention
concentration grid
exercise 402–3
concentration training 235
future directions 412–15
Confederation of Australian
Sport 542
confidence 315, 324, 409, 553
and body language 327–8
and imagery 353–5
and performance 311–37,
354–5
and success 143
as mediator between imagery
and performance 598
see also self-confidence
confidence building 223
imagery use 362
confidence states of mind 334
conflict, between coaches and
players 431
conformability 583
conscious awareness 341, 342
consciousness, and
attention 64, 65

consciousness alteration,
through exercise 444
consensus 124, 125
consistency 124, 125
consolidation theory 477
constructivism 563–4
consultants, see applied sport
psychologists
Contemporary Thought in
Performance
Enhancement 589
content analysis 581–3
contexts 563, 565, 577, 584
contingent negative variation
(CNV) 81, 82
continuity therapy 477
controllability 127, 130, 318,
365, 366
controlled aggression 292
controlled processing 66–7
controlling the
controllables 409
cooperative sport 561
coordination
losses 194, 195
COPE model 301–2
coping 288–9
complexity and variability
of 295–6
for rehabilitation after
injury 465–7
in team sports 290
stress and injury 463–5
with injury 296–8
coping confidence 332–3
coping processes 464
coping
questionnaires 299–301
coping resources 464
Coping Skills Training
(CST) 301–2
with individual
athletes 302–4
coping skills training
programs 299–301
coping strategies 288–307
as intervention
strategies 331–3
automation of 328
COPE model 301–2
development 289–90
drug use 298–9

coping strategies (*continued*)
  for children and
    adolescents 289
  future directions 305–6
  methods 290–6
  used by figure skaters 586
  used by wrestlers 586
coping styles
  and anxiety 37–8
  and different task
    demands 295
correspondent inference
  model 123–4
counsellor role, of applied
  sport psychologists 245
countering 324–5
covariation model 124–5
covert attention 78–9
credibility 583
credulous-sceptical dimension,
  of personality 14–15
cross-sectional research 597
cross-sex sport psychology
  consulting 543
crowd, *see* audience; home
  crowd
CSAI, *see* Competitive State
  Anxiety Inventory (CSAI)
cue utilisation theory 76
cues, and focused
  attention 70–2
cultural values, and social
  motivation 97

daily hassles, in sports
  injury 464–5
data analysis 581–3
data collection 581
daydreaming 342
deaf athletes, mental skills
  training programs 508
deconstruction 563
demographics, of exercise
  behaviour 440–1
denial 291, 292, 479
denial coping 296
dependability 583
dependency 561
depression 299, 460, 462, 479
design checks 584
desire for group success
  (DGS) 196, 204
  developing 196–7

detachment 291, 292
diabetes
  barriers to exercise 158–9
  exercise and self-efficacy
    in 158–60, 164
  glycemic control 159
  psychosocial factors 158,
    159
  self-care 158, 159
Diagnostic and Statistical
  Manual of Mental
  Disorders (DSM-III) 556
diet, and weight 556–7
Differential Relaxation 277
direct effects, of social
  support 293
direction, through
  goals 260–1
direction of attention 70–5,
  391
disabled athletes, *see* athletes
  with disabilities; physically
  disabled athletes
disengagement theory 477
disordered eating 555–7, 564,
  565
dissociative coping 291
dissociative thinking 443–4
dissonance theory 13–14
distinctiveness 124, 125
distraction control 390
distractions 388
dreaming 342
drive 176, 177, 179, 182
Drive Theory 49, 176, 177,
  179–80, 181
drop out 20, 58, 110–14,
  596
  and team building 429
  by adolescents 521, 596
  from children's sport 532
  internal factors 110–11
  social factors 111–12
drug prevention
  programs 299
drugs, for coping with
  stress 298–9
Dual Code Theory 357
during performance
  routines 409–10
Dutch Personality
  Inventory 441
dynamogenic factors 175–6

eating disorders 555–7
ecological validity xxviii, 73,
  343
educational concerns, of
  athletes at AIS 111–12
educational sport
  psychology 229
educator role, of applied sport
  psychologists 245
effective attention 78, 80
effective communication
  between coach and
    players 429, 430–2
  errors 431
  within teams 196, 429
effort (attribution) 126,
  133–4
effortful attention 65
ego-defensive explanation, of
  attributional bias 131,
  132
ego involvement 105–6
elation 351
electroencephalography
  (EEG) 45, 65, 81, 377,
  446
electromyography (EMG) 45,
  344, 350
elite athletes
  anxiety in 47–8
  burn-out in 275–6
  career development and
    awareness needs 486
  chunking ability 74
  competition stress 275
  components of exceptional
    performance 389–90
  in team sports 421–2
  life stress 274–5
  mood states 18, 19
  physical conditioning 221
  professionals working
    with 97, 98
  stress in 272–3
  training stress 275
elite coaches, stress
  effects 272
elitism 560
embarrassment 180, 181
emotion-focused
  coping 291–2, 297, 465
emotional/cognitive impact, of
  sport programs 562

emotional expression 495
emotionality 291, 296, 594
emotions, attributions effect on 128–9
emphasising the positive 291
employment concerns, of athletes at AIS 111–12
empowerment 427–8
encouragement 293–4
endogenous/exogenous dimension 130
enjoyment
  from sport 53, 55, 56, 58, 518, 523
  in elite figure skaters 585
environmental aspects, of sport 190
environmental factors, in team cohesion 197
epistemology xxviii, 539
equal opportunity 561
ethics xxviii, xxix
evaluation apprehension 174, 179, 182–3, 186
evaluation phase, psychological skills training (Morris model) 242
evaluations 329–31
event-related potentials (ERPs) 81, 82
exchange theory 477, 478
excitement, from sport 518, 519
exclusive athletic identity 481
exercise
  and anxiety reduction 34–5
  and heart attack rehabilitation 143–4, 157–8
  and optimal health 271
  and self-efficacy 157–60
  for coping with stress 290
  for sedentary populations 158
  for stress reduction 278–9
  in diabetes 158–60, 164
exercise adherence 158, 159
exercise behaviour
  antecedents 440–2
  consequences of 445–8
  correlates 442–5
  demographics 440–1
  stages of 441–2

exercise psychologists 438
exercise psychology 220, 437–49
  books 438
  conceptual framework 439, 440
  definition 438–9
  future directions 449
exercise-related mood enhancement 446
expanding awareness 404
expectations (of athletes), and anxiety 37
experiences 575, 588
  and coping confidence 332–3
expert practitioners 247, 251
experts/novices, use of cues, anticipation and visual scanning 71–2
expressiveness 561–2
external attention 70, 80, 391–2, 404
external awards, and intrinsic motivation 99–100
external efficacy engendering effects 294
external imagery 349–50
external locus of beliefs 294
external locus of control 318
external overloads 395
extrinsic motivation 94–103
  definition 94
  development of 101–3
extrinsic rewards, and motivation 95, 99
extroversion-introversion 8–9, 10–11
Eysenck Personality Inventory 8, 557

facilitative skills 528
facilitator role, of applied sport psychologists 245
failure
  attributional explanations 131–3
  perceptions of 136
failure avoidance, as motivational factor 103–4
failure fears, and anxiety 39
false feedback, and self-efficacy 153–4

family support
  and career transition 483, 488
  importance of 430
fatigue 272, 299, 351, 445
  and sport injury 459
faulty processes 193, 194
fear 351, 352
fear of success 39, 551, 565
feedback
  and skill improvement 56
  for children on their sporting ability 520
female athlete triad 557
females
  participation rates in sport/ administration 541–2
  see also gender; women
femininity 539, 546, 547, 561
feminism 539, 540, 560, 561, 566
fight or flight response 273
file drawer problem 180–1
film occlusion studies 71, 73
finances, influence on career transition 483
financial difficulties 112
fitness movement, feminisation of 561
Five Star Award Scheme 99–101, 106, 111
Five-Step Approach 69
flexibility of attention 76–8
flotation 326, 410
  as an aid to imagery 370, 371, 373–5
flotation REST 279, 373–5, 377
flow states
  and concentration 414–15
  at team level 206
  in elite athletes 587
  within work of applied sport psychologists 248–9
focus on what you can control 53
focusing and refocusing in the present 402–3
focusing of attention 70, 71–2, 405–6, 408
focusing on the right thing at the right time 388–90
Fool's Gold 525, 526

formulation profile   304
foundation skills   528
frame of reference   314, 315
"free flow" thought   401
Freudian approach to
    sport   91
friendships within teams   422
fun, from sport   53, 55, 106,
    518, 519
funding of research   xxxii
future issues, in sport
    and exercise
    psychology   592–603

game location   183–5
game simulations   55–6, 411
games, importance of for
    children   518
gender
  and achievement   551–3
  and men   540, 559–60
  and sport   538–66
  definition   539
  future research   560–4
  status   540–3
  stereotypes   544–5, 546, 547,
    549–50, 560, 563
gender belief systems   539,
    549–50, 565
gender order   539
gender relations   539, 540,
    543
gender role
    orientations   547–9
gender schema theory   549
gender verification tests   539
gendering   539
general dimension   582, 583
generalisability   579, 597
generality of
    self-efficacy   149–50
globality   129
goal setting   98–9, 223, 233,
    234, 236, 259–70, 410–11
  and action plans   265
  and motor learning   517
  and performance
    feedback   262
  as intervention
    strategy   321–3
  assessment of current
    position   264
  by coaches and athletes   262

effectiveness of   269
flexible approach   262
for athletes with
    disabilities   506, 510
for recovery after
    injury   467
future directions   268
in competition   266–7
monitoring of
    progress   265–6
principles   261–2
process   263–6
program   262–6
recorded in diary   262
what is it?   259–60
goal visualisation   236
goals
  and achievement
    behaviour   104
  for training   267–8
  inventory of possible   263
  priorities and
    time-lines   263–4
  programming   265
  why set them?   260–1
golden egg   594
Golf Performance Survey   295
Gordon's Test of Imagery
    Control (GTIC)   357
gradient model of
    attention   79
grief response, of injured
    athletes   465–6
grounded theory   599
group, definition   192
group dynamics, see team
    dynamics
Group Environment
    Questionnaire
    (GEQ)   203
group integration   202, 203
group performance,
    model   193–4
Group Test of Mental Rotations
    (GTMR)   357–8
group's goals vs individual
    goals   425
guilt   129, 298

habit strength hierarchies   177
habits of thinking   318
habitual attention   65
harmony   420

health beliefs, and
    behaviours   589
health psychology, attribution
    issues   137
heart rate   34, 45, 82
heavy training
  imagery to minimise muscle
    soreness after   370–1
  imagery use to assist
    recovery   363
hegemony   543, 559, 560, 562,
    564
heterosexuality   546, 558, 559
heuristic research   576
high confidence states of
    mind   334
higher-order themes   582–3
home crowd, influence on
    performance   174, 176,
    179, 183, 187
home ground
    advantage   183–5, 186–7
homophobia   558
homosexuality   540, 558
honesty   429
hopelessness-related
    emotions   128
Human Rights and
    Equal Opportunity
    Commission   558
humiliation   522
hypnosis   277–8, 282

iceberg profile, of mood
    states   18, 19
Ideal Performance State   223
ideomotor training   342
illness, and psychological
    benefits of sport and
    exercise   220
image barriers   317
imagery   223, 233, 234, 236,
    327, 328–9, 339–79, 410,
    598
  and confidence   353–5
  and mood states   352, 354
  and relaxation   371–2,
    375–6
  and self-efficacy   353, 354
  and skilled athletic
    ability   348
  for athletes with
    disabilities   505–6, 511

in self-efficacy 151, 161–2
measurement 355–9
  difficulties 355–6
  tests 356–59
motivational explanation
  of 353
theories 350–5
use during and after
  rehabilitation 369
use following
  surgery 369–70
use for gymnastics routine
  training 367–8
use for training 328
use in free-style
  swimming 368
use of flotation with 370,
  371, 373–5
use to minimise muscle
  soreness after runners
  heavy training 370–1
uses of 360–3
video modelling use 372–3,
  377, 378
imagery ability 348, 368, 377
imagery orientation 349–50
imagery rehabilitation
  program 369–70
imagery rehearsal 342, 343
imagery-relaxation
  issue 345–6
imagery training 342
  examples of use 367–72
  practice
    requirements 366–7
  when and where to use
    it 366–7
imagery training program
  athlete assessment 364–5
  commencing 363–6
  senses used 365
in vivo emotive imagery 354
in-game monitoring and
  control routine 242
independent tasks 201
individual attractions 202,
  203
individual contributions,
  recognition of in
  teams 426–7
Individual Differences
  Questionnaire
  (IDQ) 357

individual goals vs group
  goals 425
individual needs, and team
  development 425–7
individual performance
  and team member
    selection 195
  and team performance 195
individual psychological
  strategies, for
  children 528–9
individualised sport
  exercises 412
inductive methods 599
information gathering, case
  studies 281–2, 283
injured athletes, coaches'
  role 56
injury
  and career transition 482
  athlete's reaction to 466
  causes 456–7
  coping with 296–8
  imagery use to facilitate
    recovery 363, 369–70
  model 459
  prevention 217
  psychological aspects 206–7
  psychological
    factors 456–69
    explanations 459
    future directions 467–8
  psychological readiness to
    return from 217–18
  rehabilitation after 465–7
  vulnerability to,
    factors 459
injury likelihood, and
  attentional narrowing 44
inner game technique 279–80
instruments, for qualitative
  inquiry 581
intellectual accomplishments,
  sex differences 545
Intellectual Achievement
  Responsibility Scale
  (IAR) 134–5
intellectually disabled
  athletes 503, 505, 506
  mental skills training
    programs 508–9, 513
intensity, in achievement
  motivation theory 105–7

intensive aspects of
  attention 73–5
intentionality 129–30
interactional model 190
interactionist perspective xxx
interactive dependent
  tasks 201
internal attention 70, 80,
  391–2, 404
internal imagery 349–50
internal locus of beliefs 294
internal locus of
  control 318
internal narrowing,
  involuntary 395
internal overloads 395
internal/external
  dimension 125–6, 130–1
Internal/External Model 314
internality/stability, Weiner's
  attribution model 125–7
International Blind Sports
  Association Eye
  Classification System 507
International Journal of Sport
  Psychology xxiv, 227, 437
International Society of Sport
  Psychology (ISSP) xxiv,
  227
interpersonal attraction,
  among team
  members 199
interpretive methods xxxii
interpretive research 7, 577–8
inter-rater reliabilities 598
intervention plan 282, 283–4,
  304, 307
intervention strategies 311,
  312–13, 319–35, 594–5
interview data 581
interview techniques 598–9
intrinsic motivation 94–103,
  593
  and attributional
    style 133–4
  definition 94
  development of 101–3
  responsibility and
    accountability associated
    with 98
invasive research xxviii
inverted-U hypothesis 49–50,
  51, 76

involuntary internal narrowing 395
involuntary retirement 479
irrational thinking 325
isolation, of younger athletes at AIS 112

Jacobson's Progressive Relaxation 280
Journal of Applied Sport Psychology xxix, 227
Journal of Sport and Exercise Psychology 438
Journal of Sport Psychology xxiii, xxv, 227, 437, 438
journals xxv, xxix, 227, 236, 437, 438, 589

keep active, for anxiety reduction 53–4
keep things in perspective 56
kinaesthetic imagery 70, 349, 365, 513

language structures, in sport 540
lapses in concentration 387
leadership
  of teams 193, 196
  role in team cohesion 198
leadership activities, as concentration exercise 406
LEAP, *see* Lifeskills for Elite Athletes Program (LEAP)
learning approaches 248
lesbianism 558
level of self-efficacy 147–8
life after sport 218–19
Life Events Questionnaire 462
Life Events Scale for Adolescents (LESA) 460–1, 462
Life Experience Survey 461
life motivational forces 92
life stress 274–5
  and sport injury 460–3
Lifeskills for Elite Athletes Program (LEAP) 219, 489
life-span career planning 496

life-span developmental model 484–5
life-span research 596
Lifestyle Education Program 530
live training, *vs* canned programs and tapes 58
locations, for imagery training 366–7
locus of beliefs 294
locus of control 318
  and athletic injuries 457, 459
Locus of Control (LOC) Scale 348
logical positivism, *see* positivism
loneliness 133
long-term goals 261
longitudinal research 23, 595–6, 597
low confidence states of mind 334
low self-confidence, and anxiety 39
luck (attribution) 126

magnification 325
Major League Baseball, career awareness and transition needs 483–4
maladaptive coping 289, 306
  consequences of 299
males
  participation rates 541
  see also gender; men
Manifest Anxiety Scale (MAS) 33
manipulating the environment 319–20
MAPS, *see* Mental Attributes of Performance (MAPS) questionnaire
marketability of sport 561
Martens model, performance enhancement process 236–7, 239
masculinity 539, 540, 543, 546, 547, 559–60, 562, 564, 565
mass participation xxvii
massage 278
mastery models 528
maths ability 545

measurement, role in sport and exercise psychology 599
media coverage, of sport 97, 561, 564
mediator role, of applied sport psychologists 245
meditation 234, 278
membership of teams 430
men
  and gender 540, 559–60
  and sport 538–66
menstruation, and athletes' performance 564
mental advantage 221
Mental Attributes of Performance (MAPS) questionnaire 300–1, 302, 303, 306
mental blueprint 351
mental health model, of mood states 18
mental imagery 328–9
  and performance enhancement, influence of individual differences 347–8
  and physical practice 344
  definition 341–3
  future directions 376–8
  in sport 339–79
  nature of 340–1
  see also imagery
mental plans 54, 325–6
  conceptual framework 40–1
mental practice 341, 342–3, 344, 351
  and imagery 344–7
  and individuals performance enhancement 347–8
mental preparation
  for competition 390
  for swimming taper 588
  in baseball hitters 586–7
  in wrestlers 585
mental rehearsal 234, 280, 301, 304, 326, 328, 342, 405, 409–10
  for recovery after injury 466, 467
mental skills and strategies, of elite performers 589
mental skills training 223–4, 231

application to athletes with
    disabilities 504–6
disability specific 507–11
environmental factor
    consideration, with
    children 527–8
for juniors 232, 529
for teacher trainees 531–2
manuals 233
programs 413–14, 503
mental state, and peak
    performance 222–3
mental toughness 231
mental warm-up, imagery
    use 360–1
mentoring programs 488, 495
meta-analysis 181–2, 344, 351,
    545, 552
methodology xxviii, 577
Minnesota Multiphasic
    Personality Inventory
    (MMPI) 8
mood disturbance 445
in injury 297
mood states 18–19
    and exercise 445–6
    and imagery 352, 354
    in athletes with
        disabilities 503–4
moral development 518, 520
morale 420
Morris model, psychological
    skills training 240–2
motivation 90–118, 579
    and achievement
        success 551–2, 553
    and drive 183, 186
    and human behaviour 93
    and motor skill
        acquisition 517
    and sport injuries 458–9
    factors, and sport
        participation 91–2
    losses 194, 200
    personal and social
        factors 95–6
    through goals 260
    throughout life 112–14
    training 236
    see also extrinsic motivation;
        intrinsic motivation
motivational climate, for
    athletes 191

motivational interpretation, of
    imagery 353
motivational theory, relevance
    to sport 91–4
motor performance
    and effects of anxiety 41–7
    and imagery 376
    and natural imaginal
        style 349
motor skill acquisition, factors
    influencing, in
    children 517
Movement Imagery
    Questionnaire
    (MIQ) 358
movement-learning 517
movement skills, teaching of to
    children 531
multidimensionality, of
    self-concept 313
multifactor theories 594
multimedia technology 601
multiple baseline, single-case
    design 598
multiple goals 322
multiple sclerosis 460
muscle innervation 376
muscle memory 350
muscle soreness, imagery to
    minimise after heavy
    training 370
muscle tension 45
    and vulnerability to
        injury 459
mutual pretence 478

narrow attention 70, 71
narrow-external focus of
    attention 391, 392
narrow-internal focus of
    attention 391, 392–3
National Basketball
    Association 421–2
National Basketball
    League 493
National Coaching Foundation,
    mental training
    program 234–5
National Health and Physical
    Education
    curriculum 531
National Hockey
    League 483–4

National Soccer League 493
natural imaginal style, and
    motor performance 349
naturalistic inquiry 578, 586
negative self-talk 466, 467
Neuroticism scale 557
neuroticism-stability 8–9
New South Wales Rugby
    League 493
Nideffer attention
    model 391–3, 395–6
non-elite athletes
    anxiety in 47–8
    chunking ability 74
non-insulin dependent diabetes
    mellitus (NIDDM) 158
non-REM sleep 447
North American Society for the
    Psychology of Sport and
    Physical Activity
    (NASPSPA) xxiv, xxvi
novice practitioners 246
Nowicki-Strickland Locus of
    Control (LOC) Scale 348
nurturance 548, 561–2
nutrition, and eating
    disorders 557

obesity, and exercise 157
object cueing 404
object loss 460
objectivity, of research 579–80
observational research
    methods 598
occasional automaticity 68
Olympic Games 91, 96, 99,
    109, 228, 332–3, 411, 496,
    497, 541
Olympic Job Opportunity
    Program (OJOP) 19,
    487, 489, 492
    sport-specific adaptions 493
one-play-at-a-time
    technique 228
open awareness 478
optimal zones of arousal
    hypothesis 50
organised sport, for
    children 519–21
orthodox research 576, 601
osteoporosis 557
outcome expectation 146–7,
    160, 164

outcome goals   266, 267, 270
outcome value   147
overconfidence   145
overtraining syndrome   218, 299, 444–5
ownership   427, 428

pain
  coping with   298
  response to   296
Paired Psychological Skills Program   231
paradigmatic shift   602
paradigms   xxviii, 577–8
paralysis by analysis   68
"parking" thoughts   408
partial automaticity   68
participation in sport   xxiii, xxvii, 109–14, 115, 596
  adolescents' motivation   101–2, 107–9, 596–7
  and achievement motivation   588–9
  children's motivation   101
  holistic approach for youth   494
Participation Motivation Questionnaire (PMQ)   116–17, 596
participation rates, of males and females   541
passive thinking   401–2
passivity   561
pathogenic weight control   556
peak performance   217
  at team level   206
  attentional aspects   414
  components   389–90
  psychological factors   222
peer debriefer   584
peer group sport   520, 521
peers, influence on performance   182
perceived cohesion, of team members   198
perceived exertion   442–3
perceptions of success   320–1
perfectionism, and anxiety   38–9
perfectionist thinking   325

performance
  and accountability   98
  and anxiety   173–4
  and self-efficacy   155–7
  and sex differences   544–5
  and task complexity   181
  dynamogenic factors influence on   175–6
  influence of home crowd   174, 176
  influence of other contestants   174, 176
performance
  accomplishments   150, 152–3, 316
  applications   160–1
  effect on self-efficacy   294, 319, 320
performance cues   235, 236
performance
  enhancement   xxviii, 217, 225–7, 312
  and mental imagery, influence of individual differences   347–8
  and psychological skills training   220–5
  general models   236–42
  specific programs   227–33
  training materials and resources   233–6
performance-enhancing drugs   298
performance feedback, in goal setting   262
performance goals   266, 267, 269, 270
Performance Outcome Survey (POS)   136
performance planning   280–1
performance prediction   20–1
performance profiling   243–4
performance rating, MAPS questionnaire   302–4
performance skills   528
performance success, and team cohesion   205
periodisation   401, 413
persistence, in achievement motivation   107, 108
personal best performance, as goal   98–9

personal characteristics
  and gender role behaviour   548–9
  and self-confidence   327
  in team cohesion   197–8
personal constructs   13
personal development   312, 328
  as part of primary physical education programs   530–1
  through coping strategies   332
personal factors
  and motivation   95–6
  in state anxiety   37–9
personal orientation towards achievement   98–9
personal qualities, in sport motivation theory   93
personalisation   325
personality
  and injury   457–9
  and performance   20–3
  and sports behaviour   4–11
  nature of   11–14
  status of and sport research   14–16
  trait-state approaches   16–20
Personality Attributes Questionnaire (PAQ)   548
personality factor inventory   457–8
personality factors, and exercise behaviour   441
personality questionnaires   5
personality traits   546, 547, 548
  and attentional style   393
perspiration   351
persuasion   294, 354
  and self-efficacy   153–4, 161–2, 316
physical appearance   550, 554–5
physical contact sports, and children's development   522
physical education
  children's failure to thrive in   525–6
  in the school curriculum   524–5

perpetuation of hegemonic masculinity 564
problems in 524–5
versus sport 523–6
physical education lessons
and needs of individual children 523
primary teachers' perception of 524, 525
physical education programs
ad hoc approach in primary schools 525
focus on personal development 530–1
South Australian primary schools 530
physical practice, and mental imagery 344
physical self-concept 313, 448
physical self-efficacy 448
Physical Self-Efficacy Scale 163
physically disabled athletes 503, 504, 505, 506, 513
mental skills training programs 509–11
physiological arousal 316
physiological capacity 264
physiological goals 260, 269
physiological indicators, of arousal 178–9
physiological measures, of somatic anxiety 33–4
physiological processes, and somatic anxiety 45
physiological state, as self-efficacy antecendent 151–2, 154–5, 162
planning, and anxiety control 40
play opportunities, and children's sport 521–2
players' associations, role in post-sport careers 493
players' role, and selective attention 72
PMR, see Progressive Muscle Relaxation
politics, influence on career transition 482–3

POMS, see Profile of Mood States (POMS)
pool population 597
positive affirmation 233
positive focus 296
positive self-statements 304
positive self-talk 411–12, 510, 511
for recovery after injury 466, 467
positivism xxviii, 539, 563, 576–7, 578, 579, 580
research assumptions 578
positron emission tomography (PET) 82
post-game evaluations 318–19, 329–31
post-injury response 297
post-sport careers, sport management role 493
potential productivity 193
power relations 541, 543, 557
practising sport psychology 576
pre-competition routines 162, 228, 234, 236, 241, 409–10
development for golf 371–2
for athletes with disabilities 506
pre-packaged anxiety interventions 54
pre-retirement planning 482, 483
pregnancy, and athletes' performance 564
pressure, and anxiety 40
pressure to perform, in children/adolescents 289
prevention-oriented programs, for individuals experiencing transition difficulties 494
preview, imagery use 361
pride-in-team approach 196
primacy effect 125
primary prevention models 493–4
primary school, physical education programs 523, 530

primary school sport, children failure to thrive in 525–6
primary teachers
ad hoc physical education programs 525
approach to physical education lessons 523, 524
priority setting, in goal setting process 262
proactive coping 296, 301
proactive performer 182, 186, 188
proactive/reactive dependent tasks 201
problem-focused coping 291–2, 295, 296, 300
problem identification, case studies 282, 283
problem-solver role, of applied sport psychologists 245
problem-solving, imagery use 361–2
process goals 269, 270, 322
process oriented research 602
Professional Athletes Career Transition Inventory (PACTI) 483–4, 486
professional development, applied sport psychologists 246–9
professional status xxvi
professional support staff, reasons for working with elite athletes 97, 98
professional training 600
proficient practitioners 246–7
Profile of Mood States (POMS) 18–20, 230, 239, 352, 445, 503, 504
Progressive Muscle Relaxation 224, 233, 235, 277, 283, 510, 511
PST, see psychological skills training
psych-down 561
psychological capacity 264
psychological coping
and rehabilitation after sport injury 465–7
and sport injury 464
psychological goals 260, 269

psychological indicators, of arousal   177
psychological momentum   206
Psychological Performance Inventory   239
psychological screening   468
psychological skills development, imagery use   362
Psychological Skills Inventory for Sport   230, 239, 504
psychological skills training   214, 217, 345, 378
  and performance enhancement   220–5
  and program evaluation   250–1
  approaches to   225–43
  characteristics   224–5
  flexibility of operation   250
  for children   526–30
  general models   236–42
    Boutcher and Rotella   237
    limitations   242–3
    Martens   236–7
    Morris   240–2
    Thomas   238
    Vealey   237
  in schools   529–30
  limitations to use   249–50
  manuals   233–4
  peak performance based approach   226–7
  programs   233–6
  skills without a framework   226–7
  specific programs   227–33
  training materials and resources   233–6
  see also mental skills training
psychological tests, value and use of   229–30, 239
psychological trauma, after injury   465
psychometric instruments, see specific instruments, e. g. Californian Psychological Inventory
psychoneuromuscular theory   350–1, 376
psychophysiological factors   594

psychosocial factors   594
punishment, and motivation in sport   91, 92
purposeful sampling   581

qualitative methods   xxxii, 577, 578, 581
qualitative research   6–7, 575–90, 578
  examples   584–8
  future directions   588–9
  growth of   576–80
  principles   580–4
  reasons for   580
quality (of imagery)   365
quality training   390
quantitative methods   xxxii, 577, 578
quantitative research   6, 7–8
Questionnaire on Mental Imagery (QMI)   348, 357

random sampling   581
Rational-Emotive Therapy (RET) program   228
raw data themes   582
reactive coping   296
reactive/proactive dependent tasks   201
"Ready Set Go" sports program   106
reality   579
reciprocal determinism   152, 155–6, 162
reciprocal inhibition   291
recovery after illness and injury, factors   466–7
reflexive journal   584
refocus plan   40
refocusing   402, 408
reframing   325
rehabilitation
  cardiac, and exercise   143–4, 157–8, 161
  imagery use   369–70
  use of psychological coping after injury   465–7
relaxation   352
  and imagery   371–2, 375–6
relaxation-imagery issue   345–6

Relaxation Response   224
relaxation training   233, 234, 235, 277, 304
  for anxiety management   57–8
  for athletes with disabilities   505
  for coping with stress   290–1
reproductive approach to learning   248
research, future directions   21–3
research funding   xxxii
research methods   xxix, xxxii, 5–8, 581
research questions, for qualitative research   580
researcher-participant relationship   579
resignation   479
resolve coping   297
resource theories, of attention   66–70
respect   428–9
response propositions   351, 352
response set   352
response to errors   408–9
responsibility
  of individuals and coaches   98
  of individuals in team success   197
Restricted Environmental Stimulation Therapy (REST)   279, 373–5
results, through goal setting   261
retirement, definition   476
retirement from sport
  and career transitions   113–14, 218–19, 474–6
  and increased opportunities   483
  preparation for   482
  sociological ramifications   475–6, 493
reversal theory   51–2
review, imagery use   361

rewards
  and motivation in sport   91, 92
  see also external rewards; extrinsic rewards
Ringelmann effect   194–5
risk-taking   301
role conflict   546–7, 565
role modelling   315
  with children   528
role models   326–7
routine application phase, psychological skills training (Morris model)   241
routine development phase, psychological skills training (Morris model)   241–2
routines   281, 325–6, 402, 409–10
runner's high   444

safety, of organised children's sports   522
salience effect   125
sample selection   581
SARRS, *see* Social and Athletic Re-adjustment Rating Scale (SARRS)
SASI, *see* South Australian Sports Institute
satisfaction, and team cohesion   202
scanning   403
scholarships   112, 541
  for athletes with disabilities   502
  motivational value of   102, 103
school, *see* primary school
scientist-practitioner gap   576
searchlight models of attention, problems with   80
security, within teams   429–30
sedentary populations, and exercise   158
segmenting   241
selective attention   71–3, 78–9
self-assurance   301
self-attributions, and self–concept   318

self-awareness   335
self-awareness theory, and drive   179–80
self-blame   296, 298
self-comparison   334
self-concept   313–15, 317
  and exercise   448
  and self-attributions   318
  and self-efficacy   315–16
  development with age   314–15
self-confidence   144, 145, 146, 233, 235, 594
  and attributions   329–31
  and coping   331–2
  and imagery   353–5
  and personal characteristics   327
  and sporting performance   311–35
  future directions   335–6
  intervention strategies   319–35
  theories   313
self-control   301, 304
self-doubt   294
self-efficacy   144, 593
  and anxiety   156, 163
  and enhanced performance   354
  and exercise behaviour   157–60
  and exercise in diabetes   158–60, 164
  and imagery   353, 354
  and performance accomplishments   294, 319, 320
  and self-concept   315–16
  and social cognitive theory   146–7, 163, 165, 166
  and sports performance   155–7, 164, 167
  and state anxiety   156
  and task experience   156–7, 164
  antecedents   150–2, 167, 294, 353
  research on   152–5
comparison with anxiety   595

definition   145–6
  enhanced through self-talk   323–4
  future directions   162–5, 167
  generality   149–50
  level   147–7
  measurement   147–50, 162–3
  microanalytic technique   147–50, 162–3
  practical applications   160–2
  strength   148–9
self-esteem   318
  and exercise   448
  during injury   297
  in children   522
self-help attentional strategies   396
self-identity   316
self-image   316–17, 318, 409
  changing   334–5
self-monitoring   22
self-perception   315
  and exercise   448
  and intrinsic motivation   95
self-preoccupation   43
self-presentational analysis   180, 181
self-schema   22
self-serving attributional bias   132
self-talk   316, 317, 328
  control techniques   324–5
  for enhancing self–efficacy   323–4
  instructions   408
self-worth   324
sex, definition   539
sex differences   539, 543–5, 566
Sex Discrimination Act 1984 (Federal)   558
sex roles   544, 546, 558, 560
sex tests   539
sex typing   549
sexual harassment   542, 557–9, 564, 565
sexual impulses, and motivation in sport   91–2
sexuality   540, 543, 554–9, 561, 564

shame 128–9, 298, 557
shared experiences, in team cohesion 198
shifting attention 78
short-term goals 261, 321–2
Shortened Questionnaire on Mental Imagery (SQMI) 357
shyness 133
simulation activities 411
single case designs 344–5
single-thought focus 402
16 Personality Factor Questionnaire (16PF) 5, 457, 458
Sixty Something Study 159
skill acquisition 320, 326, 328
skill improvement, and feedback 56
skill learning, imagery use 360
skill level 264
skill level enhancement, and self-concept 314
skill practice, imagery use 360
skilled athletes, approach to anxiety 47–8
skimming approach to learning 248
skin conductance 176
sleep disturbance, exercise effects 447
sleep patterns, exercise effects 446–7
sleep stages 446–7
slenderness, preoccupation with 555, 556
sliding populations approach 597
slow-wave sleep (SWS) 446, 447
slump, in performance 297, 300, 302, 320, 325
Social and Athletic Re-adjustment Rating Scale (SARRS) 460
social breakdown theory 477
social cognitive theory, and self-efficacy 146–7, 163, 165, 166
social cohesion 197

social comparisons, as intervention strategies 333–4
social conditions, to trigger drive 177, 179
social death 478–9
social environment, in interactional model 190
social facilitation 173–8, 593
  current perspectives 177–85
  future directions 186–7
  historical perspectives 174–6
  practical implications of research 185–6
social factors, and motivation 95–6
social gerontological models 476–8
  criticisms 479
social learning theory 190
social loafing 195, 200–1, 428
social motivation 90–1, 93, 96, 97
social motivation theory, and drive 180
social perspective taking 304
social physique anxiety 441
Social Re-adjustment Rating Scale (SRRS) 460
social reinforcers, in sport motivation theory 93
social roles 545–50, 566
social self-concept 313
social support
  in stress-injury relationship 206–7, 464
  to influence coping 293–4
social validation 598
socialisation 544, 545, 553
socio-cultural factors 544, 552
socioeconomic status, and exercise behaviour 440–1
soft eyes–hard eyes 403
somatic anxiety 30–1, 32, 274, 594
  physiological effects 45
  physiological measures 33–4
somatypes 556

South Australian Education Department, physical education programs 530
South Australian Sports Institute
  flotation facilities 374
  goal setting workbooks 262
  sport psychologists at xxv
  sport psychology program 235–6
specific cues 408
specific goals 261
sport and exercise psychology xxix, 216
  marketing and promotion of xxxiii
Sport Anxiety Scale (SAS) 33
sport associations, selection/deselection of players 496
Sport Attributional Style Scale (SASS) 136
Sport Competition Anxiety Test (SCAT) 16, 230, 359
sport-for-women model 561
Sport Imagery Questionnaire (SIQ) 358–9
sport institutions, role in sport promotion and career transition 497
sport management, role in post-sport careers 493
sport object focusing 407
sport performance, trait and state anxiety effects 36
sport programs, graded for emotional/cognitive impact 562
sport psychologists 5, 20–1
  accreditation xxvi, xxx–xxxi
  development of athletes self-confidence 319–20, 322–3, 335–6
  evaluation procedures training 601
  future directions 600–1
  links to national sport bodies xxxi–xxxii
  overlap with exercise psychologists 438
  research opportunities xxxiii

role in relation to
clients 600–1
teaching methods 601
training xxxi
see also applied sport
psychologists
sport psychology
current status xxv–xxvii
definition 438
development xxiii–xxv
future
direction xxxiii–xxxiv
professionalisation xxv–xxvi,
xxxiii
theory and
practice xxxii–xxxiii
training xxvi, xxxi
Sport Psychology Bulletin 236
sport psychology
services 228–9
delivery to individuals and
groups 230
*Sport Psychology Training
Bulletin* 236
sport socialisation 191
sport-specific coping 305
sport-specific
measures 593
sport-specific theoretical
approach 593
sport tasks, types 201
sporting myths, in children's
sport 521–3
sporting profile, changing in
Australia 96–7
sports administrators
gender differences
in 541–2, 561
work with coaches 487–8
Sports Development Officers
Scheme 489
Sports Inventory for Pain
(SIP) 296
Sports Search
program 107–9, 115
sports studies institutes,
development of 96–9
Sports Talent Encouragement
Plan Grants 541
SportsLEAP program 112,
117, 487, 494
operation and
structure 489, 491

spotlight model of
attention 78–9
SRRS, *see* Social Re-adjustment
Rating Scale (SRRS)
stability/internality, Weiner's
attribution
model 125–7, 318
stages of loss 465–6, 479, 495
staleness 444–5
state anxiety 16, 19, 274, 594
and self-efficacy 156, 163
antecedents of 35–7
athletes with
disabilities 503
definitions 31–2
personal factors 37–9
situational factors 39–41
State institutes and
academies 103
state self-confidence 144, 594
State-Trait Anxiety Inventory
(STAI) 18, 33, 50, 503
state-trait conceptualisation of
self-confidence 144
states, and personality 11–12
steroids 208
stimulus propositions 351
stork stand 405–6
strategic research, in team/
group dynamics 207
strategy learning, imagery
use 360
strategy practice, imagery
use 360
strength of self-efficacy 148–9
stress
and arousal 185–6
and involuntary internal
narrowing 395
and sport injury 459, 461–3
cognitive-affective
model 299
coping and injury 463–5
coping strategies using
COPE model 301–2
definition 273
drug use for coping
with 298–9
in elite athletes 272–3
in elite figure skaters 585,
586
in youth golf 585
individual response to 273

on elite coaches 272
sources of 585–6
stress inoculation training 54
stress management 223, 234,
271–85, 495
approaches 276–84
case studies 281–4
future directions 284
imagery use 362
techniques 276–81
stressful life events, and sport
injuries 460–3
string and bolt exercise 363–4
strong automaticity 68
Stroop Colour Word Test 43
structural equation
modelling 595
subculture theory 477
sub-goals 264
subordination 561
substitution theory 476–7
success
and confidence 143
attributional
explanations 131–3
expectancy of 127–8
perceptions of 136
success achievement, as
motivational factor 103–4
success fears 39, 551, 565
successful experiences, as
intervention
strategies 319–21
supervised children's sport,
health and safety
aspects 522
surgery, imagery use to
accelerate healing
process 369–70
suspicion awareness 478
sweating, through anxiety 34,
45
switching, of attention 76–8
Sydney 2000 Olympic
Games 496, 497
symbolic learning theory 327,
351, 376
symbolic rehearsal 342
symbolic representation 376
Systematic
Desensitisation 224, 282,
327, 328
Systematic Relaxation 277

tactical goals   260, 269
TAIS, *see* Test of Attentional
   and Interpersonal Style
   (TAIS)
talent identification   21,
   115–16, 597
targeting   403
task cohesion   197, 201
task complexity, and
   performance   181
task difficulty
   (attribution)   126
task experience, and
   self-efficacy   156–7, 164
task focus, in MAPS
   questionnaire   301, 304
task involvement   105–6
task-oriented
   behaviour   106–7
task-specific coping   305
'tea-person' role, of applied
   sport psychologists   245
team
   and group dynamic
      studies   205–6
   attractiveness of, as a
      whole   199
   closeness of identification
      with   199–200
   effective communication
      within   196
   interaction patterns   420
   what is it?   192–3
team building   192, 420–34
   and player attrition   429
   definitions   423
   future directions   432–3
   philosophy of   423–4
team chemistry   420–1,
   422–3
team climate   199
team cohesion   193, 196, 197,
   420, 422, 429
   and collective
      efficacy   204–5
   and confidence   553
   and performance
      success   205
   and satisfaction   202
   and team
      performance   197–200,
      201–2
   antecedents   197–8

conceptual model   203
consequences of   198–9
model   202–4
team development, effective
   principles   425–32
team dynamics   190–1, 219,
   420
   and success   422
   current perspectives   200–5
   future directions   205–7
   historical
      retrospective   191–200
   strategic research
      development   207
   unit of analysis issue   205
team experiences, in team
   cohesion   198
team functioning   421, 432
team games, for children   518
team goals   425
team harmony   199–200
team leadership   193, 196
team members, and individual
   needs   425–6
team membership   193
team momentum   206
team motivation   193, 194,
   196–7, 199
team performance
   and individual
      performance   195
   and social loafing   195,
      200–1
   and team
      cohesion   197–200, 201–2
   and team process   194–5
   assumptions   193
   research   194–5
team philosophy   425
team process, and team
   performance   194–5
team selection policy   429–30
team spirit   192, 199, 420,
   422
team sport
   challenge of   421–2
   coping in   290
team success   427
team unity   430
team values   425
team work   194, 199
technical goals   260, 269
tension   351

Test of Attentional and
   Interpersonal Style
   (TAIS)   17–18, 80, 239,
   387, 396–9, 412
   attentional subscales   398
   criticisms   81, 230, 397
   effective attentional subscale
      for elite athlete   397–8
   overloaded attentional
      subscales for elite
      athlete   399
   sport-specific versions   17,
      397
thanatological models   478–9
The Sport Psychologist   xxix, 227,
   228–9, 236, 437, 509, 543,
   558, 599, 601
"The Unbendable Arm"
   exercise   363, 406–7
theme-building process   581–2
theory-practice
   nexus   xxvii–xxx, 601–2
thick description   583
think practice   53
Thomas model, performance
   enhancement process
   phases   238–40
thought-control
   techniques   233
thought distraction, and
   exercise   35
thought stopping   279, 283,
   324, 512
3 R's pre-performance
   routine   228
timing, of imagery
   training   366, 367
total mood disturbance
   (TMD)   445
training, imagery
   use   328
training diaries   262, 265, 268,
   269
training goals   267–8, 269
training materials and
   resources, for
   psychological skills
   training   233–6
training stress   275
trait anxiety   31, 32, 38, 41,
   274, 503
trait-oriented research   5, 8–9,
   10

trait-state approach, to
personality   11–12, 16–20,
22, 24
transactional model, of
coping   288–90
Transcendental
Meditation   278
transferability   583
transformational approach to
learning   248
transformed sport   561–2
transition models   479–80
Transtheoretical Model of
Behaviour Change
(TM)   496–7
travel, impact on athletes   219
triangulation   581, 583
trust   429
trustworthiness
methods   583–4
tuberculosis   460
two-dimensional model
(Weiner)   125–7
Type A characteristics, and
injury   459

uncontrolled aggression   292
under-achievement, and
motivation   108
under-performance   299
universities, and sporting
participation   102

valence of physiological
indicators   178
validation tests   599
Vealey model, performance
enhancement
process   237
verbal ability   545
verbal persuasion   151, 153,
161, 354
vicarious experience   150–1,
153, 315, 316, 326, 353–4,
372
applications   161

Victorian Institute of Sport
(VIS)   117, 486, 489,
491–2
video and computer
games   402
video feedback   412
video modelling, as an aid to
imagery   372–3, 377, 378
videotapes, for psychological
skills training   236
vigilance tasks   75
VIS, *see* Victorian Institute of
Sport
visual attention   78
visual-motor behaviour
reversal   233
visual scanning, by experts/
novices   72, 73
visual-spatial ability   545
visualisation   280, 282, 342,
365, 409, 410
techniques   236
visually impaired
athletes   503–4, 505, 506,
513
mental skills training
programs   507–8
visuo-motor behaviour
rehearsal (VMBR)   54,
280, 342, 344, 345, 346, 375
vivid imagery   350, 351
vividness   365
Vividness of Movement
Imagery Questionnaire
(VMIQ)   358
Vividness of Visual Imagery
Questionnaire
(VVIQ)   358
voluntary retirement   479

walk   327
watching the clock face   402
Ways of Coping Checklist
(WOCC)   299
Ways of Coping Questionnaire
(WOCQ)   299

Ways of Coping with Injury
(WOCI)   296
Ways of Coping with Sport
(WOCS)   295, 299–300,
302, 306, 465
weight control   555, 556,
557
Western Australian Blind
Olympic Sports
Association   507
Western Australian Disabled
Sports Association   504
what ifs   409
wheelchair athletes, *see*
physically disabled athletes
width of attention   70, 391
Wingate Sport Achievement
Responsibility Scale
(WSARS)   135
winning
coaches stressing of   55
emphasis on   289, 551, 560
in children's sport   520
wishful thinking   291, 292, 296
withdrawal from
sport   109–14, 115, 299
see also drop out
Wolpe's principle   291
women, in administrative
positions   541–3
women in sport   538–566
historical views   91, 540
women's sport
coverage of   541
success levels of   541
worry   522, 594
worst case scenario   53

youth, *see* adolescents

zone of optimal
functioning   50, 57
zoom-lens model of
attention   79
zooming of
concentration   403, 404